# Private Equity

# PRIVATE EQUITY

## JURISDICTIONAL COMPARISONS

### THIRD EDITION

GENERAL EDITORS

## CHARLES MARTIN & SIMON PERRY
*Macfarlanes LLP*

SWEET & MAXWELL

 THOMSON REUTERS

First Edition 2010
Second Edition 2014

Published in 2018 by Thomson Reuters, trading as Sweet &
Maxwell. Thomson Reuters is registered in England & Wales,
Company No.1679046. Registered Office and address for service: 5
Canada Square, Canary Wharf, London, E14 5AQ.

For further information on our products and services, visit *http://
www.sweetandmaxwell.co.uk.*

Computerset by Sweet & Maxwell.
Printed and bound by CPI Group (UK) Ltd, Croydon, CR0 4YY.
No natural forests were destroyed to make this product: only farmed
timber was used and replanted.
A CIP catalogue record for this book is available from the British
Library.

ISBN: 978-0-414-06755-4

Thomson Reuters, the Thomson Reuters logo and Sweet & Maxwell
® are trademarks of Thomson Reuters.

# Table of Contents

# Foreword

**Charles Martin & Simon Perry**   Macfarlanes LLP

The private equity landscape has changed significantly since the first edition of this book was published in 2010. Back then, the economies of many of the jurisdictions represented in these pages were in recession and the credit crisis meant that debt finance, on which so much private equity deal activity relies, was scarcely available in many places. There were other factors at work as well: fundraising was at an all-time low and, for those funds which were being raised, limited partnerships (**LPs**) had become more forthright in dictating fund terms.

The private equity industry reacted with resilience to these and other challenges and, at the time of writing, the second edition of this book in 2014 was thriving once again as economies grew, debt markets rebounded and alternative financing solutions flourished.

As the third edition of this book is published, the private equity industry has enjoyed a period of remarkable success with fundraisings and deal volumes and multiples at near record highs. However, the industry will need to continue to show flexibility and the ability to adapt if it is to remain resilient in the face of a number of recent macro-geo-political events, the consequences of which as yet remain uncertain. This comes at a time when ever larger private equity funds are being raised and those funds face competition for high-quality businesses at attractive prices from a raft of new and more specialist funds, sovereign wealth funds, family offices and **LPs** willing to invest directly.

The regulatory and tax landscapes have also continued to change as the spotlight shines ever brighter on the private equity industry. In particular, there has been an international drive in recent years to counter perceived tax avoidance and, as a result, in many jurisdictions, there has been a scaling back of the tax advantages previously enjoyed by private equity structures.

As with the previous editions of this book, we have aimed to provide a clear and comprehensive analysis of the key issues relating to private equity fundraising and deal-doing on a jurisdiction-by-jurisdiction basis, whilst picking up many of the themes referred to above.

It has been a pleasure working on this edition with some of the leading private equity practitioners at independent law firms around the world, and we would like to thank them for their hard work and collaboration. Many thanks are also due to the team at Thomson Reuters for their tireless efforts in putting this edition together.

# Austria

## Binder Grösswang Rechtsanwälte GmbH Thomas Schirmer, Markus Uitz & Philipp Kapl

## 1. MARKET OVERVIEW

### 1.1 Types of investors

In Austria, private equity is mainly driven by governmental agencies and banks but, to a minor degree, by institutional investors as an asset class. Insurance companies have recently gained increasing importance in the Austrian private equity market.

According to the latest available data (for the year 2017) from the Austrian Private Equity and Venture Capital Organisation (AVCO), the allocation between investors may be summarised as follows:

- governmental agencies: 36.4% (2016: 100%; 2015: 21.2%; 2014: 76.4%);
- banks: 31.8% (2016: 0%; 2015: 0%; 2014: 0%);
- insurance companies: 12.9% (2016: 0%; 2015: 0%; 2014: 0%);
- corporate investors: 7.6% (2016: 0%; 2015: 0%; 2014: 0%);
- unclassified: 5% (2016: 0%; 2015: 0%; 2014: 0%);
- private individuals: 4.2% (2016: 0%; 2015: 74.3%; 2014: 23.6%);
- funds of funds: 1.5% (2016: 0%; 2015: 0%; 2014: 0%); and
- family offices: 0.5% (2016: 0%; 2015: 0%; 2014: 0%).

Pension funds (2017: 0%; 2016: 0%), academic institutions (2017: 0%; 2016: 0%), capital markets (2017: 0%; 2016: 0%), endowments and foundations (2017: 0%; 2016: 0%), other asset managers (including private equity houses other than fund of funds) (2017: 0%; 2016: 0%) and sovereign wealth funds (2017: 0%; 2016: 0%) were not relevant for the Austrian private equity market.

### 1.2 Types of investments

Fundraising increased from EUR 13 million in 2014 to EUR 197 million in 2017, which is now comparable to the level of 2012 (EUR 194 million). Investments dropped from EUR 106 million in 2014 to EUR 90 million in 2017—the lowest amount since 2013 (EUR 79 million).

According to the data published by the AVCO, private equity investments have been made to the following sectors:

- ICT (Communications, computer and electronics): 39.7% (2016: 25.7%; 2015: 23.6%; 2014: 21.3%);
- financial and insurance activities: 23.9% (2016: 9.6%; 2015: 22.3%; 2014: 10.1%);
- business products and services: 18.1% (2016: 26.7%; 2015: 19.8%; 2014: 26.5%);
- consumer goods and services: 7.4% (2016: 13%; 2015: 8.6%; 2014:

13.5%);
- biotech and healthcare: 7% (2016: 5.6%; 2015: 10.2%; 2014: 13%);
- transportation: 2% (2016: 3.1%; 2015: 0%; 2014: 0.9%);
- energy and environment: 1.2% (2016: 0%; 2015: 7.7%; 2014: 12.9%);
- chemicals and materials: 0.6% (2016: 0%; 2015: 6.7%; 2014: 0.9%);
- agriculture: 0.2% (2016: 0%; 2015: 0.2%; 2014: 0%);
- construction: 0% (2016: 15.7%; 2015: 0.2%; 2014: 0.8%);
- real estate: 0% (2016: 0%; 2015: 0%; 2014: 0%); and
- other: 0% (2016: 0.6%; 2015: 0.6%; 2014: 0%).

In terms of timing, private equity has been invested as follows during the life-cycle of enterprises regarding the invested amounts:
- growth capital: 43.9% (2016: 22.8%);
- buyout: 32.5% (2016: 29.6%);
- start-up phase: 11.6% (2016: 28.5%);
- later stage venture: 8.7% (2016: 15.4%);
- seed phase: 3.4% (2016: 2.2%);
- rescue/turnaround: 0% (2016: 0%); and
- replacement capital: 0% (2016: 1.5%).

## 2. FUNDS
### 2.1 Fund structures

The typical legal structures used for private equity funds in Austria are: (1) the "GmbH & Co KG", which is a special limited partnership (*Kommanditgesellschaft—KG*) with a limited liability company (*Gesellschaft mit beschränkter Haftung—GmbH*) as the general partner (*Komplementär*) or "AG & Co KG" if the limited liability company is replaced with a stock corporation (*Aktiengesellschaft—AG*) and the investors as limited partners (*Kommanditisten*); and (2) the stock corporation. Another popular Austrian legal structure, frequently used as special purpose vehicle but less often seen for private equity funds is the limited liability company. In general, the legal forms used to structure Austrian private equity funds are similar to structures frequently used in Germany and to some extent in Switzerland but differ considerably from those used in other countries. Below is a short overview of the main characteristics of these two types of legal structures.

### Special limited partnerships—GmbH & Co KG/AG & Co KG

In a limited partnership, two types of partners may be distinguished:
- general partners with unlimited liability (*Komplementär*); and
- limited partners with limited liability (*Kommanditist*), typically the investors.

A limited partnership requires a minimum of one general partner and one limited partner. The general partner(s) is/are entitled to manage and represent the limited partnership. The involvement of limited partners is usually restricted to extraordinary business decisions such as the accession of new limited partners or the dissolution of the limited partnership. However, the articles of association of the limited partnership may contain deviating provisions.

The limited partnership's general partners are jointly and severally liable vis-à-vis third parties together with the limited partnership. The liability of a limited partner is limited to the amount determined as the partner's liability amount (*Haftsumme*) in the articles of association of the limited partnership. In general, limited partners who have provided their compulsory contribution (*Pflichteinlage*) equalling the liability amount into the limited partnership (e.g. in cash, in kind, by not withdrawing profits, set-off with claims or paying a creditor of the limited partnership) are no longer personally liable to the creditors of the limited partnership.

The main benefits of special limited partnerships are: (1) the protection of the investors under the corporate veil since only the general partner is a company with limited liability; (2) the uncomplicated transfer of shares and entry/exit of investors (no form requirement for the transfer of shares in a limited partnership, i.e. no notarial deed required (as compared to shares in a limited liability company); (3) a high flexibility with respect to corporate governance (in particular as compared to stock corporations) with few mandatory rights for investors; and (4) certain tax advantages. However, such special limited partnership features increased administrative costs for the installation and maintenance of a (at least) two tier-structure (limited partnership and limited liability company or stock corporation acting as general partner) as well as different types of partners.

Further, a special limited partnership offers certain tax advantages as it qualifies as tax transparent and, consequently, profits are taxed at the partners' level only. Further, an open fund can easily be created by using the special limited partnership for capital calls. Although there are few strings attached to the withdrawal of profits, attention must be paid to the (relatively strict) Austrian capital maintenance rules: shareholders in a limited partnership are entitled to dividend distributions and liquidation proceeds only; other payments or benefits may qualify as the repayment of capital contributions and may thus be invalid.

### Stock corporation (Aktiengesellschaft)

Stock corporations are mainly chosen for: (1) the protection of the shareholders under the corporate veil; (2) their mandatory two-tier management system consisting of a management board (*Vorstand*) acting under the supervision of a supervisory board (*Aufsichtsrat*); (3) the mandatory legal provisions ensuring a comprehensive corporate governance, a certain level of shareholder rights and transparency; and (4) the uncomplicated transfer of shares (no notarial deed required). Further, the shareholdings in the stock corporation are only publicly available in case of a sole shareholder. However, the need for a two tier-management system and extensive corporate governance provisions result in increased costs for installing and maintaining a stock corporation.

The management board is responsible for managing and representing the stock corporation. It acts basically independently from the supervisory board and the shareholders. The management board is not subject to instructions from the supervisory board, the shareholders or the shareholders' assembly (*Hauptversammlung*), whose direct influence on the operations of the stock corporation is therefore limited. Limitations may be set out in the articles of association by the supervisory board or bylaws (*Geschäftsordnung*). In addition to handling the day-to-day business, the management board prepares the financial statements and is responsible for keeping all necessary books and records of the stock corporation. The management board reports to the supervisory board: (1) on an annual basis on fundamental questions of the business policy and the asset, financial and profit situation; (2) at least once per quarter about the course of business and the company's position in comparison to the forecast calculation taking into account future developments; and (3) promptly on critical matters and circumstances which are of significant relevance for the profitability or liquidity of the stock corporation.

Members of the management board are appointed by the supervisory board of the stock corporation for a maximum term of five years and such appointment can be renewed without limitation. The appointment of a member of the management board may be revoked by the supervisory board for good cause only.

The supervisory board is responsible for supervising the management board and consists of at least three members. Any single member of the supervisory board may request a report from the management board concerning matters of the stock corporation at any time. The supervisory board may also inspect and review all books and records of the stock corporation.

Certain important business decisions (as provided for by law and potentially in the corporation's articles of association or bylaws) require the prior consent of the supervisory board.

The members of the supervisory board are appointed by the shareholders' assembly. Members of the management board of the stock corporation or a subsidiary as well as employees of the company cannot be appointed as supervisory board members. Prior to the expiration of a supervisory board member's term of office, the appointment may be revoked by a resolution of the shareholders without cause. This resolution requires a three-quarters majority of the votes cast.

Apart from an annual shareholders' meeting required by law, which deals with the approval of the annual financial statements (if the matter is referred to it by the supervisory board), the distribution of profits and the discharge of board members, shareholders' meetings must also be called if requested by a minority of shareholders.

In general, resolutions passed at a shareholders' meeting must be passed by a simple majority. A qualified majority of three-quarters is required for certain subjects, in particular, amendments to the articles of association, capital increases and decreases, changes concerning the legal form of the company, other corporate restructurings such as demergers and mergers as well as voluntary termination of the company, the issuance of authorised or conditional capital, the issuance of convertible or participating bonds, exclusion of shareholders' subscription rights on newly issued shares (*Bezugsrechtsausschluss*) and conclusion of profit transfer agreements.

A listed stock corporation has various disclosure and reporting regulations to meet the demands of the prime market of the Vienna Stock Exchange. Those regulations include, e.g. ad hoc reporting obligations, reporting regulations of the Corporate Governance Code and directors' dealing reports.

## 2.2 Regulation of fundraising and fund managers

The legal framework for private equity funds in Austria changed significantly with the implementation of the EU Directive 2011/61 on Alternative Investment Fund Managers and amending Directives 2003/41 and 2009/65 and Regulations 1060/2009 and 1095/2010 [2011] OJ L174/1 (AIFM Directive) by way of the (new) Austrian Alternative Investment Fund Managers Act 2013 (*Alternatives Investmentfonds Manager-Gesetz* or AIFMG), the abolishment of the Participation Fund Act 1982 (*Beteiligungsfondsgesetz*) and the amendment of several other Austrian laws, including the Banking Act 1993 (*Bankwesengesetz* or *BWG*), the Capital Market Act 1991 (*Kapitalmarktgesetz* or *KapitalmarktG*), Financial Markets Supervision Act 2001 (*Finanzmarktaufsichtsgesetz*), Securities Supervision Act 2017 (*Wertpapieraufsichtsgesetz*), Investment Fund Act 2011 (*Investmentfondsgesetz 2011* or *InvestmentfondsG*), the Real Estate Investment Fund Act 2003 (*Immobilien-Investmentfondsgesetz* or *Immobilien-InvestmentfondsG*) as well as certain tax laws to the extent relevant.

Most Austrian private equity funds qualify as alternative investment funds (AIFs), being collective investment undertakings which raise capital from a number of investors with a view to investing it in accordance with a defined investment policy for the benefit of such investors, without the capital serving a direct operational business and without being a UCITS (Undertakings for Collective Investments in Transferable Securities). The Austrian Financial Markets Authority (*Finanzmarktaufsicht* or FMA) is responsible for the supervision of managers of an AIF (AIFM) in Austria.

The AIFMG introduces primarily regulations on AIFMs, most importantly a requirement to obtain a licence by the FMA. However, an exemption exists for smaller AIFs whose assets under management do not exceed EUR 100 million (including assets acquired by using leverage) or EUR 500 million (for unleveraged funds with no redemption rights within five years following the date of initial investment), which need to register with the FMA only.

According to the FMA, as of 31 December 2016:

- 2,094 funds of Austrian investment companies or AIFMs were licensed for distribution in Austria;
- 21 investment fund management companies (of which 17 were licensed as AIFMs) with fund assets managed in the amount of EUR 167.10 billion existed;
- another four companies were licensed exclusively under the AIFMG and 20 registered AIFMs managed a fund volume in the amount of EUR 1.16 billion; and
- five investment companies for real estate (being alternative investment fund managers at the same time) with a managed fund volume of EUR 6.70 billion existed.

The AIFMG contains a number of structural and organisational requirements for AIFs in addition to defining their regulatory framework; for example, AIFMs need to appoint a custodian for each AIF they manage, which can in general be either a bank or a supervised securities services provider with its seat in the EU or, for AIFs with no redemption rights within five years following the date of initial investment and with the primary investment objective of acquiring control of non-listed companies, an escrow agent (typically a notary public or an attorney-at-law). The AIFMG does not provide for special training of hedge fund managers. In practice, the US qualification of a "Chartered Financial Analyst" (CFA) as well as its European equivalent "Certified International Investment Analyst" (CIIA) have become standard for private equity fund managers. Further, the Austrian "Certified Portfolio Manager" (CPM) qualification becomes increasingly recognised in the private equity sector.

Depending on the scope of activities and actual structure of private equity funds, other Austrian laws may be applicable as well; for example, private equity funds may be required to publish a prospectus according to the Austrian Capital Market Act (*KapitalmarktG*) if certain prerequisites are met.

## 2.3  Customary or common terms of funds

Private equity funds are generally categorised into closed funds and open funds. Closed funds are—either temporarily or permanently—closed to investors after the initial investment; open funds are open to further investments during the entire investment period of the fund. The incorporation of the fund is usually conditional upon a certain minimum amount of capital being aggregated in both structures.

Further, private equity funds may be differentiated into evergreen funds and closed-end funds based on their investment period and date of effective capital flow. Evergreen funds (or permanent capital vehicles) have an indefinite fund life and operate based on the principle of recycling realised investment returns back into the fund rather than distributing them to the investor. In contrast, closed-end funds have a specific fund life of 10–12 years. Closed-end funds require investors to make a capital commitment that is drawn down from time to time upon notice. At that time at which investors are admitted to the fund (i.e. at the closing), they usually do not fund any portion of their investment amount yet. As in most other jurisdictions, closed-end funds prevail considerably over evergreen funds in the Austrian private equity market.

Depending on the legal form of the private equity fund, the terms of the funds may vary to some extent but are generally similar to those in other jurisdictions. Usually, the management of a private equity fund is performed by a separate limited liability company or stock corporation. A management contract provides the details of the co-operation between the two companies and the responsibility of the management agreement as regards staffing and operation of the fund, the management of the investment process and the control of the investments. The terms of the management agreement are generally comparable to international standards.

Particularly with respect to venture capital, governmental agencies such as Austria Economic Service GmbH (*Austria Wirtschaftsservice GmbH*) and the Austrian Research Promotion Agency (*Österreichische Forschungsförderungsgesellschaft*) have also developed sample investment contracts and syndication agreements. These agreements are generally based on, and contain, contractual structures and provisions typically used in other jurisdictions.

## 3. DEBT FINANCE
### 3.1 Means of Financing

As in other jurisdictions, private equity investors typically use debt financing in Austria-related mergers and acquisitions (M&A) transactions to reduce the required equity contribution and increase their potential return on their investments. Recently, the predominant position of commercial banks as providers of acquisition financing, typically structured as syndicated loans, is being challenged by direct lending funds. These funds, while typically charging interest at levels higher than banks do, have the advantage of being able to move faster than banks and offer greater flexibility in terms of leverage, structure, repayment terms. Additionally, most direct lending deals only involve one fund which helps to streamline communication between the borrower and the lender. Since most direct lending funds only provide term debt, such funds have been seen teaming up with banks who provide working capital and ancillary facilities.

While the number of direct lending fund deals in Austria has been relatively low so far given the size of the Austrian market, the minimum ticket size of most direct lending funds being EUR 50 million plus and some legal uncertainties, the rise of this new type of financing has been a Europe-wide phenomenon with Deloitte listing 361 European mid-market deals in its Alternative Lender Deal Tracker for 2017 versus just 145 in 2013 and constantly rising since then. Out of those 361 deals in 2017, 81% involved a private equity sponsor, 65% were related to M&A transactions and 82% were structured as first lien, showing the growing importance of direct lending funds for the private equity market.

While there is clear appetite for lending into Austria by direct lending funds, there are still uncertainties around the legal framework applicable to such transactions in Austria. Although private funds are generally regulated at a European level under the AIFM Directive, it was and—for Austria it still is—unclear whether the origination of loans is permitted by AIFs.

Since 2011, the European legislator gradually issued regulations on special forms of AIFs, designed to provide finance to the real economy (European venture capital funds—EuVECA, European social entrepreneurship funds—EuSEFs and European long-term investment funds—ELTIFs). These acts clarified that the granting of monetary loans (i.e. direct lending) constitutes an eligible investment by these special funds. Absent any European legislation on direct lending by AIFs regulated under the AIFM Directive, the European Securities and Markets Authority (ESMA) has taken steps to progress a common European framework for loan origination by investment funds (ESMA, "Opinion on Key principles for a European framework on loan origination by funds", ESMA/2016/596 (2016)).

In Austria, granting of loans (on a commercial basis) generally requires a banking licenses under the Austrian Banking Act (irrespective of whether the lender also engages in deposit taking). Unfortunately, and unlike in many other jurisdictions, neither the regulator has published its view on the admissibility of direct lending of AIFs nor did the legislature issued clarifying legislatives acts. Absent any official guidance by the FMA, it can, therefore, not be ruled out with certainty that lending by AIFs in Austria does not require a banking licence (irrespective of: (1) the mentioned developments on European level and other Member States that would provide arguments why AIFs should be permitted to lend in Austria without requiring a banking licence; and (2) the mentioned ESMA opinion that contains a country annex according to which loan origination by funds is allowed in Austria without stating further details on what basis such conclusion is drawn). Clarification could be sought on a case-by-case basis by asking for the regulator's view to avoid legal risk. Alternatively, careful structuring of the debt financing may avoid the business to be qualified as constituting banking business in Austria.

Lending without a licence may have severe legal consequences which include:

- in case of natural persons (including the respective legal representative of legal persons) administrative fines of up to EUR 5 million or of up to twice the amount of the benefit derived from the breach where that benefit can be determined;
- in case of legal persons administrative fines of up to 10% of the (consolidated group) total annual net turnover or of up to twice the amount of the benefit derived from the breach where that benefit can be determined;
- any agreement on remuneration, in particular interest and commissions, associated with those transactions is void (while the transaction as such remains valid); and
- suretyships (and other accessory security interests) and guarantees associated with banking transactions conducted without the required license are legally invalid.

## 3.2 Restrictions on granting security

In the case of Austrian limited liability companies, stock corporations and partnerships, with one of the foregoing acting solely as unlimited partner (each a limited liability entity) to provide security or other financial support or assume obligations for the benefit of their direct or indirect shareholders or affiliates, the Austrian capital maintenance rules are applicable. These rules prohibit a limited liability entity incorporated in Austria from disbursing its assets to its shareholders in circumstances other than (most importantly) as a distribution of profits, by a reduction of share capital or as liquidation surplus upon liquidation.

Guarantees, share pledges and any other collateral granted by a limited liability entity to guarantee or secure the liabilities of a direct or indirect shareholder or affiliate are considered disbursements under Austrian corporate law, and thus are invalid and unenforceable if the granting of the guarantees or security interests by the Austrian guarantor or security provider were not on arm's-length terms, or for that guarantor or security provider's corporate benefit (an overall group benefit is not sufficient).

To reduce the risk of violating the Austrian capital maintenance rules and the resulting invalidity and unenforceability of upstream and side-stream security, limitation language is commonly used according to which the secured parties agree to establish and enforce the collateral against the Austrian guarantor or security provider only to the extent that such establishment and enforcement do not result in a breach of the Austrian capital maintenance provisions. It should be noted that limitation language does not enhance the value of the upstream and side-stream security but ensures that the entire security interest is not void.

The legal ramifications set out above generally do not apply to the extent that an Austrian entity secures amounts owed by itself in its capacity as borrower under the finance documents or, under certain circumstances, amounts which are on-lent and outstanding.

According to the Austrian Stock Corporation Act 1937 (*Aktiengesetz* or AktG), any agreement relating to the granting of an advance payment or a loan, or to the granting of security by a joint stock corporation to another person for the purchase of shares in the corporation or parent company of this corporation, is invalid. In addition, collateral provided by the target stock corporation for acquisition indebtedness in general violates the Austrian capital maintenance rules. Further, based on the AktG, even in cases where the capital maintenance requirements would not be violated, the participation of the target company in any financing by way of providing security interests would violate the Austrian financial assistance rules. Contrary to the capital maintenance requirements, such violation would not render the transaction null and void but it would result, at a minimum, in the potential liability of the management.

### 3.3 Intercreditor issues

Austrian law does not restrict the subordination of claims. Typical intercreditor issues encountered in other jurisdictions are therefore not relevant for Austria.

### 3.4 Syndication

Few banks are willing to take the risk of carrying out bigger deals all by themselves.

The underlying documentation is usually based on international standard documentation, in particular the standards of the Loan Market Association (LMA).

## 4. EQUITY STRUCTURES
### 4.1 Role of management

In recent years, private equity transactions in which the management is offered the opportunity to acquire (minority) shares in the target have become more frequent. Such structures are based on practical considerations since the investor usually has a strong interest in ensuring management's loyalty and commitment, in particular if the investor lacks the knowledge relevant for operating the business of the company or if the name of a management member is usually linked to the target company.

### 4.2 Common protections for investors

Typical protection mechanisms for investors (which would typically be set out in a shareholders' agreement or in the articles of association, which are publicly available) include:
- thresholds for decisions in the shareholder's meeting aligned with the

investors' stake in the company;
- nomination and removal of the management board and the supervisory board;
- transfer restrictions for other shareholders (e.g. tag along rights, rights of first refusal pre-emptive rights and anti-dilution provisions in favour of the investor);
- investment guidelines in relation to capital expenditures;
- step-in or swamping rights granting the investor additional voting rights in certain default situations;
- certain other restrictions on the management activities, including provisions for conflicts of interest; and
- reporting duties of the management on a regular basis and information rights in favour of the investor.

In order to facilitate a potential exit from any investment, drag-along rights are frequently agreed upon.

## 4.3 Common protections for management

If the management is holding shares in the target, the following provisions protecting the management may frequently be agreed upon:
- tag-along rights (enabling management members to sell their shares at the same time and under the same conditions as the majority shareholder(s));
- veto rights concerning certain important decisions; and
- anti-dilution provisions primarily designed to prevent a squeeze-out of the management (pursuant to the Austrian Squeeze Out Act 2006 (*Gesellschafter-Ausschlussgesetz*) since a 90% shareholder in a limited liability company or stock corporation may decide on a squeeze-out of the minority shareholders.

In addition, management holding a minority interest in the company will usually try to protect their function as managing directors by adapting the respective provision in the target's articles of association and/or shareholder's agreement in order to prevent the management from being revoked without factual justification.

Notwithstanding the above, the shareholder rights of managers are usually bounded.

## 4.4 Management warranties

Management's warranties do not seem to be of particular importance in Austrian private equity transactions. However, private equity investors usually expect to receive a confirmation of the correctness and accuracy of representations and warranties both from the selling entity and the management.

## 4.5 Good leaver/bad leaver provisions

Typical good leaver provisions agreed upon in Austrian private equity transactions include in particular the following triggering events:
- retirement or death of the manager;
- (lasting) occupational disability of the manager;
- ordinary termination of the manager's employment contract by the

company;
- mutual termination of the manager's employment contract; and
- extraordinary termination of the manager's employment contract for good cause by the manager.

Typical bad leaver provisions include in particular the following triggering event:
- the opening of insolvency proceedings over the manager's estate;
- termination of the manager's employment contract for good cause by the company; and
- termination of the manager's employment contract by the manager other than for good cause.

Whereas the mutual option rights of a good leaver usually provide for the market value of the shares to be paid to the manager, a bad leaver will usually only receive the initial purchase price or even book value of the shares.

### 4.6 Public to private transactions

Public to private transactions are uncommon in Austria. However, increased interest in such transactions by internationally acting private equity investors has been seen very recently.

## 5. EXITS
### 5.1 Secondary sales

A secondary sale is an exit strategy whereby a private equity investor sells its shares held in a company to another private equity investor. There exist various reasons for a private equity investor to choose a secondary sale as exit strategy. In some cases, the private investor may no longer be willing to or simply cannot finance the company anymore but the company is not yet ready for a trade sale or an initial public offering (IPO). In other cases, the company reaches the next stage of its development, requiring a larger private equity investor with sufficient financial resources to fully exploit the potential of the developing business.

### 5.2 Trade sales

Another common exit strategy is the trade sale whereby a private equity investor sells its shares held in a company to a strategic investor (i.e. someone who is operating in the same industry as the company).

A trade sale may create higher revenues for the selling private equity investor than a secondary sale due to certain synergy effects which the acquisition may create for the buyer within the same industry sector. A disadvantage of a trade sale compared to a secondary sale may be seen in the potential know-how transfer to the potential buyer being a company's competitor during the buyer's due diligence exercise.

Both secondary sales and trade sales can be carried out rather fast, whereas realised gains are usually lower than in an IPO. Most exits in the Austrian market therefore take place in the form of secondary transactions or trade sales.

### 5.3 Initial public offerings

IPOs are the preferred exit strategy for private equity investors since there are good chances: (1) to achieve a fairly high revenue; and (2) that the target's management supports the IPO (as other exit strategies would create more uncertainty for the management regarding their future employment by the company). On the other hand, an IPO requires substantial preparation both in terms of time as well as costs and entails various liability issues in connection with the prospectus. Further, due to contractual lock up provisions, private equity investors may often only partially exit from the investment by way of an IPO. Even 10 years after the financial crisis, the statistics shows that the Vienna Stock Exchange has a low level of activity but, in 2017, BAWAG Group AG had a successful stock exchange listing.

### 5.4 Refinancings
#### Leveraged recapitalisation
A leveraged recapitalisation is an exit method whereby a company being held by a private equity investor issues new debt in order to repurchase its own shares from the private equity investor. The company raises the necessary capital by taking out a bank loan or by issuing bonds. Under Austrian law, the acquisition of own shares underlies very restrictive provisions and is possible for stock companies (*Aktiengesellschaften*) only. Such exit strategy is thus very uncommon in Austrian legal practice.

### 5.5 Restructuring/insolvency
#### Liquidation
A liquidation is often used as a last resort since the selling private equity investor does not benefit from the company's going concern value. The private equity investor decides either voluntarily, or becomes forced by insolvency proceedings, to terminate the company's business and liquidate the company subsequently. Rapidly expanding companies which are not able to come up with the necessary liquidity are exposed to a high risk of ending up in liquidation.

## 6. TAX
### General
Individuals having a domicile (*Wohnsitz*) or their habitual abode (*gewöhnlicher Aufenthalt*) in Austria are subject to income tax in Austria on their worldwide income. Individuals having neither a domicile nor their habitual abode in Austria are subject to income tax only on income from certain Austrian sources. Individual income tax is generally levied at progressive rates of currently up to 50% for annual income above EUR 90,000 and of up to 55% for annual income above EUR 1 million (the 55% maximum rate is designed to be applicable until 2020).

For certain types of income, such as specific types of income from investments (*Einkünfte aus Kapitalvermögen*), special tax rates and rules for the determination of profits and losses exist.

Corporations having their place of management (*Ort der Geschäftsleitung*) or their legal seat in Austria are subject to corporate income tax (*Körperschaftsteuer*) in Austria on their worldwide income. Corporations having neither their place of management nor their legal seat in Austria are subject to corporate income tax only on income from certain Austrian sources. Austrian corporate income tax is generally levied at a rate of 25%.

Both in case of unlimited and limited (corporate) income tax liability, Austria's right to tax may be restricted by double taxation treaties.

## 6.1 Taxation of fund structures
### Investment funds

Based on the Investment Funds Act (*InvestmentfondsG*) or the Real Estate Investment Funds Act (*Immobilien-InvestmentfondsG*) in combination with the Income Tax Act 1988 (*Einkommensteuergesetz*), a domestic investment fund (or real estate investment fund) generally is subject to a special tax law regime with the core feature that the investment fund itself is not considered a taxable entity and thus not subject to taxation. Rather, the respective income of the fund is allocated to the investors that are generally taxed at that level (according to the "transparency principle").

The special tax regime is applicable if an Austrian investment vehicle actually qualifies as an investment fund or as a real estate investment fund under regulatory law. If an Austrian investment vehicle does not qualify as an investment fund, the tax treatment follows the general tax rules applicable to the respective legal form (see the following points).

As regards a foreign investment vehicle, it is decisive whether it falls within the scope of the definition of a "foreign investment fund" in the sense of the Investment Funds Act (respectively as a foreign real estate investment fund in the sense of the Real Estate Investment Funds Act). In order to ensure that the general taxation regime of an investment fund is applicable also to a foreign investment fund, the management company has to ensure that the earnings of a fund are correctly reported to the *Oesterreichische Kontrollbank*. Otherwise, a less favourable tax treatment would apply.

### Middle-Class Investment Companies (Mittelstandsfinanzierungsgesellschaften—MFGs)

After the preferential tax regime for Middle-Class Investment Stock Companies (*Mittelstandsfinanzierungsaktiengesellschaften*—MFAGs) was abolished following a ruling of the European Commission and after the subsequently issued tax regime for Middle-Class Investment Companies (*Mittelstandsfinanzierungsgesellschaften*—MFGs) ended on 31 December 2013, the Austrian legislator in summer 2017 enacted the Middle-Class Investment Companies Act 2017 (*Mittelstandsfinanzierungsgesellschaftengesetz* 2017) with which a new version of the known Middle-Class Investment Company was introduced.

Under certain requirements (at the level of the MFGs and the target), the new regime grants tax benefits to the investors in the MFGs (e.g. dividends from MFGs up to EUR 15,000 per year are tax exempt for individual investors) and the MFGs (e.g. capital gains from certain investments are tax exempt from corporate income tax).

The new provisions seek to give advantages to small and medium-sized businesses in their foundation and growth stadium. However, the Austrian Government notified the new rules as state aid with the European Commission. The new rules coming into effect, therefore, depends on the Commission's approval which has not yet been given.

## Corporations

Investment vehicles organised in the form of a private limited company or stock corporation are liable to corporate income tax at a flat tax rate of 25%, provided that a minimum annual corporate income tax in the amount of EUR 1,750 for private limited companies (with certain exceptions and reductions for newly established corporations) and in the amount of EUR 3,500 for stock corporations has to be paid if the regular corporate income tax is below such amounts. Austrian corporate tax law provides under certain conditions (e.g. parent company must own directly or indirectly more than 50% of the shares in the subsidiaries) for the possibility for two (or more) companies to form a tax group. In case of a tax group, all of the taxable results (profits and losses) of the domestic group members as well as losses of foreign subsidiaries are attributed to their respective parent, respectively the group parent. Losses of foreign group members are only attributable to the extent of 75% of the profit of all domestic group members only in the proportion of the shareholding quota in the foreign group member. They are further subject to recapture taxation at the time they are utilised by foreign subsidiary in the source state or in the moment the group member withdraws from the Austrian tax group.

Dividends distributed by an Austrian corporation are generally subject to withholding tax at a rate of 27.5% in case of distributions to individuals and of 25% in case of distributions to corporations. Dividends distributed to beneficial owners which are domestic or EU corporations (or corporations in certain European Economic Area (EEA) Member States) may be exempt from such withholding taxation (depending on the level of the shareholding and the holding period, either no withholding tax must be levied by the corporation at all, or the withholding tax must in a first step be levied, but is then credited against the corporate income tax burden of the shareholder, respectively refunded to the corporate shareholder upon request). Certain conditions and anti-abuse provisions apply. For dividend distributions to non-resident individuals and corporations, withholding tax reductions or exemptions might further be available under applicable tax treaties.

At the level of an individual shareholder, no additional income tax is levied over and above the 27.5% withholding tax levied by the amount of tax withheld (final taxation). The aggregate tax burden of profits earned by an Austrian corporation which are then distributed to an Austrian individual shareholder thus typically amounts to 45.63%.

Increases in value in the shares realizsd by the individual shareholder, such as, in particular, capital gains realised upon an alienation of shares or increases in value upon an exit of the shareholder from Austria under certain conditions are generally also subject to a special 27.5% income tax rate, unless the shareholder holds the shares as business assets and the realisation of capital gains is the main focus of such shareholder's business activity. In case of a corporation as shareholder, dividends are generally excluded from the tax base at the corporate shareholder's level. This exemption provision applies to dividends only, not to capital gains which generally are taxable if realised on the shares in an Austrian company. Capital gains realised on the shares in qualifying foreign participations might be exempt under the international participation exemption regime, subject to certain conditions.

## Partnerships

Taxation of partnerships (i.e. general partnerships or limited partnerships) does not take place at the partnership's level but at the level of the general and limited partners of the partnership only (transparency principle).

Certain differences in the tax treatment of the derived income may arise depending on whether the partnership is considered to be carrying out commercial activities (*gewerbliche Tätigkeiten*) or as merely carrying out passive asset management (*Vermögensverwaltung*). The classification of the investment vehicle depends on the individual circumstances and structuring of the partnership. Typical restructurings as well as the leveraging of transactions would, however, be considered as an indicator for commercial activities. Such distinction generally is made on the basis of the partnership's activity and does not depend on whether or not a corporation acts as general partner.

Accordingly, income from mere asset management partnerships is deemed to be income from those assets the partnership is managing. For example, dividend income from shares held by the partnership would be qualified as income from investments (*Einkünfte aus Kapitalvermögen*). Income derived from partnerships carrying out commercial activities is deemed to be income from an active trade or business (*Einkünfte aus Gewerbebetrieb*). This difference might, in particular, be relevant for the tax treatment of potential losses due to the partnerships activity.

## Silent partnerships

Silent partnerships are non-corporate legal forms in which an individual or a corporation makes a contribution in cash or in kind to the commercial enterprise of another person.

The silent partnership will not be entered into the commercial register and not disclosed to the public (except for a general disclosure in the annex to the financial statements). The commercial code only contains basic rules and grants considerable leeway for silent partnerships.

For tax purposes, one has to distinguish between typical silent partnerships (*typische stille Gesellschaft*) and atypical silent partnerships (*atypische stille Gesellschaft*).

The typical silent partner only participates in the profits of the company and does not take part in the management or representation of the company, whereas the atypical silent partner also participates in the value of the company.

From a tax point of view, silent partnerships may be compared with the partnership since taxation takes place in the asset of the investors instead at the fund level. Revenues from atypical silent partnerships may be classified as income from commercial activities (*Einkünfte aus Gewerbebetrieb*), whereas revenues from typical silent partnerships generally generate investment income (*Einkünfte aus Kapitalvermögen*). Income from silent partnerships (regardless of the qualification as typical or atypical) derived by an individual is generally subject to income tax at the regular progressive tax rates of up to 55% (and not to a special tax rate of 27.5%).

## 6.2 Carried interest

The tax treatment of carried interest depends on the structure of the respective model. Generally, all benefits received by an employee from its employment contract are, for Austrian tax purposes, treated as income which is taxed at a progressive rate of up to 55%. This applies to both monetary benefits, such as regular cash remuneration, and non-monetary benefits, such as the free or discounted issuance of shares. However, a qualification as income from capital, taxed at the special rate of 27.5%, might, under certain circumstances, be possible.

In this context, Austrian tax law provides for certain disallowances of tax deductibility which apply to management salaries and golden handshakes. Generally, the amount of salary exceeding EUR 500,000 per year is not deductible.

## 6.3 Management equity

The benefit from a free or discounted attribution of equity to employees, which generally would constitute taxable income from employment (see ss.6: "General" and 6.2 above), is, under specific circumstances, exempt from taxation up to a maximum amount of currently EUR 3,000 per year.

Under certain circumstances, the tax authorities may requalify payments intentionally made in connection with management equity, which is in the most cases taxed at the special rate of 27.5%, as income from employment taxed at the progressive rate of up to 55%. Conversely, if a manager holds a stake in a capital corporation or a limited partnership with a corporation as general partner, a consideration paid by the company to the manager which exceeds arm's-length terms could be considered as illegal repayment of capital as well as a hidden distribution of dividends.

## 6.4 Loan interest

Interest from loans granted by the investment vehicle is subject to personal or corporate income tax according to the general principles of taxation as described above.

However, interest payments to shareholders or parties related to shareholders are subject to arm's-length standards. Therefore, interest charged at excessively high rates on loans granted by shareholders or affiliates may (partly) constitute an illegal repayment of capital as well as a hidden profit distribution. If the shareholder is an individual, interest from granting loans would be taxed at the regular progressive income tax rates of up to 55% as, in the case of income from loans not subject to a banking transaction (*Bankgeschäft*), the special tax rate of 27.5% is not applicable.

## 6.5 Transaction taxes

A transfer of shares is not subject to transaction taxes under the Austrian tax regime. Further, capital duty has been abolished as per 1 January 2016. However, stamp duty (*Rechtsgeschäftsgebühr*) could be triggered in a transaction environment.

Stamp duty pursuant to the Austrian Stamp Duty Act 1957 (*Gebührengesetz*) is linked to the private law qualification of agreements. The following types of agreements, among others, are subject to stamp duty if certain conditions are fulfilled: tenancy agreements for business purposes; assignments (other than in the course of factoring arrangements); suretyship agreements; accessions to debt agreements; mortgages; and settlement agreements.

The stamp duty on loan financings, whether by shareholders or external financing entities, has already been abolished as per 1 January 2011.

Austrian stamp duty is generally only triggered if a document evidencing a dutiable transaction is either:

(1)  established in Austria;

(2)  established outside of Austria but all parties to the dutiable transaction are Austrian residents for stamp duty purposes (i.e. having a place of management, a representative office, a permanent establishment or a branch in Austria) and either: (a) the transaction concerns an asset located in Austria; or (b) one or more of the parties is entitled or obliged to fulfil its obligations in Austria (e.g. payment of the purchase price, notification of an Austrian debtor etc); or

(3)  established outside of Austria but the document is brought into Austria and either: (a) the transaction concerns an asset located in Austria; (b) one or more of the parties is entitled or obliged to fulfil its obligations in Austria (e.g. payment of the purchase price, notification of an Austrian debtor etc); (c) on the basis of the agreement, legally relevant acts are undertaken in Austria; or (d) it is used before a public authority in Austria.

A stamp duty sensitive document evidencing a dutiable transaction might not only be the agreement regarding the transaction itself (or a certified copy thereof) but any documentation (e.g. written confirmations, notifications, reports, protocols, correspondence (including e-mails and facsimile messages), notices etc) which contains certain information about the dutiable transaction, potentially even if it is only signed by one of the parties to the transaction.

## 7.  CURRENT TOPICAL ISSUES/TRENDS

In legal practice, the use of insurance in M&A transactions is gaining popularity among deal professionals in Austria. Influenced by an increasing popularity in other prominent jurisdictions, the number of private equity transactions involving warranty and indemnity (W&I) insurance also increased significantly in Austria. Most popular in auction sales and private equity secondary transactions to bridge the gap between the seller and the buyer on what gets indemnified, the length of time the seller will be liable and, of course, the maximum cap amount that can be recovered by the purchaser, such W&I insurance is also seen stapled in auction sales, i.e. the seller already provides for a specific W&I insurance in the auction process and the purchaser, to remain competitive, must assume such W&I insurance during the process and include it in its offer. The little flexibility remaining for the purchaser concerns the insurance amount as the seller will only accept a very limited (symbolic) cap amount for liability vis-à-vis the purchaser.

Due to the increasing complexity of the regulatory framework for financial institutions, many banking institutions have decreased their investment activities, leaving a gap which cannot be (entirely) closed by private equity investors. In combination with the lack of a suitable legal framework, a considerable decrease in private equity investments has been noticeable despite continuous lobbying activities encouraging the development of a suitable legal basis. After federal elections in 2017, however, the new Austrian Government declared in its government programme (which has political rather than legal relevance) its intention to strengthen the private equity sector as a part of its strategy to bolster the economic position of Austria. Vienna—as Austria's economic centre—thrives to position itself as a hub for Central and Eastern Europe (CEE) private equity activity.[1] For example, Vienna hosts the 0100 conference each year, which is a one-day event covering the range from venture capital and growth capital to buyouts and secondary transactions.

---

[1]  *Zusammen: Für unser Österreich—Regierungsprogramm 2017–2022* available at: *https://www.oevp.at/download/Regierungsprogramm.pdf* [Accessed 26 September 2018].

# Belgium

**Loyens & Loeff CVBA/SCRL** Wim Vande Velde & Henri Nelen[1]

## 1.  MARKET OVERVIEW
### 1.1  Types of investors
Private equity funds in Belgium are funded by traditional players such as:
- corporate investors (it should be noted, however, that Belgian private equity funds have a funding handicap compared with other European markets due to the very limited Belgian pension funds industry);
- banks;
- funds of funds;
- government agencies; and
- private individuals.

Recent years have shown a trend whereby wealthy individuals and/or wealthy families set up new investments funds or family offices.

The traditional players on the venture capital market are, furthermore, seeing more and more competition from university incubators and funds (both private and government sponsored) as well as business angels (although their investments are smaller).

### 1.2  Types of investments
Belgian private equity funds have been and are active in all traditional transaction types, both domestic and abroad:
- venture capital/seed capital transactions;
- growth capital; and
- buyout capital.

Compared with other European countries, Belgian private equity funds invest more in venture capital and growth capital and less in buyouts. The Belgian venture capital sector experienced intensive years in 2016 and 2017, with increased investments by both traditional venture capital players and wealthy individuals/families (some of them forming new investment funds, such as the new EUR 250 million fund Smile Invest, founded by several wealthy individuals and focused on growth companies). Past investments mainly consisted of seed and growth capital investments, with a focus on the life sciences/biotech, manufacturing and ICT sectors. One of the most notable venture capital transactions in 2017/18 was the USD 58 million (follow-up) investment by Iconiq Capital and Battery Ventures in the Belgium based enterprise data governance specialist Collibra NV.

Belgium has always seen relatively little buyout activity compared with

---

[1]  The authors gratefully acknowledge the assistance of Marc Dhaene, Linda Brosens, Eveline Hellebuyck, Robbert Jacobs and Véronique Van Eessel.

**19**

other European countries. Big buyouts of Belgian companies were mostly done by foreign private equity funds (UK and US but also, and increasingly, Dutch, French and Asian).

In terms of exit transactions, trade sales, secondary sales and, to a lesser extent, management buyouts remain popular. Compared to previous years, the Belgian mergers and acquisitions (M&A) market offered more investment and exit opportunities.

## 2. FUNDS
### 2.1 Fund structures
In Belgium, vehicles for private equity funds are usually structured as:
- a silent partnership (*gewone commanditaire vennootschap/société en commandite simple*—Comm.V/SCS);
- a partnership limited by shares (*commanditaire vennootschap op aandelen/ société en commandite par actions*—Comm.VA/SCA); or
- a (public) limited liability company (*naamloze vennootschap/société anonyme*—NV/SA);

(or a combination of the above forms if a "chain" of investment vehicles is used, which is seldom the case in Belgium).

The most commonly used structure is a (public) limited liability company directly owning the portfolio investments. However, when the concentration of the control in the hand of the founders/funds' managers is an important issue, the silent partnership and partnership limited by shares can prove to be valuable alternatives as they allow replication of the often used distinction between "general" and "limited" partners.

The above vehicles are only subject to the provisions of the Belgian Companies Code and are, as such, "unregulated".

In order to further and attract private investment activities in Belgium, the Government has set up regulated vehicles specifically aimed at facilitating the investment in private companies. These "regulated" vehicles are generally derived from any of the three aforementioned forms of companies, to which specific requirements or features are added. One of these vehicles is the Private PRICAF (private closed-ended undertaking for collective investment (UCI)—*private privak/pricaf privée*), which is a closed-ended vehicle that enjoys a specific tax treatment akin to a "look through" for the investors. Due to the burden (although limited) resulting from its regulated status, it is not widely used.

### 2.2 Regulation of fundraising and fund managers
Generally, private equity funds can be freely marketed and operated in Belgium.

In respect of fundraising, most players ensure that they do not fall into the "public" field by relying on the easily available safe harbours provided by Belgian legislation (which is based on the European directives regarding the public offering of securities). As a result, they do not have to issue a prospectus approved by the Belgian Financial Services and Markets Authority (FSMA), the financial markets regulator, when attracting funds (although the market practice is to circulate to targeted investors an offering memorandum or similar circular, the content of which is broadly the same as what would be found in a prospectus) and do not need to be authorised.

Those safe harbours are mainly provided in the Prospectus Directive.[2] Hence, fundraising is not subject to scrutiny when it: (1) is not made public (no general advertisement or promotion); (2) is limited to qualified investors/ less than 150 non-qualified investors per European Economic Area (EEA) Member State; (3) requires a participation with a nominal value of at least EUR 100,000[3]; or (4) involves a consideration payable per investor at least equal to EUR 100,000.[4]

In respect of the funds' management, the Belgian Law of 19 April 2014 on Alternative investment funds and their managers (AIFM Law) requires the authorisation of a (Belgian) management company as an alternative investment fund manager (AIFM), if such management company exceeds the thresholds provided for in art.3(2) of the AIFM Directive.[5] Management companies that do not exceed the aforementioned thresholds (small AIFMs) are subject to "notification" (instead of "authorisation"). Contrary to what is the case for authorisation, notification does not entail the obligation to comply with certain capital and organisational requirements.

As long as the marketing of the fund stays within the limits of the above-mentioned safe harbours,[6] the fund itself, whether managed by a threshold or a small AIFM, will remain unregulated. This is, however, without prejudice to Regulation 1286/2014 on key information documents for packaged retail and insurance-based investment products (PRIIPs) [2014] OJ L 352/1 (PRIIPs Regulation) which imposes the issuance of a key information document (KID) in case a fund is marketed to retail investors (even though such marketing, on the basis of the above-mentioned safe harbours, does not constitute a public offer).

For unregulated funds, the most common forms of Belgian management vehicles are the (public) limited liability company and the private limited liability company (*besloten vennootschap met beperkte aansprakelijkheid/société privée à responsabilité limitée*—BVBA/SPRL).

For regulated funds, applicable legislation usually imposes the use of a (public) limited liability company with a set share capital (higher than the minimum provided for in the Belgian Companies Code). Furthermore, the investment fund's managers must be authorised by the competent regulator before they can start (publicly) attracting investments in the regulated vehicles (a similar requirement exists for self-managed regulated funds). Managers of regulated funds (whether publicly offered or not) that can be considered to constitute alternative investment funds (AIFs) (i.e. all funds that are not

---

2   Directive 2003/71 on the prospectus to be published when securities are offered to the public or admitted to trading and amending Directive 2001/34 [2003] OJ L345/64.

3   This safe harbour is not available to open-ended funds.

4   For open-ended funds, the threshold for this safe harbor is EUR 250,000. For the sake of completeness, we note that offers with a total consideration of less than EUR 100,000 in the EEA are equally not considered public.

5   Directive 2011/61 on Alternative Investment Fund Managers and amending Directives 2003/41 and 2009/65 and Regulations 1060/2009 and 1095/2010 [2011] OJ L174/1.

6   Or the fund does not voluntarily choose to adopt one of the forms specifically designed to accommodate non-public funds investing in, e.g. private companies, such as the Private PICAF (see above).

authorised under the UCITS Directive)[7] are, in addition, subject to the aforementioned AIFM Law.

The use of other intermediaries (providing investment advice services or related investment services) to attract public investments is subject to the general applicable Belgian and European financial regulations (which, in a nutshell, require such intermediaries to be licensed before becoming active on the Belgian market or to provide services on the basis of their European passport).

### 2.3 Customary or common terms of funds

*Carried interest*: incentive and/or performance fees (upon the winding-up of the fund or at an earlier stage) in the form of the balance of distributable profits allocated to a predefined category of securities holders (often the managers of the fund(s)) provided a certain profitability target (often expressed by using a reference rate of return, so-called "hurdle rate") has been reached (and subject to the availability of net assets for that distribution).

*Catch-up*: amount representing the carried interest owed to the predefined category of securities holders once the hurdle rate is achieved.

*Hurdle rate*: reference rate (also called "preferred rate") of return on investment to be achieved before carried interests or another form of incentive become owed to the predefined category of securities holders. (Other key terms are also often used in private equity funds documentation but are as such not specific to the private equity funds industry, e.g. entrance/management/success fee, good/bad leaver, clawback, manager's commitment (amount of the management's stake in the investment vehicle), investment period, exit etc.)

## 3. DEBT FINANCE

### 3.1 Means of financing

In Belgium, private equity-backed vehicles usually obtain financing through a traditional secured term loan facility. Typical structures often involve mezzanine investors.

Instruments often used to attract equity investors include (subordinated) (convertible) bond loans, preference shares, profit certificates and warrants ("equity kickers").

The public issuance of high yield bonds solely on the Belgian market is seen but high-yield bonds are usually issued on larger markets.

### 3.2 Restrictions on granting security

According to Belgian company law, a company may only enter into transactions which are in line with its corporate purpose (as set out in its articles of association) and in its corporate interest.

The purpose clause of Belgian companies does not always expressly or implicitly allow the company to grant security or a guarantee to secure other group companies' obligations. Financing banks will therefore typically review the company's corporate purpose and regularly ask the company to amend its

---

[7] Directive 2009/65 on the coordination of laws, regulations and administrative provisions relating to undertakings for collective investment in transferable securities (UCITS) [2009] OJ L302/32.

corporate purpose to avoid any doubt.

In addition, it must be assessed whether or not a transaction is in the corporate interest of a company. This assessment is largely dependent on factual matters and any decision in this regard rests with the board of managers of the company.

The following three elements may be taken into consideration:

(1)  the security should be given for a limited period of time and should be within the financial capacities of the company;

(2)  the company should derive an actual and certain direct or indirect benefit from the transaction (the common social, economic or financial group interest can be one of the considerations in this respect); and

(3)  the benefits compared with the risks may not be disproportionate.

A security found not to satisfy the corporate interest requirement may result in civil and criminal disciplinary liabilities for the directors of the company. If the financing bank was aware (or should have been aware) that the security was granted against the corporate interest of the company, the security could be declared null and void.

Finally, a Belgian limited liability company is prohibited from engaging in financial assistance (i.e. the granting of security, loans or other means with a view to the acquisition of its shares by a third party) unless a strict procedure and a number of conditions are met. This procedure and the conditions include, without being exhaustive:

• a transaction at fair market conditions, taking into account the financial situation of the parties involved;

• approval by a qualified majority of the shareholders' meeting;

• special reporting by the board of directors in relation to the company's interest; and

• the net assets may not fall below the amount of paid-up share capital (increased with the unavailable reserves) due to the financial assistance which is granted.

In practice, this procedure is not applied frequently, since less stringent alternatives (in particular in the framework of a "debt pushdown") are conceivable and have been tried in the past.

Some examples of such alternatives are:

• the purchase of own shares by the target company prior to the sale;

• upstreaming of (available or borrowed) funds from the target company to the acquiring entity by performing a capital reduction or by distributing a (super) dividend;

• downstream or upstream merger between the acquiring company and the target company;

• the conversion of loans at the level of the acquiring company to loans at the level of the target company (at more interesting terms and conditions);

• performing an asset deal instead of a share deal (as the prohibition on financial assistance only targets the transfer of shares); and

• granting a pledge over the acquired shares in the target company.

Which alternative could be used will largely depend on the factual circumstances and the tax treatment of the transaction. Legal restraints (such as the financial assistance and corporate interest requirements) will need to be taken into account as well.

When considering the upstreaming of funds, one should therefore take into account the judgment of the Court of Appeal of Ghent of 11 April 2005, in which the security granted by a target company to secure a loan destined to finance a dividend distribution in order to allow the shareholder to repay its acquisition debt (incurred upon the acquisition of the target company), was held null and void as it would constitute an unlawful financial assistance (pursuant to the applicable rules at such time). This verdict was, however, mitigated by more recent case law (from the Court of Appeal of Mons of 16 April 2012 as well as the Belgian Supreme Court of 30 January 2015).

Furthermore, upon considering any of the above alternatives, one should always take into account the corporate interest of the target company.

### 3.3 Intercreditor issues

The Belgian rules relating to the establishment of the "ranking of creditors" in bankruptcy proceedings (*faillite/faillissement*) are quite complicated. As a general outline, one can distinguish the following ranking rules:

- costs and indebtedness incurred by the receiver during the bankruptcy (including liquidator's/receiver's salary), the "estate debts" (*dettes de la masse/schulden van de massa*) have, as a rule, the highest priority over all privileged (or secured) and unsecured claims (i.e. the so-called super priority creditors). If the receiver has contributed to the realisation and enforcement of the assets pledged (e.g. a pledge over shares or pledge over receivables) and has incurred costs in this respect, then the receiver is a super priority creditor for such costs. These costs will be paid to the receiver in priority out of the proceeds of the realised assets before distributing the remainder of the proceeds to the secured lenders:

  — security interests, e.g. a pledge or mortgage. Creditors that hold a security interest have a priority right over the secured asset (whether by means of appropriation of the asset or on the proceeds upon realisation). A prior pledge or mortgage will, in principle, rank ahead of a more recent pledge or mortgage;

  — privileges on all or certain assets including, e.g. tax, social security and employee privileges. Privileges on specific assets rank before privileges on all assets of the debtor. Certain privileges prevail over the security interests; and

- once all "estate debts" have been satisfied, and all creditors having the benefit of a security or privilege have been satisfied, the proceeds of the remaining assets will be distributed by the receiver amongst unsecured creditors who rank pari passu.

In principle, a receivable for the payment of monies (whether for principal amounts or interest) under a loan or credit facility agreement ranks pari passu with the receivables of other creditors, unless the creditor of such receivables has in any way agreed to be subordinated. Hence, the receivables under shareholders' loans or mezzanine debt are usually contractually subordinated to the receivables of the providers of senior debt finance (typically under a subordination agreement or intercreditor agreement).

## 3.4 Syndication

In Belgium, loans are syndicated either before or after the deal is done.

As to post-closing syndication, the key issue is establishing a method of transfer of the loan which will not require any formalities or extra costs and will result in the new lenders being secured in exactly the same way as if they had been original signatories to the loan.

As a general principle of Belgian law, a security is accessory to the claim it secures and, in case of a transfer of the secured claim, the security will automatically follow. However, according to art.5 of the Belgian Mortgage Act 1851, a transfer of mortgage-backed receivables requires the taking of a marginal note (*kantmelding/note marginale*) in the records of the mortgage register mentioning the assignment (in order to make the assignment of the mortgage-backed receivables effective and enforceable against third parties). Such formality triggers 1% registration duty on the amount of the transferred receivables which are secured by the mortgage. The Law of 3 August 2012 (on Certain forms of collective management of investment portfolios) on certain measures simplifying the mobilisation of receivables in the financial sector has included several exceptions to the rule requiring a marginal note when transferring mortgage-backed receivables. Transfers between non-EEA credit institutions will arguably still fall outside these exceptions.

Furthermore, recent legislation has introduced the concept of a security agent (which already existed for financial instruments and cash) into Belgian law. As of 1 January 2018, security on movables can thus be vested in favour of a security agent and it will, in principle, no longer be required for each original lender to be a party to the security agreement.

No such concept exists for real estate. Nevertheless, it is largely accepted in Belgium that multiple lenders can benefit from a mortgage through a parallel debt structure.

In a parallel debt structure, the borrower owes two debts:
(1)  the principal debt owed to the lenders; and
(2)  a separate debt for the same amount, owed to the security agent.

Any payment under the principal debt reduces the parallel debt for the same amount and vice versa. The mortgage only secures the parallel debt, which means that the security agent is the only beneficiary of the mortgage. Upon a transfer by a lender of its rights under the loan, art.5 of the Mortgage Act does not apply since the parallel debt (and therefore, the mortgage) remains with the security agent.

### Alternative means of financing

In addition to the more traditional means of financing referenced under s.3.1 above, private-equity-backed vehicles have a range of alternative means of financing to resort to. These alternatives notably include asset-based financing structures, such as borrowing-base lending, securitisation and factoring.

With the entry into force in 2018 of the Pledge Act of 11 July 2013, the setting up of asset-based financing structures has been simplified with, among others, the introduction of a register pledge. Under the old regime, the pledgor was required to relinquish possession of the pledged goods to the pledgee. The new rules allow the pledgor to remain in possession of the collateral, thus enabling them to continue operating their business. This widely welcomed reform is therefore expected to boost asset-based financing structures in the Belgian market.

The feasibility of securitisation of receivables of the investee company will depend on its assets/activities (which must have at least a constant and reliable cash flow in volumes large enough to ensure that the securitisation is profitable).

Factoring by the investee company (i.e. a financial transaction whereby a business sells its accounts receivable to a third party at a discount in exchange for immediate money with which to finance continued business) is another alternative but also depends on its assets/activities. Factoring is generally used to provide working capital to the company.

## 4. EQUITY STRUCTURES
### 4.1 Role of management

On the Belgian market, which is characterised by a large amount of small and medium sized (often family-owned) companies, management often already holds shares in the company in which the private equity fund invests and is usually already represented on the board of directors.

Management often does not have an employment agreement with the company but has a management agreement (allowing them to provide services to the company as independent workers instead of as an employee), often through their own management company.

Non-compete, non-solicitation and confidentiality clauses are typically clauses which a private equity fund will pay particular attention to (and, if absent, will want to be included in the management or employment agreement of key management). With respect to non-compete undertakings, the difference between an employment agreement and a management agreement is important. A non-compete undertaking in an employment agreement:

- may, in principle, not exceed 12 months (although exceptions are possible for companies with research and development (R&D) activities or companies conducting an international business);
- must be geographically limited to the territory where the employee can actually compete with the company (without exceeding Belgium) (although exceptions are possible for companies with R&D activities or companies conducting an international business);
- must be limited to activities which are similar to those performed by the employee; and
- must provide for a one-off payment to the employee equal to their salary during half of the period covered by the non-compete clause.

The company will not be able to invoke the non-compete clause if it terminates the employment agreement without good cause or if the employee terminates the agreement for good cause. Again, exceptions are possible for companies with R&D activities or companies conducting an international business.

In management agreements, the conditions for the validity of a non-compete undertaking are less stringent. However, to be valid, the scope of the non-compete clause in a management agreement (in terms of activities concerned, geographical scope and duration) will have to be clearly and reasonably drafted. If the scope is considered too large, the non-compete clause can be declared null and void.

The notice periods/termination payments (including "golden parachutes", if any) will also be a point of attention. For employees, the notice periods/termination payments will be determined in accordance with Belgian employment law, which, in practice, leads to rather long notice periods/high termination payments. For management agreements, parties can freely determine the notice periods and termination payments.

Especially in case of venture capital and growth capital transactions, management will often already own shares in the company at the time of the private equity investment. The private equity fund will typically subscribe to a capital increase of the company and will, in return, receive shares granting them a preferred right on dividends/liquidation proceeds, presence and veto right for key decisions at the level of the board of directors and/or veto rights at the level of the shareholders' meeting.

In the case of buyouts, management will often be encouraged to invest in the equity of the investment vehicle. Technically, management's investment in the investment vehicle can be structured in different ways:
- allocation of ordinary shares: Belgian corporate law offers great flexibility as to the rights that can be attached to different classes of ordinary shares. Hence, it is possible to grant different classes of shares in the investment vehicle to the private equity fund on the one hand and to management on the other hand; or
- allocation of other types of securities: such as warrants, certificates, bonds or granting of share options.

In order to encourage management to invest as much as possible, the cost of capital for management will often be lower than for the private equity fund ("envy factor" or "sweet equity"). Management can, furthermore, be incentivised by granting them a right to acquire additional shares if certain operational thresholds are met (ratchet). Such ratchet mechanisms are often structured through call options or warrants (exercisable if the thresholds are met).

## 4.2  Common protections for investors

Private equity funds acting as minority shareholder in a company usually try to protect their investment by obtaining control, or at least influence, over the company. Traditionally, this is done by providing for the following rights in the subscription and/or shareholders' agreement:
- right to information (periodic reporting): it should be noted that directors of a company are required by law to always act in the best interest of the company: directors may therefore not be able to comply with far-reaching information covenants requested by shareholders if these covenants conflict with the company's best interest;
- right to have one or more representatives appointed to the board of directors: as mentioned above, it should be noted that these directors will, however, be required to act in the best interest of the company at all

times; and

- right to be consulted about and/or veto certain decisions to be taken by the board of directors or the shareholders' meeting.

In order to further protect their investment, private equity funds should also include certain "exit clauses" relating to the transfer of shares in the company. The exit clauses mostly used in Belgian companies are the following:

- standstill provisions prohibiting the transfer of shares by the management: these must be limited in time and, at all times, in the company's corporate interest;
- right of first refusal: whereby a shareholder wishing to transfer all or part of its shares to a third party is obliged to first offer these shares to the private equity fund on the same conditions offered to the third party. It should be noted that, in (public) limited liability companies, such clauses may not prevent/delay the transfer of the shares for more than six months;
- drag-along clauses: whereby a private equity fund selling its shares can force the other shareholders to sell their shares to the same purchaser on the same conditions;
- tag-along clauses: whereby, in case the other shareholder(s) sell its/their shares, the private equity fund has the right to sell its shares on the same conditions; and
- put options: whereby the private equity fund can force the other shareholders to buy its shares if certain conditions are fulfilled or a certain period of time has passed, at a predetermined price.

In working out investors' protection clauses, art.32 of the Belgian Companies Code should always be taken into account. According to this article, any clause whereby the contribution of a shareholder is shielded against all losses (or whereby all benefits are allocated to a single shareholder) shall be considered null and void ("leonine pact"). This provision casts a doubt on the validity of put options whereby a private equity fund is granted the right to sell its shares at a price at least equal to its initial contribution (although recent case law somewhat limits the scope of art.32 in relation to put options).

## 4.3 Common protections for management

If management holds a minority interest in the investment vehicle, its most common protections relate to:

- the right to have one or more representatives appointed at the level of the board of directors;
- veto or co-decision rights with respect to certain key decisions to be taken by the board of directors and/or the shareholders' meeting; and
- the right to sell their shares in case of an exit by the private equity fund (tag-along right) or in case of termination of their employment agreement (good leaver/bad leaver clause; usually also requested by the private equity fund).

In specific cases, management is sometimes also granted anti-dilution protection through various mechanisms (e.g. anti-dilution warrants).

### 4.4 Management warranties

If private equity funds invest through the: (1) subscription of shares issued in the framework of a capital increase; or (2) acquisition of existing shares, warranties will be requested from the other shareholders (in case of capital increase) or the selling shareholders (in case of a transfer of shares). As mentioned above, these other shareholders will often (especially in the case of small and medium-sized companies) include management.

Such warranties have the same scope as warranties in a normal M&A transaction (title to shares, correctness of annual accounts, compliance with tax and legal obligations, correctness of the information provided to the investor during negotiations). The warranties are usually for a period between 18 and 24 months, except for tax warranties (often aligned on the statute of limitation) and, sometimes, environmental warranties (up to five or 10 years).

They are, furthermore, nearly always subject to further limitations such as a de minimis (usually between 0.5% and 1% of the investment amount) and a maximum liability cap. The maximum liability cap is usually around 30% of the investment amount for transactions up to EUR 10 million and around 15% for transactions exceeding EUR 10 million.

Specific warranties from management in the framework of a private equity investment are rather uncommon in Belgium.

### 4.5 Good leaver/bad leaver provisions

If management participates in the investment vehicle (through shares or other securities), it is common practice to provide for "good leaver/bad leaver" provisions in their participation agreement (and/or management agreement) obliging them to transfer their participation in case of (early) departure. The exit conditions (most notably the consideration) will of course be more favourable for a "good leaver" than for a "bad leaver".

Key elements in these "good leaver/bad leaver clauses" are:

- the definition of "good leaver" (e.g. illness, dismissal without cause) and "bad leaver" (e.g. voluntary resignation, dismissal for cause);
- the exercise price: in this respect, it should be noted that, under Belgian law, "good leaver/bad leaver clauses" will only be valid to the extent the exercise price is determined in the agreement or is at least determinable (without further negotiation between parties being required) on the basis of the contractual provisions; and
- the exercise conditions: e.g. obligation to exercise options immediately upon leaving the company or possibility for a good leaver to sell at a later stage; and the right of first refusal for other management members to acquire the participation of the good leaver/bad leaver.

### 4.6 Public to private transactions

Although Belgium has seen a number of public to private transactions, such operations remain very unusual in the Belgian private equity market.

In case of a public to private transaction, the key issues which must be taken into account relate to:

- the Belgian regulations on (voluntary or mandatory) takeover bids;
- the Belgian regulations on squeeze-outs (allowing a shareholder owning at least 95% of the shares of a listed company to force the remaining

shareholders to sell their shares); and

- the obligation to treat all shareholders equally (to be taken into account in the due diligence process).

## 5. EXITS
### 5.1 Secondary sales

In the case of secondary sales (which remain an important exit possibility for Belgian private equity funds and are usually structured as share deals), the exiting private equity fund will typically oppose giving warranties. However, in the Belgian M&A market, the number of secondary sales where the selling fund does not have to give any warranties remains exceptional. Usually, at least some warranties will have to be given to the buyer (as, without such warranties, the protection afforded to a buyer of shares is very limited under Belgian law).

Key issues for the exiting private equity fund in the negotiation of the share purchase agreement will therefore mainly relate to:

- limiting the scope of the warranties and their duration—the scope of warranties will of course, to a large extent, depend upon the importance of the participation held by the exiting private equity fund;
- negotiating a low maximum liability cap;
- obtaining the entire purchase price as of closing and avoiding, to the extent possible, any escrow arrangements; and
- keeping as much liberty as possible for future investments in the same business by resisting stringent non-compete and non-solicitation undertakings.

### 5.2 Trade sales

Trade sales are the most popular exit route for Belgian private equity transactions and are usually structured as share deals.

In the case of a trade sale to a strategic buyer, the exiting private equity fund will be requested to provide warranties to the buyer. The key issues will thus be the same as the ones mentioned under s.5.1 above.

An alternative to the trade sale used by Belgian private equity funds is a management buyout (MBO), whereby the management of the company acquires the company from the private equity fund.

In the framework of an MBO, the exiting private equity fund has a much stronger position in opposing (extensive) warranties as management should know (and take responsibility for) the company's operations and its financial situation.

For management, obtaining sufficient financing for the MBO will of course be a key issue. The demands of the management's finance providers may de facto complicate negotiations for the seller.

### 5.3 Initial public offerings

Initial public offerings (IPOs) remain exceptional as an exit mechanism for private equity funds in Belgium, although some investment funds successfully used this mechanism.

In a high-profile transaction which took place in June 2013, CVC exited a major part of its participation in the Belgian Post Services through a EUR 812 million IPO on the Brussels Stock Exchange. The US private equity group Apollo, which had acquired the Belgium-based chemical group Taminco in the largest buyout in Belgian history in 2011, organised an IPO of Taminco on the New York Stock Exchange in April 2013, allowing it to sell a part of its participation in the course of 2013. In 2016, another US private equity group (Lone Star) used an IPO as an exit for its investment in Balta (a Belgium-based producer of textile floor coverings). Lone Star had acquired Balta from UK private equity fund Doughty Hanson in 2015 in a secondary sale. Since its IPO, Balta's market capitalisation, however, significantly decreased.

In addition to the procedural key issues relating to an IPO (decision to offer only existing shares or not, due diligence, prospectus, price building), a private equity fund using an IPO as an exit mechanism should take into account lock-up obligations (requiring the existing shareholders at the time of the IPO not to transfer all or part of their shares during a certain period following the IPO). Such lock-up clauses (usually contained in the underwriting agreement) are valid provided they are limited in time and are, at all times, in the company's corporate interest. In case of an IPO, the lock-up clauses generally concern a period between six and 12 months.

## 5.4 Refinancings

Belgian private equity funds rarely use a refinancing as an exit mechanism.

In negotiating a refinancing, the board(s) of directors of the company/companies concerned must take the following key issues into account:

- the refinancing decisions and conditions of the refinancing must be in the corporate interest of the company/companies concerned. The board of directors must act in the interest of the company and not in the interest of its (private equity) shareholder;
- any refinancing (including a renegotiated security package) must comply with the rules on financial assistance and corporate purpose (see s.3 above); and
- granting a mortgage entails a significant cost, i.e. a registration fee of 1.3% of the amount secured thereby. Techniques exist to limit these costs (e.g. combination with a mortgage mandate). Refinancing of a loan secured by a mortgage will again entail these important costs as the mortgage will have to be granted again for the new financing. MBOs sometimes also take on the form of secondary sales, where management is backed by a new private equity investor.

## 5.5 Restructuring/insolvency

Although there have been cases where private equity funds used a restructuring as an exit (or, on the contrary, as a way to obtain control over a company by converting debt instruments into shares), this remains a rare exit mechanism for private equity funds in the Belgian market.

Key issues to be taken into account when negotiating a restructuring include:

- the restructuring must be in the corporate interest of the companies involved;
- restructuring scenarios whereby all viable/profitable assets are saved in one (spin-off) company while all other assets and liabilities are left in a

different company which goes bankrupt risk being considered fraudulent under Belgian law and will not be effective towards third parties (including creditors);

- restructurings involving a transfer and/or dismissal of employees will require information to and consultation with the Works Council (or other employee representatives body) of the company. Special legislation applies to closures or collective dismissals; and

- in the case of liquidation, the shareholders should ensure that the company is able to repay all its creditors to avoid bankruptcy proceedings. In bankruptcy, directors as well as "de facto or shadow directors" (which can include shareholders who were actively involved in the company's management) may incur specific liabilities. If a shareholder is considered to have unreasonably continued financing a loss-making company, it could also entail liability itself.

## 6. TAX
### 6.1 Taxation of fund structures
**Taxation of a regular holding company and of its investors**

A regular holding company is subject to Belgian corporate income tax but can benefit, for qualifying investments, from the Belgian participation exemption, which provides for a 100% exemption of the dividends received and of the capital gains realised, subject to the following conditions:

- the participation must amount to at least 10% of the company's nominal share capital or, alternatively, have an historical acquisition cost of at least EUR 2.5 million;

- the participation must have been held for a minimum period of 12 months. Should this minimum holding period not be reached but the below "subject to tax" requirement is met, a capital gain is subject to a taxation of 25.50%. For dividends, a commitment to hold the participation for 12 months suffices to apply the exemption regime; and

- the company in which the shares are held (and any lower tier subsidiaries) must meet the so-called "subject-to-tax requirement". That requirement is drafted in a negative way that will be satisfied if the income does not relate to a company falling within one of the exclusions, i.e.:
    (1) companies not subject to corporate income tax or subject to a common tax regime notably more advantageous than the Belgian one;
    (2) companies recognised as a Belgian regulated real estate company (B-REIT) or as a foreign REIT;
    (3) investment, financing and treasury companies enjoying a deviating tax regime;
    (4) companies receiving foreign non-dividend income that is subject to a separate tax regime deviating from the normal tax regime in their country of residence;
    (5) companies that realise profits through one or more foreign branches that are in aggregate subject to a tax assessment regime substantially more advantageous than in Belgium;

(6) intermediary companies (re)distributing dividend income of which 10% or more is "contaminated" pursuant to the above rules;

(7) companies, to the extent they have deducted or can deduct the income from their profits; or

(8) companies that distribute income that is related to a legal act or a series of legal acts, of which the tax administration has demonstrated that the legal act or series of legal acts are not genuine (i.e. that are not put into place for valid commercial reasons which reflect economic reality) and have been put in place with the main goal or one of the main goals to obtain the benefits of the Parent–Subsidiary Directive.[8]

It is, however, important to mention that common offshore regimes (e.g. Hong Kong) as well as tax holidays that are conditional and limited in time (e.g. Thailand, China) are not automatically excluded but must be assessed on a case-by-case basis.

This favourable holding regime also benefits from the absence of a specific thin capitalisation rule applying on interest expenses related to the acquisition of shares and from the extension of the dividend withholding tax exemption as provided by the EU Parent–Subsidiary Directive to all treaty countries.

At the level of the investors, dividend distributions are as a rule subject to a 30% withholding tax (including in cases of liquidation distribution). The reimbursement of paid-up capital is in principle exempt from withholding tax. For dividend withholding tax purposes, paid-up capital reimbursements are, however, deemed to derive proportionally from paid-up capital and from taxed reserves and exempt reserves incorporated into the capital. The portion allocated to the reserves is deemed to be a dividend and subject to withholding tax (if applicable).

The following domestic withholding tax exemptions may apply:

- dividends paid to foreign pension funds, which: (1) are not conducting a business or a lucrative activity; and (2) are totally tax exempted in their country of residence, benefit from a withholding tax exemption, provided that these entities are not contractually obliged to re-istribute their dividend proceeds;

- dividends paid to parent companies, which are established in the EU or in a tax treaty country (providing for exchange of information) and which are subject to corporate income tax without benefiting from a deviating tax regime, benefit from a withholding tax exemption. "Parent company" is defined as a company holding (or committing to hold) a 10% participation, in full ownership, in the share capital of the Belgian distributing company for at least one year; and

- dividends distributed by a resident company to resident and non-resident companies located in the EEA or a tax treaty country providing for exchange of information that hold a participation in the distributing company's capital of less than 10% but with an acquisition value of at

---

[8] Directive 2011/96 on the common system of taxation applicable in the case of parent companies and subsidiaries of different Member States [2011] OJ L345/8.

least EUR 2.5 million for an uninterrupted period of at least 12 months (or commitment to hold), to the extent that the receiving entity cannot credit Belgian withholding tax and both companies are subject to a corporate income tax or a similar tax and do not benefit from a regime that deviates from the common tax regime.

Dividends will not be exempt from withholding tax if the dividends are related to a legal act or a series of legal acts, of which the tax administration has demonstrated that the legal act or series of legal acts are not genuine (i.e. that are not put into place for valid commercial reasons which reflect economic reality) and have been put in place with the main goal or one of the main goals to obtain the exemption.

### Taxation of a Private PRICAF and of its investors

A Private PRICAF which assets are exclusively composed of shares the dividends of which qualify for the participation exemption or shares in one or more other Private PRICAF (certain deposits are also allowed subject to restrictions) benefit from a favourable tax regime, according to which its investment proceeds are not taxed at all in its hands.

At the level of the investors, dividends are as a rule subject to a 30% withholding tax but the following domestic withholding tax exemption may apply:
- dividends paid to foreign pension funds (see above);
- dividends deriving from realised capital gains; and
- dividends deriving from foreign source dividends and paid to foreign companies.

Based on these tax regimes, a Private PRICAF may be more interesting for investors that cannot benefit from a withholding tax exemption on distributions made by a regular holding company (e.g. individuals, tax-exempt private equity funds).

### Debt push-down

Belgian tax law does not provide in a tax consolidation system for corporate income tax purposes. Only as of 2019, Belgium will introduce a "light" tax consolidation regime in the form of a group contribution with cash compensation.

The absence of a tax consolidation combined with stringent transfer pricing regulations, makes an effective debt push-down in many cases a difficult exercise. Refinancing the equity is one of the most often used techniques. In this respect, attention must, however, be paid to recent (highly-debated) case law of lower courts denying the tax deductibility of interest expenses incurred to refinance the equity.

### 6.2 Carried interest

Belgian tax law does not provide for a specific tax regime applying to carried interest (contrary to the Netherlands, for example). Therefore, the carried interest, which is often structured as a (preferential) dividend, may benefit from the participation exemption in case it is paid to the management company of the executive and shall be subject to a withholding tax of 30% in case it is paid directly to the executive. This withholding tax is the final taxation in the hands of the executive.

However, due to the broad definition of "professional income", there is a risk of recharacterisation of the carried interest into professional income subject to personal income tax at a maximum rate of 50%. Appropriate structures can be put in place in order to at least mitigate this risk.

## 6.3  Management equity

The acquisition by managers of a carried interest in the form of equity instruments (such as preference shares) should only be taxable as professional income to the extent that the acquisition price is lower than the fair market value at the time of the acquisition, whereas capital gains should in principle be tax exempt (if realised within the normal management of private wealth).

In fund structures, the managers may receive stock options on carried interest shares. If all conditions of the stock option regime are met, the benefit of such grant is only taxable at the moment of attribution of the stock options whereby the taxable basis is determined on a lump sum basis, calculated on the fair market value of the shares. A gain realised on the exercise or on the subsequent sale of the shares is not taxable as professional income. The ruling commission has already confirmed on several occasions that the beneficial stock option regime can be applied to stock options on carried interest shares.

## 6.4  Loan interest

Interest expenses are in principle fully tax deductible—even if they are borne to acquire shares—provided that it can be demonstrated that the interest rate and the loan conditions are at arm's length. Specific non-deductibility rules apply to interest payments to tax havens. Belgian tax law provides, moreover, for two types of thin capitalisation rules:

- a 1:1 debt to equity ratio, which is only applicable in cases where the loans are granted by an individual shareholder or director of the borrower, or by a foreign company resident outside the EU, which is as such director of the borrower; and
- a 5:1 debt to equity ratio, which is applicable: (1) in cases where the beneficial owner of the interest is not submitted to tax or is submitted for this interest income to an income tax regime that is much more favourable than the Belgian one; and (2) to intra-group loans.

In implementation of the EU Anti-Tax Avoidance Directive,[9] a new interest limitation rule will apply as of 2020. The interest limitation rule foresees that exceeding borrowing costs will be deductible in the tax period in which they are incurred only up to the higher of 30% of the taxpayer's fiscal earnings before interest, tax, depreciation and amortisation (EBITDA) or EUR 3 million. "Exceeding borrowing costs" are defined as the positive difference between: (1) the amount of the deductible borrowing costs; and (2) taxable interest revenues and other economically equivalent taxable revenues that the taxpayer receives.

The standard withholding tax rate is 30%. Various domestic exemptions apply, however, as well as exemptions or reductions based on a tax treaty. The

---

9   Directive 2016/1164 laying down rules against tax avoidance practices that directly affect the functioning of the internal market [2016] OJ L193/1.

major domestic exemptions are the following:

- interest paid to a resident company;
- interest paid to a credit institution located in an EEA country or in a tax treaty country;
- interest paid on registered bonds subscribed by non-residents;
- interest paid to a company located in the EU that holds directly or indirectly at least 25% of the share capital of the Belgian paying company during at least one year (implementation of the EU Interest and Royalties Directive)[10]; and
- interest paid to a company located in the EU that is held directly or indirectly for at least 25% by another company located in the EU, which holds also directly or indirectly 25% of the share capital of the Belgian paying company during at least one year (implementation of the EU Interest and Royalties Directive).

### 6.5 Transaction taxes

The purchase of shares (even of a company the sole assets of which consist of real estate) is, in principle, not subject to transfer tax.

In real estate transactions structured as asset deals, transfer tax is levied on the transfer of ownership or usufruct of immovable property located in Belgium; at a rate of 12.5% (in the Walloon Region and in the Brussels District) or 10% (in the Flemish Region). This tax is calculated on the higher of the acquisition price or the market value of the property. The granting of a long-term lease right is subject to a 2% transfer tax.

## 7. CURRENT TOPICAL ISSUES/TRENDS

The short-term prospects for the Belgian M&A and private equity market are good: financing is still quite easily available, interest is low. The mid and long-term evolution is of course much harder to predict and will, to a large extent, depend on the international economic evolutions given the open nature of the Belgian economy and the reduced number of multinational companies with decision centres in Belgium. Based on the current situation, however, the following trends may be expected:

(1) cautious optimism exists with respect to the evolution of overall M&A activity in Belgium in the short term. Several economic indicators appear to justify a belief in a M&A activity remaining at the relatively high levels of 2016 and 2017. While industrial players are expected to continue playing an important role in M&A transactions, large international private equity funds appear to show an increasing interest in Belgium;

(2) with respect to venture capital, it is difficult to predict whether the improvement in the Belgian market seen over the last few years will be confirmed. The increasing role of wealthy individuals and families appears to be an enduring feature in any case. Attention is increasingly focused on start-ups;

(3) since Belgium is a country with a large number of small and medium-

---

10  Directive 2003/49 on a common system of taxation applicable to interest and royalty payments made between associated companies of different Member States [2003] OJ L 157/49.

sized (often family-owned) companies, smaller buyout funds are likely to remain important players in the Belgian M&A market, also taking into account the succession problems arising in many of these companies (causing current owners to sell their company). Smaller management buyout transactions with deal values not exceeding EUR 20 million are therefore likely to remain an important aspect of the Belgian M&A landscape; and

(4)  on a regulatory level, Belgium may see quite some changes in 2018–19 as both a new Companies Code and a new Civil Code are expected to be approved in the course of the second semester of 2018. For the private equity sector, the increased flexibility offered by the new Belgian Companies Code (including the creation of a new, capital-free and very flexible company type (besloten venootschap/société à responsabilité limitée) offer interesting opportunities in structuring both investments and management incentive/participation schemes.

# Brazil

**Pinheiro Neto Advogados** Álvaro Silas Uliani Martins dos Santos, Diego Alves Amaral Batista, Juliana Soares Zaidan Maluf & Luiz Felipe Fleury Vaz Guimarães

## 1. MARKET OVERVIEW

### 1.1 Types of investors

With the increased activity in the Brazilian private equity (PE) market, it is common to see all types of investors, including asset management funds, pension funds and hedge funds—both local and foreign—as well as the increased participation of Brazilian individuals qualifying as institutional investors.

International investors are leading the private equity funding in Brazil. In 2017, international investors were the source of 58% of the funding (53% in 2016 and 57% in 2015), the most important local players being pension fund and institutional investors (51%), corporate investors (13%), asset managers (8%) and governmental agencies (8%) (KPMG and ABVCAP, *Consolidação de dados da indústria de private equity e venture capital no Brasil* (2011/2012/2013/2014/2015/2016/2017)).

### 1.2 Types of investments

So far, most investments have been directed at small to medium-sized family owned companies with significant growth potential, usually in lightly regulated sectors. The consolidation opportunities available in many fragmented industries have also motivated some important waves of PE investments.

The turnover of the PE industry in 2017 was approximately USD 3.8 billion. This scenario encompasses approximately 68 invested companies with median equity values of USD 40 million per investment (KPMG and ABVCAP, *Consolidação de dados* (2011–17)).

Despite the fact that the majority of deals involves a minority stake, PE buyers are minority investors with a strong influence on decision-making, achieved by means of strong shareholders' agreements, covering corporate governance rules, registration rights and exit mechanisms.

There is no consolidated information on deal terms, especially because private transactions not involving publicly held companies are confidential. It is possible to say that PE transactions involve a share purchase agreement/investment agreement and a shareholders' agreement similar to those used in international transactions in the US and Europe, which establishes the general terms and conditions of the deal, including standard representations and indemnification clauses, voting rights, restrictions to the transfer of shares (right of first offer or refusal, tag-along and drag-along) and exit mechanisms (put, call and registration rights).

The purchase price is usually based on a discounted cash-flow valuation, and the price adjustment is usually structured as the possible variation in the position of net debt and working capital between the financial statements used in signing and closing of the transaction.

In 2017, there were nine initial public offerings (IPOs) involving Brazilian companies, out of which six involved PE portfolio companies. That evidences how PE investors can positively contribute to the growth and consolidation of Brazilian companies.

## 2. FUNDS
### 2.1 Fund structures

In Brazil, the most common method of channeling foreign PE investments is the incorporation in Brazil of: (1) a corporate entity, normally a limited liability company or a closely held company; or (2) a private equity fund (FIP) to serve as the investment vehicle.

Foreign investors are, however, also entitled to carry out PE investment directly in Brazil.

### 2.2 Regulation of fundraising and fund managers

The limited liability companies contemplated by Brazilian law are very similar to the limited liability companies, limited partnerships and closely held companies under English and US law. In Brazil, limited liability companies are governed by Law No.10,406 of 11 January 2002 (Civil Code), which has a chapter devoted to them, and, in a subsidiary manner, when applicable, by Law No.6,404 of 15 December 1976 (Corporation Law).

Closely held companies are governed by the Corporation Law and closely resemble US joint-stock companies or corporations.

FIPs are regulated by the Brazilian Securities and Exchange Commission (*Comissão de Valores Mobiliários*—CVM) Ruling No.578 of 30 August 2016, as amended (CVM Ruling 578). Additionally, where the FIP qualifies itself as a private investment fund in infrastructure (FIP-IE), which must keep at least 90% of its net equity invested in the energy, transport, water and basic sanitation, irrigation and other segments classified as priorities by the Federal Executive Branch, Law No.11,478 of 29 May 2007, as amended, and CVM Ruling No.501 of 15 July 2011 are applicable, as well as CVM Ruling 578, where such rules do not conflict with specific principles applicable only to FIP-IEs.

Similarly to other forms of Brazilian funds (and as opposed to other jurisdictions in which funds are organised as partnerships), the FIP is incorporated as a closed-end condominium of assets, without legal personality, managed and represented by an administrator registered with the CVM. Despite the fact that FIPs are not vested with legal personality in Brazil, they may hold some rights and obligations, and may act in court as plaintiff or defendant. For example, FIPs are entitled to have bank accounts and must also be enrolled with the National Register of Legal Entities for purposes of control by the federal tax authorities.

In Brazil, the Central Bank is charged with registering, monitoring and following up on foreign investments whereas the Ministry of Finance (through the Federal Revenue Office) focuses on the taxation of foreign investments. No preliminary official authorisation is required for cash investments in limited liability companies, closely held companies or FIPs.

Foreign investors must, however, be enrolled with the Federal Revenue Office, for which they must have an attorney-in-fact in Brazil, and foreign capital must be registered with the Central Bank through the Online Registration System of foreign direct investment in order to enable remittance of profits abroad, repatriation of capital and registration of reinvestments.

With regard to limited liability companies and closely held companies, if the investor is resident or domiciled abroad, it must have an attorney-in-fact in Brazil with powers to serve as a process agent. Usually, such representative also receives powers to represent the foreign investor as a partner in the Brazilian company.

Further, in order to apply for the tax benefit described in s.6.1 below, foreign investors must comply with the rules set out in Resolution No.4,373/14, issued by the Brazilian Central Bank (BACEN Resolution 4,373), which regulates the foreign investments in Brazilian financial and capital markets (foreign portfolio investments).

The participation of foreign capital is prohibited in Brazil within certain areas, such as: nuclear energy, post office and telecommunications services. Some restrictions apply to foreign investment in the ownership and management of businesses adjacent to international borders, rural properties, newspapers, magazines and other periodicals as well as in radio and television networks. The presence of foreign capital in financial institutions other than insurance companies is also subject to certain constraints.

Regarding the negotiation of fund's shares, any public offer of securities must be registered with the CVM, which is responsible for the supervision of publicly held companies and capital market transactions. Such registration is currently regulated by CVM Instruction No.400 of 29 December 2003, as amended, which sets out a series of requirements for this type of transaction. The entire process of a public offer can take from three to five months.

Nonetheless, the CVM also issued Ruling No.476 of 16 January 2009 (CVM Ruling 476) in order to ease placement of certain types of securities not directed at the public in general, thus creating a fast-track procedure that applies to restricted placements of securities (such placements are also considered public for the purposes of the CVM's regulations but are exempted from registration). This ruling was inspired in r.144A of the US Securities Act 1933.

Under the procedures of CVM Ruling 476, a maximum of 75 potential investors can be approached and the quotas of the fund can be subscribed by a maximum of 50 investors, which must be "professional investors" pursuant to the CVM's rules (i.e. investors with an initial investment in the securities corresponding to at least BRL 10 million). If this is the approach adopted, the distribution of securities is not subject to prior registration with the CVM.

The procedure determined by CVM Ruling 476 has been commonly used for the offering of quotas of FIP with a limited number of investors.

## 2.3 Customary or common terms of funds

The terms of the funds are quite flexible for all structures. For example, FIP's regulations establish that most of the operational rules, particularly those involving minimum net equity requirements, investment policy, capital calls, distributions of proceeds and duration, may be stipulated in the respective fund's bylaws.

Some of the key terms of PE funds are:

- life of fund: usually from seven to 10 years;
- investment policy: provisions defining the assets that may compose the fund's portfolio (e.g. target industries);
- investment period: rules and criteria determining the deadlines for making the investments;
- capital calls: the rules and deadline for capital calls;
- distributions: provisions on the destination to be given to the income and proceeds arising from the investment and the form of distribution or reinvestment of such resources;
- governance: provisions related to the structure and functioning of decision-making bodies (investors meetings, management and committees);
- management fees: typically, a fix management fee, which is often calculated based on the net equity of the fund or the invested capital. In some cases, a performance fee is also established;
- transfer restrictions: a fund's bylaws typically allow for an investor's interest in the FIP to be transferred conditional on other investors' right of first refusal; and
- information: rules on the information to be provided to the fund's shareholders, its regularity and format (e.g. quarterly non-audited financial statements and annual audited financial statements).

## 3. DEBT FINANCE
### 3.1 Means of financing

Normally, investments are funded through capital contributions. There is no limitation on capital increase and no minimum holding periods under Brazilian law.

The use of leverage in the industry is very limited when the interest rates in Brazil are still relatively high. Pursuant to research carried out by INSEAD–PwC,[1] another contributory factor is that funds have been able to produce satisfactory internal rates of return by focusing on operational improvements and industry consolidation.

As previously mentioned, PE funds are usually equity financed and the use of leverage is still limited, especially as a result of the relatively high interest rates and the restrictions mentioned in s.3.2 below.

### 3.2 Restrictions on granting security

In the specific case of FIPs, a CVM rule provides that FIPs: (1) may generally not contract indebtedness except in certain specific cases permitted by the CVM; and (2) are entitled to give guarantees, provided that this possibility is expressly set forth in the fund's bylaws and is conditioned to the approval of shareholders holding at least two/three of the FIP's quotas.

---

[1]   *INSEAD–PwC study on Private Equity in Brazil* available at:
   *http://www.abvcap.com.br/download/estudos/986.pdf* [Accessed 24 October 2018].

In the specific case of listed companies, a CVM rule prohibits controlling shareholders from voting on the direct or indirect transfer to a listed company of the indebtedness that has been used to acquire control of such listed company. If the acquired company remains with minority shareholders, the use of a leveraged buyout may trigger discussions regarding conflicts of interest involving the controlling shareholder, regardless of whether the invested company is public or private.

In general, companies are allowed to negotiate with their own shares in some specific cases (redemption, amortisation, to be kept in treasury) provided that such transactions comply with certain provisions of the Brazilian Corporation Law and CVM's regulation, if a publicly held company. There is no statutory provision expressly prohibiting a company from granting financial assistance in connection to the acquisition of its own shares. Notwithstanding, the granting of financial assistance could be opposed by minority shareholders based on arguments such as abuse of power of control and deviation from the corporate purpose.

Intercompany debt is sometimes used but several issues may arise if the lender is domiciled abroad, including transfer pricing and thin capitalisation rules, restrictions regarding the registration of the transaction with the Central Bank, withholding tax on interest and taxes applicable to foreign exchange transactions.

### 3.3  Intercreditor issues

With regard to equity finance, the most common structure adopted in order to set preferences among equity investors is to create different classes of shares (e.g. senior/subordinated) in the fund's bylaws. Usually, senior or preferred shares are awarded the following economic rights:
- priority in case of amortisation, redemption or payment of dividends;
- liquidation preferences; and
- higher dividends rights.

As previously mentioned, the use of leverage in the PE industry is still very limited. Nevertheless, it is possible to contractually arrange payment priorities among debt providers.

### 3.4  Syndication

As previously mentioned, the use of leverage in PE industry is still very limited. In this sense, there is no consolidated experience of syndicate loans in PE industry.

## 4.  EQUITY STRUCTURES
### 4.1  Role of management

Traditionally, Brazilian companies are family owned and managed, the shareholders often also being the managers. Because of this, it is common for the existing management to keep an equity participation in the invested company.

This situation enables a natural alignment between the FIP and the existing management. Therefore, the focus of the FIP in relation to managers is more directed to: (1) their retention (e.g. lock-up periods); and (2) the control on the definition of management compensation (e.g. veto rights).

In the case of professional managers, stock option plans have become one of the most common management incentives used to align the corporate goals and challenges with those of key members of the management. The increasing number of stock option plans in Brazil is closely connected to the development of Brazilian capital markets and the liquidity of the São Paulo Stock Exchange (B3, former BM&FBovespa), which is one of the largest stock exchanges in the world. The majority of Brazilian companies that have gone public since 2004 have had a stock option plan for key managers and employees.

Brazilian stock options are structured as a contractual call option of the eligible manager on a certain amount of shares to be issued by the company. The exercise of the stock option is subject to certain terms and conditions, such as vesting periods. The exercise price is predefined by the parties and is usually inferior to the economic value of such share.

In Brazil, stock options are implemented through a stock option plan approved by the shareholders, which sets out the general characteristics of the plan, such as the eligible participants, vesting periods, exercise procedure and limit of shares to be granted within the plan. The execution of the plan is usually incumbent on the board of directors, which decides on each specific grant of options.

### 4.2 Common protections for investors

Investors' protections are usually set forth in a shareholders' agreement and depends on the circumstances of the case, especially the corporate interest held by the relevant PE investors (e.g. majority or minority shareholder).

It is possible to say that investors typically attempt to protect their investment by having:

- seats on the board of directors;
- the right to appoint members of the executive management;
- the right to receive periodic information; and
- veto rights on certain matters.

Additionally, it is common to set forth restrictions to the transfer of shares, such as the rights of first refusal or offer, tag-along, drag-along and put and call options as well as lock-up provisions.

### 4.3 Common protections for management

In the more usual situation in which the management are also the founders of the invested company, it is more common to focus on their protection as shareholders of the invested company.

If professional managers receive stock option plans, their negotiations tend to be directed more to the vesting conditions and the amount of options as well as their compensation package.

### 4.4 Management warranties

It is not common for management to provide warranties in PE transactions. Representations and warranties, and the corresponding liabilities, are usually assumed by selling shareholders.

## 4.5   Good leaver/bad leaver provisions

Stock option plans usually grant to the company and its controlling shareholders a call option on the shares held by a manager who is leaving the company. The terms of such call option may vary depending on the cause for the relevant manager's leaving (good or bad leaving).

## 4.6   Public to private transactions

It is rare for FIPs to make offers for public companies in Brazil.

Brazilian going private transactions have generally been conducted by the controlling shareholders of the respective companies, not by FIPs. A few years ago, FIPs managed by Tarpon had taken Cremer, one of the leading Brazilian suppliers of healthcare products, private. Tarpon started investing in Cremer in 2008, when it acquired almost 6% of the company shares. Tarpon subsequently carried out a series of purchases, ultimately resulting in the acquisition of 96% of the shares issued by Cremer.

The main legal issue in connection with taking a publicly held company private is the legal tag-along right established in the Brazilian Corporation Law (s.254-A). According to this provision, the sale of control of publicly held companies is subject to a mandatory tender offer to be carried out by the buyer to acquire the voting shares owned by the remaining shareholders, the offer price for such shares being at least 80% (100% in the case of companies listed in the Novo Mercado, Nível II, Bovespa Mais and Bovespa Mais Nível II segments, furthermore, Nível II and Bovespa Mais Nível II segments allow for the issuance of preferred shares, which shall be included as target of the tender offer receiving the same amount offered to voting shares) of the amount paid for the voting shares of the controlling block.

Furthermore, the Brazilian Corporation Law and the listing rules of most of the B3 listing segments require tender offers in cases such as:

- cancellation of the publicly traded company register;
- delisting from the B3 listing segments; and
- a relevant increase in the participation of the controlling shareholder in the share capital of a publicly held company.

## 5.   EXITS

The development of a sophisticated and liquid capital market and the growth of the PE market in Brazil opened a wide variety of exit alternatives, such as IPOs, sales to strategic players (trade sales) and sales to other FIPs (secondary sales).

## 5.1   Secondary sales

The sale to another PE investor is an increasingly important exit alternative.

Depending on the circumstances of the case, the exiting FIP may structure a competitive bid or engage in a one-to-one negotiation.

Usually, the main steps involved in a secondary sale are as follows:

(1)  negotiation of a letter of intent with the potential acquirer;
(2)  performance of due diligence, covering legal, accounting and financial areas;
(3)  structuring the transaction in light of the rules concerning foreign investments and taxation;

(4) drafting and negotiation of the definitive documents, the most relevant being the share purchase agreement/investment agreement and the shareholders' agreement; and

(5) submission of the transaction to the Brazilian antitrust authorities, as the case may be.

In general, the most relevant issue relating to a secondary sale is the extent of representations and warranties granted by the exiting investor. Although it may vary depending on the specificities of each case, it is unusual for exiting investors to agree to standard warranties and the maintenance of a portion of the price in an escrow account.

## 5.2 Trade sales

The sale to a strategic investor has been the most common exit alternative for PE in Brazil.

The formal procedure to carry out a trade sale closely resembles that described above for secondary sales. However, in comparison with secondary sales, trade sales tend to:

- require fewer warranties as the strategic investor usually has greater knowledge of the business and industry;
- trigger more antitrust issues so there is usually more discussion on the provision related to the submission of the transaction to Brazilian antitrust authority; and
- generate more reluctance of the exiting investor to make available sensitive commercial information.

## 5.3 Initial public offerings

Capital market transactions are an usual exit alternative for PE investments. Exit through an IPO is well regarded among PE firms because of the possibility of higher returns. However, because of the volatility of capital markets, it is usual to pursue a dual-track process (IPO and secondary/trade sale).

The IPO process can be divided into three major steps that run in parallel:

- registration of the company with the CVM as a publicly held company;
- registration of the IPO with the CVM; and
- listing the company at B3, usually in the Novo Mercado segment, which requires the highest standards of corporate governance.

These steps require the creation of a series of documents, including a reference form (similar to Form 20-F used in the US) containing the company's main information and an offering memorandum containing the main information about the public offering of shares. The duration of the process also depends on a series of factors, mainly the level of preparation of the company regarding corporate governance and accounting controls. It usually takes between three and five months to carry out an IPO.

As an illustration of the boom in IPOs in Brazil, from 2005 to 2010 there were 182 equity offerings in Brazil, with more than BRL 320 billionraised (Bloomberg Terminal, 2011; see also M. Prahl and C. Zeisberger, "Brazilian Private Equity: Moving Centre Stage", INSEAD Working Paper 2011/74/DS (2011)). In 2010, the Brazilian oil company Petrobrás raised BRL 120 billion in a public offering of shares.

In 2011–13, 11 IPOs and three follow-ons were used as exit strategies for PE investments. Among such transactions was the IPO of Magazine Luiza SA, amounting to approximately BRL 890 million; of this, BRL 300 million was related to the sale of shares held by Capital International, corresponding to 10% of the corporate capital of the company. In 2005, Capital International acquired 12.36% of Magazine Luiza SA corporate capital, then started to participate on the board of directors and in the implementation of better corporate governance and financial management practices.

In the following years, regarding political and economic factors, the market has suffered a slowdown, which has been quickly replaced by a more optimistic scenario. After only one IPO per year in 2014–16 (Ourofino Saúde Animal, PAR Corretora de Seguros and Alliar Médicos à Frente), a boom in the IPO market was verified in 2017. Out of the nine IPOs carried out by Brazilian companies in 2017, six were PE portfolio companies (KPMG and ABVCAP, *Consolidação de dados* (2011–17)). As an example, it is possible to mention the IPO of BK Brasil Operação e Assessoria a Restaurantes SA in December 2017 (Vinci Capital Partners II B *Fundo de Investimento em Participações—Multiestratégia* and Montjuic *Fundo de Investimento em Participações Multiestratégia* as selling shareholders); and the IPO of Atacadão SA (Carrefour Group) in July 2017 (Península II Fundo de Investimentos em Participações as a selling shareholder).

It should be noted that the selling shareholder is liable for any inaccuracy or omission of relevant information in the offering memorandum. If the selling shareholder is also the controlling shareholder, it will be considered strictly liable; if a non-controlling shareholder, the selling shareholder may avoid this liability by proving compliance with its duty of diligence (e.g. hiring legal, accounting and financial assistants to conduct due diligence in the company).

### 5.4 Refinancings

Historically, refinancing has not been an exit alternative for PE investments, especially as a result of the adverse credit market conditions in Brazil.

### 5.5 Restructuring/insolvency

PE investments in financially distressed companies are still not very common in Brazil. The presence of vulture funds is still very limited. One of the few examples of this kind of transaction is the investment made in 2006 by LAEP in Parmalat, the leading producer of dairy products in Brazil.

Nonetheless, greater movement of PE activity in connection with financially distressed companies has been noticed recently, especially as a result of the consolidation of the new Brazilian Bankruptcy Law (Law No.11,101 of 9 February 2005), which has made important alternatives for the recovery of the company available, and the recent financial problems experienced by some relevant Brazilian companies.

## 6. TAX
### 6.1 Taxation of fund structures

In general, the following taxation framework will apply to limited liability companies or closely held companies and its foreign quotaholders or shareholders:

- exchange transactions related to the inflow of funds as capital contribution will be generally subject to the tax on foreign exchange transactions (IOF/Câmbio) at 0.38%;
- dividends paid to the holding company and by the holding company to the foreign investor are exempt from withholding income tax (WHT);
- capital gains earned by Brazilian holding companies upon selling of invested company interests are subject to corporate income tax (IRPJ) and the social contribution on net profits (CSL) at 34%. As a general rule, to reduce tax burden, it is possible to transfer the invested companies to the foreign investor at book value (through capital reduction) and then to sell the invested companies. This would reduce the taxation to progressive rates that vary from 15% to 22.5% of WHT or a flat 25% rate if the foreign investor is domiciled in a tax haven jurisdiction; and
- capital gains earned by the foreign investor upon selling of the shares issued by the holding company are subject to WHT at progressive rates that vary from 15% to 22.5% or a flat 25% if the foreign investor is domiciled in a tax haven jurisdiction.

The following taxation will apply to the FIP and its foreign quotaholders:

- considering that investment in a FIP is made through an institutional portfolio investment under BACEN Resolution 4,373, the foreign exchange transaction necessary for the inflow of funds to acquire FIPs quotas and for any income paid by the FIP (including redemption of FIP quotas) is currently subject to zero IOF/Câmbio. Note that the Executive Branch can increase such rate at any time;
- FIPs themselves are not subject to taxation on gains and income earned from the acquisition and disposal of assets of its own portfolio. Taxation is generally imposed at the level of the quotaholder of the FIP;
- income paid by the FIP to a foreign quotaholder (including capital gains on disposal of FIP quotas) is subject to WHT at 15%. The income may be exempted (including capital gains arising from the disposition of the FIP's shares) from WHT as long as the following requirements are observed:
  - the investment is made as an institutional portfolio investment under BACEN Resolution 4,373;
  - the FIP quotaholder does not hold, individually or jointly with related persons, shares representing 40% or more of all the FIP's shares or 40% or more of the total income of the FIP;
  - the FIP does not hold in its portfolio, at any time, debt securities exceeding 5% of the FIP's net equity;
  - the foreign investor cannot be resident or domiciled in a country defined by Brazilian law as a tax haven jurisdiction (Brazilian law defines a "tax haven" as a country where income is subject to taxation at a maximum rate below 20% but the Brazilian Federal Revenue Office has also issued a blacklist with all the countries considered as a tax haven); and
- historically, tax authorities took the position that the FIP could be organised as an "ex-dividends fund" so that dividends paid by the

invested companies to the FIP could be passed on directly to quotaholders of the FIP without WHT. However, in August 2015, Brazilian tax authorities issued new (and debatable) regulations (Normative Ruling No.1,585 of 31 August 2015), which set forth that dividends passed on by the FIP should be generally subject to the WHT at the rate of 15% (unless quotaholder is not entitled to the exemptions above). The administrator of the FIP is responsible for withholding and collecting the tax.

## 6.2 Carried interest

In Brazil, carried interest is usually structured as a performance fee. As a general rule, in order to participate in the carry distributions, the individual is required to make an equity investment in the entity that would act as the general partner, which, in turn, would also make an equity investment in the FIP.

Taking into consideration that the carry would be mostly related to a successful divestiture of the investment made by the FIP and that the Brazilian individuals would participate in the carry as a result of an equity investment made in the entity acting as general partner, there are arguments to sustain the position that the potential distribution of the carry to the Brazilian individuals through a redemption of the interest in the general partner should be taxed in the form of capital gains (progressive rates that vary from 15% to 22.5% rate) and not in the form of ordinary income (progressive rates up to 27.5%). This conclusion depends on a case-by-case analysis since the Brazilian tax regulations do not expressly address the tax treatment that should apply to carried interest distributed to Brazilian residents.

## 6.3 Management equity

As mentioned in s.4.1 above, stock option plans have become one of the most common management incentives used to align the corporate goals and challenges with those of key members of the management.

There are many tax, social security and labour issues related to stock options plans that generate consequences for management and the investment vehicle, such as whether or not the options are considered as management compensation. In general, the following aspects are indicative of the non-salary nature of the stock option:
- existence of financial cost to the employee;
- existence of risk to the worker/employee (i.e. no assured future gain); and
- acquisition of options/shares is not a frequent transaction (non-habitual).

Regarding the tax consequences to managers who are participants in stock option plans of Brazilian companies, it should be noted that:
- as a general rule, the options should not be subject to taxation at the time that they are granted since the options are usually not transferable; and
- at the time of exercise, there may be a positive difference between the fair market value of the acquired shares and the exercise price of the options.

In the event that the employee effectively acquires such shares by paying a reasonable exercise price, there are arguments to sustain that the taxation should only occur at the time that these shares are sold by the manager if he/she actually realises a gain. In this case, such possible gains would be subject to income tax at progressive rates that vary from 15% to 22.5%.

Regarding the tax consequences to the companies issuing the shares, there is a risk that possible discounts granted to employees would be considered compensation, on which all due tax and social security contributions would be applicable, as well as there being some reporting obligations on the stock option plan.

### 6.4   Loan interest

Generally, the interests paid by FIPs in connection with a loan are:

- subject to WHT at a rate of 15% (or 25% if the beneficiary is resident of a tax haven jurisdiction); and
- deductible from the calculation basis of the IRPJ and CSL, provided that the rules on transfer pricing and thin capitalisation, which may limit the deductibility, are complied with.

In case a Brazilian FIP enters into a loan agreement with a foreign creditor, note that:

- such loan shall be registered before the Brazilian Central Bank; and
- the inflow of funds is currently subject to IOF/Câmbio at the rate of 6% if that the loan is to be repaid over a term of less than 180 days. Only loans that remain unpaid for a term of more than 180 days can enter Brazil exempted from IOF/Câmbio.

### 6.5   Transaction taxes

See s.6.1 above regarding the acquisition of shares structure. When it comes to asset deals, assuming that the seller is a Brazilian legal entity, gains realised on the transaction will be generally subject to corporate income taxation at a rate of 34% (IRPJ/CSL). Moreover, sellers that carry out asset deals are also subject to Brazilian VAT taxes (Tax on Manufactured Products (IPI), Tax on Distribution of Goods and Services (ICMS), Profit Participation Program (PIS)/Social Security Financing Contribution (COFINS)) on revenues arising from the disposition of such assets.

## 7.   CURRENT TOPICAL ISSUES/TRENDS

During the past few years, Brazil has consolidated its position as a serious global player in the PE industry. However, that scenario has been impacted by the corruption scandals verified in Brazil during the last few years, which resulted in a market volatility.

The total amounts of committed and available capital by FIPs in the country have been maintained in the last three years as detailed in fig.1 below (in BRL billion) (KPMG and ABVCAP, *Consolidação de dados* (2011–17)):

FIGURE 1[2]

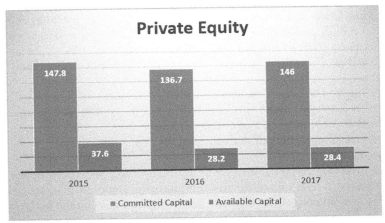

As with many other countries in the world, the global financial crisis of 2008–09 adversely affected Brazil, reducing PE investment; however, considering the favourable macro-economic scenario and the fact that the PE industry in Brazil does not rely on financial leveraging, the negative effects of the crisis on the country have been lighter than on most other developed and emerging countries, and this has enabled Brazil to rebound from the crisis relatively quickly. In 2010, Brazil experienced a significant recovery in the level of PE activity and investments reached a level even higher than the pre-crisis period. During the last few years, as a result of the continuing effect of the global financial crisis, the debt crisis in Europe, certain macro-economic changes and the political scenario (e.g. several corruption scandals involving Brazilian politicians), the market has slowed down. It has started to move again in 2017, which can be verified through the return of the IPOs.

In terms of regulatory approvals, it should be highlighted that there is no specific regulatory body to supervise the PE industry in Brazil; however, PE transactions may still be subject to regulatory supervision, depending on the characteristics of the transaction.

For example, there are several regulated sectors in the Brazilian economy. Whenever the invested company's business includes concessions, permissions or authorisations from the Government (directly or through regulatory agencies), it is likely that the PE investment will require prior authorisation from the Government or regulatory agency, to the extent that it results in a transfer of control or a change in the control structure of the invested company.

The New Brazilian Competition Law (Law No.12,529 of 2011) came into effect on 29 May 2012 and promoted significant changes to the current antitrust legal framework, the most relevant being that antitrust analysis and approval became a prerequisite to the consummation of transactions in line

---

2    Figure 1 was created by the authors using data from KPMG and ABVCAP, *Consolidação de dados* (2011–17).

with the majority of the jurisdictions worldwide.

Mergers, acquisitions, joint ventures and agreements in general must be submitted to the Administrative Council for Economic Defence when one party (considering its economic groups) has recorded gross revenues exceeding BRL 750 million in Brazil in the financial year preceding the transaction and the other party (considering its economic groups) has recorded gross revenues exceeding BRL 75 million in Brazil in the financial year preceding the transaction.

According to the New Brazilian Competition Law, if one of the parties in a transaction is an investment fund (including FIPs), its economic group should be defined as including, on a cumulative basis:

- the investment funds under common management;
- the manager;
- the investors that own, directly or indirectly, more than 20% of the quotas of at least one of the funds under common management; and
- the invested companies in which the ownership held by the investment fund (directly or indirectly) is higher than 20% of the corporate capital or voting capital.

In 2013, the *Comitê de Aquisições e Fusões* (CAF) was instituted. Inspired by the British model, the CAF supervises and regulates takeovers, mergers and other issues. Its main purpose is to ensure fair treatment for all shareholders in transactions within its scope. Submission to the CAF is not mandatory but its approval is considered by the CVM as a presumption of a fair deal.

The Brazilian PE industry has gained maturity during the last few years and it is expected to continue growing in the future, mainly as a result of:

- the size of the Brazilian economy;
- the growing middle class, which supports the enlargement of the Brazilian economy;
- the maturation of the Brazilian capital markets and the existence of liquid exit alternatives; and
- the high fragmentation of various industries and the possibilities of consolidation.

In order to improve its perception among PE investors, Brazil still needs to overcome a number of challenges, such as the complexity of its tax system and the still limited debt availability.

In terms of future trends, it is worth mentioning that CVM Ruling 578 brought benefits to the PE market and implemented several changes allowing the completion of PE transactions in a faster pace. Also, the need for infrastructure investment in Brazil and the expected wave of privatisation in certain areas may also result in an increased number of PE investments in regulated industries such as energy and transportation. The current Government has an ambitious agenda of public services concessions, especially in public transportation (airports, roads and ports).

If these issues become reality, the Brazilian PE industry should face new and challenging legal issues in the near future.

# Bulgaria

**Boyanov & Co**  Yordan Naydenov & Dr Nikolay Kolev

## 1. MARKET OVERVIEW

### 1.1 Types of investors

The private equity (PE) funds to be analysed in this chapter will be those collective investment structures that are raised privately and whose aim is to invest directly in shares (sometimes also in debt) of entitles that are not publicly traded. Therefore, the activities of such investors, like the pension funds, regulated collective investment schemes (CISs) and alike are outside the scope of this analysis, although where necessary they will be mentioned just for the purposes of outlining the differences between them and the PE funds.

The majority of the PE funds that are active in Bulgaria are not raised or originally registered in the country. However, more and more Bulgarian PE funds are getting not just registered, but also raised locally. Some of the Bulgarian PE funds operate with funds coming from other jurisdictions or were set up for the purposes of implementing various investment programmes of the EU (e.g. JEREMIE). Yet, no statistics exist as to the sources of their funding, their number, the total funds that were accumulated etc.

In late 2015, seven of the Bulgarian most active PE and venture capital funds set up the Bulgarian Private Equity and Venture Capital Association, which got registered in 2016 with the aim, inter alia, to promote and create wider awareness amongst the Bulgarian business community about the options that the PE funds offer.

### 1.2 Types of investments

Currently, the interest of the PE investors is focused mainly on the acquisition of majority shareholding in market leaders in various sectors of the economy. Certain sectors like IT, real estate or telecommunications can be said to be of particular interest.

The Bulgarian market has seen several consolidation transactions where the PE fund had initially invested in one local market leader, and has then used that leader as a platform to acquire more companies from the same business sector and thereafter to consolidate the market. The other option is to acquire a controlling shareholding in the holding company of a group of companies operating in specific economic sector.

Many of the PE fund investment transactions in Bulgaria have been highly leveraged with debt financing.

The typical sources of debt financing for PE transactions in Bulgaria are bank loans from Bulgarian or foreign banks, although their share has seen a material decrease.

## 2. FUNDS
### 2.1 Fund structures

Given that there is no specific legal framework regulating PE funds, the founding investors/managers are free to choose whatever legal structure they consider would best meet their needs. The main options are as follows:

- one of the legal structures that is appropriate for the setting up of a PE fund in Bulgaria is the joint stock company, given the free transferability of the shares and the relatively simple incorporation procedure. When raising the fund, the managers should be very careful not to make the raising a public offer of securities, which could bring the PE fund under the regulations governing the CISs. The founders could also go for a limited liability company, which is similar to the joint stock company but has a simpler management structure and its shares are always in dematerialised form. The shares in a limited liability company are more difficult to transfer as this operation would require a notarised transfer document (e.g. share purchase agreement) and mandatory registration in the state commercial register;

- a PE fund in Bulgaria could also be structured as a limited partnership or partnership limited by shares. In both cases, the investors (the limited partners) would passively invest in shares of the fund but, in the second case, they would receive share certificates that are freely transferrable, while in the first case they will just subscribe for shares that are not materialised; the general partner (who would be the manager of the fund, i.e. the fund is going to be self-managed) could be incorporated as a limited liability company, thus, the managers would also limit their liability to the amount of the contributions they would make to the capital of the general partner. There is no legal prohibition to have an individual acting as general partner but, in this case, they will be liable for the obligations of the PE fund with all of their assets;

- Bulgarian law provides also for incorporation of a holding company. A holding company shall be any joint stock company, partnership limited by shares or limited liability company, the purpose of which is to participate under any form in other companies or in their management, regardless of whether it carries on manufacturing or commercial activities of its own. At least 25% of the capital stock of a holding company must be invested directly in subsidiary companies. In fact, any joint stock company or limited liability company could perform the same functions without being specifically registered as a holding company, so there are not that many examples of registered holding companies;

- a PE fund could also take the form of a general partnership, i.e. a contractual partnership between the participants in the fund, which is not a legal entity. The participants could also set up a company to which the funds raised through the general partnership would be then transferred for management and investment. Without such a company, the management of the general partnership and its investments would be faced with certain difficulties, due to the outdated and poor legal framework applicable to this type of structure; or

- the founding investors could also set a contractual pool of assets (i.e.

without creating a general partnership) and then deliver the same to a managing company for investment purposes.

It should be noted that PE funds are not subject to any specific registration as such and therefore it is not possible to verify what forms are most commonly used.

The foreign PE funds that invest in Bulgaria usually set up sole shareholder joint stock companies or sole shareholder limited liability companies.

## 2.2 Regulation of fundraising and fund managers

As mentioned above, PE funds in Bulgaria are not subject to any special legislation and are therefore regulated by general company law.

The main legal acts that should be taken into account when setting up, raising and operating a PE fund are:

- the Commerce Act (CA): promulgated in the *State Gazette* (SG) No.48 of 18 June 1991, effective as of 1 July 1991, as amended and supplemented from time to time, which contains the general rules for the incorporation and legal status of commercial companies, rules with respect to their liquidation, distribution of profits, reorganisation, insolvency etc;
- the Obligations and Contracts Act (OCA): promulgated in SG No.275 of 1950, as amended and supplemented from time to time, which contains the rules for the establishment of general partnerships, rules with respect to the freedom of contracts, issuing of powers of attorney etc;
- the Markets in Financial Instruments Act (MFIA): promulgated in SG No.15 of 2018, as amended and supplemented from time to time, which regulates the establishment and the requirements with respect to investment brokers, markets in financial instruments etc;
- the Public Offering of Securities Act (POSA): promulgated in SG No.114 of 30 December 1999, effective as of 31 January 2000, as amended and supplemented from time to time, which regulates the legal status and requirements with respect to the publicly traded companies, the public offering of securities, initial public offerings etc;
- the Insurance Code: promulgated in SG No.102 of 29 December 2015, effective as of 1 January 2016, as amended and supplemented from time to time, which regulates the legal status of insurance joint stock companies, including rules on their investments in other companies;
- the Social Security Code: promulgated in SG No.110 of 17 December 1999, effective as of 1 January 2000, as amended and supplemented from time to time, which regulates the legal status of pension funds, including rules on their investments in other companies;
- the Credit Institutions Act: promulgated in SG No.59 of 2006, effective as of 1 January 2007, as amended and supplemented from time to time, which regulates the legal status of the credit institutions, including banks. It also contains rules regarding the participation of a bank in other companies, rules about forming exposures with respect to third parties (i.e. extending credits); and
- the Collective Investment Schemes and Other Undertakings for

Collective Investments Act: promulgated in SG No.77 of 2011, as amended and supplemented from time to time, regulates the legal status of the investment companies and CISs.

The main acts that regulate the management of a PE fund are the CA and the OCA. The requirements of the MFIA and POSA should also be taken into consideration.

The Bulgarian Parliament adopted a special act (Act on Economic and Financial Relations with Companies Registered in Preferential Tax Treatment Jurisdictions, the Entities under their Control and Their Beneficial Owners, entered into force on 1 January 2014, as amended and supplemented from time to time, commonly known as the Offshore Companies Act) which provides for certain restrictions on companies registered in offshore jurisdictions (offshore companies) and their subsidiaries to carry out certain business activities or to invest in companies performing such. The list of restricted activities covers 28 business sectors altogether, including activities requiring a licence or another type of special authorisation, or activities subject to specific legal regulations, such as credit institutions, insurance, reinsurance or insurance brokerage companies, pension insurance companies, investment intermediaries, CISs or other undertakings for collective investments and payment institutions). The result may be that any company of a corporate group that has for a direct or indirect parent an offshore company may fall under the restrictions, unless one of the exemptions under the Offshore Companies Act applies. The list of the offshore jurisdictions is to be determined by the Minister of Finance. The latest one, effective as of 1 January 2017, contained 26 jurisdictions.

The management of the PE fund and the applicable requirements will largely depend on the legal form that the investors choose. The options are:

- joint stock company: this is managed by a general meeting of shareholders (GMS), which is competent to take all major decisions that are of importance for the corporate existence of the company and could be empowered to take some major business decisions. Depending on the chosen management structure, the company would have a board of directors (one-tier management system) or a management and supervisory board (two-tier management system). The day-to-day management would be entrusted to the executive directors who are members of either the board of directors or the management board. The members of the boards can be replaced and the authority of the executive directors to manage and represent the company can be withdrawn at any time;

- limited liability company: this management structure is similar to (yet simpler than) that of the joint stock company with one-tier management system. The limited liability company is managed by a GMS, which is competent to take all major corporate decisions. Its day-to-day activities and representation are to be vested with a manager or managers, whose authority can be withdrawn at any time;

- limited partnership: in this type of company, both the management and the representation are in the hands of the general partner/partners. The limited partners may not block the decisions of the general partners. It is for that reason that this type of structure is quite appropriate for a PE fund as the general partners would manage the accumulated funds without the involvement of the limited partners;

- partnership limited by shares: the management of this structure is similar to the management of a joint stock company with one-tier management system. The shareholders (i.e. the participants with limited liability) are entitled to vote at the GMS. The general partners, even if they own shares, may participate in the GMS but may not vote. The board of directors consists of general partners only, i.e. they de facto manage and represent the company; and

- general partnership/contractual pool of assets and company managing them (we intentionally refrain from using the term "management company" as it designates a special type of joint stock company that manages mutual funds): the partners of this type of structure are free to negotiate and establish the management relations between the general partnership/contractual pool of assets and the company.

As long as the fund is "private", i.e. it is not raised through a public offering of securities/units/shares, there are neither specific requirements as to the qualification/licensing of the persons directly involved in the management of the fund, nor specific requirements as to the manner and procedures through which the fund is raised. In cases where the fund is to invest in instruments traded on the financial markets, it would need the involvement of a licensed investment broker.

In any of the structures outlined above, if the management of the investment portfolio of the PE fund is entrusted to a third party, e.g. a special company or individual, there is a risk that this third party may be viewed as someone providing investment advice or services, i.e. an investment broker, which would require a special licence.

### 2.3 Customary or common terms of funds

As mentioned above, PE funds are not subject to any specific registration as such. Furthermore, there are no reliable studies or statistics that would allow for a summary of the key terms of Bulgarian PE funds.

## 3. DEBT FINANCE
### 3.1 Means of Financing

Private equity fund deals are financed primarily through banking loans. Alternative means of financing are available as well, provided Bulgarian regulations are observed; for example, under Bulgarian law, bonds can be issued only by joint stock companies.

The CA provides for full prohibition of financial assistance to joint stock companies. Thus, if the target company is a joint stock company, it cannot provide a credit to the PE fund to be used for the acquisition of the target company's shares.

### 3.2 Restrictions on granting security

As mentioned above, the CA provides for full prohibition of financial assistance to joint stock companies and, if the target company is a joint stock company, then it cannot guarantee or provide security interests over its assets in order to secure the credit extended to its acquirer for the purposes of the acquisition.

There is no prohibition on financial assistance with respect to limited liability companies, which are the other typical form of a target company in Bulgaria.

### 3.3 Intercreditor issues

Bulgarian law contains mandatory rules for the ranking of creditors within the compulsory execution procedure and within the bankruptcy procedure. The creditors, based on the freedom of contracts principle, may conclude an intercreditor agreement to regulate the ranking of their receivables. Such agreements are common practice in Bulgaria and are usually governed by foreign law. However, in the case of a compulsory execution procedure in Bulgaria, the executive judge would be bound by the statutory provisions only and he will refuse to recognise and apply a different ranking that is based on an intercreditor agreement. In such cases, the creditors that, according to the intercreditor agreement, ranked first but did not receive payment would have a contractual claim against the creditors ranked second and below that have received payment. The same is valid with respect to the satisfaction of the creditors of a bankrupt company—the trustee of the bankruptcy will distribute the proceeds of the liquidation of the bankruptcy estate to the creditors in accordance with the ranking established by the law.

### 3.4 Syndication

Banks and financial institutions provide the option to arrange or co-finance syndicated loans for customers. Loan syndication is used for risk diversification and for securing compliance with the large exposure rules contained in the Credit Institutions Act.

The syndication may raise questions in case the provided security needs to be registered (e.g. mortgages, special pledges). The presence of many creditors could make the registration process rather painful, not to mention the difficulties should one of the members of the syndicate decide to assign its claims to a third party, including a member of the same syndicate. For that reason, the figure of registration agent becomes more and more popular. Sometimes, when the debt documentation is governed by English laws, one could also observe the use of the so called "parallel debt" concept.

It is common for the credits extended to the investee company to be refinanced after the deal as an element of the corporate and financial reorganisation to which the investee is subjected.

## 4. EQUITY STRUCTURES
### 4.1 Role of management

The management body of a PE fund represents the fund at the GMS of the investee company. Normally, representatives of the PE fund would also take seats in the management bodies, such as boards of a joint stock company, or act as managers of a limited liability company in which investments are made.

The position of board member or manager of an investee company allows the management of the fund not only to obtain direct participation in the process of taking the most important business decisions but also to receive direct information about the development of the investee company.

Certain PE funds prefer not only to have a seat on the boards but to have a majority there, which allows them to reshape the investee company in compliance with their vision for its structure and operation since quite often the Bulgarian investee companies need to implement and develop more advanced business techniques and capabilities.

Given that the majority of the PE investments in Bulgaria are made by foreign PE funds, it is not typical to see their managers holding interest in the investee company.

The management of the investee company (which is often the former majority shareholder) is often granted participation either in the investee company itself or in another structure of the PE fund. Normally, the participation is effected on the grounds of a shareholders' agreement, which provides, inter alia, for call/put options, drag/tag-along rights, achievement of certain financial results which in turn are linked to benefits and bonuses for the operational management (which, as mentioned above is often the former majority shareholder) earn-out clauses with respect to the price for the minority shares held by the management of the company etc.

## 4.2 Common protections for investors

Depending on the legal form chosen for the setting up of the PE fund, the investors have different rights. The choice of form is from the following:

- joint stock company: the investors have the right to information (rather limited, realised through submission of documents and information related to the specific agenda items of a convened GMS; the statute may provide for wider rights); the right to vote at the GMS; the right to dismiss/elect members of the board of directors/supervisory board (in the two-tier management system, the management board is elected by the supervisory board); the right to have investments above a certain value approved by the GMS; the right to sue the members of the boards; and the right to have the annual financial reports audited by an auditor different from the statutory one. Therefore, the strongest protection for the investor is to have a seat (or majority of the seats if we have a majority participation) in the board of directors or the management board of the investee company. This will allow the investor not just to receive information or vote at a GMS once or twice a year but to be directly involved in everything that the investee company is doing, to participate in the formation of the policies and even in the negotiation of specific deals. Such participation could be further strengthened by having a representative of the investor elected executive director, i.e. statutory representative, of the investee company. By implementing a dual signature system, the executive director would have hands-on control on all of the activities of the company. Given that it is typical for the members of the board of directors/management board of the investee company to distribute the various management functions between them, one would see the representatives of the PE investors responsible for or supervising the financial activities of the company;
- limited liability company: similar to those above, however, it is to be

noted that the limited liability company does not have a board so the options of the investor's options are more restricted—it should either have its representative elected manager of the company (i.e. statutory representative of the company) or have him or her elected comptroller of the company, but the latter option is really rarely used. As many PE funds prefer not to have their representatives engaged in the day-to-day management of the investee company (after all they are financial, not strategic investors), they would rather have their nominee employed as financial director of the company in order to control the financial cash flow and leave the operational management in the hands of the professionals from the respective business sector;

- limited partnership: the investors have to make sure that the company's articles of association provide for sufficient methods of protection, as none are provided in the law. Those would include primarily various information rights as the law does not allow the limited partners to interfere with the management decisions of the general partner/s;
- partnership limited by shares: the shareholders (who equate to limited partners) are entitled to vote at the GMS of the company, to request information, to carry out audits of the company etc. However, they may not participate in the board of directors as by law the latter is composed of general partners only; and
- general partnership/pool of assets and the company managing it: all protections are to be regulated by the agreement between the general partnership/pool of assets and the company.

### 4.3  Common protections for management

Various techniques have been employed by managers of an investment vehicle in order to protect their rights, especially when they are minority shareholders in the investment vehicle.

The management could seek veto rights over certain major business or corporate decisions. As an alternative to the veto rights, the management (minority shareholder) could seek a higher majority for the adoption of certain decisions that would automatically include the minority shareholder's vote. Another typical technique is the put option, as well as tag-along rights.

The minority shareholders' rights would again depend on the legal structure that the founders of the PE fund choose. Such rights are legally regulated for joint stock companies only and include:

- shareholders holding at least 5% of the shares for more than three months have the right to convene the GMS of the joint stock company and to include additional items in the agenda of the GMS convened by them;
- shareholders holding at least 10%of the shares have the right to lodge a claim on behalf of the joint stock company against the management for damages caused to the company;
- shareholders holding at least 10% of the shares have the right to request from the GMS of the joint stock company the appointment of a controller to verify the annual financial report; and
- shareholders holding at least 5% of the share capital may request from

the court the appointment of a new liquidator for the terminated joint stock company.

However, for apparent reasons, the above rights were designed in order to protect minority shareholders who are not involved in the management of the company.

The most typical tools for protection of the management's interests are the contractual ones. Through the contract, the management could be released of liability that is due to their negligence or ask for an insurance coverage in case a third party, including the state, claims damages directly from the management. The above tools would not work if the damages are caused by the management through intentional actions or omissions to act or due to their gross negligence. Furthermore, the management cannot be contractually protected in case their actions or omissions to act constituted an administrative offence or a crime under the Penal Code as in those cases they would be liable to the Bulgarian state, not to the company they manage.

## 4.4  Management warranties

Bulgarian practice in respect of management warranties expected by the PE fund is still to be developed.

Under the CA, the board members of a joint stock company deposit a guarantee for the management of the company set at an amount determined by the GMS but never amounting to less than three months' worth of gross salary. The guarantee may be in the form of company shares or bonds. Once the board members are released from their office and relieved of liability, the guarantee is returned to them.

As indicated above, the management agreement may provide for the exculpation of the managers for ordinary negligence or the limitation of their liability for ordinary negligence up to a certain amount. The liability for gross negligence or wilful misconduct may not be limited or exculpated in any way.

## 4.5  Good leaver/bad leaver provisions

The good/bad leaver clauses in a management agreement or a shareholders' agreement would be based exclusively on the freedom of contract and not on specific legal provisions or court practice.

Therefore, the good/bad leaver provisions should define in detail when the leaving manager would be viewed as a good leaver and when as a bad leaver. Special attention should be paid if the management could be discharged by a resolution of the GMS without any particular fault on the side of the management. In this case, the management would be normally considered a good leaver.

Typically, the good/bad leaver provisions would have at least the following implications: (1) compensation paid to the management in case of termination; and (2) possible compensation for damages due by the management.

Given that often the management of the investee company is the former majority or even single owner of that company, the good/bad leaver situation is also to be seen from the perspective of his/her remaining a minority shareholder in the investee company. Typically, the good/bad leaver situation would trigger the compulsory transfer of equity interest held by the management. Quite often, the price for that minority shareholding would depend on whether the leaving management is actually in a good or bad leaver situation. To secure the completion of the transfer, the management's shares are normally put in escrow and the escrow agent is entitled to transfer the shares in the event of circumstances that constitute a good/bad leaver scenario.

### 4.6 Public to private transactions

In Bulgaria, public-to-private transactions are rare, yet there have been examples of PE funds acquiring control over listed companies and then delisting them. In some of those cases, the management of the target acted jointly with the PE fund and acquired shares in the special purpose vehicle (SPV)/the target, subject to various covenants contained in shareholders' agreements.

When planning an investment in a public company, the investor needs to consider at least the following factors:

- the statutory requirements for a tender offer once certain percentage of the voting capital is acquired;
- the possibility to squeeze out the minority shareholders and delist the company once the minimum of 95% of the voting capital is acquired;
- the mandatory rules regarding the formation of the price of the tender offer; and
- the insider trading prohibition, which is of particular relevance if a data room is organised by the investee company/its majority shareholders prior to the completion of the acquisition.

## 5. EXITS

The PE funds that are most active in Bulgaria are not set up or raised locally, so it is not possible at this stage to make a generalisation as to the warranties to be provided in the case of exit or the lock-up periods during which the PE fund would be contractually prohibited from exiting through an initial public offering (IPO).

### 5.1 Secondary sales

Secondary sales are very common exits for PE funds that operate in Bulgaria.

Depending on the company type of the investee, the exit would take the form of either a sale of shares in a limited liability company (providing for notarised agreement and registration of the sale with the state commercial registry) or a sale of shares in a joint stock company (endorsement of the share certificates and their registration in the shareholders book, which is typically held by the investee in the case of materialised shares, or registration with the Central Depository AD in the case of dematerialised shares).

Depending on the percentage of shares transferred and the industry in which the investee company operates the acquirer, often assisted by the exiting PE fund and the company may need to get consents or permits (e.g. to acquire qualified participation in a bank—10% or more of the voting shares).

The purchase by the acquirer of a minority participation in the investee company does not automatically mean that no concentration clearance is needed. Various other factors are to be assessed, such as presence of a joint management agreement, presence of shareholders agreement and alike.

## 5.2 Trade sales

Trade sales are also a typical way for the PE fund to exit its investment.

A trade sale done in Bulgaria would take the same forms as the secondary sales described in s.5.1 above.

Trade sales, however, are more likely to be dependent on concentration clearance by the Bulgarian competition authorities.

Together with the transfer of control, the PE fund—seller of a majority/100% package will have to be released of all forms of control over the investee company, therefore the acquirer of the control over the investment vehicle would have to release the PE funds representatives in the management bodies not only from their positions but also from liability towards the investee company.

Depending on the industry in which the trade sale is taking place, various additional issues such as transfer of licences and registration, non-solicitation and non-competition etc need to be considered. Again, in some industries, the very transfer of control over a regulated entity is subject to regulatory clearance—e.g. banking, insurance.

One of the issues that is most difficult to deal with is that of representations and warranties as the exiting PE fund will be willing to warrant as few things as possible, while the acquirer will have the opposite interest. Very often, the acquirer would ask that a portion of the purchase price is deposited for a certain period in an escrow account as security for the compensation to be received by the acquirer in case of damages. In turn, the PE funds would fiercely oppose such a demand.

In recent years, in more and more deals, the warranties and the escrowed amount issues have been addressed by warranties' insurance policies. As a result, the exiting PE fund would be able to receive its sale price in full without any deductions or withholdings for possible future compensations.

## 5.3 Initial public offerings

IPOs are another possible exit for a PE fund that has made an investment in a Bulgarian company. However, this option is applicable only with respect to joint stock companies, therefore, prior to exiting an investment in another type of company, say, a limited liability company, the PE fund would have first to transform it into a joint stock company and make sure its shares are freely transferable (i.e. it would have to deal with the possible call/put options, drag/tag-along rights and rights of first refusal, established with respect to the investee shares).

An IPO has to be completed under the formal procedure regulated by the POSA. The investee company needs to be registered as a public company with the Central Depository, the Financial Supervision Commission and the Commercial Register and then its shares are listed on the Bulgarian Stock Exchange. IPOs are preconditioned by the publication by the investee of a prospectus approved by the Financial Supervision Commission.

The managers of the company are liable under the law for damages suffered by third parties as a result of untrue or misleading information contained in the prospectus.

## 5.4 Refinancings

This is also a possible exit under the laws of Bulgaria. However, when borrowing money in order to distribute it to the PE fund, the investee should make sure it does not get into a situation of over-indebtedness. If it does, the investee risks going into bankruptcy and its creditors may seek to reclaim the payments made to the shareholders.

## 5.5 Restructuring/insolvency

Due to the peculiarities of Bulgarian insolvency proceedings, they do not appear to be a suitable exit for an investment. Insolvency proceedings are under the control of the court and creditors so, unless the PE fund is the largest creditor of the investee, it would not have significant influence over the insolvency proceedings and the outcome of them. Cases where shareholders non-creditors have received at least a portion of their investments at the end of insolvency proceedings are rare if occurring at all.

### Voluntary liquidation

The voluntary liquidation of the investee company is a possible, yet not very popular exit for the PE fund. It would need to have, first, all of the assets of the investee company converted into cash, all claims of third parties (or of the shareholders acting as creditors) satisfied and only then could the reminder of the cash assets be distributed to the investors. In other words, depending on the scope of activities and the size of the investee company, the liquidation procedure could take from six to eight months to a couple of years. On the other hand, the taxes payable with respect to the proceeds of the liquidation are lower.

Such exits would be more typical for entities that invest in assets, like real estates, without engaging in active commercial activities, which would simplify the liquidation activities (i.e. no need to deal with termination of employees, performance of the pending third parties agreements, settlement of claims, payments, receivables etc).

## 6. TAX
## 6.1 Taxation of fund structures

The PE funds incorporated in Bulgaria are subject to 10% corporate tax under the Corporate Income Tax Act 2006 (CITA). The tax base for assessment of the corporate tax is the tax profit—the accounting financial result adjusted for tax purposes under the rules of the CITA. Certain expenses, such as representative expenses and social security expenses (e.g. for additional voluntary social security or for voluntary health insurance) are subject to tax.

Upon exiting an investment in a Bulgarian company, a PE fund that is not incorporated in Bulgaria will have to pay a capital gains tax of 10% levied over the positive difference between the selling price and the acquisition price. A double taxation avoidance treaty may provide for a more beneficial tax rate. A Bulgarian PE fund would not pay a separate withholding tax but the capital gain would become part of its annual taxable result.

Upon exiting an investment in a Bulgarian investee company through liquidation of the same, a PE fund that is not incorporated in Bulgaria will have to pay withholding tax of 5% levied over the positive difference between the amount of the liquidation quota distributed to the investor and the acquisition price of its shareholding. A double taxation avoidance treaty may provide for a more beneficial tax rate. A Bulgarian PE fund would not pay a separate withholding tax but the positive difference would become part of its annual taxable result.

No withholding tax is due if the liquidation quota is distributed in favour of the PE fund that is incorporated in any of the 28 EU Member States or in another country which is a Contracting Party to the Agreement on the European Economic Area 1994.

A company or a branch set up by foreign investors will be subject to identical taxation as those set up by Bulgarian investors.

As a rule, foreign investors (both legal entities and individuals who are not Bulgarian tax residents) will be taxed in Bulgaria on certain incomes of Bulgarian origin that they have received, provided they have no permanent establishment in Bulgaria with which the income is associated. Bulgarian investors, both legal entities and individuals who are Bulgarian tax residents (irrespective of their nationality and citizenship) will be taxed in Bulgaria on their global income.

Foreign investors will typically be subject to the following taxes:

- withholding tax on the dividends and liquidation quota: the rate is 5% but can be reduced under an applicable double tax treaty. Corporate investors from EU/European Economic Area countries will pay no withholding tax on the dividends/liquidation quota distributed by a Bulgarian company;
- withholding tax on the capital gain: the rate is 10% but can be reduced under an applicable double taxation avoidance treaty. No tax is paid with respect to the capital gains from the sale of publicly traded securities; and
- withholding tax on the interest: the rate is 10% but can be reduced under an applicable double taxation avoidance treaty. If the conditions of the Directive 2003/49 on a common system of taxation applicable to interest and royalty payments made between associated companies of different Member States [2003] OJ L157/49 are met, the income from interest shall not be subject to withholding tax in Bulgaria.

In addition, the following incomes from interests are exempt from withholding tax: (1) an income from interests' payments on bonds or other debt instruments issued by a Bulgarian resident legal person and admitted to trading on a regulated market in Bulgaria, in a Member State of the EU or in another state which is a Contracting Party to the Agreement on the European Economic Area; and (2) any income from interest payments on a loan extended by a non-Bulgarian resident person who is an issuer of bonds or other debt securities, where the following conditions are simultaneously fulfilled: (a) the issuer is resident for tax purposes in a Member State of the EU or in another state which is a Contracting Party to the Agreement on the European Economic Area; (b) the issuer has issued the bonds or the other debt securities for the purpose of lending the proceeds therefrom to a legal person who is a Bulgarian tax resident; and (c) the bonds or the other debt securities have been admitted to trading on a regulated market in Bulgaria, in a Member State of the EU or in another state which is a Contracting Party to the Agreement on the European Economic Area.

There are no tax preferences/benefits that depend on the chosen legal structure.

## 6.2   Carried interest

The law does not provide for any special tax treatment of the portion of the funds' profits that the investment managers are entitled to receive. Provided that the PE fund is incorporated in Bulgaria, the decision to distribute carried interest to the investment executives is taken by the GMS of the respective entity in compliance with its bylaws.

In cases in which the managers of a Bulgarian PE fund are Bulgarian tax residents, the carried interest forms part of their gross annual taxable income, which, upon making certain statutory deductions, is taxed at a rate of 10%.

In cases where the managers of a Bulgarian PE fund are not Bulgarian tax residents, the carried interest is subject to 10% withholding tax, which can be reduced under an applicable double taxation avoidance treaty.

## 6.3   Management equity

Taxation of management equity depends to a great extent on the specific mechanism chosen to award the equity to the manager/s. The law does not provide for specific taxation, therefore, it is taxed either as remuneration under an employment or a management contract (more likely), or as a gift (less likely). Managers are also taxed when disposing of their equity. The administrative or court practice is not sufficient to allow for the definition of clearer rules with respect to this issue.

## 6.4   Loan interest

Bulgarian PE funds are supposed to withhold tax at a rate of 10% on the interests payable to their foreign creditors. The rate can be reduced should an applicable double tax treaty provide for more beneficial terms.

See the explanation about the withholding tax on the interests payable to associated companies in s.6.1 above.

The interests paid by Bulgarian PE funds constitute a business expense for the PE fund. However, in the case of a thin capitalisation, the interests' expenses will not be recognised as such during the year of their payment. Instead, they will participate in a mechanism for regulation of the thin capitalisation providing for their expending during a period of five years.

## 6.5   Transaction taxes

Foreign tax residents pay withholding tax of 10% over the positive difference between the acquisition value and the sale price of the shares. Bulgarian tax residents have to include in their overall annual tax income, which is subject to 10%, an amount equal to the positive difference between the profit and the loss they made from the sale of shares within the respective tax year.

There is no value added tax (VAT) or similar tax on the transfer of shares or transfer of ongoing concern.

VAT is to be charged in the case of an asset deal (although the transfer of some assets could be VAT exempt). The VAT rate is of 20%.

Transaction tax is levied on the acquisition of any properties by donation and on the acquisition against payment of immovable properties, limited real rights and motor vehicles registered in Bulgaria. The tax rate for acquisition against payment is determined by every municipality independently at a rate of between 0.1% up to 3% of the higher of the transactional value or the assessed tax value. Quite often, acquisitions of real estates are structured as acquisitions of special purpose companies set up to hold the title of the real estate, yet these deals contain some additional tax risks.

## 7.   CURRENT TOPICAL ISSUES/TRENDS

Currently, the stagnation of the PE market is due mainly to the large gap between sellers' expectations and buyers' offers with respect to the equity price and the reluctance of the banks to finance such transactions.

The investors are focused on the development of their current portfolios and some of them have started to approach new investments in businesses such as shopping centres, renewable energy sources, IT, real estate, foods and beverages and agriculture.

Despite its modest size, the possibilities for growth that the Bulgarian economy offers are attracting the attention of many international PE funds. For example, 2017 and the beginning of 2018 would be long remembered for the massive acquisitions of Bulgarian shopping centres made by PE funds. Many new local players have started to participate actively in PE transactions. They cannot compete with the large international giants in terms of volume of the investments they could accumulate but their young, professional, well-educated and, above all, ambitious managers were able to produce some rather nice results for their investors.

# France

**Willkie Farr & Gallagher LLP** Eduardo Fernandez,
Grégoire Finance & Philippe Grudé

## 1. MARKET OVERVIEW
### 1.1 Types of investors

France ranks second in Europe behind the UK in terms of the amount of funds raised, with EUR 16.5 billion funds raised in 2017, 63% of which were raised from domestic sources.[1]

The funds raised in France are invested by banks, pension funds, funds of funds, sovereign funds, insurance companies, individuals/family businesses, state-owned or local public institutions and corporate investors. Among them, the main subscribers are funds of funds, insurance companies, individuals and public investors.

### 1.2 Types of investments

Private equity funds are active in France at all stages of company life, from start-up to expansion, buyout or turnaround. Buyout operations are favoured by private equity funds in terms of amounts invested, collecting about 70% of the overall amounts invested.[2] However, in terms of the number of companies invested in, buyouts represent less than 16%, innovation and development capital being generally the most important stages.

A great majority of the funds raised in France are invested in domestic companies, both private and public.

With respect to public companies, in which private equity funds are entitled to invest (subject to certain limits for certain categories of French funds as detailed below), the amount invested remain significantly lower than investments in private equity. These investments are generally made through the purchase or subscription of minority stakes, also known as private investment in public equity (PIPE) rather than public to private (or P-to-P) transactions which, as detailed below, remain rare on the French stock market.

Over the last three years, the trends have shown a great attractiveness of the French market with: (1) an increase in the number of companies invested in and, more specifically, in start-up and expansion investment; (2) increased amounts invested in each transaction; and (3) an increase in the market liquidity through successful exits.

---

[1]   See France Invest–Grant Thornton, *Activité des acteurs français du capital-investissement*, 28th edn (2018), p.4 available at: *http://www.franceinvest.eu/dl.php?table=ani_fichiers&nom_file=France-Invest-Etudes-2017-Activite-2017-VDEF.pdf&chemin=uploads/_afic* [Accessed 25 September 2018].

[2]   See France Invest–Grant Thornton, *Activité des acteurs français du capital-investissement* (2018), p.18.

## 2. FUNDS

### 2.1 Fund structures

The most commonly used vehicles by French private equity participants are FCPs (*Fonds Communs de Placement*), which are a category of alternative investment funds (AIFs) within the meaning of Directive 2011/61 on Alternative Investment Fund Managers and amending Directives 2003/41 and 2009/65 and Regulations 1060/2009 and 1095/2010 [2011] OJ L174/1 (AIFM Directive). An FCP is not an incorporated legal entity but a co-ownership of financial instruments without separate legal personality. The operation of FCPs involves three parties: (1) the investors, purchasing the interests or units (parts) of the fund; (2) a management company (the equivalent of a managing general partner in a UK limited partnership), managing the funds and taking the investment decisions; and (3) a depositary, ensuring asset custody and controlling the regularity of certain decisions taken by the management company. An FCP achieves a dissociation of equity financing from fiduciary management duties, which makes it comparable to limited partnerships.

There are two main types of FCP: FCPRs that intend to offer units to the public, the formation of which requires prior approval of the French stock market regulation authority (*Autorité des Marchés Financiers* or AMF) (named "authorised FCPRs" or *FCPRs agréés*); and FPCIs (Fonds Professionnels de Capital Investissement) that intend to offer units only to qualified investors and do not require the approval of the AMF.

Sub-types of FCPs eligible for retail investors with specific investment rules and ratios have been created by French legislators to favour investment in specific areas or to provide greater flexibility to private equity participants: FCPIs (*Fonds Communs de Placement dans l'Innovation*), dedicated to investment in innovation; FIPs (*Fonds d'Investissement de Proximité*), dedicated to local investment in designated territorial zones; and FPSs (*Fonds professionnels spécialisés*) which intend to offer units only to qualified investors who require a vehicle with greater investment flexibility than FPCIs or authorised FCPRs. Recently, the legislator has adopted new legal provisions providing for the creation of a limited partnership (SLPs). SLPs are part of the FPS and are substantially similar to the Luxembourg or Anglo-Saxon limited partnership, except for the fact that they have legal personality but are tax transparent for French tax purposes.

Another important structure used by private equity participants in France is *sociétés de capital-risque* (SCRs), regular limited liability companies benefitting from an advantageous tax regime, the exclusive corporate purpose of which is the management of securities portfolio. SCRs which fall within the definition of an AIF pursuant to the AIFM Directive are also subject to the control of the AMF.

### 2.2 Regulation of fundraising and fund managers

#### Marketing of private equity funds

##### Authorised FCPR

Units of authorised FCPRs (*FCPRs agréés*) can be subscribed by any investor, either professional or non-professional. This implies greater regulation, which explains why the creation of such FCPs must be authorised by the AMF, which shall also approve certain changes in a fund's organisation, such as a change of the management company, the custodian or the FCP auditor, or a modification in its investment policy.

### FPCIs

The creation of FPCIs, unlike authorised FCPRs, is subject to a mere declaration to the AMF. Units of FPCIs may be subscribed only by "qualified" investors or investors subscribing a minimum of EUR 100,000. French law and the AMF Regulation (General Regulation of the *Autorité des Marchés Financiers* (Order of 20 December 2017, *Official Journal* of 23 December 2017)) provides for strict control measures to ensure that units of FPCIs are subscribed or purchased by such investors only.

Any direct or indirect solicitation to subscribe or acquire units of FPCIs must be accompanied with a warning that the direct or indirect subscription, acquisition or transfer of such FPCI units is reserved for the investors described above.

The same rules apply to the creation and marketing of FPSs, provided, however, that FPSs are now also subject, as a result of the transposition of the AIFM Directive, to the obligation to publish a prospectus in addition to their internal rules, except if the FPS takes the form of an SLP.

### FCPIs and FIPs

FCPIs and FIPs are open to any investors and their creation is therefore subject to the same rules as those applicable to authorised FCPRs (AMF authorisation etc). They are, however, considered "retail" funds as their favourable tax regime makes them especially attractive to individuals with smaller investment capacity than institutional investors.

### SCRs

Any investors may purchase shares of an SCR although French law provides some equity holding limits. For instance, more than 30% of the share capital of an SCR cannot be held, directly or indirectly, by the same individual, their spouse or relatives in ascending or descending line. Fundraising in SCRs is done through share capital increases, sometimes by means of a public offer.

## Operation of private equity funds
### Authorised FCPRs or FPCIs

*Subscription*: investment in an authorised FCPR or FPCI is made through subscription to the fund units, which may be divided into several compartments or types of units with different rights in respect of the net assets or the fund's income, under conditions provided in the fund's internal rules. The applicable subscription periods are also set forth in the fund's internal rules, as outlined in more detail below.

*Duration*: although there are no legal provisions limiting the lifetime of an authorised FCPR or FPCI, the internal rules shall specify a term, which is generally between 8 and 10 years. The first years are usually dedicated to fundraising, the next years to investments and the last years to sale of investments and liquidation of the fund. The term can be extended with or without the prior consent of the investors depending on the internal rules.

*Investments*: as for the scope of assets in which authorised FCPRs or FPCIs may invest, French law provides that their assets comprise financial instruments (such as securities, convertible or redeemable bonds, warrants, units of other FCPs etc), deposits with French or foreign credit institutions, cash and shareholders' loans granted to companies in which the funds hold a participation, subject to a limit of 15% of the higher of its net assets or paid-up subscriptions. Unlike limited partnerships, authorised FCPRs and FPCIs must also comply with certain legal ratios, such as investment ratio (at least 50% of the assets of an authorised FCPR or FPCI must consist of securities issued by non-listed or, within a certain limit, listed companies), risk spread ratio (e.g. authorised FCPRs cannot invest more than 10% of their assets in securities of the same company) and level of participation ratio (e.g. authorised FCPRs cannot hold more than 35% of the share capital or voting rights of the same company).

Such constraints applicable to the assets which can be held by FCPs are not applicable to FPS or SLP which have very limited investment restrictions.

### FCPIs and FIPs

Substantially, the same rules as those applicable to authorised FCPRs apply to FCPIs and FIPs, except for the investment ratio, which is subject to further limitations: FCPIs must invest at least 70% (previously 60%) of their assets in securities of innovative non-public companies, whereas FIPs must invest at least 70% (previously 60%) of their assets in small to medium-sized businesses located within specific geographical zones.

### FPSs

*Subscription and duration*: substantially, the same rules as described above for the subscription and the duration of regular FCPs are applicable to contractual FPSs.

*Investments*: as for the scope of assets, FPSs may invest in the same instruments as the other FCPs but they are also eligible to invest notably in: (1) futures to cover the exposure of their participations; (2) securities of other French or foreign funds or investment vehicles, including vehicles mostly composed of real estate assets or debts; and (3) debts of listed or non-listed companies (without limitation).

Unlike authorised FCPRs or FPCIs, there are no specific investment, risk spread or level of participation ratios to be complied within FPSs and such ratios will result from a negotiation between investors and the management company.

### SCRs

*Subscription*: investment in SCRs is mostly made through subscription to shares via share capital increases. In addition to direct equity investment, SCRs may ask investors to lend to the SCR (through shareholders' loans or subscription of bonds) the necessary funds for the contemplated investments. This is a flexible solution for drawing down the necessary funds "just in time" for an investment but also to reimburse the funds after a divestment.

*Duration*: the term of an SCR, which is set forth in its articles of association, is generally of 8–10 years, aligned with the usual FCP life period.

*Investment*: an SCR's total debt shall never exceed more than 10% of its net assets. SCRs must also comply with certain legal ratios, such as investment ratio (substantially similar to the FCP ratio), risk spread ratio (no more than 25% of an SCR net balance sheet situation shall be invested in securities of a given company) or level of participation ratio (participation in a portfolio company must not exceed 40% of the voting rights in that company).

### Overview of any law or regulation governing how funds may be managed in the relevant jurisdiction
#### FCPs (authorised FCPRs, FPCIs, FIPs, FPCIs and SLPs)

FCPs are managed by a management company, which is an investment firm subject to the AMF's authorisation. With the AIFMD, FCPs can also be managed by any manager which is approved by any EU regulator as an AIFM. The management company represents the fund's unit holders (i.e. the investors) and must administer the fund independently and in the exclusive interest of the investors. A French management company must have its registered office and effective headquarters located in France and may choose any kind of French corporate form, subject to verification of its articles of association by the AMF and provided that its annual accounts are subject to legal control (art.312-2 of the AMF Regulation).

As regards their internal organisation, management companies must be managed by at least two persons with recognised skills and experience, and at least one of them shall be empowered to represent the company. Management companies shall also provide the AMF with the identity of its direct or indirect shareholders (whether individuals or legal entities) as well as the amount of their respective participation. The AMF will then assess the status of these shareholders in regard to the necessity of guaranteeing sound and prudent management.

Management companies must also have sufficient initial capital (at least EUR 125,000 of paid-up capital) and must maintain a securities and deposits guarantee facility (*mécanisme de garantie des titres et des dépôts*).

French management companies must establish and provide to the AMF an activities schedule for each of the services it intends to offer, which specifies the manner in which it intends to provide the investment services and indicates the type of transactions contemplated as well as its organisational structure.

As regards reporting requirements, management companies are obliged, inter alia, to: (1) disclose twice per year the composition of the fund net asset, the fund liquidating value, the leverage of the fund and the results of crisis simulation tests; and (2) publish the fund annual report at the end of the fiscal year. To ensure stability and integrity of the financial market, the AMF is also entitled to impose certain additional reporting requirements to management companies.

Finally, management companies must carry out periodical evaluation of the fund's assets, in an accurate and independent manner, either internally (provided, in such case, that the management company shall ensure the independency of the persons responsible for the evaluation) or externally through qualified experts.

### SCRs

Unlike FCPs, which are managed by an external company, SCRs are managed by the company's relevant management body, depending on the corporate form chosen. Among the different possible forms, which include *société anonyme* (SA), *société en commandite par actions* (SCA) and *société par actions simplifiée* (SAS), the SAS is currently the preferred corporate form for SCRs as it provides adequate flexibility for private equity activity. Management stability can be achieved through statutory irremovability or creation of different classes of shares, and managers are not subject to the concurrent holding-of-seats limitation existing in the SA and may therefore manage simultaneously several SCRs as a management company would for FCPs.

SCRs are regulated by general corporate law applicable to the chosen form and, for those which fall within the definition of AIF, by a number of new regulatory rules, in particular the obligations to be registered with the AMF as an AIF, to comply with periodic reporting obligations and, in certain cases, to appoint a custodian (*dépositaire*).

It should be noted that French SCRs and FCPs active in investment capital are also subject to the *Association Française de la Gestion Financière* (AFG) /*Association Française des Investisseurs pour la Croissance* (AFIC) professional code of ethics, which provides a number of compulsory rules and recommendations relating to, inter alia, conflict of interests, internal control, shareholders rights, management policy and investor relations.

## 2.3 Customary or common terms of funds

FCPs establish a document setting forth their internal rules, which is attached to the fund's authorisation request (for authorised FCPRs) or its declaration of existence (for FPCIs, FPSs and SLPs). The key terms of an FCP's internal rules that are of particular relevance for investors are as follows.

### Investment policy

Sets forth the fund's investment orientation, such as the proposed stage of investment (start-up, development, buyouts), investment scope (minority or controlling stakes), targeted economic sectors, size of target companies, territorial zones or type of instruments (shares, convertible or redeemable bonds etc).

### Co-investment

In cases where a management company manages several investment vehicles, the internal rules will provide for certain limitations and rules applicable to co-investments with the other investment vehicles under common management, in particular in respect of maximum co-invested amount, priority of certain funds etc.

### Subscription policy

This clause provides the fund's subscription policy, i.e. the periods during which investors may subscribe to the fund's units. Such subscription periods are generally defined by a limited term but internal rules may also provide that the subscription period will be closed early if certain targets are achieved (amounts subscribed, number of units issued, amount of assets invested etc) or, on the contrary, provide for the extension of the subscription period. The right for FCPs to organise a progressive call for funds by the management company to the investors, which allows availability of funds just in time for the contemplated investments, is a key element, in particular to optimise the internal rate of return (IRR) of investors.

**Reporting obligations**
  In addition to legal reporting requirements, the internal rules may provide other periodical reporting obligations, for instance, the obligation to inform investors of the evolution of the fund's portfolio companies, any contemplated investments or any completed transactions. To ensure stability and integrity of the financial market, the AMF is also entitled to impose additional reporting requirements to management companies.

**Units rights**
  The internal rules will also describe the different types of units issued by the FCP and the rights attaching thereto (voting rights, priority payment to certain units, subordination of others, units of "carried interest", as described below, capital gain allocation etc).

**Management fee and carried interest**
  The provisions relating to: (1) the proportion of capital gain (i.e. carried interest) to be allocated to the management team (usually 20%); (2) the management fees to be paid to the management company (usually 1.5–2.5%); and (3) the basis (i.e. net assets or profits of the funds, such as capital gains, dividends and interests) to which such percentages will apply are detailed in the funds' internal rules and are generally heavily negotiated between investors and managers.

**Governance**
  The provisions relating to: (1) the proportion of capital gain (i.e. carried interest) to be allocated to the management team (usually 20%); (2) the management fees to be paid to the management company (usually 1.5–3%); and (3) the basis (i.e. net assets or profits of the funds, such as capital gains, dividends and interests) to which such percentages will apply are detailed in the funds' internal rules and are generally heavily negotiated between investors and managers.

**Hurdle clause**
  Carried interest clauses are often subject to a hurdle rate which provides that a minimum interest rate shall be allocated to investors before paying the carried interest. The average hurdle rate for example for buyout funds is generally 6–8%.

**Key managers**
  Key managers clauses are considered to be particularly important by investors as they provide that investments shall be suspended until the replacement of one or more departing managers, whether the departure is voluntary or not. In certain cases, the departure of key managers will authorise

investors to require the early dissolution of the fund.

### Default clause

To avoid an investor's failure to fully pay up the amount of its subscription when called upon to do so by the management company, the fund's internal rules often provide for coercive measures, such as late payment interests or the forced transfer of units.

### Divorce clause

The insertion of a "divorce" clause, which entitles investors to replace the management company or the management team, is more and more common. If replacement is requested for breach, the management company or its management team will generally lose part of the carried interest whereas, if it is requested without breach (and subject to certain investors' majority requirements), the management company is generally entitled to indemnification and its carried interest (or a substantial part thereof).

### Ethical investment

Certain investors insist that the internal rules of the fund include an undertaking to follow socially conscious guidelines or principles, so as to favour investments that promote environmental stewardship, consumer protection, human rights and diversity.

### Side letters

Bilateral agreements or "side letters" between certain investors and the management company in respect of certain specific topics, such as reporting, co-investment rules or units transfer, are also common practice in France.

The foregoing key provisions are also relevant for the SCR fund structure, although they will be contained in the SCR's articles of association or shareholders' agreement, as the case may be.

## 3. DEBT FINANCE

### 3.1 Means of financing

Means of financing in France are generally consistent with what is available elsewhere in Europe. The main sources available to finance private equity acquisitions in France are bank financing (senior, super senior and first loss), subordinated debt (mezzanine, second lien and payment-in-kind (PIK) financing), direct lending also referred to as unitranche (in that respect please refer to the subsection titled "Alternative means of financing" below) and high yield bonds.

### 3.2 Restrictions on granting security

The ability of a financing bank to obtain security over the assets of a French target company can be restricted by the regulations on financial assistance as well as the rules governing "upstream" guarantees in France.

### Financial assistance

The French regulations governing financial assistance derive from Directive 77/91 on coordination of safeguards which, for the protection of the interests of members and others, are required by Member States of companies within the meaning of the second paragraph of Article 58 of the Treaty, in respect of the formation of public limited liability companies and the maintenance and alteration of their capital, with a view to making such safeguards equivalent [1977] OJ L26/1 (dated 13 December 1976) and are set forth in art.L.225-216 of the French Commercial Code, which states:

> "A company shall not advance funds, grant loans or grant a security with a view to the subscription or purchase of its own shares by a third party. The provisions of this article do not apply to normal transactions carried out by lending institutions or transactions completed within the framework of an acquisition of shares by employees of the company or one of its subsidiaries."

It is important to note that violation of this rule is subject to: (1) civil sanctions that can result in the cancellation of the transaction; and/or (2) criminal sanctions, which are applicable to the president, the directors and/or the managing directors who, in the name of the company, have carried out prohibited transactions.

According to applicable case law and doctrine, criminal provisions prohibiting the violation of the aforementioned article should be strictly interpreted. On that basis, a given transaction should not violate the provisions of art.L.225-216 of the French Commercial Code if:

- it is not an advance of funds or the granting of a loan or of a security; or
- it occurs after the envisaged acquisition is not considered as having been carried out "with a view to" the subscription or purchase of the target company's shares (i.e. even if the considered transaction occurred after the acquisition, such transaction must not have been envisaged beforehand).

It should be noted that civil sanctions or cancellation of the transaction can occur even if criminal sanctions are not applied. Indeed, French civil courts may have a broader construction of the provisions of art.L.225-216 of the French Commercial Code and could, for instance, decide that transactions occurring in connection with (rather than strictly prior to) the acquisition could be qualified as prohibited financial assistance.

**Upstream guarantee limitations**

Guarantees of any type (personal guarantees, independent demand guarantees, comfort letters, mortgages or pledges) issued by a French target company to meet the needs of its French or foreign parent company (or of another company controlled by its parent) may be challenged under French law if the issuance of the guarantee is: (1) not in the target company's best interests; or (2) considered a misappropriation of the corporate assets and misuse of the credit of a company (*abus de biens sociaux*), i.e. an act of using the company's assets or credit in bad faith in a manner that is contrary to the best interests of said company to bring about personal benefit or to benefit another company in which the directors hold direct or indirect interests (art.L.242-6 of the French Commercial Code), which exposes directors violating the provision to criminal sanctions.

The "best interests" concept is defined by French courts on a case-by-case basis but the criteria most often used to determine whether the guarantee is inconsistent with the target company's best interests are the same ones typically applied in criminal cases to determine whether the issuance of the guarantee constitutes an improper use of the assets and credit of the company issuing the guarantee.

The existence of a "group interest" may, subject to certain conditions, be put forward to try to justify the granting of upstream guarantees. Those conditions are: (1) the existence of a "true corporate group structure"; and (2) financial imperatives.

### Existence of a "true group structure"

Both companies (i.e. the company suffering a detriment and the beneficiary company) must belong to a group of companies that is coherent, has a common strategy, a certain degree of economic unity, i.e. with economic or commercial relationships, and brings parents and subsidiaries under the ultimate control of a holding company with control over the entire group.

### Financial imperatives

The guarantee must be in the common interest of the group and granted in the context of a group strategy, the financial capacities of the target company must not be exceeded, there must be a consideration for the target company and the guarantee must not lead to an imbalanced situation between the company issuing the guarantee and the guaranteed entity.

## 3.3   Intercreditor issues

French intercreditor agreements are generally fairly consistent with the English approach. Some specific features, however, are worth mentioning when considering or discussing intercreditor agreements, in particular the following:

- although historically, certain practitioners had concerns as to the validity and, more importantly, the enforceability of ranking provisions in intercreditor agreements, a number of court decisions have confirmed the validity of such provisions under French law over the past years. However, even though these provisions remain enforceable between parties to the intercreditor agreement, in liquidation proceedings, a court will not be compelled to take the intercreditor provisions into account when redistributing the liquidation proceeds. If certain creditors have not received what they believe they should have received, they will then need to make a claim against those who received more than such creditors believe they ought to have received, pursuant to the "turn over" provisions of the intercreditor agreement. This of course is likely to result in a fairly lengthy process as it adds another litigation to the liquidation proceedings;
- under French law, an undertaking to do or not to do a specific action is not in principle subject to specific performance. Even though a French court may order that a party take or refrain from taking an action under a penalty (*astreinte*), this is not exactly the equivalent of an English law injunction. Ultimately, the party that has been harmed by a breach of contract will be entitled to damages but there again it will require additional litigation to recover them;

- one feature that exists in typical English law intercreditor documentation and that is uncommon under French law is a power of attorney granted to the security agent to release security and/or debt of subordinated creditors if this is deemed necessary for enforcing security. The reason for this is that such power of attorney is most likely to be construed as not being in the common interest of the senior and subordinated creditors and therefore revocable under French law and as such of limited benefit in an enforcement scenario; and
- the introduction of a safeguard process (*sauvegarde*) and its subsequent amendments tend to support the efficiency of French intercreditor agreements as French law now expressly provides that the treatment of the various creditors can be different according to their specific situations, which is generally interpreted as allowing the intercreditor provisions to take effect in court-led restructuring.

## 3.4 Syndication
### Market trends

There are various ways to get banks to commit to a financing in the current environment, ranging from a "best effort" deal in which the arrangers solely advise the borrower on the terms which may be acceptable to the investors on the market to an underwritten deal in which a bank or a group of banks will commit to the entirety of the financing with a view to sell down the committed amounts in excess of their final take. Alternatively, borrowers and sponsors may proceed by way of a club deal where the share of each arranger is equal to its final take and where there is no syndication (in effect, the syndication has taken place before the deal is signed).

Where relevant syndication of bank financing is an absolute key issue which will drive the terms of the "market flex" clause, which could change the economic weight of the debt in a deal fairly significantly, hence the sponsor sensitivity to the issue. We have seen some increasing volatility on the markets depending in particular on the number of deals being presented to the market at a given time leading to the actual use of "market flex".

There is also a growing competition of unitranche financings (i.e. a deal in which all the facilities are ranking pari passu) provided by alternative non-bank investors.

### Legal aspects

Technically, syndication does not raise a lot of legal issues. The technique most generally used is a transfer by way of assignment. Such transfer no longer requires a notification to be served by a bailiff to the borrower as a perfection formality.

The French Monetary and Financial Code provides that the carrying out of "banking transactions" in France (such as lending to a borrower in France) on a "habitual" basis is only permitted for credit institutions licensed by the French banking authorities. These institutions may be French banks, French branches of foreign banks having a banking license in France, or EU credit or financial institutions which have the benefit of a European "passport". Article L.311-1 of the French Monetary and Financial Code defines "banking transactions" as including "credit operations", the latter being defined by art.L.313-1 of the French Monetary and Financial Code as, inter alia, "any act by which a person for a consideration makes or promises to make funds available to another person or assumes, on behalf of the latter, a contingent liability". This is interpreted widely and will include not only the more obvious act of lending itself, but also the provision, for example, of a commitment to lend to a French borrower.

In practice, this would prevent, for example, collateralised loan obligations (CLOs) from purchasing French debt. However, a new exception has been implemented since 3 January 2018 under which the prohibition of carrying out credit operations no longer applies to foreign entities such as credit institutions (*établissements de crédit*), financing entities (*sociétés de financement*), investment funds (*organismes de placement collectif*), pension funds (*organismes de retraite*), and securitisation vehicles (*organismes de titrisation*) as long as their activities are similar to those of the French-licensed institutions.[3] Under such new exception, French-licensed institutions are able to assign the loan receivables they hold to such relevant foreign institutions in compliance with the banking monopoly rules which will therefore ease large international syndications for French-based borrowers.

### Alternative means of financing
#### Bonds

The above-mentioned banking monopoly rules, as well as the usury interest prohibition (now mostly abrogated for corporate borrowers), historically led non-bank players on the market to use bond financing instead of bank debt-financing. Indeed, because bonds are issued by the company rather than put in place by lenders, as it is the case for regular loans, this financing structure does not fall within the scope of banking monopoly rules. mezzanine and unitranche providers therefore customarily provide their subordinated (in the case of the Mezzanine) financing structured as bonds.

#### Borrowing base facility, securitisation and factoring

Acquired companies, whose cost of financing increases significantly upon their being acquired, have pushed to negotiate debt from borrowing base facilities at a better price than revolving credit facility under the acquisition debt documentation.

For those companies whose size justified it, such borrowing base facility was sometimes replaced by a securitisation programme or, alternatively, in a case where the pool of receivables was not sufficient to justify putting in place a securitisation programme, by a factoring programme. Even though it is now more or less standard to include securitisation or factoring in the definition of "permitted financial indebtedness", it is usually on a non-recourse basis or, if with recourse, subject to a threshold and, perhaps more importantly, included in the calculation of the total net debt to compute the leverage ratio.

In addition to the pricing issue, financing based on an assignment of receivables can be a structuring issue for the lenders of the acquisition debt as

---

3    Article 2(I)(2) of Ordinance No.2017-1432 of 4 October 2017 *portant modernisation du cadre juridique de la gestion d'actifs et du financement par la dette.*

it means that one of the main assets of the group (i.e. its pool of receivables) is pledged to a separate debt provider.

### High yield bonds

High yield bonds constituted an extremely strong trend over the past few years. However, despite the great liquidity derived from that market, it has proven volatile at times closing down momentarily without much notice if any. In addition, the investment involved in structuring an initial high yield bond transaction is quite high compared to a traditional bank debt financing, not only for the initial issuance but also because of the follow-up reporting requirements.

## 4. EQUITY STRUCTURES

### 4.1 Role of management

In buyout transactions, the creation of a dual board system for the target's or investment vehicle's management structure is frequently observed, the executive powers being granted to an executive body (e.g. management committee or *directoire*) comprising one or several top managers, the decisions of which are subject to the oversight of a controlling body (e.g. supervisory board) in which the investors are represented by majority.

This system is based on a clear separation between the functions of the executive and supervisory boards: the supervisory board's mission of control and oversight over management, by the executive body, of the company's affairs excludes any participation in the management itself and vice versa; the members of the executive board are generally not members or represented within the supervisory board. Note, however, that the mere fact of qualifying as a supervisory board member does not protect said member from an extended liability if the powers vested in the supervisory board are such that they amount to an involvement in the day-to-day business of the company (or, obviously, if such limited powers are not complied with and the supervisory board member is involved in the day-to-day management). In such a case, the members of such supervisory board will be deemed de facto managers of the company and will thus bear the same liability as any "manager" (*dirigeant*).

Managers benefitting from an employment agreement with the target company would typically be expected by investors to be bound by exclusivity undertakings for the duration of the employment, as well as confidentiality, non-compete and non-solicit covenants at the expiration thereof. It should be noted that, to be enforceable, employees' non-compete covenants must be: (1) remunerated; (2) limited in scope (both as to the prohibited activity and territory); and (3) limited in time (generally to two years maximum). For non-employees, non-compete covenants may also be factored in shareholders' agreements or call options, and be granted by managers as shareholders of the investment vehicle instead of employees. In this case, less restrictive rules will apply.

In standard buyout transactions, the way private equity funds will seek to incentivise management is typically by offering equity participation in the investment vehicle. Such participation is generally made available to at least the target's top management, such as members of the executive committee, and is sometimes extended to "second-tier" and "third-tier" managers.

In primary buyout transactions (as opposed to secondary or tertiary buyout transactions), management has generally a limited amount of money available to invest in the investment vehicle. Consequently, the management investment is frequently structured with: (1) immediate access to a certain percentage of the equity at preferred conditions ("sweet" equity), such as subscription for shares at par (which can even be funded by a loan), whereas the financial investors pay a premium, and the financial investors subscribe to both shares and debt instruments; and (2) a differed access to the capital ("kicker"), through various ratchet instruments designed to grant to the management, if certain targets are achieved (e.g. the level of IRR or cash-on-cash multiple of the fund), an increased portion of the capital gain realised by the financial investors upon exit.

## 4.2 Common protections for investors

In minority investments, the funds' management company will seek to protect the investment through governance and liquidity rights.

As for governance, minority investors will ask for (and generally obtain) a board seat, as well as limitations to the powers of the executive body of the investee company, so that important decisions will require prior approval of the board, with a qualified majority.

It should be noted that, if a minority investor is granted veto rights over certain key decisions, such as determination of the budget or business plan or hiring/dismissal of the top management, it could be considered as co-controlling the investee company from an antitrust or competition law perspective and, as a result thereof, be subject to certain notification obligations vis-à-vis competition authorities.

As for liquidity, minority investors will generally ask for an anti-dilution mechanism in order to protect their level of participation against dilutive share capital increases, tag-along rights giving them the ability to exit with the majority shareholders, pari passu placement of their shares in the case of an initial public offering (IPO), put options in order to exit in certain defined circumstances (e.g. deadlock, no exit achieved before a certain date, non-compliance with the business plan) and, in certain cases, pre-emption rights over the shares of the other shareholders.

In majority investments, investors will generally seek to protect their investment by monitoring the decisions of executive management and having the ability to implement a total exit.

## 4.3 Common protections for management

Managers who hold a minority interest in the investment vehicle will generally seek to protect their position through: (1) a liquidity mechanism, such as tag-along rights in case of an exit, or put options in case they cease to hold any position in the investment vehicle or the target group, it being specified that such put options are not frequently granted by investors and usually only in the case of death, permanent incapacity or dismissal without cause of the manager; (2) anti-dilution rights to protect their participation in the investment vehicle against dilutive issuance of securities or capital increase; and (3) governance rights, limited to certain key decisions, such as change of corporate form, change of business, dissolution of the investment vehicle and related parties' transactions.

## 4.4 Management warranties

If management holds a participation in the target, and even if it is reinvesting in the purchasing vehicle as part of the buyout transaction, it is frequently required to grant the same representations and warranties (with the same limitations in terms of time period and liability cap) as the other selling shareholders pro rata to its participation or the purchase price it receives.

If management is not a seller, it is not customary in France for management to give specific warranties or indemnification undertakings in respect of the business acquired. What has been seen in the past in certain transactions is affirmation letters from management asserting that the business plan it has prepared and the assumptions contained therein are sincere.

## 4.5 Good leaver/bad leaver provisions

Other than drag-along and tag-along rights, which deal with the compulsory transfer of management shares in the case of an exit, management incentive packages generally provide for departure options exercisable if a manager ceases to be involved in the business acquired.

These departure options are generally structured as call options pursuant to which each manager participating in the investment grants to the private equity fund or the investment vehicle an option to purchase all of their interest in the investment vehicle, in case they cease to be involved in the business for any reason. In consideration for such call options, managers may be granted, in certain management investment packages, put options pursuant to which they (or their successors) have the right to force the private equity funds or investment vehicle to purchase their shares in case of death, permanent disability or dismissal without cause, at their fair market value.

The key provisions generally discussed in the foregoing options are mostly related to the price at which they are exercisable.

This price will first depend on the cause of the manager's departure. A departing manager will generally be considered a bad leaver in the case of: (1) resignation before the expiry of a certain period of time (depending on the contemplated exit time under the business plan and other vesting mechanisms); (2) voluntary retirement before the normal age legally applicable to retirement; or (3) dismissal, removal or non-renewal of employment caused by their wilful misconduct or serious fault, and a good leaver in all other cases. In good leaver cases, the manager will generally have the opportunity to sell their securities at a price equal to the securities' fair market value whereas, in bad leaver cases, the manager may be required to sell their securities at the lower of the securities' acquisition cost or their fair market value. Although this pricing difference upon the cause of departure may create certain tax and social risks (i.e. requalification of money paid to the managers as salary income or unenforceability against the employee of the lower price mechanism in the case of a bad leaver), private equity funds continue to structure most of their management incentive packages like this in France (for incentive and cosmetic reasons mostly).

Managers may also be granted follow-up rights, which generally provide that if the investment fund resells the manager's securities acquired by them through the exercise of the call option within a certain period of time (e.g. six months) for a price higher than the call option exercise price, the difference is repaid to the departed manager. Such favourable rights are generally only granted to a good leaver.

### 4.6   Public to private transactions

"Public to private transactions", defined as the acquisition of the share capital of a listed company by private equity funds (or financial investors), with or without leverage, resulting in a delisting of the company, are not common on the French stock market (an average of 5–10 transactions each year since 2005).

The main obstacles to the development of public to private transactions, in particular those structured as leveraged buyouts (LBOs), remain: (1) the threshold required to consolidate the target company for tax purposes, which is set at 95% of the target shares; and (2) the threshold required to delist the company's shares and initiate a squeeze-out takeover bid, which is also set at 95% of the target's shares and voting rights, particularly since the French regulator, the *Autorité des Marchés Financiers*, does not require takeover bids to be set at this high percentage (the maximum generally accepted is two-thirds of the target shares). These constraints can cause the success of a public to private transaction to be very expensive, if, for instance, one or several hedge funds buys more than 5% of the company's shares in order to own a blocking minority and thus negotiate an increased price for their shares.

Despite the above obstacles, there are reasonable grounds to believe that public to private transactions in France will remain an attractive option, especially for companies that have a capitalisation of under EUR 200 million, which is too low to present a real interest for market players, thus resulting in market price stagnation, absence of liquidity and difficulty in raising capital for growth.

First, in July 2015, Euronext relaxed its delisting rules: if the total amount of a company's listed securities is below 0.5% of its market capitalisation, a shareholder holding more than 90% of the voting rights is now entitled to launch a simplified public offer and delist the company's securities, even if he does not reach the 95% threshold.

Secondly, the French Government wants to simplify the public to private transaction procedure: the draft law *Plan d'action pour la croissance et la transformation des sociétés* 2018 (so-called "*loi Pacte*"), provides for a lowering of the squeeze-out threshold from 95 to 90% of the target's shares and voting rights.

## 5   EXITS

### 5.1   Secondary sales

The preferred exit route of private equity funds is secondary sales (which refers herein to the selling of a portfolio company to another private equity fund) as it provides immediate and total exit. As indicated below, this type of exit may also be favoured by the target's management as it will expect to receive a better incentive package with a private equity owner. Key issues arising in this type of transactions are the following:

- potential conflict between the private equity firm wishing a "clean" exit without contingent liabilities and the succeeding private equity firm wishing to obtain warranties on the business acquired:
  — generally, exiting private equity funds may accept a compromise on price and avoid having to give any warranties (or limiting them in time) by claiming: (1) they were not involved in management and cannot therefore grant warranties on or be liable for the way the business was managed; and (2) private equity funds need to be liquidated in a timely fashion and cannot carry contingent liabilities that survive a divestment;
  — another argument to avoid giving warranties is to claim that any material issue associated with the portfolio company would have been flagged by the selling private equity firm during its due diligence process and resolved before completion of the secondary buyout. If any issue is still outstanding, it can be clearly identified and be subject to a specific indemnity;
  — if, however, the fund is required to give warranties, it will ask the management to give the same, pro rata, to its portion of its entitlement to the purchase price. The selling fund will generally not accept joint and several liability with the other selling parties (management); and
- potential conflict of interest of the management during negotiation, especially if management is reinvesting in the secondary buyout as optimising the selling conditions for both the financial sponsors and the managers will conflict with the desire to obtain the best reinvestment terms.

## 5.2 Trade sales

Trade sales provide the same advantage for private equity funds as secondary sales: immediate and complete exit. Besides, the price obtained in a trade sale may be higher if synergies between the purchaser and the target are expected and valued and if the debt market does not allow financial investors to get sufficient leverage to offer a competitive price. The key issues arising in this type of transactions are:

- antitrust issues are more likely to arise in a trade sale than in a private equity-backed transaction;
- consenting to negative covenants such as non-compete or similar undertakings restricting the ability of the private equity firms to make future investments in the same sector. Private equity firms have specialised teams dedicated to certain selected economic areas, with the knowledge and experience necessary to provide the expertise and credibility required by investors and selling parties. It would therefore be difficult for a private equity firm to accept that, during a set period of time, it cannot engage in any business similar to the one conducted by the company sold to the corporate purchaser;
- the selling fund may wish for a "clean exit" and may therefore seek to avoid giving any warranties or indemnities or accepting earn-out mechanisms (in order to achieve a quick disposal for their investors); and

- Depending on the purchaser's strategy, management may be reluctant to favour this type of exit because of the possible effect of the change of control on its position (e.g. less autonomy and fewer incentives than in buyout transactions).

## 5.3 Initial Public Offerings

Divestment through an IPO (flotation or sales of equity) is generally not the preferred exit route for private equity funds for the following reasons: (1) it fails to provide the full liquidity required by investors; and (2) after the IPO, the funds' participation would be exposed to market volatility and analysts' predictions, which private equity managers tend to dislike.

Even if it is not a very popular choice, private equity-backed IPOs may represent a solid alternative compared to other exit routes in the actual environment, especially for the largest holdings of private equity firms, where public offerings may present the only option available to pay down debt and cash out private equity participation (at least partially). While 2017 was a good year of opportunities to sell by IPO, it was nothing compared to the boom period from 2013 to 2015.

Also, a new simplified procedure has come into force as of 21 July 2018 with respect to small IPOs: according to the new regime (new art.211-2 of the AMF Regulation), an IPO on Euronext Growth for less than EUR 8 million is now exempted from the prospectus obligation. The prospectus has been replaced by a simplified information document that is subject to review of the French regulator but not to its formal visa.

As mentioned above, the main issues that arise for private equity firms contemplating an IPO on the French market are:

- restriction to sell shares: because of the adverse effect a quick sale after the offering may have on the value of the listed company, private equity funds will generally be required by the banking institution(s) underwriting the offering to accept broad restrictions on their ability to sell their shares in the listed company. Funds are often authorised to sell only part of their shares in the IPO and are locked up for a certain period of time (generally between six to 18 months);
- warranties given by the private equity firm: the extent to which a private equity fund is required to give warranties to the underwriting banks: a private equity fund may argue that it acted as a financing party;
- reduced control over the participation: share transfer restrictions or obligations (such as drag-along, tag-along, right of first refusal) and board representation rights (and thus right to control the management of the company) are likely to terminate or be significantly re-organised upon the IPO. The continuing exposure to market risk without the protection given by the foregoing rights is an important disadvantage of the IPO exit for private equity funds (increased by the governance rules applicable to listed companies);
- dilution of the participation: the fund's participation in the listed company will also be significantly diluted as a result of the IPO;
- the amount of debt to be refinanced: depending on market conditions, the IPOs of highly leveraged companies can be difficult to achieve at an

acceptable price for the fund; and

- management co-operation: because the management will assume responsibility for the content of the IPO prospectus and will issue a statement that to its knowledge the information is correct and no material circumstances have been omitted, its active co-operation is key in any IPO process.

### 5.4  Refinancings

Refinancings can be structured so as to have the target borrow more in order to distribute to the private equity funds the proceeds of such borrowings, or as a sale and leaseback scheme whereupon assets of the portfolio company are sold to a third party and then leased back to the company and the proceeds of the sale are used to pay dividends or otherwise upstream monies to the private equity funds. A refinancing enables the fund to monetise a portion of its investment while retaining full ownership of the target and therefore gives the fund the ability to collect further profit in a secondary, trade or IPO exit. The main issues that usually arise when contemplating a refinancing are:

- corporate interest in the target: is it in the target's best interest to borrow more in order to distribute dividends to its shareholders? Would such borrowing create an abnormal burden on or risk to the financial situation of the target and can it be considered as a misappropriation of the assets of the company? Such issues need to be carefully reviewed and analysed before implementing a refinancing;
- management incentive: another issue to be considered is the effect of the refinancing on the management. Generally, management investment packages are tied to an agreed-upon set of financial targets, frequently the fund's IRR or cash-on-cash multiple, and are realised upon a sale or an IPO. If the managers are guaranteed to reach the required thresholds and realise the expected gain as a result of the proceeds received by the fund through the refinancing, whatever the future exit price, managers may lose the incentive to manage the business as efficiently as before; and
- upstreaming money to the fund: although a variety of solutions exist (disposal of reserves, payment of dividends, reimbursement of shareholders' loans, redemption of existing securities, issuance of new securities etc), the conditions under which the proceeds of the refinancing can be upstreamed to the fund and its investors will depend mostly on the existing structure and tax considerations. New constraints created by the AIFM Directive to prevent asset stripping (as detailed below) also need to be carefully considered by private-equity funds' managers before implementing any such scheme.

### 5.5  Restructuring/insolvency

An exit within the context of a restructuring or insolvency proceeding, although not ideal, is a scenario that private equity funds are more likely to face in the current environment and for which they need to be prepared. The key issues arising in a restructuring transaction can be summarised as follows.

### Debt structure

An investee company facing difficulties may request the commencement of out-of-court proceedings, either *mandat ad hoc* or *conciliation* proceedings, the aim of which is to organise an informal negotiation between the debtor's main creditors and stakeholders under the aegis of an insolvency professional appointed by the President of the commercial court (*mandataire ad hoc* or *conciliateur*). During these prevention proceedings, which are consensual and confidential, obtaining from the banks a "stand-still" period (where interest and capital reimbursements are frozen), a new repayment schedule, a debt-to-equity swap or a debt write-off requires unanimity, which might be difficult to obtain in large LBOs where the debt may be owned by a considerable number of different institutions, each with different interests. It should be noted, however, that the French Law of 22 October 2010 on Banking and Financial Regulation introduced the fast financial safeguard (*sauvegarde financière accélérée*), a new expedited procedure which allows the adoption in two months of a restructuring plan (including a debt-to-equity swap or debt write-off) binding on all financial creditors (banks and bondholders), provided it is approved by a two-thirds majority (in amounts of debt) of each category (banks and bond holders) of such creditors. This "prepack" procedure is available only to large companies which are under conciliation proceedings.

As regards regular formal in-court proceedings (safeguard and judicial recovery proceedings) which are unusual in LBO situations (where conciliation, followed as the case may be by a fast-financial safeguard, is the preferred route); since the new Ordinance (*ordonnance*) No.2014-326 of 14 March 2014 *portant réforme de la prévention des difficultés des entreprises et des procédures collectives*, creditors (to the notable exception of bonds and note-holders) are granted the ability to submit to the vote of the creditors an alternative plan to the debtor's. Although French law includes provisions enabling the cram-down of the money shareholders (yet under strict and limitative conditions), they are usually not used in LBO situations for reputational and commercial reasons as private equity funds tend to avoid holds' out to preserve their relationships with banks or other finance providers for their future acquisitions.

LBOs in which a debt push-down has been implemented can also be problematic (although a debt push-down provides a cheaper debt with better security interests): if foreign subsidiaries are borrowers, guarantors or have granted securities, it may be difficult, depending on the circumstances, to justify that their center of main interests (COMI) is also located in France and thus to open safeguard proceedings (including fast financial safeguard) in France. The enforcement of the obligations of such foreign subsidiaries will therefore not be suspended under the safeguard proceedings opened with respect to the French entities.

Structures with the top holding companies located in Luxembourg (for tax optimisation reasons) and supporting a large part of the debt or structure known as double Luxco can also be a disadvantage for funds wishing to place the distressed business under the court's protection as: (1) it will be more difficult to locate the COMI in France; and (2) it will be easier for creditors to appropriate shares under Luxembourg bankruptcy law (which provides no automatic stay for secured creditors, contrary to French law).

### Liability

One important consideration for funds forced to exit a distressed investee company involves obtaining a full release and waiver of liability from: (1) the banks; (2) the management; and (3) the investee company. This would be generally accepted in out-of-court prevention proceedings (*mandat ad'hoc* or conciliation) except if the fund has failed to be transparent with the banks on the distressed business situation. It should be noted, however, that, if the target goes into a liquidation proceedings (*liquidation judiciaire*), the risk of the private equity fund being exposed to a liability claim for asset shortfall (*action en insuffisance d'actif*) attempting to have the fund assume all or part of the distressed business liabilities as a de facto manager will be significantly increased. Contractual non-recourse provisions are in such case irrelevant. This risk is particularly significant where the distressed entity is formed as a *société par actions simplifiée* and its president is not an individual but a legal entity: in such a situation, a judge will not have to prove a de facto management and may go up to the "deep pocket" parent company (as de jure manager). Significant powers given to supervisory board (through a long list of reserved matters), on which sit representatives of the private equity funds, may also help a liquidator to re-characterise it into a board of directors with its attached liabilities. Dismissed employees may also seek to sue the private equity funds either based on tort law or on labor law (co-employment, *légèreté blamable*—where the fund can be considered to have acted unfairly and in a culpably thoughtless manner). Similarly, if the private equity funds decide to realise a distressed sale, it should be extremely cautious as regards the sustainability of the project of the purchaser. Should the company file subsequently for bankruptcy due to the fact that the business plan was not viable or the purchaser did not have sufficient financial means, the private equity funds will likely be sued by the employees on these same grounds.

### Management

Managers play a fundamental role in a distressed business situation and it is thus crucial for private equity funds to initiate discussion with them as early as possible, notably to avoid the risk of managers acting independently to favor the survival of an operating subsidiary to the detriment of the holding company or its shareholders, including by filing for safeguard (particularly since the management package generally no longer has any value). In distressed situations, the fiduciary duty of the management is towards the best interest of the company and not towards its shareholders (or the company creditors).

### Expense reimbursement

In prevention proceedings (*mandat ad'hoc* or conciliation) where private equity funds are selling their participation for no consideration, they will at least try to have the fees of advisers and management ultimately paid by the target, which is the customary practice in France.

**Kicker**

The private equity funds may be asked to sell all of their securities in the distressed target for EUR 1 but, in certain cases where existing shareholders' support is required by new sponsors, they might be offered an interest in a future exit through a kicker (e.g. warrants) or a minority stake.

## 6. TAX
### 6.1 Taxation of fund structures
**Overview**
*FCPRs or FPCIs*

FCPRs are not subject to corporate income tax. Taxes are levied only on the income of the individual or corporate investors that hold units in the FCPRs, under specific conditions.

It should be noted that the following description is limited to the tax regime of "fiscal" FCPRs or FPCIs, i.e. FCPRs or FPCIs in which at least 50% of the assets consist of stocks in non-listed European companies (or non-listed companies resident in a European Economic Area (EEA) Member State with which France has a tax treaty containing a clause on administrative assistance), that have an operational activity and are subject to corporate income tax. The tax regime of FCPIs and FIPs, whose units allow certain specific income tax benefits for individuals for contributions made before 31 December 2010 or of "non-fiscal" FCPRs is not detailed.

The tax treatment of income and capital gains varies depending on whether the same is distributed to the FPCR or the FPCI investors or not.

### Tax treatment of income and capital gains realised but not distributed by FCPRs

*Individual investors*: individual investors are not subject to taxation on the income received but not distributed by the FCPR. The same rule applies for capital gains realised but not distributed, provided that no individual investor holds, directly or indirectly, more than 10% of the units of the FCPR. If this is not the case, all individual investors may be subject to income tax at a flat rate of 12.8% increased by social taxes at a global rate of 17.2%, i.e. a global rate of 30% (applicable since 1 January 2018).

*Corporate investors*: corporate investors are not subject to tax on income and capital gains realised but not distributed by the FCPR, but they are annually taxable at the standard rate of corporate income tax (34.43% on the portion of the taxable profits exceeding EUR 500,000 and up to 28,92%, including the corporate income tax surcharge of 3.3%, on the taxable profits below this threshold) on the positive variation (the negative variation being deductible) between the fair market value of the FCPR units at the starting date and at the closing date of the fiscal year. As a consequence, capital gains to be realised upon disposal of the FCPR units are reduced or increased by the variation. Corporate investors that undertake to hold FCPR units for a five-year period are exempt from tax on the variation (which results in corporate income tax being deferred until the disposal of the FCPR units). Non-compliance with the five-year holding period triggers a 0.75% monthly tax computed on the additional amount of corporate income tax that would have been paid if such annual variation had been included in the taxable basis.

### Tax treatment of income and capital gains realised and distributed by FCPR

*Individual investors*: disposals by FCPRs are exempt from income tax (but are subject to social taxes at a global rate of 17.2%), provided that the following conditions are met. The individual investor: (1) undertakes to hold the FCPR units for at least five years; (2) reinvests in FCPR units the income distributed within this period; and (3) does not hold, directly or indirectly, more than 25% of rights in the profits of companies whose shares are held by the FCPR at any time within the five-year period. If these conditions are not fulfilled, income received by the FCPR (such as dividends, interest etc) or deriving from the disposal of the assets held by the FCPR (capital gains) and distributed to the investors is subject to income tax at a flat rate of 12.8% increased by social taxes at a global rate of 17.2%, i.e. a global rate of 30% applicable since 1 January 2018 (regarding capital gains, only on the amount exceeding the capital contribution (or the acquisition price if higher) of the investors).

*Corporate investors*: income received by the FCPR (such as dividends, interest etc) or deriving from the disposal of the assets held by the FCPR (capital gains) and distributed are subject to corporate income tax at the standard rate (34.43% on the portion of the taxable profits exceeding EUR 500,000 and up to 28,92%, including the corporate income tax surcharge of 3.3%, on the taxable profits below this threshold) but only on the taxable amount regarding capital gains. It should be noted that a favourable tax regime on capital gains applies for corporate investors holding the FCPR units for more than two years: the taxable amount is subject to taxation at the reduced rate of 15% or exempted from tax if the capital gains that are distributed derive from shares held by the FCPR for more than two years and represent at least a 5% participation.

### SCRs

Subject to a tax election, SCRs (essentially those that have at least 50% of their assets made up of stocks in non-listed European companies, representing less than 40% of the share capital of each company) are exempt from corporate income tax in most cases. Individual and corporate investors that hold shares issued by SCRs are subject to taxes as follows.

### Tax treatment of income and capital gains realised but not distributed by SCRs

Income and capital gains that are not distributed by SCRs are not subject to taxation at the investor level.

### Tax treatment of income and capital gains realised and distributed by SCRs

Taxation of individual and corporate investors on income and capital gains realised and distributed by SCRs is substantially similar to the regime described above for FCPRs.

## Differences in tax treatment between domestic and overseas investors
### FCPRs

It should be noted that overseas investors, whether individual or corporate, are subject to tax neither on income and capital gains realised by the fund that are not distributed, nor on disposals deriving from shares of foreign companies held by the fund.

Overseas investors are:

- exempt from tax on disposals of capital gains realised by the fund provided that the overseas investor does not hold, directly or indirectly, at any time during the five years preceding the disposal, more than a 25% share in the profits of the French company whose shares have been disposed of by the FCPR. Should this not be the case, such disposal would be subject to tax at the flat rate of 12.8% if the investor is an individual and at the standard rate of corporate income tax for other overseas investors, subject to the provisions of applicable tax treaties;
- subject to: (1) a 12.8% withholding tax if the overseas investor is an individual resident of a EU Member State (or of a EEA Member State with which France has a tax treaty containing a clause on administrative assistance); or (2) a 30% withholding tax for other overseas investors (individuals or corporate), on disposals of dividends received by the FCPR from a French company, subject to the provisions of applicable tax treaties; and
- exempt from tax on disposals of interest received by the FCPR, except if the account of the investor is located in a "non-co-operative state or territory", in which case the disposal should be subject to a 75% withholding tax.

### SCRs
#### Overseas individual investors

Overseas individual investors (residents of a country with which France has a tax treaty containing a clause on administrative assistance) are exempt from withholding tax, provided that the following conditions are fulfilled. The overseas individual investor: (1) undertakes to hold the SCR shares for at least five years; (2) reinvests in SCR shares the income distributed within this period; and (3) does not hold, directly or indirectly, more than a 25% share in the profits of companies whose shares are held by the SCR.

If these conditions are not fulfilled, and subject to the provisions of tax treaties, income received by an SCR or derived from the disposal of the assets held by the SCR and distributed to overseas individual investors is subject to a withholding tax at a 12.8% flat rate, subject to the provisions of applicable tax treaties.

#### Overseas corporate investors

Overseas corporate investors are exempt from withholding tax, provided that the following conditions are fulfilled: (1) the disposal derives from the disposal of shares held by the SCR for at least two years; (2) the disposal is included in the taxable basis of the overseas corporate investor but remains exempt from corporate income tax; and (3) the investor is a resident of a country with which France has a tax treaty containing a clause on administrative assistance.

If the conditions are not fulfilled, and subject to the provisions of applicable tax treaties, disposals are subject to a 30% withholding tax.

Both individual and corporate investors located in a "non-co-operative state or territory" are subject to a 75% withholding tax on disposals.

From a tax point of view, the above rules do not make one particular structure more attractive than the others. The success of the FCPR structure compared to that of the SCR is certainly due to other considerations, such as the greater flexibility it provides in terms of fundraising or fund management.

## 6.2  Carried interest

Income deriving from carried interest units of FCPRs created after 30 June 2009 or carried interest shares of SCRs issued after that date can be treated as capital gains when the following conditions are met:

- carried interest shares or units have been acquired at fair market value;
- all carried interest shares or units are similar, i.e. have the same rights;
- carried interest shares or units represent at least 1% of the total amount of capital subscriptions;
- income deriving from carried interest shares or units is effectively paid at least five years after the incorporation of an FCPR (or issuance of the shares of an SCR) and, for an FCPR, after the refund of the investors' contributions; and
- the remuneration of the investment executive is at arm's length.

If the foregoing conditions are fulfilled, individuals who are French tax residents are subject to tax at a flat rate on: (1) capital gains distributed by an FCPR; (2) dividend disposals by an SCR of income derived from capital gains; and (3) capital gains realised upon the disposal of carried interest shares or units. Should this not be the case, any income deriving from carried interest shares or units is subject to income tax as salary income at a progressive rate (highest rate: 45%, possibly increased by the temporary surcharge up to 4%) and to a specific 30% social contribution.

## 6.3  Management equity

Equity must be awarded to management on the basis of its fair market value, i.e. in compliance with the arm's length principle, except in specific schemes with a favourable tax regime, such as stock-option plans. Should this not be the case, any income derived therefrom may be treated as salary income instead of capital gains, subject to tax at a progressive rate (highest rate: 45%, possibly increased by the temporary surcharge up to 4%). In addition, such income may be subject to social taxes, borne by the employer (average rate: 40%) and the manager (average rate: 20%).

## 6.4  Loan interest
### Tax deduction of interest

As a preliminary remark, it should be noted that interest paid by a French company to a beneficiary who is a resident in a "non-co-operative state or territory", or paid on an account located in such state or territory, is no longer to be tax deductible, with certain exceptions. These rules do not apply to loans executed prior to 1 March 2010, which remain subject to less restrictive conditions.

Notwithstanding the foregoing, interest is generally tax deductible on an accrued basis. However, there are five limitations with respect to the tax deduction of interest paid to related entities.

*A limitation based on the interest rate*: interest paid by a company to related entities that exceeds a maximum legal rate, which varies each month (1.67% for fiscal years that ended on 31 December 2017), is not deductible unless the borrowing company can prove that it would not have been able to obtain a loan at a lower rate from unrelated banks under similar conditions.

Two companies are deemed to be related when one holds directly or indirectly the majority of the capital of the other or exercises a de facto decision-making power (legal management or de facto management, or majority of the voting rights) with respect to the other, or when they are under the common control of a third party according to the same tests.

*A limitation based on the thin capitalisation situation of the company*: the deduction of interest paid by a company to a related entity that exceeds the highest of the three following amounts is deferred:

(1)  interest deductible within the limitation above on interest rate × 1.5 times the net equity of the company/the average amount of loans granted by related companies during the fiscal year;

(2)  25% of the current profit before tax, after several adjustments; and

(3)  interest received from related companies.

Deferred interest according to this rule may be carried forward indefinitely, subject to a 5% annual reduction as from the second year following its payment.

In certain cases, thin capitalisation rules do not apply. For instance, interest paid to related companies within the scope of a centralised cash pooling arrangement, by the company that operates the centralised cash pooling arrangement, remains deductible. Moreover, the thin capitalisation rules do not apply if the borrowing company can prove that the debt-equity ratio of the tax group to which it belongs is at least equal to its own debt-equity ratio. Also, the interest limitations will not apply when the portion of interest deferred does not exceed EUR 150,000.

In a French tax consolidated group, interest deferred by the group members is transferred to the parent company of the tax group, which may be allowed to deduct a certain portion of the aggregate amount of the deferred interest transferred by the group members, provided that a specific ratio is satisfied.

*A limitation when a French company acquiring qualifying participations* (shares that may benefit from the parent subsidiary regime, i.e. shares representing more than 5% of the share capital and the voting rights of the subsidiary) cannot demonstrate that: (1) decisions relating to the participations are effectively made by the acquiring company or by a company established in France, or having its headquarters in the EU, or in a country of the EEA, having concluded with France a treaty aimed at combating tax fraud and evasion, which controls (within the meaning of art.L.233-3 of the French Commercial Code) the acquiring company; and (2) if a control or influence is exercised over the acquired company, that control or influence is effectively exercised by the acquiring company or by a company established in France, or having its headquarters in the EU, or in a country of the EEA having concluded with France a treaty aimed at combating tax fraud and evasion which controls (within the meaning of art.L.2333-3 of the French Commercial Code) the acquiring company or by a company established in France which is directly controlled by the same company as the one controlling the acquiring company.

For acquisition made on or after 1 January 2012, the French company must demonstrate that an autonomous centre of decisions in France exists during that financial year or another of the financial years covering the 12-month period following the acquisition.

If the French company fails to make the above-mentioned demonstration, the amount of non-deductible financial expenses is calculated as follows: interest expense of the fiscal year × acquisition price of the qualifying shareholding/amount of debt of the acquiring company of the fiscal year.

Such limitation does not apply if:

- the acquisition value of the qualifying participations is lower than EUR 1 million;
- the acquisition of the qualifying participations has not been financed through debt resulting in financial expenses incurred by the acquiring company or another company of the same group; or
- the acquiring company is able to demonstrate that, for the financial year in respect of which interest deduction may be challenged, its own leverage ratio is below the leverage ratio of the group to which it belongs.

*A general limitation on interest deduction incurred by French residents applies to both related and third party financing regardless of its purpose*: 25% of net financial expenses incurred by a company—if they exceed EUR 3 million—are no longer tax deductible. In case of a tax consolidated group, the limitation applies to net financial expenses paid by the members of the tax consolidated group to entities that are not members of the group.

Furthermore, this limitation is a permanent disallowance as there is no carry-forward mechanism of the disallowed interest.

Existing limitations on deductions apply notwithstanding this limitation.

*A limitation based on hybrid applies to interest paid by a French taxpayer* to a "related enterprise" (under the meaning of art.39.12 *du Code général des impôts*; Ordinance No.2018-470 of 12 June 2018 art.3), which is, broadly, an enterprise controlling the borrower, controlled by the borrower or under common control with the borrower.

Under this legislation, the right of the borrower to deduct the interest is subject to a requirement that the interest received by the lender is subject to a tax on profits amounting to at least a quarter of the sum that would be payable under the general law. It is for the borrower to demonstrate this at the request of the tax administration.

Where the lender is domiciled or established abroad, the tax on profits payable under the general law is to be understood as the tax that would have been payable in France if the lender had been established there.

### Withholding tax treatment on interest

Interest paid by a French borrower located in France to non-French residents is exempt from French withholding tax. However, interest paid on an account located in a "non-co-operative state or territory" is subject to a 75% withholding tax. Exemption of "loans concluded outside France" still applies to loans executed before 1 March 2010.

### 6.5  Transaction taxes
**Share deal**

Taxation of the transfer of shares of a French company will depend on the nature of the company:

- for stock companies (i.e. *société anonyme, société par actions simplifiée or société en commandite par actions*), registration duties at the rate of 0.1% of the purchase price (or the real value, if higher) will apply; and
- for other types of companies, registration duties at the rate of 3% of the purchase price (or the real value, if higher) reduced by an allowance equal to EUR 23,000 × number of shares transferred/total number of shares will apply.

Transfer of shares of a foreign company will not be subject to tax in France except if the deed is executed in France, in which case, the transfer will be subject to tax under the above rules.

In addition, it should be noted that the transfer of shares held in a French or foreign company that mainly holds real estate assets located in France is subject to registration duties at the rate of 5%, based on the acquisition price (or the real value, if higher).

**Asset deal**

Whereas contribution in kind is subject to a fixed duty and disposal of shares is subject to a transfer tax at the rate of 0.1%, the sale of a business as a going concern (*fonds de commerce*) is subject to a transfer tax of 3% on the portion of the price (or the real value, if higher) below EUR 200,000 and 5% thereafter, which makes asset deals a lot more expensive than share deals.

This is one of the reasons why a transfer of a business exceeding a certain size is frequently structured through a hive down (*apport partiel d'actifs*) to a newly formed entity, the shares of which are thereafter sold to the purchasing vehicle. However, it should be noted that French tax authorities can requalify (on the grounds of the abuse of law theory) contributions of assets immediately followed by the sale of the shares received in exchange for them as a direct sale of assets. The French Supreme Court has decided that a contribution, immediately followed by the sale of the shares, could be regarded as a sale of the assets to the beneficiary of the contribution, when the operation is realised without any economic purpose and without any risk taken by the contributing party and is, consequently, only justified by the avoidance of heavier transfer taxes. In such case, the tax reassessment is borne by the beneficiary of the contribution.

## 7.  CURRENT TOPICAL ISSUES/TRENDS

In France, 2017 was a very positive year for the entire private equity industry. It was a year of increased investment (including from foreign sources), strong exit markets and hot fundraising.

As regards exits of private equity funds, both the number of exits and the amount of capital exited increased significantly in 2017, with sale to corporates remaining the favoured exit route, but the IPO process has become a strong alternative process especially among buyout funds. The year 2018 seems to be following the same trend, with the contemplated IPO-backed of Delachaux by CVC and of Novares (ex Mecaplast) by Equistone on the Paris Stock Market.

Given the accelerating pace of the LBO market around the world, the numerous successful operations in 2017, the strong appetite of debt funds and the number of buyout funds reaching maturity that will need to exit their investments soon, private equity professionals are optimistic that the year 2018 will be favourable to LBO transactions.

As regards debt financing, especially buyout transactions, the current trend is towards a slight tightening of the market with investors being more selective on the deals, resulting in the exercise of market flex and/or a slight increase in the pricing, but the acceptable leverage remains high (north of 5.0:1 for an all senior debt).

As regards the legislative environment, there will be developments in French insolvency laws with respect to the formation of a different class of creditors and the increased ability to cram-down "out of the money" junior creditors and shareholders in formal proceedings in order to implement the draft directive dated 22 November 2016[4] on such matters.

---

[4] Proposal for a Directive on preventive restructuring frameworks, second chance and measures to increase the efficiency of restructuring, insolvency and discharge procedures and amending Directive 2012/30 COM(2016) 723 final.

# Germany

**P+P Pöllath + Partners**  Jens Hörmann, Nico Fischer & Amos Veith

## 1. MARKET OVERVIEW

### 1.1 Types of investors

The common sources from which private equity funds in Germany obtain their funding are corporate investors, private investors, public sector, banks, insurance companies, pension funds, family offices and funds of funds.

According to the German Private Equity and Venture Capital Association (*Bundesverband Deutscher Kapitalbeteiligungsgesellschaften*—BVK), in 2017, new funds in the amount of EUR 2.98 billion were raised, which was about the same amount as was raised in 2016 (EUR 2.93 billion).[1] Thus, the level of fundraising by German funds remains more or less constant and is also expected to reach a similar level in 2018. Venture capital funds could raise EUR 1.49 billion which is slightly more than in 2016. The fundraising of buyout funds dropped from EUR 1.46 billion in 2016 to EUR 0.94 billion in 2017.

Due to the German pension system, fewer pension funds exist in Germany than in other countries. Thus, pension funds have a less important role as investors in private equity funds in Germany compared to their roles in other countries.

### 1.2 Types of investments

According to the BVK, the private equity investments in German target companies reached EUR 11.31 billion in 2017, which made 2017 a record year in which two thirds more than in 2016 (EUR 6.77 billion) have been invested in German private equity target companies. German investment companies invested EUR 8.18 billion and foreign investment companies EUR 3.13 billion of the total investment volume of EUR 11.31 billion in Germany in 2017.

As in previous years, the bulk of investments were made in buyouts (79%). The buyout volume totalled EUR 8.94 billion. Furthermore, of all transactions in which private equity funds invested in Germany during 2017, 9% were venture capital (seed, start-up and later-stage venture capital) and approximately 12% growth capital.

In 2017, the largest portions were invested in industrial products (39%), followed by biotechnology/healthcare (16%), and information and communication technology (15%).

---

[1] All data in s.1 has been taken from: Presentation, "BVK-Statistik 2017" (February 2018), unless otherwise indicated.

## 2. FUNDS
### 2.1 Fund structures

The domestic legal structure most commonly used as a vehicle for domestic private equity funds is the "GmbH & Co KG". This is a limited partnership (*Kommanditgesellschaft* (KG)) with a private limited liability company (*Gesellschaft mit beschränkter Haftung* (GmbH)) as the general partner and with the investors as the limited partners. In order to establish non-business status of the partnership for German tax purposes, the partnership must have a managing limited partner, who typically is affiliated with the general partner/sponsor. The partnership is formed in accordance with the provisions of the German Commercial Code (*Handelsgesetzbuch* (HGB)).

Occasionally, other legal structures such as a limited liability company (*Gesellschaft mit beschränkter Haftung* (GmbH)), a public limited company (*Aktiengesellschaft* (AG)) or a partnership limited by shares (*Kommanditgesellschaft auf Aktien* (KGaA)) are used as a vehicle for domestic private equity funds. Under German law, a very specific investment company (*Unternehmensbeteiligungsgesellschaft*) exists (*Gesetz über die Unternehmensbeteiligungsgesellschaft*—UBGG) but due, to various constraints, it is an unpopular legal regime.

The German limited partnership has certain advantages over other legal entities, e.g.:

- the assignment of interests in the partnership does not require notarisation (while the filing to the commercial register requires a notarial certification);
- the accession of new investors as limited partners is uncomplicated and cost-efficient;
- the partnership agreement is not publicly available;
- the rights of the limited partners are restricted by law to certain information rights; and
- there are beneficial tax rules if the partnership is not engaged in business activities for German tax purposes (tax transparent status).

Beside domestic legal structures, foreign legal structures are often used as vehicles for private equity funds investing in Germany, such as limited partnerships, in particular based in Luxembourg, Guernsey or Jersey.

### 2.2 Regulation of fundraising and fund managers

The regulatory framework for private equity funds in Germany changed immensely with the transposition and implementation of Directive 2011/61 on Alternative Investment Fund Managers and amending Directives 2003/41 and 2009/65 and Regulations 1060/2009 and 1095/2010 [2011] OJ L174/1 (AIFM Directive) into national law. The German Capital Investment Act (*Kapitalanlagegesetzbuch*—KAGB) became effective on 22 July 2013 and replaced the German Investment Act 2004 (*Investmentgesetz*). The KAGB is now the main legal framework for all German fund structures (including closed-ended funds).

The introduction of the KAGB has increased the administrative burden for market participants. All alternative investment fund managers (AIFMs) wishing to manage and/or market funds in Germany are nowadays subject to registration or authorisation requirements and hence under the supervision of the German Federal Financial Supervisory Authority (*Bundesanstalt für Finanzdienstleistungsungsaufsicht*—BaFin).

## Management

As a general rule (and subject to the exemption for so-called sub-threshold managers which is currently still made use of by most German resident AIFMs; see discussion below), AIFMs with their principal place of business in Germany seeking to manage an alternative investment fund (AIF) are required to obtain a full licence from BaFin prior to the commencement of management activities. The licence requirements include, among others, the following:

- internal organisation and risk management requirements, including conduct rules and reporting requirements;
- capital maintenance rules;
- asset stripping prohibition;
- remuneration rules;
- depositary requirements; and
- disclosure obligations towards investors.

An exemption exists for German managers of so-called "Spezial-AIF", i.e. funds in which only professional or semi-professional investors are invested, provided certain thresholds regarding the assets under management are not exceeded. Those thresholds are:

- EUR 100 million (including assets acquired through use of leverage); and
- EUR 500 million when the portfolio only includes unleveraged funds with no redemption rights within five years following the date of initial investment.

If these requirements are met, the German AIFM is only subject to a registration with BaFin and is exempt from most of the requirements applicable to fully licensed AIFMs.

The "semi-professional investor" mentioned above is a type of investor which Germany opted to include in the KAGB beside the professional and retail investors mentioned in the AIFM Directive. Semi-professional investors are persons for whom there are certain requirements (e.g. minimum commitment, sufficient knowledge and experience) and, in many instances, they are treated very similarly to professional investors.

If an AIFM has received a full licence from BaFin, it may, unlike a merely registered sub-threshold AIFM, also raise and manage funds on a cross-border basis in other EU countries (passport option), provided that the fund is marketed to professional investors only.

## Marketing

All AIFMs wishing to market funds in Germany will need to obtain marketing approval from BaFin or—in the case of an EU AIFM marketing an EU AIF—from its EU home authority, prior to conducting any marketing activity in Germany.

"Marketing" is defined as any direct or indirect offering or placement of fund interests at the initiative of the fund manager (or on behalf of the fund manager) to investors domiciled or having a registered office in Germany.

The requirements which must be fulfilled to obtain marketing approval vary depending on whether the AIF and AIFM is domiciled in or outside the EU/European Economic Area (EEA) as well as the kind of investor at which the AIF is aimed (retail/semi-professional/professional).

With regard to marketing AIFs by non-EU AIFMs to professional investors, Germany has implemented art.42 of the AIFMD but has gold-plated the requirements in one aspect: the non-EU AIFM must appoint a "depositary-lite" that performs the depository functions set out under art.21(7)–(9) of the AIFM Directive for the relevant AIF.

With regard to marketing AIFs to semi-professional investors by non-EU AIFMs, full AIFMD compliance is required. Marketing to typical retail investors ("private investors") requires in addition compliance with the burdensome rules on German retail funds.

Requirements include:

- non-German AIFMs (i.e. EU and third-country AIMFs) must be subject to public regulation for investor protection purposes;
- non-German AIFMs must have their registered office in the same country as the non-German AIF;
- non-German AIFMs and the management of their AIFs must comply with the requirements of the AIFM Directive;
- non-German AIFMs must appoint a representative and a paying agent in Germany:
- AIFs must comply with the product rules of the KAGB; and
- the marketing documents must be translated into German language.

German also has specific new requirements for third-country AIFs. For example, if a third-country AIF is marketed to professional investors only, the third-country AIFM must not only comply with the requirements under art.42 of the AIFM Directive but must also appoint a "depositary-lite", i.e. one or several persons or entities assuming the depository functions set out under art.21(7)–(9) of the AIFM Directive for the third-country AIF. In addition, the third-country AIFM must also abide by the anti-asset-stripping provisions implemented in the KAGB. The requirements are more burdensome if the marketing is addressed to semi-professional or even retail investors.

The KAGB now also provides for a lighter regulatory regime for EU sub-threshold AIFMs, under which they can market their AIFs to professional and semi-professional investors in Germany on a cross-border basis provided that all of the following apply:

- they are registered as a sub-threshold AIFM in their home Member State;
- marketing of AIFs managed by sub-threshold AIFMs is allowed under the rules of the home Member State and is not subject to stricter requirements than those under the KAGB ("reciprocity requirement"); and
- the sub-threshold AIFM has notified the intended marketing to BaFin.

Reciprocity exists for instance with regard to Luxembourg and the UK but not with regard to Austria.

## 2.3 Customary or common terms of funds

The customary or common terms of German private equity funds are similar to those in other jurisdictions and typically address the same issues that investors know from other jurisdictions.

## 3. DEBT FINANCE

### 3.1 Means of financing

Most transactions include a great variety of debt instruments: senior loans provided by banks, second-lien loans, mezzanine instruments provided by banks or specialised lenders in general with equity kickers or similar remunerations, and payment-in-kind (PIK) instruments.

If the financial structuring is only possible after the transaction, senior loans can be provided as working capital facilities or bridge loans.

Mezzanine finance is usually structured as a junior loan. Alternatively, other forms of mezzanine finance are used, such as vendor loans, usufruct rights (*Genussrechte*), silent participations and bonds, including high-yield bonds in large transactions.

### 3.2 Restrictions on granting security

German law contains several provisions that restrict financing banks of the purchaser to use the assets of a target company to collateralise debt financing. In particular, stock corporations and private liability limited companies established under German law are subject to provisions dealing with the raising and maintenance of capital.

In a stock corporation, the contribution of a shareholder must not be returned (s.57 para.1 of the Stock Corporation Act 1937 (*Aktiengesetz—AktG*)). Therefore, stock corporations are prohibited from giving any benefit to the shareholder unless it is from the profit retained or exceptionally permitted by law. Consequently, the stock corporation must usually not give any loans to shareholders or other securities to collateralise loans of a shareholder for the purpose of acquiring shares of the stock corporation by such shareholder.

In a private limited liability company, the regulations of raising and maintaining capital are less strict. However, according to s.30 of the Limited Liability Company Act (*Gesetz betreffend die Gesellschaft mit beschränkter Haftung—GmbHG*), the stated share capital (*Stammkapital*) must not be paid out to the shareholders. Thus, loans to the shareholders are forbidden if the redemption claim is not fully adequate and the stated share capital is affected by it. These capital maintenance rules, however, do not apply to shareholders with whom the GmbH has entered into a domination and profit and loss transfer agreement.

Section 30 of the Private Limited Liability Company Act also applies analogue to a GmbH & Co KG.

If the target company is a general partnership (*offene Handelsgesellschaft—OHG*) or a limited partnership, the use of the assets of the target company as collateral for debt of a partner is not directly addressed by law but may be limited under the provisions of the partnership agreement.

### 3.3 Intercreditor issues

Similar to other jurisdictions, intercreditor agreements determine the ranking of claims of different creditors. Such an agreement may, inter alia, address the following issues:

- declarations of some creditors to subordinate their claims to other creditors' claims;
- prohibition for junior creditors to amend or change their loan agreements with the banks to the detriment of the senior creditors;
- declarations by junior creditors not to satisfy their claims unless the senior creditors' claims are executed—usually, the accruing interest is exempt from this provision;
- suspension of some rights of junior creditors until the fulfilment of the senior creditors' claims, such as the termination of credit contracts, the prohibition of an offset or a debt settlement, or to file for insolvency;
- warrant of special rights to the senior creditors in the case of insolvency of the debtor or the guarantor;
- duty of senior creditors to sweep payments wrongly received; and
- sole power of enforcement of the security trustee and the use of the proceeds by the security trustee.

When formulating intercreditor agreements, s.489 para.4 of the German Civil Code (*Bürgerliches Gesetzbuch*—BGB) should be considered. According to this provision, the debtor's right of termination may not be excluded or impaired by contract.

## 3.4 Syndication

Credit institutions may syndicate their loans during or after a transaction.

The legal structure of syndication with a third party is usually the partial assumption of rights and obligations under a facility agreement from the old creditor to the new creditor. The assignment of loan claims to a new creditor is permitted by law but might be limited by the terms of the loan agreement.

In the case where the loan is assigned to another credit institution that already participates in the consortium, this is legally considered an amendment of the agreement and thus needs the permission of all parties. Often the agreement already provides the permission for these types of syndications.

To simplify syndications, many loan agreements between banks and debtors are drafted in accordance with the standards of the Loan Market Association (LMA). The LMA developed a sample loan agreement in accordance with German law. This results in loans which are subject to German law being more fungible.

## 4. EQUITY STRUCTURES
### 4.1 Role of management

Obviously, the management of the target company plays a significant role. Hence, in addition to restrictive covenants on non-compete, non-solicitation and confidentiality, managers' service agreements often provide for, among other compensation components, variable payments in order to incentivise the management. The variable payments usually depend on the performance of the target company or the individual performance of the manager. For determining the amount of the bonus, the payments may be related to key financial figures, such as earnings before interest, taxes, depreciation and amortisation (EBITDA) or the economic value added, or to the fair market value of the target company.

When determining the remuneration of the management board of a stock corporation, s.87 para.1 of the AktG and s.4.2 of the German Corporate Governance Code (the Code) must be complied with. According to these rules, the supervisory board of the stock corporation has to ensure that the aggregate remuneration bears a reasonable relationship to the duties of the members of the management board as well as the condition of the company, and that it does not exceed standard remuneration without any particular reasons. Pursuant to s.4.2.3 of the Code, the amount of compensation shall be capped, both overall and for variable compensation components.

## 4.2  Common protections for investors

A private equity fund commonly seeks to receive statutory and contractual control over the activities of the target company.

If the target company is a GmbH, the shareholders can largely instruct the managing directors to take or refrain from taking certain measures. The shareholders can also remove the managing director at any time.

In addition, the management of the target company is often bound by the rules of procedure adopted by the shareholders of the target company. These rules subject certain business activities to the prior consent of the shareholders' meeting or, if any, the shareholder's committee.

If contractually agreed, delegates of the private equity funds can take seats in the target company's body, such as in the supervisory board, the advisory board or the shareholders' committee.

Due to German corporate law, the corporation's articles must be filed with the commercial register and are open to the public. Thus, protective provisions are often inserted into a confidential private shareholders' agreement and not into the articles of association itself (see below).

## 4.3  Common protections for management
### Management participation

The management also usually benefits from an equity participation in the target or acquisition company. Such equity participation is often indirect through a tax transparent common vehicle which pools the interests of management and which is controlled by the private equity investor.

The equity participation is always subject to a shareholders' agreement providing:

- control of the private equity investor over shareholder decisions relating to the target company;
- sometimes, veto positions for the management with regard to substantial decisions to be taken in the shareholders' meeting;
- anti-dilution protection for the management, in particular with respect to future financing and/or refinancing (recaps);
- for a prohibition of the management to dispose of its shares without the consent of the private equity investor;
- exit provisions such as tag and drag-along rights; and
- a good leaver/bad leaver scheme (discussed further in s.4.5 below).

## 4.4  Management warranties

Private equity funds usually request comprehensive protections from the sellers and management through warranties which cover all relevant aspects of the target company. While sellers' warranties usually include information about the past and the current business, management warranties may also refer to the future development of the target company.

The management of the target company usually develops a business plan prior to the transaction. Therefore, the investors may expect a management warranty that the business plan was prepared thoroughly and in due manner. However, it is typically not expected to be warranted to reach the goals of the business plan. Besides the business plan, manager warranties can also reference other information provided by the management, such as management presentations, due diligence documents, vendor due diligence reports or buyer due diligence reports if known to the management.

By receiving these management warranties, investors attempt to obtain complete and correct information prior to the purchase of the target company. The damage compensation in the case of a breach of such warranties is usually limited to the amount of the participation of the respective managers in the company and the private assets of the manager are not affected or only affected to a limited degree. Claims based on a warranty breach are usually subject to the statute of limitation, typically 12–24 months following the transaction. Legal proceedings concerning the breach of management warranties are rare.

### 4.5    Good leaver/bad leaver provisions

One of the most important elements of a management participation programme (as discussed in s.4.3 above) is the leaver scheme, which makes provisions concerning the compulsory transfer of the manager's shares if the manager ceases to be active for the company. Technically, this is structured by call and/or put options. If, for example, the manager terminates his/her service contract or resigns as the managing director of the target company, the private equity investor is granted the right to acquire the (indirect) share of the respective manager in the target company. Further option events are insolvency of the manager, execution measures against the manager, breach of contractual obligations by the manager and disability of the manager. Sometimes the manager is granted a put option to be exercised in case of disability or death.

The purchase price payable to the leaving manager usually depends upon the circumstances of the leaver event. A "good leaver" is commonly a manager who leaves the company because of retirement, death, disability or termination without fault of the manager. A "bad leaver" departs because of termination through the company with good cause or termination by the manager themselves during a specified initial period.

The calculation of a manager's compensation often depends on the acquisition costs and the market value of any shares acquired by the manager as part of the transaction or management contract. A good leaver usually receives the market value of the shares; a bad leaver typically receives the lower of acquisition costs of the shares and fair market value. Under German corporate law, compensation clauses that do not consider the market value of the shares are not always enforceable. In particular, courts have decided that clauses may not be valid if they provide compensation only in the amount of the book value of the company. Such jurisprudence should be considered when formulating good leaver/bad leaver provisions. Furthermore, compensation clauses could be found to be void if, at the time of the agreement, the market value of the shares clearly exceeded the amount of the compensation. If compensation clauses are valid at the time of the agreement but invalid at the time of the departure of the manager, courts may also adjust the compensation clauses.

For the determination of the amount of the compensation, other parameters than the good leaver/bad leaver provisions may be taken into account, such as time vesting or performance vesting.

### 4.6 Public to private transactions

Public to private transactions have become a common way for private entities to invest in public listed companies.

Going-private transactions often involve a transformation of the legal form from a stock corporation to a limited liability company and thereby permitting greater flexibility and tighter control by the new owners over management. Additionally, costs for complying with stock exchange requirements can be avoided.

Another important device for a public to private transaction is the domination and profit and loss transfer agreement. This instrument allows the majority shareholder to control the management of a publicly listed stock corporation, including the right to give specific instructions to management regarding certain business transactions. In deviation from the standard model, the management of the stock corporation loses its relative independence vis-à-vis its shareholders.

Both a transformation and a domination and profit and loss transfer agreement require an offer to minority shareholders of the dominated company to acquire their shares against payment of a consideration in cash.

Prior to the above, public to private transactions are typically affected by the Takeover Act 2002 (*Übernahmegesetz*—WpÜG). This Act regulates all public offers whereby a bidder wishes to acquire substantial stakes in a publicly listed target company. Thus, it provides a detailed schedule for the going-private transaction: for example, provisions for how a bidder can make an offer to acquire shares of a target company, how the minimum purchase price is to be calculated, what other formal requirements a bidder must comply with (providing offer documents, securing sufficient financial resources etc) or when a bidder must issue a mandatory offer.

There are also disclosure issues in connection with going-private transactions. The requirements of the Securities Trading Act 1994 (*Wertpapierhandelsgesetz*—WpHG) must be complied with. According to the Securities Trading Act, whenever an investor ownership reaches, exceeds or falls below 3%, 5%, 10%, 15%, 20%, 25%, 30%, 50% and 75% of the voting rights in a listed company, a notification to both the company and the Federal Financial Supervisory Authority is required.

## 5.  EXITS

According to the BVK, exits of German target companies in 2017 amounted to a volume of EUR 5.42 billion, which is an increase of nearly

50% compared to 2016 (EUR 4.36 billion).[2] Most relevant exit routes in 2017 were trade sales constituting 50.1% of all exits followed by secondary sales (40.4%). In contrast, initial public offerings (IPOs) have not played any significant rule in 2017 (as in the year before).

## 5.1 Secondary sales

A secondary sale is the sale of the target company from a private equity investor to another financial sponsor. A secondary sale may be an exit option if a second stage of development can be started in the development of the target company with another financial sponsor. Consequently, the target company should have enough potential to warrant to the new investor an increase in value by operative improvement. For a successful secondary sale, the management should also be willing to invest a substantial amount of its proceeds received in the exit together with the new investors (roll over).

## 5.2 Trade sales

A trade sale is the sale to a strategic investor. The purchaser usually expects to benefit from synergy effects. As a result, it is necessary for the purchaser to acquire a controlling interest in the target company. In this case, the private equity investor may make use of its drag-along rights vis-à-vis minority shareholders, e.g. management.

## 5.3 Initial public offerings

IPOs in Germany usually command higher costs and more effort than secondary and trade sales but often create better overall returns. Furthermore, IPOs allow spreading the divestment over time, whereas other sales allow a full immediate divestment.

Thus, IPOs were often the preferred exit channel. However, due to the environment, the market for IPOs has not been very active in Germany at all.

For an IPO, it is required that the target company is organised in a structure capable of sale of shares in capital markets. A common method is a tax-neutral reorganisation into a stock corporation or a partnership limited by shares according to the German Law on the Regulation of Transformations 1995 (*Umwandlungsgesetz*—UmwG). If the IPO involves an increase of capital, a shareholder resolution is mandatory. If the IPO involves only the existing shares and no new shares are issued, a shareholders' resolution might still be necessary. According to a decision of the German Federal Supreme Court, a withdrawal from the stock market requires a shareholders' resolution. It can be argued that a shareholders' resolution is needed for an IPO as well. It is debated if a simple shareholders' majority is sufficient for such a resolution.

To be permitted into the regular market, a prospectus in accordance with the Takeover Act 2002 (*Übernahmegesetz*—WpÜG) approved by the Federal Financial Supervisory Authority has to be issued. Additionally, the requirements of the German Stock Market Act 2007 (*Börsengesetz*), the listing regulation (*Börsenzulassungsverordnung*) and s.35 of Regulation 1278/2006 on a special intervention measure for oats in Finland and Sweden for the

---

[2] All data in s.5 has been taken from: Presentation, "BVK-Statistik 2017" (February 2018), unless otherwise indicated.

2006/07 marketing year [2006] OJ L233/6 must be fulfilled. For instance, the annual financial statements of the last three years need to be disclosed, a sufficient spread of the shares need to be shown etc. The listing regulation requires a written application for permission with some attachments, e.g. excerpts from the public register and articles of association.

If the shares should not be traded on the regular market but in the unofficial market instead, the guidelines of the respective stock exchange must be met.

### 5.4 Refinancings

Refinancing is referred to as the new structuring of debt. Recapitalisation (recap) is the repayment of equity in part or in total to the financial sponsor.

The recapitalisation allows a private equity fund to realise a partial exit from an economic point of view. After a certain period of time, the private equity fund uses the improved operative results to receive a return financed by debt through surplus dividends, repayment of shareholder loans or repurchase of shares. Important features of the recapitalisation process are the increase of cash flows, the degree of debt relief and the leverage arbitrage.

### 5.5 Restructuring/insolvency

In the case of insolvency, the Insolvency Code (*Insolvenzordnung*—InsO) determines the order of priority in insolvency proceedings. Both debt providers and shareholders are insolvency creditors. Debt providers are generally given priority over shareholders unless a creditor agreed to subordinate their claim to all other forms of financing. However, in insolvency proceedings, the creditors typically only realise a marginal portion of their claims.

Sometimes, financial investors specialising in turnaround situations and restructurings are interested in buying an insolvent target company, either immediately before or during insolvency proceedings.

## 6. TAX
### 6.1 Taxation of fund structures

The German investment taxation system faced a high level of complexity coupled with systemic issues as well as ongoing concerns regarding the free movement of capital based on European law. Therefore, the German Investment Tax Act (*Investmentsteuergesetz*) has been modified substantially by the German Investment Tax Reform Act with effect as of 1 January 2018.

The German Investment Tax Act, as amended, distinguishes now between investment funds (*Investmentfonds*) on one hand and the newly introduced sub-category special investment funds (*Spezial-Investmentfonds*) on the other.

Within the meaning of the German Investment Tax Act, investment funds are open-ended funds (typically Undertakings for Collective Investments in Transferable Securities—UCITS), while special investment funds are limited to a maximum of 100 investors and fulfil certain other criteria, including a specific tax product regulation. As a result of the investment tax reform, regular investment funds have been subject to a system change. Under the new investment taxation system, regular investment funds are liable to German corporation tax on their German dividend income, real estate income and so-called other income. Special investment funds and their investors on the other hand may opt to be subject to a special tax regime under the German Investment Tax Act that is similar to the previous system and remain hence transparent for tax purposes; this tax regime has not materially changed.

Due to their investment policies and the fact that they do not grant redemption rights to investors, private equity funds typically do not qualify as either investment funds or special investment funds. Thus, we will not dwell on the details of their taxation.

The vast majority of private equity funds are structured as limited partnerships. In general, partnerships are excluded from the scope of the new German Investment Tax Act. Therefore, partnerships and their investors are subject to the general rules of taxation for partnerships and their investors.

These rules are summarised below.

Private equity funds set up as a limited partnership allow investors from different jurisdictions to invest in a fiscally "transparent" structure for tax purposes. To be regarded as fiscally transparent, it is required that the activities of the private equity fund are limited to passive asset management rather than to business activities. From a German tax point of view, certain criteria must be met in order to avoid the private equity fund qualifying as a business. In order to qualify as passive asset management rather than as a commercial business, a private equity fund has to be managed, at least partly, by one or more of its limited partners if only a corporation (or a so-called deemed-business partnership) is acting as its general partner. Furthermore, the fund limited partnership may not hold an interest in a partnership, which in turn performs actual business activities or qualifies as a deemed business for German tax purposes (unless the investment is made indirectly through a corporation); and it has to qualify as not being engaged in a trade or business pursuant to the guidelines provided by the German Federal Ministry of Finance (*Bundesfinanzministerium*) in its administrative pronouncement dated 16 December 2003.[3] Due to this circular, a qualification as private asset management requires:

- not to use bank loans (except for short-term bridge loans);
- not to have an extensive organisation to administer the fund's equity;
- to use the equity funds' expertise only for inserting on its own account;
- only to administrate and realise investments for its own account;
- not to have short-term holdings;
- not to reinvest sale proceeds (except as cover for investors' capital initially used to pay managing fees);
- not to be actively involved in the management of target companies; and
- not to have entrepreneurial investments in the target company.

If a private equity fund fulfils these requirements, the German fund vehicle is neither subject to German corporate income tax nor subject to German trade tax. All income is immediately allocated to its partners and taxed at the

---

3    German Federal Ministry of Finance, "Circular regarding classification of venture capital and private equity funds for income tax purposes; differentiation between income from private asset management and business income [*Schreiben betr. einkommensteuerliche Behandlung von Venture Capital und Private Equity Fonds; Abgrenzung der privaten Vermögensverwaltung vom Gewerbebetrieb*]" (16 December 2003).

level of the partners. The taxation of each partner depends on its individual tax status.

In a decision of 24 August 2011,[4] the German Federal Tax Court raised, in an obiter dictum, doubts whether the criteria for private asset management set out in the aforementioned administrative pronouncement are too generous but did not explain these doubts in more detail. The German tax authorities have not announced that they will cancel or amend the criteria for private asset management as set out in the administrative pronouncement and representatives of the Federal Finance Ministry informally confirmed in seminars that it is indeed not intended to do so. As a consequence, the criteria for private asset management as summarised above should continue to apply.

Thus, if the partner in the German non-business fund vehicle is a German individual, since 1 January 2009, the income (capital gains, dividends, interest) is subject to a flat tax regime (*Abgeltungssteuer*) in the amount of 25% plus a solidarity surcharge thereon at a rate of 5.5% and—where applicable—church tax. It is discussed presently (e.g. in the coalition agreement) that the flat tax regime applying to capital income of individuals shall be abolished in relation to interest income. Instead, the standard tax rates (progressive tax rates) shall apply. For dividends or capital gains such changes are not discussed. The flat tax may be (partially) refunded if a double taxation agreement is applicable. Nonetheless, a withholding tax of 15% will usually remain applicable in Germany to dividends under the relevant double taxation agreements.

If the partner of a German non-business fund vehicle is a domestic corporation, such as a GmbH or an AG, it is subject to corporate income tax and trade tax, regardless of its shareholders. This implies that 95% of the dividend received and capital gains from the sale of a shareholding of the fund are generally exempt from corporate income tax, provided in respect of dividend income that such partner holds—indirectly through the fund—10% or more of the target company's share capital as of the beginning of the calendar year (or at the time of the acquisition of such participation). In addition, 95% of the dividends are generally exempt from trade tax if the corporation indirectly holds 15% or more of the target company's stated share capital from the beginning of the assessment period. Special tax rules apply to capital gains realised by companies active in the financial and insurance sectors as well as by pension funds.

If the partner is a foreign individual or a foreign corporation, (subject to non-resident taxatin, e.g. on dividends from German corporations), it is generally not taxed in Germany but in its home jurisdiction. However, if the foreign individual or the foreign corporation (in)directly holds 1% or more of a German target company's stated share capital, capital gains are subject to German taxation in the same manner as a German individual or a domestic corporation, unless it has protection under an applicable double taxation treaty.

If the private equity fund is qualified as a generating business income for German tax purposes, it is subject to trade tax (with the income allocated to

---

4    I R 46/10, BFHE 234, 339.

its German permanent establishment). Additionally, if the partner of the German business private equity fund is a German or foreign individual, according to the partial income system (*Teileinkünfteverfahren*), 60% of the capital gains and dividends received by the partner are taxable. Interest and other income of the business private equity fund is fully taxable. If the partner of the German business private equity fund is a domestic or foreign corporation, the corporation is subject to corporate income tax as described above but not to trade tax on its level (with the exception of companies in the financial and insurance sectors and pension funds). (Special rules and restrictions for the trade tax exemption apply in case of non-German partnerships.)

## 6.2 Carried interest

In Germany, it was in dispute for a long time whether carried interest qualifies for tax purposes as remuneration for service or as partnership income. Finally, in 2004, the Act for Promotion of Venture Capital came into force. Under this Act, carried interest is qualified as remuneration for services if the interest is paid by a private equity fund partnership that is not engaged in a trade or business.

Following this, 40% of the carried interest received from such a private equity partnership can be tax exempt from German income tax. For private equity funds set up before the end of 2008, 50% of the carried interest can be tax exempt.

It is debated whether the same rules apply for carried interest that is paid by a private equity fund engaged in business, or structured as a corporation.

In the international context, the qualification of carried interest as remuneration for services can cause double taxation issues.

## 6.3 Management equity

The basic tax consideration of the management participation programme is that the management receives capital gains and dividends are distributed tax exempt. This requires that the management has economic ownership straight away with its participation, meaning that the managers bear real value risks from the investment. If this is not the case, the appreciation is subject to taxation as ordinary income from employment and subject for wage tax (for which the employer has a liability). Otherwise, the following tax rules apply.

The taxation of capital gains depends on whether the shares were acquired before or after the end of 2008. Concerning the sale of shares acquired before the end of 2008, capital gains are tax exempt if the holding period of the shares is at least 12 months and if the total investment in the target company is less than 1%. Otherwise, according to the part-income tax rule (*Teileinkünfteverfahren*), 60% of the capital gains are taxable.

Concerning the sale of shares acquired after the end of 2008, capital gains are subject to tax of 25% plus a 5.5% solidarity surcharge (and—where applicable—church tax) if the management total investment in the target company is less than 1%. Otherwise, the part-income tax rule as described above, applies as well.

Dividends are generally subject to tax of 25% plus a 5.5% solidarity surcharge (and—where applicable—church tax) and if cases of distributions by German corporations are subject to withholding tax at the aforementioned tax rate.

Due to a change in the administrative practice of German tax authorities, since the beginning of 2008, the management fees paid by a private equity fund to its manager are subject to value added tax (VAT) regardless of whether such management fee is structured as a priority profit share in the balance sheet profit of the receptive partnership. Thus, the fees are regarded as an additional fee, not as part of the contribution as partner or shareholder.

### 6.4  Loan interest

The interest payable on straight-line (i.e. non-hybrid) loans to the private equity fund is usually not subject to German withholding tax.

Interest expenses of the target company are partly tax deductible. Since 2008, the interest barrier regulations (*Zinsschranke*) limit the tax deductibility of interest expenses of German companies. This rule is complex. In short, the deductibility of interest expenses is capped at 30% of the EBITDA of the relevant company. However, companies are able to build up an EBITDA reserve in business years where 30% of the EBITDA exceeds the negative interest balance. This reserve can be used in the following five business years if the negative interest balance exceeds 30% of the EBITDA in one such business year. The restrictive provisions (and the EBITDA reserve) do not apply if the interest expenses do not exceed the interest income by more than EUR 3 million.

### 6.5  Transaction taxes

Under German tax law, the sale of all of a company's assets as a going concern (*Geschäftsveräußerung im Ganzen*) is not subject to VAT. However, in the case of the sale of the company's assets other than by sale of all assets as a going concern, VAT is applicable.

The purchase of shares of a company is exempted from VAT.

If an asset deal includes the transfer of property, land transfer tax (*Grunderwerbssteuer*) is raised in the amount of 3.5–6.5%. The tax is based on the proportional purchase price.

In a share deal, land transfer tax is only raised if the purchaser acquires or consolidates 95% or more of the shares of a corporation or a partnership that owns property in Germany. The 95% will not only be reached if the fund holds the interest in the company directly or indirectly but also if the fund is only beneficial to the owner of the interest. The tax is based on the fiscal property value.

The same tax rules apply if 95% or more of the partners of a partnership that owns property change within five years. To avoid land transfer tax, a purchaser might acquire less than 95% of the partnership shares and receive a call option for the rest of the shares that can be exercised five years later. There are currently discussions to lower the thresholds to 90% and the relevant period for changes identity to partnerships to 10 years.

## 7.  CURRENT TOPICAL ISSUES/TRENDS

According to the latest market outlook of the BVK, investors are focusing increasingly on Germany and private equity as an asset class. Nearly 50% of the respondent investment companies are basically optimistic about the asset class private equity and Germany as a preferred investment location for private equity investors. This is also reflected in their mainly positive expectations on the development of their investment activity in Germany.

Better macro-economic conditions than in previous years, large amounts of committed capital ("dry powder"), historic low levels of interest rates and improvements to the legal framework conditions for investment companies in Germany are factors that indicate an increase in investment activities in Germany. Furthermore, the positive economic prospects and the expected short to mid-term interest rate policy of the European Central Bank (ECB) might facilitate further improvements in financing conditions in the near future.

The German transaction landscape is expected to be dominated by acquisitions of and divestments in small and medium-sized companies. In this context, according to the BVK, secondary buyouts, carve outs and minority and majority shareholdings in family-owned companies are considered to be the most attractive sources of investment. The preferred industries for investments are anticipated to be software/IT, internet/media/ communications and biotechnology/pharmaceuticals/medicine.

The exit environment may be dominated by trade sales, i.e. sales to strategic investors. Other exit channels, such as secondary sales/secondary buyouts and IPOs, are expected to trail behind considerably. In respect of taxation, legislative changes (e.g. base erosion and profit shifting (BEPS), multilateral instrument (MLI)) are in the discussion, which may affect both deal and fund structuring.

# Italy

**CBA Studio Legale e Tributario**  Giuseppe A. Galeano
& Emanuela Sabbatino

## 1. MARKET OVERVIEW
### 1.1 Types of investors
The typical structure for private equity investments in Italy is represented by a management company/closed-end investment fund reserved to qualified investors or hedge funds (asset management company/*società di gestione del risparmio* (SGR)/*fondo chiuso riservato*/*fondo speculativo*).

The periodic survey of the Italian private equity and venture capital market, conducted by the Italian Private Equity and Venture Capital Association (AIFI), in co-operation with PricewaterhouseCoopers (Pwc),[1] shows that, in 2017, the number of operators investing, disinvesting or raising capitals grew by 5% with respect to the previous year (139 operators against 133 of 2016). The buyout market is the segment with more active investors (56 operators, out of which 26 are international players).

In 2017, the resources collected in the Italian private equity market increased by 283% for an amount equal to EUR 5,063 million against EUR 1,313 million of the previous year. Such positive trend is the result of some institutional investors' activity, which led to the closing of operations for an amount of EUR 4,110 million. Conversely, fundraising activity pursued by private operators decreased by 29% (EUR 920 million against 1,298 million of the previous year). It must be noted that, in compliance with international practice, these figures do not include the resources of EUR 1.075 million deriving from international operators that are based in Italy. Should such resources be included, the total amount of economic resources collected in 2017 would amount to EUR 6,138 million.

Moreover, in 2017, the geographical distribution of funds raised continued to be under the predominance of Italian resources (72% of the market, equal to EUR 527 million in comparison with 28% of foreign sources, equal to EUR 201 million). As regards the sources of investment, in 2017 individual investors and family offices have been the primary source of investment in Italy (27%), followed by private funds of funds (FoFs) (17%), and public sector and sovereign funds (14%), which grew significantly by 11 points. Likewise, sources deriving from banks increased by five points.

### 1.2 Types of investments
The 2017 private equity deals represent the third highest value registered in the last decade in the Italian market after the economic crisis with a total value of investments equal to EUR 4,938 million (40% less than in 2016, the

---

[1]   This survey is the reference for all statistics throughout this chapter, unless otherwise indicated.

year in which a significant boost was favoured by several large deals for an amount of EUR 8,191 million). As regards the number of deals, 2017 recorded 311 transactions compared to 322 in 2016 (3% less).

During 2017, buyout transactions continued to represent the biggest investment segment as far as resources (EUR 3,444 million), followed by infrastructure investments (EUR 659 million) and expansion transactions (EUR 338 million). In terms of the number of investments, early stage transactions continued to be the most frequent category (133), followed by buyout (90) and expansion transactions (45).

The average value of investment per transaction decreased in 2017 with respect to the previous year (EUR 15,9 million against EUR 25,4 million in the previous year). Such result was partly due to the lack of investments in mega deals and a contraction of investments in large deals (EUR 1,598 million against EUR 6,081 million in 2016) which nevertheless represented 74% of the transactions carried out in the market.

The highest number of investment transactions were made in the field of industrial products and services (16%, corresponding to 51 transactions) followed by investments in ICT (Information and Communication Technology) (just under 16%, corresponding to 49 transactions) and medical (11%, corresponding to 35 transactions). In terms of value, the highest investments were also made in the field of industrial products and services (26%), followed by manufacturing—fashion (11%) and energy and environment (9%).

In general, the use of leverage in Italy is low due to the increasing use of alternative financing instruments (as regards the access to leverage, see s.3 below).

## 2. FUNDS
### 2.1 Funds structures

The most common vehicle for private equity investments in Italy is the common investment fund (in particular, the closed-end investment fund reserved to qualified investors), which is typically managed by an asset management company known as *società di gestione del risparmio* or SGR, whose assets are separated from the fund's assets. Under the Italian legislation, funds may be also structured as companies, i.e. fixed capital investment companies (SICAFs) or variable capital investment companies (SICAVs).

The basic rules governing private equity funds are contained in Legislative Decree No.58/1998 (Consolidated Financial Act or TUF) and its implementing provisions, such as, inter alia, Ministerial Decree No.30 of 5 March 2015 and the Bank of Italy's Regulation of 19 December 2015, as amended by the decision of 23 December 2016 (the Regulation).

Under the TUF, as amended by Legislative Decree No.44/2014, an "investment fund" is defined as an undertaking for collective investment (UCI) set up in the form of an enterprise with independent equity, divided into units and managed by a fund manager (art.1(1)(j) of the TUF), which, in accordance with a recent ruling of the Milan Court (N.7232/2016), should be considered as an entity endowed with legal personality. The funds are managed by SGRs (art.36(1) of the TUF), which must be authorised to operate by the Bank of Italy, after consultation with Consob (the National Commission for Companies and the Stock Exchange Market) (art.34(1) of the TUF) and registered in a special list held by the Bank of Italy (art.35(1) of the TUF).

SGRs must be incorporated in the legal form of a joint-stock company and have their registered office and their head office in Italy (art.34(1)(a)–(b) of the TUF). The minimum corporate capital requirement for an SGR is EUR 1 million (art.34(1)(c) of the TUF and Title II Ch.I s.II.1 of the Regulation). Such amount is reduced to EUR 500,000 for SGRs managing closed-end reserved alternative investment funds and to EUR 50,000 for SGRs falling below certain thresholds (Title II Ch.I ss.II and VII of the Regulation). In addition, the Regulation sets out specific provisions concerning the minimum SGR's asset requirements (the so-called *patrimonio di vigilanza*) and the obligation for SGRs falling below certain thresholds to hold/invest approximately 20% of their minimum corporate capital in specific assets (Title II Ch.V s.V of the Regulation).

The fund's assets shall be deposited with a custodian (an Italian bank, Italian branch of an EU bank and a bank of non-EU countries, an investment firm or an Italian branch of an EU Investment company and a company in non-EU countries, other than banks) whose duties are governed by art.48 of the TUF. The custodian shall be in charge, inter alia, of verifying the legitimacy of the operations of sale, issue, repurchase, reimbursement and annulment of the fund units, as well as the appropriation of the UCI's revenues. It shall be liable towards the UCI manager and investors for any loss suffered by them as a result of its failure to perform its obligations. In all cases in which the custodian becomes aware of any irregularity in the management of the SGR—and/or the funds—it shall promptly inform the Bank of Italy and Consob.

## 2.2 Regulation of fundraising and fund managers

Apart from, and in addition to, the TUF and the Regulation, the operations of a fund are also subject to the fund's own rules, which must, however, comply with the requirements set forth in the TUF (in particular, arts 36-37), in the Decree of the Ministry of Finance No.228/1999 and in the Regulation. The fund's rules shall define the features of the fund and govern its functions, identify the manager and the custodian and their functions, and establish, inter alia:

(1) the name and the duration of the fund;
(2) the procedures for participation in the fund, the terms and procedures for the issue of the certificates, for reimbursement of units and for the liquidation of the fund;
(3) the bodies responsible for the investment choices and for the criteria for dividing the investments according to those choices;
(4) the type of assets, financial instruments and other valuables in which the capital of the fund may be invested;
(5) the criteria for the determination of the income and of the management results and any systems for the sharing and distribution of the same;
(6) the expenses borne by the fund and those borne by the asset management

company;

(7)  the amount of, or the criteria for determining, the fees owed to the asset management company and the costs charged to investors;

(8)  the means for publishing the unit value; and

(9)  whether the fund is a feeder fund.

Article 13 of the TUF, as replaced by Legislative Decree No.72/2015, establishes that the individuals responsible for the SGR's administrative, managerial and control functions are deemed to be suitable for their appointment when they: (1) meet the requirements of professionalism, integrity and independence; (2) meet the criteria of competence and fairness; and (3) devote the time necessary for the effective performance of their duties. Such requisites, as specified by Decree of the Ministry of Finance No.468/1998, shall be assessed by the corporate administration and control bodies, which are entrusted with the strategic supervision and are responsible for the documentation of the process of analysing the suitability of the aforementioned individuals (Title IV Ch.II.1 of the Regulation). Whoever should not meet such requirements shall be disqualified from the office, as determined by the corporate body, within 30 days from the appointment or from awareness of the relevant circumstances.

## 2.3  Customary or common terms of funds

As mentioned above, closed-end funds are the most commonly used type of funds for private equity investments because these structures grant gains from the investment and facilitate the investors' exit from the fund at predetermined dates. Pursuant to the Regulation, closed-end funds are subject, inter alia, to the following rules:

•  the fund cannot invest more than 20% of its net assets in unlisted financial instruments issued by the same entity (Title V Ch.III s.V.3.1 of the Regulation);

•  an SGR cannot hold, through the funds that it manages, more than 10% of the voting rights in a listed company. This limitation can be only derogated in the scope of those transactions which aim at increasing the value of the shareholding with the purpose of transferring it in a timeframe which is coherent with the investment policy of the fund (Title V Ch.III s.V.6.1 of the Regulation);

•  the fund can take out debt up to the maximum amount of 10% of its total net assets and it can create securities over its assets only if the security is instrumental to, or connected with, the performance of the fund (different thresholds and rules apply to the real estate closed-end funds) (Title V Ch.III s.V.6.2.2 of the Regulation); and

•  the fund can grant loans only if they are conducive to, or connected with, the acquisition of shareholdings in target companies. The amount of the loan is compounded for the purposes of the 20% limit indicated in the first bullet point above (Title V Ch.III s.V.6.3 of the Regulation).

## 3.  DEBT FINANCE

### 3.1  Means of financing

The Italian private equity market has been traditionally characterised by the Italian companies' dependence on bank loans. However, after the financial crisis, banking institutions, which had been saddled with a large bad loan pile, reduced their lending to enterprises by selecting more carefully their investments and finance transactions to the point that, by 2013, credit to Italian businesses dropped by 40% compared to the volumes of 2008. This notwithstanding, Italian companies still depend significantly on bank financing, which accounts for more than 60% of the overall financial debt (20 points above the European average). In fact, by the end of 2017, lending to the non-financial private sector grew by 1.8%—with a particular increase in loans granted to manufacturing firms (2.6% over the preceding twelve months) and a positive trend for service firms (0.7%). The investments are directed mainly at the mid-market, in line with the structure of the Italian economy. In light of the above, the funds tend to invest in small and medium-sized industrial companies, which they keep in their portfolios for a longer time.

Due to the difficulties in obtaining bank loans that Italian companies faced during the recession, the legislator focused on reforming the lending market in order to facilitate access to liquidity. For instance, Law Decree No.83/2012, as converted into Law No.134/2012, promoted new financing instruments by allowing the issuance of short-term financial notes and bonds (the so-called "Minibonds") by unlisted Italian companies for an amount not exceeding, on aggregate, twice the amount of the corporate capital, the legal reserve and other available reserves resulting from the last approved financial instruments. Likewise, following the 2014 legislative measures, which allowed direct lending by Italian alternative investment funds (AIFs), the legislator improved the TUF's regulatory framework by specifying that AIFs may lend only to subjects other than consumers and by allowing direct lending to non-consumers by EU AIFs under certain conditions and limitations.

Besides the mentioned reforms to increase access to financing, according to a recent trend in Italian private equity, Italian enterprises privilege the issuance of hybrid instruments which stand between shares and bonds, such as those admitted by the Italian Civil Code (the Code) under art.2346(3) and art.2411(3) (the so-called *strumenti finanziari partecipativi*). Such instruments do not give to the subscriber the status of shareholder in the issuer (the right to vote in the general shareholder meeting is excluded) and grant economic rights and limited administrative powers (such as the option right in the event of issuance of new hybrid instruments and the right to vote in a special assembly).

### 3.2 Restrictions on granting security

General rules concerning financial assistance are contained in arts 2357, 2358 and 2474 of the Code.

If the target company is a joint-stock company (SpA), it is not allowed to grant loans or provide guarantees for the purchase or subscription of its own shares, unless certain conditions are satisfied, such as, inter alia (art.2357–2358 of the Code):

- the transaction is authorised in advance by the extraordinary shareholders' meeting;
- at least 30 days prior to the shareholders' meeting, the directors draw up

a report describing the transaction and highlighting, among others: (1) the transaction's terms and conditions; (2) the economic purposes of the transaction; (3) the specific interest of the company in the transaction; (4) the risks of the transaction associated with the company's solvency and liquidity; (5) the price for the purchase or subscription of the shares; and (6) whether the transaction will be carried out at arm's length;

- the resolution of the shareholders' meeting and the report are filed with the companies' register; and
- the aggregate amount of the loans and guarantees does not exceed the dividends distributable and the reserves available resulting from the last financial statements.

Moreover, due to the amendment to art.2357*ter* of the Code by Legislative Decree No.139/2015, the purchase of own shares is considered as a reduction in the value of equity. Hence, a special purpose non-distributable reserve is required to be entered in the company's financial statements for an amount equal to the price paid.

If the target is a limited liability company (Srl), no loans can be given, or securities made, by the target for the purchase of its stock (art.2474 of the Code).

Specific rules apply to merger leveraged buyouts (MLBOs). Pursuant to art.2501*bis* of the Code, an MLBO is defined as a merger between two companies, one of which incurred debt for the purchase of the other, whereby, as a result of the merger, the assets of the target become a generic security for the reimbursement of the debt. This kind of transaction is legitimate only when it is carried out in compliance with the following formal and substantive requirements:

(1) the merger project indicates the financial resources necessary to the company resulting from the merger to repay the debt;

(2) the board report outlines the reason underlying the transaction and it contains a sound economic and financial plan with the indication of the financial resources and the description of the purposes of the transaction (in this respect, it is worth noting that many scholars have stressed that the reasons in question must be of real business nature and may not consist of the mere need to repay the acquisition debt);

(3) the appraisals' report confirms that the indications contained in the board report are reasonable; and

(4) a report by an auditing company of the target or the purchaser is attached to the merger project.

## 3.3 Intercreditor issues

Larger private equity transactions are generally characterised by a complex financial structure (that typically includes senior and mezzanine lending), which requires the parties to enter into one or more intercreditor agreements, when more than one lender is involved. The main purpose of such agreement is to establish the security rankings and payment subordination of the lenders, both at the ordinary and extraordinary level (e.g. in the case of bankruptcy). In addition, by intercreditor agreements, the lenders usually disclose to each other the terms and conditions of the existing loans (in particular, collateral and covenants). In certain cases, mainly when the mezzanine lender is a bank that acted as the arranger of the transaction and which intends to place the debt in a secondary market, intercreditor agreements can also contain provisions concerning the transfer of the loan.

### 3.4 Syndication

Syndication of loans basically depends on the amount of the financing required. Generally speaking, in the case of high amounts, banks tend to syndicate the loan, both prior to and after the completion of the deal.

## 4. EQUITY STRUCTURES

### 4.1 Role of management

The role of management varies based on the type of private equity transaction.

So, for example, in early stage transactions, the contribution of the entrepreneur/manager is mainly represented by their knowledge of the business, while their involvement in the capital is usually rather limited.

In such transactions, private equity investors usually contribute the most relevant part of the capital and retain majority control in the target company. The entrepreneur/manager, who usually serves on the board of directors (most often as CEO), acts under the strict control of the majority shareholder. The chairman of the board and the other director(s) are normally designated by the private equity investor.

In expansion transactions regarding family businesses, private equity funds usually invest in a minority stake, while the majority is retained by the family members, who tend to continue to manage the business, and are generally encouraged to do so by the private equity investor. Typically, the private equity investor exercises full control over the financial part of the business acquired, through a CFO of its own choice. Suffice it to say for these purposes that, while funds can be somewhat flexible regarding the governance and management of the company in which they invest, in these cases, the fund's exit strategy and possibilities of dismissing its investment must simply have no limitations.

In buyout transactions, the control of the target company is normally acquired by the private equity investor, who manages the investment based on a pre-determined business plan and monitors permanently the economic performance of the business. It is not uncommon to involve the managers in stock incentive packages (stock options, managers' stock and waterfall profit arrangements with the other shareholders, if any).

### 4.2 Common protections for investors

Based on the type of private equity transaction, the investors seek different types and grade of protection of their interest. Control at board level is usually very strong in the case of buyouts or early stage transactions, while it is weaker in expansion deals. Obviously, lower level powers in the board are frequently balanced by veto rights on certain relevant matters concerning the management of the company. Investors are normally protected also by strong, no-limits type exit clauses, and include pre-emption or at least offer matching rights, put option, drag-along and tag-along mechanisms, the right to withdraw from the company under certain circumstances (which is typical of Italian corporate law) and full ratchet rights. In cases where the investors do not play a hands-on role in the company, attention shall be given to the possibility that the investor is perceived as a shadow executive and, as a result, can be faced with issues of corporate direction and control, which are very relevant in terms of their legal implications and consequences. Moreover, in order to increase protection for investors, foreign insurance companies have started to promote specific warranty and indemnity (W&I) policies which provide covering to investors for losses resulting from breaches and/or inaccuracies of representations and warranties concerning the target company or its business made in the context of a private equity transaction. Such policies, which are becoming popular in the Italian market for fund to fund sales, provide protection to either the seller (the insurance cover losses resulting from valid claims brought by the investors for a breach of warranty) or the buyer (the insurance cover losses resulting from breaches of warranties which are recoverable from the seller). Generally, W&I policies provide for the payment of a premium calculated on the basis of the deal value and for the performance of a full diligence on the target and indemnify the beneficiary in relation to undisclosed events (however, issues resulting from the target's due diligence are not covered).

### 4.3  Common protections for management

Some of the basic protection instruments briefly described in the s.4.2 above (seat on the board, veto rights, tag-along clauses) can be also applied in favour of the managers who own a stake in the company. In a case where the managers are not shareholders of the company, the following instruments can protect their economic interest: (1) stock option plans (SOPs); (2) variable compensation schemes that recognise premiums and bonuses to the manager depending on the economic performance of the company (earnings, turnover, sales trends and net income); and (3) other benefits (i.e. the provision of a specific amount to be paid as an indemnity in case of termination of employment between the target company and the manager without just cause).

### 4.4  Management warranties

The so-called "legal" warranties (i.e. those contemplated under the Code), in case of acquisition of a company's shares, are extremely limited and only cover the title to the shares (in the case of eviction) and the absence of hidden faults in the shares themselves (i.e. no warranty covers the assets represented by the transferred shares). Therefore, in line with the practice of common law systems, acquisition agreements in private equity transactions contain a wide range of warranties concerning the company, its business, operations and assets. Generally speaking, Italian practice features warranties that can be divided into two groups: (1) those concerning the shares (full title, no encumbrances, no limits on circulation etc); and (2) those relating to the company. In private equity transactions, the representations and warranties concerning the companies are analytical and even stronger in scope than those used in typical mergers and acquisitions (M&A) deals. They range from good-standing of the company and full title to the company's tangible and non-tangible assets, to the existence and recoverability of the receivables, full compliance with the applicable laws and regulations (including on tax, environmental, security and other matters), possession of all the necessary authorisations and licences, no material default in respect to business agreements, no current material litigation or threatened and others. Indemnity systems' thresholds (de minimis, basket caps etc) also tend to be more buyer-friendly than they would be in ordinary M&A transactions.

### 4.5    Good Leaver/bad leaver provisions

The manager's competence and personal experience is extremely important to private equity investors. The marketing activity relating to the acquisition vehicle is often based on the reputation and qualities of the manager, who, consequently, must be granted effective powers to conduct the business. Therefore, clauses concerning the conditions of early termination of the management relationship are frequently inserted into agreements with managers. Such clauses may concern the stake in the company already held by the manager as well as the treatment of any stock options. The consequences of a manager's early termination depend on its underlying reasons.

In bad leaver clauses (such as, for example, dismissal of the manager by the company for just cause or voluntary resignation of the manager, save, therefore, for cases of death or physical or mental inability to work deriving from illness or accident), the investor may be entitled to exercise a call option right over the manager's stock or, alternatively or simultaneously, the stock option granted to the manager may be forfeited.

In its ruling No.16601 of 5 July 2017, the Italian Supreme Court established that foreign judgments providing for the payment of punitive damages are enforceable in Italy notwithstanding the incompatibility of such category of damages with the Italian system (damages are paid as a compensation for losses or harms suffered by the injured party) upon condition that such rulings must derive from a legal system which recognises them.

Hence, punitive damages should be considered by Italian companies operating in Italy and abroad which are now more exposed to higher potential risks on being convicted to payment of punitive damages.

On the contrary, in a good leaver situation (e.g. dismissal without just cause or voluntary resignation, or the cases of death or physical or mental inability to work deriving from illness or accident), the consequences of early termination usually depend on the duration of the activity of the managers and the state of the investment (generally, in these cases, the managers can, to a certain extent, exercise their stock option rights in proportion to the results achieved prior to termination). Sweet equity arrangements and incentive plans in general can give rise to relevant issues of a tax and employment law nature.

### 4.6    Public to private transactions

Public to private transactions are not very common. They are usually rather complex, costly and time consuming as it is necessary to meet the requirements of the public takeover regulatory framework. Therefore, private equity funds tend to invest in public companies only if the conditions are particularly profitable, with the purpose of delisting the company, increasing its value and listing it again upon divestment. Public to private transactions are usually carried out through a takeover bid (*offerta pubblica d'acquisto* or OPA) launched by a Newco incorporated by a private equity investor and the management of the target company. The purpose of the OPA is to acquire all the shares of the public company, with a consequent delisting. Alternatively, if, following an OPA, the Newco acquires the majority necessary to control the extraordinary shareholders' meeting of the public company, delisting can be realised by merging the latter with a non-listed company.

OPAs are governed by arts 101*bis* –112 of the TUF. They shall be carried out under the surveillance of Consob and are subject to strict communication and disclosure obligations.

The Italian public companies that are the target of an OPA must obtain the approval of the ordinary or extraordinary shareholders' meeting before taking any defensive measures against a hostile bid (art.104 of the TUF). However, the company's bylaws can derogate from this requirement. Any derogation must be communicated to Consob and to the supervisory authorities for takeover bids in member countries in which the company's securities are admitted to listing on a regular market or in which admission to listing has been requested. Likewise, such derogation must be promptly disclosed to the public.

If indicated in the bylaws of the Italian public target companies, during the offering period, any limitations on the transfer of the shares under the bylaws or on the voting rights in the shareholders' meetings set forth in the bylaws or in the shareholders' agreements are not effective (art.104*bis*(1)–(2) of the TUF).

In addition, if the bylaws so provide, where the offeror acquires (following an OPA) at least 75% of the shares of the target company with voting rights in the resolutions concerning the appointment or revocation of directors or members of the management or surveillance bodies, in the first shareholders' meeting which follows the closing of the offer (called to amend the bylaws or to revoke or appoint directors or members of the management or surveillance bodies), the multiple-voting shares confer only one vote and the following restrictions are not effective: (1) limitations on the voting rights under the bylaws or the shareholders' agreement; (2) any special right concerning the appointment or revocation of directors or members of the management or surveillance body, under the bylaws; and (3) the additional votes due pursuant to art.127*quinquies* of the TUF (art.104*bis*(1), (3) of the TUF). In the case of a positive outcome of the OPA, the offeror shall indemnify the shareholders whose rights became ineffective as a consequence of the application of the above described provisions.

In certain cases, the OPA is mandatory. Generally, this happens when the same shareholder holds, following various acquisitions, more than 30% of the shares of a public company. In this case, such a shareholder shall launch an OPA for the purchase of all listed shares (the so-called "totalitarian mandatory OPA" or "global takeover bid"). However, in certain cases indicated in the TUF (e.g. temporary transactions, gratuitous transactions, transactions aimed at saving a company in crisis etc), the OPA is not mandatory even if the 30% threshold is exceeded. In companies other than small and medium-sized enterprises (SMEs), the OPA is mandatory when a shareholder comes to hold more than 25% of the shares of the company and provided that there is no other shareholder with a higher stake. Issuers qualifying as SMEs can provide in their bylaws a different threshold other than 30% as long as it is not lower than 25% and not greater than 40%. The price of the totalitarian mandatory OPA shall not be lower than the highest price paid by the offeror in the 12-month period prior to the date when the OPA is communicated to Consob. If no shares were purchased by the offeror in the period in question, the price shall not be lower than the average market price of the previous year (art.106 of the TUF).

If following the totalitarian OPA the offeror acquires more than 95% of the company's shares, the remaining minority shareholders have the right to sell out their stake in the company, for the price of the previous totalitarian OPA (art.108 of the TUF). Likewise, art.109 of the TUF provides that, when purchases are made by persons acting in concert and exceed the thresholds established under arts 106 and 108 of the TUF, then a mandatory OPA is triggered. For such purpose, "persons acting in concert" are defined as persons co-operating on the basis of a specific or tacit agreement, verbal or in writing, even valid or without effect for the purposes of acquiring, maintaining or strengthening control over the issuer or to counteract achievement of the aims of a takeover bid or exchange tender offering. Article 111 of the TUF contains a squeeze-out provision, which grants to the offeror who holds, following a totalitarian OPA, more than 95% of the corporate capital of the target, the right to purchase the remaining shares within three months from the expiration of the term for acceptance of the offer, provided that the offeror indicated the intention to avail itself of the squeeze-out right in the offering memorandum.

## 5.  EXITS
### 5.1  Secondary sales
In 2016, secondary sales to other private equity investors represented the main divestment strategy as regards the divestment amount (54%) and they accounted for 24% of all divestment transactions.

When the private equity investor is a minority shareholder, this kind of exit strategy (replacement) is frequently used where the company has concluded a particular stage of its corporate life (e.g. start-up) and needs to initiate a new phase with a new partner that has different characteristics (e.g. expansion). The same can also occur at the end of a turnaround financing or when relationships among the management, entrepreneur and investor are not particularly positive. In these cases, the replacement is usually not very profitable for the exiting investor because—unlike the trade sales—it rarely has a strategic importance for the purchaser. Therefore, the price tends to be rather low.

The issue is different when the exiting investor is a majority shareholder (or holds 100% of the company's capital) (secondary buyout). In these cases, the sale is frequently carried out by means of a bidding procedure in which private equity and industrial investors may concur.

Secondary buyout transactions are generally performed at the end of the cycle of the first buyout, i.e. when the debt accrued for the acquisition of the company has been substantially repaid. This kind of transaction is normally used in stable business fields, where it is possible to generate constant cash flow over time. The structure of such transactions is substantially the same as that of normal buyouts, except for some particular features. First, in secondary buyouts, there are private equity funds on both sides of the sale (as buyer and as seller). In addition, such transactions present a risk of conflict of interest for the managers of the target company with regard to their duties towards the company, their willingness to complete the transaction and their future plans regarding the Newco. Last, but not least, in secondary buyout transactions, the buyer normally does not manage to obtain the same level of warranties and indemnities as in a standard buyout because the seller's (private equity fund's) presence in the company was limited to a relatively short period of time, with the consequent difficulties in assuming long-term indemnification obligations.

## 5.2  Trade sales

In 2016, trade sales were the most common way for a private equity investor to exit a company in Italy in terms of number of transactions (37%). As regards the volume, they accounted for 34% of all disinvested amounts (against 23% in 2015).

In Italy, trade sales typically concern at least the majority and more often the entire corporate capital of the company. They can be triggered in various ways, which are normally established in advance at the time of investment, in the target's bylaws or shareholders' agreements (e.g. drag-along rights).

A trade sale is generally carried out either by private negotiation or by means of a bidding procedure (auction sale). Generally speaking, in Italy as in other countries, the main advantage of the trade sale compared to the secondary sale consists in the possibility of obtaining a higher price from an industrial investor than from another private equity fund because industrial investors usually have a strong strategic interest in the acquisition. In the case of SMEs, it is normally preferred to an initial public offering (IPO) because IPOs are long, complex and expensive procedures.

As indicated above in respect of secondary sales, the problem of trade sales is often represented by the difficulty for the buyer to obtain appropriate warranties and indemnities.

## 5.3  Initial public offerings

The number of divestments carried out in Italy in 2016 by means of IPOs accounted for 3% of all transactions and for 2% in terms of volume.

IPOs are mostly used for bigger enterprises, due to the relevant complexity and expensiveness of the procedure. It shall be noted, however, that the presence of an institutional investor in the company reduces to a certain extent the "traumatic" impact of an IPO on the company. Indeed, when private equity funds acquire a shareholding in the company, they impose on the company certain rules of corporate governance (such as the certification of financial statements, periodic reporting, clear separation between the assets of the family and the company) which then facilitate the implementation of the procedures required to comply with the rules of a regulated market.

In certain cases, the exit of the private equity investor by means of an IPO is agreed upon and governed by the shareholders' agreement, which normally provides for the right of the fund to initiate an IPO within a certain time frame, without the possibility for the other shareholders to impede such a procedure, unless they decide to personally purchase the investor's shares.

In Italy, an IPO normally follows the steps outlined below:

- resolution concerning the listing to be adopted by the corporate bodies of the company;
- appointment of the advisor, sponsor, global coordinator, communication company and legal advisor;
- issuance of the information memorandum and price determination;
- placing of the shares; and
- listing on the Stock Exchange.

Private equity investors frequently use Alternative Investment Market (AIM) Italia, a segment of the Italian Stock Exchange, which specialises in SMEs in which, by the end of November 2017, 90 companies had listed. In fact, AIM Italia is an attractive segment for Italian companies due to its flexible regulation and easy implementation that does not have specific requirements as regards the corporate governance of the company or the minimum or maximum capitalisation levels. In order to increase the overall level of market transparency, some amendments to the AIM Italia segment rules were introduced, with effect from January 2018, both on the admission phase and on the post-admission phase such as, inter alia:

- the requirement of shares' subscription by at least five institutional investors for the satisfaction of the minimum free float of 10%;
- the requirement for promoters of special purpose acquisition companies to be persons with proven experience and/or who hold management positions in the areas of: (1) transactions on the primary capital market; (2) private equity transactions; (3) management of mid-sized companies; and/or (4) the investment banking sector; and
- the cancellation of certain provisions within the AIM Italia segment rules, which could generate overlaps with the regulatory framework on market abuse regarding inside information and disclosure requirements.

## 5.4 Refinancing

In some cases, private equity funds releverage their investment with the purpose of cashing out the equity invested in a target company by leveraging the company with new debt. This kind of transaction is carried out by means of a sale of the target's shares by the fund to a Newco, which is incorporated by the same fund (sometimes with another minority shareholder) and which uses leverage to finance the buyout. The use of releverage gives rise to a number of issues under Italian civil and tax law. In the first place, in many cases (mainly when 100% of the Newco is held by the private equity fund and no other shareholder participates in the transaction), the subsequent merger between the Newco and the target is not possible because of breach of the financial assistance rules (see s.3.2 above). This, of course, generates problems concerning the availability of the funds for the reimbursement of the financing and the guarantees to be offered to the lender. There is also the risk that the tax authorities challenge the deductibility of the financial interest if they believe that the transaction was not based on valid economic reasons. Therefore, releverage exit transactions need to be restructured and carried out in a careful and appropriate manner in order to avoid or reduce the risks in question.

### 5.5   Restructuring/insolvency

If the company suffers losses, which exceed one-third of the corporate capital but do not affect the minimum corporate capital requirement, the directors are inter alia obliged to convene a shareholders' meeting to resolve upon the reduction of the corporate capital or to carry forward the losses. If, at the end of the next financial year, the losses are not reduced below one-third of the corporate capital, the shareholder's meeting shall reduce the corporate capital (arts 2446 and 2482*bis* of the Code). Where the losses exceed one-third of the corporate capital and, at the same time, the corporate capital decreases to below the minimum capital requirement, this is considered an automatic cause for winding-up the company, unless the company is recapitalised or transformed into another company with a lower capital requirement (arts 2447, 2482*ter* and 2482(1)(4) of the Code). The same occurs when the entire corporate capital is lost. To avoid winding-up, private equity funds tend to privilege working with investors specialised in turnaround in order to conclude restructuring agreements as provided by the Italian Bankruptcy Law (Royal Decree 16 March 1942 No.267, as subsequently amended and supplemented). Such kinds of agreements provide, inter alia, for the conversion of the whole outstanding debt into equity or hybrid instruments as well as the possible refinancing by the lenders to allow the company to achieve the envisaged business goals.

If winding-up is not avoided, the kind of losses mentioned give rise to the total or partial depreciation of the relevant shareholding in the portfolio of the private equity funds (write-off). In 2016, write-offs stabilised at 8% in terms of number of transactions and 1% in terms of value.

## 6.   TAX
### 6.1   Taxation of fund structures

The tax regime of investment funds has been modeled with the aim of making the Italian tax rules applicable to funds compliant to other countries' regulations and promoting this type of investment structure.

Investment funds, which are not resident for tax purposes in Italy, are not subject to taxation in Italy. On the contrary, where a fund is "resident" for tax purposes in Italy (i.e. it was incorporated in Italy and it is managed by an Italian SGR or by a foreign management company), it is considered to be subject to taxation in Italy. The funds resident in Italy are divided into two categories, which imply different tax treatments.

Where both the following conditions are satisfied, i.e.: (1) the fund (or the management company) is subject to prudential supervision; and (2) the fund is qualified as a "collective investment management form", the income of the fund (excluding real estate investment trusts or REITs) is exempt from the corporate tax (*Imposta sui Redditi delle Società* or IRES). In such a case, save for certain exceptions, the capital income realised is in general subject to a definitive withholding tax at source of 26%.

If one (or both) of the above-mentioned conditions are not satisfied, the fund is subject to IRES and is consequently taxed at 24%; therefore, the same tax regime provided for joint-stock and limited liability companies is applied.

The qualification of an entity as an "investment fund" for tax purposes does not depend on the legal form of the fund but, rather, on its functions and on the provisions concerning the investment of any collected financial resources. Consequently, such qualification shall be made on a case-by-case basis.

As regards the tax regime of the quota holders of the funds that are exempt from IRES, the capital gain (arising from the difference between sale price and historical purchase price) is taxed by applying a 26% withholding tax. The taxation is "at source" for individuals who are resident in Italy and "in advance" for companies; the taxation regime of non-resident quota holders shall be determined by applying the treaties on double taxation.

## 6.2  Carried interest

Recently, the Italian Tax Authority has introduced new measures (art.60 of Law Decree of 24 April 2017) to define the Italian taxation of carried interest. In general, the so-called "carried interest" is the remuneration received by employees and directors of (private equity or other) fund management companies and deriving from shares, quotas or other instruments endowed with privileged interests on equity. It has introduced a non-rebuttable presumption that qualifies the carried interest as financial income rather than employment income. For such purpose, the following requirements ought to be met:

- the overall investment commitment of employees and directors entail an actual disbursement of 1%, at least, of the aggregate investment made by the collective investment undertaking or of the net equity in case of companies or other entities;
- the proceeds from shares, quotas or financial instruments endowed with the above-mentioned privileged interests on equity only accrue after all the other investors or participants to the collective investment undertaking have received a minimum predefined return on their capital investments, as provided by the bylaws or by a regulation; or, in case of change of control, the sale price received by all other unitholders or participants to the investment is at least equal to the invested principal amount plus the aforesaid minimum return; and
- the shares, quotas or financial instruments endowed with privileged interests on equity are held by employees and directors (or, in the event of their death, by their heirs) for, at least, five years or, if earlier, until the date of change of control or replacement of the asset manager.

The issuer of the shares, quotas or other instruments endowed with privileged interests on equity must be resident for tax purposes in Italy or in a state that allows an adequate exchange of information with Italy.

If all the above-mentioned requirements are satisfied, the proceeds derived from carried interest are generally subject only to a 26% withholding tax, rather than the harsher progressive tax regime applicable to employment income.

## 6.3 Management equity

The awarding of shares is subject to taxation at the ordinary rate applicable to the beneficiary. On the date when the option right is exercised, the difference between the normal value of the shares (approximately, the fair value) and the amount paid by the employee for the exercise of the option right (where a price is provided) contributes to form the employee's income. However, if the issuing company is an "innovative start-up", the awarding of stocks and stock options to employees is not taxed, subject to certain conditions.

As for the company, the cost incurred is generally deductible. However, the aspects concerning the deductibility of the cost vary on the basis of the accountancy principles applied by the company.

Award of equity is not relevant for the purposes of social contribution.

Thereafter, dividends and capital gains arising from such shares are subject to a 26% withholding tax, upon certain conditions.

## 6.4 Loan interest

In general terms, passive interest paid is subject to withholding tax. However, by way of derogation from the general rule, no withholding tax is due upon the occurrence of the following conditions:
(1) the paying company is resident for tax purposes in Italy and it is not entitled to any tax relief;
(2) both companies take one of the forms listed in the Annex of the Directive (Directive 2003/49 on a common system of taxation applicable to interest and royalty payments made between associated companies of different Member States [2003] OJ L157/49);
(3) the controlling company has a minimum holding of 25% of the voting rights in the controlled company, that has been maintained for an uninterrupted period of at least 12 months;
(4) the company, which benefits of the interest exemption, complies with certain specific requirements (including the residence for tax purposes in an EU Member State) and it is the beneficial owner of the same; and
(5) before the payment of the interest, the paying company obtains a certificate from the competent foreign Tax Authority concerning the residence of the actual beneficiary and a declaration of the beneficiary confirming compliance with the above requirements. These documents must be kept by the paying company and shown to the Italian Tax Authority in case of a tax assessment.

The Italian Tax Authority pays particular attention to the verification of the presence of conduit companies to establish the actual beneficiary of the income.

Similar rules are applicable to dividends (the withholding tax is generally applicable but it is not applied subject to certain conditions).

The amount of passive interests paid to the foreign holding can be subject to the verification of congruity of the applied interest rate in accordance with the transfer pricing rules. An interest rate which exceeds the arm's-length amount can be challenged by the Italian Tax Authority (with the consequence of non-deductibility of part of the passive interest paid by the financed company).

Ultimately, we should note that companies can deduct financial interest (net of the active interest) during the financial year in which the interest has accrued only within the limits of 30% of the *gross operative profit* (which approximately corresponds to earnings before interest, taxes, depreciation and amortisation (i.e. EBITDA)). The interest which is not deducted in one financial year can be carried forward and deducted in the following financial years, if and to the extent to which the 30% of gross operative profit exceeds the net passive interest of such financial year.

## 6.5  Transaction taxes

Based on various types of both group structure and transactions, different tax consequences are applicable.

Assuming that both: (1) the target (OpCo); and (2) the vehicle (Holding) are resident in Italy for tax purposes and are liable to IRES, the most common types of structures are the following.

*Purchase and subsequent transfer of the participation:*

- direct tax (advantageous): it is possible to apply the mechanism of the participation exemption. If certain requirements are satisfied (non-interrupted possession for 12 months, classification of the participation in the category of fixed financial assets from the first financial statement drawn up after the purchase, residence of the participated entity in a country which is not considered a "tax haven" by Italian Tax Authority and exercise by the same company of business activities during the three financial years preceding the disposal), the capital gain arising from the sale of the participation is exempt, for the 95% of its amount, from IRES;
- indirect tax (advantageous): fixed registration duty (EUR 200). The transaction is VAT-free; and
- other aspects:
    (1)  the company can continue to deduce its previous tax losses (advantageous);
    (2)  the purchased entity remains responsible for the tax liabilities which arose prior to the purchase (disadvantageous).

*Transfer of the going concern:*

- direct tax (disadvantageous for the seller): the difference between the value recognised for tax purposes of the assets of the going concern and the final purchase price is subject to taxation. On the side of the purchaser, the fiscal value of the net assets purchased is equal to the price paid;
- indirect tax (disadvantageous): proportional registration duty (the rate varies based on the nature of the transferred net assets); and
- other aspects:
    (1)  tax losses are not transferable together with the going concern;
    (2)  the responsibility of the transferor for tax liabilities can be limited under certain conditions (advantageous).

*Contribution of the going concern and transfer of the shareholding:*

- direct tax (advantageous): taxation at 5% on the capital gain arising from the transfer of the shareholding when the participation exemption regime

is applicable;
- indirect tax (advantageous): fixed registration duty (EUR 200); and
- other aspects: tax losses may not be contributed together with the going concern (disadvantageous).

*De-merger and transfer of the shareholding:*
- direct tax (advantageous): taxation at 5% on the capital gain arising from the transfer of the shareholding when the participation exemption regime is applicable;
- indirect tax (advantageous): fixed registration duty (EUR 200); and
- other aspects:
    (1) subject to certain conditions, the company can continue to deduce its previous tax losses (advantageous);
    (2) the implementation of the procedure of de-merger is rather complex as regards tax and civil law aspects (disadvantageous).

In respect of all the above-mentioned kinds of transactions, it shall be noted that the tax savings obtained by the taxpayer can be challenged by the Italian Tax Authority where it deems that the structure of the transaction is not justified by valid economic reasons and that it aims exclusively at eluding obligations or prohibitions set forth by tax laws and at obtaining undue tax savings.

## 7. CURRENT TOPICAL ISSUES/TRENDS

The private equity market in 2017 confirms the growth trend undertaken in the last two years.[2] Only in 2006, 2007 and 2008 has the analysis recorded similar activities.

Regarding supply side, the number of active operators in Italy stands at 92, considering both lead and co-investors (+8% in comparison to 2016).

In 2017, foreign investors confirmed their absolute significant position (50% of operations have been closed by non-domestic funds, in a slight decrease from 53% in 2016).

With reference to the investment stages, during 2017, the market confirmed the trend of the previous years, with a high prevalence of buyout operations (67% of preferences), although decreasing in respect to 2016 (77%). Expansion deals have increased their percentage, with a share of 25%, in comparison to 22% in 2016 and 35% in 2014. The residual 8% of the market is mainly constituted by turnaround (6%, with a marked growth respect to 1% in 2016), while replacement constitutes 2%.

In terms of deal origination, private and family business, recording only a slight decrease of preferences (67% in 2017 in comparison to 70% in 2016), continues to represent the greater part of investment opportunities. The disposal of business units from national groups has decreased from 8% to 5%.

Secondary buyouts highlight a meaningful increase in respect to 2016 (24% v 16%). Compared to the past, the sale of minority shares between operators and the disposals from foreign groups slightly decreased (together, they represent 4% of the market).

---

[2] All data is taken from the *Private Equity Monitor Report* (2017) available at: *http://www.privateequitymonitor.it/attach/pem_2017.pdf* [Accessed 24 October 2018].

With reference to the industry, the market players preferred the traditional compartment of industrial products, with 38% of the whole market, showing a marked growth in comparison to 2016 (27%).

Consumer goods confirm their second position in the investors' preferences (19%), increasing their share with reference to the previous year (14%). These two sectors together represent more than 55% of the whole market.

The third and fourth sectors are tertiary (professional services, except for financial ones) with 8% (v 7% in 2016), and food and beverage (7% v 10% in 2016).

Regarding economic and financial characteristics of target firms, the median value is EUR 41.7 million, with a slight increase in comparison to the 2016 value.

Furthermore, with reference to the sales classes, 60% of investments are addressed towards firms which do not exceed EUR 60 million; a decrease in respect of 2016 (69%). On the contrary, it has been possible to detect an increase of firms with revenues between EUR 60 and 300 million (34% v 23%).

With regard to the legislative framework, with the introduction of specific rules concerning carried interest matters (art.60 of Law Decree of 24 April 2017), Italy has also decided for the first time to specifically regulate this type of incentive instrument. As with any first-time rule adoption, the application of this rule in the future may lead to doubts and misgivings but, given the high potential of the incentive, further clarification is expected.

Furthermore, the tax authorities have finally accepted the deduction of interest arising from the LBO transaction without any connection with the inherence clause, considering the inherence of such interest implicit in the structure of the acquisition.

# Japan

**Nagashima Ohno & Tsunematsu** Ryo Okubo &
Takashi Miyazaki

## 1. MARKET OVERVIEW
### 1.1 Types of investors
Common sources from which private equity funds obtain their funding in Japan are institutional investors, such as pension funds, insurance companies, banks, trust banks and funds of funds. Foreign investors, including foreign institutional investors, foreign individuals and sovereign wealth funds, have also been active in Japan.

### 1.2 Types of investments
Typical transactions in which private equity funds invest in Japan are secondary buyouts, public to private transactions, divestment/spin-off transactions, management buyouts, reorganisation transactions and private investment in public equities.

## 2. FUNDS
### 2.1 Fund structures
The legal structures most commonly used as vehicles for private equity funds in Japan have been limited partnerships organised under foreign law, such as Cayman Islands law, and limited partnerships for investment business (*toshi jigyo yugen sekinin kumiai* or LPS) organised under the Limited Partnership Act for Investment Business (Act No.90 of 1998). Historically, international private equity funds operating in Japan have mainly used overseas limited partnerships and domestic private equity funds have mainly used either overseas limited partnerships or LPSs. Overseas limited partners are formed under various jurisdictions, such as the Cayman Islands, Ireland and Delaware, US. For the purpose of this chapter, however, we assume that the overseas limited partners are Cayman limited partnerships.

Other possible structures include: a general partnership (*nin-i kumiai* or NK) under the Civil Code (Act No.89 of 1896); an anonymous partnership (*tokumei kumiai* or TK) under the Commercial Code (Act No.48 of 1899); or a limited liability partnership (*yugen sekinin jigyo kumiai* or LLP) under the Act on Limited Liability Partnerships (Act No.40 of 2005). These alternative vehicles are pass-through entities under Japanese tax law but are used less commonly as vehicles for private equity funds for various reasons. In the case of a NK, a partner of a NK may not assert a limitation on liabilities provided in the partnership agreement and owe unlimited liabilities against bona fide third parties. Secondly, in the case of a TK, TK investors are subject to withholding tax of 20.42% regardless of whether the TK investors are domestic or overseas investors. In addition, the managed assets of a TK belong to the TK operator, which is equivalent to the general partner of an LPS, and, accordingly, is subject to the TK operator's credit risk. Finally, in the case of a LLP, the amount of a LLP's losses that may be passed through to LLP investors are subject to a certain limit, the calculation of which is based on the investment amount of the LLP investor. In addition, one of the basic rules of LLPs is that a LLP's operation requires the consent of all partners unless the relevant decisions have been entrusted to one or more partners; and not all decisions of a LLP may be entrusted to one or more partners. Conversely, a LPS's operation may be conducted by the general partner without the consent of limited partners.

In the following sections, we assume that the fund is organised as a LPS unless we specifically refer to another type of vehicle.

## 2.2 Regulation of fundraising and fund managers
### Private placement rule

The offering of interests in a LPS (or an overseas limited partnership) that invests more than 50% of its contributed funds into securities requires an onerous public offering process, including the filing of a securities registration statement unless it satisfies the following private placement requirements under the Financial Instruments and Exchange Act (Act No.25 of 1948, the FIEA):

- the number of investors in Japan who acquire the fund interests (the interests) through the offer must be fewer than 500. As long as the number of investors in Japan who ultimately acquire the interests as a result of the offer is fewer than 500, the number of the offerees may be 500 or more. However, if the total number of investors in Japan who hold the interests is 500 or more as of the end of a business year, due to multiple offerings or transfers, the general partner may be subject to a continuous disclosure obligation, such as the filing of an annual report; and

- notification must be made to investors upon solicitation that: the offering complies with the requirements for a private placement of the interests and is not registered under the FIEA; and the interests fall within a certain right provided in a certain provision of the FIEA. A document describing such matters must be submitted to the investors upon or prior to the acquisition of the interest.

### Securities business regulations

To solicit the interests, the (ultimate) general partner of the fund that is a corporation must comply with the securities business regulations under the FIEA. In essence, the general partner is required to be registered as a "type 2 financial instrument business provider" under the FIEA unless it satisfies the following exemption requirements (*tekikaku kikan toshika tou tokurei gyomu*) provided in art.63 of the FIEA on an ongoing basis (it should be noted that the exemption requirements were substantially tightened due to the amendment to the FIEA that came into effect in 2016):

- the number of non-qualified institutional investors in Japan (non-QII investors) is 49 or fewer;
- the non-QII investors meet certain qualifications (Specially Permitted

Business Qualified Investor);

- at least one of the investors in Japan other than the general partner is a qualified institutional investor (QII investor);
- no fund of funds or other investment vehicle that has non-QII investors as its own investors is included in the partners, with certain exceptions;
- the general partner submits a certain notification to the Director of the Local Finance Bureau pursuant to art.63 of the FIEA in advance; and
- the limited partnership agreement provides that: (1) any interest initially solicited to be sold in Japan and acquired or purchased by a QII investor may not be transferred to another person or entity in any manner other than by transfer of such interest to another QII investor; and (2) any interest initially solicited to be sold in Japan and acquired or purchased by a person who is a Specially Permitted Business Qualified Investor may not be transferred to another person or entity in any manner other than by transfer of such interest in whole to one QII investor or Specially Permitted Business Qualified Investor.

As an alternative measure, the general partner may outsource the entire marketing activities to a licensed firm to avoid its registration requirement. However, as the definition of "solicitation", which triggers the registration requirement under the securities business regulations, is broad and may include any communication between the general partner and potential investors, avoiding the registration requirement is usually difficult for the general partner of the fund. Accordingly, the above exemption is commonly used by the general partners of funds if the general partners can satisfy the requirements for the above exemption.

### Fund management regulations

In managing and operating the funds contributed by holders of interests in a LPS (or an overseas limited partnership) by investing more than 50% of the funds into securities or derivative transactions, the (ultimate) general partner of the fund that is a corporation must comply with the fund management regulations under the FIEA. In essence, the general partner is required to be registered as an "investment management business provider" under the FIEA unless it satisfies the requirements of one of the exemptions provided in the FIEA. Commonly used exemptions are as follows:

- art.63 of the FIEA provides an exemption from the fund management regulations (*tekikaku kikan toshika tou tokurei gyomu*) subject to the same requirements (except for the last point) for the exemption from the securities business regulations described above;
- the general partner may be exempted from the above registration requirement by outsourcing all of the investment management activities to an investment manager who is duly registered as investment management business provider in Japan pursuant to an investment advisory agreement, subject to certain additional requirements; and
- for an overseas limited partnership, a special exemption is in place. In essence, this exemption is available when: (1) the direct investors in Japan are limited to QII investors or persons who have submitted a notification under art.63 of the FIEA to be exempted from the fund management regulations; (2) the indirect investors in Japan (which is defined in the

law) are limited to QII investors; (3) the number of direct and indirect investors in Japan is fewer than 10; and (4) the amount invested from direct investors in Japan is one-third or less of the total invested amount of the fund.

As the exemption provided in art.63 of the FIEA may exempt the general partner from both the securities business regulations and the fund management regulations, it is a commonly sought exemption.

## 2.3 Customary or common terms of funds

The Ministry of Economy, Trade and Industry (METI) has published on its website a model limited partnership agreement for a LPS. Key terms of the limited partnership agreement are similar to those in other jurisdictions.

For example, the purpose and investment strategy, including an investment guideline, are stated and certain types of investments, such as an investment in the form of a hostile acquisition or investment in antisocial forces, may be prohibited. Borrowings and derivative transactions may also be prohibited. As to the method of investment, the capital call method is common and the procedures to make a capital call are provided in the agreement. A no-fault divorce provision and key person provision may be added. Where an investment committee, an advisory board and/or a partners meeting are provided for, the authority and process relating to these bodies are also provided for. In this respect, due to a limitation under the law that limited partners of a LPS may not operate the business of the LPS, and in light of the tax implication explained in s.6.1 below, these bodies usually retain only advisory power. Provisions setting forth the mechanism of carried interest may include a hurdle rate, catch-up provision and claw-back provision similar to those provided in other jurisdictions.

## 3. DEBT FINANCE

### 3.1 Means of financing

Private-equity-backed vehicles typically obtain financing through a traditional secured term loan facility from banks. It is becoming more common to include mezzanine financing, especially in large-scale deals. Mezzanine financing typically consists of one or a combination of preferred shares, subordinated loans and warrants as a sweetener, and is provided by mezzanine funds or lease companies. Subordinated corporate bonds have also sometimes been used. Only rarely have seller financings and the securitisation of a business been used. High-yield bonds have yet to be used for financing in private equity transactions in Japan.

### 3.2 Restrictions on granting security

Unlike in EU jurisdictions, there is no statutory financial assistance restriction in Japan. However, granting security interests or providing guarantees or loans to certain shareholders at the expense of other shareholders will contradict the general fiduciary duty of directors. Accordingly, the provision of a guarantee or the grant of a security interest by the investee company is usually suspended until the investee company becomes wholly owned by the investment vehicle as the result of the closing of the stock sale and purchase transactions or completion of a post-closing squeeze-out (in the case of a two-step public to private transaction). The investee company's wholly owned domestic subsidiaries may also provide guarantees or grant security interests after the investee company becomes wholly owned by the investment vehicle. In order for the investee company's partially owned domestic subsidiaries to provide a guarantee or grant a security interest, they must obtain the consent of their other shareholders for the same reason (i.e. directors' fiduciary duty to the other shareholders) even after the investee company becomes wholly owned by the investment vehicle. For foreign subsidiaries, whether or not financial assistance or any other restrictions exist under the local laws should also be checked. Following achievement of 100% ownership of the investee company by the investment vehicle, the debt is often pushed down to the investee company through a post-acquisition merger between the investee company and the investment vehicle.

Japanese law does not have a convenient method to create and perfect security interests over different types of assets in one common procedure. For example, shares, inventory, trade receivables, bank deposit accounts and real estate need to be pledged and perfected in very different manners. In addition, while it is possible to create security over certain types of floating assets, such as inventory and trade receivables, identification of the scope of the pledged assets is strictly required. Further, in certain cases, such as where trade receivables are being pledged and the underlying trade agreement has a non-assignment clause, the consent of third-party obligee(s) may also be required to create security interests. Accordingly, creating security interests over substantially all of the assets of the investee company and perfecting them is often a time-consuming and costly process as compared to that in the US or UK, and therefore the scope of the security package tends to be limited as the result of negotiations between the lender and the borrower in light of time and cost.

### 3.3 Intercreditor issues

For mezzanine financing, preferred shares and subordinated loans are the most commonly used structure. In the case of a subordinated loan structure, an intercreditor agreement is entered into to provide for the priority of the senior lender. In the case of a preferred shares structure, the mezzanine financer, as an equity holder, is structurally subordinated to the senior lender, as creditor. Still, it is common that an agreement is entered into to set forth the rights and interests between the senior lender and the mezzanine financer, and a shareholder agreement is entered into to set forth the rights and interests between the sponsor, who is the common shareholder, and the mezzanine financer. Given the preferred shares structure, key issues that are typically encountered when agreeing on and documenting such agreement among the relevant parties and its ancillary documents, such as a preferred shares subscription agreement and the terms of the preferred shares, include: when the payment of dividends to the preferred shareholder should be suspended; restrictions on the borrower's call option to purchase the preferred shares; restrictions on the preferred shareholder's put options to sell the preferred shares to the issuer (i.e. borrower) in exchange for cash or common shares; the terms of the preferred shareholder's tag-along rights vis-à-vis the sponsor; the terms of the sponsor's drag-along rights vis-à-vis the preferred shareholder; the extent to which the preferred shareholder has veto rights with respect to the management of the investee company; and restrictions on assignment of the preferred shares, common shares and syndication of senior loans.

### 3.4  Syndication

In large-scale transactions, lenders commonly syndicate their loans. Lenders usually syndicate their loans after the closing of the acquisition transaction partly because of the lack of sufficient time prior to the closing for negotiation of the terms of the loan among all syndication banks, and partly because it is preferable to avoid unnecessary information leaks. In some cases, banks request a clear market provision and a market flex provision in the commitment letter that are similar to those in other jurisdictions. A clear market provision is a provision that requires the absence of other similar debt instruments issued by the borrower during a specified period to facilitate syndication; and a market flex provision is one that gives the arranger the right to modify the terms agreed to between the arranger and the borrower to facilitate syndication when the syndication market is tight. Key issues both for the banks and for the investee company include: when the borrower or the mezzanine financer must obtain the consent of the majority lenders, super-majority lenders or all lenders; the definition of the majority lenders and super-majority lenders; and the time period and the scope of permitted assignees with respect to the assignment of loans for the purpose of syndication, the cost of which is usually borne by the borrower (i.e. permitted syndication).

## 4.  EQUITY STRUCTURES

### 4.1  Role of management

In a traditional Japanese company, the management consists of the directors of the company. In the case of management buyouts, each management member typically enters into a management agreement with the sponsor and retains a board seat. The management agreement usually provides that the management member exclusively engages in the management of the investee company to achieve the business plan as agreed between the sponsor and management. The remuneration of management typically includes a fixed portion and a performance-based portion. Management may be removed by the sponsor in the event of a violation of the management agreement by management or, in some cases, their underperformance.

The management agreement usually provides for a certain period of non-competition following the termination of the office of management.

Management typically receives an equity participation in the investment vehicle in the form of shares, stock options or interests in a share ownership association or a combination of those. Stock options are issued as stock acquisition rights under the Companies Act of Japan (Act No.86 of 2005). A share ownership association is traditionally organised in the form of a NK.

## 4.2 Common protections for investors

The sponsor usually holds a majority of the voting rights and, accordingly, may pass an ordinary resolution and block the passage of a super-majority resolution at a shareholders meeting. As the appointment and removal of directors are subject to an ordinary resolution unless otherwise provided in the investee company's articles of incorporation, the sponsor having the majority of voting rights controls the board seats. In addition to this appointment and removal right, the sponsor typically seeks to control the individual directors through the above-mentioned management agreement. Further to the above-mentioned provisions, the management agreement usually provides that management report periodically and, additionally, at the request of the sponsor, the condition of the investee company. The sponsor may also seek to send its representatives as observers to the meetings of the board of directors or other internal meetings of the investee company.

For shares and stock options held by management, the sponsor usually enters into a shareholders' agreement with management to provide for such matters as restrictions on the assignment of the shares and stock options by management and the sponsor's drag-along rights for the exit.

## 4.3 Common protections for management

The sponsor's drag-along rights are often coupled with management's tag-along rights so that management may collect their investment at the time of exit by the sponsor. In some cases, management retain a majority of the board seats as long as they achieve a certain business performance level agreed to between management and the sponsor.

## 4.4 Management warranties

Generally speaking, management warranties are not very common in Japan. In most traditional Japanese companies, as the management members are former employees of the company who have been promoted to management, they tend to have no or only a small portion of shares of the investee company and would not be able to afford the indemnity liabilities, even if they provided management warranties. However, in cases of management buyouts where management members have a large portion of the shares of the investee company as the founding-family members, the sponsor, as the seller, will seek such shareholder management to provide warranties regarding the investee company.

## 4.5 Good leaver/bad leaver provisions

Where management participates in the equity in the investment vehicle, a shareholders' agreement between the sponsor and management and/or a stock option grant agreement between the investment vehicle and management are usually entered into. These agreements commonly include provisions that deal with the compulsory transfer of their shares and stock options if they cease to be involved in the investee company. The reasons that trigger such compulsory transfer are provided in the agreements on a case-by-case basis but, typically, termination of employment for cause and violations of the agreements are included among such reasons. Where such compulsory transfer is triggered, the shares are sold at market price or at the originally issued price and the stock options are renounced.

## 4.6 Public to private transactions
### Mandatory tender offer requirements

It is common for private equity funds to make offers for public companies in Japan. Where the investee company is listed, the private equity funds must follow the mandatory tender offer rules under the FIEA that apply to the following acquisitions:

- acquisitions in off-exchange transactions where, after the acquisition, the holding ratio (as defined in the FIEA) is more than 5% but less than one-third, except acquisitions of such shares from 10 persons or less within 61 days (the "5% rule");
- acquisitions in off-exchange transactions where, after the acquisition, the holding ratio exceeds one-third (the "one-third rule");
- acquisitions in off-exchange transactions where the holding ratio before the acquisition exceeds 50% and the holding ratio after the acquisition is two-thirds or less, except acquisitions of such shares from 10 persons or less within 61 days; and
- acquisitions within three months of 10% or more of the total issued voting shares in total (whether in off-exchange or on-exchange transaction, or whether already issued or newly issued shares), which includes acquisitions of 5% or more of the total issued voting shares in off-exchange transactions (except for acquisition through tender offer) where the holding ratio after the acquisition exceeds one- third (the "speed acquisitions rule").

In addition, where the holding ratio reaches two-thirds or more after acquisition, a tender offer is always required and the tender offeror must purchase all classes of equity securities of the investee company offered in the tender without setting any maximum number on such purchase or any limitation on the class of shares to be purchased (the "two-thirds rule").

To launch a tender offer, the tender offeror must file a tender offer registration statement with the regulator describing a wide variety of matters including: (1) the purpose of the transaction, including the management policy following the completion of the transaction, the terms of the second step of the transaction, such as a squeeze-out scheme; (2) how the tender offer price was calculated, including the method of the calculation (e.g. the discounted cash flow (DCF) method) and the calculated range of the price, the ratio of the premium added, how the price was negotiated with the investee company and its principal shareholders, whether or not a stock price valuation report was obtained from a third party, and how such opinion was reflected in the tender offer price; (3) agreements between the tender offeror and the investee company or its management; and (4) in the case of management buyouts, the measures to secure the fairness of the tender offer price. In connection with (4) above, METI has recommended certain measures, such as use of a third-party special committee, in its *Guidelines on Management Buyouts for Enhancement of Enterprise Value and Securement of Fair Process* (2007). Certificates from financial sources, including the sponsor, senior lender and mezzanine financer, that evidence the existence of funds to close the tender offer must be attached to the tender offer registration statement.

### Restriction on financing-out/material adverse change-out

Under the FIEA, events that allow a tender offeror to withdraw a tender offer after it has been launched are very restricted. In particular, neither a failure of financing nor the occurrence of a material adverse change (MAC) is permitted as a reason to withdraw a tender offer (i.e. no financing-out and MAC-out are permitted). However, the bank commitment letters usually provide many conditions precedent to extending loans, including business MAC and market MAC. Accordingly, even if the lenders walk away due to a MAC event, the investment vehicle must still close the tender offer by raising the necessary funds from other financing sources, including equity, or it will default. No default cases have yet occurred in Japan although there have been some close cases. In this regard, on 31 March 2010, the Financial Services Agency of Japan (FSA) published (in an addition (amendment) to "Q&As on Tender Offer Bids of Shares etc") its view that the certificates from financial sources that are attached to tender offer registration statements must be supported by a certainty of funding and provided examples of what will be required of such certificates in order to support a certainty of funding. The FSA also requires full disclosure on the certificates from banks, which are attached to tender offer registration statements, of the conditions precedent provided in the commitment letters. Generally speaking, the FSA's view on certainty of funding is much less restrictive than the "certain funds" requirements in the UK and other EU jurisdictions. In particular, business MAC and market MAC provisions usually included in the commitment letters from banks are not viewed as impairing the certainty of funding in general. Accordingly, such view of the FSA has not reduced the risk of default due to a failure of financing, such as when a MAC event occurs. In addition, while conditions precedent are disclosed in the current practice in accordance with the view of the FSA, the FSA has permitted summarisation of conditions precedent that contain sensitive or confidential information as well as blackening out financial figures included in conditions precedent. Such treatment is intended to address the lenders' concern that disclosure of sensitive or confidential information may have adverse effects on the target company's business.

### Legal risks relating to squeeze-out transactions

There are a couple of typical methods to squeeze-out minority shareholders following a tender offer. One method uses a consolidation of shares (*kabushiki heigo*) or, if the controlling shareholder's holding ratio reaches 90% or higher (special controlling shareholder), a right to request the sale of shares and stock acquisition rights (*kabusiki tou uriwatashi seikyu*). The other method uses a cash-out merger or cash-for-stock swap. To implement each of these methods, a special resolution at a shareholders' meeting (the voting requirement with respect to which is usually two-thirds) is required (except where using a special controlling shareholder's right to request the sale of shares and stock acquisition rights, in which case only a board resolution is required). Thus, it is customary for a tender offeror hoping to carry out a squeeze-out transaction to set the minimum requirement to close the tender offer at two-thirds of the total voting rights of the investee company.

Even though a squeeze-out transaction can be procedurally completed by securing two-thirds, it does not necessarily mean that the transaction will not be blocked by minority shareholders. While no reliable court precedents exist in this regard yet, the general understanding is that a cash-out transaction can be blocked if the relevant shareholders' resolution was made as a result of an abuse of rights of the majority shareholders thereby making such resolution extraordinarily unfair. The most important factor to measure such extraordinary unfairness is the fairness of the purchase price offered to the minority shareholders. A high holding ratio of the majority shareholders after the tender offer would also be a significant factor. In this regard, a holding ratio of 90% or higher has been considered safe among practitioners, although no court precedents exist on such number.

Giving appraisal rights under the Companies Act of Japan (Act No.86 of 2005) to the minority shareholders is another significant factor and the most practical recourse for minority shareholders who are not satisfied with the purchase price is an appraisal right. With an appraisal right, minority shareholders may request the investee company to purchase their shares, and a fair purchase price is determined by the courts if no agreement is made between the minority shareholder and the investee company (in the case where using a special controlling shareholder's right to request the sale of shares and stock acquisition rights, a minority shareholder has an appraisal right to request the court to determine the fair purchase price for the sale). Usually, in a squeeze-out transaction, the investee company or the special controlling shareholder, as the case may be, sets a purchase price that is equal to the tender offer price. In July 2016, the Supreme Court held (decision of 1 July 2016, 70(6) MINSHU 1445) that, as long as the tender offer was conducted under generally accepted fair procedures, the share purchase price in the squeeze-out transaction should be equal to the tender offer price unless there are exceptional circumstances where the basic facts for the transaction have unexpectedly changed. Since this Supreme Court decision, private equity funds have become able to stably implement a squeeze-out transaction in Japan.

## 5. EXITS

### 5.1 Secondary sales

Secondary buyouts and trade sales have been the most common method of exiting in Japan. In full exits, all of the shares of the investee company are sold to an operational company in the same business field or another private equity firm. In partial exits, a strategic partner or another private equity fund invests equity in the investee company. In either case, the private equity firm is usually unwilling to give warranties regarding the investee company and the range of warranties is decided on a case-by-case basis in negotiations between the parties.

### 5.2 Trade sales

Please refer to s.5.1 above.

## 5.3 Initial public offerings

In recent years, less than 10% of exits have been made by way of an initial public offering (IPO). In an IPO, private equity funds may sell a part of the shares of the investee company held by them at the time of the IPO. In addition, lock-up periods are usually provided in a lock-up agreement to avoid sudden drops in the stock price on the market. Accordingly, an IPO is an appropriate method of exit only where the total market value of the investee company is large enough to expect a large transaction volume of its shares after the shares are listed and the private equity funds can expect to secure the capital gains by selling all of their remaining shares after the lock-up period is over. When an IPO is planned, private equity funds commonly implement a capital policy prior to the IPO to lower their holding ratio by way of a partial sale or an issuance of new shares to third parties.

## 5.4 Refinancings

In some cases, recapitalisation coupled with refinancing has been used by a sponsor to enjoy better financing terms and achieve a partial exit with additional leverage prior to the IPO. Recapitalisation may be implemented by way of distribution of surplus cash or repurchase of shares or, alternatively, by way of the sponsor setting up a new acquisition vehicle to purchase the shares of the target company from the sponsor itself.

## 5.5 Restructuring/insolvency

There are few cases of restructuring and insolvency of investee companies reported in Japan but restructuring or insolvency could occur as a result of the investee company's failures to comply with the covenants of loans or its failures to refinance them. In restructuring and insolvency cases, because private equity funds as the common shareholder are subordinated to lenders, the private equity funds usually cannot recover their investments.

# 6. TAX

## 6.1 Taxation of fund structures
### Permanent establishment

A LPS is a pass-through entity under Japanese tax law and, accordingly, income and losses for an LPS are treated as income and losses for each partner, pro-rated based on the investment ratio of each partner or in accordance with a profit and loss distribution ratio otherwise provided in the partnership agreement. Overseas investors in a LPS are deemed to have a permanent establishment (PE) in Japan for purposes of Japanese tax law and, accordingly, their income attributable to the PE, including capital gains, is subject to general Japanese corporate tax as well as tax withholding unless they satisfy the following requirements for an exemption of income attributable to the PE:

- the overseas investor is a limited partner;
- the overseas investor does not perform the operation of the LPS;
- the holding ratio of the overseas investor in the LPS is less than 25%;
- the overseas investor does not have any special relationship with the general partner of the LPS;
- the overseas investor does not have a PE in connection with any business other than the business of the partnership; and

- the overseas investor submits an application for this exemption to the relevant tax bureau, to which a copy of the limited partnership agreement of the LPS must be attached.

METI has published a guideline (*Concerning "the act specified by Cabinet Order as the execution of operations" within special provisions for taxation on foreign partners and special provisions for taxable income of foreign partners having no permanent establishments*) on what kinds of activities on the part of overseas investors contradict the second requirement and it should be noted that giving consents to the general partner regarding the operation of the LPS is generally considered to contradict such requirement.

### 25% holding rule

Even when a LPS's overseas investor does not have a PE in Japan, where a LPS's overseas investor and its "related persons" hold 25% or more of the shares of a company at any time within the most recent three years, and sell 5% or more of the shares of a company, capital gains from the sale are subject to Japanese tax, except for possible exemptions under the relevant tax treaties. In this regard, the definition of "related persons" includes the other investors of the LPS in which the overseas investor invests in general. However, tax reforms in 2009 introduced an exemption from this rule to the effect that such an LPS is excluded from the definition of "related persons" if, generally speaking:

- the LPS satisfies the requirements for the exemption of income attributable to the PE mentioned in the first point above;
- the LPS has held the shares for at least one year; and
- the overseas investor submits an application for this exemption to the relevant tax bureau, to which a copy of the limited partnership agreement of the LPS is attached.

### Real estate holding companies

Even when a LPS's overseas investor does not have a PE in Japan, where a LPS's overseas investor and its "related persons" hold and sell 5% (in the case of listed companies) or 2% (in the case of non-listed companies) of the shares of a company, deriving at least 50% of its value from real estate in Japan, capital gains derived through the LPS are subject to Japanese tax, except possible exemptions under the relevant tax treaties.

### In the case of a Cayman limited partnership

A Supreme Court decision in 2015 (judgment of 17 July 2015, 69(5) MINSHU 1253) established a standard for classification of foreign entities for the Japanese tax purposes and concluded that a Delaware limited partnership constitutes a corporation (opaque). Under this standard, as well as taking into account that the Supreme Court refused on the same day the appeal made by the Japanese Government in another case in which classification of a Bermuda limited partnership was at issue (Tokyo High Court's judgment of 5 February 2014, 2235 Hanrei jihō 3), it is generally understood that a Bermuda limited partnership would constitute a partnership (transparent), though case-by-case analysis may still be necessary. Given the similarity between a Bermuda limited partnership and Cayman limited partnership, though likewise should be subject to case-by-case analysis, a Cayman limited partnership would also constitute a partnership (transparent) in many cases. As long as neither it nor its partners have any PE in Japan, capital gains are generally not subject to Japanese tax, while dividends are subject to Japanese withholding tax of 15.315% (in the case of dividends paid by listed companies) or 20.42% (in the case of dividends paid by non-listed companies) with a possible reduction under relevant tax treaties. The 25% holding rule mentioned above and the special rules for real estate holding companies mentioned in the third point are also applicable in the case of a Cayman limited partnership (in the same way as an LPS as long as a Cayman limited partnership is treated as a pass-through entity).

## 6.2 Carried interest

Carried interest is usually provided in the form of contingent fees to the general partner in the limited partnership agreement. It should be noted, however, that generally all of the taxable income of a company is aggregated for purposes of Japanese corporate tax regardless of whether such income is classified as capital gain or ordinary income, and the difference between ordinary income and capital gain has no substantial meaning as long as the general partner is a Japanese corporation.

## 6.3 Management equity
### Stock options

Stock options are issued as stock acquisition rights under the Companies Act of Japan (Act No.86 of 2005). From the perspective of the individual management member (i.e. individual director), stock options are categorised into tax-qualified stock options and non-tax-qualified stock options. The general tax treatment is that, for non-tax-qualified stock options that are assignable at any time, the grant of the stock options is a taxable event and for non-tax-qualified stock options that are non-assignable, the grant of the stock options is not a taxable event but the exercise of the stock options is a taxable event. On the other hand, for tax-qualified stock options, neither the grant nor the exercise of stock options is a taxable event and tax is deferred until the sale of the shares that were obtained through the exercise of the stock options. In order for stock options to be tax-qualified, the following requirements provided in art.29-2(1) of the Act on Special Measures Concerning Taxation (Act No.26 of 1957) must be provided in the relevant grant agreement:

- the stock acquisition rights shall be exercised between two and 10 years following the date of the resolution granting the stock acquisition rights;
- the total amount of the exercise price with respect to the exercise of the stock acquisition rights for one calendar year shall not exceed JPY 12,000,000;
- the exercise price per share with respect to the exercise of the stock acquisition rights shall be equivalent to or exceed the price per share of the shares of the company at the time of execution of the grant agreement;
- the stock acquisition rights shall be non-assignable;
- delivery of the shares upon exercise of the stock acquisition rights shall not be made in violation of the offering terms approved in the resolution

granting the stock acquisition rights; and
- pursuant to an agreement entered into in advance between the issuer and a financial instrument business provider (e.g. securities firms and trust banks) in connection with the exercise of the stock acquisition rights, when the grantees acquire shares upon exercise of the stock acquisition rights: (1) transfer of such shares shall be recorded in the "book of transfer account" (*furikae kouza-bo*) opened at the financial instrument business provider; (2) such shares shall be delivered to the financial instrument business provider for custody; or (3) such shares are entrusted for administration to the financial instrument business provider.

From the perspective of the investee company or investment vehicle, the general tax treatment is that the value of stock options granted to directors are deductible, to an extent not inappropriately high, only where the stock options are non-tax-qualified and are granted in consideration for the services provided by the director and such stock options are restricted in transfer and satisfy certain other statutory requirements.

### Shares

From the perspective of the individual director, as long as the shares are issued at the fair market price, acquisition of shares is not a taxable event.

From the perspective of the investee company or investment vehicle, the issuance of new shares is a capital transaction that is not a taxable event as long as they are issued at the fair market price. However, unless the investee company or investment vehicle is incorporated as a legal entity other than a stock corporation (*kabushiki kaisha*), such as a limited liability company (*godo kaisha*), at least 50% of the paid-in amount must be allocated to increase the paid-in capital and such increased capital is subject to a registration and licence tax at the rate of 0.7%.

### 6.4   Loan interest

From the lender's perspective, it should be noted that, for purposes of Japanese corporate tax, generally all of the taxable income is aggregated and subject to an effective tax rate of approximately 30%. Accordingly, interest is also aggregated into taxable income. In addition, generally speaking, interest on loans extended by a non-resident lender to a Japanese company in connection with its business conducted in Japan is subject to Japanese withholding tax at the rate of 20.42%. Most of the income tax treaties provide that the withholding tax rate for interest is reduced generally to 10% and some of them even exempt withholding tax on interest received by financial institutions under certain conditions.

From the borrower's perspective, interest may generally be deducted as an expense. However, the borrower may be denied a deduction of the interest that it paid to a non-resident lender for Japanese corporate tax purposes if the thin capitalisation rules under Japanese tax law, which, roughly speaking, set the maximum debt-to-equity-ratio at 3:1, or the earning stripping rules under Japanese law, which, roughly speaking, deny deduction of interest in excess of 50% of income before interest, apply.

### 6.5 Transaction taxes

Japan has stamp tax, and it applies, in particular, to real estate sales agreements, intellectual property sales agreements and business transfer agreements at the maximum amount of JPY 0.6 million per agreement and to receivables sales agreement at JPY 200 per agreement. Such stamp tax is not applicable, however, to share purchase agreements and purchase agreements on most movable assets, such as inventory or machines.

Japan also has value added tax, namely a consumption tax and local consumption tax, the current aggregated rate of which is 8%. Taxable transactions for the purpose of the consumption tax and local consumption tax include transfers of goods or other assets for consideration within Japan. However, certain categories of transactions, such as transfers of land and transfers of securities, are excluded from taxable transactions. As such, share purchases are not subject to the consumption tax and local consumption tax but asset purchases are subject to these taxes with certain exceptions.

In addition, for real estate sales, a real property acquisition tax is applicable at the rate of 3% for land or residential building sales and 4% for other building sales.

## 7. CURRENT TOPICAL ISSUES/TRENDS

In recent years, especially in 2016 and 2017, the private equity fundraising market has been very active. Private equity deals in recent years have also been active and the total volume of the deals in 2017 would mark a record high, with a relatively large number of large-scale deals (over JPY 100 billion).

Japanese banks continue to be active in providing debt financings. Japanese banks are also becoming more active in providing debt financing for outbound cross-border transactions by Japanese companies.

Private equity has gradually taken root in the Japanese market, with an increasing number of participants over the past 20 years, and, during this time, relevant laws and legal practices surrounding private equity funds have been maturing. Accordingly, it is expected that the Japanese private equity market will continue to grow.

# Luxembourg

**Loyens & Loeff Luxembourg Sàrl** Marc Meyers, Jérôme Mullmaier & Maude Royer

## 1. MARKET OVERVIEW
### 1.1 Types of investors

Luxembourg private equity investment vehicles, whether they are formed as regulated or unregulated vehicles, generally obtain their funding from institutional investors, professional investors or sophisticated private individuals. The lightly regulated investment company in risk capital (*société d'investissement en capital à risque*—SICAR), specialised investment fund (*fonds d'investissement spécialisé*—SIF) and the unregulated reserved alternative investment fund (*fonds d'investissement alternatif réservé*—RAIF) in particular are targeted at so-called "well-informed investors", meaning any institutional, professional or other investor which: (1) has confirmed in writing that it adheres to the status of "well-informed investor"; and (2) either invests a minimum of EUR 125,000 in the company or has obtained an assessment made by a credit institution, investment firm or management company certifying its expertise, experience and knowledge in adequately appraising the risks entailed by an investment in such a vehicle.

In particular, Luxembourg has for many years been the jurisdiction of choice for many of the world's best known and most reputable private equity houses for the structuring of their investments as it offers some of Europe's most customised fund regimes for private equity. As at 17 July 2018, the number of SICARs that are specifically dedicated to private equity increased to 283. As for RAIFs, 439 of them have been established within the two-year period since the introduction of this new fund regime. Many of these RAIFs are focused on private equity strategies (but the exact number cannot be confirmed as RAIFs are not required to be dedicated private equity investment vehicles). Over the past few years, unregulated fund structures such as the RAIF or the special limited partnership (SCSp) got real momentum as they allow to establish Alternative Investment Fund Managers Directive (AIFMD)[1] compliant unregulated funds. Unregulated fund structures are often preferred by fund sponsors unless investors demand or legal or tax considerations drive the structuring phase towards a regulated fund (such as a SICAR or SIF).

It is also worthwhile mentioning that more managers of private funds have been opting for Luxembourg as their funds domicile in recent years. In an "AIFMD compliant" context, the recognition of Luxembourg as a well-regulated and well-known funds centre plays an important role in fundraising and, ultimately, in the process of selecting the fund's domicile. With the

---

[1] Directive 2011/61 on Alternative Investment Fund Managers and amending Directives 2003/41 and 2009/65 and Regulations 1060/2009 and 1095/2010 [2011] OJ L174/1.

selection process being more investor-driven than ever, Luxembourg has thus been gaining significant ground against offshore centres, mostly at investors' request.

## 1.2 Types of investments

While private equity real estate and technology are most popular for SICARs having a focused investment strategy, there has been a general confirmation of the trend for "clean-tech" and infrastructure Luxembourg-based private equity structures, with the setting up and launch of a significant number of private equity funds investing in alternative and renewable energy projects (wind, solar and water) and related new technologies. Numerous SICARs have also been used for the purpose of providing mezzanine financing.

## 2. FUNDS
### 2.1 Fund structures

When opting for Luxembourg as their investment hub, private equity initiators (or promoters or sponsors) generally opt for either an unregulated ordinary commercial company (Soparfi) or for one of the following fund regimes:

- a SICAR, based on the Law of 15 June 2004, as amended, relating to the investment company in risk capital (SICAR Law) (the SICAR is a vehicle specifically dedicated to private equity and venture capital investments, whether diversified or not);
- a SIF, based on the Law of 13 February 2007, as amended, relating to specialised investment funds (SIF Law); or
- a RAIF, based on the Law of 23 July 2016 relating to reserved alternative investment funds (RAIF Law).

Although the SIF Law does not prescribe any quantitative, qualitative, geographical or other type of investment restrictions, the Luxembourg Supervisory Commission of the Financial Sector (CSSF) has issued a circular (Circular 07/309), pursuant to which a SIF should generally not invest more than 30% of its assets or commitments in securities of the same kind issued by the same issuer. Certain exemptions may apply to this rule (e.g. in the case of a feeder fund structuring). While it is not subject to any direct regulatory approval or supervision, it is generally considered that a RAIF must comply with similar diversification rules. To the extent such restriction makes the SIF and the RAIF incompatible with non-diversified private equity investments strategies, an initiator would instead either opt for the Soparfi, taking advantage of a flexible and efficient fiscal and legal framework, for the SICAR or for the RAIF with a corporate object restricted to investment in risk capital assets (within the same meaning as for SICARs), thereby allowing no diversification requirements to apply.

The Soparfi and the SICAR can only be formed as a corporate form having a legal personality separate from that of their investors (except if the Soparfi or the SICAR is established as a SCSp which does not have legal personality), whereas the SIF and the RAIF may, as referred to above, in addition, be organised as a common fund (*fonds commun de placement*—FCP) managed by a Luxembourg-based management company. It is important to stress that the

Soparfi, SICAR, SIF and RAIF acronyms do not refer to specific legal forms but merely to a specific set of legal, regulatory and tax provisions with the actual investment vehicle or entity being formed as one of the following:
- a public limited liability company (SA);
- a private limited liability company (SARL);
- a partnership limited by shares (SCA);
- a co-operative company in the form of a public limited liability company (Coop-SA);
- a common limited partnership (SCS);
- a SCSp; or
- solely in respect of the SIF and the RAIF, an FCP.

The SCA, SCS, SCSp and FCP deserve special attention. The SCA, SCS and SCSp are formed by agreement between one or several general partners with unlimited liability and general management powers, together with limited partners who participate in any profits and share in any losses, generally pro rata with their participation in the partnership and up to the amount of their commitment or contribution, as the case may be. Unlike the SCSp, which does not have legal personality, the SCA and SCS have full legal capacity distinct from that of their partners. The SCA, SCS and SCSp will further allow the initiator to structure the acquisition vehicle by using common law-style partnership concepts, well known to the international investor and initiator base. The SCS and SCSp can implement capital account mechanisms which are customary for common-law limited partnerships. Under this mechanism, each limited partner has, typically, an account reflecting its contribution to the partnership which is adjusted over time to reflect its participation to profits and losses of the partnership. This mechanism does not require the issuance of securities of any kind to the limited partners. The full significance of the limited partnership as an investment vehicle can be further appreciated when looking at its fiscal treatment (see s.6 below).

The FCP is similar to a unit trust in the UK or a mutual fund in the US. It is organised as a co-proprietorship whose joint owners are only liable up to the amount they have committed or contributed. The FCP does not have a legal personality and must be managed by a Luxembourg-based management company.

## 2.2 Regulation of fundraising and fund managers

The regulatory landscape applicable to fund managers is preliminary made up of the Luxembourg AIFMD implementing Law of 12 July 2013 on alternative investment fund managers (AIFM Act). The AIFM Act has notable effect in terms of both fundraising and fund manager regulation. Other sets of regulations may come into play on the fundraising side when offers to the public and/or to retail investors are contemplated (Law of 10 July 2005 on prospectuses for securities (Prospectus Law) and Regulation 1286/2014 on key information documents for packaged retail and insurance-based investment products [2014] OJ L352/1 (PRIIPS Regulation) regimes, as defined below).

### Applicable fundraising legislation

As far as private equity vehicles are concerned, the applicable fundraising regime mainly consists in three sets of legislation:

- the Luxembourg private placement rules;
- the AIFMD marketing regime as implemented under the AIFM Act;
- in case of marketing of AIFs to retail investors, the PRIIPs Key Investor Information Document (KIID) regime as set out under the PRIIPs Regulation; and
- in the case of offers of closed-ended funds to the public, the Prospectus Law.

The potential application of the above rules will have to be checked ahead of any Luxembourg offering (irrespective of the type of fund being offered, i.e. a SIF/SICAR or unregulated fund). For present purposes, we have assumed that the vehicles on offer are not open ended.

### The Luxembourg private placement regime

Luxembourg private placement rules consist in various pieces of legislation, most notably, laws on:

- the protection of consumers (contained in the Consumer Code);
- commercial practices and unfair competition; and
- door-to-door sales, itinerant trade, display of goods and canvassing for orders.

### The Alternative Investment Fund Managers Act marketing regime

As a preliminary remark, the AIFMD marketing regime only applies to the marketing of investment vehicles qualifying as AIFs and fund managers falling within the scope of the AIFM Act.

As a general principle, Luxembourg-based alternative investment funds managers (AIFMs) licensed under the AIFM Act benefit from a European passport to market EU AIFs within the meaning of the AIFMD to professional investors across the EU. AIFMs licensed in other EU countries could also benefit from the passport for the purpose of their Luxembourg offering. The passport would not be applicable to Luxembourg-based sub-threshold AIFMs solely registered (and not licensed) with the CSSF (unless they have decided to fully opt in to the AIFMD regime). Further, the passport is not yet available in respect of non-EU AIFs and non-EU AIFMs. At this stage, marketing of AIFs without a passport to Luxembourg professional investors by non-EU based AIFMs is subject to a prior notification to the CSSF and compliance with the conditions set forth under the AIFMD (namely, compliance with the AIFMD transparency requirements, co-operation agreements between the CSSF and the relevant third-country regulator, and non-registration of the relevant country on the Financial Action Task Force (FATF) non-co-operative territories list). It is worthwhile noting that marketing is permitted from the moment the notification form has been filed with the CSSF. In addition, the marketing of foreign AIFs to Luxembourg retail investors is subject to prior authorisation from the CSSF which is reliant on the following conditions: appointment of a Luxembourg-based paying agent, monthly calculations of subscription/redemption prices, sufficient risk spreading (which threshold depends on asset class and instruments invested in) and some borrowing limitations (which level depends on the asset class invested in). "Retail investor" is defined as any investor who is not a professional client under Directive 2014/65 on markets in financial instruments and amending Directive 2002/92 and Directive 2011/61 [2014] OJ L173/349 (MiFID II), it being understood that the CSSF authorisation will not be required with respect to any marketing directed to Luxembourg-based: (1) "well-informed investors" as defined above; or (2) other investors meeting the eligibility standards of the European Long-Term Investment fund (ELTIF), European Venture Capital Funds (EuVECA) and/or European Social Entrepreneurship Funds (EuSEF) regimes.

### The packaged retail and insurance-based investment products regime

The PRIIPs Regulation imposes on so called PRIIP manufacturers (board of the fund or the AIFM, as the case may be) to produce a KID if and before a PRIIP is made available to retail investors within the European Economic Area (EEA) after 31 December 2017. The definition of PRIIPs is broad as to include investment funds. Accordingly, KIDs will have to be produced even for many investment funds which look and feel like non-retail products, e.g. because they require high minimum investments and/or specific investor characteristics. The "person selling a PRIIP" within EEA (Point of Sale) will need to provide the KID to retail investors in good time before those retail investors are bound by any contract or offer relating to that PRIIP. Grandfathering provisions may apply in some cases to AIFs. The aim of the KID is to provide potential retail investors with a standard document being clear and easy to understand. The KID is a pre-contractual document of no more than three A4 pages. The KID contains seven sections requiring specific input (name of product/what is the product (legal form, objective etc)/risk overview/what happens if the PRIIPs manufacturer is unable to pay out/costs overview/recommended holding period/complaint procedure). The KID is finally subject to a yearly review process.

### The Prospectus Law regime

Besides the AIFMD marketing rules, the marketing of closed-ended funds may, in the case of an offer to the public, be subject to the Prospectus Law, which has implemented Directive 2003/71 on the prospectus to be published when securities are offered to the public or admitted to trading and amending Directive 2001/34 [2003] OJ L345/64 (Prospectus Directive). Under the Prospectus Law, any communication to persons, in any form and by any means, which presents sufficient information on the terms of the offer and the securities to be offered to enable an investor to decide to purchase or subscribe to these securities constitutes an offer to the public falling within the scope of the Prospectus Law. An exemption from publishing a prospectus under the Prospectus Law, however, applies in case of offers targeted only to "qualified investors" (e.g. professional investors under the AIFMD/MIFID II), to fewer than 150 persons or legal entities per EU or EEA Member State other than qualified investors, or when the offer is for a total of at least EUR 100,000 per investor or each security has a nominal value of at least EUR 100,000.

### Regulation of fund managers
#### *Managers of unregulated funds*

Since the AIFMD regime came into life, unregulated funds (any investment vehicle not subject to the supervision of the CSSF, potentially a Soparfi) could now fall within the scope of the AIFMD regime if they qualify as an AIF and their manager subsequently becomes subject to registration or authorisation under the AIFM Act.

An AIF is defined by AIFMD art.4(1)(a) as

> "a collective investment vehicle, including investment compartments thereof, which raises capital from a number of investors with a view to investing it in accordance with a defined investment policy for the benefit of those investors and does not require authorisation under the Directive 2009/65 (the UCITS Directive)".

Being subject to regulatory supervision/authorisation is not a requirement to qualify as an AIF. The CSSF confirmed that it is the responsibility of the management body of the collective investment vehicle to self-assess if it qualifies as an AIFM and, hence, if it manages one or several AIFs.[2] This self-assessment is not necessary for RAIFs which are AIFs by law and need to be established as fully AIFMD-compliant products.

Assuming AIFs are being managed and none of the exemptions under the AIFMD are available, then an AIFM licence shall be applied for should the AIFMD thresholds of assets under management be met. The standard threshold is set at EUR 100 million, including assets acquired through the use of leverage, but this is increased to EUR 500 million when the portfolio of assets managed consists of AIFs that are not leveraged and have no redemption rights exercisable for a period of five years following the date of the initial investment in each AIF. The AIFM licence can be applied for either internally by the AIF itself (where the legal form of the AIF permits internal management) or externally by its manager (such as the general partner of a SCSp. Alternatively, the AIF sponsor may also have recourse to a third-party AIFM (in Luxembourg or in another EU jurisdiction) if it does not want to go through the AIFM application process. This route is particularly popular among medium-sized fund managers. Fund managers, who would, at least initially, not be prepared to establish the required substance (including staff etc) in Luxembourg are also increasingly looking at appointing third-party AIFMs.

Falling below the above thresholds does not mean a full exemption from the AIFM Act requirements. Sub-threshold managers established in Luxembourg are required to register themselves with the CSSF, disclose the AIF that they manage (and their investment strategies) and regularly report to the CSSF the principal instruments in which they trade and relating investment exposures. That said, it remains an option for sub-threshold managers to elect to fully subject themselves to the AIFM Act requirements (especially if they want to

---

[2] CSSF, "Frequently Asked Questions concerning the Luxembourg law of 12 July 2013 on alternative investment fund managers as well as the Regulation 231/2013 supplementing Directive 2011/61 with regard to exemptions, general operating conditions, depositaries, leverage transparency and supervision", Version 12 (14 August 2018), p.5, Question 1(a).

benefit from the EU passport attached to the licence). The threshold test will be irrelevant for RAIFs which need to be fully AIFMD compliant and then appoint an external AIFM which can either be established in Luxembourg or in another EU/EEA jurisdiction.

### *Managers of specialised investment funds/investment companies in risk capital*

Managers or directors of SIFs and SICARs must be authorised by the CSSF. The same approval requirement applies to management companies of SIFs set up as a FCP. In practice, the Luxembourg-based management of SIFs or SICARs delegates the investment advisory function, under its responsibility, to advisers located outside Luxembourg. The CSSF will only authorise the delegation of the discretionary investment management power if the investment manager is regulated and subject to equivalent supervision by another authority.

The AIFMD regime and related registration/licensing obligation can also be applicable to managers of SIFs/SICARs should the latter qualify as an AIF. In this context, the AIFM Act has amended the SIF and SICAR laws to establish two types of SIFs/SICARs, namely those managed by an AIFMD-compliant manager and those managed by an AIFMD non-compliant manager.

### 2.3   Customary or common terms of funds

The following terms mainly apply to private equity vehicles structured as regulated SIFs/SICARs, unregulated RAIFs or limited partnerships (such as SCSs/SCSps):

- funding process: commitment or subscription-based;
- investment policy, investment period, diversification of investments (if applicable), leverage ratio;
- relations between investors and management: powers of the management, removal of management, good/bad leaver;
- organisational/operational expenses; and
- fee structure and distribution waterfall: carried interest and distribution rules are provided for in the vehicle's documentation. It is also possible to have a high watermark mechanism. Carried interest is usually channeled through the carried interest special investment vehicle. Management fees and sometimes performance fees also apply. A typical waterfall would feature a structure of distributions, starting with a return on the capital contributions or drawn-down commitments by investors, plus the preferred return (with a hurdle rate of around 8%on the investors' drawn-down commitments or capital contributions), then the catch-up of the carried interest for the management team (special investment vehicle) and an 80/20 split between investors and management thereafter.

## 3.   DEBT FINANCE
### 3.1   Means of financing

Along with the traditional means of financing, such as senior, mezzanine and high yields bond financings at the level of Luxembourg private equity holding entities, the number of financings at the level of Luxembourg private equity sponsors (the funds) has increased notably since 2014. Indeed, concurrently with the surge in the AIF market, Luxembourg has seen a significant development in fund finance activity, supported by the possibility of implementing efficient security packages in the context of credit facilities for funds, which are typically secured by the unfunded capital commitments of the funds' investors. The more common security package comprises: (1) a pledge by the fund of its rights in and to the unfunded capital commitments of the investors and the claims against the investors in relation to those commitments; and (2) a pledge over the bank account into which investors are required to pay their contributions.

### 3.2 Restrictions on granting security

Under art.430-19 of the Luxembourg Law of 10 August 1915 on commercial companies (Company Law), a Luxembourg company may only advance funds, make loans or provide security interests, directly or indirectly, with a view to the acquisition of its shares by a third party, if the following conditions are fulfilled:

- the transaction must take place, on the responsibility of the board of directors, at fair market conditions, especially with regard to the interest the company receives and the security interest provided to it for the loans and advances in question;
- the board of directors must submit the proposed financial assistance for prior approval by the general meeting of shareholders;
- the board of directors must present to the general meeting of shareholders a written report stating the reasons for the transaction, the company's interest in entering into it, the conditions on which the transaction is made and the risks involved;
- the aggregate financial assistance granted to third parties may at no time result in the reduction of the company's net assets below the amount of the share capital plus the non-distributable reserves;
- the company's balance sheet must include among its liabilities a non-distributable reserve of the same amount as the aggregate financial assistance;
- when a third party, by means of financial assistance from a company, acquires that company's own shares or subscribes to shares issued in the course of an increase in the subscribed capital, this acquisition or subscription must, in addition to all other conditions, be made at a fair price; and
- in certain circumstances, a special auditor's report on the envisaged operation must be provided to the general meeting of shareholders, notably when members of the parent's management are parties to one of the operations falling under the financial assistance rules.

Whereas the rules relating to financial assistance apply to SAs (*sociétés anonymes*) and partnerships (*sociétés en commandite*), there are certain uncertainties whether such rules apply to SARLs (*sociétés à responsabilité limitée*). Due to residual terminology left in certain provisions (including provisions in respect of criminal sanctions) of the Company Law following the entry into force of the Luxembourg Law of 10 August 2016 (2016 Law) amending the Company Law, there is a possible discrepancy between such provisions and the fact that the financial assistance prohibition contained in the Company Law is not expressly mentioned as being applicable to SARLs. Pursuant to the parliamentary works in respect of the 2016 Law, it seems that the intention of the legislator was not to apply the financial assistance prohibition rules to SARLs. Due to the provisions referred to above, it can however not completely exclude that a Luxembourg court could apply such prohibition to Luxembourg SARLs.

Unlawful financial assistance results in the guarantee or security interest being void and triggers the civil/criminal liability of the company's directors.

In addition to the financial assistance issue, certain corporate benefit issues may arise when a Luxembourg company has to grant up or cross-stream guarantees (security interests). While it is generally accepted that downstream guarantees may be provided by a Luxembourg company without any limitation, legal practitioners are more reserved when it comes to cross or upstream guarantees. However, based on current Belgian case law (to which Luxembourg courts are likely to refer in this context), and provided that the corporate object allows the granting of guarantees to secure obligations of group companies, a Luxembourg company may in principle validly assist other group companies if:

- a group exists;
- it can be demonstrated that the company derives a benefit from granting such assistance; and
- the assistance is not, in terms of the amounts involved, disproportionate to the company's financial means and the benefits derived from granting the assistance.

It is for the board or management body of a Luxembourg company to determine whether an action such as providing a guarantee is in that company's best corporate interest. Practitioners usually insert some guarantee limitation language in up or cross-stream guarantees so as to have some assurance that the guarantor will not be declared bankrupt by performing its obligations under the guarantee.

In any event, the corporate benefit of the guarantor/security provider should be taken into account.

### 3.3  Intercreditor issues

The company's creditors (and therefore also debt providers) generally have priority over the shareholders, who are residual claimants only. In addition, there may be contractual (through the use of intercreditor arrangements) or structural subordination (through the use of multi-layered corporate structures).

In the vast majority of cases, first-ranking security interests are granted in favour of the senior lenders.

Under Luxembourg law, certain creditors of the insolvent party have rights to preferred payments arising by operation of law, some of which may under certain circumstances supersede the rights to payment of secured creditors and most of which are undisclosed preferences (*privilèges occultes*) arising by operation of law. They include in particular the rights relating to the insolvency official's fees and costs, as well as any legal costs, the rights of employees to certain salary amounts, the rights of the Treasury and certain assimilated parties (namely social security bodies) as well as certain other rights. These preferential rights may extend to all or part of the insolvent party's assets.

### 3.4 Syndication

In Luxembourg, loans are syndicated either before or after the deal is done. The transfer of the debt has to be notified to or accepted by the debtor.

The transfer of the security interests and other rights accessories to the loans may require further notifications, acceptances and formalities.

Security interests which fall within the scope of the Luxembourg Law of 5 August 2005 on financial contractual arrangements, such as securities held through an account located in Luxembourg, bearer securities physically located in Luxembourg or registered securities issued by a Luxembourg issuer, shares in Luxembourg companies, claims (*créances*) governed by Luxembourg law (including unfunded capital commitments of the investors of the Luxembourg funds) or owed by an obligor (*débiteur*) located or deemed to be located in Luxembourg, or bank accounts opened with banks located in Luxembourg, may be granted to a security agent/trustee. In such cases, if a loan is transferred without a change in the holder of the security interest (i.e. the security agent/trustee), the transfer will not require additional formalities (except if provided otherwise in the security interest documentation).

With regard to mortgages over Luxembourg real estate and pledges over business, Luxembourg law does not explicitly recognise the possibility of having a security agent/trustee and the transfer of loans secured by such mortgages/pledges will require further notifications, acceptances and formalities.

## 4. EQUITY STRUCTURES
### 4.1 Role of management

Management typically participates in an investment by either directly or indirectly taking an equity stake in the buyer, i.e. in the Luxembourg private equity investment vehicle. Some managers may be offered a board seat, which provides them more information on and power over the strategy to be applied to the target. In this case, the target and the managers enter into management agreements instead of employment agreements as they give both parties more flexibility. Employment agreements are subject to the stricter rules of labour law: for example, non-competition clauses then need to be geographically restricted, specific to the activity which is the subject of the clause (e.g. in a specific sector), reasonably limited in time and providing for adequate compensation, and termination clauses also need to be carefully drafted.

Both a management agreement and an employment agreement would contain clauses relating to non-competition, which must be limited in time and space and be specific, as well as non-solicitation and confidentiality clauses. Clauses whereby the manager commits to remain in the management for a certain period of time or spend a certain amount of time on managing the investment may also be included. Restrictions on the transfer of equity owned by the managers, such as lock-up periods before transfers are allowed, are also used as an incentive to retain management.

Management is often entitled to a carried interest, the payment of which will be subject to each investor first receiving the full amount of its capital contribution and preferred return on its capital contribution. Management will either subscribe to a specific class of shares of the investment vehicle entitling it to carried interest directly, or to shares of a dedicated carry vehicle which is itself a shareholder of the investment vehicle. In the latter case, the carried interest is distributed as a dividend on the shares of the carry vehicle.

At the investment level, the managers participate by acquiring shares in the target's share capital, convertible bonds, or options and warrants in relation to such shares. Management incentive plans are also sometimes included in deals.

These participations in the equity of the target company allow for a better alignment of interests between the management and investors.

## 4.2 Common protections for investors

Depending on the level of their shareholding in the Luxembourg investment vehicle, the investors concerned will be more or less successful in obtaining some level of control or influence over the vehicle. This can be achieved by providing the following rights:

- rights to be appointed or have a representative appointed to the management body of the investment vehicle, or to an advisory or investment committee, whose opinion may be of either a purely consultative or binding nature;
- information rights with respect to financial data in addition to the information that must be made available to shareholders under Luxembourg law; and
- "exit clauses" relating to the transfer of shares may also be foreseen, including standstill provisions, rights of first refusal, lock-ups, tag and drag-along rights or clauses allowing for a sale to affiliates, put options and good and bad leaver provisions.

## 4.3 Common protections for management

If management with a minority interest in the investment vehicle is at the origin of its setting up, it will usually set up the Luxembourg fund under the legal form of a (common/special limited or corporate) partnership, in which management would be the sole or controlling shareholders in the managing general partner/unlimited shareholder of the partnership. In addition, the constitutional documents of the Luxembourg investment would provide for only very limited and restrictive circumstances under which the managing general partner could be dismissed by the investors.

If management has no final say in the legal form to be used for the investment vehicle, it would generally negotiate its protection, taking into account the right to appoint one or more representatives to the management body, certain rights in connection with important decisions and certain exit rights.

## 4.4 Management warranties

Private equity funds would usually ask to obtain certain warranties with respect to the underling investment, including from management, particularly in connection with the correctness of the legal, tax and financial information provided and on the basis of which an investment decision has been made. The typical time period for these kinds of warranties would be from one to two years, subject to the relevant statute of limitations applying to specific matters.

### 4.5 Good leaver/bad leaver provisions

In the case of management participation at the level of the investment vehicle, good leaver and bad leaver provisions are generally included in a shareholder's agreement. The key terms of those provisions are the definitions of a good and bad leaver. Good leavers would typically leave for reasons of permanent incapacity or illness, or dismissal without cause; bad leavers would be dismissed for cause or resign voluntarily.

The purchase price of the shares of good leavers would usually be the fair market value of the shares they own, whereas bad leavers would typically be offered at most the lower of the initial subscription price and the fair market value of the shares, or even a small nominal amount. Evaluation of the shares, if provided for, is usually to be performed by independent valuers and arbitration clauses may apply.

Measures for enforcing good leaver/bad leaver provisions, including compulsory transfers, are usually provided for and may include call options on the managers' shares as described under s.4.2 above.

### 4.6 Public to private transactions

Luxembourg is mainly a financial centre where deals are partly structured but offers for public companies are very rare, especially from private equity funds, due to the limited number of targets available.

The Luxembourg law on takeover bids implementing the EU Takeover Directive (Directive 2004/25 on takeover bids [2004] OJ L142/12) provides for compliance with a set of rules as well as the principle that all shareholders are to be treated equally, which is of paramount importance in the context of Luxembourg law.

## 5. EXITS
### 5.1 Secondary sales

Exit from an investment by way of a secondary sale would typically involve a requirement for the usual representations and warranties by new investors from the selling private equity fund as well as additional representations and warranties from the managers staying in the investment. These sales are realised by the sale of the shares the private equity fund holds in the investment and involve the negotiation of limitations on the representations and warranties, liability, payment of the purchase price by instalments and any non-competition undertakings by the seller.

### 5.2 Trade sales

In the event of a trade sale, the same issues arise for the selling private equity fund as in a secondary sale; the negotiating power of the purchaser being potentially strengthened by its position as a strategic investor. Financial arrangements also have to be taken into account and may be an additional source of formalities to be complied with when structuring the deal.

## 5.3    Initial public offerings

Given the size of the local markets, there are not many exits including initial public offerings (IPOs) in Luxembourg. These kinds of exits are usually structured in other jurisdictions as many underlying investments are located abroad. Although there are some listings on the Luxembourg stock exchange of shares of SIFs and SICARs, these listings have not been motivated by any exit opportunity, rather, the driving factor has been a requirement by one or more investors to invest in securities which are listed.

## 5.4    Refinancing

Refinancing may be used as an exit route in which case the interest of the target company has to be taken into account as the notion of group interest in Luxembourg law is not recognised as such, contrary to the corporate interest of the company itself, which must be respected at all times for fear of liability issues with the company's management. The financial assistance rules must also be complied with.

## 5.5    Restructuring/insolvency

The restructuring of an investment would typically involve other jurisdictions more directly than Luxembourg. In Luxembourg, the applicable rules concerning financial assistance, the fate of employees (very few of them being directly employed by the Luxembourg structure) and corporate interest also apply.

Liquidations of companies may not result in a fraudulent attack on third parties' rights and bankruptcy rules should also be taken into account, as fraudulent bankruptcy entails criminal and civil liability for those concerned, including the shareholders, who may also have further liability due to their actions as de facto managers as their intervention in the company's management leads to the piercing of the corporate veil.

## 6.    TAX
### 6.1    Taxation of fund structures

The analysis of the tax features of Luxembourg private equity investment vehicles requires a schematic approach. By and large, the available investment vehicles can be divided into vehicles that are in principle (if they are considered opaque) subject to general taxation rules on the one hand (a Soparfi, SICAR or RAIF SICAR, as referred to below) and vehicles that are generally exempt from tax on the other hand (a SIF or the standard RAIF). Within each category, we furthermore need to distinguish between entities that are fiscally opaque (SARLs, SAs and SCAs) and those that are fiscally transparent (e.g. an SCS, SCSp or FCP).

#### Unregulated ordinary commercial company

A Soparfi, whether in the form of an SA, SARL or SCA, is an ordinary fully taxable commercial Luxembourg resident company subject to income taxation (namely, corporate income tax plus an employment fund surcharge and municipal business tax) on its worldwide income (combined rate for the city of Luxembourg in 2018 is 26.01%), subject to specific domestic or treaty exemptions and indirect taxation (e.g. VAT). However, exemptions apply as regards income and capital gains derived from qualifying participations (the participation exemption).

A Soparfi is also subject to a 0.5% net wealth tax on its net asset value as of 1 January of each year (0.05% tax rate for net assets exceeding EUR 500 million). Exemptions apply as regards, inter alia, qualifying participations. Soparfis are subject to a minimum net wealth tax ranging from EUR 535 to EUR 32,100 (depending on the size of their balance sheet). A Soparfi whose assets comprise at least 90% of financial assets is subject to a minimum net wealth tax of EUR 535 or EUR 4,815 (depending on the size of its balance sheet).

Dividend distributions by a Soparfi are generally subject to Luxembourg dividend withholding tax at a rate of 15%, although this rate may be reduced, often to zero, by the application of Luxembourg double tax treaties or the exemptions provided under Luxembourg tax law (notably, Luxembourg's implementation of the Parent-Subsidiary Directive[3] or the withholding tax exemption available for certain shareholders that are resident in a country with which Luxembourg has a tax treaty in force and are subject to a corporate income tax considered as comparable to the Luxembourg one).

Liquidation surpluses distributed by a Soparfi to its shareholders are not subject to withholding tax in Luxembourg.

### Investment company in risk capital

The SICAR can, generally speaking, be described as a tax-neutral vehicle for private equity investments.

### Taxation of the investment company in risk capital—fiscally opaque

The SICAR regime for fiscally opaque entities (such as a SA, SARL or SCA) follows the ordinary income tax regime of the Soparfi with a few risk capital-specific adjustments. The SICAR is thus also subject to corporate income taxes and to specific domestic or treaty exemptions, and should qualify as a resident company for domestic and Luxembourg tax-treaty purposes. However, such a type of SICAR benefits from a specific, objective, unconditional risk capital exemption to the extent that income from securities as well as income derived from the transfer, contribution or liquidation thereof (namely, bonds, shares, other transferable securities as well as negotiable instruments giving the right to acquire the aforementioned securities) are exempt. Temporarily invested idle funds may also benefit from this exemption, provided that these funds are effectively invested in risk capital investments within a 12-month period.

All other income is fully subject to ordinary Luxembourg direct taxation rules.

Fiscally opaque SICARs are exempt from net wealth tax. However, they are

---

3  Directive 2011/96 on the common system of taxation applicable in the case of parent companies and subsidiaries of different Member States [2011] OJ L345/8.

subject to a minimum net wealth tax in the same way as Soparfis.

### Taxation of the investment company in risk capital—fiscally transparent

A SICAR formed as a fiscally transparent SCS allows for the replication of a common law-type limited partnership vehicle. Although the limited partnership has its own legal personality separate from that of its partners, it is itself not liable for direct taxation or net wealth tax in Luxembourg. The same applies to the SICAR formed as an SCSp with the difference that the SCSp has no legal personality of its own.

### Taxation of distributions by the investment company in risk capital

The SICAR regime distinguishes itself from the rules applicable to Soparfis in that it always permits fiscally neutral (namely, without source taxation) profit repatriations: neither dividends nor liquidation proceeds distributed by a SICAR to investors are subject to withholding tax.

### Specialised investment fund

Generally speaking, the SIF is characterised by its tax neutrality:

- it is exempt from tax on income or capital gains;
- it is also exempt from net wealth tax; and
- distributions (including dividends and liquidation surpluses) made by a SIF to investors are not subject to withholding tax in Luxembourg.

However, the SIF is subject to an annual subscription tax of 0.01%. The taxable basis of the subscription tax is the aggregate net assets of the specialised investment fund as valued on the last day of each quarter. Certain money markets and pension funds or SIFs investing in other funds, which are already subject to subscription tax, are exempt from subscription tax.

### Reserved alternative investment fund

RAIFs are also characterised by their tax neutrality. The default tax regime applicable to RAIFs mirrors the SIF regime. This means that the RAIF will only be subject, at fund level, to an annual subscription tax levied at a rate of 0.01% of its net assets calculated on the last day of each quarter. Depending on the investment assets, some exemptions from subscription tax apply in order to avoid a duplication of this tax. Irrespective of the legal form chosen for the RAIF, it is wholly exempted from corporate income tax, municipal business tax and net wealth tax, and distributions of profits by the RAIF do not give rise to a withholding tax.

However, RAIFs whose constitutive documents provide that their sole object is the investment in risk capital assets (the RAIF SICAR) are taxed according to the same tax rules as those applicable to SICARs.

Under these SICAR-mirroring tax rules, a RAIF SICAR that takes a corporate legal form (like the SA, SARL or SCA) is fiscally opaque and is a normally taxable entity for corporate income tax purposes but with an exemption for any profits and gains derived from securities (see above). Fiscally opaque RAIF SICARs are also exempt from net wealth tax but subject to a minimum net wealth tax (as SICARs).

Likewise, a RAIF SICAR that takes the form of a partnership (the SCS or SCSp) is tax transparent (see above).

### Tax treaties

Luxembourg is currently a party to 81 tax treaties covering most industrialised nations, according to data provided by the Luxembourg tax authorities on their official website (available at: *https://impotsdirects.public.lu/fr/conventions.html* [Accessed 26 September 2018]), with some 16 additional treaties (including new treaties with countries having an existing treaty with Luxembourg) under negotiation or pending entry into force. Soparfis and fiscally opaque SICARs and RAIFs (the corporate object of which is limited to investments in risk capital), in principle, should be entitled to benefit from all the treaties currently in force. Insofar as SIFs and RAIFs are concerned, they might be able to do so for those countries for which the Luxembourg tax authorities state that investment companies with variable capital and investment companies with fixed capital can benefit from the respective tax treaty, which are the treaties with Andorra, Armenia, Austria, Azerbaijan, Bahrain, Barbados, Brunei, China, Croatia, the Czech Republic, Denmark, Estonia, Finland, Georgia, Germany, Guernsey, Hong Kong, Isle of Man, Indonesia, Ireland, Israel, Jersey, Kazakhstan, Laos, Liechtenstein, Macedonia, Malaysia, Malta, Moldova, Monaco, Morocco, Panama, Poland, Portugal, Qatar, Romania, San Marino, Saudi Arabia, Serbia, Seychelles, Singapore, Slovakia, Slovenia, Spain, Sri Lanka, Tajikistan, Taiwan, Thailand, Trinidad and Tobago, Tunisia, Turkey, United Arab Emirates, Uruguay, Uzbekistan and Vietnam. For Bulgaria, Greece, Italy and Korea; the applicability of the tax treaty is not clearly derived from its wording.

In June 2017, Luxembourg formally signed the Organisation for Economic Co-operation and Development's (OECD's) Multilateral Instrument (MLI) developed as part of BEPS (base erosion and profit shifting) Action 15. The MLI will implement in the tax treaties (between its signatories) certain recommendations arising from the BEPS project, e.g. the prevention of treaty abuse and anti-hybrid rules. Luxembourg has not excluded any of its bilateral tax treaties from the scope of the MLI but has made a series of reservations regarding specific provisions. On 15 June 2018, the Government approved a bill of law for the ratification of the MLI.

### Capital duty

The capital duty on capital contributions to a Soparfi, SICAR, SIF or RAIF is set at EUR 75 per incorporation or additional subsequent capital contribution.

## 6.2 Carried interest

The Luxembourg taxation rules define "carried interest" (*l'intéressement aux plus-values*) as a share in the profit of an AIF paid to employees of AIFMs or employees of management companies of an AIF. The carried interest must be paid on the basis of an incentive right, which is granted based on the employees' status and the AIF's performance.

The tax law distinguishes between two categories of carried interest income earned by the employees of AIFMs or management companies of AIFs:

(1) carried interest not structured under units, shares or representation issued by an AIF; and

(2) carried interest structured under units, shares or securities issued by an AIF.

The return on the first type of carried interest arrangement is taxed at the progressive income tax rate with a maximum set at 42% (subject to a surcharge of up to 9% on the income tax due for allocation to the employment fund leading to a combined rate of maximum 45.8%). Capital gains on the second type of carried interest realised are subject to the same progressive income tax rate. However, if the gain is realised after a period of six months, it is not subject to taxation unless the carried interest represents a substantial stake in a tax-opaque AIF. Such a substantial stake is generally present if the carried interest directly or indirectly represents more than 10% of the AIF's capital. In this case, gains are taxed at half the applicable progressive income tax rate. To ensure that the income paid under the second type of carried interest arrangement benefits from this exemption, the carried-interest holder should dispose of its carried interest, which would generally entail a buy-back of carried units by the AIF.

## 6.3 Management equity

Equity awarded to managers, e.g. shares attributed for free or preferential shares, may be considered as taxable income in-kind granted to the manager and/or may be redefined as professional income for the manager.

The Luxembourg taxation on the granting of shares will mainly depend on the capacity for which managers receive such shares. If the recipient is an employee or manager and if he/she is subject to Luxembourg tax on his/her employment/management income, the granting of those shares might qualify as being deemed employment income or deemed directors fees. The granting of shares can only be qualified as employment income if the director is also an employee of the company or is a director in charge of the day-to-day management of the company and receives the said shares in counterpart of those functions.

In either case, it is taxable at progressive tax rates up to 42%. Subsequent income from the awarded equity should be considered as income from movable property such as dividend income and is taxed as investment income. In principle, this income is also subject to progressive tax rates up to 42%. Nevertheless, as mentioned in s.6.2 above, amounts paid as investment income to a Luxembourg resident executive might be taxed beneficially (compared with professional income).

## 6.4 Loan interest

As a general rule, (at arm's length) interests are fully taxable at the normal rate set forth above at the level of the recipient and deductible from the tax base of the distributing entity for Luxembourg tax purposes. SIFs and RAIFs are however exempt of any taxation and should not be concerned by this rule which is only relevant for Luxembourg fully taxable entities such as Soparfis.

Note that interest derived from loans used to finance participations that are exempt under the participation exemption are not tax deductible or subject to a further claw-back mechanism.

Interests paid by a Luxembourg company to an entity with legal personality or a foreign individual are not subject to withholding tax except in case of profit-sharing interest. Repayments of principal on indebtedness are furthermore not subject to Luxembourg withholding tax. Interest paid to a Luxembourg individual is subject to a 20% flat taxation. A draft bill was submitted to Parliament in June 2018 to implement the measures of the EU anti-tax avoidance directive, to come into effect as from January 2019. It introduces an interest limitation rule:

- borrowing costs should be entirely deductible at most up to the amount of the interest (and assimilated) income received; and
- other borrowing costs should be deductible at most of up to 30% of the taxpayer's earnings before interest, taxes, depreciation and amortisation (EBITDA) (with a minimum lump sum deduction entitlement amounting to EUR 3 million).

The draft law provides some exceptions, such as full deduction for standalone entities and a carve-out for regulated financial undertakings. Financial undertakings are, among others, regulated SICARs, AIFs and Undertakings for Collective Investment in Transferable Securities (UCITS).

### 6.5 Transaction taxes

To the extent that SICARs, SIFs or any kind of AIF (including RAIFs) typically rely on the services of specialist investment managers or advisers, a specific VAT exemption, in principle, applies to fund management services in accordance with art.44.1.d of the Luxembourg VAT Law (Law of 12 February 1979 on Value added tax) implementing art.135.1.g of the EU VAT Directive 2006/112.[4] This exemption may also cover some of the administrative services generally provided to funds to the extent they are specific to and essential for the management of the funds. The case law of the European Court of Justice (*Abbey National Plc, Inscape Investment Fund v Commissioners of Customs & Excise* (C-169/04) EU:C:2006:289) confirmed that fund investment advisory services can be covered by the exemption, even when delegated to a third party, and irrespective of whether the fund investment adviser has a power of decision for the investment fund.

Although the question has not been formally addressed by the Luxembourg VAT authorities—or any judicial body—it appears that fund management services supplied to RAIFs should benefit from the same exemption.

Luxembourg VAT legislation foresees that funds benefitting from the VAT exemption for fund management services qualify as VAT taxable persons. Although this does not per se trigger an obligation for the SICARs, SIFs, RAIFs or other AIFs to register for VAT, the latter may have to do so, should they receive VAT taxable services from suppliers located outside Luxembourg. This is often the case as the investment funds generally have to reimburse different parties for specific expenses.

SICARs, SIFs, RAIFs and other AIFs are in principle not able to recover VAT incurred on their costs. However, thanks to the broad application of the VAT exemption of art.44.1.d of the Luxembourg VAT Law, this VAT leakage is in practice limited to the VAT due on services such as custodian, notary, auditor or lawyer services. Moreover, the Luxembourg VAT rate is the lowest

---

4    Directive 2006/112 on the common system of value added tax [2006] OJ L347/1.

in the EU (17% since 1 January 2015, compared with an average of 21% in the EU (20% in the UK and 23% in Ireland)).[5]

## 7.   CURRENT TOPICAL ISSUES/TRENDS

Luxembourg continues to strengthen its ranking as the world's second largest fund domicile after the US as the assets under management of Luxembourg domiciled funds have in 2017 for the first time crossed the bar of EUR 4 trillion and stood at EUR 4.271 trillion as at 31 May 2018. Such increase is not only based on the growth of traditional Luxembourg-domiciled UCITS funds but is also due to the continued strong growth in respect of alternative investment funds, including in the areas of private equity.

The modernisation of the Luxembourg partnership regime (which was implemented together with the transposition of the AIFMD) has led to offering private equity houses and other fund initiators accustomed to Anglo-Saxon partnerships a new onshore alternative of fund structuring, regulated or not regulated as a product, linked to an EU-based AIFM, to access the AIFMD distribution passport to EU investors. This has been a significant driver for the success of Luxembourg as a European hub for the structuring of AIFs. There is no reason to doubt that this trend, which has been sustained by the increasing success of the new RAIF regime, will continue.

---

5   European Commission, "VAT rates applied in the Member States of the European Union" (2018) available at: *https://ec.europa.eu/taxation_customs/sites/taxation/files/resources/documents/taxation/vat/how_vat_works/rates/vat_rates_en.pdf* [Accessed 26 September 2018].

# Mexico

## Berdeja Abogados, S.C.  Teófilo G. Berdeja Prieto[1]

## 1. MARKET OVERVIEW

In the past four years, the private equity industry in Mexico has seen an increasing level of deal activity, with financing available and a fair number of deals getting closed. Bank willingness to provide financing for leveraged buyouts continues to improve and liquidity in the market is coming from both traditional and non-traditional sources. A gradual improvement in the Mexican economy has been noticeable during such period. The current situation, combined with the traction being gained by structural reforms in telecommunications, energy and electricity, among others, opens up the way for significant opportunities for investment by private equity funds in Mexico.

### 1.1 Types of investors

The most common sources from which private equity funds obtain their funding in Mexico are corporations, individuals and banks. Pension funds, insurance companies and the government have, so far, a fairly limited participation as sources of funding since, under current regulations, the same can invest mainly in securities listed on the Mexican Stock Exchange.

### 1.2 Types of investments

Private equity funds invest for the most part in Mexico by way of minority investments in private or public companies. They have occasionally taken a majority position in private companies with a view towards restructuring the same and exiting the investment. In fewer instances, private equity funds have invested in start-up companies, management buyouts or buy-ins and public to private transactions.

In several instances, the above transactions have been leveraged.

## 2. FUNDS
### 2.1 Fund structures

In organising and operating an emerging markets fund, a private equity sponsor will typically consider—in addition to the risk profile of potential investments in the fund's target market—legal, tax and other factors.

There would appear to be three basic categories for a fund's level of presence in Mexico. There are, of course, several variations of the same. A first category would consist of the organisation of a fund outside Mexico, without any presence in Mexico. This may involve the private offering of participations in the fund to Mexican residents from outside Mexico.

[1] The author gratefully acknowledges the assistance of the following persons: Ivan Moguel Kuri and Marco Polo Carrillo Chávez (Chevez, Ruiz, Zamarripa y Cia).

Investors should be contacted on a one-to-one basis. The sale should be made on an unsolicited basis. The fund should not offer or sell the securities through a public offering in Mexico; a step that would trigger application of the regulatory framework for such offerings. Each potential investor should be previously identified and directly approached so that there are no mass communications. Care should be taken to domicile the fund in a jurisdiction which is not considered a tax haven under Mexican regulations. This may subject Mexican residents to special reporting requirements and rules to determine taxable income relating to investments in the fund.

A second category would involve a reduced presence of the manager of the fund, which would have employees in Mexico that can assist the manager in sourcing local deal opportunities for the fund and getting transaction approvals from the fund's investment committee, among other things. Under this category, the fund typically does not have investors in Mexico, will not be offered from Mexico to investors in other countries and will not invest in Mexican securities with a view to a distribution of the same. Under this category, it is advisable to incorporate a Mexican vehicle that will hire required employees and will interpose a separate entity between the manager of the fund, on the one hand, and Mexican corporations that will receive investments from the fund, on the other. This avoids an implication that either the manager or the fund has a permanent establishment in Mexico, which might subject them to Mexican taxes in respect to income attributable to Mexico. Care should be taken to make sure that the fund will underwrite transactions from abroad and that the Mexican vehicle will not be doing so on behalf of the fund in Mexico so as to avoid an implication that the Mexican vehicle would act as a permanent establishment of the fund in Mexico.

A third category would involve incorporation of a fund in Mexico. The best structure to be adopted would depend on a host of factors, including the investor base, relevant tax treaties and internal tax policies of Mexico at the time. Under Mexico's network of tax treaties, a foreign investor's capital gain is generally exempt from Mexican tax so long as the investor owns less than 25% of the Mexican company. Some funds deal with this by setting up multiple alternative investment vehicles and dividing fund limited partners among them to bring each vehicle's ownership below the applicable percentage. Others have organised a series of parallel funds from the outset, an approach that can be problematic in the event of default by investors in one of the parallel funds as the resulting reallocations can no longer be done within a single vehicle but instead require selling securities between the funds; a potential taxation event.

## 2.2 Regulation of fundraising and fund managers

The regulation of fundraising and fund managers is included in federal statutes and implementing regulations; mainly, the Securities Exchange Act 2005 (SEA).

Any securities subject to a public offering or intermediation are regulated securities under the SEA.

The SEA defines as a public offering that which is made in Mexican territory, through any means of mass communication and to an unspecified person, to subscribe, purchase, sell or transfer securities for any consideration (art.2-XVIII). A public offering subjects the issuer to the approval registration process of the SEA, which is intended to afford the investing public adequate safeguards and information concerning its investment decision. A public offering requires the previous approval of the National Banking and Securities Commission and the registration of the relevant securities with the National Securities Registry as a precondition for the listing of such securities with the Mexican Stock Exchange.

As long as fundraising for a private equity fund is conducted privately, it is not subject to the requirements established by the SEA for a public offering of securities.

The SEA provides a safe harbour to determine when an offering is private; as long as any of the following requirements is complied with: (1) it is made exclusively to institutional or qualified investors; (2) it consists of an offer of shares of a company, or equivalent securities, to less than 100 persons, regardless of whether there is one or several classes or series of shares; (3) it is made under a valid employee plan that grants employees of a company the right to hold shares of the company or the right to subscribe to a pro rata portion of a capital increase in the company or affiliates of the same; and (4) it is made to shareholders or members of institutions that conduct their activities primarily with the same (for example, a sports club) (art.8).

Trading of securities is regulated as "intermediation" under the SEA. Brokerage firms are the only entities authorised to act as fully fledged intermediaries under the SEA (art.2-XV). Other institutions may carry out certain intermediation activities. The rest of the public must conduct trading and other intermediation through brokerage firms.

The activities of the fund manager of a private equity fund do not involve intermediation with securities as long as the manager confines its activities to advising the fund as to how to administer its investments in portfolio corporations. The manager of a private equity fund does not need to be authorised by any financial services authority.

Under a separate article, the SEA establishes a number of requirements to be complied with by investment advisors. "Investment advisors" are defined as persons that render discretionary portfolio management services in a professional and regular capacity (art.225). Although investment advisors are not deemed to conduct intermediation with securities, the same are required to register with the National Banking and Securities Commission and comply with a number of requirements established under the SEA. A private equity fund manager should not fall within such a category as long as the manager advises only the private equity fund that it is managing and refrains from rendering portfolio management services to other persons.

### 2.3 Customary or common terms of funds

Customary terms of funds in Mexico track closely terms used for private equity funds internationally.

## 3. DEBT FINANCE

### 3.1 Means of financing

Traditional secured term loan facilities are generally available as a means to obtain financing. Both commercial and development banks are the types of institution that would typically provide such facilities.

The market for non-investment grade bonds in Mexico is almost non-existent, given the reluctance from investors to accept the high risk involved in issuances of such bonds and the various legal and regulatory impediments, such as restrictions on pension funds looking to purchase non-investment-grade bonds. Thus, the use of high-yield bonds as a means of financing for private equity vehicles is very limited in Mexico. However, Mexican regulators issued a relatively recent set of rules that allows private equity vehicles to raise capital from Mexican pension funds (*Sociedades de Inversión Especializada en Fondos para el Retiro*) through the issuance of securities denominated *Certificados de Capital de Desarrollo* (Development Capital Certificates or CKDs) and *Certificados Bursátiles Fiduciarios de Proyectos de Inversión* (Investment Project Trust Certificates or CerPIs) placed through the Mexican Stock Exchange.

CKDs are securities issued by trusts established by companies that wish to finance specific projects the profitability of which is linked to the underlying assets or activities of portfolio companies or projects, thus, the profitability of CKDs is linked to the success of the specific project or company to be financed as the issuer of CKDs is under no obligation to repay any amount as principal or interest. The issuance of CKDs may be structured to finance various projects or companies, or just one specific company or project. Currently, the issuance of CKDs does not require a credit rating by a rating agency. In an attempt to accommodate the concerns of the private equity industry, applicable regulations have set corporate governance and disclosure requirements that are not as strict as those applicable to publicly traded companies.

Securitisation, invoice discounting and structured finance in general are available as alternative means to obtain financing. However, in those instances where securitisation entails a public offering of securities, the costs associated with the regulatory regime required to implement the same (see s.2.2 above) can be substantial.

## 3.2   Restrictions on granting security

Generally, there are no prohibitions on financial assistance in Mexico as there are in other jurisdictions, that is, a Mexican target company may act as guarantor and provide security interests over its assets to financial institutions providing lending facilities to an acquirer of such a target company's shares. Mexican law contemplates security interests which may cover various rights and assets of the target company and provide certainty and flexibility to creditors. Such security interests include industrial mortgages (in essence, floating lien on the entire business unit of the mortgagor), guarantee trusts and pledges without transfer of possession. Certain limitations may apply to the granting of industrial mortgages. There is a line of thought in the sense that industrial mortgages are reserved to Mexican banks as such types of mortgage are regulated under the Credit Institutions Act 1990 (CIA) (art.67). However, the CIA does not restrict the granting of industrial mortgages to those granted for the benefit of Mexican banks. The principle of freedom of commercial contracts, recognised by Mexican law, supports the position that industrial mortgages can be established for the benefit of foreign financial institutions. Some state civil codes, such as the Civil Codes of the states of Mexico and Jalisco, expressly contemplate the possibility of granting mortgages over the entire business unit, similar to the industrial mortgage, for the benefit of any creditor, thus allowing the granting of such security interests to foreign financial institutions (Civil Code for the State of Mexico art.7.1100; Civil Code for the State of Jalisco art.2518).

Lenders should be mindful of bankruptcy provisions that allow a bankruptcy court to void security interests as fraudulent conveyances if the target company is declared insolvent generally within 270 calendar days after the granting of such security interests by the target company, as provided for under the Commercial Bankruptcy Act 2000 (CBA) (art.112).

A longer preference period, which may reach up to three years before the target company is declared insolvent, may be determined upon the occurrence of certain circumstances by the bankruptcy court.

### 3.3 Intercreditor issues

The ranking of the interests of providers of debt and equity finance will depend on the type of financial instruments used to structure the transaction. Generally, the equity instruments used in private equity transactions include common stock, preferred stock and stock options. Debt instruments generally include a combination of senior and subordinated bank loans. It is common to see hybrid instruments, including both debt and equity components, such as loans convertible into common or preferred stock.

Lenders will generally require a comprehensive security package from the acquirer and the target company. The security package will protect the lenders and provide priority over other creditors in an insolvency scenario. Senior loans will usually benefit from first ranking security interests and will have priority of repayment, while subordinated loans may benefit from second ranking security interests and will rank behind the senior loans in terms of priority of repayment. In an insolvency scenario, equity instrument holders will rank behind debt instrument holders in terms of repayment of its respective investments and common stock is typically the last among equity holders. Tax and labour obligations generally enjoy priority over both debt and equity holders.

In a typical transaction involving both debt and equity financing, there would be an intercreditor agreement regulating key issues such as priority of claims, enforcement of security interests, subordination on insolvency, permitted payments and amendments to agreements. The conflicting interests of debt and equity holders are also regulated by extensive covenants in loan agreements which generally protect lenders (e.g. prepayment events, financial ratios, negative pledges and change of control provisions), and the granting of protection rights to equity holders (e.g. pre-emptive rights, right of first refusal, tag-along and drag-along rights).

Provisions which limit the voting rights of equity holders should be reflected, to the extent possible, in the bylaws of the relevant company, as well as structured as events of default in the relevant agreements, so as to ensure enforceability of the same. This complies with the provision of Mexican corporate law which provides that, as a general rule, contract covenants which restrict the freedom of vote of shareholders should be included in the bylaws of the corporation (Business Corporations Act 1934 art.91-VI–VII). This is not a point of concern, however, in the case of a special type of corporation called investment promotion business corporation (*sociedad anónima promotora de inversion*), a transition vehicle that may be created to facilitate the transformation from a closely held corporation to a publicly held one, since such types of contract covenants are valid when stipulated among shareholders of the same (although such provisions are not valid vis-à-vis the corporation, unless enforcement of the same is mandated by a court order).

### 3.4   Syndication

Generally, when the loan amount in a transaction is above a certain level, arrangers and underwriters of debt financing will seek to syndicate the loan with other financial institutions. The legal documentation will include provisions to facilitate the syndication of the loan. An information memorandum will generally include investment considerations, a preliminary term sheet, an industry overview and financial information of the target company. Commitment letters will include provisions describing the type of syndication and the conditions under which the arrangers would effect syndication. Loan agreements will typically include provisions regulating the voting requirements for lenders to approve amendments or changes to the loan agreement. Finally, loan agreements will include provisions regarding secondary loan sales.

## 4.   EQUITY STRUCTURES
### 4.1   Role of management

Management due diligence in private equity transactions has become increasingly challenging in the current competitive deal market. A thorough management due diligence process can help determine the most effective way to align the economic interests of the private equity fund with those of the management of a portfolio company.

Management do not typically have board seats, although occasionally they do have the same. Employment agreements are relevant. However, such agreements are not as important as the actual terms of employment. The latter prevail over any written agreement by operation of law. This cannot be waived by party agreement. It is therefore of the essence to carefully review employment terms, including scope of work, terms of remuneration, social security registrations, the period of employment in the company that will give rise to seniority payment in the case of employment termination, accrued holidays, accrued and unpaid overtime etc.

Senior management would typically receive an equity participation in the portfolio company. This can be achieved in essence through shares, share options and/or an employee benefit trust. When granting such equity participation through shares or share options, it is advisable to grant the same through an agreement separate from the employment agreement. This allows for the structure of such an agreement as a commercial agreement that can provide, for example, for call rights of the private equity fund upon termination of employment with the portfolio company. A commercial agreement of this type would enhance enforceability of the same by the private equity fund, whilst call rights included in an employment agreement may be more difficult to enforce given the public policy provision of Mexican labour law which provides that an employee's rights cannot be waived by party agreement.

From a tax standpoint, the granting of an option, the exercise of an option or the acquisition of beneficiary rights under a trust are subject to income tax payable by the employee which can currently reach up to 35% where employees are placed in the highest income bracket. The most common approach is for management to purchase restricted shares or shares subject to vesting and call provisions.

### 4.2 Common protections for investors

Investors typically seek to protect their investment through super-majority requirements necessary to adopt certain key resolutions at the shareholders' or board of directors' levels. They also utilise information rights, drag-along rights, tag-along rights, put and call rights, or call and reverse call rights.

All protections of this type, relating to voting rights, should be included in the bylaws of the portfolio company. Otherwise, as discussed before, the same may be unenforceable if left exclusively as a covenant in a party agreement (see s.3.3 above).

### 4.3 Common protections for management

The fundamental protections for management are found in their actual terms of employment, employment agreements and equity participation in the portfolio company, if applicable. Management would not normally enjoy board seats, veto rights, tag-along rights or drag-along rights, although occasionally they may do so.

### 4.4 Management warranties

Management warranties are fairly unusual in private equity investments in Mexico. The fundamental reason is that, as a general rule, an employee may not be made subject to additional responsibilities that go beyond adequate performance of its employment duties. Warranties are normally sought from the sellers of a target company or from a portfolio company and the majority shareholders of the same.

### 4.5 Good leaver/bad leaver provisions

Where management participates in the equity in the portfolio company, it is advisable to execute an agreement, separate from the employment agreement, pursuant to which shares are subject to call rights from majority shareholders which can be exercised at any time. In practice, such rights would be exercised at the time an employee would leave the company, should majority shareholders wish to do so. The reasons for a separate agreement are summarised in s.4.1 above.

### 4.6 Public to private transactions

It is not common for private equity funds to make offers for public companies in Mexico. However, there are a few instances in which such transactions have been carried out.

The fundamental issue involved in this type of transaction is the mandatory requirement that a tender offer be launched by the acquirer of 30% or more of a listed company as well as the subsequent requirement, which applies in conjunction with the delisting of a company, to set up a trust for a period of six months after the delisting of the company, during which shareholders of the target company will be able to sell their shares to the trustee at the same price of the tender offer (SEA arts 98, 108).

Other issues are the terms of the consulting agreement, if any, to be executed with the fund, the structure of contractually mandated nomination rights, the disposal (or simplification) of anti-takeover provisions, the simplification of board committees and the revision of existing corporate governance rules to adjust the same to the new reality of the company.

Public to private deals can be beneficial to all parties involved. Public shareholders get immediate liquidity and management teams, in some instances, may retain significant equity stakes in the ongoing success of their companies.

## 5.  EXITS
### 5.1  Secondary sales

Although not a common exit alternative, private equity investors do participate in the secondary market for the sale of partnership interests in Mexican private equity funds. Investors in private equity funds may sell partnership interests before the end of the period originally envisaged for their investment for a variety of strategic and financial reasons, including the need for liquidity and reduction of overall exposure to private equity assets. Investors in Mexican private equity funds are predominantly foreign institutional investors (i.e. pension and insurance funds, financial institutions etc), although highly capitalised investors also have a relevant participation.

There are certain legal considerations involved in the sale of partnership interests by limited partners (investors) in the secondary market, affecting the fund and particularly the general partner (private equity firm). If the fund documents grant a right of first refusal to limited partners with respect to transfers of limited partnership interests in the fund, the general partner may be under the obligation to provide right of first refusal notices to the limited partners and provide guidance to them on the process; alternatively, the general partner may collaborate with the prospective seller and buyer to obtain waivers to such a right from the other limited partners. If the right of first refusal is exercised by one or more limited partners, the general partner and the limited partners will have to negotiate the division of the partnership interest among the various buyers.

### 5.2  Trade sales

Private equity funds in Mexico typically exit their investment through trade sales, particularly via selling equity share participations in portfolio companies to strategic buyers. Generally, strategic buyers are foreign companies interested in entering the Mexican market or larger local companies wishing to expand their market share. The legal provisions associated with this exit alternative are tag-along and drag-along rights, put and call rights, or call and reverse call rights.

Private equity funds also exit their investments by selling back the shares to the company or the original shareholders through negotiated sales or, as mentioned before, through the use of put option agreements. However, portfolio companies are often reluctant to accept put option provisions so this exit alternative is not as common as sales to strategic buyers.

## 5.3  Initial public offerings

The capital market in Mexico is small and particularly focused on large well-established companies: although initial public offerings (IPOs) represent an exit alternative to private equity funds, they are not often used as an exit option in practice. The costs involved in taking a company public, as well as those related to corporate governance and transparency obligations, are also seen by investors as factors that induce them to consider other exit alternatives.

Mexican portfolio companies may conduct a local or an international IPO. In Mexico, companies may sell their stock to the general public through a public offering on the Mexican Stock Exchange (see s.2.2 above). Mexican portfolio companies may also be taken public in foreign markets, especially when investors in the corresponding private equity fund are well-known institutional investors in the jurisdiction where the IPO is intended to take place. Given the fact that portfolio companies are in many instances exporters with strong links to the US, transaction documents often provide for a right of the fund to list the Mexican company in US public markets. Alternatively, Mexican portfolio companies may establish a US holding company which may conduct an IPO directly on a US public market.

Transaction documents may include lock-up period provisions requiring certain stockholders to temporarily waive their right to sell their shares after an IPO. Such stockholders may include strategic partners, management and directors of the portfolio company. Such provisions may be coupled with a trust established on the relevant shares as a means to ensure enforcement of lock-up provisions.

## 5.4  Refinancings

Although not a common exit strategy, private equity funds may recoup all or part of their investments in portfolio companies through the replacement of all or a significant part of the original acquisition financing before its scheduled final maturity date. Refinancing debt may be used to repay any kind of investor debt or to fund a reduction of share capital and other distributions to shareholders. This type of refinancing would generally take place when the target company business has grown to the extent that it can bear the increased debt burden and reduction of share capital derived from the refinancing.

Typically, the original acquisition financing documents would include provisions restricting the ability to incur new indebtedness. The various providers of the original acquisition financing would have different interests and expectations to be managed in a refinancing. Senior lenders would be more inclined to approve the incurrence of additional debt than junior debt holders that may see additional debt obligations ranking ahead of their own claims.

There would be certain costs involved in completing a refinancing, such as prepayment fees, new arrangement fees, hedging break costs and due diligence costs, particularly if new lenders are not acquainted with the borrower and the business of the portfolio company. Finally, borrowers and equity investors would try to negotiate more flexible covenants and to provide fewer guarantees and security interests than those provided for in the original financing transaction documents.

## 5.5   Restructuring/insolvency

Private equity investors would only have a residual claim in the event of an involuntary exit derived from bankruptcy proceedings resulting in the liquidation of a portfolio company. Holders of preferred stock generally enjoy a liquidation preference so that, upon liquidation, merger or sale, they are entitled to reimbursement of their shares before any payment is made to holders of common stock. However, holders of both preferred and common stock shall be entitled to reimbursement of their contribution only after all debt creditors have been repaid in full. Private equity investors would often request the issuance of preferred stock convertible into common stock at any time at the request of the instrument holder at a specified price per share. It is common to see hybrid instruments in private equity transactions such as loans convertible into common or preferred stock.

Anticipating restructuring scenarios, private equity investors typically request pre-emptive rights and right of first refusal provisions to protect themselves from dilution, should new investors be brought in, or from unwanted shareholders, should other existing shareholders offer their shares to a third party. Preferred stock holders would generally request the right to vote as a class, separately from common stock holders, in relevant issues such as mergers, acquisitions and changes of control.

## 6.   TAX
### 6.1   Taxation of fund structures
**Mexican legal entity as vehicle for private equity fund**

Legal entities resident in Mexico are subject to income tax at a rate of 30% with respect to all income obtained regardless of the location of the source of wealth from which such income derives.

The income tax basis named "taxable result" is computed by reducing taxable income (including capital gains, which comprise, among others, those related to shares listed in the Mexican Stock Exchange) by giving effect to deductible items, which in general include necessary expenses, depreciation and amortisation of fixed assets and intangible assets as well as the cost of sales and employees' profit sharing paid (discussed below).

Net operative losses calculated by taxpayers in a tax year can be offset in the following 10 years, until full utilisation.

The Mexican Income Tax Act 2013 does not provide a specific regime for capital gains, since said income is part of the general taxable base (taxable result).

Nevertheless, there are certain specific rules that limit the deduction of capital losses (i.e. losses on the sale of shares) against capital gains obtained from such sales.

Mexican tax regulations include transfer pricing rules based on an "arm's length" principle and the utilisation of comparables.

In the event that non-resident pension and retirement funds are shareholders of Mexican legal entities which obtain at least 90% of their income from the sale or lease of immovable property situated in Mexico and from the sale of shares the value of which derives in more than 50% from immovable property located in Mexico, such Mexican legal entities will be exempt from income tax purposes, in the proportion that the non-resident pension and retirement funds participate in said Mexican legal entities, provided they meet certain requirements contained in tax laws.

In addition, Mexican law establishes an obligation for legal entities to pay 10% of yearly taxable profits to their employees (this mandatory profit sharing is known as PTU per its acronym in Spanish).

Mexican legal entities are obliged to determine a tax account for control purposes named net-after-tax-profit account (CUFIN per its acronym in Spanish), which includes profits (netted from income tax) in respect to which income tax has already been paid at the corporate level. The main purpose of such an account is to allow profits that are distributed as dividends arising from said account not to pay additional income tax at the corporate level.

Any dividend distributed exceeding the referred account, that is, arising from profits not taxed yet, would be taxed at a corporate level on a grossed-up basis (42.86% rate). Mexican resident legal entities are entitled to credit the referred income tax paid against their own income tax due in the same year or against that payable within the following two years.

Starting in 2014, dividends paid by a Mexican legal entity to a foreign resident or to a Mexican individual resident are subject to a 10% income tax withholding. Such withholding tax applies only to profits generated beginning in 2014. For these purposes, Mexican legal entities are obligated to keep a CUFIN account starting in December 2013 and create a new CUFIN account starting in 2014.

For investment stimulus purposes, so-called Temporary Validity Provisions of the Mexican Income Tax Act provide that Mexican legal entities may apply a tax credit equal to the 1%, 2% or 5% of distributed dividends or profits generated in the tax years 2014, 2015 and 2016, provided that the dividends or profits are distributed to Mexican individual residents in tax years 2017, 2018, 2019 and onwards, respectively. Therefore, the effective applicable withholding tax rate for dividends or profits distributed in tax year 2017 equals 9%, for tax year 2018 equals 8% and finally for 2019 and onwards equals 5%.

## Foreign resident entity as vehicle for private equity fund

Foreign resident entities that have a fixed place of business in Mexico through which they carry out business activities are deemed to have a permanent establishment in Mexico.

A foreign resident with a permanent establishment in Mexico will be subject to income tax on the same terms and with the same obligations as those of an ordinary Mexican legal entity, with respect to income attributable thereto.

Accordingly, if a foreign resident entity incorporated as a vehicle for a fund has a fixed place of business in Mexico, it may have a permanent establishment exposure in Mexico, thus being subject to the income tax obligations referred to in the subsection titled "Mexican legal entity as vehicle for private equity fund" above.

The 10% income tax required to be withheld from dividend distributions also applies to distributions made by permanent establishments in Mexico to their head office or to another permanent establishment.

### Foreign resident investors

In general terms, foreign residents are subject to income tax in Mexico on income obtained in cash, goods, services or credit arising from sources of income located within Mexican territory.

The circumstances that give rise to a source of income located in Mexico and the applicable income tax depend on the type of income obtained by foreign residents. As a general rule, income tax is withheld by the person who makes a payment deemed as taxable income, when it qualifies as a Mexican resident.

Non-resident pension and retirement funds are exempt from income tax purposes in Mexico with respect to income arising from interest, capital gains and leasing real estate situated in Mexico, as long as they fulfil a series of requirements provided in Mexican regulations, such as being exempt for income tax purposes under the law of its country of residence.

### Capital gains

Foreign residents are subject to income tax on the sale of shares or securities representing title to property when: (1) a Mexican resident is the issuer; or (2) more than 50% of the book value of the shares or securities arise directly or indirectly from real estate located in Mexico, regardless of the place of residence of the issuer.

Income tax is determined by applying a 25% rate on the gross amount of the transaction or 35% on the net profit (income reduced by the adjusted tax cost basis of the shares or securities), subject to fulfilment of certain requirements.

However, a reduced 10% rate shall apply to the sale of shares traded on the Mexican Stock Exchange, provided that the sale is made in such a market and the investor does not sell 10% or more of the shares representing the capital stock of the issuer, through one or several transactions within a 24-month period. The corresponding tax shall be withheld by the Mexican broker-dealer involved in the transaction.

Mexico has entered into over 50 treaties to avoid double taxation with other countries, which contain rules that may reduce or eliminate the tax impact on the sale of shares or securities.

In general terms, tax treaties entered by Mexico exempt the gain arising from the sale of shares issued by Mexican companies, provided the seller held a participation of less than 25% of the issuer during a 12-month period preceding such a sale, to the extent the book value of the shares is not arising from the ownership of Mexican real estate.

Under Mexican tax law, even though a sale of shares deriving from a corporate restructuring triggers income tax, if a particular ruling from the Mexican tax authorities is obtained before the corporate restructuring, the payment of such tax is deferred until a future sale of shares out of the relevant corporate group takes place. Under some tax treaties, payment of such tax is altogether dispensed with.

The sale of immovable property situated in Mexico is also taxable in Mexico either by applying a 25% rate on the gross amount of the transaction without deductions or a 35% rate on net gains, provided certain requirements are met.

### Services

Income obtained by foreign residents for rendering independent services is subject to income tax in Mexico when the services are provided in the country. Income tax is levied at a 25% rate applicable to gross income, without any deduction.

However, this type of income generally falls within the scope of the "business profits" provision contained in tax treaties entered into by Mexico, thus being exempt from income tax, except for income considered as a royalty.

### Dividends

As discussed above, dividends paid by Mexican resident entities to foreign residents are subject to a 10% income tax withholding. Such withholding tax applies only to profits generated beginning 2014.

### Interest

The treatment of interest payments is discussed in s.6.4 below.

### Mexican resident investors

In general, Mexican resident investors, either legal entities or individuals, are subject to income tax with respect to any worldwide income obtained: payments received from capital gains, interest (reduced by inflationary effects) and services, among others, are taxable.

Mexican legal entities are subject to a 30% corporate income tax rate and Mexican individuals are subject to a rate that reaches 35% when placed in the highest income bracket.

Dividends received by a Mexican legal entity paid by another Mexican legal entity are not deemed taxable income and, consequently, are not subject to any type of income tax withholding in Mexico.

In the event that dividends are paid to Mexican individual shareholders, those amounts will be considered taxable income and, as discussed above, are subject to an additional 10% income tax withholding whenever the distribution corresponds to profits generated on or after 2014.[2] Such Mexican individual shareholders can claim a credit equivalent only to the income tax

---

[2] As mentioned before, Mexican legal entities may apply a tax credit equal to the 1%, 2% or 5% of distributed dividends or profits generated in the tax years 2014, 2015 and 2016, provided that the dividends or profits are distributed to Mexican individual residents in tax years 2017, 2018, 2019 and onwards, respectively. Therefore, the effective applicable withholding tax rate for dividends or profits distributed in tax year 2017 equals 9%, for tax year 2018 equals 8% and finally for 2019 and onwards equals 5%.

paid at the corporate level by the company that paid the dividend. However, the additional 10% tax withheld, if applicable, is deemed a non-creditable tax.

As a result, Mexican resident individuals may be required to pay additional income tax in respect to dividends received since they are subject to a tax rate that may reach 35%, depending on their income level, while only being able to credit the corporate income tax paid (at a 30% rate) by the entity distributing the dividends. As mentioned above, the determination of a suitable structure for a private equity fund in Mexico is related to the activities to be undertaken, the nature of the investors and the exit alternatives.

Consequently, a case-by-case analysis should be made before deciding the structure of a fund (see s.2.1 above).

### 6.2 Carried interest

Under Mexican law, any amount paid by a Mexican resident entity that is regarded as a participation in the taxpayer's profits, or that is conditioned upon the generation of profits, is deemed a non-deductible item for income tax purposes.

As a general rule, any payment falling under the concept of "carried interest" that is structured in such a way that is related to the profits of the entity making the payment will be regarded as a non-deductible item.

In view of the aforementioned restriction, these types of payments are usually structured in Mexico as service payments, the determination of which is based upon formulas that are not directly related to the entities' profits.

In general terms, residents abroad or individual residents in Mexico who obtain this kind of income shall be subject to income tax on the gross income received. The tax is levied through withholding at a rate of up to 40%, which may vary depending on the legal nature of the recipient and the amount of income earned.

It is advisable to review both the nature of the payment and the country of residence of the beneficiary in order to determine whether it would be possible to claim the benefits contained in any of the tax treaties entered into by Mexico.

### 6.3 Management equity

The granting of options by a Mexican resident entity employer, or by a related party, to its employees residing either in Mexico or abroad, in order to acquire shares or securities that represent the ownership of goods issued by the employer or a related party at no cost or at a cost lower than the market value of the shares, is deemed salary income.

The income is determined by considering the difference between the fair market value of the shares or securities representing the ownership of goods as of the date on which the acquisition option is exercised by the employee and the price agreed upon the granting of said option. The tax is levied at a rate of up to 35%, which varies depending on the level of income of the taxpayer.

### 6.4 Loan interest

For income tax purposes, Mexican resident entities are entitled to deduct interest payments made by the same, without any adjustments, provided certain requirements are met. The proceeds from a loan must be invested in the business's purposes, certain capitalisation rules must be observed, the interest rate and other loan conditions must be consistent with fair market conditions and the required tax withholdings must be complied with, among others.

The decision to provide funding to a Mexican vehicle through debt or equity is complex since the benefit of deducting interest accrued is limited by the following factors: (1) Mexican tax law considers the inflationary effects related to debts and credits granted to the taxpayer, which implies from an economic standpoint that only real interest (reduced by inflation) is deductible; and (2) foreign exchange effects on capital taken as a loan in foreign currency are treated as interest.

Foreign residents that receive interest payments on loans granted to Mexican legal entities are subject to payment of income tax in Mexico. Withholding must be carried out by the payer by applying rates that range from 4.9% (applicable to foreign banks located in a country with which Mexico has entered into a tax treaty) to 40% (applicable to related parties whose income is subject to a preferential tax regime—in essence, tax haven countries). Such rates are levied on the gross amount of interest paid by the Mexican resident, without any deduction.

The applicable tax rate depends on the nature of the loan that gives rise to the payment of interest, the payer as well as the person that is the effective beneficiary of the payments.

Tax treaties entered into by Mexico establish a reduced withholding tax rate on interest paid abroad, which generally is 5% of interest paid to banks and ranges from 10% to 15% of interest paid to other recipients, which most of the time represents a significant reduction over the rate applicable in respect to residents of countries with whom a treaty has not been executed.

## 6.5 Transaction taxes

In Mexico, there are three principal transaction taxes. The value added tax established in respect to sales of goods, the rendering of independent services, the granting of the use or temporary enjoyment of goods and the importation of goods or services that takes place in Mexico, levied at a general tax rate of 16%. A special tax on production and services is imposed on the sale and importation of certain items, including alcohol, alcoholic beverages, sugar-based beverages, high caloric value food, fossil fuels, pesticides, cigarettes, petrol and diesel as well as gambling, raffling and telecommunications activities. The tax rate varies depending on the type of product or service involved. There is a local tax, named real estate transfer tax, which taxes individuals and legal entities that acquire real estate located in Mexico at a rate that does not exceed 5% generally, over the higher of the recorded value, the appraisal value of the property or the value of the transaction.

# 7.   CURRENT TOPICAL ISSUES/TRENDS

As mentioned before, new deals are being structured and debt funding for the same is gradually becoming available again.

Exits, although still limited, are being achieved through combinations of IPOs, secondary sales and trade sales. Significant opportunities are becoming available for investment by interested private equity funds.

The prospects for fundraising and deal-doing are clearly increasing.

The most recent relevant regulatory changes occurred when the Mexican President signed into law new telecommunications, energy, electricity and fintech laws, which create significant opportunities for investment by private equity funds (for a summary of the amendments, see: Berdeja Abogados, S.C., "*Client Update: Telecommunications Reform Implementation*" available at: *http://berdeja.com.mx/memos/Memo-Telecommunications-Implementation.pdf*; Berdeja Abogados, S.C., "*Implementation Energy Reform*" available at: *http://berdeja.com.mx/memos/implementation-energy-reform.pdf*; Berdeja Abogados, S.C., "*Planning Ahead: Progress in Implementation of Mexican New Electricity Market*" (2016) available at: *http://berdeja.com.mx/memos/Mexican_New_Electricity_Market.April.19.16.pdf*; Berdeja Abogados, S.C., "*Client Update: Mexican President Submits Bill For Fintech Act to Congress*" (2017) available at: *http://berdeja.com.mx/memos/ Mexican_President_Submits_Draft_FinTech_Act_to_Congress.NOV6B.17.pdf* [All accessed 18 September 2018]).

Implementing regulations relating to the above-mentioned laws are in the process of being prepared at a rapid pace.

# The Netherlands

**Loyens & Loeff NV** Bas Vletter, Joep Ottervanger, Mark van Dam & Marco de Lignie[1]

## 1. MARKET OVERVIEW
### 1.1 Types of investors

The information in this chapter has been derived from *Ondernemend Vermogen*, the Dutch private equity and venture capital market in 2017 (a report about the Dutch private equity market in 2017) by the Dutch Private Equity and Venture Capital Association (*Nederlandse Vereniging van Participatiemaatschappijen*) (NVP).

2017 has been a strong year for the Dutch private equity and venture capital market, with EUR 4.4 billion in total raised funds, EUR 514 million of which was raised for venture capital and EUR 3.9 billion was raised for private equity, mainly obtained from:

- individuals and family offices (EUR 539 million, forming 12.25% of total private equity investments);
- banks (EUR 238 million, 5.41%);
- funds of funds (EUR 1.272 billion, 28.9%);
- pension funds (EUR 1.152 billion, 26.19%);
- academic institutions (EUR 25 million, 0.57%);
- insurance companies (EUR 240 million, 5.45%);
- public sector (EUR 158 million, 3.58%);
- sovereign wealth funds (EUR 195 million, 4.43%);
- other asset managers (EUR 72 million, 1.64%);
- corporate investors (38 million, 0.85%);
- endowments and foundations (232 million, 5.27%); and
- others (EUR 16.8 million, 0.38%).

### 1.1 Types of investments

In 2017, typical transactions in which Dutch and foreign private equity funds invested in the Netherlands were buyouts (68% of total private equity investments), early-stage financing (0.68%), start-up financing (3.91%), later-stage financing (3.42%), growth (10.27%) and other transactions such as replacement capital (13.58%). These percentages and the following numbers refer to the investments of these private equity funds in Dutch companies.

In 2017, Dutch and foreign private equity funds invested EUR 2.7 billion in buyouts, a decrease of approximately 3.6% from the EUR 2.8 billion invested in 2016. The number of realised buyouts in 2017 (92) is the highest since 2007. A large number of the 92 realised buyouts by Dutch and foreign

---

[1] This chapter was originally written by Bas Vletter, Joep Ottervanger, Mark van Dam and Marco de Lignie and has been updated by Mark van Dam and Milad Feroegh.

private equity funds in the Netherlands (42) involved an investment in small and medium-sized enterprises (SMEs) with a maximum investment amount of EUR 15 million. The total number of buyouts involving an investment of EUR 15 million up to EUR 50 million was 49, which is an increase of 19 compared to the peak in 2007 (30).

Investments in venture capital have reached record highs, with a total of 233 investments and a total amount of EUR 320 million invested in 2017, compared to a maximum of EUR 212 million in previous years.

Lastly, the market for replacement capital financing shows an increase with investments amounting to EUR 543 million in 2017, compared to 289 million in 2016. For the avoidance of doubt, it is noted that these figures do not include any investments by or in (private equity) real estate funds.

## 2. FUNDS
### 2.1 Fund structures
In the Netherlands, vehicles for private equity funds are usually structured as:

- a limited partnership (*commanditaire vennootschap*—CV);
- a private limited liability company (*besloten vennootschap met beperkte aansprakelijkheid*—BV);
- a public limited liability company (*naamloze vennootschap*—NV);
- a Dutch fund for mutual account (*fonds voor gemene rekening*—FGR);
- a co-operative (*coöperatie*); or
- a combination of the above.

### 2.2 Regulation of fundraising and fund managers
**Authorisation**

Following the implementation of the Directive 2011/61 on Alternative Investment Fund Managers and amending Directives 2003/41 and 2009/65 and Regulations 1060/2009 and 1095/2010 [2011] OJ L174/1 (AIFMD) in the Netherlands, the management or marketing of private equity funds in the Netherlands by "large" managers, i.e. managers which, directly or indirectly, manage portfolios of private equity funds whose assets under management amount to EUR 500 million or, when open ended or leveraged, EUR 100 million (the threshold) or more, triggers an authorisation requirement in the Netherlands, with the following exceptions:

- non-European Economic Area (EEA) based managers are able to continue managing and marketing their funds, absent Dutch authorisation, which under the AIFMD is still possible, subject to compliance with the Dutch national placement regime;
- EEA-based managers may, when authorised in their home state, manage or market their funds in the Netherlands subject to compliance with the passporting conditions as introduced by the AIFMD (as implemented in the Netherlands); and
- the management of intra-group or captive funds is not captured by the authorisation requirement in the Netherlands provided the conditions of the AIFMD are complied with.

A manager is deemed to manage a private equity fund in the Netherlands if it is established in the Netherlands or if the fund managed by it is established in the Netherlands.

The term "fund" as used above corresponds with the notion of an alternative investment fund (AIF) as used in the AIFMD by means of an incorporation by reference to art.4 of the AIFMD.

### Sub-threshold managers

Sub-threshold managers established in the Netherlands may voluntarily apply for authorisation in the Netherlands, provided they comply with the AIFMD requirements (as implemented into Dutch law) in their entirety.

Alternatively, Dutch sub-threshold managers may manage and market their funds without Dutch authorisation in the Netherlands, provided that:

- the sub-threshold manager manages portfolios whose assets under management in total do not exceed a threshold of EUR 100 million or, if the fund is unleveraged and there are no redemption or repayment rights exercisable with respect to interests in the fund during a period of 5 years, EUR 500 million;
- the fund's units or shares (limited partnership interests) are exclusively offered:
    — to professional investors within the meaning of s.1:1 of the Dutch Act on the Financial Supervision 2006 (*Wet op het financieel toezicht*—AFS) (e.g. banks, insurers, pension funds, brokers, fund managers, funds or qualifying large corporations); or
    — the fund's units or shares are offered to fewer than 150 persons or have a nominal value of, or are offered for a consideration payable per investor of, at least EUR 100,000 and provided a banner or selling legend as to the fund manager's unregulated status (in a predefined size and layout) is printed on the fund's offering documents; and
- the relevant sub-threshold manager is registered with the Dutch competent authority, the Financial Markets Authority (*Autoriteit Financiële Markten*—AFM).

The aim of said registration is to ensure that the AFM can assess whether or not the sub-threshold regime is legitimately relied upon and to effectively monitor any build-up of systemic risks. Dutch sub-threshold managers are due to disclose to the AFM, amongst others, information on the main instruments in which the funds are trading, on the principal exposures and on the most important concentration of the funds managed.

Finally, it is noted that, considering that funds making private equity investments are not excluded from the scope of the venture capital regulation (Regulation 345/2013 on European venture capital funds [2013] OJ L115/1—EuVECA), EU-based managers of (EU) funds which comply with the conditions of the EuVECA may benefit from a passport as introduced therein for the marketing of units or shares to potential investors that are, or on request may be, treated as professional clients (within the meaning of Directive 2014/65 on markets in financial instruments and amending Directive 2002/92 and Directive 2011/61 [2014] OJ L173/349—MiFID II) or to investors investing at least EUR 100,000 on the condition that they have confirmed their awareness of the risks associated with their investment. As per March 2018, the EuVECA has been revised so as to broaden the qualifying investments to any company that has fewer than 499 employees, making the EuVECA registration a very attractive alternative to an AIFMD license, provided a manager can comply with its requirements.

Note that the Dutch legalisation implementing the AIFMD does not permit other European sub-threshold managers to manage Dutch funds or market in the Netherlands. As a consequence, Dutch sub-threshold managers are also barred from marketing Dutch funds in certain countries (particularly Germany).

### Dutch national placement regime

Non-EEA-based managers may manage and market their funds, absent Dutch authorisation, in the Netherlands subject to compliance with the transparency requirement of the AIFMD as implemented into Dutch law, notably the pre-investment disclosures as set out in art.23 of the AIFMD, provided that:

- the fund's units or shares are exclusively offered to qualified investors (i.e. a professional investor or eligible counterparty unless it opted not to be treated as a professional investor in accordance with MiFID II or an investor which opted to be treated as a professional investor in accordance with MiFID II) and provided a selling legend is included in the fund's offering documents;
- the country where the manager is located is not listed on the Financial Action Task Force (FATF) list of non-co-operative countries;
- an agreement between the AFM and the local supervisor of the manager providing for the exchange of information is in place; and
- a notification is made to the AFM by filling out a notification form of the AFM; pursuant to the notification form, an attestation must be included from the home state regulator, confirming that it will effectively comply with the co-operation agreement between it and the AFM.

Authorised EEA-based managers may market their non-EEA funds in the Netherlands subject to full compliance with the operating conditions and organisational requirements of the AIFMD, including the depositary requirement, as implemented into applicable law, provided:

- the fund's units or shares are exclusively offered to qualified investors (i.e. a professional investor or eligible counterparty, unless it opted not to be treated as a professional investor in accordance with MiFID II, or an investor which opted to be treated as a professional investor in accordance with MiFID II);
- the country where the fund is located is not listed on the FATF list of non-co-operative countries; and
- an agreement between the local supervisory authority of the manager and the local supervisory authority of the state where the fund is established has been concluded on the exchange of information.

### Passport for non-European Economic Area managers and funds

The passport for the marketing by non-EEA managers of their funds, or by EEA managers of their non-EEA funds (such to include EEA feeder funds of non-EEA master funds), in the Netherlands is not yet available.

## Grandfathering

In light of the introduction of the AIFMD, certain grandfathering provisions were agreed upon among Member States to ensure that certain existing funds would not be captured by the AIFMD.

A grandfathering provision that is typically relevant for private equity funds is that managers of closed-ended funds which do not make "additional investments" (limited financial injections arising out of existing commitments or investments, and only to the extent that they represent a negligible percentage of the fund's portfolio and are aimed to preserve or maintain the value of the portfolio, may be disregarded) after 22 July 2013 may continue to manage these funds in the Netherlands without Dutch authorisation.

With the passage of time, this grandfathering provision becomes less and less important, although there are still some funds that rely on it.

## Retail top-up

The Netherlands has implemented the Member States' option of the AIFMD to allow AIFMD-authorised managers to manage or market funds that are open to retail investors on the condition that stricter requirements apply to the business operations, disclosures to investors and regulatory authorities, the depositary and the treatment of investors.

## 2.3 Customary or common terms of funds

The terms used for Dutch private equity and/or venture capital funds (or for funds marketed in the Netherlands) mostly conform to UK-style private equity customary terms, including in particular:

- terms of 8–12 years during which no redemption rights are exercisable by investors (three–five-year investment period);
- a capital first distribution model (20/80% split of net proceeds, taking into account an 8% preferred return and a usually full catch up);
- clawback obligation for the manager in relation to "excess" carried interest (usually supported by an escrow arrangement with the escrow account being an account in the name of the fund and not with an escrow agent);
- management fees ranging usually from 1% to 2% over commitments (with a step down to invested capital after the investment period);
- key man: an automatic suspension or termination of the investment period following the departure of one or more key members of the management team (usually subject to replacement arrangement);
- for cause removal of the manager/management team with usually simple majority of the investors' by commitment;
- not-for-cause removal of the manager/management team with usually 75–85% of the investors' by commitment;
- at least 1% co-investment by the manager/management team;
- reinvestment options are generally limited to investments realised within 12 months and/or amounts drawn for management fee and costs and expenses;
- transaction fees are generally fully offset against management fees;
- exclusivity arrangements vary but usually stipulate that successor funds cannot be launched before at least 70% of the commitments are invested,

committed, reserved or expended;

- investor representation on the fund's advisory board (advisory board deals among others with conflicts or potential conflicts of interests);
- liability of investors is limited to their committed capital to the fund (subject to a limited partner give back);
- give-back obligations of investors limited in time; and
- International Financial Reporting Standards or Dutch Generally Accepted Accounting Principles (annual valuation and reporting mostly conforms to Invest Europe principles).

## 3. DEBT FINANCE
### 3.1 Means of financing

Among the means by which private equity backed vehicles obtain financing for making investments other than through a traditional secured term loan facility (senior, junior, mezzanine debt) are vendor loans and earn-outs. Vendor loans form part of the purchase price as a result of which the vendor becomes a creditor of the purchaser. The issues in connection with vendor loans are based on the correlation between any such vendor loans and the loans provided by the banks. Typically, questions arise as to what the interest rate on the vendor loans in comparison with the loans of the banks may amount to, when the vendor loans can be repaid and whether they may be repaid prior to repaying the loans of the banks.

Even though an earn-out is more often used to bridge the gap between the valuation of the company by the vendor and the valuation of the company by the purchaser, it is sometimes also used as an alternative means of financing, where the purchaser is allowed to settle the purchase price over an extended period of time.

### 3.2 Restrictions on granting security

As a consequence of the implementation of the AIFMD, alternative investment fund managers (AIFMs) may not facilitate, support or instruct any portfolio company to engage in asset-stripping before the end of the period expiring 24 months following acquisition of control, provided that the portfolio company is within the scope of the asset-stripping prohibition (which is not the case if the portfolio company is, for instance, a real estate special purpose vehicle or a SME). However, the effects of the asset-stripping prohibition as it now stands may currently be parried by structures that were commonly used to parry financial assistance in the past:

- a bridge/take-out structure. Using this structure, the acquirer takes out a loan to buy the target. Debt is pushed down as the target takes out a loan to make loans to the acquirer. Subsequently, the acquirer uses the upstream loan to repay its own loan. Once the aforementioned 24-month period has lapsed, the asset-stripping prohibition no longer applies and distributions that were within the scope of prohibition can be made to the acquirer to settle the upstream loan; and
- a legal merger between target and acquirer.

In addition, the Dutch Civil Code provides that any dividend distribution by a private limited liability company, regardless of the way such distribution is financed, may only be approved by the board of directors of the company if they know or reasonably should have anticipated that the company would not be able to meet its (future) obligations. Also, the recipient of such distribution that knew or should have reasonably anticipated that such distribution would result in the company failing to meet its (future) obligations is required to return the distribution.

### 3.3 Intercreditor issues

Generally, the company's creditors (and therefore also debt providers) have priority over the shareholders. Shareholders are the ultimate residual claimants. Preferred shareholders are repaid before the ordinary shareholders. However, it is often contractually provided that shareholder loans and holders of preferred shares rank equally and without preference.

Debt providers often require security in the form of a right of pledges on shares, receivables, stock and other assets. Banks usually require subordination of the other debt providers. Therefore, intercreditor agreements are concluded where the priority of payment of all debt providers is set out. In addition, a multi-layered corporate structure is often designed to result in structural subordination of the non-bank debt provider.

### 3.4 Syndication

In the majority of private equity investments in the Netherlands, private equity funds do not syndicate their investments. Recently, however, co-investments and club deals are on the increase, in part as some large institutional fund investors seem keen on pushing down effective fund management fees by engaging in co-investments.

## 4.  EQUITY STRUCTURES
### 4.1  Role of management

Management is frequently offered an equity interest in the buyer. Equity interests give management a greater feeling of co-ownership of the company and form an incentive for managers to perform well. Usually, management will participate on beneficial term (with a so-called envy factor). It is customary that management also co-invests (in order to provide skin in the game).

In addition, management usually enters into (or continues) an employment arrangement with the target or the buyer (through either an employment agreement or a service agreement). To protect the investor's interest, the following clauses are typically part of the arrangement: non-compete; non-solicitation; and confidentiality. Furthermore, the early voluntary termination by a manager of its employment arrangement with the target usually has an impact on the manager's equity stake.

The latter arrangement is normally included in the shareholders' agreement, which provides that management:

*   is obliged to offer its shares and/or certificates in the company for a certain price if it ceases to be involved with the target (good/bad leaver provisions, see s.4.5 below);

and which may also provide that management:

*   is not allowed to transfer its shares within a certain time frame (lock-up);
*   must stay with the company for a certain period of time on an exit; and

- is the only party to give operational-type representations and warranties in the context of such exit.

## 4.2   Common protections for investors

Investors usually do not take a place in the management board of the investment vehicle. In order to protect their investment, it is more common for investors to take a place on the supervisory board (in a two-tier board structure) or to act as non-executive directors (in a one-tier board structure). Additionally or alternatively, the shareholders' agreement and/or the portfolio company's articles of association may provide for (any of) the following:

- approval for key management decisions: certain matters, such as borrowing, acquiring or divesting assets, entering into contracts of employment or other contracts above certain thresholds, filing a winding-up petition or entering into a long-term collaboration with another company, require prior approval of the shareholders;
- information rights: shareholders usually seek to obtain information in the form of interim balance sheets, interim overviews of cash flow and debt positions, overviews of pending legal proceedings and any deviations of the business plan;
- resolution of conflict of interest matters and valuation issues;
- lock-ups, drag along rights and the possibility to sell shares to affiliated companies; and
- good and bad leaver provisions.

## 4.3   Common protections for management

Management usually seeks to protect its position through board seats and tag-along rights. Furthermore, management holding a minority interest in the investment vehicle usually ensures that the shareholders' agreement provides for limited veto rights with regard to matters directly concerning their position. Common examples of such matters are any changes to the articles of association, the emission of unissued capital and the dissolution of the company.

## 4.4   Management warranties

When private equity funds exit their investment by means of a buyout, they want to limit their future exposure under representations and warranties as much as possible and potential buyers may envisage obtaining further reaching warranties of the selling managers in addition to the limited warranties of the selling private equity fund. In addition, often existing management will be expected to roll-over proceeds from the sale into the new holding vehicle (often again at favourable terms)

The warranties given by the management usually relate to information provided to the buyer, to the correctness of the assumptions forming the basis of the business plan that is prepared by the buyer and the management together and to the correctness and completeness of the most important findings of the buyers in their contemplated due diligence. Managers may be persuaded in advance to give these warranties to a potential buyer at an exit.

With respect to representations and warranties in general, there has been an increase of cases in which the exposure thereunder is insured by the buyer (or in some cases the seller) taking out warranty and indemnity insurance.

## 4.5   Good leaver/bad leaver provisions

Leaver provisions, under which managers are obliged to offer their shares and/or certificates in the company if they cease to be involved, usually contain the following terms. In most cases, bad leaver provisions contain the clause that the manager receives the lower of: (1) the market value of their shares as determined by a corporate body or an independent expert; and (2) the price the manager paid for the shares. Good leaver provisions usually entail that managers receive the market value of their shares. A manager is usually a bad leaver if they terminate their employment prior to a certain moment in time; if their employment ends because of urgent or serious reasons; or if the manager is personally declared bankrupt. In any other cases, the manager usually is a good leaver.

Furthermore, the above-mentioned good leaver/bad leaver provisions also apply to the management team of the AIFM managing the fund regarding their entitlement to carried interest distributions of the AIF. Bad leavers are usually forced to sell their interest in the carried interest vehicle at the lower of (1) and (2) above. Most AIFMs have a vesting scheme in place pursuant to which a good leaver is required to sell part of its interests in the carried interest vehicle. The size of such part of interests depends on the number of years that the good leaver was appointed as a manager.

## 4.6   Public to private transactions

There is a continuing interest in public to private transactions in the Netherlands. The rules regulating the bid process are, with a few exceptions, exclusively governed by the AFS, which is supplemented by a decree (*Besluit openbare biedingen Wft* of 12 September 2007). The AFM monitors compliance with the AFS—including applicable insider trading rules—and is, inter alia, empowered to impose penalties and issue public warnings. Infringement of the AFS may also qualify as an economic offence and may therefore be subject to criminal sanctions as well.

Specific additional Dutch requirements are the consultation of, and disclosure obligations to, the trade unions and works councils of Dutch target companies, as set forth in the SER Merger Code (*SER-besluit Fusiegedragsregels* 2000), a quasi-legislative code of conduct and the Works Councils Act 1971 (*Wet op de ondernemingsraden*). In addition, Dutch corporate law contains general rules of conduct that are to be observed by the relevant (Dutch) target in respect of, inter alia, its stakeholders, including its minority shareholders, and by its shareholders amongst themselves; these rules also apply to a public takeover bid situation. Finally, bids resulting in concentrations exceeding certain thresholds must be notified to the competent Dutch or European anti-trust authorities and may require their approval.

The AFS in particular contains certain rules which apply to bids, including rules on: the timelines of the bid; the contents of an offering document and a position statement; public announcements in respect of the bid; and mandatory offers.

## 5. EXITS
### 5.1 Secondary sales

When private equity funds exit their investment by means of a secondary sale, potential buyers normally envisage obtaining further reaching warranties from the selling managers in addition to the limited warranties from the selling private equity fund. These further reaching warranties are envisaged by potential buyers in the context of the opportunity of the selling managers to partially invest the proceeds of the sale in the buying vehicle, as referred to in s.4.4 above.

### 5.2 Trade sales

The further reaching warranties of the selling managers are also envisaged by potential buyers in trade sales. However, as it is quite uncommon for the selling managers to invest the proceeds of the sale in this scenario, the relative bargaining positions of the parties are decisive in this regard.

### 5.3 Initial public offerings

In comparison with the numerous cases of private equity funds exiting their investments by means of private sales, exits by means of initial public offerings (IPOs) are relatively rare in the Netherlands.

### 5.4 Refinancings

Refinancings regularly occur in the Netherlands and continue to be a means for private equity funds to boost their returns.

### 5.5 Restructuring/insolvency

In an insolvency scenario, an exit can be realised by way of an asset transaction or alternatively by way of debt for equity swaps. Pre-packs do occur in the Netherlands. However, pre-pack bankruptcy and sales of assets in connection therewith have come under closer legal scrutiny.

## 6. TAX
### 6.1 Taxation of fund structures
**Corporate entities**

The BV, the NV and the co-operative are opaque entities and, in principle, subject to the regular corporate income tax regime (see the rest of s.6.1 below).

Subject to certain conditions, the BV and the NV may be eligible for the special corporate income tax regime for fiscal investment institutions (*fiscale beleggingsinstellingen*—FBIs). The FBI is subject to corporate income tax at a rate of 0%. The Netherlands also offers a tax-exempt regime for collective investment institutions (*vrijgestelde beleggingsinstellingen*—VBIs). However, as private equity funds do not usually qualify for the aforementioned regimes, a detailed description of these regimes goes beyond the scope of this chapter.

**Limited partnerships and contractual entities**

A limited partnership (CV) and a fund for mutual account (FGR) can be structured as tax transparent or opaque entities. A CV is considered tax transparent if the transfer of a limited partnership interest, any change in the relative interests of the limited partners and the admission to the CV of a new limited partner is subject to the prior consent of all partners (limited and general). A similar rule applies for the FGR.

In addition, the FGR is tax transparent (without the need for unanimous approval of the investors) if the interests in the fund may only be transferred to the fund (pursuant to a redemption).

Tax transparent CVs and FGRs are not subject to corporate income tax and are not obliged to withhold dividend tax upon profit distributions (opaque CVs/FGRs are subject to the regular corporate income tax regime).

### Corporate income tax regime

Transparent private equity funds are ignored for corporate income tax purposes. Any income derived by these funds is directly allocated to the investors.

Private equity funds that are subject to the regular corporate income tax regime are generally taxed on their worldwide income at a rate of 20–25% (2018). However, under the participation exemption regime, income and gains from qualifying participations are exempt from corporate income tax. Investments in Dutch and foreign companies qualify for the participation exemption, if both: the investment represents at least 5% of the paid-up nominal share capital of a subsidiary with a capital divided into shares; and this subsidiary is not held as a passive investment.

If the subsidiary is held as a passive investment, the participation exemption nevertheless applies if either the so-called "asset test" or the "subject-to-tax test" is met.

*Passive investment*: a subsidiary is considered a passive investment if the taxpayer's objective is to obtain a return that may be expected from normal asset management. Subsidiaries (indirectly) held by a shareholder with an active management function (for example, private equity funds) should generally not be considered passive investments.

*Asset test*: the asset test is met if less than 50% of the subsidiary's assets is comprised of low taxed passive investments. Generally (subject to certain deeming provisions), low taxed passive investments are investments that are not reasonably required for the business operations of the subsidiary holding the assets and are not subject to a "realistic levy" in accordance with Dutch standards (see below). The test is applied on the fair market value of the aggregate assets, including non-capitalised goodwill, held by the subsidiary and its participations in which the subsidiary holds at least 5%.

*Subject-to-tax test*: this test is met if the subsidiary is subject to a "realistic levy" (that is, a profit-based tax with a regular statutory rate of at least 10%) in accordance with Dutch standards, meaning that no special tax base deviations such as tax holidays, deductible dividends or a significantly broader participation exemption regime than applicable under Dutch law should apply.

### 6.2 Carried interest

Carried interest arrangements typically fall within the scope of the so-called "lucrative interest" regime. This tax regime applies to certain shares, receivables or other rights with similar economic characteristics that qualify as "lucrative interests". The income derived from lucrative interests will either be taxed as ordinary income against the progressive rates up to 51.95% (2018) if the lucrative interest is held directly, or as income from capital against a flat rate of 25% if the lucrative interest is held through an entity in which the taxpayer holds a substantial interest (i.e. an interest of 5% or more).

A lucrative interest is present if the taxpayer has acquired shares, receivables or rights with similar economic characteristics that are deemed to be granted with the intention to form a remuneration for services (to be) rendered by the taxpayer or certain related persons. Shares may constitute a lucrative interest if: (1) there are various classes of shares and the shares held by the executive are subordinated to other classes of shares, while the class of shares held by the executive constitutes less than 10% of the aggregate paid in capital (including share premium and shareholder loans); or (2) the shares are preference shares with a preferred dividend of at least 15% per annum.

Market standard carried interest schemes of private equity funds generally fall within the scope of the lucrative interest regime and, if structured appropriately, the individual asset manager will pay tax in respect of the carried interest received by him or her at an effective rate of 25% (2018).

### 6.3 Management equity

In principle, the award (for a consideration below fair market value) of equity is subject to wage tax at progressive rates up to 51.95% (2018) in the hands of the individual manager (not the investment vehicle).

### 6.4 Loan interest

The acquisition of Dutch target companies by private equity funds is often structured through a so-called acquisition holding, which finances the acquisitions of the Dutch target company with (third-party and group) debt. By forming a fiscal unity between the acquisition holding and the Dutch target, the interest expense on the acquisition debt can be used to set off against the operating profits of the Dutch target, thus reducing the Dutch tax base. There is no withholding tax in this regard.

However, certain anti-abuse rules apply that may effectively limit the interest deduction. One of these anti-abuse rules specifically applies to acquisition debt. The "interest deduction limitation rule for acquisition debt" as implemented in the Corporate Tax Act 1969 (*Wet op de vennootschapsbelasting*) on 1 January 2012 entails that, after the formation of a fiscal unity between the acquisition holding and the target company, the interest on the debt related to the acquisition of the target company cannot be set off against the own taxable profit of the acquisition holding and not against the profits of the target company.

As an exception to this rule, an amount of up to EUR 1,000,000 interest on the acquisition loan is deductible, regardless of the own taxable profit of the acquisition holding. Interest in excess of this threshold is not deductible unless the second exception can be applied. Under the second exception, acquisitions will not be considered to be financed with excessive debt if the acquisition loans do not amount to more than 60% of the acquisition price of the target companies at the end of the year in which the target companies are included in the tax consolidation. In subsequent years, for acquisition loans to be considered not excessive in respect of those acquisitions, the applicable percentage is reduced by five percentage points per year down to 25% (which implies that 25% of the acquisition debt may thus remain outstanding in later years without resulting in excess acquisition debt).

In addition, effective from 1 January 2013, the deduction of "excessive" interest on loans taken up for investments in participations qualifying for the participation exemption may be (partially) denied.

Excessive interest is determined as the interest due by the taxpayer in a taxable year multiplied by a certain fraction. As a general rule, the numerator of the fraction comprises the positive difference between: (1) the aggregate historic cost price of qualifying investments; and (2) the fiscal equity of the taxpayer, and the denominator comprises the aggregate amount of loans taken up by the taxpayer.

The above restriction only applies to interest in excess of EUR 750,000, i.e. interest up to this threshold is, as a general rule, deductible. Acquisitions of or capital contributions to participations are disregarded to the extent the taxpayer can argue that they relate to an increase in operational activities of the group. This is an important exception in the context of private equity acquisitions.

Further, certain other interest deduction restrictions could apply if loans are taken up from related entities.

It should be noted that a new EU interest limitation rule (known as the earnings stripping rule under the Anti-Tax Avoidance Directive (Directive 2016/1164 laying down rules against tax avoidance practices that directly affect the functioning of the internal market [2016] OJ L193/1), needs to be implemented in Dutch law no later than 1 January 2019. In brief, under the earnings stripping rule the deduction of net borrowing, costs will be limited to the highest of: (1) 30% of the earnings before interest, tax, depreciation and amortisation (EBITDA); and (2) an amount of EUR 1,000,000. In view of the introduction of the earnings stripping rule, it is currently considered by the Dutch legislator to abolish one or more of the existing interest deduction limitation rules.

### 6.5  Transaction taxes

The purchase of assets is subject to value added tax (VAT), which is in principle chargeable by the supplier. The acquisition of shares is not subject to VAT. Often, VAT paid in connection with the purchase of assets is reclaimable. If the assets qualify as Dutch real property, property transfer tax at a rate of 6% may be payable (2% for residential property). If such transfer is structured through shares, property transfer tax could also be payable.

## 7.  CURRENT TOPICAL ISSUES/TRENDS

Dutch private equity funds attracted EUR 4.4 billion in new commitments in 2017—a substantial increase in comparison to the EUR 2.4 billion in 2016. The following market trends can be identified in the Netherlands:

* a substantial increase in Dutch venture capital investments;
* an increase in buyouts; and
* as a result of Brexit, it is expected that several financial institutions shift their focus to, inter alia, the Netherlands, which is expected to result in an increasing amount of (private equity) funds to be established in the

Netherlands in the future.

International private equity funds investing in the Netherlands are gradually increasing in number, as shown by the various bids of the past year; this is supported by the number of transactions (411), which is an increase of 46 compared to 2016.

Due to the increasing numbers for fundraising and private equity and venture capital investments in the Netherlands, we notice a growing attention and appreciation for fund formation and fund financing in the Netherlands.

# Poland

## WKB Wierciński Kwieciński, Baehr sp.k. Ben Davey, Jakub Jędrzejak, Klaudia Frątczak & Łukasz Czekański[1]

## 1. MARKET OVERVIEW

Among the countries which have joined the EU since 2004, Poland has the largest economy and is the top destination for private equity investment. According to data published by Eurosat (available at: *https://ec.europa.eu/ eurostat/tgm/table.do?tab=table&init=1&language=en&pcode=tec00115 &plugin=1* [Accessed 14 September 2018]), after avoiding recession and sustaining more than respectable levels of growth during the period from 2008 to 2013, Poland's gross domestic product (GDP) grew by an annual average rate of 3.675% in the period from 2014 to 2017. During the same period, the GDP of the eurozone grew by a comparatively modest annual average rate of 1.95% (figures take from Invest Europe, *European Private Equity Activity Report 2017* (2017) available at: *https://www.investeurope.eu/ media/711867/invest-europe-2017-european-private-equity-activity.pdf* [Accessed 11 September 2018]). Poland has the advantage not only of strong fundamentals but, like other former communist countries that have been reintegrated, it also has a compelling macro-convergence story to tell. In addition, it has high levels of education, plenty of entrepreneurial talent, comparatively cheap and flexible labour markets, relatively low levels of corporate tax, reasonably strong corporate and government balance sheets as well as a rapidly developing consumer culture supported by increasing levels of disposable income. Importantly, Poland has many well-regarded local and regional private equity managers and is attracting ever-increasing interest from foreign private equity funds. But despite all this, private equity fundraisings and investments as a proportion of GDP still remain low compared to the rest of Europe and other emerging markets (especially emerging Asia). According to the *European Private Equity Activity Report 2017* prepared by Invest Europe, the annual average private equity investment activity in Poland in the period 2013 to 2017 was just over 0.2% of the GDP, compared to the European annual average in the same period of just below 0.35%. Clearly, Poland could do a better job at selling the message that, as an investment destination, it provides emerging market opportunities, with the risk profile of a developed market.

### 1.1 Types of investors

In general terms, there are two types of private equity funds operating in the Polish market: local funds, originating from and/or concentrating their

---

1   The authors gratefully acknowledge the assistance of Robert Makowski, Daria Prygiel, Katarzyna Kozak, Janusz Szlanta and Karol Filipiuk.

activity in Poland (and/or other Central and Eastern Europe (CEE) countries); and big international funds, for whom Poland is just one of many markets around the world.

For both types of funds, it is difficult to indicate the prevailing source of their investment finance as most funds do not reveal such information to the public.

The sources of financing for the local funds include, among others, pension funds, insurance companies, banks, foundations, corporations and individuals as well as other big international private equity funds and funds of funds. However, the local pension funds are not major investors in private equity funds as they are in many other countries. There are a number of regulatory reasons for this, including: (1) restrictions on investments in alternative assets (discussed further in s.2.2 below); and (2) restrictions on investments abroad, which limit the ability to invest in "local" private equity funds that raise funds through foreign structures or in foreign currencies (currently, a Polish pension fund may not invest more than 30% of its portfolio in assets denominated in a currency other than Polish zloty and, within that limit, only in assets denominated in currencies of EU Member States or members of the European Economic Area and/or the Organisation for Economic Co-operation and Development (OECD)). Having regard to the low levels of support from local pension funds, the local private equity funds, like the international players operating in Poland, raise a significant proportion of their funds internationally rather than in Poland. As such, the manner of their fundraising falls outside the scope of this chapter.

## 1.2 Types of investments

In Poland, private equity funds usually invest in mature businesses, particularly in the mid-market. The predominant investments are buyouts (both management buyouts and management buy-ins) and equity injections (growth capital) by way of expansion, rescue and replacement capital. However, there are increasing levels of venture capital investment (e.g. seed, start-up or high-risk technology transactions). Public to private transactions are and were quite rare. The take-private transaction in respect of one of Poland's leading vodka producers—Polmos Lublin—that occurred in 2006/07 probably still remains one of the most prominent transactions of that type on the Polish market. More recently, in 2012, Eko Holding (which owns a chain of grocery stores) was taken private by Advent International after a tough battle with Mid Europa. There is no reliable data available on minority investments by private equity funds but, in general terms, they are not especially popular in Poland. To a large extent, this is because many funds investing in Poland will only invest if they can obtain a majority position in the target. There are several mezzanine funds that are active in Poland. However, in recent years, potential funding gaps that might otherwise have been filled by mezzanine financing have often been closed by equity investors providing more equity or senior lenders providing slightly more senior debt.

In general, private equity investments in Poland are significantly smaller in comparison to private equity markets in larger and more developed economies. The average equity investment for a typical buyout deal is between

EUR 15 million and 30 million. However, in the last few years, there have been some notable exceptions. For example, Mid Europa, Cinven and Permira bought Allegro (an online e-commerce platform often referred to as the "Polish eBay") from Naspers for USD 3.25 billion (one of the largest acquisitions ever on the Polish market), CVC Capital Partners bought a chain of convenience stores called "Żabka" from Mid Europa for EUR 1.1 billion, Bridgepoint and Cornerstone bought Smyk Group (a chain of stores selling children's apparel, toys and accessories) from Empik Media & Fashion for approximately EUR 245 million and Emest Investments acquired 100% of GetBack (a debt collection company) from Idea Bank for approximately EUR 190 million. Other high-profile transactions include the acquisition of Piotr i Paweł (a supermarket chain) by TFI Capital Partners, the acquisition by Abris Capital Partners of a majority stake in Velvet Care (a manufacturer of hygiene products) from Avallon, the acquisition by Mid Europe of a stake in Hortex (a leader in the frozen fruit and vegetable market) and the acquisition by Macquarie Infrastructure of a majority interest in INEA (a Polish cable network operator) from Warburg Pincus.

Looking to the future, there are prospects on several fronts. In particular, many businesses in Poland are still in their first generation of ownership and management, often without any obvious family successor, potentially making them ideal candidates for management buy-ins. Also, there has been considerable interest from Asian investors, particularly from China, especially in the electrical engineering, automotive and energy sectors. The fast-moving consumer goods sector is considered to be ripe for consolidation. Other sectors which remain popular for investment include TMT, business services, healthcare, pharmaceutical and retail. Further, venture capital investors now have a major ally in the Polish Development Fund (*Polski Fundusz Rozwoju*) which, among other things, acts as a fund of funds to boost venture capital investments into start-ups and early stage companies in Poland.

### Use of leverage in the above transactions

There is not much data available on the use of leverage in recent private equity transactions in Poland. In general terms, the availability of leverage in Poland reduced during the global financial crisis, even though the Polish economy did not suffer greatly and Polish banks remained in relatively good condition because they had not invested significantly in risky financial instruments on the US and other markets. Also, the leverage ratios in Poland tend to be relatively conservative. Having said that, debt finance is usually available, especially for investments in well-managed mature businesses, and the situation seems fairly stable. According to a survey conducted by Deloitte ("Maintaining momentum: Private Equity Confidence Survey Central Europe" (2018) available at: *https://www2.deloitte.com/content/dam/Deloitte/ce/Documents/about-deloitte/ce-private-equity-confidence-survey-summer-2018.pdf ?nc=1* [Accessed 11 September 2018]), as at May 2018, 74% of respondents expected the availability of debt finance in the CEE region to remain unchanged, with 10% anticipating that debt finance will be more readily available and only 17% expecting a decrease in the availability of debt. In cases where private equity investors faced difficulties obtaining debt financing, some financed their investments 100% from equity, sometimes with a view to introducing leverage at a later point in time. Clearly, this is only possible for smaller ticket deals.

## 2.  FUNDS
### 2.1  Fund structures

Poland is not a jurisdiction in which private equity managers would normally locate their fund structures. In most cases, Poland is only used as a jurisdiction in which target companies are acquired and, for these purposes, funds usually use Polish limited liability companies (LLCs) as special purposes vehicles (SPVs). Other types of vehicles used from time to time as SPVs (although much less frequently) are Polish joint stock companies (JSCs) and limited liability partnerships (LLPs).

**Polish limited joint stock partnerships**

In recent years, there has also been increased use of Polish joint stock limited partnerships (JSLPs). JSLPs are a hybrid vehicle with a general partner that is liable for the partnership's liabilities and obligations in full, and other participants that are shareholders (as if it were a corporate entity). However, subject to some transitional arrangements which have now expired, JSLPs ceased to be tax transparent starting from 2014 and are now treated as separate taxpayers whose income is taxed in the same manner as for companies (i.e. LLCs and JSCs). In light of that, the use of JSLPs in investment structures has become and is expected to remain relatively uncommon. Nevertheless, these entities may still be used as potential vehicles for venture capital investments and this type of a partnership can act as an alternative investment company (AIC) (see s.2.2 below).

**Polish limited liability companies (sp. z o.o.)**

A Polish LLC is the most commonly used type of SPV vehicle in Poland for many reasons. First of all, a Polish LLC is the simplest type of company which, at the same time, imposes no direct liability on its shareholders for the company's actions, obligations and liabilities. For example, in terms of internal governance, a Polish LLC, unlike a JSC, is not required to have a supervisory board in addition to its management board (although an LLC is not prohibited from having a supervisory board).

In addition to simplicity, Polish LLCs are also preferred as SPVs for acquiring target companies and/or businesses because there are practically no financial assistance limitations and they may easily provide upstream security for external transaction financing (for details, see s.3.2 below).

On the other hand, the means of providing equity are less flexible than for a JSC (where instruments such as an authorised or conditional share capital increase as well as bonds or warrants convertible into shares, or with pre-emption rights, are available). However, there are low minimum share capital requirements with respect to Polish LLCs (the minimum is PLN 5,000, i.e. approximately EUR 1,150).

**Polish joint stock companies (S.A.)**

A Polish JSC is the only type of Polish company that can be publicly listed. Consequently, they are usually the SPVs of choice for target companies with respect to which the acquiring fund has already planned (or is considering) an exit through an initial public offering (IPO). There are higher share capital requirements for JSCs than for LLCs (the minimum is PLN 100,000, i.e. approximately EUR 23,250).

On the other hand, Polish JSCs offer more diverse ways of financing than Polish LLCs. For example, a Polish JSC may increase its share capital by decision of the board (within the limits set by the shareholders). In addition, unlike an LLC, it is also possible to increase the company's capital conditionally (e.g. conditional upon specified persons or entities agreeing to take up shares). Finally, a Polish JSC may issue bonds and/or warrants that are convertible into shares or which provide for a right of pre-emption with respect to newly issued shares. On the other hand, a JSC is subject to certain financial assistance limitations that do not apply to LLCs (for details, see s.3.2 below).

### Polish limited partnerships

Polish LLPs are less frequently used as transaction SPVs in Poland. First of all, at least two partners are required to form and maintain a Polish LLP, while both JSCs and LLCs can have just one shareholder. Further, Polish LLPs are not typical companies in that they do not have a legal personality in the true sense, although they can acquire rights and take up obligations (as well as sue and be sued) in their own name. Finally, the shareholders (or rather partners) of a Polish LLP may be held responsible for its liabilities. In particular, at least one of the partners in an LLP must be a general partner, who is fully liable for the obligations of the LLP, and at least one of the partners in an LLP must be a limited partner, who is liable only up to a specific sum as set out under the LLP's articles of association.

The practical impact of the partner liabilities can be mitigated to a large extent. For example, a newly established Polish LLC could be the general partner of the LLP (and have a relatively low, or even minimal, share in profits) while the fund could be a limited partner in the LLP (and have a low level of liability and a high share in the LLP's profits). Under such arrangements, the only partner who is fully exposed to the LLP's liabilities is the LLC, which at the same time gains limited profits from the underlying business.

### Establishment or acquisition of Polish special purpose vehicles

From a practical perspective, it is worth mentioning that each of the SPVs referred to above may take from three to eight weeks to establish (depending on the competent registration court and other authorities dealing with the formation of the SPV). However, each type is readily available for acquisition as a shelf vehicle from reputable firms providing such services.

## 2.2  Regulation of fundraising and fund managers

Poland has many mature private equity managers with sizeable and stable teams, well-defined investment policies and broad investor relationships. Investors seeking exposure to Poland have a good choice of buyout, expansion venture capital and turnaround funds (as well as mezzanine funds), offering regional, sub-regional or national geographic focus. Most of the investment goes towards buyout funds and expansion funds (as well as mezzanine funds). There is considerable support for the sector in Poland from government agencies and the Polish Development Fund (*Polski Fundusz Rozwoju*), a group of state or state-owned financial and advisory institutions supporting companies, local governments and individuals and investing in the sustainable social and economic development of Poland, the European Bank for Reconstruction and Development and, increasingly, foreign investors. Since September 2017, Abris closed its third fund with commitments of EUR 500 million, and Enterprise Investors had a first and final closing of its Polish Enterprise Fund VIII at EUR 498 million, exceeding its proposed cap of EUR 450 million. In late 2018, Value4Capital announced a first close of its Poland Plus fund at EUR 80 million with a target of EUR 150 million and, in April 2018, Innova Capital had a first close of its sixth fund at EUR 194 million, putting it on track to reach the proposed size of EUR 325 million.

Parts of the AIFM Directive (Directive 2011/61 on alternative investment fund managers and amending Directives 2003/41 and 2009/65 and Regulations 1060/2009 and 1095/2010 [2011] OJ L174/1) and the UCITS V Directive (Directive 2014/91 and amending Directive 2009/65 on the coordination of laws, regulations and administrative provisions relating to undertakings for collective investment in transferable securities (UCITS) as regards depositary functions, remuneration policies and sanctions [2014] OJ L257/186) were implemented in Poland by way of amendment of the Investment Fund Act 2004 (which is now called the Investment Fund and Alternative Investment Fund Management Act) (Investment Fund Act). The amendments, which came into force on 4 June 2016, introduced the concepts of an AIC and an alternative investment fund (AIF) into Polish law. However, the National Private Placement Regime part of the AIFM Directive has not been implemented in Poland. As such, non-EU funds or EU funds managed by a non-EU entity (for which passporting is not available) may only really be marketed by way of reverse solicitation.

Under the definitions used in the Investment Fund Act, an AIF is a collective investment institution whose object of activity (including activity as part of a separated sub-fund) is collecting assets from multiple investors in order to invest them in the interests of such investors in accordance with a specified investment policy. An AIC is an AIF other than a specialised open-ended investment fund or a closed-ended investment fund. An AIC may conduct its activity in the form of an LLC or JSC as well as a limited partnership or a limited joint-stock partnership in which the sole general partner is a company.

As a result of the amendments to the Investment Fund Act, private equity and venture capital funds have now been brought under the supervision of the Polish Financial Supervision Commission (FSC).

The FSC is also responsible for granting permission for the creation, as well as ongoing oversight, with respect to Polish investment funds, i.e. a special type of legal entity with legal personality that can be created pursuant to the Investment Fund Act, and may be: (1) an open-ended investment fund; (2) a closed-ended investment fund; or (3) a specialist open-ended investment fund.

Under the Investment Fund Act, a Polish investment fund may be created only by an Investment Fund Committee (the Committee). Apart from its role of establishing a Polish investment fund, the Committee is also a corporate body of the fund, which represents and manages the Polish investment fund. Such Committee may operate only in the form of a JSC, with its seat in the territory of Poland, and requires the consent of the FSC for conducting activity as a committee of a Polish investment fund. If the Committee is supposed to have just one shareholder, only a legal person may become the sole shareholder of the Committee. Subject to some exceptions, the management board of the Committee must consist of at least two members with an upper education degree or who are licensed financial advisors who have work experience of at least three years in managerial or other independent positions in financial market institutions or performing functions in authorities of such institutions.

Certain restrictions apply with respect to selling shares in the Committee. A proposed dealing under which a person reaches, exceeds or goes below 10%, 20%, 33.3% (one-third) or 50% of the votes at the Committee's general meeting must be notified to the FSC, which can object to the transaction.

If a Polish investment fund's portfolio includes at least 80% non-publicly traded instruments, such fund may operate as a non-public assets fund. This type of fund may be closed-ended or specialised open-ended, for which, among other things, the rules governing the management, as well as the information and disclosure obligations, are much less restrictive than in the case of open-ended investment funds.

There are certain restrictions on the instruments in which pension funds and insurance companies can invest, and those limitations also apply to investing in private equity. These limit the flow of capital to the private equity sector in Poland. However, a pension fund can invest in a private equity fund operating in the form of a Polish investment fund, provided that the total investments of the pension fund in closed-ended investment funds does not exceed 10% of the value of the assets of the pension fund and, together with investments in specialist open-ended funds, does not exceed 15% of such value. Also, the Committee of a non-public assets fund does not need to hire licensed financial advisors.

Apart from the above restrictions, the private equity market is highly diversified and there are no common rules which govern the management of private equity funds.

The MIFID 2 Directive (Directive 2014/65 on markets in financial instruments and amending Directives 2002/92 and Directive 2011/61 [2014] OJ L173/349), which came into force on 3 January 2018 and has not yet been implemented in Poland, seeks to impose further requirements in respect of investment funds. Importantly, the new requirements are intended to restrict the remuneration model for distribution of products and, in particular, to reduce the incentive to pressure investors into particular products based on the amount of fees paid to the distributor. In the absence of these requirements, distribution fees of up to 70% of the management fee were seen on the market. The directive seeks to limit the distribution fees to

5% of the amount to be invested (with such fees being deducted from such amount in a manner that is transparent to the investor).

### 2.3 Customary or common terms of funds

As noted above, private equity funds operate on the Polish market through a number of different types of entities. Most fund vehicles are not domiciled in Poland and have terms governed by laws of foreign jurisdictions. However, the terms of funds that originate in Poland and operate in the form of investment funds are governed by the Investment Fund Act.

Under the Investment Fund Act, the main terms of an investment fund shall be included in its statutes. The Investment Fund Act requires that the statutes of an investment fund specify, among other things:

- the terms of the investment policy of the fund;
- the rules on payment of profits to the investors (if payable prior to repurchase of the participation units);
- the types, maximum value and methods of calculation of the costs and expenses of the fund, including the management fee; and
- the frequency of evaluation of the fund's assets or methods and rules for such evaluation.

## 3. DEBT FINANCE

### 3.1 Means of financing

In Poland, there are no specific alternative means by which private equity-backed vehicles typically obtain financing other than through a traditional secured term loan facility. The covenant light, bullet only and deep subordination lending practices that were seen in some countries during the mid-2000s never really took hold in Poland. As a result, the terms of financing have not changed greatly over the last decade, except that these days the debt to equity ratios are lower than in the past, the financial covenants are a bit tighter and, generally, to the extent possible, the banks try to be even more protective (especially in terms of the covenants, undertakings and security packages that they demand of a borrower).

In recent years, bond financing has become increasingly popular. Corporate bonds issued under Polish law are quite common for smaller and local deals. However, larger corporate financings under Polish law have been buoyed by an amendment to the Polish Bond Act 1995 that took effect in July 2015. The amendment lifts limitations on the maximum interest and allows the terms of issue to be prepared in English, provided that each individual bond has a nominal value of at least EUR 100,000. For big ticket deals, there may be foreign (mainly New York law, high-yield) bonds issued as a means of financing (possibly to refinance bridge financing provided in the interim by banks).

### 3.2 Restrictions on granting security

In Poland, there are certain limitations which impact on the ability of a financing bank to receive full security over the assets of a target company. The most important limitation applies to Polish JSCs and might be characterised as a financial assistance limitation. The other applies to LLCs and can be characterised as a capital preservation limitation.

## Financial assistance

In Poland, financial assistance limitations apply only to JSCs. In general terms, financial assistance is allowed under Polish law—though with certain limitations. A JSC may, directly or indirectly, finance the acquisition of its own shares, in particular through the issuance of loans, making advance payments and/or establishment of security, only under the following conditions:

- the financing is on market terms, especially with respect to: (1) the interest received by the company; and (2) the security established to the company's benefit in respect of the financial assistance it provides in the form of loans and/or advance payments, and such financial assistance is granted only after the solvency of the debtor has been analysed;
- if the financing is being given for the purposes of the acquisition of, or the taking-up of shares in, the target company, such acquisition or taking-up of shares shall be in exchange for fair consideration;
- before the financial assistance is provided, the target company has to create a reserve fund (capital) for the purposes of the financing, with such fund being created from sums which can be subject to distribution as dividends (i.e. in general terms, profits); and
- the financing shall be approved by a general shareholders' meeting of the company and the relevant resolution shall be made on the basis of a report from the management board describing the purpose of the financing, the company's interest in providing the financing, the terms of the financing and its influence on the company's cash flows.

Most of the above limitations do not apply to services provided within a financial institution's ordinary course of business and/or to services provided to a company's employees (or employees of an affiliate of the company) which aim at enabling the acquisition by such employees of the company's shares.

As can be seen from the above, the "whitewash" procedure for a JSC to provide financial assistance is rather cumbersome and time-consuming and, for those reasons, it is not generally applied in practice. Rather, if the target is a JSC, for the purposes of providing the initial acquisition financing, the security is usually given only over the shares to be acquired, with an undertaking of the buyer and/or its parent, that the JSC and the buyer (most often an LLC) will be merged (with the buyer being the surviving entity) or that the JSC (or the buyer, following such merger, if it is not an LLC) is transformed into an LLC within a specified timeline. Following such merger and/or transformation, the limitations relating to financial assistance do not apply.

## Limitations on capital distributions in limited liability companies

A limitation that applies to Polish LLCs and which may, under certain circumstances, have an impact on security being issued to financing banks applies to payments to the benefit of the Polish LLC's shareholders. Shareholders in an LLC may not receive any payments under any legal title (i.e. of any nature), if such payments are to be made from assets which are required to fully cover the company's share capital. The precise scope of such limitation is open to interpretation and debate. However, it is generally considered that it applies to any payments following which (if they were made) the overall value of the company's assets would be less than the nominal value of the company's share capital.

The above limitation could be of some importance if the target company's nominal share capital was of significant value. In such circumstances, it can have a bearing on the scope and value of security issued to the financing banks since such security is usually provided to support some guarantee-type arrangement where the target company guarantees the acquiring entity's debts and, consequently, payments made on the basis of such security could be treated as payments made for the benefit of the LLC's shareholders.

### Guarantee limitations

As stated above, typically, when security is being issued by the target company to secure the financing of its acquisition, it is done under some sort of guarantee arrangement whereby the target company guarantees the debts of the acquiring entity. Consequently, an additional limitation on the ability to provide guarantees (and effectively also security) may also apply as a result of the operation of the Polish Bankruptcy Law 2003. Specifically, a Polish company is insolvent not only when it does not pay its debts as they fall due but also when the overall value of its liabilities (regardless of whether they are due and payable or not) exceeds the overall value of its assets. For that reason, and in order not to risk that the target company will be found insolvent as a result of issuing security, the value of the security provided by a Polish target company is usually contractually limited to such value that, at a given time, will not cause the target company to be regarded as insolvent.

However, amendments to the Polish Bankruptcy Law which took effect on 1 January 2016 have significantly reduced the problem (Restructuring Law 2015). For the purposes of the balance sheet insolvency test, the period during which the value of liabilities must exceed the value of assets in order for a company to be regarded as insolvent has now been extended to 24 months. Also, contingent liabilities (e.g. guarantees) have been expressly excluded from the calculation. As a result, guarantees given in respect of acquisition debt financing which, by nature are contingent liabilities, are unlikely to result in the technical insolvency of the guarantee provider (at least until the liability crystallises and, even then, only if the liability impacts the balance sheet for more than 24 months).

### 3.3 Intercreditor issues

A key issue when agreeing and documenting the relative ranking of interests of any providers of debt and equity finance in respect of a typical investment in Poland is the decision about whether separate sets of security shall be established for various types of creditors (senior, mezzanine etc) and, consequently, whether more than one security agent will be appointed for each creditor group or whether just one set of security will be established for all. In the latter case, the financing documents confirm that the security is being established in favour of one entity (usually the senior security agent) but to secure the claims of all of the lenders. In such a case, the financing documents also set out the seniority of the claims of the various creditors (as, with one set of security, the ranking of the various claims is not reflected in the security documents). Although this method provides for a simplified structure and limits the number of transaction (especially security) documents, it can be applied only to a transaction where there is trust between the lenders and where the security holder is a highly credible entity because the remaining creditors have no direct interest in the security established by the borrower and their rights arise only under agreement with the security holder.

On the other hand, in transactions where separate sets of security are being established to the benefit of each type of lender (senior, mezzanine etc), the senior lenders may be concerned about the second and further ranking lenders' entitlement to enforce their security. Although such other lenders rank behind the senior lenders in terms of satisfaction from the subject matter of the security, they are entitled under law to initiate enforcement proceedings on their own and without the need to wait for the senior lender to do the same. For this reason, senior lenders require stand-still periods and other related provisions which require the lenders who rank behind the senior lenders to notify them of any default under their financing documents and to withhold from any enforcement actions whatsoever for a certain period of time after a default has occurred.

Finally, in many international financings with multiple creditors and/or multiple facilities and/or other financings (e.g. bonds) secured by one set of security, it is usually necessary to apply a parallel debt mechanism in order to create a single claim that can be easily secured by one set of Polish security documents (for details, see s.3.4 below).

### 3.4 Syndication

There was a decline in syndicated loans in the years immediately following the global financial crisis. However, currently, given the size of recently contemplated investments and the value of the facilities required, the conclusion of syndicated facility agreements has become an important and prestigious achievement for banks.

A significant proportion of syndicated facilities in Poland is related to infrastructure projects (e.g. construction of motorways, railways or pipelines) rather than private equity investments.

Syndication can take the form of a statutory regulated syndication as provided for under the Polish Banking Law 1997. A Banking Law-governed syndication is a syndication among banks only. The banks enter into an agreement under which they set out the conditions for granting the facility and the terms of securing the facility, and appoint a bank that is empowered to conclude the facility agreement on behalf of others. According to the Banking Law, the risk connected with the facility is divided between the banks in proportion to their commitments. Granting a syndicated loan by entities other than banks or by a syndicate of banks and other entities (e.g. mezzanine funds) is not specifically regulated by Polish law. However, it is allowed based on the general principle of freedom of contract.

From the banks' perspective, one of the most significant issues relating to syndicated financing is proper securing of receivables. For many years, Polish law did not specifically allow for securing receivables of more than one creditor with just one security. Various means (e.g. a power of attorney) were used to address this, although many were less than ideal. However, for quite a few years now, Polish law has recognised the necessity of enabling just one entity to secure other parties' claims. First, a pledge administrator was allowed to be appointed (from among the creditors) to administer registered pledges (including over shares or assets). In addition, an amendment in 2009 to the Law on Land and Mortgage Registers 1982 that came into effect at the beginning of 2011 allows for a mortgage administrator to be appointed who can administer mortgages over real estate established to secure the claims of a group of creditors (and who does not need to be one of the creditors). Despite this, the above structures are not ideal and, in many instances, especially in the case of international financings, a parallel debt concept is implemented. Specifically, under the foreign-law-governed finance documents (as parallel debt is not a concept known to Polish law), a single claim to the benefit of the security agent is created which reflects, represents and equals the sum of all underlying secured claims. Such parallel debt is an abstract undertaking which at all times mirrors the underlying secured claim such that each repayment of the secured claim decreases the parallel debt and vice versa. By virtue of this arrangement, Polish-law-governed security documents can secure a security agent's own and single claim.

As for the company to which the loan is being made, the issues mainly relate to co-ordinating the negotiations and actions of the syndicating creditors because agreeing a syndicated financing may be a time-consuming and costly exercise.

## 4. EQUITY STRUCTURES
### 4.1 Role of management

The roles of management in an investment are usually twofold.

First, a member of management typically has a seat on the management board of the target company. This is usually regulated under agreements that the members of management enter into with the target company. A management contract, being a more flexible form of contract than an employment contract, is usually chosen. The parties to such contract may freely establish the principles of remuneration, tasks and goals to be achieved, terms and conditions of termination of the contract etc.

Any disputes between the company and the manager are decided by the civil court (as opposed to labour law courts, which tend to be more favourable to employees and which are competent for disputes relating to employment contracts).

Secondly, a member of management is usually entitled to some sort of equity participation in the investment. Generally, for tax optimisation, as well as the fact that most types of Polish company (including the most popular, i.e. the LLC) do not provide for appropriate means to implement equity participation which is supposed to change over time (e.g. based on the company's results), the members of management often acquire shares or other financial instruments in one of the holding companies, usually a company which is a direct or indirect holding company of the target and which has its registered office in another jurisdiction (often, with some tax preference). The equity participation is usually structured in the form of initial equity at the beginning of the investment, with options to acquire additional equity depending on the results of the underlying business. In some instances, the equity participation takes the form of "phantom" shares (i.e. a contractual entitlement to receive an additional bonus, the value of which is linked to the market value of the target's shares rather than actual share or option ownership).

Equity participation can sometimes also take the form of participation in share option schemes, which is more likely if the equity participation takes the form of shares in a public company.

## 4.2   Common protections for investors

Investors typically protect their investment by controlling the appointment procedure of the target company's management board. This usually also includes the right to appoint a large enough number of members of the management board so that, if necessary, the investor can control the majority of votes on the board. With respect to the information rights and the decision-making process, investors usually require management to inform the investor of matters which meet a materiality threshold as set out by the investor. Investors also require a right to be informed about meetings of the board and usually have a right to participate in such meetings as an observer. Ordinarily, management is required to provide the investor with management accounts on a monthly and/or quarterly basis. Investors also tend to have veto rights with respect to decisions which are material to the business of the target company, including approval of annual budgets or of material changes to the company's strategy. Furthermore, investors protect their investments through drag-along rights allowing them to require that management exits the investment together with the investor, and by putting other limitations on management's dealings in shares, including a ban on selling and/or encumbering their shares in the investment vehicle, and stipulating a set of restrictive covenants.

## 4.3   Common protections for management

A member of management, on the other hand, would typically seek to protect its position, particularly if it holds only a minority interest in the investment vehicle, first and foremost by assuring itself a seat on the management board of the target company. Further, where its influence over and control of the business of the company is limited by the investor's veto rights, a member of management can sometimes seek a right to exit the investment and be treated as a good leaver if the investor blocks management's ability to implement its own strategy for the underlying investment (although this is rarely accepted by investors). In such a case, management usually seeks to have a put option enabling it to require that the investor buys out management's shares in the investment vehicle. Finally, management usually seeks a tag-along right enabling it to exit the investment together with the investor and, generally, on terms and conditions as close as possible to those offered to the investor. Sometimes, management also requires the investor to undertake not to dilute management's investment by way of additional capital increases (e.g. to finance capital expenditures or add-on investments of the target) without management's consent.

### 4.4 Management warranties

Management is usually quite reluctant to give warranties in addition to those given by the seller. Investors, on the other hand, usually expect each member of management to confirm that, according to its knowledge, the warranties given by the seller are true, accurate and not misleading. Investors may also ask management to provide warranties with respect to the company's historic accounts as well as with respect to the target's business, assets and operations.

The management warranties are usually given for a period of between one and three years. Longer warranty periods may be agreed with respect to specific matters like taxes or environmental protection. The members of management usually seek to cap their liability at the level of their investment and to require that any potential warranty claims be satisfied primarily from their shares held in the investment vehicle.

### 4.5 Good leaver/bad leaver provisions

In cases where management participates in the investment vehicle's and/or the target's equity, the investment agreements usually include provisions which deal with the compulsory transfer of shares if a member of management ceases to be involved in the management of the target company. In such cases, in some transactions, a differentiation is made between a bad leaver (generally a manager who ceased to be involved with the business as a result of its own fault, dishonesty, fraud, bankruptcy, conviction for a criminal offence and/or material breach of the investment agreement) and a good leaver (generally a person who is not a bad leaver).

A good leaver is usually allowed to benefit fully from its investment, while a bad leaver's right to realise its investment is either limited or, depending on the underlying circumstances, excluded.

### 4.6 Public to private transactions

Private equity funds do not often make offers for public companies in Poland.

There are some key issues that must be taken into account in public to private transactions. First, there are certain thresholds of shareholding which, if exceeded, require a shareholder to announce a tender offer for a certain number of shares. For example, the threshold of 33%, at which point an offer needs to be made for 66% of the company's shares or for all the remaining shares in the company, and the threshold of 66%, at which point an offer needs to be made for all the remaining shares in the company. Exceeding the above thresholds can only be done by way of a tender offer. When planning a public to private transaction, investors usually seek to reach a 90% shareholding, which allows delisting of the company and squeezing out of minorities.

Another issue is the difficulty in payment of a control premium to a significant or majority shareholder exiting a public company. In general terms, all shareholders of a publicly held company shall be offered the same price for the same type of shares, although there are ways in which investors try to pay a control premium to sellers anyway.

Finally, investors contemplating a public to private transaction have limited ability to run a due diligence exercise with respect to the target. In general terms, due diligence processes are limited to information that was already disclosed to the market or which management considers non-material and, consequently, not subject to a disclosure obligation.

## 5. EXITS

Private equity funds typically exit their Polish investments through sale to an industry player, less frequently by sale to another private equity fund or another type of financial investor, and least often by way of an IPO. Some of the recent high-profile exits include the sale of DUON (an energy company) by AKJ Investments and TFI Capital Partners to Fortum Holding in early 2016, the sale of Zabka Polska (a network of convenience stores) by Mid Europa to CVC Capital Partners for EUR 1.1 billion (one of the biggest exits in Poland) in early 2017 (as mentioned in s.1.2 above), the sale by Enterprise Investors in April 2017 of its stake in Dino Polska (which operates a chain of small supermarkets) for EUR 376 million in the largest private equity IPO in the CEE, the acquisition by management of RUCH S.A. (a network of kiosks and convenience stores) from Eton Park Capital Management in mid-2017, and the acquisition of a portfolio of 28 hotels by Chariot Top Group, a company co-managed by Griffin Real Estate, from funds managed by Ares Management L.P., Axa Investment Managers—Real Assets and Apollo Rida.

### 5.1 Secondary sales

Generally, the level of warranty protection that may be expected is lower in a secondary sale, especially when the selling fund is close to the end of its life and is seeking to minimise both the amount and the duration of any substantive warranties it offers in order to allow final distributions to its investors with the minimum risk of clawback. Having said that, private equity bidders are almost always invited to participate in any competitive sales process and secondary sales are increasing.

Occasionally, where there is some debt financing from the investor still in place in the target at the time of sale, or where external debt financing is secured over the shares or through undertakings and/or commitments of the selling investor and is not being refinanced as part of the transaction, a secondary sale might involve a new financial investor taking over from the former. Such substitutions (which involve transfer of both rights and obligations, including the financial/investment obligations) potentially involve numerous issues connected with the transfer of the former investor's rights and obligations under the finance and security documents.

The transfer of the selling investor's receivables and related security (if any) usually requires entering into additional amendment and accession agreements with, or obtaining waiver letters from, other financing entities involved in the initial transaction, such as banks or mezzanine lenders.

Nonetheless, apart from the above issues, there are no specific legal issues which would prevent or significantly limit exiting an investment in Poland through a secondary sale.

## 5.2 Trade sales

Trade sales seem to be the most favourable and desired method of exiting an investment for private equity funds in Poland. Usually, such deals have less complex structures and bear less transaction completion and related risks than other exit methods. This is particularly due to the fact that the purchasing entities in a trade sale transaction are likely to have an in-depth knowledge of the market in which the target company operates and, consequently, are more likely to undertake their due diligence and reach decisions faster, and be less demanding in terms of the breadth and duration of the representations and warranties.

On the other hand, a trade sale to an industry player active in the same or related market to that of the target company may raise competition law issues and the transaction itself may require a longer and more complex antitrust clearance procedure. This can result in a significant delay to the process compared to a sale to a financial investor, with the Polish competition authorities potentially taking several months (or longer) to consider a clearance application where the buyer's and the target's businesses overlap. Finally, there are also recent examples of deals where private equity funds have shown their ability to move faster and demand less strict transaction documents (especially in terms of representations and warranties, interim covenants and terms of liability) than trade buyers, while at the same time offering comparable financial terms.

## 5.3 Initial public offerings

There are two markets in Poland on which shares in a target company may be sold publicly. The main market is the Warsaw Stock Exchange, which is the largest stock exchange in the CEE and attracts the larger scale offerings. The alternative trading market, NewConnect, is used for offerings of smaller companies.

Despite strength in the public markets, IPO exits have been relatively subdued in recent years and remain the least attractive exit route for private equity. In fact, it is becoming more and more common for companies to leave the public markets for a variety of reasons, including the high costs, stringent disclosure obligations and pressure from shareholders for short-term performance (sometimes at the expense of longer term strategies). This may open up opportunities for public to private transactions.

## 5.4 Refinancings

Some activity has been seen in refinancing of private equity funds' portfolio companies in recent years. This type of refinancing was focused on extending the maturity date and/or improving the terms (including the margins) of the financing initially obtained for the transaction and/or of the current account and/or revolving credit facilities for the target. On many occasions, such refinancing simply involved amending the existing facility agreement and, potentially, amendments to the existing or the establishment of some additional security but did not result in a change of lender(s). Refinancings involving a change of a lender are still quite rare in Poland.

## 5.5 Restructuring/insolvency

In general terms, the insolvency of a portfolio company is a last resort for a private equity fund to exit an investment and may only be beneficial to those funds whose investment constituted or was structured at an appropriate level as debt finance to the company and was well secured by the company's assets. For a typical equity investment, an insolvency is hardly ever an opportunity for a profitable exit. However, some recent changes in the law may provide private equity investors with some opportunities. In particular, a new Polish Restructuring Law came into force and the Polish Bankruptcy Law was substantially amended, each with effect from 1 January 2016.

The new Restructuring Law contemplates four types of restructuring proceedings, one of them being proceedings for approval of an arrangement. Within such proceedings, the debtor presents its creditors with an arrangement proposal and collects the votes for its adoption under the auspices of a qualified restructuring advisor who supervises the process. After the required majority of creditors (both in terms of value and number) vote in favour of the arrangement, the debtor files a motion for approval of its terms. These sorts of proceedings may help struggling businesses to turn the ship around.

The amendment to the Bankruptcy Law introduced the "pre-pack" sale concept to the Polish legal system. Under this procedure, a motion for a declaration of the bankruptcy of an entity may be accompanied by a motion for approval of the terms of sale of its enterprise. There has been increasing interest in and use of the "pre-pack" procedure in recognition of its key benefit, namely, the acquisition of a distressed business without liability for debts accrued before the transaction date and free from encumbrances (unlike under an ordinary process for acquisition of an enterprise).

On the other hand, the application of the "pre-pack" procedure has its limitations. In particular, it may be difficult to undertake a "pre-pack" where the enterprise or its assets are subject to a registered pledge. Also, there is always a risk that the court will deny the approval of the terms of sale and instead rule to open regular bankruptcy proceedings. In addition, the creditors of the enterprise may appeal the court's decision to approve a "pre-pack" until one week after its announcement in the *Court and Commercial Gazette*. An appeal may cause the process to last several months, if not longer.

Nevertheless, the use of "pre-packs" is expected to continue to grow in popularity and, in turn, become a possible path to exit from some private equity investments, and a potential opportunity for new investments, particularly for private equity funds with a distressed asset or turnaround mandate.

## 6. TAX
### 6.1 Taxation of fund structures

As mentioned above, private equity funds are not usually domiciled in Poland. However, the entities which are used by private equity funds as SPVs for investments in Poland are frequently Polish companies (i.e. LLCs and

JSCs) and LLPs.

## Companies

Under Polish law, the amounts of taxable income from different sources of revenue have to be calculated separately. The taxable income from a source of revenue for a given tax year is the total taxable revenues earned from the source for that year less the total deductible tax costs attributable to that source for that year. However, in certain cases, tax is simply imposed on revenues (e.g. payment of dividends, where no tax-deductible costs are recognised).

The Polish Corporate Income Tax Act 1992 treats capital gains (e.g. revenues from the redemption or sale of shares in another legal person) as a separate source of revenue form, for example, revenue generated from operating activities. In the case of calculating the taxable income from the disposal of shares, the amount of the tax-deductible costs depends on the method of acquisition of the shares. If the shares were purchased/taken up for cash, the expenses incurred in acquiring the shares (including the purchase/subscription price, notarial fees, court fees, stamp duty etc) shall be treated as tax deductible costs. However, these expenses are not recognised as tax-deductible costs until the moment of disposal of the shares for consideration.

If, with respect to any source, the tax-deductible costs are higher than the taxable revenues, the difference is a tax loss for such source of income. A tax loss may be carried forward over five consecutive years, however, the taxpayer may not deduct more than 50% of the loss in any particular tax year. Moreover, a tax loss for one source of income will not decrease the taxable income for any other source.

The corporate income tax rate in Poland is 19% (or 15% for small businesses and taxpayers in their first year of business) of taxable income or revenues calculated on the basis of these rules.

The main difference in tax treatment between domestic investors and foreign investors is that foreign investors are not generally treated as Polish tax residents. As such, taxation of the profits made in the territory of Poland mainly depends on the terms of the applicable double tax treaty. Generally, income from the sale of shares is not subject to tax in Poland but in the country where the seller has its registered office. There are exceptions to this rule in the case of double tax treaties which include the so-called "real estate clause" (such as the Luxembourg–Poland Double Tax Treaty 1955), where capital gains realised on the disposal of shares which directly or indirectly derive more than 50% of their value from immovable properties situated in Poland are subject to taxation in Poland.

A similar principle also applies under the Polish Corporate Income Tax Act 1992 and Polish Personal Income Tax Act 1991. In particular, income earned by a foreign tax resident shall be taxed in Poland to the extent it arises from the transfer of ownership of shares in a company, the rights and duties in a partnership, or ownership title in respect of an investment fund, a collective investment institution or another legal person or on account of the receivables resulting from holding of those shares, rights and duties or ownership titles, if immovable properties located in the territory of Poland or rights to such immovable properties constitute at least 50% of the value of the assets of the relevant company, partnership, investment fund, collective investment institution or other legal person. However, this rule only applies to foreign investors from a country with which Poland has not concluded a double tax treaty. Otherwise, the relevant double tax applies instead.

A payment of dividends is taxed at 19% unless an applicable double tax treaty provides otherwise. Based on the EU Parent–Subsidiary Directive (Directive 2011/96 on the common system of taxation applicable in the case of parent companies and subsidiaries of different Member States [2011] OJ L345/8), however, dividends payable by a Polish subsidiary to its parent based in Poland or another EU or European Economic Area (EEA) Member State are exempt from withholding tax provided the parent has held at least 10% of the shares in the Polish subsidiary for at least two years. This exemption applies whether the two-year period of continuous shareholding is satisfied before or after (or partially before and after) the date on which the dividends are paid.

Entities from other countries may only benefit from the preferential withholding tax rates provided in the respective double tax treaties. Payments of dividends by a Polish company directly to a parent located in a state with which Poland has not concluded a double tax treaty (mainly places such as Hong Kong and Monaco) are subject to 19% withholding tax in Poland. For this reason, private equity funds having their seat in such places generally do not invest in Poland directly but via EU subsidiaries or Polish subsidiaries held by EU subsidiaries.

### Limited partnerships

An LLP is transparent for income tax purposes, which means that it is the partners, not the partnership itself, that are recognised as taxpayers. As a result, a partner in a limited partnership which is a company will be subject to corporate income tax and a partner who is an individual will be subject to personal income tax (PIT), in each case, in respect of its share of the limited partnership's income.

The revenues from participation in a partnership should be added to each partner's revenues in proportion to its share in the partnership. This principle applies also to the tax-deductible costs, expenses not recognised as tax-deductible costs etc.

The resulting income will be taxed at the partner's level.

In certain situations, limited partnerships may be preferred over companies from a tax perspective, especially for partners who are individuals (natural persons) and not companies.

In general, the Polish tax authorities assume that participation in a Polish partnership gives a foreign partner a permanent establishment in Poland. Consequently, a foreign partner's share of the profits from an LLP will be subject to taxation in Poland. However, depending on the relevant double tax treaty, a foreign partner's income from the sale of its participation in an LLP may be taxed only in the seller's country, unless the relevant double tax treaty includes the above-mentioned "real estate clause" with regard to the sale of such interests (as is the case with the UK–Poland Double Tax Treaty 2006) or, in the absence of a double tax treaty, the similar provisions under Polish corporate and PIT laws apply, in which case, the income may be taxed in Poland.

## 6.2   Carried interest

The provisions of Polish tax law do not provide for a special regime of taxation of private equity funds. As a result, there is no special regime for carried interest (i.e. profit entitlements of investment executives that are designed to align their interests with those of the private equity fund's investors and provide incentives for the executives to maximise the fund's performance). Discussed below are three options for structuring carried interest. The taxation of interests arising by virtue of contributions to/investments in the fund by such persons is not discussed here.

First, direct payment of carried interest to a Polish individual from a domestic fund may be subject to PIT on a general basis (i.e. on a progressive tax scale of 18–32%). There are arguments supporting the view that, to the extent that carried interest is distributed as a share of a limited partnership's income resulting from sale of shares, the applicable rate is 19%.

Secondly, carried interest might also be paid on the basis of a consulting agreement concluded between a domestic private equity fund and an individual acting as a sole entrepreneur. If the carried interest is treated as a fee for performance of intangible services (advisory, consulting etc), the individual may benefit from a 19% PIT rate (after fulfilment of other formal criteria).

Finally, carried interest may be paid to the executive via an overseas fund/company located in a country with a preferential tax regime, which would allow reduction of the tax burden connected with payment of the carried interest directly to the Polish executive.

In principle, taxation of carried interest paid to a foreign individual depends on the basis of payment of the carried interest and the relevant double tax treaty.

## 6.3   Management equity

There are various issues related to stock option plans or other mechanisms under which management is awarded with shares and/or an option to acquire shares in the investment vehicle (for consideration or free of charge).

The Polish Personal Income Tax Act 1991 provides for preferential tax treatment of revenue from participation in certain incentive plans. In particular, revenue from participation in a qualifying incentive plan in respect of the shares in a joint stock company is only treated as arising at the time of sale of shares. Generally, in order to qualify, the incentive plan should be a remuneration system established by way of a resolution of the general meeting of the joint stock company and the participant must be an employee of the stock company (or an employee of a company of which the joint stock company is a dominant entity). Also, the joint stock company must be located in an EU/EEA country or a country with which Poland has a double taxation treaty.

The taxable income from the sale of shares acquired under a qualifying incentive plan will be treated as capital gains and taxed at 19% PIT. For this purpose, the taxable income is calculated as the difference between the revenue earned from such sale and the tax-deductible costs. In that regard, expenditure incurred in respect of the acquisition of the shares may be recognised as a tax-deductible cost but no tax deductible cost will be recognised to the extent the shares were acquired free of charge.

However, revenues obtained under an incentive plan which does not meet the above criteria may be taxed at two stages, i.e. the point at which the participant exercises the relevant right and acquires the shares, to the extent that the participant acquires the shares below market value, and at the moment of sale of the shares.

As with sale of shares acquired under a qualifying incentive plan, the taxable income at the second stage will be treated as capital gains and taxed at 19% PIT. However, the taxable income arising from the first stage is not treated as a capital gain. Similarly, benefits received in cash or other benefits in kind, and not arising by way of subscription for and disposal shares, are not treated as capital gains (e.g. proceeds under a phantom share scheme). In such cases, the taxable income is taxed according to different rules depending on its source. Generally, such taxable income will be taxed on the progressive tax scale of 18–32%. However, revenues arising from rendering services as an entrepreneur are taxed at the personal income rate of 19%.

### 6.4 Loan interest

Interest paid to a private equity fund that is a Polish legal entity constitutes part of its business income and is subject to tax in accordance with general rules (it is not subject to withholding tax calculated, withheld and paid by the borrower).

Interest paid to foreign private equity funds is generally subject to 20% withholding tax in Poland, unless the applicable double tax treaty provides otherwise.

However, it should be noted that, provided certain conditions set out under Polish law are satisfied, interest paid to EU/EEA companies may be exempt from withholding tax (e.g. provided the parent has held at least 25% of the shares in the Polish subsidiary for at least two years; similar to the situation in respect of dividend payments, this exemption applies whether the two-year period of continuous shareholding is satisfied before or after (or partially before and after) the date on which the interest is paid).

### 6.5 Transaction taxes

Generally, a purchase of shares is subject to 1% civil transactions tax (CTT) paid on the market value of the shares subject to sale. However, if the sale of shares in a JSC is executed through a brokerage house, a CTT exemption would apply.

A sale of assets by a value added tax (VAT) payer usually constitutes a supply of goods or provision of services (e.g. licences) within the meaning of the Polish VAT Act 2004 and, as such, is subject to VAT. The basic VAT rate in Poland is 23% (although there are preferential rates for certain supplies, e.g. the supply of food). In certain cases, a supply of goods (e.g. buildings or land) may be VAT exempt. The supply of a business (including by way of sale or in-kind contribution) which is a going concern or an organised part of a going concern is not subject to VAT. Rather, such a transaction is subject to CTT (calculated at the rate of 1% or 2% of the market value of the underlying assets, depending on the category).

## 7. CURRENT TOPICAL ISSUES/TRENDS

In terms of the legal framework, an amendment to the Act on Shaping the Agricultural System 2003 in 2016 has introduced provisions aimed at limiting the direct or indirect acquisition of agricultural land other than by natural persons with relevant qualifications who will actually farm it. Importantly, the Act generally gives the National Support Center for Agriculture a pre-emptive right in respect of shares in companies which own at least 0.3ha of agricultural land (whether or not the company is engaged in agriculture and regardless of the ratio of the value of the agricultural land owned by the company to the value of all its assets). A transaction which is undertaken in breach of the new rules will be invalid. On their face, the new rules would not seem to be particularly relevant to most private equity transactions. However, it is quite common in Poland for companies with real properties which are primarily industrial to also have small parcels of real property that remain designated as agricultural (e.g. operators of warehouses, logistics centres, service centres or manufacturing facilities on the outskirts of a city). Potentially, for transactions involving target companies in this situation, it may be necessary to sell the agricultural land before the broader transaction. Alternatively, if the agricultural land is not actually being used for agriculture, it may be appropriate to seek a change of the designation of the land before a direct or indirect sale occurs. Either of these approaches could affect the timetable for the transaction. Further, in many cases, the invalidity of a transaction may not be immediately apparent at the time. For this reason, careful review of historical transactions that may have been subject to these rules is becoming an important part of due diligence on a prospective target, even if the relevant company no longer holds the affected assets.

Also, the Government is seeking to take back majority ownership of several previously state-controlled businesses, including financial institutions, and has been prepared to intervene to block foreign ownership in other cases, particularly in the energy sector. In particular, the Control of Certain Investments Act 2015 (which came into force on 1 October 2015) imposes a requirement to notify the Prime Minister or the Minister of Energy about a planned acquisition of a significant interest (including, for example, 20% of the voting rights) in a relevant company operating in certain specified strategic business areas (generally in the energy, oil and gas, chemical, armament and telecommunications sectors). The relevant Minister may prevent the acquisition if it would threaten, among other things, the independence of Poland, the integrity of its territory, the freedoms or rights of people in or citizens of Poland, national security or public order. The notification requirement only applies if the relevant company is included on the list contained in the Regulation of the Council of Ministers regarding the list of entities subject to protection of 6 December 2017. However, the list can be amended or extended at any time. For example, PKP Energetyka (the electricity distributor to the Polish railway network) was placed on the list in July 2016 after being acquired by CVC Capital Partners in 2015 (which may limit the exit opportunities for CVC given the expectation that the government wishes the asset to be returned to state-owned hands). Also, EDF and Engie's Polish assets were put on the list after press reports about their potential sale and, in December 2016, the Polish Government used the Act to block a restructuring ahead of the potential sale of EDF's district heating assets to IFM Investors and its Rybnik power plant to Czech utility EPH, and the assets were eventually sold to PGE (a state-owned energy company).

The Crisis Management Act 2007 also gives the Government scope to block transactions which concern certain critical infrastructure and systems, including energy infrastructure, telecommunications infrastructure, financial systems, food and water supply systems, healthcare infrastructure and systems, transport infrastructure, rescue services and facilities for production, transport, storage, warehousing or use of chemical and radioactive substances. The scope to block a transaction only applies if the relevant target has been notified by the Government that it is subject to the Act.

As regards factors other than changes to local law, there is increasing concern over various sources of instability that might affect the world and European economies. These include increasing political tensions between the US and the EU and between the US and China, the potential for damaging trade wars, uncertainty over the form and impact of Brexit, rising oil prices and uncertainty about the future of the euro. Nevertheless, for the time being, most quality businesses are finding buyers. Having said that, transaction processes are often fragile or prolonged and caution still prevails over exuberance.

# Russia

**Egorov Puginsky Afanasiev & Partners** Arkady
Krasnikhin, Vyacheslav Yugai & Roman Malovitsky

## 1. MARKET OVERVIEW
### 1.1 Types of investors
Russian private equity funds receive funding from a range of investors,
including:
* Russian financial institutions;
* high net worth individuals;
* the investment divisions of Russian corporates;
* family offices;
* foreign private equity investors;
* foreign pension funds; and
* development bodies (e.g. the European Bank of Reconstruction and
  Development).

Russian government investment programmes, including RUSNANO and
the Russian Direct Investment Fund (RDIF), are also sources of investment
capital.

Russian pension funds and insurers are not yet a major source of funding
(although regulatory reform may change this position).

### 1.2 Types of investments
Historically, the majority of private equity investment in Russia has been at
the expansion stage of investment, providing additional capital to enable the
business to develop to a point where an exit can be contemplated, whether by
sale to a strategic investor or, less commonly, via an initial public offering
(IPO). Private equity investors commonly take a minority interest with the
founders retaining operational control, although investors are often granted
options to increase their stake (sometimes to a controlling interest) over time.
Leveraged buyouts of mature businesses are uncommon. Venture capital
funding has become more prevalent recently, particularly in the technology
sector, backed by Russian government initiatives such as RUSNANO and the
Skolkovo Foundation.

Investments have been made across a wide range of sectors, with notable
recent deals involving technology, media and telecommunications, consumer
goods and services, and infrastructure. Federal Law No.57-FZ on Foreign
investments in legal entities of strategic importance to the national defence
and state security of the Russian Federation of 29 April 2008 (Strategic
Investment Law) places limitations on investment by foreign entities in a
range of strategic sectors (notably natural resources) and imposes a consent
procedure which makes these sectors less attractive for private equity
investment, particularly given that the majority of private equity funds are

offshore vehicles.

Investments tend to be non-leveraged, consistent with the minority positions taken by private equity investors, but the injection of private equity capital is often a precursor to debt financing, enhancing the credibility of the portfolio company from the lenders' perspective.

## 2. FUNDS
### 2.1 Fund structures
Domestic private equity funds in the Russian Federation can be established in the form of: (1) joint stock investment funds (an incorporated fund); (2) closed unit investment funds (an unincorporated mutual fund); or (3) investment partnerships.

### Joint stock investment fund
A joint stock investment fund is a legal entity in the form of a joint stock company, the exclusive activity of which is fixed by its charter as investing in assets in line with standards set out in its investment declaration.

The investment declaration must be approved by the general meeting of shareholders of the joint stock investment fund (but the charter may reserve this power to its supervisory board). The investment declaration also has to be filed with the Central Bank of Russia (CBR). The joint stock investment fund is entitled to pursue its activities only under a licence issued by the CBR.

The property of the joint stock investment fund is divided into property designated for investing (investment resources) and property designated for supporting the operations of the fund.

The investment resources of the joint stock investment fund are transferred to a management company on a trust management basis. Trust management means that the management company manages the investment resources on behalf of the joint stock investment fund, must hold the assets separately to its own and, in its dealings with fund assets, must specify that it acts in the capacity of trust manager. The management company must meet the requirements set out in Federal Law No.156-FZ on Investment funds of 29 November 2001 (Investment Funds Law) and requires a licence issued by the CBR to act as trust manager of a joint stock investment fund.

A joint stock investment fund is not entitled to issue securities other than ordinary registered shares. The charter of a joint stock investment fund may or, where it is established by regulatory acts of the CBR, must provide that the securities of the fund may be owned only by qualified investors.

### Unit investment fund
Unlike joint stock investment funds, a unit investment fund is not a legal entity but an unincorporated mutual fund.

A unit investment fund comprises property transferred by investors (usually cash for investment purposes) to a management company to be held in trust management on the condition that this property will be pooled with the property of other investors and property acquired in the course of the life of the fund.

A share in the right of ownership of the fund is certified by a security (unit) issued by the management company. The rights of unit holders include the right to demand proper trust management from the management company, to participate in the general meeting of unit holders and to receive monetary compensation on termination of the fund.

Russian law provides for three types of unit investment funds: open, stock, interval and closed. Private equity funds can be established in any form of unit investment funds. Closed funds differ from the other three types of unit investment funds in that the unit holders of a closed unit investment fund are not entitled to demand termination of the trust management agreement prior to expiration of its term (except in cases stipulated by law). All unit holders of private equity funds shall be qualified investors.

The relationship between the management company and the investors in the fund is established by trust administration rules, which must be registered with the CBR. The management company carries out all transactions with the fund's property in its own name but must indicate that it is acting in the capacity of a trust manager (and will otherwise be liable in person and with only its own property).

The management company must meet the requirements set out in the Investment Funds Law and is entitled to pursue its activities only under a licence issued by the CBR.

### Investment partnership

Federal Law No.335-FZ on Investment partnership of 28 November 2011 (Investment Partnership Law) introduced the investment partnership. This is a contractual arrangement enabling two or more partners to arrange collective investments without establishing a separate legal entity.

Activities of an investment partnership may include both equity investment (acquisition and/or sale of non-publicly traded shares and participatory interests) and non-equity investment (such as acquisition of bonds and derivative financial instruments).

An investment partnership comprises two types of partners: (1) managing partners, which are responsible for the management of the investment partnership; and (2) ordinary partners. Managing partners are allowed to make both cash and in-kind contributions to the investment partnership but ordinary partners are required to contribute cash. Managing partners may receive a management fee for their management activities.

An investment partnership is established by an investment partnership agreement, which may include provisions on the following:

- rights and duties of partners and the managing partner;
- remuneration of the managing partner;
- the size and type of partners' contributions;
- capital call procedures;
- conduct of the investment partnership's business (management and decision-making procedures, or establishment of an investment committee);
- distribution of profits;
- apportionment of the partners' shares upon a creditor's demand; and
- exit rules.

There is no requirement to register an investment partnership agreement with the CBR.

The partners' common property must be accounted for in a separate balance sheet to the property of the managing partner(s).

Partners (other than the managing partner) may transfer their interests in the investment partnership to other partners or third parties subject to pre-emptive rights for the other partners.

Partners are liable on a joint and several basis with all their property for non-contractual obligations and contractual obligations assumed in relation to non-commercial parties. Ordinary partners are liable for the contractual obligations of the investment partnership assumed in relation to commercial parties to the extent of the value of their respective contributions to the partners' common property. If the common property is insufficient, the managing partners bear subsidiary liability for such obligations of the investment partnership on a joint and several basis. Any agreement of the parties to the investment partnership agreement purporting to exclude or limit the partners' liability as described above will be null and void.

## 2.2 Regulation of fundraising and fund managers

The following laws and regulations govern the manner in which private equity funds can be marketed and operated in Russia:

- the Investment Funds Law provides the legal framework for establishment and operation of joint stock investment funds and unit investment funds. The Investment Funds Law specifies requirements for investors, management companies and investment funds, procedure of formation, reorganisation and liquidation of investment funds, rules of circulation of equity interests, raising of funds and other basic issues connected with the activity of investment funds;
- Federal Law No.208-FZ on Joint stock companies of 26 December 1995 (Companies Law) regulates issues concerning establishment, reorganisation and liquidation of joint stock companies, their legal status, and the rights and obligations of their shareholders. The provisions of the Companies Law are applied in relation to joint stock investment funds subject to the specific requirements of the Investment Funds Law;
- the Investment Partnership Law, in compliance with the Civil Code of the Russian Federation, regulates investment partnerships;
- various regulatory acts of the CBR, which is the federal executive body in charge of the securities market (i.e. CBR Directive No.4129-U of 5 September 2016 on composition and structure of assets of joint stock investment funds and unit investment funds); and
- various regulations of the Federal Financial Markets Service (FFMS; although the FFMS has ceased to exist and its authority has been transferred to the CBR, its regulations continue to apply) specify requirements for investment funds, including but not limited to: (1) the amount of a joint stock investment fund's own resources and procedure for their calculation (FFMS Order No.09-32/pz-n of 13 August 2009); (2) the minimum value of property which constitutes a closed unit investment fund (FFMS Order No.125/pz-n of 2 November 2006); and (3) additional requirements for preparation, convocation and holding of a general meeting of the holders of equity interests (FFMS Order No.08-

5/pz-n of 7 February 2008).

The following laws and regulations govern the management of private equity funds in Russia:

- the Investment Funds Law stipulates requirements for the management company, its rights, obligations and responsibilities, certain rules concerning remuneration of the management company and restrictions on its activities; and
- various regulations of the CBR and FFMS specify certain requirements for the management companies of investment funds, including but not limited to:
  — the requirements as to the amount of own resources of the management company (CBR Directive No.4075-U of 19 July 2016);
  — the requirements as to the procedure for determining the amount of remuneration of the management company (FFMS Order No.08-31/ pz-n of 29 July 2008); and
  — the procedure, terms and requirements for obtaining licences by management companies (CBR Regulation No.481-P of 27 July 2015 and CBR Guidance No.166-I of 29 June 2015). Pursuant to Russian law, the management company of a private equity fund can be only a joint stock company or a limited liability company incorporated under the legislation of the Russian Federation. The management company is entitled to carry out its trust management activities only on the basis of a licence issued by the CBR.

In case of revocation of the management company's licence, the rights and obligations of such management company under the trust management agreement shall be transferred to another management company within three months from the date of revocation, otherwise, the closed unit investment fund shall be terminated.

Under Russian law, the management company is not entitled to simultaneously manage and own the property of the private equity fund. Therefore, the management company is required to transfer the fund property into the custody of a licensed Russian custodian (depositary).

Starting from 28 January 2018, all senior managers of the management companies (i.e. CEO, chief accountant, their deputies, board members, compliance and AML (anti-money laundering) officers) shall meet the requirements of business reputation established by the CBR. The candidacies of CEO, chief accountant, their deputies and chief compliance officers shall be agreed with the Central Bank. Such persons are prohibited to hold these positions in any other financial organisations.

A more restrictive approach is envisaged for shareholders of the management companies. No one offshore company is allowed to dispose or control (directly or indirectly) more than 10% in the charter capital of the management company. Potential investors of the management companies shall also meet the requirements of financial position and business reputation established by the CBR. Failure to do so leads to reduction of the voting rights under 10% of votes. Acquisition of more than 10% of the shares of the management company is to be agreed with the Central Bank as well. All joint stock investment funds and management companies shall be the members of a self-regulatory organisation.

### 2.3 Customary or common terms of funds

Russian law provides for the following key terms and requirements for domestic private equity funds:

- private equity funds established in the territory of the Russian Federation may be in the form of a joint stock investment fund, a closed unit investment fund or an investment partnership;
- private equity funds organised in the form of a joint stock investment fund, as well as the management company of private equity funds, are entitled to carry out activity only on the basis of a licence issued by the CBR;
- the own resources of a private equity fund in the form of a joint stock investment fund as at the date of submitting documents for receiving a licence shall be not less than RUR 35,000,000 (about EUR 460,000);
- the minimum value of property which constitutes a private equity fund in the form of a closed unit investment fund is RUR 25,000,000 (about EUR 330,000);
- the assets of such private equity funds as joint stock investment funds for qualified investors and combined unit investment funds may include any property, except for cash; and
- the term of trust management agreement in respect of the closed unit investment fund shall be not less than three years and not more than 15 years starting from the date of its formation.

## 3. DEBT FINANCE

### 3.1 Means of financing

Leveraged buyout transactions are not very common in Russia but, as noted above, debt finance is very often part of the medium-term development plan for a portfolio company which will be initiated by the private equity investment.

Financing in the form of a traditional secured term loan facility remains the predominant form of financing in Russia. Loan facilities are generally extended by banks, and the major state-owned Russian lenders, VTB, Sberbank and Vnesheconombank, have become prominent lenders in recent years as the major international banks have to some extent retrenched from lending in Russia due to sanctions.

Usually, a loan is extended under a bilateral facility agreement using the template employed by the particular lender. No common template is widely recognised in the Russian debt market, although the use of English-law documentation in line with Loan Market Association (LMA) standards is common, even among the major Russian banks which frequently lend through offshore subsidiaries.

Bonds are used much less frequently than bilateral facilities. Bond issuance tends to be used by mature companies with predictable cash flows rather than the growing companies which are typically the target of private equity deals in Russia. Further, bond issuances are subject to a more restrictive regulatory regime than facility agreements. High yield bonds are rarely used in the context of private equity investments in Russia.

Until recently, securitisation was limited solely to debt securities secured by mortgage portfolios. However, new regulations in respect of securitisation have recently been introduced which broaden the asset classes that may back the securities issued and it is expected that securitisation will become more widespread in Russia. This may offer an alternative to a standard loan facility for portfolio companies within certain sectors, notably energy and technology.

## 3.2   Restrictions on granting security

No general restrictions limiting the grant of security exist in Russia and lenders usually secure loans by pledges over assets and shares.

However, if a lender, whether through voting powers in respect of shares or otherwise, can control a company whose shares are pledged, anti-monopoly clearance may be required for the grant and/or enforcement of the pledge.

Further, if a lender is a foreign person (company or natural person) or is directly or indirectly controlled by a foreign person, the grant and enforcement of the pledge may require the consent of the authorised governmental bodies under the Strategic Investment Law. Such consent may be required if the company that has pledged its shares is a strategic company. A company is treated as strategic if it conducts any of the activities listed in the Strategic Investment Law or holds a land plot of national importance.

A pledge may be challenged if entered into in anticipation of the insolvency of the pledgor. This risk needs to be carefully considered by lenders as Russian law specifies a wide list of situations when a pledgee is deemed to be aware of the weakened financial position of a pledgor.

## 3.3   Intercreditor issues

The lack of regulation of intercreditor priority, together with imperative provisions of the Civil Code envisaging priority of pledgees on a strict chronological basis, used to be one of the key challenges for structuring complicated financial transactions. However, the Civil Code has recently been amended to address this issue and the priority of pledgees can now be changed by agreement between the pledgees (or between the pledgees and the pledgor). However, these new provisions of the Civil Code have not yet been tested in any cases and there is a risk that the Russian courts may take a restrictive approach to their interpretation.

Subordinated loans are expressly permitted by Russian law only for credit organisations acting as borrowers. An unsecured loan granted to a company which is not a credit organisation will be treated pari passu with all other unsecured loans if insolvency proceedings against the borrower are commenced.

The priority of creditors in the course of insolvency is strictly regulated by Russian law. Different rules apply to the insolvency of credit organisations and certain other companies but, generally, non-voluntary creditors, such as injured individuals or employees, enjoy priority over other creditors. Claims of a pledgee will be satisfied from the proceeds of sale of the pledged property but in an amount not exceeding 70–80% of such proceeds (depending on the secured obligations).

## 3.4 Syndication

Whilst syndication does exist and its use has been developing in recent years, the syndicated loans market remains relatively small in the Russian Federation for both commercial (absence of risk management standards appropriate for syndication) and legal reasons.

However, regulation of syndicated loans is developing in line with expectations of market participants. New Law on Syndicated loans has been effective since 1 February 2018. Though, these new syndication regulations have not been tested by the courts and there are still a number of grey areas (for example, whether facility agent may act on behalf of all the creditors in the course of insolvency proceedings; whether lender may assign its rights under syndicated facility agreement to the other non-credit entities).

The lack of standard Russian documentation for syndication and sub-participation leads lenders to use LMA forms, which are not entirely consistent with Russian legislation.

## 4. EQUITY STRUCTURES
### 4.1 Role of management

The majority of private equity investment in Russian companies operates on a joint venture model. The founding shareholders will continue to hold equity (typically a controlling stake) in the portfolio company, usually through an offshore corporate vehicle, and will be party to a shareholders' agreement with the private equity investor(s). Board representation for the managers is likely to be derived from the equity ownership of the founding shareholders (and reflect the founding shareholders' controlling stake) rather than specific rights in their capacity as managers.

The wider management team would not usually be given equity directly in the investment company (whether in the Russian operating entity itself or any offshore holding company) but may hold shares in the founding shareholders' investment vehicle. However, to align the interests of the management team with the shareholders, it is common for there to be a performance-related bonus scheme. This may take the form of a phantom equity arrangement, whereby the managers are entitled to a percentage of any uplift in the value of the company based on a deemed equity holding. Alternatively, a formula-based remuneration scheme linked to the achievement of key investment milestones or the internal rate of return (IRR) achieved by the private equity fund may be used.

Management would usually be employed under Russian law employment contracts, the terms of which are closely prescribed by Russian law.

The key management appointment in any Russian company is the general director (CEO), who has extensive management authority under Russian law, including the ability to conclude transactions on behalf of the company and sign agreements binding the company without any additional authorisation (except as stipulated by the company's charter) or any power of attorney. The controlling shareholder is likely to insist on having the right to nominate the general director but an investor with a significant minority stake will want to ensure that the shareholders' agreement puts in place appropriate checks and balances on the general director's authority.

## 4.2 Common protections for investors

Protections will vary depending upon the size of the shareholding to be acquired by the private equity investor but will typically include:

- board representation: the investor would expect at least one director. Note that, in the case of direct investment in a Russian joint stock company, cumulative voting will apply for board appointments and the appointments procedure will need to take this into account;
- veto rights: a requirement for investor consent to specific actions should be documented in any shareholders' agreement and hardwired into the Russian operating company via its charter. Veto rights would range from blocks on fundamental changes to the company's business or actions that may result in value leakage (for an investor with a sub-20% holding) to some involvement in material operational matters (where the investor has a 25–50% holding);
- limits on the authorities of key personnel: constitutionally, in employment contracts or through some form of "two key" approval system. For a majority or significant minority investor, there may also be a hardwired right to appoint or at least remove the general director (CEO), the chief financial officer (CFO) and other key personnel, which rights should be enforceable and backed by hard commitments;
- transfer provisions: lock-in applicable for agreed investment period, rights of first offer/refusal on share transfers, tag-along right (for minority shareholders) and drag-along right (for majority shareholders). Put and call options may apply (typically at a discount to fair value) in the event of a default by a shareholder (e.g. change of control or material breach of the shareholders' agreement). Private equity investors need to be aware of the potential for transfers to be frustrated by requirements to obtain regulatory consents (from the Federal Antimonopoly Service and under the Strategic Investment Law);
- information rights: rights to receive audited accounts, monthly management accounts and other key information, particularly information required to enable the private equity fund to make required disclosures to its own investors. The private equity investor may also have the right to appoint the CFO as a means to access information at operating level. Investors will also normally insist upon the appointment of a "Big 4" auditor; and
- adequate recourse against the founding shareholders for breach of commitments through guarantees, pledges and rights over depositary accounts.

The investor should be prepared for the possibility that there will be deadlock or the partner will turn hostile in the future. In addition to economic alignment, solutions are a clear secured exit (put or put–call if it is realistic that the partner could ever be a forced seller) and possibly the right to syndicate to bring in a third-party investor who could calibrate the position with the partner.

The way that value is stripped out of Russian companies is through contracts with related parties, transfer pricing schemes and remuneration. These need to be tightly controlled with vetoes and rights of appointment/removal over key personnel, backed up by strong financial controls (and, for example, a financial controller or a "two key" system in respect of certain matters). The consequences for breach need to be loss of economic alignment and triggering of secured exit rights (or lawful penalties in lieu).

Items like business plan, respective obligations (including OPEX and CAPEX), the path to exit (IPO, buyout, trade sale), dividend policy and outside financing expectations need to be clearly agreed at the outset.

### 4.3   Common protections for management

To the extent that the managers are also the founding shareholders and hold equity in the portfolio company, they will enjoy the same protections as described for the investor. In addition, if the founding shareholders maintain a controlling stake in the company, they will seek protections to ensure that they have full operational control at the Russian level. The founding shareholders will wish to keep the powers of the general director (if such person is appointed by them) as unrestricted as possible. The balance between the founding shareholder's operational control and the investor's veto rights is often a critical negotiating issue, particularly where returns for the founding shareholders have a performance-related component (e.g. the right to retain an above-pro-rata share of profit once the investor's IRR has been achieved).

Save where they act in the dual capacity as managers and shareholders, management will not usually be given any specific protections other than rights under employment contracts and any bonus-plan agreements.

### 4.4   Management warranties

The investor would expect to be given comprehensive business warranties from the founding shareholders. Warranties regarding title to shares and assets, tax, accounts, permits/licences (depending on the sector) and litigation are all critical. Managers who are not also founding shareholders would not generally give any warranties to the investor. Limitation periods for warranty claims are typically up to three years for title and tax claims, and from one to two years for all other warranty claims. De minimis (individual and basket) thresholds and caps are commonplace.

### 4.5   Good leaver/bad leaver provisions

As noted above, it is rare for the wider management to be given equity in the portfolio company and, as such, management departures do not usually trigger any obligations regarding equity transfers. However, it is fairly standard for the bonus scheme applicable to management to include good leaver/bad leaver provisions. The grounds for dismissal of an employee are heavily circumscribed by Russian law and, as such, there can be a conflict with the bonus scheme agreements, which will seek to make "bad leaver" a much broader concept.

### 4.6   Public to private transactions

Public to private transactions are rare in Russia, but any such transaction would need to comply with the takeover rules under the Companies Law.

A mandatory offer must be made to the target company's shareholders to acquire all other voting shares in a public joint stock company, and securities convertible into such shares, at their market price when a bidder acquires more than 30% (as well as over 50% and 75%) of the target company's shares.

A bidder is entitled to squeeze out the minority shareholders of a public joint stock company if both: (1) the bidder demanding the squeeze-out owns more than 95% of the total number of the target company's shares (together with its affiliates); and (2) at least 10% of the shares owned by the bidder were acquired through a mandatory or voluntary public offer.

The consent of the Federal Antimonopoly Service is likely to be required for any acquisition. Depending on the sector in which the target company operates, consent under the Strategic Investment Law may also be required.

## 5. EXITS

### 5.1 Secondary sales

Secondary sales (the sale by a private equity fund of one or more portfolio companies to another private equity fund or financial institution) have not been, and are not, very common in Russia.

### 5.2 Trade sales

Trade sales, to either financial or strategic investors, are the most commonly used means of exit in Russia.

Lock-in periods are commonly included in shareholders' agreements between founders and private equity investors, often in the range of three–five years. There is often a reasonable endeavours obligation on the parties to work towards an exit (third-party sale or IPO) after that date and, in the absence of such exit, the private equity investor would be free to sell its stake subject to any applicable transfer restrictions.

Rights of first refusal or first offer are often included in the shareholders' agreement and, for a minority shareholder, a sale to a majority shareholder who wishes to assume sole control may represent the most viable exit.

Tag-along rights and drag-along rights are common so, if a majority shareholder elects to exit, this will usually result in a 100% disposal.

The private equity investor is not normally excluded from the obligation to give warranties to a third-party purchaser on an exit, save in situations where it is compelled to sell pursuant to an exercise of a drag-along right (in which case only title warranties are usually expected).

### 5.3 Initial public offerings

IPO exits are frequently contemplated by shareholders' agreements for private equity investments but are rarely realised. Whilst there have been several notable recent IPOs of companies with private equity investment (Lenta, Tinkoff Credit Systems, Europlan, Globaltruck Management and Detsky Mir), trade sales are likely to remain the primary exit mechanism for private equity investments.

## 5.4 Refinancings

Refinancing as a means of exit is not commonly used by Russian private equity funds.

## 5.5 Restructuring/insolvency

Restructuring/insolvency as a means of exit is not generally used by Russian private equity funds.

# 6. TAX

## 6.1 Taxation of fund structures

As described above, trade sales are the most common exit strategy in the Russian private equity market.

The Russian tax system does not include an express capital gain tax. Investors' capital gains on a sale of shares are subject to corporate profit tax (20%) or personal income tax (13% tax for residents/30% tax for non-residents), depending on whether the taxpayer is a corporation or an individual. Capital gains on shares are not subject to VAT or other special transaction taxes.

Unit investment funds and investment partnerships are not separate legal entities and are tax-transparent so that, for tax purposes, all income (including exit proceeds of any investment) is received at the investor level only. A joint stock investment fund is a separate taxpayer and has a two-tier taxation structure, which means that the fund first pays tax upon exit from portfolio companies and then investors pay tax upon exit from the fund. This makes a joint stock investment fund less attractive from a tax perspective.

The corporation tax regime applicable to capital gains derived by resident entities and foreign entities which carry out business activity in Russia through a permanent establishment (should such capital gains be attributed to the Russian permanent establishment's activity) is the same.

The general rule is that the tax base is determined as income from the sale or redemption of shares less deductible expenses (acquisition expenses, brokerage and management fees). It is important to note that, for tax purposes, the income from the sale of shares is not always determined as being equal to the agreed sale price. This is primarily relevant for shares which are not publicly traded, the price of which for tax purposes is determined as capital per share. Tax obligations should be fulfilled through a self-assessment mechanism (quarterly submission of tax returns).

Capital gains from the sale of shares in either Russian investment funds or companies which are received by foreign legal entities not operating through a Russian permanent establishment (or where the capital gain is not attributable to such permanent establishment) are exempt from (withholding) taxation unless more than 50% of the disposed fund's or company's assets is represented by Russian real estate. In some cases, this national limitation to the general exemption rule may be overridden by the application of a double tax treaty. However, most double tax treaties are now being renegotiated in order to close this loophole and bring them into compliance with national tax rules. Note also that the above exemption applies only to capital gains from sales of shares and does not cover the redemption of shares, which is taxed at source (withholding taxation) at a standard rate of 20%.

Capital gains derived by individual investors are generally taxed in the same way as those derived by corporations except that overseas individual investors are not entitled to exemption of capital gains through a double tax treaty (unlike corporate investors).

A number of funds provide for interim payments, which are treated as non-operational income and are usually taxed on a cash flow basis. Russian tax rules provide for a special dividend tax rate, which is 13% for residents and 15% for non-residents (corporates and individuals). If dividends are paid to overseas investors, the rate of taxation may be reduced or eliminated subject to application of a double tax treaty.

Considering the above, it may be more tax advantageous to invest in Russian funds and companies through foreign special purpose vehicles (SPVs). This investment structure can not only eliminate withholding taxation of capital gains in Russia but can also decrease the overall tax burden on the return on investment. However, the use of an SPV, and the choice of jurisdiction in which to incorporate such SPV, will need to be carefully considered in view of the controlled foreign company legislation which has been effective in Russia since 2015.

## 6.2 Carried interest

Russian tax law does not recognise carried interest as a special type of income and does not provide for any special taxation rules in this regard. The management company will pay corporate profit tax on carried interest and/or other types of management fees in case of a mixed fee arrangement. For tax purposes, carried interest is treated as regular operational income of an investment manager and is subject to corporate profit tax at a rate of 20%.

## 6.3 Management equity

Specific tax aspects related to the equity that is awarded to management usually arise in closed funds, where the investment declaration allows the transfer of non-monetary assets to the management. Despite the fact that the fund property is managed on behalf of the investors, the management company is liable to pay VAT and substantive taxes (e.g. property tax and land tax) in respect of the managed property. Special rules with respect to payment of property tax and land tax at the level of the management company have been introduced in order to prevent tax avoidance schemes whereby assets are transferred to a captive fund (usually a closed unit investment fund) in order to avoid taxes. The relevant taxes are paid by the management company on behalf of the equity holders.

## 6.4 Loan interest

Under the general rules, loan interest (if paid to an overseas lender) is subject to withholding tax at a rate of 20%. In certain cases, the withholding tax may be eliminated or reduced by the application of a double tax treaty.

Loan interest payable to a Russian entity would not be subject to withholding tax.

Generally, interest is deductible by the payor for its profit tax purposes. However, with respect to loans that are considered controlled transactions (e.g. between related parties), interest may be deducted only within certain limits (i.e. based on the CBR's refinancing rate for rouble-denominated loans; and EURIBOR and LIBOR for EUR and USD-denominated loans respectively).

Note that, in respect of a unit investment fund, Russian legislation prohibits a management company from entering into a loan or other credit facility arrangement save where the management company lacks the funds for redemption of the equity interest. In this case, a short-term debt financing may be obtained (for a term of not more than six months) and the overall amount of such financing must not exceed 20% of the unit investment fund's equity capital. This restriction does not affect joint stock investment funds or investment funds with limited circulation shares.

## 6.5 Transaction taxes

As mentioned above, Russian legislation does not provide for any special transaction taxes (such as a financial transaction tax or similar).

## 7. CURRENT TOPICAL ISSUES/TRENDS
### De-offshorisation

Historically, the preference has been for investments in Russian assets to be structured via an offshore holding company in a jurisdiction with a favourable double tax treaty with Russia and which permits the putting into place of an English law shareholders' agreement (including the typical bespoke international protections). The investor would then seek to "hardwire" the protections granted at the offshore level in the Russian operating company through amendments to the charter.

However, the "de-offshorisation" agenda signalled by President Putin in 2013,[1] including the impending introduction of controlled foreign company tax rules, has been picking up momentum and seems likely to continue to cause significant changes in transaction structuring. The trend towards onshore investment will undoubtedly also be accelerating by the EU and US sanctions in relation to Ukraine, and the desire of Russian parties to avoid any of their assets being blocked in the future.

Investors are likely to remain under increasing pressure to make investments directly into Russian portfolio companies under Russian law (rather than through an offshore SPV). Russian corporate law has improved significantly in recent years (e.g. permitting the use of shareholders agreements in respect of Russian companies and moving to introduce warranties and representations) so this is not as problematic as it once may have been. However, Russian law does not yet offer the flexibility of an English law shareholders' agreement and workarounds are likely to be developed to find a way to provide international protections in the context of an onshore deal (e.g. holding Russian equity through a depositary so that a foreign law shareholders' agreement can be used).

---

[1] "President Putin instructed the Government to develop measures aimed to encourage voluntary de-offshorisation" (2013) available at: *http://www.finmarket.ru/main/article/3221494* [Accessed 25 September 2018].

## Funding

The EU and US sanctions on certain Russian individuals and companies resulted in a "pause" in new investments from the EU and the US. In any event, the major Western private equity funds (with some exceptions) have not been significant investors in Russia in recent years, and the private equity funds of the state-owned banks (VTB and Sberbank) and RDIF (the Russian sovereign wealth fund), as well as the portfolio investment divisions of the oligarchic groups, have tended to be the dominant players.

There has been a developing trend towards a co-investment model, with non-Russian private equity investing alongside Russian funds and benefiting from their market knowledge and local execution abilities. RDIF is notable in this regard as its strategy is expressly based on co-investment and attracting at least matching funding for each investment in a portfolio company.

This co-investment seems likely to continue, although perhaps with a geographical shift in the pool of investment capital. Funding from Asia and the Middle East seems likely to figure more prominently, reflecting the increasing economic strength of these regions and the pivot towards Asia that has been signposted by the Russian Government. RDIF's funds established with China Investment Corporation, Korea Investment Corporation, Mubadala Development Company and Abu Dhabi's Department of Finance may be suggestive of how the investment landscape will look in the near future.

# Spain

**Gómez-Acebo & Pombo** Fernando de las Cuevas & Iñigo Erláiz

## 1. MARKET OVERVIEW
### 1.1 Types of investors
In consonance with the size of investment, financial institutions (through their stakes in private equity institutions), private investors, funds of funds, pension funds and public investors are the main investors in the private equity sector in Spain. In addition, several huge funds are in the process of being created as a consequence of the high levels of liquidity in the market and the demand of the investors for attractive returns. During the last few years, investments made by financial institutions have represented a major part of the total investment in funds in Spain.

### 1.2 Types of investments
As the financial markets continue to recover, there has been an increase in the number of leveraged buyout (LBO) transactions. However, said transactions are being carried out using less leverage than at the onset of the economic crisis. Highly LBOs have taken place in Spain recently, such as the acquisition of 100% of Pronovias by BC Partners (the former has accrued a total debt of EUR 313 million after its acquisition by BC Partners).

A growing number of investments in companies in the expansion phase of their development can be seen in the Spanish market but there is also an increase in late stage private equity investments, given the excellent investment opportunities on offer in the market and the potential return offered as a consequence of the improvement in the market conditions and the rise of consumption.

In sectorial terms, the sectors with the highest investment volumes are IT, consumer-related products, renewable energies and healthcare.

## 2. FUNDS
### 2.1 Fund structures
Private equity companies (VCC) and private equity funds (VCF), which are regulated by Law 22/2014 (GP), of 12 November 2014, governing private equity entities and their management companies, are the legal structures used in Spain for private equity investments. As opposed to the previous law of 2005, the GP does not differentiate between common regime and simplified regime private equity entities (VCEs). The current GP now differentiates between ordinary VCEs, Pyme VCEs and European VCEs, which have the following requirements and particularities:
- ordinary VCEs: are those whose main purpose is the temporary participation in non-financial and non-real estate companies, which, at

the time of the investment, are not listed in any stock markets;

- Pyme VCEs: these are a special type of VCE which must invest in certain kinds of companies (non-listed companies with less than 250 employees and less than EUR 50 million of annual turnover etc) with a minimum capital of EUR 900,000 (in the case of VCCs) and EUR 1,650,000 (in the case of VCFs), along with other specific requirements; and
- European VCEs: are those VCFs that wish to use the designation of "European Private Equity Fund" for their commercialisation in the EU.

VCCs must be public limited companies (SA). Their way of operating does not differ greatly from any other type of trading company but most have the particular characteristics stipulated in the GP (minimum capital, corporate purpose etc).

Unlike VCCs, VCFs are non-legal entities, which involve a large number of investors and are based on Anglo-Saxon limited partnership structures. Management companies, whose operating rules and codes of conduct are also set out in the GP and which play a role similar to that of general partners in limited partnerships, are responsible for the management and representation of these VCFs.

VCCs must obtain prior authorisation for their incorporation from the Spanish Securities and Exchange Commission (CNMV), have the incorporation of the company recorded in a public deed and registered at the Commercial Registry (these are optional requirements in the case of VCFs), and be registered in the relevant CNMV register before being allowed to start operations.

As explained in greater detail in s.6.1 below, both VCCs and VCFs benefit from advantageous tax regimes.

## 2.2 Regulation of fundraising and fund managers

The GP sets out the regulation of capital contributions in VCEs (VCCs and VCFs), including requirements for minimum capital that must be invested in VCCs (EUR 1,200,000) and in VCFs (EUR 1,650,000), the minimum amount which must be paid up initially (50% of the minimum initial equity in VCCs but 100% in VCFs) and the nature of the contributions (which may not consist of fixed assets in the case of VCFs).

The operating rules and codes of conduct for VCEs' management companies are also contained in the GP and require prior authorisation from the CNMV. The GP stipulates a minimum initial share capital for management companies of EUR 125,000 and for self-managed collective investment companies of EUR 300,000. In both cases, the initial share capital must be fully paid upfront. The management companies are also required to be properly organised and have sufficient resources to carry out their corporate purpose, meaning that they must have adequate administrative, accounting, human and technical resources for their business and turnover. They must also draw up binding internal rules of conduct to govern the actions of their administration bodies, managers and employees.

It is also obligatory for management companies to provide the CNMV with any and all information required of them as well as information as to the history of the funds they manage and the level of compliance with the various legal requirements (including asset investment ratios, patrimony and liquidity ratios, positions in the management company's group, a list of purchase and sale transactions etc).

## 2.3 Customary or common terms of funds

The routine requirements included in limited partnership agreements are set out in the management regulations, which stipulate how the funds operate: duration of the fund, conditions for subscription and redemption of the shares, regularity with which valuations of the shares have to be calculated, rules for administering, managing and representing the fund, the way in which profit and loss is determined and allocated, rules for the winding-up and liquidation of the fund, the form in which the management company is remunerated (basically, by means of a placement, management, investment or success fee), investment policy, disinvestment formulas, types of financing granted to subsidiaries, and formulas that allow the management companies to participate in investee companies and in their administration bodies. In general, the way in which these matters are dealt with is similar to those of other European countries. The management rules usually establish a limited duration for the fund (normally between seven and 10 years), a placement fee (around 2.5% of the value of each subscribed share), a management fee (approximately 2.5% of the subscribed equity per annum) or a success fee (which is usually established at 20% of the profit obtained by the VCF) as well as the minimum guaranteed return for the participants, which generally fluctuates between 6% and 8% of the participants' contributions. It is usual for an investment committee and a supervisory board to be established, made up of representatives from among the participants in the VCF and independent professionals, if applicable.

## 3. DEBT FINANCE

### 3.1 Means of financing

Besides the conventional forms of financing for private equity transactions (mainly (1) external debt funding by obtaining loans and/or bank credits, which in the larger transactions are structured as senior and mezzanine; and (2) funding contributed by the shareholders of the Newco), funding can be obtained in Spain through the issuance of high-yield bonds. They are not very frequent in private equity transactions, partly because the issuance of bonds in Spain is subject to considerable restrictions, such as the limitation established by the Spanish Capital Companies Law (*Ley de Sociedades de Capital*), prohibiting the issuance of bonds for an amount higher than the issuing company's capital plus its reserves. Funding by means of the issuance of high-yield bonds usually delays completion of the funded transaction by several months, although the problem of delays involved in the issuance of bonds is usually solved by a bridge loan from a bank, which subsequently handles the issuance and placement of the bonds.

Equity loans which are usually granted by the VCCs to their subsidiaries for periods that vary between three and five years are another form of financing used in Spain. This type of loan is regulated in Royal DecreeLaw 7/1996 and is characterised by its having a variable interest rate linked to different factors that indicate the company's economic situation (e.g. net profit, business turnover or the company's total assets), although it is also customary to establish a fixed interest rate which is generally low. Equity loans are considered by company law to be net assets for the purposes of share capital reductions and liquidations and, in the order of loan priority, they place the parties making them behind common creditors, i.e. as subordinate creditors.

## 3.2 Restrictions on granting security

In Spain, the financial assistance regime is more restrictive than in other European countries. Without exception, no company may advance funds, grant loans, give guarantees or provide any type of financial security to enable a third party to acquire its shares or shares in its controlling company. For this reason, with the LBOs, it is necessary to design structures that do not violate the prohibition on granting financial security. In this respect, both case law and the few existing court rulings on matters of this nature (specifically, Madrid Provincial Court Decision 2007/53501 of 9 January 2007) provide that the merging of Newco—a new company specifically incorporated to acquire the target company—and the target, after the acquisition and prior to commencing the repayment of the existing debt, is the appropriate procedure to avoid the application of the rules on financial assistance, on the understanding that a merger sufficiently protects the interests of the parties that could be affected by these transactions (mainly shareholders and creditors). For this reason, forward and reverse merger LBOs have been used almost exclusively in Spain as the mechanisms for carrying out these transactions.

Mergers carried out within the framework of an LBO are governed by Law 3/2009, which specifies the information requirements and calls for a report from an independent expert so that duly informed creditors and minority shareholders can exercise their rights in the merger process pursuant to the law. There is a widespread view that Law 3/2009 should be interpreted as meaning that a merger precludes the applicability of the Spanish regulations prohibiting the granting of financial assistance.

## 3.3 Intercreditor issues

An agreement governing the relationship between financing parties and establishing the debt hierarchy is essential in high-volume private equity transactions when a number of different financing parties are involved. From a legal point of view, it is a question of including mechanisms in the agreements to guarantee that the financing party assuming less risk will receive a lower return than the financing party assuming the greater risk in the transaction. This is not always as simple as it appears, as there are different cases, particularly those related to Spanish insolvency law, in which variations and changes in the hierarchy can be agreed and accepted by the parties. Consequently, the main issues to be considered when recording the debt hierarchy should focus on maintaining the agreed risk-return model. To do this, it is common practice to negotiate stand-still, cross-default or step-up clauses. In the case of LBOs, it is usual to add pari passu, negative pledge, material adverse change or financial covenants to these clauses.

The provisions of Insolvency Law 22/2003 (IL) also need to be taken into account since the order of payments foreseen in the IL may differ from the order stipulated in the agreement between the financing parties to the transaction. To protect the economic model, the order recorded in the agreement must be made consistent with the legal order and thereafter mechanisms provided to effect an eventual variation. For example, the IL considers creditor loans that are made by parties related to the debtor, such as group companies of the debtor and their shareholders, to be subordinate loans. It is therefore important for the financing parties to look through their portfolios and rule out the risk of becoming subordinate creditors.

## 3.4 Syndication

It is usual for the debt financing parties to syndicate their loans in the case of transactions that require a large investment. To ensure the success of syndicated loans, it is essential to guarantee that the system for notifying and adopting resolutions between the agent bank and the rest of the financing parties is appropriate, thereby avoiding undue inefficiency or delays in decision taking. In this respect, the system of majorities for the adoption of specific resolutions that affect all the members of the syndicate of financing parties is in force in Spain. The relatively recent introduction of the majority rule has proven to be more satisfactory than the unanimity rule which prevailed previously and which frequently led to consortiums with a large number of participants being unable to operate. Along with the majority rule, it is crucial that the agent bank should diligently fulfil its duties, especially its duty as notification agent.

In addition to the aspects mentioned above, gross-up clauses, clauses relating to the fixing of commissions, unexpected cost increases, supervening illegality, financial covenants and early maturity clauses in the event of a decrease in guarantees, deterioration of the borrower's solvency or cases of cross default are extremely important.

## 4. EQUITY STRUCTURES

### 4.1 Role of management

Senior members of the management team of the acquired company usually participate in the target company by continuing in a management capacity as a member of the board of directors or as a member of the executive committee, as applicable. Additionally, in start-up and seed capital transactions, and in the case of management buyouts (MBOs), management buy-ins (MBIs) and buy-in management buyouts (BIMBOs), the managers usually also participate in the company's capital by becoming shareholders and participate in the taking of decisions by attending the general shareholders' meeting.

The main contractual clauses relating to the management team are those that impose a non-compete obligation, which may not exceed two years, and the continuance obligation in the event of sale to a third party, without prejudice to all those clauses common to senior executive contracts.

In start-up and seed capital transactions, MBOs, MBIs and BIMBOs, the managers receive a participation in the share capital of the target company in exchange for their tangible or intangible contribution. This participation is in excess of their cash contribution because it also includes the managers' know-how, and consists of the acquisition of privileged shares/participations and the granting of the right to subscribe either without a premium at face value or with a lower premium, or by granting qualified voting rights for specific matters in the administration bodies.

Other formulas for the participation of the management team relate to their continuance and the obtaining of results or profit, such as equity ratchets, vesting systems or stock option plans. The structure of these incentive arrangements will depend in particular on tax issues.

### 4.2 Common protections for investors

A due diligence process will be carried out by investors before a deal is entered into to help establish the correct price. Once established, the sale and purchase agreement (SPA) is likely to contain clauses related to financial representations and price adjustment mechanics.

A VCF investment is protected during the life of the investment by specific clauses, such as shareholders agreements and bylaws of the investee company. The main clauses in this respect are: those protecting confidentiality, those requiring the consent of the investor before any actions can be taken, setting out pre-emption rights and mechanisms aimed at ensuring their validity (e.g. the requirement of a qualified majority for the exclusion of pre-emption rights, the fixing of the price by a third party in the case of disagreement), restrictions imposed on the managers in relation to the free transfer of shares and participations, and pre-emption rights with respect to the distribution of dividends.

There are several clauses that afford investor protection when investors exit the company. In a liquidation, it is frequent to see preference clauses which operate by creating preferred shares or participations, paid for from a special reserve; an undertaking to vote in favour of distributing the special reserve following the sale; and, in the event of selling 100% of the company, an agreement that grants the investor a pre-emption right over the shares being sold. Tag-along and drag-along clauses are usual if the sale is to a third party, and repurchase or buy-back clauses are common place if the sale is to the rest of the shareholders. Finally, if the exit is by way of an initial public offering (IPO), the pre-emption rights in the listing, registration rights, temporary restrictions (usually from three to six months) on a future sale of shares, the elimination of the restrictions on free transfer and the reinforced voting majorities, and the automatic conversion of the preferred shares to common shares are all very common.

### 4.3 Common protections for management

Clauses defining issues that are confidential or subject to a qualified majority are fundamental protection mechanisms for managers as well as the adoption of anti-dilution mechanisms to maintain the ratio of political power vis-à-vis possible capital increases (for example, increase conditional upon their being executed with a share premium, or by granting veto clauses or qualified majority clauses to managers to be able to decide on such increase).

In the event of an unexpected need for further funding, clauses could be established according to the issuance of promoted stock to the managers, without a premium and in favourable conditions. Likewise, preference clauses are usually included in the event of distribution of dividends, especially if the company profits exceed certain thresholds. With respect to the managers' exit from the company, there are the typical tag-along clauses (the aptness for registration of which or their non-applicability to third parties raises problems under Spanish law), lock-out clauses and clauses that accelerate vesting if the liquidity event occurs prior to the consolidation.

### 4.4　Management warranties

The management team is required to provide guarantees to cover any and all risks arising from an incorrect evaluation of the company and from its potential contingencies. Consequently, the representations and warranties (R&Ws) required are those that are usually included in SPAs (warranties that cover administrative, labour, tax, environmental, intellectual property, real estate, contractual and corporate risks etc). Thus, the managers will be liable not only for the management of the target company but also for the management of the acquired company, insofar as it has led to a change in the sale price.

The liability of the management team is generally established, in Spain, for a period of between one and two years after the transaction has been completed, except when liability arises from obligations that are subject to a statute of limitations, in which case the temporary limitation will usually be broader. The casuistry relating to the liability cap is very broad, there being no consistent criteria under Spanish law. In any event, the established liability caps are usually standard for this type of transaction.

### 4.5　Good leaver/bad leaver provisions

Spanish equity-based incentive schemes usually contain clauses that link the managers' participation in the company's capital to their continuance in the company. If a manager holding shares leaves the company before the investor has exited, this will give rise to a buy-back right in favour of the company or other shareholders. Voluntary resignation breaching a continuity obligation, fair dismissal and breaches of contract is normally considered a bad leaver scenario, whereas unfair dismissal and full permanent disability or severe disability will fall within good leaver scenarios. Managers are required to undertake more severe commitments (generally non-compete obligations) for the event of bad leaver scenarios.

### 4.6　Public to private transactions

It is not customary in Spain for VCFs to make offers for listed companies. Until the GP, the corporate purpose of the VCCs did not actually include public to private (P2P) transactions. Since the former GP came into force, a number of these kinds of transactions have taken place, such as those involving the companies Recoletos, Amadeus and Cortefiel; however, these were specific cases, and transactions of this kind are not frequent in Spain, where the natural private equity market is the middle market.

When carrying out a P2P transaction, the main factor to be considered is that, under Spanish law, when a company decides to delist its shares, it must launch a mandatory buyout bid for delisting within 12 months following the acquisition of the participation. This generates the need for a greater degree of transparency and information with respect to the shareholders and competent authorities (in Spain, the CNMV). Finally, it is important to include in the purchase agreement clauses related to break fees, undertakings to launch a takeover bid (TOB) or the non-acceptance of competing TOBs and, if applicable, clauses that allow the acceptance of a competing TOB if it improves on the price of the former by an agreed minimum amount after paying the relevant penalty.

## 5. EXITS

### 5.1 Secondary sales

The most common disinvestment mechanism in Spain is that of selling to a third party. Some of the reasons that have led to the rise in secondary buyouts as an exit mechanism, used by the market operators with high liquidity and scarce good investment opportunities, are precisely the above-mentioned lack of maturity of the secondary market, the regulatory obstacles and, in general, the difficulties in carrying out an IPO. The negotiation process and the agreements (between parties with common interests and concerns) in secondary buyouts are usually simpler and without R&Ws, or with very delimited and clear areas of responsibility for the seller.

### 5.2 Trade sales

Trade sales continue to be the most common exit mechanism. The purchaser's knowledge, and his/her capacity to identify risks in the target company and reflect this in the price, results in SPAs also usually having limited R&Ws, consistent with the fund's interest in limiting eventual liabilities to the period of its duration.

### 5.3 Initial public offerings

IPOs continue to be a seldom-used exit mechanism. There are basically two reasons for this: the complexity of and costs associated with an IPO; and the difficulties of ensuring a successful exit in an uncertain, immature secondary market. Despite this, in Spain, IPOs contain clauses that are common to this type of process (lock-ups for around six months' duration, elimination of restrictions on majorities and voting rights, conversion of preferred shares into common shares, registration rights etc).

### 5.4 Refinancings

Refinancing has rarely been used as an exit mechanism. Notwithstanding the foregoing, in the context of a refinancing, a new investor might be sought to replace a former private equity investor, or the debt cancellation or replacement may allow the investor to partially liquidate its investments.

### 5.5 Restructuring/insolvency

As a result of the risks in insolvency law (principally revocatory actions and the demanding of liability if the judge hearing the insolvency proceedings considers that the transaction is detrimental), turnaround transactions are seldom carried out in Spain, even when they should be commonplace in an economic environment such as that of a few years ago, when several companies became insolvent.

## 6. TAX
### 6.1 Taxation of fund structures

VCCs and VCFs are subject to taxation in accordance with the general corporation tax regime, with the special feature that the proceeds generated by the sale of shares/participations in companies in which the VCEs invest VCC or VCF money (provided that the transfer is carried out after the commencement of the second year of possession from the moment of acquisition or delisting, and up to the 15th year inclusive) benefit from a partial exemption of 99%. However, the exemption is not applicable when, among other reasons, the acquiring entity is linked to the VCC or is resident in a tax haven.

Transactions to incorporate companies and increase the share capital of those VCEs that fulfil the criteria in the GP are exempt from stamp and transfer tax.

To offset internal double taxation of dividends, dividends or participation in profit received by residents in Spain from promoting companies will be subject to a 100% deduction or total exemption, irrespective of their shareholding percentage in such companies or the length of time that they have possessed such shares.

Dividends and participation in profit received by the VCCs are treated as not having been obtained in Spain in the case of individuals who are shareholders or entities subject to non-resident income tax without a permanent establishment in Spain and, consequently, they will not be subject to taxation in Spain (this will not be applicable if the income is received through a country or territory classed as a tax haven).

### 6.2 Carried interest

A share of any profits that the general directors of VCFs receive as compensation, motivating them to work towards improving the fund's performance, is known as a carried interest. If the carried interest consists of remuneration or salary, the person receiving it would be subject to personal income tax. However, if the said income (bonus for example) has been generated over more than two years, only 70% of it is taxable (subject to an overall limit of EUR 300,000 per annum) as it would be irregular income.

If, however, it is profit on a real investment made by the executive, then a capital gain is generated, which is subject to taxation at a maximum rate of 23%.

### 6.3 Management equity

In the specific case of free distribution of shares to executives, the distribution will be exempt from tax up to an annual share value of EUR 12,000 per annum, provided that the shares are held by the executives for no less than three years, that the offer is made with the same conditions to all employees and that the employees, together with their relatives, do not own more than 5% of the share capital of the company or of another company.

An alternative that could offer certain tax advantages if certain criteria are met is that of granting share/stock options to the directors or other employees (including managers, as long as they are considered employees). The main tax advantage, in addition to the one explained above, is that the income derived from the exercise of the share options held by the directors or other employees benefits from a reduction of 30% (subject to restrictions on limit), only 70% of it being taxable.

### 6.4 Loan interest

Interest on the loans when paid to a credit entity in Spain will not be subject to withholding tax. However, if the interest is paid to a non-bank financial institution, it will be subject to a withholding tax, as explained below.

Loan interest paid to a non-resident other than a company resident in another Member State of the EU will be subject to taxation in accordance with the non-resident income tax regime, at the general rate of 19%, and tax agreements entered into by Spain with other countries will be applicable, thereby avoiding double taxation.

Interest paid by a company resident in Spanish territory to a company resident in any other Member State of the EU will not be subject to withholding tax in Spain.

### 6.5 Transaction taxes

No VAT or transfer tax will be levied on the acquisition of shares by VCCs. However, if the shares are acquired from companies principally related to real estate, the acquisition could be subject to transfer tax (generally at the fixed rate of 7%) or VAT (at the rate of 21%)—depending on the type of real estate transaction used for the acquisition of the shares—on the value of the property owned by the target company.

The transaction would be subject to VAT (at the rate of 21%) if the acquisition relates to a company's assets rather than its shares. If the acquired assets constitute a branch of activity (tangible and intangible assets that constitute an independent economic unit capable of developing a business or professional activity on their own), the transaction would not be subject to VAT.

If the acquirer is an entrepreneur or professional established in Spain for VAT purposes and the acquisition is related to his/her economic activity, and if the transaction is subject to VAT, the input VAT paid in the acquisition could be deductible (against output VAT) or refundable (if input VAT exceeds output VAT at the end of the tax period) for the acquirer. The transfer tax, however, is never deductible for the taxpayer.

## 7. CURRENT TOPICAL ISSUES/TRENDS

Private Equity in Spain is in the process of consolidation and Spain has been positioned as one of the most attractive and promising countries of the European market over the last few years. During 2017, the private equity market in Spain reached a record in terms of volume and number of investments which, according to estimates from the Spanish Private Equity and Private Equity Association (ASCRI), amount to approximately EUR 4,900 million (679 investments). The main explanation for this positive outlook derives from Spain´s solid economic growth, the intense investment activity carried out by international funds (which implied a significant rise in the number of megadeals) and the dynamism of the middle market.

Barcelona and Madrid continue to be the two main hubs of private equity investments in Spain as these two regions are Spain's centres for innovation and entrepreneurship and, therefore, the majority of the VCEs and start-ups are concentrated in these regions.

Fundraising for investments is on the increase and this pace is expected to continue as a consequence of international institutional investors' growing confidence in Spanish GPs and the high rates of liquidity together with the low interest rates and government programmes structured through funds of funds such as Innvierte and FOND ICO Global, which are managed by CDTI and Axis/ICO, respectively.

The forecast for the coming years continues to be positive: the maturity and variety (in phases and economic sectors) of Spanish start-ups is increasing (73 investments were made in late stage phase over the last year), the local VCFs have even more resources and experience and the foreign investors continue to be interested in investing in Spanish private equity.

# Switzerland

**FRORIEP** Dr Marcel R. Jung, Dunja Koch, Laetitia Meier-Droz & Jérôme Pidoux

## 1. MARKET OVERVIEW

### 1.1 Types of investors

In line with the global trend, Switzerland continues to be attractive for private equity investments, although, in 2017, the investments in Swiss companies flattened.

The types of investors who invest in Swiss companies remain heterogeneous and include corporate and institutional investors, and increasingly family offices, entrepreneurial families and private individuals.

Domestic academic institutions, Federal and Cantonal governments (directly or through Cantonal banks) and Swiss pension funds remain comparatively marginal investors. This is due to a number of reasons, which include fragmentation of the market (with 26 Cantons primarily promoting, individually, their local businesses, and different regional innovation clusters being set up and sponsored locally) as well as regulatory limitations and constraints (such as the absence of a simple and suitable vehicle for private equity investments, as described further below). Despite recent relaxation of regulatory limitations, pension funds remain reluctant towards private equity investments—an attitude which is understandable, given the solidity of other investment categories, such as the local real estate market and Swiss "blue chip" listed companies. Within private equity, in Switzerland, there are substantial differences with regard to the most common sources of funding in the different market segments (venture capital (VC), growth and buyout).

Finally, capital is increasingly raised through initial coin offerings (ICOs), although, just like crowd lending, this is not really relevant in the context of private equity.

### 1.2 Types of investments

Switzerland has a strong start-up and VC industry with an increased involvement in the high-tech sector. In 2017, new record levels were achieved in the overall investment and the number of financings rounds according to the *Swiss Venture Capital Report* (2018) (available at: *https:// www.startupticker.ch/uploads/File/Attachments/VC%20Report%202018_WEB_ v.pdf* [Accessed 19 September 2018]). Biotech and ICT were growth drivers. The invested capital rose from approximately CHF 300 million in 2012 to CHF 938 million in 2017, although, compared to 2016, it has flattened.

Indeed, traditional VC financings have suffered in the last 18 months since the emergence of ICOs. Not only start-up companies but also later-stage ventures, including those active in non-blockchain related industries, such as biotech companies, have been entering the ICO market to seek additional funding, sometimes even after having completed initial VC rounds. The attraction for the existing shareholders in such ICO companies obviously is the ability to find funding in ICOs without diluting their equity stakes. The crowdfunding element attached to ICOs allows for significant capital raising through large numbers of investors, in most cases, investing significantly less than EUR 1,000 each. VCs have meanwhile also complained that some good investment opportunities have moved into the ICO sphere. Having said that, there has been a cooling off in the success rate ICOs have had during the last quarter. We believe that ICOs will move towards offering more interesting economic rewards than has been the case in the past. We likewise believe that VCs will consider investing into ICOs on a broader basis than this happened in the past as the ICO market matures. Proof of this is the fact that the significance of fiat currencies raised in token sales is increasing compared to the sales proceeds raised in cryptocurrencies, in particular, in the private and pre-sale phases.

There is a very broad and heterogeneous spectrum of transactions, ranging from seed to start-up and later-stage ventures. Public to private transactions remain less common, although a few players specialise in this segment. Minority investments in public companies are rather unusual in Switzerland, while the last few years have seen a number of transactions going public by way of reverse merger with listed companies.

## 2. FUNDS
### 2.1 Fund structures

Swiss fund structures and fundraising in or from Switzerland are governed by the Federal Act on Collective Investment Schemes of 23 June 2006 (CISA) and the Federal Ordinance on Collective Investment Schemes of 22 November 2006 (CISO).

The CISA distinguishes between: (1) open-ended structures (contractual investment funds and investment companies with variable share capital (*société à capital variable* or SICAV)), where investors have the right to redeem their shares at net asset value; and (2) closed-ended structures (limited partnership and investment companies with fixed capital (*société à capital fixe* or SICAF)), where redemption rights are limited or not available at all (distributions are only made upon divestments of the portfolio or final dissolution).

By the nature of their investments (illiquid mid to long-term investments), private equity funds are typically set up as closed-ended structures. The two closed-ended structures available under the CISA are: (1) the limited partnership for collective investment (LPCI); and (2) the SICAF.

### The Swiss limited partnership for collective investments

An LPCI must invest in ""risk capital" and has been specifically created for alternative investments, private equity, real estate or infrastructure projects. It can invest either directly or through other investment structures. The CISO defines "risk capital" as the capital used for direct or indirect financing of companies and projects which offer the possibility of generating above average returns with above average risks. Investments may be made out of the LPCI's equity, third-party financing or by a mixed form of financing, such as mezzanine financing. Pursuant to the CISO, LPCIs are permitted to invest in two other types of assets, namely: (1) real estate, constructions and infrastructure projects; and (2) alternative investments. To fulfil their purpose, LPCIs may take control of companies and place representatives on the board of its portfolio companies in order to further the interests of their investments.

The structure of the LPCI is similar to the typical limited partnership organised under the laws of Anglo-Saxon jurisdictions: (1) its sole purpose must be collective investment; and (2) its members shall consist of: (a) at least one general partner who is subject to unlimited liability; and (b) limited partners who are only liable up to a set amount (the limited partners' contribution).

The general partner must be a Swiss company (*société anonyme/ Aktiengesellschaft*) with a minimum paid-in share capital of CHF 100,000 and which may only act as general partner for one LPCI.

LPCIs must obtain a licence from the Swiss Financial Market Supervisory Authority (FINMA) prior to any activity and is subject to FINMA's ongoing supervision. The general partners must also fulfil the general authorisation requirements under the CISA, which include in particular the following:

(1) all persons responsible for the management and the business operations of the general partner must: (a) have a good reputation; (b) guarantee proper management; and (c) possess the required professional experience;
(2) all significant equity holders of the general partner must have a good reputation and not exert their influence to the detriment of prudent and sound business practice;
(3) it must have in place internal regulations and appropriate organisational structure; and
(4) it must have sufficient financial guarantees.

All limited partners must be Qualified Investors within the meaning of the CISA. The circle of Qualified Investors includes, among others, institutional investors and certain high-net-worth individuals (see definition of "Qualified Investors" below).

An LPCI may only manage its own investments and is prohibited from providing management services to third parties or carrying out a commercial activity. It must appoint a custodian bank and a paying agent in Switzerland. In addition to the CISA and its ordinances of application, the LPCI is also governed by the provisions of the Swiss Code of Obligations relating to limited partnerships in general.

The limited partnership's agreement and the prospectus of the LPCI must contain information regarding the investments, investment policy, investment restrictions, risk diversification, risk associated with investments and investment techniques used by the LPCI.

The general partner of the LPCI may delegate the investment decisions of the partnership to a third party, provided that it is in the interests of an efficient management of the LPCI and further provided that such delegation is made to persons sufficiently qualified to carry out such tasks. In any event, the general partner remains responsible for instructing and monitoring the persons to whom duties have been delegated and for controlling the due performance of such duties.

The relationship between the general partner(s) and the limited partners is governed by a partnership agreement, which generally benefits from contractual freedom subject to certain mandatory provisions. Partnership agreements typically include provisions on the following matters:

(1)  capital commitment and possible extension;
(2)  repayment of capital;
(3)  duration of the LPCI and possible extension;
(4)  management and representation of the LPCI;
(5)  management fees;
(6)  investment policy, investment restrictions, risk diversifications, investment techniques;
(7)  reporting, right to receive information;
(8)  conditions for admission of new and withdrawal of existing investors, and transfer of participations;
(9)  participation rights and voting rights of the limited partners; and
(10) distribution of income.

LPCIs must in addition issue a prospectus. The Swiss Funds and Asset Management Association and the Swiss Private Equity and Corporate Finance Association have published a template prospectus, which has been acknowledged by FINMA for the purpose of licensing proceedings.

Until now, notwithstanding the efforts of the Swiss legislator to create a new type of vehicle to accommodate private equity investments, the success of LPCIs as structures to set up Swiss private equity funds has been limited. Indeed, as of June 2018, only 18 LPCIs have been registered with FINMA. They have essentially the purpose to invest in real estate and infrastructure projects, medicine and life science or have been set for VC.

**The SICAF**

The SICAF is the second closed-ended structure available under the CISA that could be used to set up a private equity fund. In short, a SICAF is an investment company with fixed capital: (1) which takes the form of a Swiss company (*société anonyme/Aktiengesellschaft*); (2) whose sole purpose is collective investment; (3) whose shareholders do not need to be Qualified Investors; and (4) which is not listed on a Swiss stock exchange. Swiss companies whose shareholders are exclusively Qualified Investors or whose shares are listed on a Swiss stock exchange are not subject to the CISA and therefore may not qualify as a SICAF.

Like the LPCI, in addition to the CISA, SICAFs are governed by the provisions of the Swiss Code of Obligations relating to companies.

SICAFs must have a custodian bank and a paying agent in Switzerland. Their articles of association and internal regulations must contain rules regarding the investments, the investment policy, the investment restrictions, risk diversification and the risks associated with investments.

Due to, among other things, the applicable tax regime (see below), since the entry into force of the CISA, not one single SICAF has been registered as a private equity structure.

## Conclusions

With the exception of a few private equity LPCIs, currently, the vast majority of private equity funds active in Switzerland are set up outside Switzerland, mainly as offshore funds. Switzerland remains, however, an important market for fundraising. Therefore, the regulation on fundraising plays an important role for private equity funds.

## 2.2 Regulation of fundraising and fund managers
### Fundraising

The Swiss legal framework of fundraising is based on the concept of "distribution". If an activity is deemed a distribution in or from Switzerland, it falls within the scope of and is subject to the requirements of the CISA, unless the CISA provides an exemption. "Distribution" is defined as any offer or advertisement for funds in view of obtaining subscriptions, which is not exclusively directed at "Regulated Qualified Investors" (see definition below). It encompasses any proposal or marketing aiming at the acquisition/subscription of any fund regardless of the means.

Distribution of foreign funds to non-qualified investors requires a prior authorisation from FINMA. Private equity funds are typically not directed at retail investors. Due to their characteristics (in particular their investment policy, closed-ended structure, low diversification and absence of domestic supervision recognised as equivalent to that required in Switzerland), none of the offshore funds could obtain authorisation by FINMA for distribution to non-qualified investors.

As a result, the raising of capital by private equity funds may only be made in or from Switzerland under exemptions provided by the CISA or to Qualified Investors.

The following activities are not deemed distribution and do not fall within the scope of the CISA:

(1) the distribution of foreign funds to regulated financial intermediaries subject to the supervision of FINMA such as banks, securities dealers, fund management companies, regulated asset managers of collective investment schemes and central banks ("Regulated Financial Intermediaries") and regulated insurance institutions (together with Regulated Financial Intermediaries, "Regulated Qualified Investors");

(2) the provision of information and the offer of funds at the instigation or request of the investor (reverse solicitation);

(3) the provision of information and the offer of funds to investors under a written asset management agreement entered into with a Regulated Financial Intermediary;

(4) the provision of information and the offer of funds to investors under a written advisory agreement entered into with a Regulated Financial Intermediary (provided that the written advisory agreement contemplates an advisory relationship for a financial consideration and is entered into on a long-term basis); and

(5) the distribution of funds under certain employee participation plans.

Distribution directed at "Unregulated Qualified Investors" falls within the scope of the CISA and triggers certain obligations regarding the funds and the distributors.

The following categories of investors are considered "Unregulated Qualified Investors":

(1) public entities and pension funds with professional treasury operations;
(2) companies with professional treasury operations;
(3) certain high net worth individuals within the meaning of the CISA and the CISO (generally with assets of at least CHF 5 million or, alternatively, financial assets of at least CHF 500,000 and market knowledge based on individual education and professional experience or similar experience to assess the risks of the investment) may request in writing to be treated as qualified investors; and
(4) investors that have entered into a written asset management agreement with a Regulated Financial Intermediary or a recognised independent asset manager pursuant to art.3(2)(c) of the CISA and have not declared that they want to be treated as non-qualified investors ("opt-out"), provided that the Regulated Financial Intermediary or the recognised independent asset manager is involved in the distribution from the outset.

"Qualified Investors" refer to both regulated Qualified Investors and Unqualified Investors.

In case of distribution to Qualified Investors, foreign funds are not required to obtain an authorisation from FINMA but they are subject to certain requirements, which include in particular:

(1) the appointment of a Swiss representative and a Swiss paying agent prior to any distribution activity in Switzerland;
(2) the name of the foreign fund must not be confusing or misleading; and
(3) the documentation of the foreign funds must be adapted to include Swiss specific disclosure and information.

Swiss and foreign financial intermediaries who contemplate distributing foreign funds to Qualified Investors must be subject to an appropriate supervision (i.e. Swiss financial intermediaries must be authorised as distributors by FINMA or benefit from an exemption based on their regulatory status and foreign financial intermediaries, who distribute on a cross-border basis, must be authorised to distribute funds in their home jurisdiction and be appropriately supervised).

They are subject to further requirements, which include in particular:

(1) they must enter into a distribution agreement subject to Swiss law with the Swiss representative(s) of the fund(s) which they distribute;
(2) they use fund documentation which comply with the requirements of Swiss law and in particular which indicates the details of the Swiss representative and the paying agent, the jurisdiction of origin of the fund, the place of jurisdiction/performance and the place where the fund documents can be obtained free of charge (i.e. the Swiss representative), as well as certain information and disclosure on fees and costs, retrocessions and rebates pursuant to the Guidelines on Duties Regarding the Charging and Use of Fees and Costs of 22 May 2014 issued by the Swiss Funds and Asset Management Association; and
(3) they comply with Swiss regulations on distribution of collective

investment schemes.

### Operations of private equity funds

Under the CISA, "fund management companies" (responsible for the overall management and administration of a collective investment scheme) are treated differently from "asset managers" of collective investment schemes (which are only responsible for managing the assets and/or the risks of funds). Under the CISA, any entity responsible for the management of collective investment schemes, or the safe keeping of the assets of collective investment schemes, must obtain an authorisation from FINMA. "Fund management companies" may delegate the asset management and/or risk management activities to a third party. Swiss asset managers of Swiss and non-Swiss collective investment schemes must also obtain an authorisation from FINMA, except if investors of the fund(s) which it manages are Qualified Investors and: (1) the assets under management, including the assets acquired through the use of leveraged finance, do not exceed CHF 100 million; or (2) the assets under management do not exceed CHF 500 million and consist in non-leveraged collective investment schemes where investors are not permitted to exercise redemption rights for a period of five years from the date of their first investment.

### 2.3 Customary or common terms of funds

With regard to terms of a Swiss LPCI, please see the corresponding sub-section of s.2.1 above.

## 3. DEBT FINANCE

### 3.1 Means of financing

Companies can issue bonds which, if the offer is to a limited circle of individuals only, will be deemed a private offer. As a rule of thumb, an offer to more than 20 individuals is considered to be public if it is offered to investors that are not selected and approached on an individual basis. It has to be noted that even an offering made to all customers of a bank is a public offering as the investors contacted are not individually chosen.

Whilst the market for domestic and international bonds in Switzerland is on the lower side given the low interest rates, there seems to be an appetite by investors for C-Graded Bonds.

The other form of financing combining debt and equity is mezzanine financing, where debt and participation rights of the lenders can be relatively freely agreed upon. Depending on the terms, this will result in the debt financing being considered as equity from a corporate law point of view. Finally, capital is increasingly raised through crowd lending, although this is not really relevant in the context of private equity.

### 3.2 Restrictions on granting security

There are certain restrictions in Swiss corporate law on Swiss companies granting a benefit to group companies other than their own subsidiaries. In finance transactions, these upstream benefits could typically arise if a Swiss company grants a security interest to a lender to secure obligations of its parent or other group company. Guarantees and other security interests granted by a Swiss subsidiary or other group companies may therefore require different actions to be taken, such as:

- making sure that the transaction is covered by the company purpose and, if not, amending the articles of association to include the right to grant upstream and cross-stream loans, guaranties, security and other benefits;
- reminding the directors that they must at all times act in the best interests of the company. There is no concept of interest of a group of companies under Swiss corporate law and, hence, companies must enter into transactions that are in their own interests rather than in any "group interest". Granting security for the benefit of a parent company and/or other group companies could be null and void if such a security is not given at arm's length or would result in the disposal of essential operating assets of the Swiss subsidiary or obviously exceeds its economic capacity; and
- inserting a specific limitation language in the facility agreement or each security agreement. Such language is required as a security granted by a Swiss subsidiary to secure obligations of a parent and/or group company may be considered as a redemption of equity contribution, distribution of legally protected reserves or constructive dividend and could violate withdrawal regulations under Swiss corporate law.

Given these withdrawal restrictions, transaction agreements usually provide that any payment by the Swiss company shall be limited to its free reserves and profits available for distribution to shareholders at the time of the enforcement of such a security. The mechanics for payment require the Swiss company to arrange for an audited interim balance sheet and resolutions of the board of directors and shareholders to make an amount available for payment from the free reserves available for distribution.

Even in the event that there is no prohibited return of equity as set out above, the security granted could represent a hidden distribution of dividends. A benefit granted in favour of a parent group company qualifies as a hidden distribution of dividends if—according to the standard of "dealing at arm's length"—there is a manifest disproportion in the consideration which is to the detriment of the Swiss subsidiary. A hidden distribution of dividends may trigger withholding tax at the current rate of 35% (subject to any applicable double tax treaty), whereby there is an additional risk of the tax being "grossed-up" (i.e. the distributed sum is considered to be merely 65% of the dividend).

According to case law, in the context of cash pooling, an up or cross-stream loan blocks the freely disposable equity of a company as a result of which dividends can only be paid out to the extent that there is an excess of disposable equity.

### 3.3 Intercreditor issues

Syndicated lenders are all treated as pari passu creditors of a Swiss company in bankruptcy or debt moratorium provided that they have a direct claim against the latter. Sub-participants are not able to exercise direct claims against the Swiss company and there is no possibility under Swiss insolvency law for lenders to split the claim and/or the vote with their sub-participants. The only way for the sub-participant to exercise any right in bankruptcy or debt moratorium proceedings is to agree with the lender to transfer the debt by way of assignment.

## 3.4 Syndication

Loans can be syndicated before or after the transaction is completed. If before, syndicated loan agreements governed by English law usually provide for a security agent or security trustee acting as agent or trustee for all the lenders. For Swiss law governed security, security agents and security trustees typically act as agents of the finance parties. Should the loan be syndicated after the deal is done, it triggers the following issue with respect to security arrangements governed by Swiss law: some security interests (e.g. pledges) created under Swiss law are considered as a collateral security (*akzessorische Sicherheit*) conditional upon the existence of a valid claim. Such a security has the priority provided for under the agreements as long as the secured obligations have not been invalidated, discharged, novated, waived or otherwise expired, lapsed or terminated. If the syndicated loan agreement allows a lender to transfer its claims by way of novation, there is a risk that the security would lapse automatically with the transfer (by novation). Parallel debt wording is therefore typically inserted into the facility agreements with the aim of mitigating or eliminating this risk but the concept of a parallel debt has never been decided on by a Swiss court. There is, theoretically, a remote risk that the parallel debt provision could be attacked on the grounds of so-called simulation.

Syndication may also trigger tax issues to be considered in all syndicated transactions, including those allowing sub-participations. In principle, if there are more than 10 so-called non-bank lenders participating in the facility by way of assignment, transfer, novation or sub-participation or, if the Swiss company has more than 20 non-bank creditors, interest payments become subject to withholding tax at the current rate of 35%. For the purpose of the threshold of non-bank creditors, private placements ("club-deals") are counted as one per formal written instrument of debt acknowledgement (tranche) and, under certain circumstances, where the refinancing of a bank is such that the bank appears to be only interposed and not acting in its own economic interests, the lenders to that bank would also count for the threshold of non-banks.

## 4. EQUITY STRUCTURES
### 4.1 Role of management

Management is key to the success of a company and, as such, it is usually also key to a private equity investment and its development. In this respect, Switzerland provides a favourable legal framework and cultural environment for management to thrive. Indeed, the flexibility of the Swiss legislation in the areas of labour and contracts laws, as well as its comparatively low personal taxation level, provides an auspicious environment for the management team to be adequately incentivised.

The role of management that is typically experienced in Switzerland is the following: the management—and in particular the Chief Executive Officer (CEO)—will, generally, sit on the board of directors. Other members of top management, such as the Chief Fnancial Officer (CFO) or the Chief Operational Officer (COO), are also sometimes offered board membership, although in practice this is less common.

### Employment agreements

In employment agreements for the management, a common feature is the insertion of incentives for the achievement of certain goals (in the form of variable salaries, cash bonus payments and/or participation plans) in order to strengthen long-term involvement of the management in the cause of business. Such employment agreements often also provide for incentives and may also include other provisions, which are usually considered important from an investor's perspective, such as: (1) non-competition obligations (limited by statute as to scope and duration) and non-solicitation undertakings; (2) assignment of intellectual property; as well as (3) minimum terms of employment or long notice periods (in particular for key management, an initial term of one to two years and/or notice periods of six months to one year are not unusual).

In addition, Swiss law allows an ample degree of flexibility in terminating an employment agreement. Except in special circumstances, employment agreements can be terminated within the contractually agreed notice period and without any indemnification or additional payment. Moreover, it is generally possible to send an employee on garden leave during the notice period.

### Participation of management

It is usual for management to be offered a participation in the company up to a certain minority percentage (usually around 3–5%, although the percentage may vary, e.g. be somewhat higher—and the salary lower—in start-up and early-stage companies). Such participation is often structured by way of grants of shares and/or share options (which entitles the holder of shares to both economic benefits and voting rights), and sometimes as profit participation certificates (which usually give only economic benefits). Management participation is usually achieved through company shares/share option plans, sometimes also by means of individual share purchase agreements or—much less frequently—of indirect participation rights (i.e. participation in a special purpose vehicle which holds shares or other participation rights in the company).

Phantom shares (i.e. the allocation of a merely virtual share in the company which is not incorporated in any security or title) are quite unusual. Share option plans typically contain deferred grants and vesting periods (sometimes of several years—it is usual for a company at growth stage to have a vesting period of between one and three years while, for companies at a start-up stage, the vesting period can be much longer) in order to secure managemen"s long-term involvement. The exercise of options is very often determined by adherence to a shareholders' agreement imposing limitations on voting rights and restricting the disposal of shares; continued employment is also a common condition for the exercise of good leaver and bad leaver provisions.

Cliff vesting is often provided in the event of a trade sale, an initial public offering (IPO) or the achievement of certain milestones.

## 4.2 Common protections for investors
### Investment agreements

Investment agreements typically contain initial investment protection, in particular with regard to representations and warranties given by companies and/or management. Since a company"s representations and warranties coupled with monetary indemnification may violate the legal prohibition on redemption of capital contributions, investment protection towards companies must be structured accordingly, e.g. through compensatory capital increases or similar provisions of indirect indemnity.

### Shareholders' agreement

The basic and long-term protection of investors and their investments are implemented through a shareholders' agreement, which will usually include a number of provisions ensuring that any new shareholder will adhere to and fall within its scope of application. To some extent, the provisions of a shareholders' agreement can be further strengthened in the company's articles of association and in regulations of the board of directors. Common investment protection instruments include: (1) the issue of preferred shares; (2) anti-dilution provisions; and (3) transfer restrictions in the form of rights of first refusal and pre-emption rights. Shareholders' agreements also often contain call options exercisable against a party in breach of contractual obligations. Statutory subscription rights under Swiss company law, coupled with the fact that all share capital increases must be resolved or authorised by the shareholders, also provide anti-dilution protection as well as protection for minority shareholders, or control over future share capital issuances. Quorum requirements at the level of shareholders and voting obligations are also common protection instruments.

### Directors and information rights

In addition to those mentioned above, other investment protection tools include the right for sizeable investors to appoint their own representatives on the board of directors, or at least observers, as well as provisions regarding composition of the board of directors. It is also usual to include reporting requirements and information rights (on financial and other issues) and direct supervision over management. It is worth mentioning that directorship can sometimes be a double-edged sword for investor representatives, especially in early-stage companies or in restructuring and turn-around situations, since the members of the board of directors have an obligation to act solely in the interest of the company, while failure to do so may trigger personal liability.

### Rights to exit

Investors typically secure a successful exit strategy (IPO, trade sale etc) by means of strong drag-along clauses. The deposit of issued share certificates with an escrow agent, who is provided with corresponding instructions, may further secure the investors' right and the possibility to effect exit transactions in a short timeframe, especially against inactive or opposing minority shareholders.

### 4.3 Common protections for management
#### Protection of minority rights

Management members do not always have board seats and, if they do, they usually do not enjoy any veto rights. Nevertheless, minority rights of management and/or their position may be protected through appropriate provisions in a shareholders' agreement but outright veto rights are unusual rather than qualified majority selected matters. Pursuant to Swiss company law, statutory subscription rights for shareholders in capital increases grant a certain degree of anti-dilution protection to minority shareholders (although it is not rare that these rights are waived in shareholders' agreements). Usually, management's position is further secured through tag-along rights and sometimes through obligations of investors to allocate a certain percentage of the capital to management and/or key employees (a pool of 12–15% is common for start-up and early-stage companies, while this percentage is usually lower for growth-stage companies).

#### Termination of employment

Share option plans and shareholders' agreements often provide for favourable conditions if employment is terminated for convenience by the company (e.g. good leavers clause in case of a change of control). Inversely, the termination of a manager's employment may lead to a right for other investors to purchase their shares by means of pre-agreed price mechanism.

### 4.4 Management warranties

The fund normally expects the management to give far-reaching warranties. The warranties cover in particular those aspects of which the management has better knowledge than the shareholders and the board of directors.

#### Typical warranties

The warranties that are solicited usually cover the target company's financials and current and future business, including the plans and the circumstances that may lead to future risks. In particular, the management will typically guarantee: (1) the correctness and the completeness of the due diligence; (2) the absence of adverse changes for the time period ranging from the last audited financial accounts to the closing; (3) the availability of the intellectual property rights, permits and authorisations necessary to carry on the target company's business; (4) the absence of claims, actions, investigations or proceedings pending or threatened; and (5) compliance with applicable laws, tax and social security obligations and pension plan requirements.

#### Time-limit and caps

Usually, warranties contain both a time-limit and a cap. The time-limit usually depends on the business field of the target company, i.e. how easily risks can be discovered after the target company's acquisition. As a general rule, one might expect an average warranty period of 12 months. While the warranties pursue the objective of obtaining full disclosure by the management, the liability cap achieves a counterbalance effect to the extent it limits the financial risks for the members of the management. Usually, the liability cap amounts approximately to annual one-year compensation of the respective individual. Consequently, the managers of a company might each be eligible for different warranty caps. Additionally, there is a minimal threshold under which no claim shall be raised. Such threshold amounts in general to one-sixth of the annual compensation of the respective individual.

## 4.5 Good leaver/bad leaver provisions
### Bad leavers
If a member of the management leaves the target company as a bad leaver, the other shareholders will typically be entitled to exercise a call option within a timeframe of at least one month to purchase the shares of the bad leaver in proportion to their respective participations in the target company. If some shareholders renounce their call option rights, the others will be entitled to purchase additional shares. The price of the shares amounts to either: (1) the market value; or (2) the lower of the market value and the price which the member of the management paid for the shares.

### Good leavers
A good leaver might be either: (1) entitled to keep its shares, usually while continuing to be bound by the shareholders' agreement; or (2) required to sell them in case the other shareholders desire to exercise their call options. However, in this case, the price for the shares generally amounts to either: (1) the market value increased by a premium; or (2) the higher of the market value and the price which the member of the management paid for the shares.

The calculation of the market value is also defined in the shareholders' agreement. Where there is disagreement among the parties, the market value will typically be finally established by an appraiser. The procedure for the appointment of the appraiser and the party that bears the appraisal costs are usually regulated in the shareholders' agreement as well.

## 4.6 Public to private transactions
It is not common in Switzerland for a private equity fund to make offers for public companies.

## 5. EXITS
The nature of private equity investments is that they are pursued for a limited period of time, usually between two and seven years, with a maximum of up to ten years. The primary motivation being financial, their main goals can be distilled down to two basic points: obtaining the highest possible profit from their investment and a successful exit. This means that private equity investors will only invest if they are confident that there are several different options available to them to achieve a successful exit. Despite its relatively small size and number of players, the Swiss market offers good exit options and is comparatively liquid", as has been demonstrated in recent years by the partially substantial and successful exits of private equity investors, notably in the areas of life sciences, biotech and pharmaceuticals.

Exit options available to investors in the Swiss market are: secondary sales (s.5.1 below); trade sales (s.5.2 below); IPOs (s.5.3 below); refinancings (s.5.4 below); and restructuring or liquidation (s.5.5 below).

## 5.1   Secondary sales

The buyer in a secondary sale is generally another private equity investor. Though it is true that sophisticated players tend to prefer lengthier agreements which compare with international standards, sale and purchase agreements with respect to stockholdings in Switzerland can be drafted in a few pages and indeed this is usually practice. Swiss statutory provisions foresee very short notice periods to claim a misrepresentation or breach of warranty. Sale and purchase agreements therefore make stipulations to exclude the application of such statutory provisions.

In addition, Swiss law provides very limited protection with respect to damages incurred within the target company. Consequently, sale and purchase agreements must expressly foresee rules according to which the buyer can recover the damage incurred by the target company.

A final important point is that statutory representations and warranties imposed under Swiss law where there is a sale of shares of an undertaking are very limited. Accordingly, it is standard practice for the buyer to request that all representations and warranties which are customary and appropriate for the individual sale transaction be listed in the sale and purchase agreement.

## 5.2   Trade sales

In Switzerland, this exit option is often the most attractive one for investors since it gives them the opportunity to sell all their stock in a transaction, without being limited by the kind of lock-up provisions otherwise present in an IPO (see s.5.3 below), while being able to take advantage of any contractual exit preference such as partial exit possibly with earn out provision. Furthermore, from a tax perspective, this exit route may result in a tax-free capital gain for corporate and individual investors.

### Drag-along/tag-along provisions

To secure this exit option, the equity investor should set out drag along/tag along provisions in the investment agreement or shareholders' agreement which will compel/enable other shareholders to sell their shares along with the investor. Such provisions, which are acceptable and in principle enforceable under Swiss law, significantly increase the liquidity of the investment. It is also important for the investor to provide for a right of first offer, which will allow them to control the entry of future shareholders and to secure a possible trade sale.

### Exit preference

Parties can also set forth in the agreement that the investor shall have a preferred position with respect to the proceedings of a trade sale ("exit preference"). This rule cannot be included in the articles of association of Swiss companies but can be inserted into shareholders' agreements. Swiss law allows for some leeway in the drafting of such provisions. Hence, legal engineering is available where sophisticated parties require it.

## 5.3   Initial public offerings

In Switzerland, a listing is possible at the SIX in Zurich or at the Berne eXchange (BX) in Berne.

A listing may be an exit option of interest to an investor since it increases the liquidity—and thus the price—of the securities' trades and simultaneously enhances the reputation of a company. Obvious as the advantages may be, it is nevertheless worth mentioning that a listing is a very long process (about six months) and that it is expensive, both in terms of management time and of legal and financial advisers' fees.

In this context, a relevant development is that, since 1 January 2014, listed companies must organise a mandatory and binding shareholders' vote on the aggregate compensation allocated to the board of directors and to the senior management each year, including the payment of golden parachutes and signing-on bonuses for the governing bodies of the company.

An IPO will also often compel the company to change its equity structure. Where private equity investors hold preferred shares, as is often the case in Switzerland, these rights must then be adapted for an IPO. With this in mind, it is advisable to draft in the investment agreement a provision according to which the preferred shares shall be converted into ordinary shares if and when the shares were to be listed so that this hurdle may be avoided.

One of the main inconveniences of an IPO for the investor is that a quick and complete exit is seldom possible given the prevalence of investment agreements concluded in Switzerland which impose lock-up obligations on investors. The most common formulation of such an obligation prevents the investor from selling its shares during a period of six months. For young companies, this kind of prohibitions can also be mandatory as per the directives of the SIX. Another issue with IPOs is that new shares are often issued. Under Swiss corporate law, existing shareholders are protected from capital dilution in the case of a share capital increase. However, these protective rights of shareholders can be limited or withdrawn if it is justified by a fair reason and if all shareholders are treated equally. In addition, shareholders' agreements often contain the possibility for dilutions.

Under Swiss law, unless the articles of association of a company give power to the shareholders' meeting or the organisational regulations give power to the management, the decision to list a company does not lie with the shareholders but rather with the board of directors. In the event that the shareholders do have the right to decide on this item, a majority vote is then required. To secure this exit route, a minority investor could negotiate a contractual right to decide by itself on a resolution with regard to the listing.

As for the issue of price setting—for instance, through a book-building process—it is important for the investor that has not secured a majority of board seats to have set out in the shareholders' agreement that the decision on price requires its agreement, such a rule being admissible under Swiss law.

### 5.4 Refinancings

Refinancing or recapitalisation allows a change of the capital structure of a company through the substitution of debt for equity. When this process is initiated by the company itself, it is called a leveraged recapitalisation. For the investor, a leveraged recapitalisation is not a real exit option since it remains shareholder of the company but such a process can instead be considered the preamble to a subsequent exit.

It is worth mentioning that under Swiss law, the articles of association can provide that holders of preferred shares—which need not be in the form of registered shares—may benefit from a priority or higher dividend than common shareholders.

## 5.5  Restructuring/insolvency

The insolvency option is often the least appealing option for a private equity investor since the assets of the company will be sold at their liquidation value, which is generally substantially less than the continuation value. However, in some cases, liquidation may be a good means for the investor to redeem the capital and the reserves since, in this situation, Swiss law does not set out any particular rules for the protection of capital. The threat of liquidation can also prove a useful negotiation tool for the investor to convince the management to find a buyer for the company.

Where the investor does not hold a majority of the share capital but wishes to trigger the liquidation process, a duty should be negotiated in the shareholders' agreement for the other shareholders to vote for the liquidation in certain circumstances.

As a final note, the articles of association of Swiss companies can provide holders of preferred shares with an advantage on the liquidation proceeds.

## 6.  TAX
### 6.1  Taxation of fund structures
#### Swiss income and capital taxes

Contractual investment funds (FCPs), SICAVs and LPCIs that were approved by the Swiss supervisory authority in accordance with the CISA are not treated as taxpayers for Swiss income and capital tax purposes. In this respect, these collective investment schemes are transparent. Income from units of these collective investment schemes is fiscally attributed on a pro rata basis to the unit holders irrespective of whether the income is distributed (*Ausschüttungsfonds*) or accumulated (*Thesaurierungsfonds*). The Swiss resident unit holder is subject to Swiss income tax on dividends, interest etc realised by these collective investment schemes. Swiss income tax arises at the moment the distributed income becomes due (*Ausschüttungsfonds*) or the accumulated income is credited, i.e. at the moment of debiting in the account of reinvestment (*Thesaurierungsfonds*).

Capital gains upon the sale or redemption of units in these collective investment schemes are income tax-free in the hands of the Swiss resident individual unit holder if he or she holds the unit as private assets (i.e. the unit is not related to a business activity). The redemption of units is taxable insofar as the liquidation proceeds include income that has not yet been taxed in the hands of a Swiss resident individual unit holder.

The LPCI is a limited partnership. The Swiss resident unit holders (limited partners) of an LPCI are subject to Swiss income and wealth taxes on the income and the assets of the LPCI. As capital gains derived from movable assets that are held as private assets and do not relate to a business activity are income tax-free, capital gains realised by the LPCI are not taxed in the hands of the Swiss resident individual unit holders. The holding of units of a LPCI as limited partner does not itself qualify as a business activity of the Swiss resident individual unit holder.

As an exemption, FCPs, SICAVs and LPCIs are treated as taxpayers for Swiss income and capital tax purposes to the extent they own Swiss or foreign real estate, irrespective of whether the income is distributed (*Ausschüttungsfonds*) or acccumulated (*Thesaurierungsfonds*). These collective investment schemes are subject to a particular (lower) corporate income tax rate. Income from Swiss and foreign real estate is exempted at the level of the Swiss resident unit holder as this income is subject to Swiss corporate income tax at the level of the FCP, SICAV and LPCI.

In contrast, SICAFs are always treated as taxpayers for Swiss income and capital tax purposes, irrespective of whether they own Swiss or foreign real estate. The unit holder realises dividend income upon distribution that is subject to Swiss income taxes. Capital gains realised by SICAFs are converted into taxable income in the hands of a Swiss resident individual unit holder. A SICAF is entitled to participation relief on dividend and capital gains derived from qualifying participations.

The reason for the different Swiss tax treatment between SICAVs and SICAFs is the right of the SICAV unit holder to redeem units at their net asset value. This right brings the legal relationship of a SICAV economically into the scheme of a FCP that is treated as transparent.

A Swiss resident individual unit holder is not entitled to shareholder relief on dividends from qualifying participation in SICAFs. Capital gains upon the sale of units in a SICAF are income tax-free in the hands of the Swiss resident individual unit holder if he or she holds the unit as private assets (i.e. the unit is not related to a business activity). A Swiss resident corporate unit holder is entitled to participation relief on capital gains and dividends from qualifying participations in SICAFs.

In the hands of a Swiss resident individual unit holder, the redemption of units is taxable in so far as the liquidation proceeds exceed the nominal value and the paid-in capital of the participation.

Due to the economic double taxation of corporate profits (taxation of corporation profits and taxation of distributed dividends) in Swiss taxation and the conversion of capital gains realised by SICAFs into taxable income in the hands of a Swiss resident individual unit holder, SICAFs were not previously attractive as collective investment schemes. However, due to the lowering of the corporate income tax rates in the past, the disadvantage of non-transparency has been significantly reduced. Further, as capital gains upon the sale of units in a SICAF are income tax-free in the hands of the Swiss resident individual unit holder if he or she holds the unit as private assets (i.e. the unit is not related to a business activity), a cumulating SICAF (*Thesaurierungsfonds*) may provide tax advantages. However, the Swiss withholding tax (Swiss WHT) on dividends paid by the SICAF is a significant obstacle for non-Swiss resident investors.

### Foreign withholding taxes

FCPs, SICAVs and LPCIs are not treated as Swiss resident persons for treaty purposes. Therefore, these collective investment funds are not entitled to relief from foreign withholding taxes under an applicable double tax treaty between Switzerland and a source state. The Federal Tax Administration has agreed a number of Mutual Agreements with foreign treaty states that entitles FCPs, SICAVs and LPCIs to ask for relief from foreign withholding taxes on behalf of their Swiss resident unit holders. Switzerland has agreed Mutual Agreements with Austria, Canada, Denmark, France, Germany, the Netherlands, Norway, Spain, Sweden, and the UK and Ireland. Australia, Japan and Canada grant withholding tax relief at source also in relation to SICAVs on grounds of Swiss address.

If no Mutual Agreement is applicable, the Swiss resident unit holder has to ask for treaty relief from foreign withholding taxes in accordance with the applicable treaty provisions.

SICAFs, however, are treated as Swiss resident persons for treaty purposes. Therefore, this collective investment scheme is entitled to relief from foreign withholding taxes under an applicable double tax treaty between Switzerland and a source state in accordance with the applicable treaty provisions.

## Foreign collective investment schemes

The rules of Swiss taxation of income from units of foreign collective investment schemes in the hands of Swiss resident unit holders are the same as for Swiss collective investment schemes. A foreign collective investment scheme is compared to Swiss FCPs, SICAVs, LPCIs and SICAFs and treated accordingly for Swiss tax purposes. It is of significance that foreign collective investment schemes report information in accordance with the rules of Swiss income taxation in order to avoid adverse discretionary Swiss income taxation.

Foreign collective investment schemes may be subject to Swiss taxation if they lack substance abroad and are effectively managed in Switzerland.

## Withholding tax

Switzerland has not become a preferred international jurisdiction for the establishment of collective investment schemes. There is a tax reason for this: income from units in Swiss collective investment funds are subject to Swiss WHT. The Swiss WHT levied on income of Swiss collective investment schemes is a significant obstacle for non-Swiss resident investors and the reason that Swiss international financial institutions use offshore partnerships and offshore corporations in international fund structuring.

FCPs, SICAVs and LPCIs that are approved by the Swiss supervisory authority in accordance with the CISA are treated as taxpayers for Swiss WHT purposes. In this regard, these collective investment schemes are not transparent. Income from units of these collective investment schemes is subject to Swiss WHT at a rate of 35% irrespective of whether the income is distributed (*Ausschüttungsfonds*) or accumulated, i.e. at the moment of debiting in the account of reinvestment (*Thesaurierungsfonds*).

Swiss WHT arises at the moment the distributed income becomes due (*Ausschüttungsfonds*) or the accumulated income is credited (*Thesaurierungsfonds*). The collective investment scheme is obliged to withhold the Swiss WHT from the gross income and to pay it to the Federal Tax Administration.

If the collective investment scheme demonstrates that income will be sourced continuously from foreign sources to a minimum of 80%, it may ask the Federal Tax Administration to be exempted from Swiss WHT to the extent that income is paid or credited to a foreign resident unit holder ("affidavit procedure").

Exempted from Swiss WHT are capital gains and income from Swiss and foreign real estate that is directly owned by the collective investment scheme and repayment of paid-in capital if the income is distributed by the FCP, the SICAV or the LPCI to the unit holder by means of a separate coupon.

Swiss WHT may be refunded fully or partially according to Swiss domestic tax law or an applicable double tax treaty. In accordance with Swiss domestic tax law, a Swiss resident unit holder is entitled to a full refund of the Swiss WHT. Foreign resident unit holders are entitled to a full refund of Swiss WHT if the income is sourced from foreign sources to a minimum of 80% ("Affidavit Procedure"). If a double tax treaty between the resident state of the foreign resident unit holder and Switzerland is applicable, the foreign unit holder is entitled to full or partial refund of the Swiss WHT.

In contrast to FCPs, SICAVs and LPCIs, SICAFs are always treated as taxpayers for Swiss WHT purposes, irrespective of whether they were approved by the Swiss supervisory authority in accordance with the CISA. Income from units of this collective investment scheme is treated as dividend and subject to Swiss WHT at a rate of 35% if distributed. The repayment of paid-in capital is not subject to Swiss WHT. The Affidavit Procedure is not applicable.

## 6.2 Carried interest

In the field of private equity investments, it is common that the fund manager participates in the profit of the collective investment scheme. This profit participation is called carried interest. The Swiss income taxation of the carried interest depends on the legal form of the Swiss resident fund manager and the particular collective investment scheme. Income from fund management qualifies as income from self-employment activity in the hands of a Swiss resident individual and as taxable profit in the hands of a Swiss resident company. If Swiss resident fund managers who are employed with the fund management company hold their own units in the collective investment scheme or participation in the fund management company, such units and participations generally qualify as private assets and are not imperatively related to a business activity of the fund manager. In that case, capital gains from the sale of the units and/or the participation are treated as income tax-free.

If the fund management is provided by the fund manager individually or as a partner of a partnership (rather than through a fund management company) on a contractual basis, and the fund manager or the partnership has the right to profit participation, the units in the collective investment schemes and the participation in the partnership qualify as business assets. Capital gains, income and carried interest are taxable income from self-employment activity in the hands of the Swiss resident individual fund manager.

## 6.3 Management equity

The tax treatment of equity participations and options to obtain equity participations in the collective investment scheme granted to management follows the Swiss tax law provisions for employment income, in particular those on the taxation of employee participations. Equity participations and options to obtain equity participations are generally taxable at grant. Taxable employment income corresponds to the difference between the fair market value of the equity participations and the options respectively as well as the acquisition price, if any. A discount of 6% per annum is applicable for equity participations with selling blocking period. Options that are subject to a selling blocking period and options to obtain shares of unlisted equity participations respectively are taxed at exercise. Taxable income corresponds to the difference between the fair market value and exercise price. The capital gain upon the sale of the equity participation generally qualifies as private tax-free capital gain in the hands of a Swiss tax resident manager. Equity participations and options to obtain equity participations that are subject to vesting are taxable at vesting or exercise respectively.

### 6.4 Loan interest

Switzerland does not levy Swiss WHT on interest paid on individual loans. However, interest paid by a Swiss borrower to Swiss or foreign lenders for the purpose of collective financing or on bank deposits is subject to interest withholding tax at a rate of 35%. A collective financing is present if a Swiss borrower issues a bond. A bond consists of written debt acknowledgments with fixed amounts that are issued either in more than 10 tranches at comparable conditions (*Anleihensobligationen*) or more than 20 tranches at variable conditions (*Kassenobligationen*). Bank deposits include more than 100 interest-bearing deposits without fixed amounts that are issued on a continuous basis. Swiss and foreign banks are not taken into account for the calculation of the Swiss-borrower 10/20/100 Non-Bank Rule. Switzerland does not levy issuance stamp duty on the issuance of bonds.

The question as to whether commercial agreements qualify as loans, in particular bonds or bank deposits, is answered under Swiss tax law on a substance over form approach.

In order to avoid Swiss WHT on interest, a Swiss borrower and the lender jointly agree to include in credit facilities so-called Swiss borrower language according to which the lender may not assign any of its rights and benefits (including sub-participations) or transfer (by way of novation or assumption of contract) any of its rights, benefits and obligations to another person without prior written consent of the Swiss borrower.

### 6.5 Transaction taxes

Units issued by FCPs, SICAVs and LPCIs are not subject to Swiss federal issuance stamp duty and not subject to Swiss federal turnover stamp duty. The sale and purchase of units is, however, subject to Swiss federal turnover stamp duty at a rate of 0.15% if a Swiss securities dealer (e.g. a Swiss bank) is involved either as party or intermediary. Redemption of units is not subject to Swiss federal turnover stamp duty.

Units issued by SICAFs are subject to Swiss federal issuance stamp duty at a rate of 1% but not subject to Swiss federal turnover stamp duty. The sale and purchase of units is subject to Swiss federal turnover stamp duty at a rate of 0.15% if a Swiss securities dealer (e.g. a Swiss bank) is involved either as party or intermediary. The sale and purchase of units is subject to Swiss federal turnover stamp duty at a rate of 0.3% if a Swiss securities dealer (e.g. a Swiss bank) is involved either as party or intermediary. Redemption of units is not subject to Swiss federal turnover stamp duty.

Units issued by foreign collective investment schemes are not subject to Swiss federal issuance stamp duty but subject to Swiss federal turnover stamp duty at a half rate of 0.15%. The sale and purchase of units is subject to Swiss federal turnover stamp duty at a rate of 0.3% if a Swiss securities dealer (e.g. a Swiss bank) is involved either as party or intermediary. Redemption of units is not subject to Swiss federal turnover stamp duty.

## 7.  CURRENT TOPICAL ISSUES/TRENDS

The Swiss investment environment remains very attractive despite the strength of the Swiss franc. Switzerland remains a typical "buyer's market" with many companies that are in search of funds. This global trend appears to be driven by the situation in the US and, although the local market is showing a certain resistance, there is a comparatively strong pressure on pre-money valuations in Switzerland too. Furthermore, the skills and quality of the employees are often perceived as an additional asset by private equity funds when investing in Switzerland.

Currently, there is a positive environment in Switzerland for exiting investments. There have been a number of exits. Usually, exits have been achieved through trade sales/merger and acquisition transactions, including a number of research and development/intellectual property transactions. It is interesting to note that exits have also been achieved at earlier stages than usual and that trade sales have not been limited to large companies but have included a number of medium-sized investments.

Swiss start-ups have attracted attention in recent years, particularly through sales to larger companies. One downside is that investment from Swiss capital, such as through domestic pension funds or traditional banks, remains very low. The gap can be partially offset by foreign investors but domestic 'pioneer' investors would benefit even more from the potential available.

According to a recent study by Dealroom.co for 2015–17, Switzerland also has the lowest ratio of all European countries: on average, only a quarter of the capital ultimately invested in startups over the entire period was collected through Swiss VC funds. (*Swiss Venture Capital Report* (2018)).

The trend continues that a couple of transactions involve a listing on the stock exchange and/or listed companies. Exits by way of IPOs are not so common due to the substantial risks of loss of value during lock-up periods. However, particularly in the biotech sector, exits by way of IPOs on the SIX Swiss Exchange and the US Nasdaq have been seen in the last few years.

The worldwide increase in regulations is expected to continue to have a strong impact on how private equity is carried out.

In this context, the private equity structure developed by legislation in Switzerland, i.e. the LPCI (see s.2.1 above), may become attractive, the more so if the current interesting investment environment can be maintained. Much will, however, depend upon the ability of Switzerland to develop transparent and attractive rules for the taxation of performance fees of general partners/managers. Adaptation to the upcoming regulatory developments in

Europe will also be key.

The rapid evolution in FinTech has not only attracted the attention of FINMA but eventually pushed the Swiss Government to propose FinTech-specific amendments to the Banking Act of 8 November 1934 and other financial laws. A new Banking Ordinance entered into effect on 1 August 2017 designed to reduce barriers to entry for FinTech firms and to strengthen the attractiveness of the Swiss financial markets.

The new regulation sets out a legal framework suitable for all existing and future FinTech companies as well as other actors satisfying the legal conditions. The three major amendments are:

(1)  deadline extension for settlement accounts for the period to 60 days to suit crowdfunding models;

(2)  an exemption for innovative companies from requiring such a banking licence. They should be able to take more than 20 deposits from the public provided that the total amount held does not exceed CHF 1 million; and

(3)  introduction of a new category of banking licence, the so-called "FinTech licence".

It remains to be seen whether these modifications will increase FinTech start-ups and stimulate their development in the next few years.

# United States

**Paul, Weiss, Rifkind, Wharton & Garrison LLP** David Lakhdhir, Ramy Wahbeh, Brian Grieve & David Carmona

## 1. MARKET OVERVIEW

Fundraising and deal flow in the US private equity market have been robust in recent years, as cash-rich but yield-starved investors flock to the asset class in search of higher returns. US-based private equity firms closed on USD 232.7 billion in fresh capital commitments in 2017 and (US) private equity acquirers closed over 4,000 acquisitions in the US with an aggregate deal value of USD 538.8 billion. Threatened changes in tax law to end the favourable treatment of "carried interest" were not implemented and other tax law changes held out the prospect of heightened corporate after-tax earnings. In short, the US private equity market has thrived. But it is not without challenges.

On the fundraising side, 2017 also saw over half of private equity funds close well above their initial target size and in shorter than projected timeframes. Sponsors with strong track records capitalised on the investor demand, with 75% of follow-on funds in 2017 larger than their predecessors. Despite record fundraising however, the market remains slanted towards larger, more established firms. As investors look to consolidate their dollars in fewer funds to increase efficiencies, capital flowed disproportionately to established funds with strong brand recognition and strong historic returns. So, while large amounts were raised by the largest funds, only 247 US private equity funds held final closings in 2017, the lowest number since 2012, and the median fund size climbed from USD 225 million in 2016 to a record high of USD 292.5 million in 2017.

On the buy-side, target valuations are high, leading to fewer traditional investment opportunities and—when combined with the burgeoning amount of private equity "dry powder" described below—resulting in intense competition. The S&P 500 hit a five-year high in January 2018, continuing the second-longest bull market on record and thus limiting the attractiveness of many listed companies. And privately held companies were also often no bargain. Due to the strong economy and accessible credit markets, the average earnings before interest, tax, depreciation and amortisation (EBITDA) multiple paid to acquire a company in the US in 2017 was above 10x.

In regard to financing, while funding for leveraged buyouts was often available on good terms, in 2013, US federal regulators (including the Federal Reserve, the Office of the Comptroller of the Currency—OCC and the Federal Deposit Insurance Corporation—FDIC) introduced guidance steering banks away from financings that would push the debt-to-EBITDA multiple above 6x, although recently some regulators are reportedly considering revisiting that guidance.

While the booming stock market might suggest a corresponding boom in public market exits, in reality, the pace of exits continued to slow in 2017, decreasing by 16.3% since 2015 and falling below the five-year mean. Average holding periods have thus increased to record heights as sponsors struggle to find new investments and make swift and profitable exits from existing investments entered into at elevated multiples. As of 2017, 34% of private equity sponsored companies were acquired more than five years ago.

With capital raising continuing to outpace both deployment and returns, dry powder reached an unprecedented level of USD 641 billion in March 2018 and, if present trends continue, will continue to grow.

In part to sidestep the overheated auction market, private equity firms now often attempt to distinguish themselves by highlighting their demonstrated operational expertise, flexible management fees or specific sector focus. Even formerly generalist private equity firms now often develop industry specific vehicles with deep specialty expertise to rival strategic buyers. Firms also increasingly enter into private equity-strategic partnerships on sizable transactions to compete with well-funded strategic buyers. Another emerging strategy is for private equity firms to front-run full auctions by leveraging relationships to submit bids ahead of time, by asking for "VIP auctions" (in which selected firms receive advance access to the data room) or by completing due diligence early in the process.

As the days of relying mainly on financial engineering and leverage to generate value have passed and finding operational efficiencies has become a necessity in order to drive value for investors, private equity funds are increasingly taking far more active roles in their investments. Buy-and-build strategies remain a popular way to generate returns in the otherwise low organic growth environment, with even large sponsors entering the middle market in search of fragmented industries and roll-up opportunities. Direct investments by larger limited partners (LPs) into existing portfolio assets have also become more commonplace, as LPs continue to seek lower fees and transparency into their investments, while private equity funds aim to deliver higher returns to their investors and foster goodwill.

**Types of funds**

Over 2,700 private equity funds headquartered in the US closed fundraising in 2016–17 and many more were formed or raised additional capital across the "alternative asset" management spectrum. These asset management firms manage a wide range of investment funds, including: traditional leveraged buyout (LBO) funds; venture capital (VC) funds, which typically invest in start-ups and high-tech companies; and hedge funds, a large and often ambiguously named category that includes investors with a wide range of investment strategies including global macro-funds, long–short equity funds, event driven funds and relative value funds. There is also a substantial amount of capital invested in "funds of funds", which are collective investment vehicles that pool and channel money into other alternative asset funds, including private equity funds, to diversify investment risk.

These fund categories can be further sub-divided. While some of the traditional LBO funds still avoid engaging in unsolicited—or in US parlance "hostile"—takeovers, many are now willing to be more aggressive. One reason for this shift is a reduced incentive on the part of traditional funds to be viewed as management friendly, due in part to the curtailed ability of management to influence sales following the Delaware Chancery Court's recent emphasis on conflicts of interest in going private transactions. "Activist" funds are able to take significant positions in potential target listed companies and then seek to cause a change in management or strategy, including by making an offer to buy the company. Some funds—known broadly as "credit funds"—acquire securities across the capital structure but with an emphasis on debt securities or derivatives based on debt instruments. Credit funds can be sub-divided further, with some focused on distressed investment situations, often buying up debt positions as a precursor to pursuing an acquisition, while others focus on a specific strata of the capital structure (e.g. mezzanine debt).

VC funds can be divided based on the stage of development that they typically finance: early stage investors will invest in the early rounds of financing while late stage investors will wait to invest until later financing rounds, when the underlying technology and/or business plan has been more fully developed. In the VC world, there is often sectoral differentiation, with funds specialising in—for example—the life sciences, telecommunications technologies, computing or alternative energy technologies.

## 1.1 Types of investors

Equally wide is the range of investors that participate in private equity funds in the US. Due to the long investment horizons, higher returns associated with private equity come at the expense of liquidity. Investors therefore tend to be those that are comfortable locking up large amounts of capital for long periods of time. Key investor categories include public pension funds, union pension funds, funds of funds, insurance companies, university and charitable endowments and foundations, corporate pension funds and other corporate investors, sovereign wealth funds, government agencies, financial institutions and wealthy (or "ultra-high net worth") individuals and their feeder funds, so-called "family offices".

US pension money (public, corporate and union) is the largest aggregate component, comprising about 46% of the capital invested in the asset class in recent years. Many pension funds turn to private equity in today's low interest rate environment in response to unique pressures to generate high returns to meet their obligations. In the US, however, corporate and union pension investors are subject to a number of special rules.

Sovereign wealth funds, insurance companies and endowments/foundations also play important roles as investors in private equity funds, accounting for approximately 10% of total private equity investments respectively. While endowments and foundations famously pulled back on their private equity investments in the wake of the credit crisis, they have turned their attention back to private equity because of its ability to produce high returns relative to lacking yields from other asset classes in recent years.

Funds of funds are now also a substantial component of capital in many private equity funds' capital base, particularly in the VC field. Investment and commercial banks, however, generally no longer play a significant role in organising or funding private equity and hedge funds in the US since the implementation of the "Volcker Rule" (from the Dodd-Frank Wall Street Reform and Consumer Protection Act 2010—Dodd-Frank Act) in 2014.

## 1.2  Types of investments

In the early years of US private equity investing, funds tended to make two types of investments. Traditional LBO funds acquired companies using their own equity capital, with significant leverage provided by bank loans and in many instances one or more layers of subordinated debt. Traditional VC funds made non-controlling equity investments in start-up and developing technology companies, often in the form of convertible preferred stock instruments.

Private equity firms have branched out to engage in a much broader range of investments. Particularly in recent years, sponsors have been forced to design creative investment strategies due to high asset valuations and the increasing level of competition in the market for investment opportunities. The only material limitations constraining the investment creativity of private equity fund managers in the US are imposed by the investment parameters in their fund documents and by the fund managers' desire to achieve returns on investment consistent with the strategies presented to investors.

Funds invest in non-controlling equity investments, including in listed companies, in high-yield "mezzanine" acquisition debt instruments (often issued with conversion rights or common stock purchase warrants) and consortium investments, to name a few alternatives. Private equity firms in the US also sometimes make non-controlling private investments in public equity securities (often called PIPES). These investments are sometimes made to finance the equity component of acquisition financing or to provide emergency financing to a company in financial distress, and occasionally for other reasons. PIPES are often structured as shares of convertible preferred stock, taking advantage of the ability of many US companies to issue new series of preferred stock with only the authorisation of the board of directors (and not the shareholders). Neither US state corporation laws nor the articles of incorporation of most US companies provide shareholders with pre-emptive rights, so a board of directors of a listed company can agree to issue shares solely to a private equity fund and shareholders' approval is only required under New York Stock Exchange (NYSE) and NASDAQ rules if shares with 20% or more voting power are issued. The issuing company receives a fresh injection of equity capital and can close the investment relatively quickly as neither a Securities and Exchange Commission (SEC) review nor a road show is required.

Private equity/strategic partnerships and club deals have surged in popularity under current market conditions. Rather than lose out to cash-rich strategic buyers, some private equity firms prefer to team up with strategic buyers or other private equity firms to bid on sizable assets together. Moreover, buy-and-build strategies, whereby private equity firms merge their existing portfolio companies with smaller companies from outside of their portfolios in similar industries, remain popular in today's low-organic-growth environment. This strategy has several advantages: it accelerates portfolio companies' growth by acquisition; it enables private equity firms to realise strategic synergies similar to corporate investors; it reduces the original purchase price multiple and therefore increases return; and it enables private equity firms to secure higher exit prices by creating large targets that become interesting for large corporations who would have ignored smaller players.

Larger LPs also increasingly make direct investments in private equity fund assets, for example, by co-investing in deals with private equity firms or acquiring minority ownership of existing portfolio assets. Co-investments are attractive to LPs because they offer transparency into the funds in which they invest and because they often include lower or no fees and higher returns than investing in funds. Occasionally, LPs have also acquired minority stakes in existing portfolio companies. Private equity funds may agree to these types of transactions because they deliver higher returns to investors and create additional goodwill between the sponsor and the LP.

### Public to private transactions

Since the early 1980s, private equity funds have often—and in some instances famously—acquired US listed companies. US terminology in this area differs slightly from that used in Europe. While listed companies are in US parlance called "public companies" (because they are listed, not because of their form), the term "public to private" or "P2P", while understood, is used less in the US than in Europe. What Americans call a "going private" transaction is only a subset of what in the UK would be called a public to private transaction. The term "going private transaction" is in US parlance often understood to include those transactions which are defined in the SEC's r.13e-3 of the US Securities Act 1933 (Securities Act) to be "Rule 13e-3 transactions", namely transactions in which insiders at or an affiliate of a listed company directly or indirectly acquire(s) the company, which is delisted or otherwise "taken private".

Under the SEC's rules, because there are heightened risks of conflicts of interest in a Rule 13e-3 transaction between the affiliated acquiring company or group and the acquisition target, the SEC requires a more robust set of public disclosures, including a detailed recitation of the communications and negotiations that were the "background" to the transaction and a statement as to the fairness of the transaction to unaffiliated shareholders. Delaware law (under which a majority of US listed companies are organised) similarly imposes a higher standard of review of the terms of such a transaction. Instead of deferring to the board's "business judgement" absent a breach of fiduciary duty, a Delaware court will assess the "entire fairness" of a transaction of this nature.

Because of the enhanced disclosure standard and stricter standard of review, in transactions of this nature, the target will be advised to follow procedures designed to insulate board members from allegations of conflict of interest in the consideration and approval of the deal and to retain independent advisors that provide advice solely to the "independent committee of the board" established to consider the transaction. Similarly, where senior management has agreed or is expected to play a significant role in the proposed buyout, management will usually be excluded from the board's or special committee's consideration of the fairness of the transaction.

## Takeover rules

There are two means of acquiring a US listed company: a merger under state law; or an offer (called a "tender offer" in the US). Mergers are usually "triangular" in the sense that the acquiring company organises a subsidiary in the same state as the company to be acquired (often Delaware), which is then merged with the target company resulting in the acquiring company owning 100% of the target. In Delaware, a merger must be approved by the board of directors of each merging company and then approved by a majority (50.1% in Delaware; two-thirds in some other states) of shareholders in a subsequent meeting of shareholders. The consideration paid can be shares of the acquiring parent company, cash, notes or even other forms of consideration. Mergers where the consideration paid is entirely cash are common. The mechanics of effecting a merger are governed by the applicable state law (usually Delaware) but the form of proxy statement sent to shareholders to solicit their approval, and the disclosure requirements if shares are the merger consideration and the proxy statement is also a prospectus, are set by federal law and supervised by the SEC.

Tender offers are actually less common, as a means of acquiring a listed company in the US, than triangular mergers. In theory, a tender offer can be used to acquire a US public company without its board's approval but the board's ability to interpose takeover defences will often mean that, as a practical matter, its approval is needed for an offer to succeed. In some cases, a tender offer may also allow an acquisition to be completed more quickly than would be possible through a triangular merger but this advantage will often disappear if there is a need to obtain a number of competition or other regulatory clearances in advance of completion of the offer.

The US rules impose fewer hurdles to private equity acquisitions of US listed companies than is the norm in Europe but this is offset by the ability that boards of directors have in the US to resist offers that they determine not to be in the best interests of the company and its shareholders. There is, for example, no requirement under US law that an offer or merger proposal be fully financed. To the contrary, a private equity fund can in theory make a takeover bid with no financing commitments, so long as it believes in good faith that the financing can be arranged. Similarly, under US law, a person making a tender offer can impose whatever conditions it wishes and a person seeking to acquire a company through a triangular merger can impose whatever conditions the target's board are willing to accept. There is also no legal requirement that a controlling (e.g. 30%) shareholder make an offer to acquire the balance of a company's shares. And the percentage ownership required to "squeeze out" minority shareholders is usually a simple majority, or in some states two-thirds, not the 90% or 95% that is required in most countries in Europe.

This regulatory flexibility is offset by the negotiating power of US corporate boards. Target boards are likely to reject acquisition proposals that lack financing or are overly conditional, to block persons seeking to acquire de facto control without making an offer to all shareholders and to block offers made at a price the board deems inadequate. The ability of a board to engage in defensive measures, including the adoption of shareholder rights plans (often called "poison pills") that effectively preclude a would-be acquirer from purchasing more than, for example, 15% of a company without its board's approval, provides US corporate boards with the ability to negotiate for better terms from a position of relative strength. The fact that the law allows the flexibility to structure acquisitions and their conditions as the acquirer and target board may agree, however, will often prove useful to a private equity fund acquirer.

## 2. FUNDS

### 2.1 Fund structures

US private equity funds were traditionally formed as domestic limited partnerships, usually in Delaware. In recent years, a majority of US-advised funds have organised certain parallel funds (described further below) as limited partnerships in the Cayman Islands or occasionally other non-US jurisdictions, such as Luxembourg, for a range of reasons including more recently to facilitate compliance with AIFMD (Directive 2011/61 on Alternative Investment Fund Managers and amending Directives 2003/41 and 2009/65 and Regulations 1060/2009 and 1095/2010 [2011] OJ L174/1, described further below). A corporation is almost never used as the legal vehicle for private equity funds, as it will attract US corporate tax, whereas a limited partnership or limited liability company (LLC) will almost universally be viewed as tax-transparent, at least for US federal income tax purposes, although the LLC form is rarely utilised.

Many US private equity funds contemplate the creation of parallel funds to accommodate the tax, regulatory or other technical requirements of particular investors, such as non-US investors (including "sovereign wealth fund" investors) and US tax exempt entities. Thus, a private equity fund generally, upon closer inspection, actually consists of two, three or more parallel funds or parallel investment vehicles that are similarly named and invest side by side on virtually identical and pro rata terms, except to the extent that tax, regulatory or other technical requirements dictate otherwise. The key distinction amongst parallel funds is typically the structuring vehicles that are utilised to facilitate investments; the parallel fund through which US state and local pension funds (which generally take the position that they are not subject to any taxation) will not typically invest in portfolio companies through corporate entities as otherwise such investors are subject to an extra level of taxation without realising any associated benefit, whereas the parallel fund through which non-US investors invest will interpose non-US corporate entities so as to isolate any US tax filing obligations within the corporate entity.

A limited partnership can be formed in Delaware in less than a day by preparing and filing a short certificate of limited partnership, listing basic information about the partnership, including its name and the name and address of the general partner and registered agent. Unlike in many other jurisdictions, the partnership agreement and the names of the LPs are neither required to be filed or made publicly available, nor are limited partnerships required under Delaware law to file financial statements publicly. A similarly efficient process applies in forming Cayman Islands limited partnerships. The formation of a Luxembourg limited partnership is much more involved however.

A private equity fund structured as a limited partnership will typically have a single general partner and many LPs. The partnership will typically enter into an advisory or investment management agreement with an investment manager, which is usually an affiliate of the fund's general partner. Each of these plays a distinct role:

- the general partner has overall management responsibility and retains ultimate control over investment decisions, although it delegates varying degrees of its authority to the investment manager. The general partner has unlimited liability for the partnership's debts and generally owes a fiduciary duty to the LPs (which can be modified or eliminated under Delaware or Cayman Islands law, for example). The general partner is typically a single purpose entity (i.e. it serves as general partner to only one private equity fund), organised in a juridical form that enjoys limited liability;

- the LPs are the primary investors in the fund. They are typically passive investors but they will have varying rights to information, some of them will often have the right to designate representatives to an advisory committee and all of them will have the right to vote on specified major issues relating to the fund (such as termination or suspension of the investment period, the removal of the general partner or the dissolution of the fund, though whether these items are voted on by the advisory committee or the LPs generally is subject to negotiation during the fund formation process). Under Delaware law, LPs are able to designate representatives to an advisory committee and/or to vote on major issues of this nature without jeopardising their limited liability status, so long as they are not engaged in the management or control of the partnership's business;

- a US private equity fund or its general partner is typically advised by an investment manager, which is typically engaged as an independent contractor and employs (or is affiliated with the entity that employs) the individuals who source and negotiate investment opportunities, supervise and serve on the governing bodies of portfolio companies, facilitate disposition/exit events and otherwise advise on fund investments;

- the general partner or management company will usually have an investment committee, which reviews and approves investment decisions (e.g. acquisition, financing, restructuring and disposition); and

- in virtually all recent funds, there is an advisory committee composed of representatives of the LPs (typically those that invest large amounts of capital or are well-respected in the investing community), which may be asked to review and (in some cases) approve transactions that present material conflicts of interest or that the general partner otherwise feels should be discussed or disclosed (or is required or prudent to discuss and disclose) with representatives of the investors. Decisions made by the advisory committee are binding on all of the fund's partners.

As noted above, the structure of the fund and its related entities is significantly influenced by the tax consequences of that structure and the tax considerations of the individual investors. Fund vehicles are generally treated as partnerships for US federal income tax purposes and, thus, the fund itself is not subject to US tax on its gains and income. As a result of this "pass-through" treatment, the partners recognise their allocable share of the gains and losses of the fund. Limited partners of the fund, whether US taxable investors (e.g. banks), US tax exempt investors (e.g. pension funds), US and non-US high net worth individuals or non-US institutions, are each sensitive to different tax issues. For example:

- LPs that are otherwise tax exempt, like private pension funds or endowments, must pay taxes on income derived from trade or business activities, including those operated through a pass-through vehicle in which the fund holds an interest (such as a US LLC), that are unrelated to the exempt purpose of the LP (also referred to as unrelated business taxable income or UBTI) and on income and gains from investment assets that are debt-financed at the fund level (i.e. the fund and not the portfolio company is the borrower of such indebtedness);
- non-US investors are taxed, and subject to withholding, on any income effectively connected to a US trade or business. This effectively connected income, or ECI, is generated by fee income, certain real estate investments, loan origination and other business activities, including those operated through a pass-through vehicle in which the fund holds an interest. As a general matter, there will be withholding tax owed on any ECI allocable to a non-US investor regardless of whether there is an associated distribution of cash to such investor; and
- non-US investors that are "sovereign" in nature may recognise income that is derived from the conduct of any US or non-US "commercial activity" (CAI).

Steps to avoid or minimise these and other adverse tax consequences should be considered when creating the fund structure. The limited partnership agreement may, for example, require the fund to minimise UBTI, ECI and CAI and/or may grant LPs the right to opt out of a particular investment that would give rise to specified adverse tax consequences for that investor.

## 2.2 Regulation of fundraising and fund managers

The US has a robust set of laws governing investment companies, investment advisors and the offering of securities. Because private equity funds are private limited partnerships (or similar investment vehicles) that usually attract capital only from large, sophisticated investors, they have in the past largely avoided direct regulation by the SEC and other US regulatory bodies. This has changed to a great extent as a result of legislation (including changes to existing law) in response to the financial crisis of 2007–08, including, among other things, the SEC's requirement to eliminate certain exemptions from registration for investment advisers to private equity funds and rules imposed by the Dodd-Frank Act that, among other things, restrict bank holding companies from investing their proprietary capital in, and managing, private equity funds.

### Investment company regulation

The US Investment Company Act 1940 (ICA) imposes a strict regulatory regime on "investment companies" (a term that is broadly defined to include trusts, partnerships or any other type of investment vehicle) that attract investment from US persons. Almost all private equity funds fall within the broad definition of "investment company" under the ICA but nearly all are exempted from its registration requirements by one of the following exemptions:

- s.3(c)(1) of the ICA exempts from the definition of "investment company" an investment vehicle that has no more than 100 security holders (excluding knowledgeable employees and, if a non-US fund, non-US LPs) and does not make or propose to make a public offering of its securities; or

- s.3(c)(7) of the ICA exempts from the definition of "investment company" an investment vehicle if all of its US security holders (excluding knowledgeable employees) are "qualified purchasers", a term that includes individuals with at least USD 5 million of investments and entities with at least USD 25 million.

Qualifying for one of these exemptions is important because most private equity funds would not be able to exist in their current organisational or fee structure if they were required to register under the ICA. The largest and most successful private equity funds rely exclusively on s.3(c)(7) of the ICA to maximise the fund's capital raising ability.

### Regulation of fund management

Investment advisers in the US are regulated under the Investment Advisers Act 1940 (Advisers Act) and are subject to substantive regulatory requirements as well as registration and disclosure requirements. State level regulatory requirements may also apply but typically do not govern with respect to private equity firms whose managed funds offer securities on the basis of, and rely on exemptions from registration with the SEC under, the private placement exemptions afforded by reg.D of the Securities Act ("Regulation D"), in which case state level regulatory requirements imposed on such funds are limited to notice filings with certain states in which the fund's securities were offered and sold.

Since 2011, investment advisers to most US private equity funds have been required to register with the SEC under the Advisers Act. Some investment advisers are able to avoid SEC registration by advising solely private funds and having aggregate assets under management of less than USD 150 million; but these may be subject to state regulation instead. Similarly, there is a limited exemption available for "foreign private advisors", which may exempt an advisor that has no place of business in the US, has fewer than 15 clients (i.e. fund vehicles) and investors in the US, has aggregate assets under management attributable to clients and investors in the US of less than USD 25 million, and neither holds itself out generally to the public in the US as an investment adviser nor acts as an investment adviser to any investment company registered under the ICA or to a US business development company (BDC). There is also an exemption for VC funds but this exemption, too, is unlikely to offer any help to managers of large-scale private equity funds as

VC funds are restricted in their use of leverage.

An investment manager required to register under the Advisers Act is subject to the registration and regulatory requirements of the Advisers Act, including filing a Form ADV (Pts 1 and 2) with the SEC, reporting and disclosure to clients, complying with the custody rule, establishing compliance programmes, personal securities trading and a code of ethics, appointing a chief compliance officer and becoming subject to periodic audits by the SEC. As discussed further below, in recent years, the SEC has moved aggressively to regulate fund managers, with a specific focus on the extent to which registered investment advisers have disclosed to their investors all material facts pertaining to their business practices.

In light of the strict requirements of this exemption, many management companies to major European private equity funds are also required to register with the SEC, which is consistent with the expectations of US investors. Conversely, US private equity fund managers are now required to register their offerings and/or make filings with or provide notices to the Financial Conduct Authority (FCA) in order to comply with AIFMD and market their funds in certain jurisdictions in the EU (including the UK).

### Offerings of fund interests

Unless an exemption applies, any company that offers or sells securities publicly in the US must register the offering with the SEC and deliver to each purchaser a prospectus that complies with the requirements of the Securities Act. Limited partnership interests are considered securities under the Securities Act. Avoiding registration for private equity funds is critical, not only to avoid the cost and disclosure requirements of being a publicly traded company but also to qualify for the exemptions from the ICA described above. Private equity funds must therefore offer and sell limited partnership interests in a manner that complies with the private placement exemption under the Securities Act. US private equity funds typically structure their fundraising activities to comply with s.4(a)(2) of the Securities Act generally but more specifically rely almost exclusively on the safe harbour afforded by Regulation D of the Securities Act.

Section 4(a)(2) of the Securities Act exempts an offering from the registration and prospectus requirements of the Securities Act if the transaction does not involve a public offering. The term "public offering" is not defined in the Securities Act. There is case law that sheds light on the term's meaning but determining whether the transaction is a private placement depends on the circumstances of the specific transaction, including the absence of any public sales efforts, the limited number of offerees and the level of sophistication of the offerees and their relationship with the issuer.

Regulation D under the Securities Act provides a "safe harbour" exemption designed to avoid the uncertainty of relying on s.4(a)(2) on its own. Generally, a fund complies with the safe harbour requirements under s.506 Regulation D if it:

- offers its interests in the US to "accredited investors" and not more than 35 other investors (but only if those investors receive prospectus level disclosure);
- does not conduct any general solicitation or advertising (defined

broadly);

- ensures that none of the following are "bad actors" (as defined): the issuer, its predecessors, affiliated issuers and individuals affiliated with the issuer; beneficial owners of 20% (or more) of the issuer's voting securities; investment managers and affiliated individuals; promoters and affiliated individuals; and placement agents and other persons soliciting investors, and affiliated individuals; and
- files electronically a Form D with the SEC in advance of, or within the 15-day period following, the first sale of securities by the fund.

Because the level of disclosure required to provide to a fund's investors under Regulation D if one offers to persons who are not accredited investors is similar to the level required for a public offering of securities, interests in private equity funds are almost never offered to non-accredited investors. Every private equity fund manager will prepare and distribute a "private placement memorandum" or similar offering document to potential investors that contains, among other things, the manager's strategy, management team, investment history and conflicts of interest, and the private equity fund's terms, risk factors and tax attributes.

Limited partnership interests that have been sold in a private placement under s.4(a)(2) of the Securities Act or Regulation D may not be resold unless the resale is registered under the Securities Act (which will never happen unless a private equity fund itself engages in a registered offering) or an exemption from resale is available. To ensure compliance, the fund will demand representations and warranties from all investors that they are acquiring the interests for their own account and not for resale, and will also impose contractual restrictions on resale.

The Employee Retirement Income Security Act 1974 (ERISA) and VC operating company (VCOC) rules are also relevant to private equity fund formation in the US. Under the regulations of the US Department of Labor, the assets of an employee benefit plan investing in a private equity fund will be treated as a portion of the underlying assets of the fund unless an exemption applies. If the fund's assets are treated as plan assets, the sponsors of the fund may be deemed fiduciaries of the employee plan and subject to certain responsibilities and potential liabilities under the ERISA, including duties of prudence and compliance with the plan's governing documents. Moreover, the general partner's carried interest in the fund may violate the ERISA's self-dealing or prohibited transaction rules. Those organising a private equity fund (in the US or overseas) will therefore want to ensure that its assets are not ERISA plan assets. In general, a fund will not be deemed to hold plan assets if:

- participation in the fund by "benefit plan investors" (a defined term) is not "significant", meaning that such investors have invested less than 25% of the value of any class of interests in the fund; or
- the fund qualifies as a VCOC by ensuring that its first investment and at least 50% of the fund's assets overall on an annual basis are invested in operating companies and the fund has direct management rights (e.g. appointment of a director or access to rights to information) from such operating companies.

Because it is possible inadvertently to fail the first "significant participation" test and the consequence of failure is material to both fund and investors, many funds seek to satisfy both tests by keeping benefit plan investor investment below 25% and qualifying as a VCOC. However, once compliance with the "significant participation" test is assured, a private equity fund will rarely not take advantage of this; otherwise, VCOC compliance will limit the fund's flexibility, which is particularly important with respect to funds that invest in debt securities (e.g. in situations where a prospective portfolio company is experiencing distress and control is sought through acquisition of debt), where it is very difficult for a lender to obtain the requisite "management rights" imposed by VCOC regulations with respect to a borrower.

## 2.3 Customary or common terms of funds

Although there is a great range of US private equity funds and significant variation in terms across funds, some useful generalisations concerning the customary or common terms of private equity funds can be made. However, the spectrum of terms across the latest, most established private equity funds, on the one hand, and the middle market, less established or newly established private equity funds, on the other hand, greatly differs. Further, the current state of the fundraising markets is quite robust, such that, notwithstanding pressure from investors for more investor-favourable terms (including through industry organisations, such as the Institutional Limited Partner Association (ILPA)), general partners of private equity funds (in particular the "mega" and larger buyout funds) generally have more bargaining power.

### Investment term

Private equity funds are typically established for a fixed term (e.g. 10 years). The general partner may have some leeway to unilaterally extend this period, however, it is typically subject to advisory committee or LP approval. The reason to include the term is typically to permit the fund to continue to protect and preserve existing investments before having to commence the orderly disposition of assets following the end of that period. LPs are focused on term extensions in order to determine if the manager of the private equity fund can justify the continuing receipt of management fees during the extended term.

### Capital commitments

Each LP will make a specific capital commitment to the fund, which is drawn down in cash over the "commitment" or "investment" period for purposes of making new investments. The commitment period of a US private equity fund is typically five–six years. At times, this period may be extendable but rarely without advisory committee or LP approval.

### Sponsor commitment

Sponsors of private equity funds will generally commit in the aggregate between 1% and 10% of the aggregate third-party capital committed to the private equity fund. Typically, a de minimis portion of the sponsor commitment will flow through the general partner and the balance of the sponsor's investment will come in through a "special" limited partnership interest in an effort to minimise the sponsor capital that is subject to unlimited liability, but there is some variety in practice in this area. The sponsor's commitment is typically funded through a combination of the management company and its owners, and the employees of the sponsor. The sponsor commitment typically does not bear management fees or carried interest. In recent years, due to increased scrutiny by the Internal Revenue Service (IRS), fewer sponsors are utilising "management fee waivers" to fund their sponsor commitments.

### Closings

In most cases, LPs are admitted during a 9–12-month period, although in recent years, in light of the pace of deployment of capital, investment allocations made by investors and a general consolidation of the industry (generating greater concentration of capital in fewer private equity funds), offering periods have reduced or been limited to a "one and done" closing. Investors that are admitted after the initial closing are typically required to pay their share of any prior capital contributions made by existing LPs to fund investments, management fees and expenses, plus a cost of carry thereon (e.g. the preferred return rate reflected in the fund's distribution waterfall or, less often, the "prime rate" maintained by US financial institutions, plus 2% thereon) and the existing investors receive a refund on those capital contributions plus the cost of carry (typically other than the portion allocable to management fees, which is paid to the manager).

### Diversification requirements and investment restrictions

Most funds have limits on the percentage of total committed capital that can be invested in any one company or transaction (typically 15–25%), in any geographic area, in additional or follow-on investments (typically 15–25%) following the expiration of the commitment period and, less often, in any one sector. Fund documents will also allow certain investors who are subject to policies, laws, rules or regulations that prohibit or limit their investments in particular industries (e.g. banking or media companies) or assets (e.g. gambling, munitions, pornography, alcohol or tobacco) to be excused from participation in such prohibited asset classes, in which case the investors who are permitted to invest in such investments make up the shortfall (up to an agreed-upon monetary cap).

### Distribution waterfall; calculation of carried interest and clawback

Most US private equity funds employ distribution methodologies, and calculate the carried interest payable to the fund's general partner, on a deal-by-deal basis. This means that each investor in the fund must receive a return of its invested capital with respect to a given investment, management fees and expenses allocable such investment as well as such amounts with respect to any other investments that have been significantly written down in value or disposed of at a loss, plus a preferred return on such amounts (typically at 8% per annum), before the general partner is entitled to carried interest distributions or a portion of the fund's profits. Once this preferred return has been distributed, there is typically a "general partner catch-up", in which the general partner is distributed an enhanced percentage of profit so as to cause the general partner to have been distributed 20% of all profits to date. Thereafter, further profits are usually allocated 20% (or some similar percentage) to the general partner and the balance (i.e. 80% in the typical case) to the LPs. The deal-by-deal distribution methodology is distinguishable from the European-style or "All Capital Back" distribution methodology, whereby investors recover all capital contributions with respect to all investments, management fees and expenses before the general partner is entitled to receive any carried interest distributions.

The LPs will request, and the general partner will virtually always acquiesce to, mechanisms to ensure that, on a cumulative basis, the general partner does not receive more than the intended percentage of carried interest over the life of the fund. These mechanisms include "clawbacks" (supported by sponsor or individual guaranties) and "holdbacks" or "escrows". Where investment returns are calculated on a cumulative basis, early exit transactions may result in interim distributions on the general partner's carried interest that are no longer justified at a later date. To avoid an overpayment on the carried interest, the general partner will typically agree to return any amounts previously distributed to it as carried interest to the extent such amounts exceed the portion to which it is ultimately entitled, measured on a cumulative basis over the life of the fund (calculated net of tax liabilities previously incurred by the general partner or indirect partners of the general partner (e.g. investment professionals associated with the fund sponsor) with respect to the earlier gains).

Typically, the clawback is calculated at the end of the life of the fund, although a number of private equity funds employ interim clawbacks that are calculated, for example, after five or six years (following the end of the investment period). As stated above, some sponsors will escrow a portion of the carried interest (typically 20–50%) until a specified rate of return (taking into account realised and unrealised appreciation of investments) has been achieved or a certain number of years have passed. In recent years, carried interest deferrals and the reduction or elimination of the preferred return have become more common.

## Management fees

In addition to the general partner's carried interest, the investment manager will also typically receive a fee in the range of 1.5–2% per annum of the fund's capital commitments (during the investment period) or invested capital (following a "step down" upon the earlier of the end of the investment period and the investment manager's right to receive management fees from a successor fund) to cover ongoing overhead expenses of the investment manager (employment compensation, rent, utilities). The management fee is typically paid quarterly.

In recent years, investors have focused on management fees to ensure that it is not a "profit center" for the investment manager; in particular, some investors would typically rather "pay for performance" and bear an increased carried interest in exchange for a reduction in management fees, or otherwise invest a larger amount or participate at a first or early closing to receive a reduced management fee. Some private equity funds have included these features in recent fundraisings. The payment of management fees is recoverable through the distribution waterfall in any event. However, certain investors will ask private equity funds to return all management fees (and perhaps all expenses, described further below as if the distribution waterfall were "European-style", rather than allocable management fees (in the case of a deal-by-deal distribution methodology), through the distribution waterfall prior to the general partner becoming entitled to carried interest distributions.

### Expenses

In recent years, private equity fund managers have endured certain scrutiny from investors and the SEC as to the types of expenses that the private equity fund (and therefore the investors), rather than the private equity fund manager, are bearing. Although investors in the private equity fund are entitled to a return of all of their capital contributions funded to pay expenses plus the preferred return thereon, investors are focused on reducing their economic burden with respect to expenses (thereby increasing their returns) and obtaining as much transparency as possible with respect to expense allocations and amounts. Whereas it is understood that the private equity fund bears virtually all investment-related expenses, investors are particularly focused on the private equity fund bearing an amount of "reasonable" organisational expenses and non-investment related operating expenses, which is highly difficult to ascertain given the extent to which investors negotiate fund documents and the complexities associated with organising fund structures that are tax-efficient for investors. While no private equity manager can guarantee the total amount of organisational expenses and operating expenses that can be incurred, in response, private equity managers have vastly expanded the disclosure in this regard in the fund's private placement memorandum and limited partnership agreement, and the manager's Form ADV on file with the SEC. Private equity fund managers have also increased transparency with regards to expenses at advisory committee meetings and regular reporting to investors.

### Transaction Fees

Transaction fees (including break-up fees, directors' fees, advisory fees, consulting fees and similar fees) are often paid to private equity fund managers in connection with actual or contemplated investments. Several years ago, only a portion (50–80%) of these types of fees was applied to reduce the amount of management fees that the investors would otherwise owe to the manager. In recent years, due to investor requests and the regulatory climate, it is almost universally accepted (certainly in the case of the more established private equity funds) that 100% of such fees are applied to reduce management fees.

### Investor withdrawals

In traditional private equity funds, investors have no right to liquidity or to withdraw from a private equity fund (except when required by law, rule or regulation). With the permission of the general partner (which may be refused at the general partner's discretion), an investor may transfer its limited partnership interest and funding commitment to a new investor. These transfers are typically subject to a number of conditions, to enable the general partner to avoid subjecting the fund to adverse regulatory or tax consequences depending on the identity of the transferee, the size of the transfer and the frequency of transfers.

### Commitment termination

LPs also generally have no right to terminate their capital commitments during the commitment period but in a number of funds there are exceptions. For example:

- a "key person" provision may address the potential turnover of senior professionals of the investment manager. These clauses are typically triggered by the departure of key professionals, or failure by an agreed number or group of the key professionals to dedicate the agreed amount of time to the particular private equity fund or the manager's business in general. If triggered, the commitment period will be automatically suspended or terminated; if suspended, then investors generally have the right with a super-majority vote (66.6–75%) of the commitments to cause the commitment period to terminate;
- a "no fault" termination provision sometimes gives the investors the right at any time by super-majority vote (75–85%) to cause the commitment period to terminate or to terminate the fund; it is relatively uncommon for investors to retain the right to remove the general partner "without cause"; and
- "cause-based" provisions—e.g. triggered by wilful misconduct by or criminal conviction of the fund sponsor—which give investors, by majority vote or super majority vote (e.g. 50–66.67%), the right to terminate the commitment period, remove and replace the general partner and/or terminate the fund. If a general partner is removed for cause, it will only be entitled to carried interest distributions with respect to investments made or committed to prior to its removal, subject to a reduction or "haircut" (typically in the range of 20–50%).

### Borrowings

Typically, private equity funds that engage in a LBO strategy will cause portfolio companies to incur indebtedness in connection with their acquisition. This indebtedness is typically incurred by the portfolio companies and not by or with recourse to the private equity funds themselves. In addition, some private equity funds will incur indebtedness at the fund level that is recourse to the private equity fund and collateralised by the LPs' capital commitment. This credit facility (known as subscription line financing) allows the private equity fund to make efficient use of cash by calling capital less frequently. While credit facilities have many benefits for the fund and the LPs, some LPs may perceive credit facilities as having adverse effects (such as the incurrence of UBTI by US tax-exempt investors associated with such indebtedness) or request transparency associated with the use of credit facilities (such as reporting that assumes that investments that were funded using the credit facility were instead funded using capital contributions). The ILPA has recently focused on the usage of borrowings by private equity funds.

### Co-investments

In recent years, private equity funds and their LPs have focused on offering and obtaining access to co-investment opportunities. A co-investment is an opportunity for an investor (typically an existing investor in the private equity fund) to invest an incremental amount of capital in a single portfolio company in which the private equity fund is also investing. Typically, an investor will bear a reduced (or no) carried interest or management fee in connection with a co-investment and will have the opportunity to diligence the portfolio company itself, rather than committing "blindly" to the investment. These enhanced economic terms will allow an investor to "blend-down" the overall amount of management fees and carried interest that it is bearing with respect to a given private equity fund manager. As such, at the outset of the fundraising process and throughout a fund's investment period, investors are actively seeking co-investment opportunities.

The SEC has recently focused on co-investments and has sought visibility with respect to the manager's process associated with offering and allocating co-investment opportunities to investors. In response, many private equity fund managers have sought to maintain maximum flexibility with respect to their processes associated with the offering and allocating of co-investment opportunities. Co-investments have also generated attention with respect to allocation of expenses—that is, whether the manager, the private equity fund or the co-investor(s) should be liable for expenses associated with a transaction that is not ultimately consummated.

## 3. DEBT FINANCE
### 3.1 Means of financing

Private equity buyers will often seek sources of financing both inside and outside the traditional bank market. Non-traditional lenders (such as hedge funds, mezzanine funds and private equity debt funds) are less constrained by, for example, the 6x leverage lending guidance which traditional banks tend to observe. Financing structures sought by private equity purchasers regularly include high-yield senior secured, senior unsecured or senior subordinated notes (commonly issued in r.144A of the Securities Act on private placement).

High-yield securities typically carry a relatively high interest rate (whether in cash, payment-in-kind or a combination of the two) but may offer significant flexibility in terms of cash flow management and covenants (though so-called "covenant-lite" bank loans have been steadily moving toward high-yield style covenant flexibility with a clear convergence between bond terms and bank terms, similar to the phenomenon occurring in Europe). High-yield bond offerings typically require the delivery of an offering memorandum 20–30 days prior to closing in order to allow for a marketing period (or road show). Additionally, in recent years "unitranche" financings have made their appearance in the market, mostly in middle-market transactions or bespoke structures. Unitranche products combine senior and subordinated debt into one instrument, typically with a blended interest rate that falls between the senior debt and the subordinated debt.

### 3.2 Restrictions on granting security

In the US, senior debt to finance acquisitions are typically secured by a lien on substantially all the assets of the acquired company and its material subsidiaries. The acquired company, and in most cases its material US subsidiaries, will also guarantee the loans through upstream guarantees, which are often secured by the assets of the guarantor. This is permissible in the US because there is no prohibition of "financial assistance" (or any similar doctrine) that would prevent the assets and cash flows of an acquired company to be used to support an acquisition.

There is also no prohibition on upstream guarantees or grants of security in the US. However, if a subsidiary providing an upstream guarantee or granting an upstream security interest is insolvent at the time of said guarantee or grant, or is rendered insolvent thereby, the guarantee or security interest may later be voided on the grounds that the issuance of the guarantee or the grant of the security interest is a "fraudulent transfer" or "fraudulent conveyance". While the terminology differs depending on the state; the concept is similar to the English law concept of a transfer at undervalue. In the context of a LBO, the primary concern is that the guarantees and grants of security interests given to the lenders would be transfers for less than fair value but there are other aspects of a LBO that may also be voided as fraudulent transfers and thus must be analysed carefully.

To guard against fraudulent transfer claims, lenders will often seek to structure the financing transaction in a manner that minimises the risks, and demand representations and warranties—and in some cases opinions of third-party valuers—that the borrower and its subsidiaries are not insolvent (or close to insolvent). Guarantees will also typically be limited to a percentage of the guarantor's net worth so that it can be demonstrated that the upstream guarantor was not—at least in a balance sheet sense—rendered insolvent by the contingent liability represented by the guarantee.

For US tax reasons, non-US subsidiaries typically will not guarantee acquisition loans made to their US parent or grant a lien on their assets in support of the loan. For similar reasons, a US borrower will usually not pledge as security more than 65% of the shares of a non-US subsidiary or any shares of a minor subsidiary that is not held directly by a US obligor. This practice generally survived after the tax reforms signed into law in December 2017 by President Trump.[1]

## 3.3   Intercreditor issues

Intercreditor arrangements allow creditors with divergent claims and interests to order their relations from a credit and operational standpoint so that, if a debtor goes into default or otherwise experiences trouble managing its debts, the creditors have agreed in advance how their rights interact, including allocating priority of repayment and rights to pursue the debtor for recovery.

In general, there are three primary types of subordination in the US:

*   *structural subordination*: de facto subordination is achieved by the

---

[1]   See "Trump's tax bill: US Senate passes reform legislation" (20 December 2017), *BBC News* available at: *https://www.bbc.com/news/world-us-canada-42421821*; An Act to provide for reconciliation pursuant to titles II and V of the concurrent resolution on the budget for fiscal year 2018 (H.R.1—115th Congress, 2017–18) available at:
*https://www.congress.gov/bill/115th-congress/house-bill/1/text* [Accessed 26 September 2018].

extension of credit at different levels in a corporate structure, with (for example) junior indebtedness residing at the holding company level and senior at the operating company(ies). Structurally subordinated creditors rely on dividends for repayment (which the structurally senior debt may regulate), usually mature later than the senior debt at their subsidiaries and, in many cases, may be paid interest in-kind (or PIK interest), at least initially;

- *payment subordination*: the order of payment recovery is created through contractual arrangement. A well-drafted subordination agreement will specify what type of defaults on senior debt (e.g. payment only, or also covenant defaults, and if the latter for how long) will block payments to subordinated creditors and require payments received by junior creditors to be paid over to the senior creditors. In many cases, there will be agreed "standstill" periods (ranging from 30 days to unlimited duration) in which the subordinated creditors are precluded from accelerating payment or taking action to enforce their loans, to give the senior lenders time to try to work out the borrower's financial issues without the involvement of other classes of creditors; and

- *lien subordination*: the order of payment recovery is created by the priority of secured lenders over the unsecured or by order of priority of lien as between senior secured and junior lien secured creditors. Lien subordinations as between secured creditors that share collateral typically are implemented in part through contractual arrangements that provide that the senior secured creditors receive proceeds from realisation of the collateral prior to the junior secured creditors. There may also be a standstill period during which junior secured creditors cannot enforce liens unless and until the senior liens are discharged. Intercreditor agreements with lien subordination often address insolvency situations covering permitted enforcement rights for junior creditors, access to "debtor-in-possession" (DIP) financing, waivers of rights such as the use of cash collateral, waiver of objections to s.363 of the US Bankruptcy Code on sales of the debtor and waiver of voting rights with respect to reorganisation plans.

In sponsor financings, particularly for large LBOs, intercreditor agreements typically do not provide for payment subordination but only lien subordination. This is the principal difference between US-style and UK-style intercreditor agreements. US intercreditor agreements sometimes include an overall limit on the volume of senior indebtedness and specify whether additional classes of debt can be layered between senior and junior creditors. Junior creditors are sometimes given the right to buy out the claims held by senior creditors within 10–20 days following an acceleration of the senior debt for 100% of the underlying principal plus any accrued and unpaid interest.

Under the US Bankruptcy Code, a subordination agreement is enforceable within bankruptcy if the agreement is enforceable under applicable non-bankruptcy law. Under state law, subordination provisions that are clear and unambiguous are usually enforceable. Some bankruptcy courts have, however, limited the enforceability of intercreditor agreements to matters regarding the distribution of payments, taking the view that the Bankruptcy Code guarantees certain secured creditors rights and neither public policy nor congressional intent support a finding that intercreditor agreements can alter US Bankruptcy Code protections. These decisions do not undermine the utility or enforceability of intercreditor arrangements as between creditors but they do demonstrate the limits to the enforceability of these arrangements in the face of the wide discretion of US bankruptcy courts. Indeed, the availability of US Bankruptcy Code protections makes unnecessary certain contractual protections (e.g. relating to distressed disposals) that senior lenders need to provide for in European intercreditor agreements.

### 3.4  Syndication

A substantial majority of large loans to finance US private equity acquisitions are "syndicated" to a group of banks recruited by one or more leading banks which serve as the agents or lead arrangers. The lead arranger(s) will typically be responsible for the negotiation of the term sheet as well as the credit agreement between the private equity fund and the borrower. The lead arranger(s) will then seek to assemble a lending group, if possible, in advance of the signing of the credit agreement or, in some cases, between the signing and the initial draw-down of funds and sometimes (although less frequently in the current market) after the extension of credit.

The syndication can be accomplished on either a "best efforts" or a "firm commitment" basis. The lead arrangers under a best efforts syndication do not commit to provide the facility and agree to use reasonable efforts to secure commitments from other financial institutions. In a firm commitment syndication, the lead arranger commits to fund the entire facility, even if the loan cannot be successfully syndicated by the arranger. However, the parties will typically include a "flex" provision in the agreed term sheet, which allows arrangers to modify, within pre-agreed limits, the pricing and other terms as determined by "market conditions" at the time of closing in order to facilitate syndication of the credit. In the context of an acquisition, the private equity buyer will typically seek committed financing in order to provide certainty of funds to the seller.

Even where the lead arrangers of a financing have firmly committed to provide financing, they will often insist on being provided a 10–15 business day "marketing period" to allow them to syndicate the facilities prior to the completion of the acquisition. This marketing period will commence once the arrangers have been provided with sufficient marketing materials, including reasonably current financial statements, an offering memorandum and sometimes financial projections for the target, to allow them to syndicate the facilities. As a result, US private equity purchasers will often insist on including, within the acquisition agreement, both the right to obtain the financial statements and other information and seller co-operation necessary to meet the requirements of its financing sources and flexibility in respect of the closing date that accommodates the need to provide its financing sources with the required marketing period prior to closing.

## 4. EQUITY STRUCTURES

### 4.1 Role of management

A private equity acquirer will typically offer employment agreements to one or more key executives, and some combination of the opportunity to invest in the company alongside the fund and/or some form of stock option/profits interest, restricted stock unit, restricted stock or phantom stock plan to retain and motivate key executives.

A private equity acquirer will typically also invite one or a few of the senior members of management (e.g. the CEO (Chief Executive Officer) and sometimes the CFO (Chief Financial Officer)) to sit on the board of directors of the target or its new parent, together with representatives or independent nominees of the private equity investor. Unlike in many other jurisdictions, US boards serve primarily an oversight and guidance function. Day-to-day operations and the representation of the company (including the signing of contracts) are typically handled by executive officers, not directors, although the two groups can overlap. Non-executive appointees of the private equity firm—who may be employees of the management company or independent directors—are likely to constitute a majority of the board of directors of the controlling company.

Key executives will often request employment agreements, the terms of which are usually negotiated with the private equity investor before it makes its investment. Apart from addressing salary and bonus opportunity, such agreements will often cover equity-based incentive compensation, termination and severance protection, and any special benefits granted to the executive. These contracts may also provide a senior executive with the right to serve as a director while they remain, for example, president and CEO of the company. The board can terminate any executive at any time, however, and a controlling shareholder can remove them from the board. In such a case, the employment agreement will determine the monetary compensation payable to the terminated employee.

Because US executives can resign at any time, and employment-related non-competition agreements are difficult to enforce (and in some states, such as California, are enforceable only in limited circumstances), employment agreements provide asymmetrical benefits. The executive obtains economic protection for the term of the agreement but the employer has no assurance that the employee will remain if he or she obtains a better offer elsewhere. Comfort in this regard will typically flow only from the terms of a well-constructed incentive programme that provides significant incentives to remain with the company.

When a private equity investor makes only a minority investment, the nature of management's equity participation and the degree of influence of the private equity investor over the terms of that participation will depend on the nature of pre-existing management incentive programmes, the nature and size of the investment and the type of company. Minority investments in listed companies in the US usually do not give the private equity investor significant influence over the terms of employment or equity participation in the company.

### Management equity participation

A range of mechanisms have been developed to facilitate meaningful levels of management equity participation and to provide other means of motivating management through equity-linked incentive arrangements. Management equity participation arrangements include:

- management co-investment;
- restricted stock programmes;
- stock option plans or grants of profits interests; and
- restricted stock unit, phantom stock and similar plans.

Each of these has the objectives of encouraging retention, motivating performance and aligning interests of the fund and its portfolio company, while at the same time minimising the tax and accounting burden on the individual executive and portfolio company. Other things being equal, employees desire to avoid or minimise the realisation of income on the award or vesting of incentive shares, stock options or other similar equity-based compensation, while facilitating the recognition of capital gains (rather than ordinary income from employment) on the appreciation in value of their shares or other interest in the portfolio company. These considerations will often compete with the desire of the portfolio company to deduct as compensation expense the cost of share awards, stock options and similar equity-linked incentive schemes. A balancing of these considerations will require a review of projected taxable income and the likely availability of other corporate tax deductions. As noted above, profits interests do not give rise to compensation deductions.

When acquiring a portfolio company, both the fund and members of management will often desire, and may insist, that management purchase equity in the company alongside the fund. If the senior managers already own a stake in the company, then they and the fund will often have a common interest in allowing their existing investment to be "rolled over" into the new company. A rollover of all or a portion of any existing equity holdings may permit a deferral of the capital gain that management would have realised in the transaction, and reduces or eliminates the need for management to fund the purchase with cash. It is sometimes also possible to roll over equity incentive awards such as stock options, restricted stock and similar interests on a tax advantaged basis. Any such rolled equity should be taken into account in determining the appropriate size of any new equity granted to management by the portfolio company post-closing.

Funds take different approaches to the structuring of their own equity investments as well as that of the management team of the acquired entity. The UK model of an extremely thin layer of ordinary shares supported by much larger "loan stock" investment, in which management do not invest, is not common in the US. Instead, management is likely to invest in the same equity interest as the fund, either directly or through a limited partnership or LLC through which management receives an enhanced interest in profits. In other cases, management may invest on identical terms to the fund but will be granted an additional interest through the grant of "restricted stock", which are shares that are nominally owned by the executive, or "restricted stock units", which are entitlements to shares or their economic equivalent but do not confer ownership in any shares at issuance, or stock options. In each case, these supplemental grants will be subject to forfeiture based on a vesting schedule that may be tied to continued employment, attainment of specified performance measures or both.

Some equity incentive programmes provide a participation interest in the appreciation of value only. This may be structured through the issuance of stock options, in the case of a corporation, or a "profits interest" in the case of a partnership or LLC. It is not uncommon, for multi-jurisdictional programmes, for profits interests to have no tax at grant in the hands of a US person but to be subject to tax in the hands of a taxpayer in another country based on the value at the time the profits interest is transferred to the participant.

Participation in the upside potential of a company may also be structured through the use of "phantom stock", which is a derivative designed to mimic the value of the underlying shares without requiring their issuance, at least initially. These grants are in each case likely to be subject to time vesting conditions, which require the equity holder to be employed with the company for a specified period of time (e.g. three years), with the options, profits interest or phantom stock vesting at intervals during that period or only vesting at the end of the period (known as "cliff" vesting). Phantom stock may raise special tax issues for employees subject to tax in the US, particularly those who terminate employment with vested units. It is common to have vesting accelerate, or the equity forfeited, in the event of the employee's termination, depending on the reason for termination, as discussed in more detail below. Vesting is often accelerated upon a sale transaction or other exit event, although in such cases vesting of equity awards with performance conditions sometimes depends on the investor realising a minimum return on its investment. The term "sweet equity" is somewhat loosely defined but typically applies to an equity interest provided to management on terms more favourable than those applicable to third-party investors (e.g. as a bonus), on the basis that such sweet equity has value to management only if certain performance or service measures are attained.

Management equity programmes (MEPs) that provide management resident in multiple countries with the opportunity to participate in growth in the company's equity value commonly present issues that require close coordination. If the MEP contains restrictive covenants that must be agreed as a condition to participation, as discussed above, the covenants likely will not be equally enforceable in all jurisdictions in which participants are located, requiring input from local counsel and co-ordination with employment agreement obligations. The tax treatment of the receipt of the MEP interests may differ significantly across jurisdictions, with some participants not subject to any tax at grant and those in other countries being taxed on the fair market value of the award at grant depending on local rules. Fund managers will want to consider what is intended if new hires join a MEP after the initial participants, for example, with regard to multi-year performance measures that must be attained for the MEP interests to vest. Jurisdictions may also have different laws regarding the rights of a spouse, affecting the advisability of signing a spousal consent when a MEP interest is awarded. Further, MEPs may require co-ordination between a shareholders agreement and articles of association, which structure may be unfamiliar to US participants. For grants of profits interests, US fund managers will often want all participants to make so-called "protective" US Internal Revenue Code s.83(b) elections not later than 30 days after the receipt of their LP interest, to ensure that the participants will be respected as partners from the inception of their participation and will not be subject to additional tax upon vesting. While such elections will not subject non-US participants to income tax in the US, the process of securing the elections can be somewhat cumbersome and requires explanation.

Co-investments and equity incentive participations are usually subject to transfer restrictions, drag-along provisions and call rights under the company's shareholders' or members' agreement and/or the equity incentive programme.

## 4.2   Common protections for investors

Where there are multiple investors, they will usually enter into a shareholders' agreement (or a partnership or members' agreement), which will deal with governance, restrictions on transfer and other issues designed to regulate the relationship among the investors. Where funds have invested together in a consortium, a primary purpose of this agreement will be to allocate board seats among the investors and specify what actions (if any) will require agreement among the consortium members.

The terms of the shareholders' agreement will depend on whether the private equity investor has a controlling or minority position, its relative percentage ownership interest compared with other investors and whether the company is public or private. Minority investors may through these arrangements seek a number of complementary governance protections, including the right to appoint directors, veto rights over certain company actions (e.g. change of control transactions, capital raising transactions, significant investments, related party transactions, executive officer appointments) and rights to receive information about the company.

Rights designed to provide the investors with liquidity are typically considered critical. These include tag-along rights, registration rights (which are rights to demand that the company initiate a public offering of the investor's shares by registering them for public sale under a registration statement with the SEC or to "piggy-back" on the demand rights of other investors), and put rights and mandatory redemption rights (which require another investor or the company to purchase the investor's shares in certain circumstances). Other rights sought by minority investors include pre-emption rights in connection with future issuances of equity and rights of first offer or rights of first refusal in respect of proposed sales of shares to a third party.

## 4.3   Common protections for management

Although the management team in a US private equity transaction will typically have a minority investment, it is unusual for that interest to confer much if any control over the governance of the company or its strategic direction. The primary protections for management are likely to be contained in employment agreements for the most senior executives. The type and level of protections given to management as a minority investor will vary significantly depending on the level of the investment but it is relatively unusual for management's investment to be sufficiently high to obtain much if any control in their capacity as investors.

### 4.4 Management warranties

As a general rule, in a US private equity transaction, the target's management will not provide personal warranties about the company. This practice, while common in Europe, is often viewed with surprise by US executives and their US legal advisors. Instead, in US transactions, the seller(s) will typically give or at least be responsible for representations and warranties about the target company and its business. Some of these representations and warranties will, however, be given to the knowledge (actual or constructive) of key members of management.

### 4.5 Good leaver/bad leaver provisions

Management investors are generally subject to tight restrictions on their ability to transfer their equity interests in the investment vehicle, and the company and/or private equity fund often retains the right to "call"—that is, to require the sale of—an executive's equity if they leave the employment of the company.

Call rights on management's equity awards are generally triggered upon termination but will often depend on the reasons for termination. The executive may be terminated for "cause" or may resign without "good reason": in other words, the executive is a "bad leaver". The corollary is where the executive is terminated without "cause" or resigns for "good reason": the executive is a "good leaver". It is also common to distinguish between "purchased" equity and equity awarded to management through an equity incentive plan, with call rights being more common and/or robust in the case of equity awards.

A bad leaver will generally lose all rights to unvested equity awards. Vested equity awards may sometimes be retained by an executive who resigns without good reason but are generally forfeited by an employee terminated for cause. To the extent the private equity investor has the right to call management's purchased equity, the right will usually be triggered only for bad leavers, although in some cases the right will extend to all cases but the call price will differ depending upon the circumstances of the departure.

A good leaver will often forfeit all unvested equity awards but, in some cases, an executive who is terminated without cause may become entitled to additional vesting of his or her then unvested equity awards. Vested stock options that are unexercised will often expire within a short time, usually between 30 and 90 days, following good leaver terminations. For purchased equity, management will occasionally be granted the right to require the company to buy their equity in connection with a good leaver termination.

Definitions of "cause" and "good reason" vary but there are common themes. "Cause" is often defined to include acts of fraud or criminal activity by the executive, intentional wrongful acts or gross negligence that harm the company, the failure of the executive to follow reasonable instructions of the company's board or the executive's material breach of an employment agreement or other agreement with the company. "Good reason" will generally include reductions in the executive's base compensation or duties and responsibilities, forced transfers of the executive's workplace to another location and adverse changes in the executive's title or reporting responsibilities.

## 4.6 Public to private transactions

Clarifying senior management's post-acquisition role, including its prospective equity participation, in public to private transactions can be complicated, particularly in respect of any members of management who serve on the board of directors of the target company (often only the CEO but sometimes the CFO or other executives). Senior management personnel in these situations is deemed to have a clear conflict of interest in considering any acquisition proposal, and if on the board will have to disclose their conflicts to the board, and if among the highest compensated will have to disclose the terms offered to them to shareholders considering a proposed offer or merger proposal. An executive on the board will, in some situations, have to recuse him or herself from at least some board deliberations. And if the termination provisions in senior managements' employment arrangements would lead to so-called "parachute payments" subject to special excise tax, these issues can become even more complex.

It is customary in US public to private situations to leave negotiation of the specific terms of continued employment and of any equity (or other) incentive plans until after agreement is reached on the terms of the offer or merger. This reduces the extent to which senior management will appear to have been induced to support a transaction by their prospective terms of employment and equity participation but leaves a private equity buyer with less than full certainty that it will be able to retain the full senior management team on mutually satisfactory terms. There is thus often a carefully orchestrated dialogue around these issues, designed to avoid legal pitfalls while assuring the buyer that management will remain on acceptable terms.

## 5. EXITS

The pace of US exits has slowed continuously since peaking in 2015, with only 1171 exits in 2017 (a 16.3% decrease compared to 2016). Secondary sales decreased by 15.5% during 2017, while corporate sales decreased by 5.5%. The average private equity holding period for US-based companies thus now exceeds six years, the highest level since the end of 2014. These prolonged hold times are reflective of a challenging environment in which high acquisition prices have made generating returns increasingly difficult.

## 5.1 Secondary sales

A private equity investment will often be made with a view to selling the portfolio company in a subsequent sale of corporate control, often to a trade buyer but perhaps also to another private equity house. Sales of this nature may take place after the portfolio company has been "cleaned up" (where there are financial or operational problems), expanded through organic growth or augmented by add-on acquisitions.

Historically, secondary sales of portfolio companies from one fund to another were relatively unusual in the US. This is no longer the case. To the contrary, secondary buyouts (SBOs) are becoming the go-to exit option for private equity firms in the middle market. As some private equity funds come under strong selling pressure, particularly in respect of underperforming or even distressed assets, or because they are approaching the end of their fund's life, they may seek to sell to another fund at or near the beginning of its investment period. Challenging initial public offering (IPO) conditions and recession worries have further driven the sponsor-to-sponsor channel in recent years. Private equity funds are now frequent bidders in secondary auction processes, with SBOs driving the median exit size to an all-time high of USD 221.5 million in 2017. Dual track processes have also gained in popularity, with many general partners simultaneously exploring the IPO and secondary sale options. The trend towards private equity-to-private equity transactions is expected to become even more of an industry norm as firms look for both liquidity and deal flow in the current market environment.

## 5.2 Trade sales

Private equity sellers typically try to limit their exposure to liability from breaches of representations and warranties and other indemnities after the closing. Historically, US private equity sellers were sometimes willing to take on some contingent liability for these items, for a limited duration and with a modest cap on the seller's maximum liability absent fraud (e.g. 10–15% of the purchase price), for example, through an escrow fund or a deferred payment arrangement.

In today's robust mergers and acquisitions (M&A) market, representations and warranties (R&W) insurance has generally become market practice in most industries as buyers look to make their offers more attractive to sellers by ensuring that they retain most of the net proceeds after the deal closes. By shifting the risk associated with breaches of representations or warranties to third-party insurers, buyers are able to let sellers off the hook without taking the liability on in its entirety. R&W insurance thus generally makes deals more likely to happen, particularly in transactions with private equity sellers or when companies are carving out divisions or business units. While R&W insurance can in theory be taken out by either party, buy-side policies are far more prevalent, in part because there are legal advantages to buyers to place the insurance themselves. Insurance policies are subject to a deductible (or "retention") and coverage is limited to a specified maximum. The cost of the policy is a percentage (usually approximately 2–3%) of the coverage amount desired. Management may need to play a role in obtaining this insurance, as the insurer will want to confirm that the representations and warranties are true to the knowledge of the target company's senior management. Known risks generally require special coverage apart from the R&W insurance, thus, a buyer should rely on due diligence and the advice of counsel in determining exposure to both known and unknown risks.

## 5.3 Initial public offerings

Traditionally, IPOs were viewed as a logical exit mechanism for companies that were bought in a development stage and "groomed" for a listing. In the case of a family owned middle-market company, for example, or a number of small competitors in an industry that are "rolled up" into a larger player or the spin-off of a division into a standalone company whose missing elements (initially supplied by the seller under transition services agreements) are replaced through the efforts of the new owner, there was a strong story behind the graduation of the privately held portfolio company to listed company status. A more difficult case surrounds a portfolio company that had been taken private (perhaps based in part on the ostensible cost savings from the avoidance of the costs of public ownership, including expenses associated with Sarbanes–Oxley Act 2002 compliance), which is then reoffered to the public in an IPO at a significant premium to its take-private price.

In a US IPO, a registration statement must be filed with the SEC containing the prospectus to be used in the offering together with a variety of exhibits and other information. This is publicly available from the date of filing, in the case of US issuers, and is subject to comment by the SEC staff. The staff usually responds in about 30 days and between a few additional days and a few additional weeks are typically needed to deal with any comments that the staff may have. Once the document has been cleared by the staff (not "approved" by the SEC; to say that it has been is a violation of law), the registration statement can be declared effective and sales can begin. Most US IPOs are effected on an underwritten basis, based on a book-building process so, once the underwriting agreement has been signed, only in the most extraordinary circumstances will the offering not be completed.

Sales of shares in an IPO can be either primary (in other words, by the company) or secondary (by the private equity owner and/or its co-investors, including management). The allocation of shares between these tranches will typically depend upon the issuer's need for capital and the underwriters' assessment of market conditions. Where the issuer's use of proceeds is to reduce indebtedness, a primary sale of shares is likely to predominate and the underwriters may "cut back" all other shares in the offering in order to maximise value. Registration rights agreements, under which private equity funds and other investors in a US deal will typically have the right to demand the registration of the sale of their shares in the event of an IPO, will usually provide the issuer and/or underwriters the ability to cut back secondary sales in this manner.

After the completion of an IPO, the listed company's former private equity owners will usually remain as substantial shareholders in the newly listed company, required by the underwriters not to sell their holdings for a "lock-up" period of between 90 and 270 days. Its representatives will often stay on the board of directors for a period of time, not as of right but due to their knowledge of the company and its management. Over time, the fund will usually sell out of its investment entirely, thus completing the fund's realisation upon its investment, but the timing and method of sale of its shares will be somewhat constrained for so long as its representative(s) remain on the board.

IPO activity has generally been sloping downward since peaking in 2014. While the number of sponsor-related IPOs increased by 45% in 2017 relative to 2016 (amounting to a total of USD 14 billion), the total IPO count in 2017 remains approximately 25% lower than the post-financial crisis

(2010–16) average. This prolonged slowdown of IPOs, despite a strong market environment, might be reflective of the widely accessible credit markets as well as broader challenges with both the IPO process and the regulatory and operational challenges of public companies.

## 5.4   Refinancings

Particularly in the current low interest rate environment, many private equity funds will also explore opportunities to recapitalise their investments by borrowing more money and distributing the proceeds of the incremental borrowing to the fund and other investors. Some funds seek to structure their investments from the outset with a view to pursuing an interim distribution of this nature, while others consider refinancings as an alternative to a sale or IPO.

## 5.5   Restructuring/insolvency

While schemes of arrangement, which were originally contemplated as means of facilitating a financial restructuring, are utilised in many countries as an exit technique, there is no direct equivalent under US law.

## 6.   TAX

Tax considerations play a central role in the structuring of US private equity funds and their portfolio investments.

## 6.1   Taxation of fund structures

Most US private equity funds are structured as partnerships or other entities that are treated as partnerships for US federal income tax purposes. Partnership treatment is generally desirable to avoid fund-level US taxes and also facilitates the tax efficient structuring of the general partner's carried interest arrangements.

Both US (e.g. Delaware) and non-US (e.g. the Cayman Islands) partnerships are widely used, based on the fund manager's preference and a range of deal-specific considerations with a noticeable recent trend towards using exclusively non-US partnerships in order to address certain US tax considerations. Non-US corporate entities that have been organised in jurisdictions that do not impose material tax on offshore investments (e.g. Luxembourg) may also be used as it is usually possible to make a "check the box" election for such corporate entities to be treated as partnerships for US federal income tax purposes. In some cases, fund managers will organise non-US corporate entities (or partnerships that "check the box" to be treated as corporations for US tax purposes) as "blockers" to address the particular tax sensitivities of US tax-exempt investors and some non-US investors. These "blockers" may be feeder funds into the main fund vehicle or parallel funds that invest alongside the main fund vehicle.

## 6.2   Carried interest

The general partner's carried interest is generally structured as an enhanced participation in profits after the other investors have received a return of capital and a minimum return (i.e. a preferred return or hurdle rate). Under current law, the carried interest is generally not taxed upon grant (if at that point it only represents an interest in profits of the fund above the value of fund investments at the time of grant) and, if the fund's gain on sale of an investment is a capital gain, then the general partner's share will flow through as a capital gain. In general, funds will seek to structure investments to maximise capital gains, as opposed to other forms of income, because the US federal income tax rate on the former (currently 20% plus 3.8% on net investment income not taking into account any applicable state/local income taxes) is lower than the marginal federal tax rate for individuals on ordinary income (currently 37%, plus 3.8% in some instances not taking into account any applicable state/local income taxes). Not all fund income will constitute capital gains, however, as funds may hold a range of investments that generate interest, dividend or business operating income.

The 2017 tax reform in the US took a limited step in the direction of treating carried interest as ordinary income by changing to three years (rather than the usual one year) the length of time an investment must be held before earnings on its disposition are eligible for the favourable capital gains tax rate for owners of the fund sponsor receiving the carried interest. The full impact of this change on private equity fund sponsors remains uncertain, however, given that the investment horizon for most private equity investments is typically longer than three years.

In addition to the carried interest, the fund manager will also earn a fee based on investor commitments and invested capital, which will usually be taxed as ordinary income.

### 6.3  Management equity

As discussed above, senior executives in individual portfolio companies may participate in the investment through a wide range of incentive programmes and instruments, including equity co-investments, stock options and restricted stock plans. While the individual executives will generally prefer to invest through structures which are designed to provide capital gains treatment for any appreciation in value, the relevant portfolio company may prefer to structure the equity participation in a manner that, while resulting in ordinary income to the executive, provides the company with a compensation deduction. In some cases, the current value of the corporate deduction may outweigh the benefit of the tax rate differential between capital gains and ordinary income; careful consideration of the most tax-efficient management equity participation will therefore be necessary in each transaction.

If the portfolio company is a partnership or a LLC, it may be able to grant its management team profits interests that entitle their holder to deferred taxation and capital gains treatment, but such interests do not provide the portfolio company with a compensation deduction. Profits interests programmes can also be complicated to structure for a management team, who may prefer not to be treated as partners for tax purposes and may be more familiar with stock options, restricted stock units or restricted stock.

If a portfolio company is public, annual compensation in excess of USD 1 million (whether cash or equity) paid to its CEO, CFO and certain other top-paid executives is not deductible under s.162(m) of the Internal Revenue Code and a performance-based compensation exception to that rule was eliminated with the 2017 tax reform.

### 6.4 Loan interest

Although fund managers are increasingly using fund-level credit facilities backed by the capital commitments of investors to the fund to meet short-term cash needs and ongoing operating expenses, US private equity funds still will typically not borrow money themselves to fund deals but will instead cause their deal-specific investment vehicles to incur debt for particular investments. This is in part for reasons of risk diversification but also results from tax issues that would arise for US tax-exempt investors if they invest through a leveraged partnership (at least without a "blocker").

While in the UK (for example) it is typical for private equity funds to invest a substantial percentage of their invested funds in portfolio companies in the form of "loan stock", in general, this structure is avoided in the US as it will generate significant amounts of "phantom" or "dry" "deemed" interest income for LPs while not giving rise to offsetting tax or other benefits. Interest payments by US portfolio companies to non-US investors may, moreover, be subject to withholding, thus further reducing the tax efficiency of this structure for non-US investors.

### 6.5 Transaction taxes

A wide range of tax considerations come into play in structuring individual fund investments, often requiring a careful balancing of the interests of buyer and seller and, in some instances, also senior management. Special consideration often must be given to the interests of non-US investors and also of US investors with specific tax attributes (such as pension plans and other tax-exempt investors). Non-US investors will, for example, be subject to US withholding tax on certain types of income (dividends, some interest income and the sales of shares in US companies a significant part of whose value relates to US real estate assets) and an effort generally is made to avoid or minimise this. On the other hand, some non-US investments may create special issues for US investors under US rules relating to controlled foreign corporations as well as other anti-deferral rules.

The complexity of these and other tax considerations render impossible a comprehensive treatment of even a fraction of the range of tax issues that must be considered. The centrality of tax planning to nearly all private equity investments made by private equity funds with US sponsors or investors is, however, hopefully clear from the foregoing superficial overview.

## 7. CURRENT TOPICAL ISSUES/TRENDS

Private equity firms, which have only been subject to SEC review since 2011, faced a process of rigorous SEC investigations and enforcement actions beginning in 2012. Areas of particular concern to the SEC were the inappropriate allocation of fees and expenses, the lack of transparency and hidden fees, the differing valuation methods used in marketing materials and presentations to investors, the practice of setting up separate accounts and side-by-side investment arrangements and the presence of so-called "zombie" advisors (managers that are unable to raise additional funds but may seek to continue to manage legacy funds long past their expected life). The examinations led to a number of enforcement actions and had many ripple effects on the US private equity industry, including increased transparency and more vigilant regulatory compliance measures. Remaining contentious issues and evolving trends in the industry include the following.

## Carried interest

The tax rate that applies to fund managers on profits on investments, which is colloquially referred to as "carried interest" or simply "carry" (which derives from the investors' "carrying" the investment professionals by putting up the money on which the profits distributed to the fund managers are earned), is the subject of considerable discussion. Carried interests are "profits interests" for US income tax purposes that are not subject to tax at grant in the hands of a US person based on the rationale that such interests have value only if the partnership granting them appreciates in value after the date of grant and any distributions on such profits interests are funded by such appreciation. Another way of explaining the rationale for the zero US income tax at grant is that, if the granting partnership were to liquidate on the date of grant, the holder of a profits interest would not be entitled to any proceeds.

In the US, fund managers' management fees are taxed at ordinary income tax rates, usually in the highest tax bracket (currently 37% plus 3.8% in some instances and not taking into account any applicable state/local taxes). Carried interest earnings, on the other hand, generally are eligible for long-term capital gains treatment based on the character of the underlying realisation at a reduced tax rate (currently 20% plus 3.8% and not taking into account any applicable state/local taxes). The treatment of carried interest distributions as investment earnings has been criticised by some as a loophole that permits fund managers to pay an unfairly low tax rate on earnings that should be taxed as compensation income. Others say that the earnings being taxed are investment gains by a partnership and whether the partners' contribution to the partnership is the investment of capital or time, the underlying assets are capital investments and should be eligible for capital gains treatment.

The 2017 tax reform took a limited step in the direction of treating carried interest as ordinary income by changing to three years (rather than the usual one year) the length of time an investment must be held before earnings on its disposition are eligible for the favourable capital gains tax rate for owners of the fund sponsor receiving the carried interest. The full impact of this change on private equity fund sponsors remains uncertain, given that the investment horizon for most private equity investments is typically longer than three years. In addition, several US states are considering legislation that would increase the effective rate of tax on carried interest. Because they constitute distributions of investment earnings, distributions on profits interests, such as carried interests, do not entitle the distributing partnership to a compensation deduction.

## Investor sophistication and direct investments

Investors have evolved and become increasingly sophisticated in recent years, leading to a shift in the types of investments which powerful LPs seek out. Direct investments and co-investments have emerged as popular investment vehicles in recent years, primarily because they offer an effective way for investors to reduce fees and increase transparency into their investments.

Some LPs have taken this strategy even further by integrating a portion of their investment management activities in-house, bypassing the traditional private equity structure and associated fees altogether. Sovereign Wealth Funds and Canadian Pension Funds have acted as trailblazers in this regard, luring away top talent from private equity firms and circumventing general partners in hard-to-reach illiquid markets such as infrastructure, private credit and buyouts. Such in-house teams are becoming more common and could reshape the future of the private equity industry, with many LPs potentially becoming direct competitors of traditional private equity firms for both investments and talent.

### Standardisation of fee reporting

With competition in the sector at all-time highs, investors seek those administrators that provide good returns but also enhanced transparency throughout the investment cycle. In January 2016, the ILPA published a "Fee Reporting Template". While adoption of the template is not mandatory for most funds, it was designed to increase transparency by showing investors exactly how money is collected by general partners, and how costs are accounted for and offset. Key fund managers were early adapters of the guidelines, paving the road for broader standardisation in the industry. To date, over 160 fund managers have submitted fee information using the template and the ILPA aims to focus on identifying best practices for its future uses, including guidance for maintaining oversight of the data and recommendations to ensure compliance with the agreements struck between investors and private equity firms.

# Contact Details

## General Editors

Charles Martin & Simon Perry
Macfarlanes LLP
20 Cursitor Street
London EC4A 1LT
T: +44 20 7831 9222
F: +44 20 7831 9607
E: charles.martin@macfarlanes.com
simon.perry@macfarlanes.com
W: *www.macfarlanes.com*

## Austria

Thomas Schirmer, Markus Uitz &
Philipp Kapl
Binder Grösswang Rechtsanwälte
GmbH
Sterngasse 13
Vienna 1010
T: +43 1 53480 340
F: +43 1 534808
E: schirmer@bindergroesswang.at;
uitz@bindergroesswang.at
kapl@bindergroesswang.at
W: *www.bindergroesswang.at*

## Belgium

Wim Vande Velde & Henri Nelen
Loyens & Loeff CVBA/SCRL
Rue Neerveld 101-103
Brussels 1200
T: +32 2 743 43 43
F: +32 2 773 23 89
E: wim.vande.velde@loyensloeff.com
henri.nelen@loyensloeff.com
W: *www.loyensloeff.com*

## Brazil

Álvaro Silas Uliani Martins dos Santos,
Diego Alves Amaral Batista, Juliana
Soares Zaidan Maluf & Luiz Felipe
Fleury Vaz Guimarães
Pinheiro Neto Advogados
Rua Hungria 1100
01455-906 Sao Paulo
Brazil
T: +55 11 3247 8995
F: +55 11 3247 8600

E: asantos@pn.com.br
W: *www.pinheironeto.com.br*

## Bulgaria

Yordan Naydenov & Dr Nikolay Kolev
Boyanov & Co, Attorneys at Law
82 Patriarch Evtimii Blvd.
Sofia 1463
T: +359 2 8055055
F: +359 2 8055000
E: y.naydenov@boyanov.com
n.kolev@boyanov.com
W: *www.boyanov.com*

## France

Eduardo Fernandez, Grégoire Finance &
Philippe Grudé
Willkie Farr & Gallagher LLP
21-23 rue de la Ville l'Eveque
Paris 75008
T: +33 1 53 43 45 00
F: +33 1 40 06 96 06
E: efernandez@willkie.com
gfinance@willkie.com
pgrude@willkie.com
W: *www.willkie.com*

## Germany

Jens Hörmann, Nico Fischer & Amos
Veith
P+P Pöllath + Partners
Rechtsanwälte und Steuerberater mbB
Hofstatt 1
80331 München
T: +49 89 24 240 278
F: +49 89 24 240 996
E: jens.hoermann@pplaw.com
W: *www.pplaw.com*

## Italy

Giuseppe A. Galeano & Emanuela Sabbatino
CBA Studio Legale e Tributario
Galleria San Carlo 6
20122 Milan
Via Guido D'Arezzo n. 18
00198 Rome

T: +39 02 778061
F: +39 02 76021816
E: giuseppe.galeano@cbalex.com
emanuela.sabbatino@cbalex.com
W: *www.cbalex.com*

## Japan

Ryo Okubo & Takashi Miyazaki
Nagashima Ohno & Tsunematsu
JP Tower, 2-7-2
Marunouchi, Chiyoda-ku
Tokyo 100-7036
T: +81 3 6889 7000
F: +81 3 6889 8000
E: ryo_okubo@noandt.com
takashi_miyazaki@noandt.com
W: *www.noandt.com*

## Luxembourg

Marc Meyers, Jérôme Mullmaier &
Maude Royer
Loyens & Loeff Luxembourg Sàrl
18-20, rue Edward Steichen
Luxembourg L-2540
T: +352 466 230 1
F: +352 466 234
E: marc.meyers@loyensloeff.com
jerome.mullmaier@loyensloeff.com
W: *www.loyensloeff.lu*

## Mexico

Teófilo G. Berdeja Prieto
Berdeja Abogados, S.C.
Av. Santa Fe No. 170 - 4o Piso
Col. Lomas de Santa Fe
01210 Mexico, D.F.
T: +52 55 5292 2730
F: +52 55 5292 2740
E: tberdeja@berdeja.com.mx
W: *www.berdeja.com.mx*

## The Netherlands

Mark van Dam & Marco de Lignie
Loyens & Loeff NV (Amsterdam office)
Fred. Roeskestraat 100
1076 ED Amsterdam
T: +31 20 578 5785
E: mark.van.dam@loyensloeff.com
marco.de.lignie@loyensloeff.com

## Poland

Ben Davey, Jakub Jędrzejak, Klaudia
Frątczak & Łukasz Czekański
WKB Wierciński, Kwieciński, Baehr
sp.k.
Plac Małachowskiego 2,00-066
T: +48 22 201 00 00
F: +48 22 201 00 99
E: ben.davey@wkb.pl
jakub.jedrzejak@wkb.pl
klaudia.fratczak@wkb.pl
lukasz.czekanski@wkb.pl
W: *www.wkb.pl*

## Russia

Arkady Krasnikhin, Vyacheslav Yugai &
Roman Malovitsky
Egorov Puginsky Afanasiev & Partners
40/5 Bol. Ordynka Str.
119017, Moscow
T: +7 495 935 80 10
F: +7 495 935 80 11
E: arkady_krasnikhin@epam.ru
vvy@epam.ru
roman_malovitsky@epam.ru
W: *www.epam.ru*

## Spain

Fernando de las Cuevas & Iñigo Erláiz
Gómez-Acebo & Pombo
Castellana, 216
Madrid 28046
T: +34915829100
E: abogados@gomezacebo-pombo.com
W: *www.gomezacebo-pombo.com*

## Switzerland

Dr Marcel R. Jung, Dunja Koch, Laetitia
Meier-Droz & Jérôme Pidoux
FRORIEP
Bellerivestrasse 201
8034 Zurich
T: +41 44 386 60 00
F: +41 44 383 60 50
E: dkoch@froriep.ch
W: *www.froriep.ch*

## United Kingdom

Charles Martin, Simon Perry & Stephen
Pike
Macfarlanes LLP

20 Cursitor Street
London EC4A 1LT
T: +44 20 7831 9222
F: +44 20 7831 9607
E: charles.martin@macfarlanes.com
simon.perry@macfarlanes.com
stephen.pike@macfarlanes.com
W: *www.macfarlanes.com*

## United States

David Lakhdhir, Ramy Wahbeh, Brian

Grieve & David Carmona
Paul, Weiss, Rifkind, Wharton & Garrison LLP
10 Noble Street
London
EC2V 7JU
T: +44 207 367 1600
F: +44 207 367 1650
E: dlakhdhir@paulweiss.com
W: *www.paulweiss.com*

# Evidence-Informed Practice for
# Social Workers

# SOCIAL WORK SKILLS IN PRACTICE

## Series editors:

**Ruben Martin**, *Honorary Senior Lecturer in Social Work, University of Kent*
**Alisoun Milne**, *Professor of Social Gerontology and Social Work, University of Kent*

## About the series:

The social work profession is constantly evolving and adjusting to changes in the policy, professional and care contexts and to wider issues such as demographic and structural shifts. The *Social Work Skills in Practice* series aims to explore core skills and knowledge needed to practise effectively as a social worker. Initiatives to address perceived challenges and concerns within the profession have included reforms, new standards and reviews of social work education. The foregrounding of evidence-informed practice and recognition of the complex nature of social work will be increasingly important in the future. There is therefore a need for textbooks addressing new and developing requirements and expectations that will help practitioners respond to practice requirements in an informed, effective, agile and critical way. This series is targeted at Masters level students, Newly Qualified Social Workers (ASYE and CPD), professionals and undergraduate students in their second placements. All books in the series adopt a critically reflective lens on the development and deployment of social work skills, are theoretically grounded and address issues of relevance to all service user groups, families and carers, different settings and sectors and the increasingly varied context of social work practice.

## Titles in the series:

*Professional Writing Skills for Social Workers*: Louise Frith and Ruben Martin
*Diversity, Difference and Dilemmas: analysing concepts and developing skills*, Kish Bhatti-Sinclair and Chris Smethurst (eds.)
*Social Work Skills with Networks and Communities*: Martin Webber

# Evidence-Informed Practice for Social Workers

Hugh McLaughlin and Barbra Teater

Open University Press

Open University Press
McGraw-Hill Education
8th Floor, 338 Euston Road
London
England
NW1 3BH

email: enquiries@openup.co.uk
world wide web: www.openup.co.uk

and Two Penn Plaza, New York, NY 10121-2289, USA

First published 2017

A catalogue record of this book is available from the British Library

ISBN-13: 978-0-335-22694-8
ISBN-10: 0-33-522694-9
eISBN: 978-0-335-22695-5

Library of Congress Cataloging-in-Publication Data
CIP data applied for

Typeset by Transforma Pvt. Ltd., Chennai, India

Fictitious names of companies, products, people, characters and/or data that may be used herein (in case studies or in examples) are not intended to represent any real individual, company, product or event.

Printed and bound by CPI Group (UK) Ltd, Croydon, CR0 4YY

# Praise for this book

*"This book is an excellent introduction to the subject for social work students and social workers. It sets out in a very accessible style the ways in which social workers can develop understanding of key features of, and practical ways to make use of, Evidence-Informed Practice, within a real appreciation of the social work role and its values. I would advise all social work students and social workers to read it."*

Brian Littlechild, University of Hertfordshire, UK

*"This book should probably be seen as and become an essential tool for good and effective social work practice. The authors provide a detailed and painstaking guide to the process of accessing, assimilating, critically analysing and applying the best evidence available to support social workers in undertaking their roles in an informed and insightful manner. It oozes the accumulated wisdom of these expert writers, whilst remaining fundamentally practical, and it thus renders itself virtually indispensable."*

Roger Smith, Professor of Social Work, Durham University, UK

Barbra would like to dedicate this book to her students at the College of Staten Island.

Hugh would not only like to recognize his students, but also Catherine for her continuing support and forbearance, and James and Eleanor, who still keep him young at heart!

# Contents

# About the authors

**Hugh McLaughlin** is Professor of Social Work at Manchester Metropolitan University, where he is Head of the Faculty Research Degrees and module leader for MA Practice and Social Work Research dissertation module. Prior to entering academia, with Salford University, he worked as a social worker, team manager, area manager and assistant director (children and families). His research interests include the involvement of service users in social work education and research, critical professional practice, and the creation of learning organizations. He currently maintains links with practice as the Chair of the Trustee Board for After Adoption, and is editor-in-chief of *Social Work Education: The International Journal*. Hugh has over 100 publications, including *Understanding Social Work Research*. When not working, Hugh likes to run or scuba dive, particularly in warmer waters than the UK.

**Barbra Teater** is Professor of Social Work at the College of Staten Island, City University of New York, where she is director of the Master of Social Work (MSW) programme and coordinator of the Disability Studies minor. She previously spent eight years in social work education in the UK at the University of Bath and the University of Bristol. Barbra currently teaches research methods to MSW students. Her research interests include social work education, the social work academic workforce, and health and well-being among older adults. Barbra has published over 40 journal articles and book chapters, and authored or edited a number of textbooks, including the bestselling text: *An Introduction to Applying Social Work Theories and Methods*. When Barbra's not writing, you can find her running in Central Park or along the Hudson River in New York City.

# About the editors

The series is edited by Ruben Martin and Alisoun Milne.

**Ruben Martin** is Honorary Senior Lecturer in Social Work at the University of Kent, where he was Director of Studies for the BA (Hons) Social Work programme for seven years. He has been a probation officer and national training officer for a voluntary organisation. Since his retirement from his full-time academic post in 2010 he has continued work as part-time lecturer and tutor, consultant, freelance practice educator, writer and editor.

**Dr Alisoun Milne** is Professor of Social Gerontology and Social Work at the University of Kent's School for Sociology, Social Policy and Social Research. She has managerial responsibilities for, and contributes to delivering, the university's undergraduate and postgraduate social work qualifying programmes. Alisoun is widely published in both academic and practice-related journals. Her key research interests are: social work with older people and their families; older carers; mental health in later life; and long-term care. Before becoming an academic in 1995 Alisoun worked as a social worker and team manager in two London boroughs. She is a member of the Standing Commission on Carers, the Association of Professors of Social Work, and was on the Executive Committee of the British Society of Gerontology from 2009 to 2015. She is registered with the Health and Care Professions Council.

# Series editor's foreword

The social work profession is constantly evolving and adjusting to changes. The *Social Work Skills in Practice* series, to which this book is a welcome addition, aims to explore core skills and knowledge needed to practise effectively as a social worker. Initiatives to address perceived challenges and concerns within the profession have included reviews of social work education. In one of them, referred to in Chapter 1 of this book, Professor David Croisdale-Appleby puts forward three constituents to a social worker role: those of practitioner, professional, and social scientist. It is arguably this third component that is difficult to achieve and easily neglected.

In this book, Hugh McLaughlin and Barbra Teater promote ways of enhancing the 'social worker as a social scientist' responsibility, and suggest how the three role components can be integrated into 'evidence-informed practice' (EIP). The authors go beyond the probably more familiar and narrower concept of 'evidence-based practice' (EBP) by putting forward an EIP process that includes consideration of best available evidence; practitioners' own knowledge and expertise or 'wisdom'; and service users' and carers' values, wishes, and circumstances.

In keeping with distinctive features of books in this series, the authors achieve a reader-friendly and engaging style, while putting forward well-argued practice-based ideas. Completing activities within each chapter, considering case examples, and reflecting when prompted will help you engage with the material. The authors acknowledge that deciphering various types of knowledge and evidence can feel like working with a foreign language. They demystify some of the intricacies of research and make the book practical and relevant in a variety of ways, not least by outlining specific EIP steps and concrete ways of implementing it. They also explore ethical challenges and aspects of interprofessional practice.

The authors bring their own considerable professional and academic expertise, UK and international experience. They refer to a variety of relevant sources, and suggest further reading and other resources for information. In keeping with its message, the book itself is evidence-informed. It will provide an innovative contribution to social work education and practice aimed at the achievement of high standards. It should challenge you as a social work student or practitioner to pursue EIP, whatever your work setting or service user group.

**Ruben Martin**
Honorary Senior Lecturer in Social Work
University of Kent

# Acknowledgements

Barbra and Hugh would like to thank Ruben Martin for his continued support throughout this project, and Caroline Prodger, Richard Townrow and Karen Harris, from the publishers, for seeing the project through.

# Part 1

## Overview of, and basis for, evidence-informed practice

# 1 Introduction: The call for evidence-informed practice

> **Chapter overview**
>
> By the end of this chapter you should have an understanding of:
>
> - The rationale for incorporating evidence-informed practice in social work.
> - The history and evolution of evidence-informed practice.
> - The definition of evidence-informed practice and how this differs from evidence-based interventions.
> - The layout of the book.

## Introduction

The social work profession is currently facing a series of challenges. These challenges and their resulting issues, including increasing social worker workloads, a lack of public trust and concerns about the nature of social work, have led Higgins (2015: 4) to claim that we are currently involved in a battle for the 'soul of social work'. It is the premise of this book that if we accept that there are daily challenges facing practitioners in working with some of the most vulnerable and disadvantaged people within society in situations of complexity, contradiction and ambiguity, it then becomes essential, if not also ethically imperative, for social workers to work in an evidence-informed way. The rest of the book will seek to justify this claim in greater detail, but it is our position that if we want to ensure the effective use of limited resources – particularly social work time – to make a difference in the lives of service users and carers, social workers have to become evidence-informed practitioners. It is worth noting that we use the terms 'service users' and 'carers' throughout, although other authors may use terms like 'clients', 'experts by experience' or 'citizens' to signify those with whom social workers interact.

In England, public confidence concerns over child protection led to the Social Work Task Force (2008–9) and the setting up of the Social Work Reform Board (SWRB) with its final report in 2012. In parallel to these developments, Professor Eileen Munro undertook her review of child protection in 2011, and concluded that the bureaucratization of social work tasks de-skilled social workers. The SWRB developed a new Professional Capabilities Framework (PCF), which sets and describes the level of capability required for social work students and practitioners at all the stages of their career. These though have been added to with the introduction of separate key Knowledge and Skills Statements for approved child and family social workers (DfE 2014) and adults' social workers (DH 2015).

Additionally, the Health and Care Professions Council (HCPC) took over as the social work regulator in 2012 from the previous regulator, the General Social Care Council (GSCC), and published *Standards of Proficiency: Social Workers in England* (HCPC 2017), which stipulates the threshold standards for social workers when they finish their training and start practising within the profession. At the time of writing, government has indicated there will be a new social work regulator, focused solely on social work, from 2018. Initially, the Children and Social Work Bill 2016 suggested that the government would directly regulate social workers, but following significant opposition the proposed new regulator, Social Work England, will be independent of government but accountable to Parliament (Community Care 2016). How independent this will be remains an open question. Importantly, this represents the third regulator of social work in England in six years.

Despite such initiatives, concerns have remained about the education of social workers, and in 2013 the Secretary for State for Education asked Sir Martin Neary to undertake an independent review of the education of children's social workers (Neary 2014), which was followed by Professor David Croisdale-Applebys review, commissioned by the Department of Health, on the education of both adult and children's social workers (Croisdale-Appleby 2014). While there are fundamental differences between these two reports, there are areas of agreement including a proposal for a more meaningful engagement with service users and carers, reconnecting with the skills and knowledge needed for good practice, and the foregrounding of evidence for practice. Croisdale-Appleby underlined the importance of a social work profile:

> comprised of three components: **the social worker as a practitioner, the social worker as a professional, and the social worker as a social scientist.**
>
> (Croisdale-Appleby, 2014: 15 – bold in original)

These initiatives have not been restricted solely to England; in Scotland there has been the publication of a new vision for social work by the Scottish Government (2015) and ten-year strategies in both Northern Ireland (Department of Health, Social Services and Public Safety [DHSSPS] 2012) and Wales (Welsh Assembly Government [WAG] 2007). These programmes have taken place against a background of 'fiscal austerity' resulting in public sector funding cuts, as well as growth in the older population, entrenched social inequalities, the uncertainties of Brexit (Dennison 2016) – now triggered – and the growth in market-orientated and risk-averse public sector practice (Scottish Social Services Council [SSSC] 2015). This has all occurred in a period of neo-liberal challenges to the welfare state resulting in a return to the notions of the 'deserving' and 'undeserving' poor, and a decrease in the support for spending more on welfare benefits from 61 per cent in 1989 to 30 per cent in 2014 (NatCen 2016).

The requirement for social workers to become evidence-informed practitioners demands that they are not merely research consumers or research literate, but begin to conceptualize their interventions as 'experiments'. This requires social workers to be clear about the purpose and nature of their intervention and also clear about the intended outcomes evaluating whether this has been achieved or not, and why. Such practitioners can then aggregate these outcomes with similar cases and begin to develop an awareness of which approaches are effective under which conditions. As Cabot, the then president of the American National Association of Social Workers, beseeched social workers in 1931:

> I appeal to you, measure, evaluate, estimate, and appraise your results in some form, in any terms that rest on anything beyond faith, assertion and the 'illustrative case'. Let us do this ourselves before some less knowledgeable and less gentle body takes us by the shoulders and pushes us into the street.
> (Cabot 1931: 6, quoted in Sheldon and Chilvers 2000: 1)

We will explain later in this chapter what we mean by evidence-informed practitioners, but first we want to explore the support for the use of research in social work.

---

### Activity 1.1

**What informs your practice decisions?**

Think about a case from your recent professional or practice experience and answer the following questions:

1. What was the identified problem/reason for receiving social care services?
2. What informed your assessment?
3. What informed your choice of intervention?
4. To what extent did you consider: (a) the service user's or carer's values and wishes; (b) your practice knowledge and past experiences; and (c) research evidence?
5. Was the intervention successful? How do you know?

---

## Professional capabilities, key skills: research and evidence-informed practice

The International Federation of Social Workers (IFSW) and the International Association of Schools of Social Work (IASSW) agreed an updated definition of social work in 2014 that stated:

> Social work is a practice-based profession and an academic discipline that promotes social change and development, social cohesion, and the empowerment

and liberation of people. Principles of social justice, human rights, collective responsibility and respect for diversities are central to social work. Underpinned by theories of social work, social sciences, humanities and indigenous knowledges, social work engages people and structures to address life challenges and enhance well-being.

(IFSW 2014)

Importantly for our purposes, social work's core mandate embraces social change, social development, social cohesion and the liberation of people. From a research-informed perspective, how would you know if your practice has promoted social change, social development, social cohesion or the liberation of people without evaluating or researching the impact of your practice? The definition also highlights that social work is based at the practice–academic intersection where research and theory inform practice and practice challenges and further develops theory and research. Over our careers, we have interviewed students for social work courses, students for social work posts, social workers for management positions, and managers for senior management posts, and throughout of all this there has been a motivational thread of wanting to 'make a difference', to challenge social injustice, and to advocate for service users and carers. It is our contention that to do this effectively requires an evidence-informed approach. We do however recognize there is often a disconnect for students between research and practice resulting in what Harvey et al. (2013: 12) describe as 'research anxiety' due to student concerns about their ability to understand the foreign language of research, or to understand alternative ways of conceptualizing the world and acting in it.

The need for social workers to use research and implement evidence-informed practice is recognized internationally. The Global Standards for Social Work Education, which is supported by IASSW and IFSW, calls for social workers to have knowledge of research, skills in the use of research methods, the consideration of ethics in research, and the critical appreciation of the use of research and different sources of knowledge that can influence social work practice (IFSW/IASSW 2014). The IAASW/IFSW (2004) also issued a separate statement on research and its need to influence, and be influenced by, practice and teaching to promote a research-informed professional culture informed by a critical standpoint and anchored in the principles of social justice.

In England, the PCF specifies the use of research, evidence, and evaluation across three of the nine capabilities. For students at the end of their final year placement/qualifying level, the following capabilities are listed under the domain of 'knowledge' (BASW 2016: 4):

Demonstrate a critical understanding of the application to social work of research, theory and knowledge from sociology, social policy, psychology, and health.
Recognise the contribution, and begin to make use of research to inform practice.
Demonstrate a critical understanding of research methods.

Under the domain of 'critical reflection', the following capabilities include (BASW 2016: 5):

Inform decision-making through the identification and gathering of information from multiple sources, actively seeking new sources.
With support, rigorously question and evaluate the reliability and validity of information from different sources.
Know how to formulate, test, evaluate, and review hypotheses in response to information available at the time and apply in practice.
Begin to formulate and make explicit, evidence-informed judgements and justifiable decisions.

Finally, under the domain of 'intervention and skills', the following capability is specified (BASW 2016: 5):

Select and use appropriate frameworks to assess, give meaning to, plan, implement and review effective interventions and evaluate the outcomes, in partnership with service users.

In England, both the children's and adults' Chief Social Workers' key Knowledge and Statements (DfE 2014; DH 2015) also contain support for the importance of research for practice in promoting the text in italics appears in both statements:

*a critical understanding of the difference between theory, research, evidence and expertise and the role of professional judgement* within that; how to utilize research skills in assessment and analysis; how to identify which methods will be of help for a specific child or family and the limitations of different approaches; and how to make effective use of the best evidence from research to inform the complex judgements and decisions needed to support families and protect children.

(DfE 2014: standard 10)

The extent to which these aims are integrated into social work education and practice varies by country. For example, the United States requires students to engage in 'research-informed practice' and 'practice-informed research' (CSWE 2015: 5), which involves demonstrating the following behaviours:

use practice experience and theory to inform scientific inquiry and research. . .;
apply critical thinking to engage in analysis;
use and translate research evidence to inform and improve practice, policy, and service delivery.

The Australian Association of Social Workers (AASW 2015) specifies that social workers should apply research knowledge and skills to inform and develop practice and to execute and disseminate research-informed practice. Social work graduates are expected to have achieved the following learning outcomes (AASW 2015: 12):

> The ability to undertake research to further inform and influence organisational goals and social policy.
> The ability to undertake evidence informed practice in all interventions.
> The ability to plan and execute project work and/or a piece of research and scholarship with some independence.
> The ability to apply research knowledge and skills to undertake research congruent with social work values and ethics.
> The ability to utilise research in practice to address the needs and aspirations of individuals, groups and communities in society in particular vulnerable populations.
> The ability to explore complex and sensitive social issues and problems to achieve socially just outcomes.

As demonstrated, there is a global expectation for social workers to have the skills necessary to participate in evidence-informed practice to ensure they are practising safely and effectively. Therefore, there is a need to support social work students and social workers to address the requirements and expectations of social work practice and, particularly, to practise using evidence-informed practice. We aim to enhance social workers' use of evidence-informed practice through this text by focusing specifically on developing and supporting the skills and knowledge needed to identify, critique, and apply research in social work practice, while taking into consideration service users' and carers' wishes and circumstances, and the social worker's own knowledge and experiences.

---

**Activity 1.2**

### Your definition of evidence-informed practice

Write down your definition of evidence-informed practice. What do you see as the essential elements of evidence-informed practice? What would make it possible for you to combine these elements in your practice?

---

## Evidence-based medicine: the precursor for evidence-informed practice

Evidence-informed practice (EIP) evolved from evidence-based medicine that was originally developed and defined by Sackett et al. (1996: 71) as:

> The conscientious, explicit, and judicious use of current best evidence in making decisions about the care of individual patients. The practice of evidence-based medicine means integrating individual clinical expertise with the best available external clinical evidence from systematic research. By individual clinical expertise we mean the proficiency and judgement that

individual clinicians acquire through clinical experience and clinical practice. [. . .] By best available external clinical evidence we mean clinically relevant research, often from the basic sciences of medicine, but especially from patient centred clinical research into the accuracy and precision of diagnostic tests (including the clinical examination), the power of prognostic markers, and the efficacy and safety of therapeutic, rehabilitative, and preventive regimens.

Evidence-based medicine was a response to the perceived problem in medicine that there was excessive reliance on 'the authority of teachers, texts and hierarchical superiors rather than the practitioner's own informed and independent judgement' (Evans and Hardy 2010: 41). The basic premise behind evidence-based medicine was to 'do no harm'. This was achieved by ensuring a thorough consideration of the research available regarding the patient's condition, their specific circumstances, while equally critiquing and considering this information based on the clinician's experiences and knowledge. The integration of evidence-based medicine insinuated an acknowledgement that there was no 'one size fits all' in working with patients who are variable, but, rather, that each individual encounter with a patient meant the clinician would engage in a process of decision-making that involved two elements: (1) best available research evidence; and (2) clinician's knowledge and experience.

Since Sackett et al.'s (1996) seminal work, the principles of evidence-based medicine have been applied to other settings, including education, nursing, management, policy-making and social work. With the expansion of evidence-based medicine to other settings, there has been the development and more common usage of the term 'evidence-based practice' (EBP). Social workers' use of EBP was seen as an improvement on traditional ways of working. Social workers would now utilize the best scientific evidence currently available in making practice decisions, such as the choice of intervention, and share this information with services users and/or carers, such as the efficacy of interventions, in order to engage the service users and carers in making practice decisions (McNeece and Thyer 2004). In this process, the evidence-based practitioner, according to Persons (1999: 2), participates in the following tasks:

- Provides informed consent for receipt of the intervention.
- Relies on the efficacy data (especially from RCTs [randomized control trials]) when recommending and selecting and carrying out interventions.
- Uses the empirical literature to guide decision-making.
- Uses a systematic, hypothesis-testing approach when implementing the intervention in each case.

Persons (1999: 2) goes on to state that the process:

- Begins with a careful assessment.
- Sets clear and measurable goals.
- Develops an individualized formulation and a care plan based on that formulation.
- Monitors progress towards the goals frequently, and modifies or ends the intervention as needed.

The integration of EBP was viewed as an improvement to 'traditional' ways of making practice decisions, which did not rely on research evidence of the efficacy of interventions. EBP continued as a growing trend, particularly due to the demands from government agencies and funding bodies for social care organizations and agencies to have more accountability, efficiency, and effectiveness (Pope et al. 2011). Likewise, as we demonstrated above, using research evidence is a key domain among the social work education regulatory bodies across various countries, as well as within the Global Standards for Social Work Education.

The early introduction of EBP in social work closely followed a medical model with the emphasis upon clinicians and interventions. Both doctors and social workers work with people who have complex problems and need to access a range of theoretical and research-based evidence to decide upon interventions or courses of action. Here, EBP can help with decision-making in providing frameworks for assessing the quality of the evidence and how different sources of knowledge may interact. However, there are significant differences between medicine and social work, as one of the authors has written elsewhere (McLaughlin 2012: 101). The intervention of social workers in people's lives is not the same as the prescription of drugs or a surgical operation by a doctor. While the two disciplines work primarily with people, the focus in medicine is upon the physical and biomedical aspects of individuals (General Medical Council 2009). This is not to say that medicine is not also concerned with the social and psychological aspects of people, but these are not its primary focus (Evans and Hardy 2010). Social work, on the other hand, is embedded in the social and psychological aspects of people's lives, working 'at the nexus of individual distress often created by preventable life inequities fostered by economic, political and social policies' (Gambrill 2016: S110). Social work is not purely a technical activity, but also a moral, social and political one where social workers have to learn to live with uncertainty, change, and paradox. Again, this is not to say that social workers are not concerned with the physical and biomedical aspects – they obviously are; but these are not their primary focus.

## Evidence-informed practice for social work

Sheldon and Chilvers (2000: 2) acknowledge an uncomfortable truth for social work (and medicine) that:

> It is perfectly possible for good hearted, well-meaning, reasonably clever, appropriately qualified, hard-working staff, employing the most contemporary approaches available to them, to make no difference at all and even on occasions to worsen the conditions of whom they seek to assist.

To address this they advocated for evidence-based social care (Sheldon and Chilvers 2000) arguing that social work should focus on 'what works', with minimal adverse circumstances for the service user or carer and at minimal cost. This elevated the importance of empirical evaluations with a downgrading of the importance of critical refection, ethics, and issues of power as being non-scientific. Sheldon (2001) and Sheldon and McDonald (2008) have argued that what was needed was greater scientific awareness based upon a privileging of quantitative research approaches and, particularly, randomized control trials (RCTs) (we return to these in Chapter 7), which are viewed as the 'gold standard' minimizing bias and demonstrating causal links between practice and outcomes. However, Sackett et al. (1996: 71) have stressed that evidence-based medicine is not a 'cookbook' and that:

> External clinical evidence can inform, but can never replace, individual clinical expertise, and it is this expertise that decides whether the external evidence applies to the individual patient at all.

Thus, the particular perspective of the evidence-based social care advocated for social work projected a narrower view than that of medicine wherein the social work version downplayed practice wisdom or practice expertise. In recent years, the importance of the patient's perspective has been acknowledged by evidence-based medicine (Gredig and Marsh 2010). This inclusion of the perspective of service users and carers is important, particularly as social work is a profession that espouses the importance of *'working with'* service users and carers, rather than *'doing to'*. In social work, issues of personalization and agency are integral to practice, while service users and carers have played a mandated role in the provision, delivery and accreditation of social work education in the UK since 2003. This role includes involvement in the admissions process, curriculum design, curriculum delivery, assessment, programme management and the approval and re-approval of social work qualifying programmes. This has also been spreading across the globe (Driessens et al. 2016; McLaughlin et al. 2016).

The inclusion of service users' and carers' perspectives suggests that social workers should incorporate the best available evidence with their practitioner knowledge and expertise *and* the service user's and/or carer's values and wishes in order to conduct an assessment, develop a care plan, and evaluate practice interventions. 'Best available evidence' refers to research from basic and applied research studies, including practitioner research, particularly from studies that evaluate the outcomes of social work interventions, or establish the reliability and validity of assessment measures (McNeece and Thyer 2004). 'Practitioner knowledge and expertise' refers to the knowledge, skills and values gained through social work education, and through experiences of practising social work and delivering and evaluating interventions in social work practice. Finally, 'service users' and carers' values and wishes' are defined as the 'unique preferences, concerns, and expectations each client brings to a clinical encounter with a social worker, and which must be integrated into practice decisions if they are to serve the client' (McNeece and Thyer 2004: 9). We might also want to add here the importance of a strengths-based approach to service users and carers, viewing them as not merely problems to solve, but as people with strengths and insights who have

**Figure 1.1** Three elements of the EBP process

something positive to offer the process. The three elements that encompass EBP are depicted in Figure 1.1, which involves the elements as separate categories, yet each is explored, critiqued, and subsequently applied to the decision-making process of social work practice. What is important here is that the three elements are separate, yet connected, and together inform and challenge the other and form the basis, integration and power of evidence-informed practice.

Based on these three elements as depicted in Figure 1.1, the definition of EBP in social work is as follows:

> a decision-making process integrating best research evidence, practitioner experience, and client and/or community characteristics, values, and preferences in a manner compatible with the organizational systems and context in which care delivery occurs.
>
> (Manuel et al. 2009: 614)

And as:

> a process of lifelong learning that involves continually posing specific questions of direct practice importance to clients, searching objectively and efficiently for the current best evidence relative to each question, and taking appropriate action guided by evidence.
>
> (Gibbs 2003: 6)

We would like to note the distinction between EBP as a *process* (or a verb) and EBP as a *product* (or a noun). As a *process*, EBP involves social workers engaging in the three elements depicted in Figure 1.1 in which they assess and identify the problem, evaluate the best research evidence that reports on the effectiveness and efficacy of interventions, take into account the service user's and/or carer's values, wishes, and circumstances, and evaluate all the information against their knowledge, values, and experiences (Williams and Sherr 2013). EBP as a *product* is in reference to 'empirically validated treatment', 'evidence-based interventions', or 'an intervention protocol' that has been empirically tested and shown to be an effective intervention (e.g. Cognitive Behavioural Therapy [CBT]) (William and Sherr 2013). Although empirically validated intervention protocols are part of the EBP process in terms of being considered among the 'best research evidence', it only serves as one element in the EBP process. Because EBP can often be used to describe both a process (as a multi-factorial approach to the decision process) and a product (single factor in the decision process) (Jaynes 2014), we have chosen to use the more recently accepted term of 'evidence-informed practice' (EIP). EIP more clearly specifies that social workers are not basing their decisions purely on research evidence ('evidence-based'), but, rather, that they are using evidence to 'inform' their decisions, along with information from service users and/or carers and their own practice knowledge and experience. It also seeks to distance itself from an overly medical view of evidence challenging the primacy of quantitative approaches in all situations. While randomized control trials (RCTs) can be seen as particularly important as an evidential source in medical research, this does not mean to say the same hierarchy of knowledge for medicine should just be transposed to social work. As we have already noted, social work is not the same as medicine and requires both the same and different research methods to answer the questions of practice. This is not to say that quantitative methods are not important to social work – they are; but they should not act in such a way as to diminish the importance of qualitative research. As Trinder (2000: 158) noted:

> The benefit of evidence-based practice is that it has brought a welcome emphasis on research and effectiveness. The potential danger is that the rhetorical force of the work evidence, particularly evidence defined as that based on RCTs, can offer seductively simplistic messages for practitioners and managers.

It is also worthwhile noting that in February 2016, 76 senior healthcare academics from 11 countries wrote an open letter to the editors of the *British Medical Journal* (BMJ) to bring attention to their policy of rejecting qualitative research as a 'low priority' or of little 'practical value' (Greenhalgh et al. 2016: 1957). The research question should drive research design, not the other way round. EBP has helpfully focused attention on the importance of research, but has become firmly associated with a particular form of biological evidence that only partially transfers to the social world and the questions social workers face in their daily practice.

Social work has tended to become more associated with EBP as a noun rather than as a process. While EBP in social work appears to promise a degree of certainty and to answer the question of 'what works', this has been often been on the basis of inflated claims of effectiveness, while neglecting the importance of individual circumstances and service user or carer characteristics (Gambrill 2016). This simplicity has been attractive to managers struggling to balance budgets and service demands, but is unhelpful to practitioners who struggle with practising in an ethically informed way within a contested and contestable field balancing competing demands, ambiguity, and complexity in emotionally demanding situations. Therefore, to emphasize the processual nature of EBP, to highlight the unique features of social work, and to distance our work from an over-reliance on quantitative hierarchies, we will use EIP throughout the remainder of this book.

**Revisit your definition of EIP**

Look at your definition of EIP that you recorded in Activity 1.2. To what extent has your definition and its key elements changed or remained the same? If it has changed, write a new definition in your own words.

We believe that social work and social care are very challenging and rewarding vocations which seek to 'work with' some of the most vulnerable in society; thus, this demands that those who engage in this work in an ethically honest way should use all the tools available to them to promote human rights, social justice, problem solving in human relationships, and the empowerment and liberation of service users and carers. To do this requires an evidence-informed practice approach that integrates practitioner, service user or carer, and research knowledge and evidence to provide high-quality services reflecting the needs, values and choices of those whom social workers seek to serve. To neglect any of these three aspects is to potentially deliver a less-than-quality service to those who most rely on the skills and interventions of social workers.

These arguments will be revisited in this book and applied to the role of the social worker in practice; but before we go any further we would like to highlight the aim and organization of the book and the key areas to be addressed in each chapter. While the order of the book has been developed to build on chapter by chapter, we are aware that readers may only wish to dip into particular sections and hope that whichever type of reader you are you find information to inform, to make you think, to make you consider alternative approaches, and to help you become a more effective social worker.

## Aim and organization of the book

Through this book we aim to address the concerns regarding the skills necessary for social workers to practise effectively with service users and carers. In particular, we cover the skill of 'evidence-informed practice' (EIP), which requires social workers to be able to assess a service user or carer's situation, and determine the best course of action by balancing the research on the effectiveness of interventions (given the service user's or carer's specific characteristics and needs), the service user's or carer's past experiences and wishes, and the social worker's experiences and practice wisdom. In this chapter we established the need to practise using EIP, covered the history of EIP, and explored the definition of EIP in relation to social work. In the remainder of book we review more specific skills needed in order to apply EIP to social work practice, and the challenges in doing so. In Chapter 2 we introduce the different types of knowledges that help to inform social work practice and provide an introduction to the assumptive worlds behind major paradigms of quantitative, qualitative, and mixed-methods approaches. Chapter 3 reviews ethics in practice and research, and provides examples of the ethical nature of practice, how ethics are governed and managed in research, and the challenges of acting ethically within an evidence-informed practice. Chapters 4 and 5 review the barriers and facilitators in applying EIP in social work practice – for example, through multi-agency practice, the culture of organizations, and practice–research partnerships. We then turn more towards the development of practical skills. In Chapter 6 we provide an overview of the specific steps in applying EIP to social work practice; Chapter 7 reviews skills needed to identify, assess, and critically appraise the different types of evidence; and we conclude with Chapter 8, which explores how to implement and evaluate EIP in your own practice.

## Summary

Through this chapter we have provided a rationale for the incorporation of EIP in social work practice. We explored numerous government initiatives and reviews that call for the integration of research and evidence in social work practice, and the Global Standards for Social Work Education and various social work regulatory bodies that stipulate research and EIP principles to be embedded throughout social work education to create future evidence-informed practitioners. The history of evidence-based practice was presented as well as its development within the social work profession, and the difference between evidence-based interventions (as a product) and EIP (as a process). EIP within social work involves the consideration of the best available evidence, together with the practitioner's knowledge and expertise and the service user's and/or carer's values, wishes, and circumstances.

### Key points

- Social workers should work in an evidence-informed way, particularly given the daily challenges they face in working with some of the most vulnerable and disadvantaged within society.
- There is a global expectation for social workers to have the skills necessary to participate in evidence-informed practice to ensure they are practising safely and effectively.
- Social workers should incorporate the best available evidence with their practitioner knowledge and expertise *and* the service user's and/or carer's values and wishes in order to conduct an assessment, develop a care plan, and evaluate practice interventions.
- Evidence-informed practice (EIP) specifies that social workers are not basing their decisions purely on research evidence ('evidence-based'), but, rather, that they are using evidence to 'inform' their decisions along with information from service users and/or carers and their own practice knowledge and experience.

## Further resources

Evans, T. and Hardy, M. (2010) *Evidence and Knowledge for Practice.* Cambridge: Polity Press.

Gambrill, E. (2016) Is social work evidence-based? Does saying so make it so? Ongoing challenges in integrating research, practice and policy, *Journal of Social Work Education*, 52(Suppl. 1): S110–25.

Gredig, D. and Marsh, J.C. (2010) Improving intervention and practice, in I. Shaw, K. Briar-Lawson, J. Orme and R. Ruckdeschel (eds) *The Sage Handbook of Social Work Research.* London: Sage.

# 2 Research knowledges

**Chapter overview**

By the end of this chapter you should have an understanding of:

- The differing types of knowledges that help to inform social work practice.
- An understanding of the assumptive worlds of the major research paradigms.
- An awareness of key research methods and their potential for practitioners.

## Introduction

As the previous chapter highlighted, evidence-informed practice (EIP) consists of three knowledge sources coming together to identify potential social work interventions; but where do busy social work practitioners access evidence from research, their service users, carers, and their own experience? This chapter will begin to answer these questions by first identifying Pawson et al.'s (2003) typology for social work knowledge, the philosophical underpinnings of different knowledge paradigms, and identifying key research methods, including their strengths and weaknesses.

### Activity 2.1

**Where can you gain knowledge?**

Before reading any further, write down where you believe it is possible for you to gain knowledge to help you to identify potential intervention plans for a particular case that has been causing you some concern.

## Types and quality of knowledge in social work

Pawson et al. (2003) identified a five-part classificatory framework for knowledge sources within social work and social care. These five knowledge sources included:

- *Organizational knowledge*: this refers to knowledge gained from governance and regulation activities in the organization of social work processes. This may include agency policies or protocols.

- *Practitioner knowledge:* this covers the knowledge that you, as the practitioner, have gained from your experience in your day-to-day role as a social worker. This knowledge source tends to be personal, tacit, and specific to particular context.
- *Service user and carer knowledge:* this knowledge is also often tacit and personal and is the knowledge gained from being on the receiving end of social worker interventions. Traditionally, this knowledge has been undervalued and under-represented.
- *Research knowledge:* this is knowledge gathered systematically within accepted recognized parameters that is often explicit and made available in journal articles, books, reports, and/or evaluations.
- *Policy community knowledge:* this knowledge comes from the wider policy community, and may include knowledge that comes from think tanks, agencies, or the civil service.

While the five sources of knowledge above are presented as distinct entities, they often overlap. In particular, we can recognize that practitioner knowledge and service user and carer knowledge impact upon each other. Service users' and carers' views of a proposed intervention or interference in their life is likely to be influenced by their previous experience, if any, with social services. Similarly, social workers' perspectives of a particular intervention are likely to be influenced by their previous experience, if any, with service users and carers who may have had a similar issue. Social work and service user and/or carer encounters are not neutral encounters. Past contacts on both sides of the relationship are likely to influence future ones.

At this point, we are going to look at practitioner and service user and carer knowledge in more detail before moving onto research knowledge. It is also worth identifying the differences between knowledge and evidence, although the two are often used interchangeably. Gilgun (2010: 282) defines knowledge as:

> information and understandings that researchers and practitioners develop from their professional practices as well as from their personal and professional values and personal experiences.

The *Oxford English Dictionary* online identifies evidence as a 'ground for belief; testimony or facts tending to prove or disprove any conclusion' (OED 2016). From these two definitions it is clear the two concepts are related. Evidence in social work aims to be able to prove (or disprove) whether a form of intervention has been successful or not. Effectiveness is concerned with what works, and which intervention or interventions are likely to achieve a desired result. Knowledge contributes to identifying evidence by providing the building blocks for constructing the evidence, while evidence helps to confirm or challenge our claims to knowledge. Trevithick (2008) also reminds us that knowledge can be classified into three overlapping headings: theoretical knowledge, factual knowledge, and practice/personal knowledge. Trevithick's (2008) framework argues that all three types are important and should be used to guide a social worker's understanding and action. A skilled practitioner will thus rely on more than just research knowledge or evidence.

## Practitioner knowledge

Practitioner knowledge, or practitioner wisdom, is an essential part of becoming an effective practitioner. As Fouche (2015: 14) acknowledges, being 'a skilled practitioner relies on more than research to inform practice decisions, assessments and interventions'.

---

**Activity 2.2**

### Practice and theoretical knowledge

1. Do you consider practice knowledge to be more important than theoretical knowledge in delivering your social work practice effectively? If so, why? If not, why?
2. How do you make sense of your practice experience?
   a. What role does supervision play in this?
   b. What role do colleagues play in this?
   c. What role do agency colleagues play in this?
   d. What role do service users play in this?
   e. What role do carers play in this?

---

Fouche's quote begs the question: 'What more?' How do you as a social worker know you have achieved the outcome you set out to achieve, or at least have done 'no harm'? Is it always possible to do 'no harm' in social work? It could be argued that in certain circumstances, for example, removing a child from their family home may ensure the child's physical safety, but may cause emotional harm to both the child and the family. How do you as a social worker know you have made the best decision?

We would like to suggest that one important source of knowledge for a practitioner is the role of supervision in social work. It is no surprise that supervision has been highlighted as a key offer to newly qualified social workers in the Assessed and Supported Year in Employment (ASYE) in England, and the Assessed Year in Employment (AYE) in Northern Ireland. Employers in England also have the responsibility to 'ensure that social workers have regular and appropriate social work supervision' (LGA 2014: Standard 5). In his enquiry report into the death of Victoria Climbié, Lord Laming (2003: 211) claimed that: 'Effective supervision is the cornerstone of safe social work practice. There is no substitute for it.' Beddoe (2012) notes that two key features differentiate supervision in social work as opposed to other professionals in that a) it continues throughout the social worker's career – not just in training, and b) it is delivered in-house. Traditionally, there have been tensions within supervision being criticized as overly focused on the management of cases neglecting individual professional development (Moriarty et al. 2015); while Davys and Beddoe (2010: 220) have gone even further and suggested supervision has become 'part of a system of surveillance of vulnerable and dangerous populations'. In a review of previous studies of supervision, Carpenter et al. (2012: 3) found supervision's primary functions to be:

administrative case management
reflecting on and learning from practice
personal support
mediation, in which the supervisor acts as a bridge between the individual staff member and the organisation
professional development.

For our purposes, the significance of the second bullet point is important: 'reflecting on and learning from practice'; although it could also be argued that an indicator of professional development would be the ability to work effectively with service users and carers. It is common for social work students or practitioners to consider themselves as reflective practitioners, although it is not uncommon for them to be uncertain about what they are claiming to be. Reflective practice is closely associated with Schön (1983), who regarded reflective practice as practice followed by 'thinking-in-action' or 'thinking-on-action' and becomes 'thinking-for-action'.

**Activity 2.3**

**Assessing your reflections**

Think of a challenging personal or professional situation you have faced, or are facing. This could include an interview/meeting, case conference, or even a phone call where you were aware of 'reflecting-on-action' or 'reflecting-in-action'? What types of things informed your reflections? For example, these could include personal prior contact, something a colleague said, or something you read in a file.

At its most basic, reflection involves thinking holistically, embracing 'facts and feelings, artistic and scientific understanding, and subjective and objective perspectives. All sources of knowledge need to be recognized and drawn on' (Wilson et al. 2008: 12). Reflective practice acknowledges that for professionals, like social workers, who work with people, there is never a simple answer to the issues or problems faced by service users and carers, as everyone is an individual and everyone will experience the same situation differently.

Wilson et al. (2008: 13) suggest that Schön's reflection-on-action or reflection-in-action can be compared to the 'conversations in our heads' that happen in practice.

Often, while relating to service users, social workers are thinking or feeling things that are pertinent to the encounter but they fail to articulate them. It is only afterwards that while reflecting on the encounter that they are able to make explicit this internal conversation. As a social worker becomes more skilled in their practice the capacity to reflect-in-action becomes greater. With heightened awareness of the processes and dynamics at work in an encounter, reflective practitioners can make them explicit in the course of the interaction and use them to inform subsequent actions.

Social work can be a confusing experience as the authors well remember from practising social work. It is quite easy to feel confused about what a service user or carer was telling us, wanting to believe what we were hearing, but being uncertain whether what we were being told was what the service user or carer believed, or had achieved, or what they thought we wanted to hear. This can create feelings of guilt or anxiety, while feelings of frustration, anger, uselessness, or even pleasure, may also be typical. These internal conversations keep intersecting with the external focused conversation providing an ongoing inner debate. In seeking to unpack and make sense of these dual conversations, Ruch (2002) identifies four types or levels of reflection. These consist of technical reflection, practical reflection, critical reflection, and process reflection.

1. *Technical refection* – This revolves around the questions, 'What did I do?' and 'Could I do it better?' This includes thinking about both what you did and, conversely, what you didn't do. Technical reflection tends to focus more on reflection-on-action and is a post-encounter exercise. It should include both theoretical and research components. However, technical reflection is not totally dependent on these; it also needs to include service users' and/or carers' perspectives on their situation, and how it might be improved.
2. *Practical reflection* – Wilson et al. (2008: 15) claim that, 'practical reflection understands knowledge to be more relative, constructed, contextual and inter-subjective'. Practical reflection thus involves both formal (e.g. theoretical influences) and informal sources of making sense, including personal experience and intuition. Practical reflection challenges us to re-examine our assumptions, both personal and professional, to enhance our understanding of our professional practice while considering alternative practice approaches. This approach demonstrates a social worker's willingness to try new options, while recognizing his or her own professional prejudices.
3. *Critical reflection* – Critical reflection goes beyond the two previous levels of refection whereby the social worker may be able to identify why they undertook a particular course of action, and what they might do differently next time. However, critical reflection challenges the worker to consider how the prevailing structural, political, and social conditions have contributed to the condition arising in the first place.

Fook (2002: 41) comments on the differences between being reflective and being critically reflective:

A reflective stance points up the many and diverse perspectives that can be taken on knowledge itself, and the shaping of knowledge. The important difference is that critical reflection places emphasis and importance on an understanding of how a reflective stance uncovers power relations and how structures of dominance are created and maintained.

For Fook, critical refection requires an anti-oppressive standpoint informed by a moral stance based on social work values (of which more will be discussed in Chapter 3) promoting anti-oppressive practice within a social justice framework. It will not surprise the reader that this will place the social worker at odds with dominant discourses about the 'deserving' or 'undeserving poor', the stigmatization of service users or carers, understanding austerity as a feature of neo-liberalism, and the widely accepted view that the reduction of welfare expenditure is a 'good thing'. Critical reflection not only asks the practitioner to think about what they did and if it could have been done better, but should they have been doing it all. For example, what should be the social work role in working with migrants and asylum seekers? The challenge of the critical perspective can be seen in the development and growth of the Social Work Action Network (SWAN) (http://www.socialworkfuture.org/who-we-are/constitution) in the UK, and the promotion of Macro Matters (https://macrosw.com/about/) in the USA.

4. *Process reflection* – According to Wilson et al. (2008: 15) 'the distinctive feature of process reflection is the importance it attributes to unconscious aspects of refection'. Process reflection thus draws on psychodynamic approaches which emphasize the unconscious processes operating in interpersonal encounters and our abilities to think and to feel. This distinguishes process reflection from technical, practical, and critical reflection by its emphasis on the affective dimensions of reflection, as much as the cognitive ones.

---

**Activity 2.4**

**Assessing the service user and/or carer perspective**

1. In the light of the discussion above, consider how a critical standpoint might help you to enhance your understanding of the perspective of service users and/or carers?
2. You might want to think about those who use drugs, experience mental issues, use food banks, or are homeless.

---

These four types of reflection contribute to a holistic model of reflection, although it is not clear how a practitioner would privilege one form of reflection above others. It should also be noted that reflection is a contested concept, and debate is ongoing. Ixer (1999) titled one of his articles, 'There's no such thing as reflection', based on our lack of agreement of what reflection is, and how it can be evidenced.

Schön (1983) highlighted the importance of thinking-on-action and thinking-in-action. It could also be argued that it is just as important to consider thinking-for-action, returning to the importance of supervision research.

While supervision is important to help a social worker, at whatever level within an organization, to improve their performance and become more effective, this effectiveness also concerns thinking about what to do next in a particular case, group or community work – thus thinking-for-action.

Supervision is an essential component of social work. Carpenter et al. (2012) found that while supervision is correlated with perceived worker effectiveness, can increase critical thinking, and should contain opportunities for supporting the emotional nature of practice, there is currently little evidence on the impact or outcomes of supervision on service users and carers. This does not suggest that we should stop providing supervision, but that the subject has been rarely studied and should be a priority for the future. As Carpenter et al. (2012: 1) comment, 'overall, the empirical basis for supervision in social work and social care in the UK is weak. Most of the evidence is correlational and derives from child welfare services in the US.' What is important for us to consider here is the transferability of knowledge and experience between countries. Just because something works in the US, it does not mean to say that it will not work in the UK; but it also does not mean that it will work. There are significant similarities and differences between the UK and US. UK social work has benefited from the social work expertise from different countries, including the US, Canada, Australia, Norway, etc., but also from indigenous knowledges such as the Maori in New Zealand, and the development of family group conferences which are now being used in over 20 countries (Family Rights Group, online). The point being made here is that just because an intervention works in one country, it does not necessarily work somewhere else as it may be dependent upon the nature of that country's welfare state, culture, or even the training and support provided to the social workers within that nation.

On a positive note, Carpenter et al. (2012: 1) also noted that 'good supervision was correlated with perceived worker effectiveness'. While supervision is usually connected to a one-to-one relationship between the supervisor and supervisee, group supervision, where you have one supervisor and a number of supervisees, has been shown to increase critical thinking.

Practitioner knowledge can also be developed in a number of other ways in which social workers can work together, learning with and from each other. This may include the use of team meetings to explore particular types of cases, and potential alternative ways of working with these. This can be particularly helpful where similar types of cases can be aggregated and alternative approaches considered which may result in a group work as opposed to an individual approach being considered. We have tested out such approaches in our own practice using the team as a source of referrals and as a critical friend. This can develop further into practitioner research, of which more will be said in Chapter 8.

## Service user and carer knowledge

Having considered the importance of practitioner knowledge, it is important we now consider the role of service user and carer knowledges. Within this text we refer to a service user as someone who is at the receiving end of service provision provided by social work and social care practitioners. A carer is similarly:

> anyone who cares, unpaid, for a friend or family member who due to illness, disability, a mental health problem or addiction cannot cope without their support.
>
> (Carers Trust n.d.)

Like service users, they experience the delivery, or non-delivery, of social care services. These services may be provided voluntarily or involuntarily, by the statutory sector including local government and health trusts, charity bodies like Barnardo's or Age UK, or the independent sector, involving organizations like fostering agencies or elderly person's homes providers. It is essential to note that we are not implying a dualism between those who supply services and those who use them; it is possible to be both a service user or a carer and a practitioner, not to mention being a service user or a carer and academic, or practitioner and academic. Also, even if you, or your family, have not needed to use services up to this point in your life does not mean to say that you will not need them in the future. Thus, if only for this selfish reason, we all have a stake in the quality and appropriateness of services on offer to service users and carers, and if we can learn with and from them we need to do so.

We should also seek to problematize the concepts of service user, client, or expert by experience (McLaughlin 2009). For the benefit of this book we have used the term 'service user', but accept that it contains difficulties: the term identifies someone by her or his dependency on services, and neglects other possible identities, such as being a parent, school governor, or academic.

Pawson et al. (2003) described service user knowledge as undervalued, tacit and personal, and derived from the experience of being on the receiving end of service provision. As Beresford (2000: 493) has noted:

> One key quality distinguishes such (service user) knowledges from all others involved in social care and social policy provision. They alone are based on *direct experience* of such policy and provision from the *receiving end*, service users' knowledges grow out of their personal and collective experience of policy, practice, and services. They also explicitly emphasize this. They are not solely based on an intellectual, occupational, or political concern.
>
> (italics in original)

## Activity 2.5

### Service user and carer knowledge

1. How does the above quote make you feel?
2. Do you feel it is accurate?

3. How do you seek to engage the views of your service users and carers and how do you know you do this in a non-oppressive way?
4. What do you do if a service user or carer disagrees with your assessment of what is needed to change a situation?

What is important here is the acknowledgement that service users' and carers' knowledge is based on their experience of being on the receiving end. As such they experience both the intended and unintended consequences of social workers' actions. We, as social workers, might identify a task-centred approach as part of an approach to a particular situation, but the service user may not experience it in the way we had hoped and may even view it as oppressive. Service users are thus in an important and privileged position to know what is required to change a particular situation. Service users have traditionally argued that services have all too frequently been organized for the benefit of service providers, not the service user (Branfield and Beresford 2006).

In an attempt to redress this imbalance there has been an increasing interest and advocacy for co-production. Co-production works from a strengths-based approach in that it assumes that service users have expertise and assets, not necessarily money, that can be utilized to contribute to meeting their own needs, or the needs of others. Co-production also emphasizes the role and expertise of the practitioner and how positive outcomes can come from a respectful and sustained relationship that increases the influence of individuals, groups, and communities (Powell and Dalton 2003).

Needham and Carr (2009) identified three different types of co-production: compliance, intermediate, and transformation.

- *Compliance level* – This refers to co-production that takes place at the stage of service delivery whereby service users and carers collaborate with practitioners to achieve individual outcomes. However, this is viewed as mere compliance as it does not involve service users and carers in the problem definition, only in contributing to solutions to already identified problems.
- *Intermediate level* – This level refers to a much greater recognition and valuing of all those who can contribute to co-production. It may include involvement in the training of professionals or recruitment of managers. However, it may also lead to greater expectations on service users and carers whereby co-production may be experienced as a form of manipulation or successful exploitation of service user and carer labour (Wilson 1994).
- *Transformative level* – This level of co-production raises the service user or carer to the level of expert asking what assets they can offer to collaborative relationships to transform policy, provision, and practice. At this level, both practitioners and service users or carers are empowered; however, we need to remember that some people are already active citizens, whereas others may be disadvantaged socially and personally, and it is important not to forget the importance of social justice and a fair distribution of outcomes.

**Figure 2.1** Different types and levels of co-production in social care
*Source*: Based on Needham and Carr (2009: 8).

It is important to note that different levels of co-production may be appropriate, given the nature of the task. For a high-risk child or adult abuse case compliance may be more appropriate than the transformative level, although there may be occasions where an intermediate or transformative approach is more appropriate. Similarly, the involvement of front-line staff and service users and/or carers in reviewing service provision, strategies, resources, outputs, and outcomes is potentially transformative. For co-production to work it requires the empowerment of service users and/or carers and practitioners. Service users and/or carers need to know they are not being viewed as the problem or a 'deficit', but as someone with assets who can share their perspective in achieving agreed goals. Practitioners, on the other hand, need to be confident in their ability to share power that is expected by their employer and value service user and carer expertise. Co-production, and the opportunities it provides for collaboration between practitioners and service users and carers, can be seen as a key aspect in helping to develop an evidence-informed practice. The third part of this triangle involves research knowledge, and this is where we move onto next. But just before we do, please complete Activity 2.6.

---

**Activity 2.6**

**Views and access of research evidence**

1. How do you usually react when someone mentions research evidence?
2. Can you identify an example of research that you have used in your practice?
3. How and where do you access research evidence in practice?

---

## Research knowledges

Research knowledge plays an important role within practice, although it is often hidden. Research knowledge may be reflected in informing national legislation, policy, or agency guidance, as well as being implemented by social workers in practice. Social work is an applied discipline, and as such social work research by its very nature is undertaken to improve social work practice and outcomes for service users and carers. This is not to eschew basic research, as this may lead to theoretical insights that contribute to social work practice, but to acknowledge that social work is primarily about engaging with people to improve lives. As such, social work practice should influence research, just as research should influence social work practice.

Social work, as we have mentioned, is a complex and challenging calling which utilizes a number of academic disciplines to generate knowledge, including: psychology, sociology, psychiatry, social policy, politics, philosophy, arts, mathematics, and economics. While the first set of these disciplines will be recognized by most readers, it is also important to include the last three. The arts, such as poetry, pictures and writing, are all effective mediums for working with service users (Huss 2015). Mathematics is important, although a frequent criticism of social workers is their dislike of numbers, which Webber (2015) attributes to social work entrants being more likely to have a humanities background than a science one, making them less familiar with empirical methods than colleagues in clinical psychology or psychiatry. Lastly, economics has become more and more important; as we face reduced resources it is important that we consider the cost benefits of our practice interventions. Traditionally, social work has shied away from costing its activities; but it is essential that we do this, rather than leave it to others who may identify indicators that mean less to practitioners and service users and carers, and are likely to be process rather than outcome driven. It is also important to include costings; if two interventions are equally effective, and one costs a great deal more, it is important that the cheaper intervention is implemented so that resources are not wasted that could be used in other cases.

It is worth noting that there is no universal agreement as to what research is, and there are thus as many definitions of research as there are research textbooks. At one level, research is about finding out something we did not know before, and is an activity we all engage in every day. At a different level, the Department of Health (DH 2005: para 1.7) defines research 'as the attempt to derive generalizable new knowledge by addressing clearly defined questions with systematic and rigorous methods'. The ideas contained within the DH definition highlight the importance of systematic investigation to address clearly defined questions which will generate generalizable knowledge for sharing with others. It is interesting that the last research quality exercise for universities went for a broader definition, viewing research as 'a process of investigation leading to new insights effectively shared' (Higher Education Funding Council for England [HEFCE] 2012: 48). What is new here is the addition of the insights of research being shared effectively, and for the research quality exercise this has been captured by the idea of impact. This is good news for social work and requires researchers to consider how their research can impact upon policy and practice.

## Philosophical underpinnings of knowledge

In seeking to understand research knowledge it is important to understand the underpinnings of different research positions without having to be a slave to their antecedents. The philosophy of science is often split into ontology, epistemology and methodology. Ontology refers to the study of being, and Snape and Spencer (2003: 11) identify three key questions:

> Whether or not social reality exists independently of human conceptions and interpretations.
> Whether there is a common, shared social reality or just multiple context-specific realities.
> Whether or not social behaviour is governed by 'laws' that can be seen as immutable or generalisable.

This highlights the two key ontological positions. The first is realism, which argues that social reality exists independently of ourselves and is out there waiting to be discovered. The second is idealism, which challenges this perspective and argues that social reality is only understandable through social meanings known through the human mind. These two positions are viewed as mutually exclusive.

In recent years, both positions have been viewed as too extreme, and some writers have tried to identify less extreme positions. Hammersley (1995) has argued for subtle realism, and Bhaskar (1979) for critical realism; both represent variants of realism influenced by the ideas of idealism in that, while there may be something that is an external reality, it can only be knowable through the human mind and socially constructed representations. Similarly, there are also variants of idealism, subtle idealism, and relativism. Subtle idealism suggests that reality can only be knowable through socially constructed meanings, but that these meanings are shared, allowing for a collective meaning (McLaughlin 2012); while relativism also accepts that meaning can only be known through socially constructed meanings, but that there is no single meaning, only multiple meanings (Crotty 2003).

Having highlighted the two extremes of the ontological spectrum, we move onto epistemology or the nature of knowledge (Crotty 2003). Epistemology is concerned with how we can philosophically ground the claims we make about reality. In particular, we will identify positivism and interpretivism, and you may want to consider how they relate to realism and idealism.

### Positivism

Positivism has a long intellectual history in social science research, with Augustus Comte (1798–1857) often considered the first to proclaim positivism, suggesting the social sciences could be studied using the same logic as the more established natural sciences. Giddens (1977: 28–9) identifies the four major claims of positivism:

- Reality consists of what is available to our senses.
- Science is the primary discipline.
- The natural and social sciences share a common unity of method.
- There is a fundamental distinction between fact and value.

Positivists regard facts as objective and superior to values, which are seen as subjective and relative. For positivists, the world is essentially measurable through the use of a neutral observation language to establish 'facts' which are directly verifiable, thus suggesting a correspondence theory of truth. The core concern here is to be able to describe and account for regularities in social behaviour that can be expressed as associations between variables and can be explored through systematic, repeated and controlled experiments. Karl Popper (1902–94) moved positivism forward with his assertion that no theory can be accorded more than provisional acceptance in that:

> There can be no ultimate statements of science; there can be no statements that cannot be tested, and cannot in principle be refuted, by falsifying some of the conclusions that can be deduced from them.
>
> (Popper 1980: 47)

Popper's post-positivistic stance suggested that all theories are by nature tentative, indicating that his own theory should also be subject to the same cautionary note. He also suggested that all scientists should set out to disprove their theories. While this might be an idealistic stance, in our experience most academics set out to prove their theories, not to disprove them. This does raise an important point whereby our publishing bias looks to report on research that proves something works, rather than the intervention has been a failure, even though we can often learn as much from things that do not work as do work.

### The interpretivist/constructivist response

Vico (1688–1744) reacted to the positivist paradigm by suggesting it has an insufficient conception of human beings; people are not like atoms and cannot be studied using the same methods as the physical and natural sciences. The interpretivist and constructivist position argues that human beings and social life cannot be reduced to a set of statistics, although what makes human life distinctive is open to question, but is likely to include: choice, moral and political concerns, and the self (McLaughlin 2012). This reaction to positivism has led to approaches that acknowledge that people construct and maintain their own daily lives, thus leading to interpretivism and/or constructivism. These approaches allow researchers to work with the subjective understandings, interpreting and constructing meanings. A wide range of theorists have contributed to these perspectives, and they are often used as umbrella terms, as they are here. Bell (2017: 25) provides a helpful distinction between the positivist paradigm and interpretivism and constructivism, although both are often conflated.

- Both believe there is a fundamental difference between the natural and social sciences.
- The social researcher should attempt to understand the subjective meanings of social action (**interpretivism**).
- Researching social issues needs an understanding of the social world derived from the ways in which people construct and maintain everyday social reality in different contexts (**constructionism**).
- Pure observation cannot produce theories, since all observation is 'theory laden'.
- Social reality is pre-interpreted (in contrast to physical reality).
- Research focus tends to be on words and accounts (qualitative data) or visual data, rather than on measurement.

To this, we could add that the interpretivist and constructivist eschew the notion of a neutral observation language, suggesting that language, like observation, is imbued with meaning. Interpretive or social constructionist approaches thus acknowledge that the researcher and the social world impact upon each other. For them, facts and values are not distinct but are linked. In comparison to the positivists they use inductive as opposed to deductive logic, and work with much smaller samples emphasizing depth and detail. This also leads to the importance for qualitative researchers to be able to identify their own position; they are not neutral observers and need to identify the analytical lens by which they seek to interpret or construct the world.

The interpretivist and social constructivist positions are, like positivism, not without their challenges. In particular, how can the interpretivist or social constructionist claim that their view should have prescience over the layman, as both share the same social reality and have access to the same tools to understand it. This has led to the criticism of social relativity, as Hammersley (1995: 17) notes:

> To the extent that sceptics or relativists seek to claim . . . that there is no universal truth or reality, they are hoist by their own petard . . . the argument undermines itself. If it is true that the validity of all valid claims is not universal but relative to some framework of assumptions, then for the relativist this is true of relativism as well. And this means they must recognize their position as false when viewed from other points of view.

### Pragmatism

At a philosophical level it could be claimed that positivism, with its quantitative methodology, and interpretivism and social constructionists with their qualitative methodologies, are not only incompatible but also incommensurate. To hold one as true is, by definition, to view the other as false. However, this is patently not the case in practice. In practice, it is possible to use both qualitative and quantitative approaches together without thinking you are a fraud. This has led to what Creswell (2003) has called pragmatism. Pragmatism is not committed to any one particular philosophical position, allowing members to have a choice of methods, processes or techniques with which to engage. In particular:

- Pragmatists do not see the world as an absolute entity.
- Truth is what works at the time.
- Pragmatists privilege the 'what' and 'how' questions of research.
- Pragmatists accept that research always occurs in social, hierarchical, political, and other contexts (Creswell 2003: 12).

Pragmatists would argue that we should stop debating philosophical positions and let the research question drive the design. It is argued that, by using both qualitative and quantitative approaches the researcher is able to enhance the quality and rigour of their study. Recent research of social work academics in the UK and US (Teater et al. 2016) found that there has been a move towards mixed methods approaches in both countries. In the UK, this has been a move from qualitative approaches to mixed methods, while in the US the direction of travel has been from quantitative approaches towards mixed methods.

Thus, both quantitative and qualitative approaches can be used to inform the other. However, it should be noted that just because a research study uses both methods, it does not mean it is a better study; additionality and complementarity are not guaranteed. Any mixed methods study needs to justify how combining the two approaches will better answer the research question.

It is also worth sounding a note of caution here. While we support the development of mixed methods approaches, using mixed methods in our own research does not mean that we should ignore the philosophical underpinning of our research approaches. It is important to understand the differing ontological and epistemological traditions, but not to be hidebound to them. On the other hand, it is important not to view research as purely instrumental, stripping out the philo- sophical underpinnings and value statements – such a position potentially leads to research being conceived as merely technical competence, and that is dangerous!

### Activity 2.7

#### Philosophical underpinnings of knowledge

This section of the book covers an area that students traditionally find difficult to understand – we are told it often seems like a foreign language. Where do you stand in relation to the positivism, interpretivism/social constructionism, pragmatism debate? Why? How do you think someone from each of the three different approaches might research the experience of a young person leaving care, or an older person suffering from dementia who wishes to remain in their own home?

## Data collection methods

Having looked at the philosophical underpinnings of research we move onto some of the key research data collection methods, including randomized con- trolled trials, interviewing, surveys, focus groups, documentary analysis, and photo-elicitation.

### Activity 2.8

#### Data collection methods

Do you consider the following quantitative, qualitative, or mixed methods?:

- Randomized controlled trials.
- Interviewing.

- Surveys.
- Focus groups.
- Documentary analysis.
- Photo-elicitation.

None of the approaches identified are inherently qualitative, quantitative, or mixed methods as it depends on the nature of the questions or data to be collected, and whether these include open or closed questions. Closed questions require the respondent to choose from a fixed number of possibilities (e.g. 'Did you vote for Brexit?'). The range of answers can only be: 'Yes', 'No', a spoiled vote, or did not vote. Open questions have no one correct answer, but require an explanation (e.g. 'What is your view of the government's position on adoption?'). This allows interviewees to identify the government's position, say whether they agree with all or part of this, and why.

### Randomized control trials

Randomized control trials (RCTs) are often viewed as being the 'gold standard' for measuring efficacy. RCTs reduce bias and require people with an identified need to be randomly selected to be part of a group to receive an intervention, and a control group who receive no intervention. The two groups can then be compared in terms of outcomes, and any differences would then not be the result of chance, but would be explained by the intervention. Ideally, the intervention group would be split into two, whereby one half of the group would receive a placebo to ensure that just the attention of being part of a research project was not the reason for any improvements.

RCTs have a simple logic, and are much admired in medicine, but are much less common in social work. They are also more common in the US than in the UK. As Jessiman et al. (2016) note, RCTs of social work interventions are generally difficult and expensive to carry out. Jessiman et al. also recount some of these difficulties and challenges in an RCT of therapeutic intervention for sexually abused children in the UK, while Dixon et al. (2014) note that RCTs have been viewed as both impractical and unethical in social work. (See Chapter 7 for more information on RCTs.)

### Interviewing

Interviewing is a skill that is very familiar to social workers and is often viewed as the method of choice for qualitative researchers. Interviews are usually conducted in a one-to-one situation to explore a topic of interest in depth. This is particularly so for studies which seek to identify a detailed understanding of an interviewee's subjective meanings, attitudes, or beliefs. It is possible to identify an interview schedule based on closed questions, although the most common form is the semi-structured interview. This includes both open and closed questions. The closed questions usually focus on demographic identifiers, and may on occasion include some rating scales to allow for future comparisons;

while the open questions allow interviewees to identify their positions in depth. Interview schedules also include prompts as a reminder to the interviewer of the ground they wish to cover. Interviews are good at understanding and interpreting the meanings people make of their lives in natural settings, but are not good at making causal statements or demonstrating statistical significance between variables, and are therefore not generalizable.

### Surveys

We have all experienced surveys, either being stopped in the street to respond to questions about some product, or through the internet after making a purchase. Surveys are generally considered quantitative in their approach, seeking to study 'the prevalence or correlations of variables within a population' (Taylor et al. 2015: 165). This means they collect data from a particular sample of the population in a standardized form, allowing it to be codified, and causal deductions are then made from the relationships between the variables. Surveys are usually undertaken with larger sample sizes than interviews, often when the interviewer is not present, making it important that the questions are clear and unambiguous. They can help in making policy decisions when statistics are aggregated from large samples, but they are not very effective in understanding processes or the meanings that people attach to situations.

### Focus groups

Focus groups are a popular method of data gathering in qualitative research. They may be used in their own right, but are often combined with other methods. Focus groups are often used prior to both interviews and surveys to identify key topics for questions, and, as Cronin (2001: 165) explains, are managed group discussions:

> A focus group consists of a small group of individuals, usually numbering between six and ten people, who meet together to express views about a particular topic defined by the researchers. A **facilitator** or **moderator** leads the group and guides the discussion between the participants.
>
> (bold in original)

The strength of the focus group is that it allows the researcher to collect a large amount of data for little financial cost, or the researcher's time (Hardwick and Worsley 2011). The interactive nature of the focus group members helps participants clarify their own views, but also opens them to alternative perspectives while providing the opportunity to challenge others' views, and being challenged on their own views. As such they encourage elaboration and theorization but, like interviews, are limited in their generalizability and very dependent upon the selection of group members and the facilitator's skill.

### Documentary analysis

Unlike the previous data collection methods, which involve primary data, documentary analysis depends on secondary data, which is data collected by someone else, rather than the researcher. Documents can include client or staff records, case conference minutes, or agency reports. These types of documents are, of course, confidential, and may be difficult to access. Other documentary sources may be easier to access and include government publications, local authority or voluntary sector services information on websites, think tank reports, serious case reviews, newspapers, blogs, or other media. Documentary analysis can be undertaken as either a qualitative or quantitative approach. As Smith (2009: 110) recognizes, whatever its source, 'documentary material will be a "secondary source", that is, it represents a construction of social reality, which is then subject to a further categorization and interpretation by the researcher'. However, researchers need to be aware of the purposes for which the original documents were produced, acknowledging that they may have included some issues and excluded others depending on the objective for which they were written and, as such, documents cannot be taken at face value. They must also be located contextually and spatially at the time at which they were produced.

On the positive side, this method of data collection offers the opportunity for a systematic inquiry of situations where it may be impractical, methodologically unsound, or unethical for a researcher to be present. Documentary analysis can be the data collection process for a particular study, or used in combination with other approaches.

### Arts and visual methods

Bell (2017) claims there has been a renaissance of creative methods using arts-based and visual methods in social work research. Arts-based methods may include such things as dance, puppetry, play, or drama, while visual methods may include the use of photographs or videos, paintings to express feelings or to make a point, or the group or community production of posters or films. It should be of little surprise that such techniques are becoming more popular as they have been used in therapeutic social work approaches for many years.

Visual images may be supplied by the researcher or by the research subjects. For example, young people may be asked to view pictures of their local area or be asked to use their own phone (or be provided with a camera) to take pictures of places where they may feel happy, sad, safe, or threatened, which then acts as the focus of an interview with the researcher. Huss (2012) describes how visual methods can be used in social work research, crossing the boundaries between the humanities and social sciences and acting as a means to bring communities, service users' and carers' perspectives to the fore of the research.

## Summary

This chapter has covered a wide range of issues in trying to introduce differing types of knowledges by building on the identification of EIP in Chapter 1. Following acknowledgement of Pawson et al.'s (2003) typology of knowledge sources, we identified the importance of practitioner wisdom and service user and carer knowledge, as well as research knowledges. Research evidence was also explored in terms of its philosophical underpinnings and key research methods. The next chapter will examine the importance of ethical issues for social work and social work research, and suggest you cannot have good social work practice or social work research that is unethical.

---

**Key points**

- There is more than one type of knowledge.
- Supervision and critical reflection are important in understanding practitioner knowledge.
- Service user and carer knowledge is based on being on the receiving end of social policy and social work practice – both its intended and unintended consequences.
- Research knowledges based on realism, idealism and pragmatism come from differing philosophical underpinnings about the nature of the world and how it can be known.
- There is a range of data collection methods that can be used, including randomized control trials, interviews, surveys, focus groups, documentary analysis, and arts and visual methods.

---

## Further resources

Crotty, M. (2003) *The Foundations of Social Research*. London: Sage.

Pawson, R., Boaz. R., Grayson, L. et al. (2003) *Types and Quality of Knowledge in Social Care*. London: SCIE.

Webber, M. (ed.) (2015) *Applying Research Evidence in Social Work Practice*. London: Palgrave.

# 3 Ethical challenges and evidence-informed practice

---

**Chapter overview**

By the end of this chapter you will have an understanding of:

- The importance of ethical issues to social work practice and research.
- The basis of ethical codes.
- The key ethical issues for research.

---

## Introduction

Fenton (2016: 18) acknowledges that 'social work is not a neutral profession, operating in a vacuum and unaffected by political and social developments'. Consider the challenging debate on how we should care for the increasing numbers of people with dementia, the international response to refugees and asylum seekers, the way many governments in the West have tried to redefine disability to reduce individual entitlement, and the re-emergence of the 'deserving' and 'undeserving poor'. Such considerations reflect one of Shardlow's (2013: 98) enduring ethical questions, 'Who should be helped?', while the second question concerns 'How should social workers behave?' While, in this chapter, we primarily focus on the second of these, we cannot ignore the first, and in many situations the two may well overlap. We accept that social work is an inherently ethical and value-laden activity. In this chapter we will identify ethical principles and codes, examples of the ethical nature of practice, how ethics are governed and managed in research, and how the challenges of acting ethically in evidence-informed practice (EIP) can be managed.

### Activity 3.1

**Your ethical practice**

1. In your personal life, how do you know if you have acted ethically? How do you know if you have acted unethically?
2. In your professional life, how do you know if you acted ethically? How do you know if you have acted unethically?

## Ethical practice

Your answers to the first question in Activity 3.1 may have included a 'gut feeling' of satisfaction or dissatisfaction, depending on whether you felt you had made the right decision or not. Other sources of evidence might be from the response of family or friends. For the second question, it might include a 'gut feeling', but in a professional context you may have discussed the decision with colleagues or your manager. One other aspect that will impact on both positions will be the outcome of our decisions. This reminds us that ethical decisions can have material effects, and as social workers we need to be aware that our actions and inactions have outcomes that will have consequences for others.

### Activity 3.2

#### Assessing values

1. List and consider what you believe to be the most important values that inform your practice.
2. Having completed your list, are you able to rank your value positions?
3. What happens if two of the values are in conflict?

While ethical practice is often lauded as the foundation of social work practice, it may surprise you to know that 'there is no universally accepted definition of what is meant by "ethical practice" in social work today' (Papouli 2016). At one level this is quite disturbing, but at another level we should not be surprised. Ethical questions concern what should happen in particular circumstances and, as such, can be contestable. One way professions have sought to socialize their members to adopt particular normative behaviours is to publish codes of ethics that state 'required, expected and prohibited behaviours' (Shardlow 2013: 99).

The International Federation of Social Work (IFSW) and the International Association of Schools of Social Work (IASSW) published a joint statement of ethical principles in 2012 (online at http://ifsw.org/policies/statement-of-ethical-principles/) with three key principles: human rights and human dignity, social justice, and professional conduct, which are then divided into 21 subsections. The IFSW and IASSW acknowledge that these are very general principles, intended to support ethically informed decision-making, but there is no obligation for social workers to abide by the code. On the IFSW website above, there is also a link to 22 countries' social work ethical codes, including Australia, Canada, the UK and US, but also Japan, Russia, Singapore, and South Korea. However, there is not a legal obligation in all of these countries for social workers to abide by the code; in some countries the ethical code can be viewed as aspirational.

Since 2005, the occupation of social work has been regulated in the UK – in England, since 2012, by the Health and Care Professions Council (HCPC). The HCPC covers 16 professions, but social work is in the process of being moved again to a single professions regulator – Social Work England. In Scotland, Wales, and Northern Ireland the situation has been more stable, with the Scottish Social Care Council, the Care Council for Wales, and the Northern Ireland Social Care Council respectively. These bodies all retain a register of all suitably qualified candidates, although all except the HCPC include student social workers. While these bodies have developed ethical codes for social workers, it is worth noting that there is no similar requirement for employers. Papouli (2016: 158) notes that the purpose of ethical codes is to 'guide professional behaviour, protect clients from abusive practices, and delineate standards for ethical practice, as well as safeguard the reputation of the profession'. While being aware of the code is an important first step, it does not ensure ethical practice. To practise ethically requires more than ethical code compliance, as the code cannot be reduced to routine; and morally engaged practitioners – and we would also add researchers – cannot hide behind the code, and must retain the accountability for their own professional practice (Husband 1995) or research.

### Ethical codes for practice

Most codes draw on utilitarian or deontological theories. Utilitarianism is associated with the nineteenth-century British philosophers and social reformers Jeremy Bentham and John Stuart Mill. Utilitarianism argues that the right action is the one that produces 'the greatest good for the greatest number'. Banks (2012) notes that this has led to 'consequentialism', whereby what matters is the outcome of the actions, not the actions themselves. While this may seem initially attractive to social workers, it sanctions unjust and discriminatory acts if you can justify that the majority benefit from such actions. So it could be argued that intentionally discriminating against certain groups – for example, the disabled or drug users – supports the greater good by encouraging others to avoid being identified as stigmatized as members of these groups. Such a position also allows members of these groups to be seen as 'undeserving', allowing society to treat them differently and more harshly than they otherwise would. It could be agued that utilitarianism contains an assumption that some groups – probably those who social workers work with – should lower their life expectations to allow others to have higher expectations. Fenton (2016) argues that the notion of the 'greater good' is also undeveloped in social work where the emphasis is upon relationships, equal worth, and social justice.

The other major approach to ethical codes, deontology, is associated with Immanuel Kant (1724–1804), a German philosopher. Deontology is associated with doing one's duty, and is concerned with 'rules' and principles that must be followed. It is based on a rational model, which, unlike utilitarianism, treats people as ends in themselves, and not just as means. Deontology argues that we should only do something if we believe that it should be a universal law (Banks 2012). As such, Carey and Green (2013) argue that it is the most influential approach within social work. 'Respect for persons', 'user self-determination' and 'empowerment' can all be seen to be categorical imperatives, often included within codes that can be traced back to the seminal work of Father Biestek (1961). Biestek's work was focused on casework and took a very individualistic and Christian stance towards social work and, in particular, casework. This has certain limitations in that, for example, empowerment is often seen as a key value for social workers. Social workers should empower their service users and carers, but can you empower someone else? At best you can create the conditions in which they can empower themselves. As Lorenzetti (2103) also notes, to support a service user or carer to successfully access a food bank does nothing for challenging structural problems and inequalities that make food banks a necessary part of our social fabric.

### Virtue ethics

In recent years, there has been a growth in virtue ethics which is concerned with 'the quality of the person, rather than the "rightness" of the act itself' (Fenton 2016: 67). While the notion of the virtuous social worker, and having an alternative to the lists of deontology and utilitarianism, are to be welcomed, this does not mean that virtue ethics are not without their difficulties. Clifford (2103) critiques virtue ethics for its focus upon individual practice, ignoring how organizations and management may create oppressive conditions in which to act virtuously becomes very difficult. He also highlights that, if we believe that society is divided and unjust then virtue will be defined by those with power, and it will necessarily favour retaining the status quo and their hold on power.

## The seven tensions

Shardlow (2013) has helpfully eschewed the normal way of considering ethical codes for guiding social work practice to identifying seven key tensions within practice. The seven are:

- Professional boundaries.
- Dual relationships.
- Conflicts of personal values and professional ethical requirements.
- Conflicts of interest.
- Confidentiality and data protection.
- Whistle-blowing and unacceptable professional practice.
- Mental capacity, best interests, and risk.

### Activity 3.3

**Your experience with the seven tensions**

1. Identify three of the seven tensions and see if you can identify situations in social work practice where each of these tensions has been relevant to you.
2. Having identified these tensions, how did you resolve them?
3. Would you have been comfortable discussing your rationale for your actions with your manager or supervisor?

### Professional boundaries

Professional boundaries suggest that there is a line between those behaviours that can be seen as suitable to social work practice and those which are undesirable. This can range from whether social workers should give service users and carers their own mobile number, the type of posts they make on their Facebook page, engaging in activism, to sexual relationships with service users and carers or a member of the service user's or carer's family. Inappropriate relationships with service users and carers is often a reason why social workers have been struck off the HCPC register (HCPC 2016) where social workers are deemed to have overstepped the boundaries between professional and personal relationships. At one level, having a relationship with a service user or carer can be seen to be wrong; but how long after someone stops being a service user or carer would a relationship not be deemed to be in breach of professional boundaries? Three months, one year, two years . . . ever?

### Dual relationships

Dual relationships are closely related to professional boundaries and can occur when a social worker enters into a second relationship with a service user or carer. This could be, for example, as a babysitter, handyman, sexual partner, or minister, and is generally viewed as unacceptable as it potentially compromises the nature of the professional social work relationship. However, this again is not clear-cut, and Shardlow (2013) notes that Pugh (2009) indicates such a separation is not always possible in rural communities where there is an increased risk of contact purely by being a member of the community. Such dual relationships may also be more likely within community social work contexts, and the focus on reciprocity and equality of relationships. A social worker faced with this tension should at least discuss the dual relationship with their supervisor.

### Conflicts of personal values and professional ethical requirements

A conflict of personal values and professional ethical requirements is typically exemplified by the tension for social workers who hold the sanctity of life as sacrosanct and who are asked to advise a woman who has unwillingly become pregnant. In these instances, social workers can adopt a relativist view where they seek to compartmentalize their personal view and professional responsibilities, or they may need to identify another social worker to counsel the woman. Alternative examples might have included tensions caused by faith-based or politically aligned social workers being asked to engage in activities in opposition to their firmly held beliefs.

A conflict of interest may occur in a family that has differing needs for support, and to meet the needs of one parent, for example, may disadvantage the other parent or children. This may, on occasions, require the social worker to seek another social worker to advocate for other members of the same family.

### Confidentiality and data protection

The confidentiality of service users and carers is usually taken as sacrosanct in social work. No service user or carer should expect details of their circumstances to be made public without granting permission, although it should be noted that communications between social workers and their service users and carers is not privileged in the same manner as that between a doctor and patient, or lawyer and client. Within the UK, the Data Protection Act (1998) provides a legal framework regulating who may have access to which data, and also what sanctions may be brought against those who breach the regulations. Of particular note is the explosion of smartphones, tablets and laptops which, with the availability of Wi-Fi and social network sites, has resulted in the ability to handle large amounts of data on the move, which presents confidentiality issues for social workers and managers to consider.

### Whistle-blowing

A whistle-blower is a social worker or social work student who raises a concern about safe or illegal practices in the workplace. All social work organizations should have a whistle-blowing policy, and any potential whistle-blowers should consult this; you should also not be treated unfairly or lose your job because 'you blew the whistle'. However, this is not as easy as it sounds. Kline (2009), reporting on a survey of 500 social workers, found that, too often, raising concerns with their employer, never mind whistle-blowing, was a bad career decision. Social workers were most concerned about victimization and career damage as a result of whistle-blowing. Thus, while whistle-blowing may be the right thing to do, if you spot illegal or unethical practices, it may come with a personal cost for the individual.

### Capacity, best interests and risk

One of the complexities of social work practice is where a social worker has to deal with an individual who may pose a risk to themselves, and others. On occasions, this may require the support of the police; but Shardlow (2013: 110) also notes that, at other times, this may happen when social workers are involved in multi-agency decision-making where they are 'not blessed with greater degrees of prescience than any other profession'. In cases of risk where the risk turns out satisfactorily, nothing will be said; but when things do not work out the social worker will be held individually accountable and open to blame. This fear has been especially evident in child protection work and has created a situation where practitioners may fear for their future and engage in a defensive practice to reduce the risk (Whittaker and Havard 2016). While social workers cannot escape the possibility of risk, they need to be able to recognize the different levels of risk and positively engage in actions to reduce the levels of risk-identifying ways that can be managed within the multi-agency team. However, the very nature of risk, and its association with probability, suggests that if they engage in enough decisions at some time they will experience an adverse outcome to their risk management.

Risk is not only an issue for children's services; it is also inherent in adult services, where increasing levels of dementia and Alzheimer's disease within the older population has led to issues of mental capacity. These have often focused on how to support people to live the lives they want without placing themselves, or others, in danger. In England and Wales, this has been recognized by the Mental Capacity Act (2005) (in Scotland, the Adults with Incapacity Act (2008) is very similar) which provides legislation for working with those who are deemed to not have the capacity to make a decision for themselves, and works from the basis that people should be assumed to have capacity unless it can be proved otherwise. The legislation also recognizes that capacity may be permanent or temporary; for example, it may be due to learning difficulties, dementia, brain injuries, or may be the result of substance use or mental health problems. The legislation in England and Wales requires researchers to obtain approval from an appropriate research ethics committee if researching in this area. University ethics approval is not considered sufficient to balance the importance of properly conducted research with the needs and interests of proposed participants with mental incapacity or impairing conditions. In England, the ethics committee has to be one approved by the Secretary of State, and in Wales recognized by the Welsh Assembly Government. This legislation also provides guidance on research participants whose capacity to provide informed consent may diminish during the research.

In seeking to manage these tensions, Shardlow (2013) suggests two approaches. The first involves sharing the tension with your practice supervisor or manager. However, he does not say what should happen if you should disagree with your supervisor. The second suggestion is 'look to external reference points that confer additional legitimacy' (Shardlow 2013: 112). This could include the Universal Declaration of Human Rights (United Nations 1948) and/or the UN Convention on the Rights of the Child (United Nations 1989). However, both these valuable documents are easier to understand in a theoretical rather than practical sense.

So far, we have sought to show that ethical issues and tensions are inherent in social work practice. The use of ethical codes may suggest a way in which ethical concerns might be managed, but we need to remember that 'doing things right is not the same as doing the right thing'. Social workers thus need to develop strategies and have the confidence and the moral courage to face these dilemmas; it would not be social work if these dilemmas were not present. We now move on to looking at issues involved in ethics in research.

## Ethics in research

Like practice, research is neither neutral nor intrinsically beneficial and takes place within a social and political context with many unethical experiments having been done in the name of research. Between 1940–44, doctors performed inhuman experiments in Nazi concentration camps. From 1932–72, the US Public Health Service used 600 African-American men as guinea pigs to study the progress of syphilis. Of these, 399 had contracted syphilis and 201 had not. The 399 were not treated, although effective medical treatment was available to manage the disease. During the experiment 40 men died and wives and children also became infected (Brandt 1978). In 1955, Willowbrook State School, a New York school and institution for children with developmental disabilities, was the site of an experiment in which 700 children were intentionally infected with hepatitis without their consent. The researchers wanted to follow the course of the disease while testing the effectiveness of gamma globulin (Pence 2000). At Alder Hey Hospital in the UK, there was a scandal concerning the retention of babies' organs for research purposes without the parents' knowledge or consent (Redfern 2001). Redfern's review into this practice also noted that many of the parents indicated that, if they had been asked, they would have given their permission.

The examples above could all be justified within a utilitarian framework where the suffering of the few should be weighed against the good that they will achieve for everyone else. This begs the question about who should decide who should be sacrificed, such as African-American men or children with developmental disabilities, so that others may benefit? Plomer (2005) suggests such questions are about power in that the African-American men, the children with developmental disabilities, or the parents of the babies did not have power to resist the medical paternalism or professional self-interest.

While we have been using bioethical examples we, who research in the social sciences, should not become complacent. Homan (1991) calls Laud Humphrey's study into the behaviour of homosexual men in public toilets one of the most unethical methodologies in the history of the social sciences. Humphreys acted as 'watch queen' or lookout, coughing when strangers appeared, thus alerting the men inside. Not only did he observe the events, he also recorded the men's age, dress, and car registrations, which he later used to trace their home addresses. Then, in a later public health survey, he visited 50 of these subjects at their home after changing his dress and hairstyle. Orme and Shemmings (2010: 47–8) argue that:

> The risks associated with social work research are more subtle, in that engagement with those who are experiencing disadvantage and poor social conditions can lead to raising the hopes of those with whom the researcher is in touch. Social work research also involves making contact with those who for a variety of reasons are isolated and excluded. This can lead to unrealistic expectations of the research relationship.

It is also worth noting that randomized control trials (RCTs) (see Chapter 7), which are often considered to be the 'gold standard' for evidential validity, also have significant ethical concerns built into their structure. RCTs compare the effectiveness of an intervention between an experimental group, a group that has a placebo, and a control group. It has to be questioned ethically who decides which individuals should be placed in which group as only one group receives the intervention. What are the impacts of non-intervention for a group of young people who have been sexually abused, never mind the suggestion of a placebo whereby they are deceived to think they are receiving the intervention but are actually receiving an inferior intervention? How would this address either group's problems, or promote their well-being? Also, what about the experience of an older person who is being abused by a member of their family? How could you decide to allow a control or placebo group in such situations. This is not to say that RCTs cannot be ethical, but there are serious challenges to be addressed, especially in relation to social researchers' 'duty of care', and an awareness that the likely benefits of such interventions are unlikely to be experienced by those involved in the research study.

In response to the range of concerns about the ethical nature of research, there has been a move, like in practice, to codify research ethics.

**Principles of a social work code of research**

Before going any further, please write down what you consider would be the key principles for a social work code of research?

These codes include, among others, social work research (Butler 2002), Social Research Association (SRA 2003), and the British Psychological Association (BPA 2010). Butler reminds us that professional ethical codes are more than mere statements of ethical positions; they also represent a form of professional claims-making and self-interest, staking out a boundary between those who can and cannot be included. We should not mix up having a social work code of research ethics with asserting only social work academics can do social work research. Such a position is obviously untenable, and other disciplines can add value to social work research, including research from psychology, sociology, economics and law, to name but a few.

Beauchamp and Childress (1989), working from a biomedical ethics perspective, are generally regarded as identifying the key principles for guiding ethical research. In particular, they identified the importance of respect for autonomy, beneficence, non-maleficence, justice, and scope. Respect for autonomy is probably the ethical position most familiar to social workers in that it requires researchers to treat research respondents as 'ends' in themselves, and not a 'means to an end'. This principle predicts the importance of informed consent, to preserve confidentiality while prohibiting duplicity or dishonesty. Beneficence and non-maleficence are usually referred to as 'doing good' and 'not doing harm'. In medicine, this can be reduced to a rational calculation whereby short-term pain is traded for long-term gain. All research is potentially harmful – for example, interviews for seemingly uncontentious issues may trigger painful memories, causing emotional distress. Researchers need to be aware of these possibilities and have previously identified a protocol as to how they should manage such situations. Justice refers to the moral responsibility to deal fairly with competing claims – for example, about who receives an intervention. It also demands that researchers do not put their own interests in front of others – for example, not allowing a respondent to answer a question or finish an interview without giving a reason. It is also possible to combine the principles, and Butler (2002) notes that the combining of respect for autonomy and beneficence infers the moral duty to act in ways that increases autonomy and promotes empowerment. The Economic and Social Research Council (ESRC), a UK research council, has developed six key principles of ethical social research. All social science researchers applying for funding from the ESRC need to address these principles in their research bids:

Research participants should take part voluntarily, free from any coercion or undue influence, and their rights, dignity and (when possible) autonomy should be respected and appropriately protected.

Research should be worthwhile and provide value that outweighs any risk or harm. Researchers should aim to maximise the benefit of the research and minimise potential risk of harm to participants and researchers. All potential risk and harm should be mitigated by robust precautions.

Research staff and participants should be given appropriate information about the purpose, methods and intended uses of the research, what their participation in the research entails, and what risks and benefits, if any, are involved.

Individual research participant and group preferences regarding anonymity should be respected and participant requirements concerning the confidential nature of information and personal data should be respected.

Research should be designed, reviewed and undertaken to ensure recognised standards of integrity are met, and quality and transparency are assured.

The independence of research should be clear, and any conflicts of interest or partiality should be explicit (ESRC 2015: 4).

It is quite easy to see how these have their roots in the work of Beauchamp and Childress (1989).

How do these six principles compare with the ones you identified earlier? You probably identified the importance of voluntary participation, informed consent, and anonymity, but we would be surprised if you also identified that the research should be worthwhile and of value to outweigh any harm or risk, the integrity of the research design, and the importance of identifying any conflicts of interest. While the ESRC's framework is a useful starting point to assess ethical issues, the extent to which researchers consider ethical issues varies between academic disciplines, and is a contested topic. Social work, with its emphasis upon respect for persons, and promoting dignity and human rights, may require stronger ethical positioning than other social science disciplines.

Dominelli (2005) goes a stage further and claims there is a difference between social work and non-social work researchers. She argues that the key features of social work researchers is their commitment to change, a more egalitarian attitude between the researchers and the subjects of the research, accountability to service users and carers, and a holistic engagement with the different aspects of the people they are researching. While these initially suggest a different approach, having discussed this with colleagues of other professions, it is probably more about differences of degree rather than of kind.

### Research governance

Research governance is sometimes confused with ethics, but refers to the administrative processes established by universities, charities, and health and social care agencies to quality assure research proposals and research integrity. Its purpose is to protect research participants, researchers and other staff, financial probity, and to ensure that the research is ethical. For university researchers, this usually requires them to obtain university approval and, depending on where they wish to undertake the research, may also require separate approval of the agency/hospital in which the research is undertaken. Some agencies, depending on the nature of the research, may just accept the university approval; but many will not. When reading any research article or report, it is important to consider whether the research has been given ethical approval, and how the risks from the research have been mitigated. Most peer-reviewed journals require authors to identify this process; this may be a problem in certain countries which do not have a developed research governance system, but even in those situations the ethical issues, and how they were addressed, should be identified.

In the UK, there remains an anomaly in that the research governance approaches for children and adults in social services are different. This is a result of the split of children's and adults' social services between the Department for Education and the Department of Health, just after the initial framework for research governance was published in 2001 (DH 2005). This has resulted in a national framework for adult services and a piecemeal approach by children's services. McLaughlin and Shardlow (2009) identified a range of approaches undertaken by local authorities, ranging from where adult social services only were covered, both adults and children were covered, and where the research governance framework was introduced across all local authority services. Boddy and Oliver (2010) undertook a scoping study for children's work on behalf of the Department for Education, and identified the need for a national approach which acknowledged the increasing range of integrated children's services; but we still await this guidance, during which time children are potentially afforded less protection than adults in England. At this stage, we would like to consider the position of children in research.

## Activity 3.5

### Ethical considerations in research

a) Thinking about the ethical issues involved in research with children:
   1. Can you identify ethical issues that are particularly important when considering research with children and young people?
   2. How might you address these issues to minimize any risk?

b) Thinking about the ethical issues in working with adults with a mental health diagnosis:
   1. Can you identify ethical issues involved that are particularly important when considering research with adults with a diagnosed mental health condition?
   2. How might you address these issues to minimize any risk?

c) Now compare and contrast your answers to a) and b) and consider similarities and differences in ethical issues for children and adults.

### Ethical research with children and young people

Much of what we have described so far concerns adults, and while the issues for children are similar there are some distinctive features. In keeping with the UN Convention on the Rights of the Child (1989), we will use the term 'children' to refer to children and young people under 18 years of age. This is not to suggest that children are a homogenous group – they certainly are not; children in the early years of school do not think similarly to teenagers. Children are also subject to the same intersectionalities as adults, where differences may be due to gender, ethnicity, disability, sexuality, class, religion, whether one lives in the country-side or city, and so forth. As such, childhood can be viewed as a social construct that can, and should, be problematized. Article 12 (1) (UN 1989) supports the view of children as social 'actors' in their own right, both created by and creating their own social world.

When children are involved in research as either research respondents or co-researchers, issues of age, maturity and ability are important for the researcher to consider. It may well be that the researcher first has to approach a gatekeeper – for example, a parent, social worker, or school teacher – to gain access to the children in the first place. This creates an immediate dilemma, as Balen et al. (2006: 32) capture in highlighting the balancing act between exercising a duty of care against the responsibility to allow children to develop.

> In what circumstances does adult gatekeeping become interference in the rights of children to impart information through their participation in research? Given that parents are seen as the 'natural' protectors of their children, to what extent does bypassing parental consent (albeit in pursuit of according children greater autonomy) deprive children of their parent's protection?

This conundrum has no simple answer. At the extremes of the age range we would probably all agree that those under 5 years old require parental protection, while 16- to 18-year-olds do not. However, if the 16- to 18-year-olds are subject to a care order, their local authority's permission will be required. Shaw et al. (2011) argue that a parent's or carer's consent should also be sought if the 16- to 18-year-old is deemed vulnerable – for example, if they have a learning disability, or if the interview was to be conducted in the carer's or parent's home.

Children in the middle years are more complex in that it is possible to invoke 'Gillick competence', following Lord Scarman's judicial decision that children under 16 have the right to consent confidentially to request contraceptive advice if they have sufficient knowledge or understanding to make their own decision. This immediately raises the question as to who decides if a child has sufficient knowledge and understanding? Also, it could be argued that a parent's consent would not be required, as it would contravene the child's right to confidentiality in situations where a researcher wanted to research children's drug use or sexual activity confidentially (Shaw et al. 2011). Once a gatekeeper is made aware of a research proposal they cannot be made unaware of it.

Children have the same rights as adults in relation to being research participants. They have the right to 'informed consent' or 'assent', a term sometimes used to express willingness to participate in research by people who are, by definition, too young to give informed consent, but who are old enough to understand the proposed research and its demands upon them. As such, the methods for obtaining consent, or assent, may need to be undertaken in a different way for children than adults, with the possibility of using cartoons or pictures to clarify what the researcher expects of the child. Their confidentiality should also be protected as long as a child protection concern does not arise, and that their anonymity be assured in any publication. Also, depending on the country, researchers researching children, and any other vulnerable group, should be required to have had a police check to assure parents, carers, schools, or other providers that there are no reasons why they should not be alone with children. Lastly, any data from children, like adults, should be stored in a secure place like a locked cabinet or on a password-protected computer.

Having looked at the issues of ethics in practice and research, we now move on to the importance of these for EIP.

## Ethics in evidence-informed practice

The point to make here is that research that is not ethical can hardly be the basis for the development of EIP. As has already been argued, ethics are an integral part of both practice and research. This means that practitioners need to assure themselves as to the ethical veracity of any research project they wish to include within their practice. Researchers should include with their reports where their research received research governance approval, but more importantly the ethical issues of the research, including the risk of harm to research respondents and how these risks were reduced. However, just like practice, research rarely follows a linear path, and unexpected ethical issues may arise which have to be addressed on site.

Researchers should also identify details of those aspects of their research that were successful, as well as those which were not. There is a publishing bias in that you will find it harder to identify examples of research that did not work. This is disappointing as such research can be very beneficial in preventing others wasting their time on practices that do not work. When speaking to a director of social services, one of the authors was told that of their research: 'If it tells me what I want to hear I'll publicize it far and wide. If it doesn't, it will just gather dust on the bookshelf!' However, it is common for researchers to note that there are limitations to their work, requiring further research to fully understand or prove whether something works or not.

## Summary

In this chapter we have identified how ethics is integral to practice and research. We have identified the principles on which social workers and social work researchers have developed codes of ethical behaviour, but that these codes do not mean that practitioners, or researchers, can abrogate their responsibility to act ethically. We identified how unethical research had been undertaken in the name of science, and the particular ethical issues you should expect to be addressed in reading research articles.

## Key points

- Neither practice nor research is morally neutral.
- Professions have sought to socialize their members into particular normative behaviours and increase public confidence through the development of ethical codes. However, to practise ethically requires more than ethical codes compliance; it requires morally engaged practitioners and researchers.
- Most codes draw their philosophical underpinnings from utilitarian and deontological principles.
- Shardlow has identified seven key tensions for practice.
- Research councils, commissioners, and journals expect research to receive ethical approval prior to contact with human subjects.
- Research with children requires further consideration of: gatekeepers, duty of care versus the right to develop, maturity, and understanding.
- Research you want to implement in your practice should identify the ethical risks in the research, and how these may be mediated.

## Further resources

Butler, I. (2002) A code of ethics for social care and social work research, *British Journal of Social Work Research*, 32(2): 239–48.

ESRC (2015) *ESRC Framework for Research Ethics: Updated January 2015*. Swindon: ESRC. Available at http://www.esrc.ac.uk/files/funding/guidance-for-applicants/esrc-framework-for-research-ethics-2015/ [Accessed 7 February 2017].

IFSW and IAASW (2012) *Statement of Ethical Principles*. Available at http://ifsw.org/policies/statement-of-ethical-principles/ [Accessed 3 February 2017].

Shardlow, S. (2013) Ethical tensions in social work, in J. Parker and M. Doel (eds) *Professional Social Work*. London: Learning Matters.

Shaw, C., Brady, L.-M. and Davey, C. (2011) *Guidelines for Research with Children and Young People*. London: National Children's Bureau.

# 4  Interprofessional practice and evidence-informed practice

> **Chapter overview**
>
> By the end of this chapter you will have an understanding of:
>
> - The importance of multi-agency practice to current social work practice and research.
> - The potential advantages and disadvantages of multi-agency working.
> - The key elements of effective practice.
> - The issues to address in providing evidence of the effectiveness of your own multi-agency working.

## Introduction

Interprofessional practice has, as one of the authors claimed, become a bit like 'motherhood and apple pie' (McLaughlin 2013a) whereby it is often feted as not only the best way of practising social work, but also the only way. In this chapter we will look at the mandate for interprofessional practice by identifying the strengths and challenges of this approach, including how it potentially relegates the role of the service user or carer, and also examine its evidence base and its implications for evidence-informed practice (EIP). But, before we begin we will try to clarify what we mean by interprofessional working.

### Activity 4.1

**Your experience of working interprofessionally**

Before we begin to discuss interprofessional practice, you might want to consider what you mean when you talk about working interprofessionally. Think about a case you have worked on and:

- List all the people with whom you worked.
- Were they all professionals?
- Who made the decisions as to what each of you would do?

- Did it work well? If so, how did you know?
- If it did not work well, how did you know?

## Interprofessional practice

Leathard (2003: 5) has eloquently described interprofessional practice as a 'terminological quagmire'. Terms like 'interprofessional collaboration', 'multi-disciplinary working', and 'interdisciplinary working' all inhabit the same bog, and it is not uncommon for the different terms to be become conflated. Banks (2010) has claimed that we used to use the term 'multi-professional working' to signify different professionals working alongside each other, but that this has increasingly become replaced by 'interprofessional working', signifying that different professionals were working closely together towards an agreed common goal with the potential of an interchangeability of individual roles.

Banks' definition is important here as it reminds us that interprofessional practice is not static, but dynamic; its continuum can include cases where a social worker and health visitor share a case, to situations where the team around a child might include a social worker, a family support worker, an occupational therapist, a teacher, a special educational needs coordinator, a foster carer, a drugs worker, a GP, and a paediatrician. While the first situation may be managed informally, the second will require a much more formal coordination and review process to ensure each of the professions identified know their role in the overall plan, and also whether their plan is working or not. This also begs the questions, who decides who will do what and whose role is it to coordinate the 'team'? We will return to these questions later.

For the purposes of this book we are using the term 'interprofessional practice' to cover this continuum.

## Initial thoughts and rationalizations for interprofessional practice

The failure of professions to work together has been a common theme of child abuse inquiries in the UK from Maria Colwell (1974) to Peter Connolly (Baby P, 2007). While much of the emphasis has been on child protection, there have also been adult inquiries, including Christopher Clunis (Ritchie, 1994) concerning mental health services, and Steven Hoskin (Flynn, 2007) who had a learning disability. Wilson et al. (2008) have noted that adult services, like children's services, have also experienced a similar drive to improve interprofessional working.

Smith (2013: 12) notes that interprofessional practice and collaboration between practitioners is not something recently discovered, but believes that 'in some form or other has always been the norm'. Certainly, both authors can identify with this from their own practice experiences. Smith also usefully highlights that the development of interprofessional practice can be compared to the developments in industrial production, often associated with F.W. Taylor (1856–1917). Taylor is viewed as the father of 'scientific management', believing that not only was there 'one best machine' for every job, but also 'one best way' to undertake any job (Mullins 1989). Taylor was concerned with finding more efficient and productive methods for working by identifying all the work processes, analysing and breaking them down into discrete tasks, and then, by using the scientific method, streamlining them into straightforward tasks to maximize performance.

Smith (2013) notes that similar trends can be identified in the development of the welfare state, with an increasing number and range of specialists, often with responsibilities that can only be achieved with the support of others. This has resulted in the development of a number of 'newer' professions, like social work, which have fought hard for recognition and sought to identify a distinctive remit informed by a distinctive value and knowledge base. This can also be viewed as a position of political self-interest in which the different professions seek to secure their own boundaries and, in the process, stop other professions claiming the same territory. These hard-won territorial claims can thus raise issues for effective collaboration, as differing professionals may well have to give up some of their 'own' territory to work together effectively. We can see that this is further complicated when we remember that we are assuming that all those who work together are, or consider themselves to be, 'professionals'.

**Activity 4.2**

### What defines a profession?

Which of the following do you consider to be a profession?

- Family support worker.
- Youth justice worker.
- Independent domestic violence advocate.
- Children's social worker.
- Adults' social worker.
- Approved mental health practitioner.
- Housing officer.
- Carer.
- Foster carer.

Can you identify the reasons why you have considered some of these roles to be professional ones, and others not?

It is not the purpose of this book to explore the nature of professionalism, but it is important to be aware that the use of the term 'interprofessional practice' potentially obscures or marginalizes the perspectives of those who are not considered to be professional. In practice, this also makes it more difficult for interprofessional practice to be effective when members of the interprofessional team's insights and experiences are considered of less importance.

When one of the authors started working in local authority social work in the 1970s, he worked as a generic social worker with childcare, youth justice, mental health and adult cases. These have since all become areas of individual specialization with separate management structures, whereby it could now be argued that interprofessional practice happens when a children's social worker works with a youth justice worker, an approved mental health practitioner and adult social worker, in a situation where a young person has committed an offence and whose parents have mental health needs, and where there is child-to-adult violence. This becomes even more problematic when we consider the position of carers and service users in these types of situations, and their opportunities to engage, influence, and be influenced by the interprofessional collaboration (McLaughlin 2013a). (More about this will be said later in the chapter.)

These two distinct and mutually supporting trends of increasing specialization and professionalization have contributed to the changing work environment in health and social care. Tasks have increasingly become more specialized, and often at the same time routine, creating tensions and barriers as different professions have sought to defend and expand their own areas of influence. These tensions have been recognized by successive governments, with the Department for Health (DH) (1998: 3) neatly summarizing their impact:

> All too often when people have complex needs spanning both health and social care, good-quality services are sacrificed for sterile arguments about boundaries. When this happens, people, often the most vulnerable in our society . . . and those who care for them, find themselves in the no man's land between health and social services. This is not what people want or need. It places the needs of the organization above the needs of the people they are there to serve.

This concern about interprofessional working by the government purports a view that, all too often, professionals wanted to deliver services in a way they felt was needed, rather than what the service user or carer recipient wanted. The push for interprofessional practice also supports the increased managerialism in professional services, whereby professionals become employees and professional autonomy is viewed as a problem in delivering efficient and consistent services. 'Managers become privileged and workers are employed to implement what the manager decides' (McLaughlin 2013a: 960).

Alongside the push towards interprofessional practice is a growing acknowledgement that 'social work services do not have all the answers' (Roe 2006: 8). As such, it becomes both imperative and vital that social work services, or for that matter any other human service, work with fellow agencies. It can also be argued that interprofessional practice is important for improving efficiency, which can be supported by co-location, making communication easier and faster for differing professionals working in the 'same team'. This also potentially provides a greater range of skills that can be called upon to address a service user's or carer's issues, or problems leading to a more 'holistic' service supporting different agencies to work more collaboratively, helping to encourage a situation where the interventions of one agency do not dilute the impact of another. Ideally, interprofessional practice creates a situation whereby 'the whole is greater than the sum of the parts'. Smith (2013) also claims that interprofessional practice can support innovation, promote creativity, and lead to a greater likelihood of user-centred services.

Interprofessional practice is not only considered essential for day-to-day practice, but also for the 'wicked' social problems that are beyond the ability and scope of any one agency. It should not, therefore, also be a surprise that successive governments have come to view professional boundaries as barriers to meeting service user, carer, and patient needs.

Galvani (2008: 105) provides a compelling case for interprofessional work when she highlights the position of people with drug using problems:

> Many have a number of problems that precede, coincide with and/or result from problematic substance use. These problems commonly include experiences of child abuse, domestic violence, financial problems, housing problems, trouble with the police, family breakdown, loss of employment, and physical and mental health problems. No one agency can be an expert in all these things.

## Organizations and interprofessional work

We have already noted that interprofessional practice is neither a static state, nor a homogeneous term, but is dynamic and can move backwards and forwards within a continuum in the same case. This situation is reflected in the nature of interprofessional collaboration between organizations, where Glasby (2007) has identified the following hierarchical formations ranging from the two organizations being merged into one entity, to the minimal position of sharing information that could be described as collaboration:

- Formal merger between the two organizations.
- Partner organization.
- Joint management.
- Coordinating activities.
- Consulting each other.
- Sharing information between organizations.

From the range of organizational arrangements above it is possible to claim interprofessional practice within a wide range of circumstances. However, it should not be assumed that the higher up the scale one is, the better it is for service users or carers. A formal merger does not guarantee a better service, and by itself structural change rarely changes anything (Peck et al. 2002; Glasby 2007). The degree of collaborative organizational arrangements required will depend on the purpose of the configuration. For example, as McLaughlin (2013b) points out, the police are a critical partner in the safeguarding of adults and children, but no one has suggested that children's and adults' services should be formally merged. Within the UK there have been several attempts to merge health and social care, with the introduction of Care Trusts (DH 2000) that aimed to promote an integrated approach around the patient or service user, within a single management structure, with multi-disciplinary co-located teams and the potential for financial flexibility to allow resources to be vired between the different services.

Cameron et al. (2014) identified that successful agency collaborations required attention to organizational, cultural, and contextual issues. The organizational issues included challenges such as the joint understanding of aims and objectives and their role in achieving this, as well as the need to establish flexible roles, effective communication, co-location, strong management, and adequate resources. The cultural issues included the need to manage differing philosophies and values, building trust and respect with and between workers, and team building. Contextual issues included the need for a good relationship between agencies, and preferably a history of joint working and financial stability.

The recent UK coalition government continued with this policy, even though, as Cameron et al. (2014) point out, the evidence base for collaborative working between health and social care is weak. In 2010, a White Paper set out the government's aim of extending the use of the Health Act 'flexibilities', making it easier for agencies to implement the partnership arrangements as a means to 'unlock efficiencies' that are perceived to exist (DH 2010a). This was further supported by the government's vision for adult social care that emphasized the intention to remove barriers, preventing the pooling of budgets, while also encouraging the involvement of social enterprises and user-led organizations in the provision of care (DH 2010b).

While policymakers' focus has changed over time, Rummery (2009) argues that the reasons for government interest in interprofessional collaboration remains the same, which is the concern about a rising demand for services and a need to reduce public expenditure. We could also add that this has become all the more imperative following the financial crisis of 2009, the resultant austerity measures, and their continuing financial impact.

## Interprofessional education

Interprofessional education, like interprofessional practice, is bedevilled by definitional inexactitude, but can be viewed as 'occasions when two or more professionals learn with, from, and about each other to improve collaboration and the quality of care' (Freeth et al. 2005: 11). HCPC (2017: 10), the current regulator for social work in England, requires social work qualifying students and registered social workers as part of their Standards of Proficiency (SoP) to be able to:

- Work in partnership with others, including service users and carers, and those working in other agencies and roles (SoP 9.6).
- Contribute effectively to work undertaken as part of a multi-disciplinary team (SoP 9.7).

Sharland et al. (2007) undertook a systematic study of research studies on interprofessional education in social work qualifying education programmes. They found that there was a wide diversity in the studies which often used different methodologies and were often flawed, thus making it difficult to compare results or say with any certainty whether interprofessional education made a difference or not. Zwarenstein et al.'s (2005) review of post-qualifying education was more positive. They found a growing body of evidence that suggested it was possible to evidence positive effects on service delivery, although these were not evident in all settings. While this evidence does not provide a robust endorsement of interprofessional education and practice, this does not mean that we should not practise interprofessionally, or educate for interprofessional practice.

Barr (2013), a leading figure in interprofessional education (IPE), has commented that IPE has moved from the 'margins to the mainstream', where it has now become embedded in professional qualifying programmes like social work. However, it again has to fight for space within an increasingly crowded profession-specific curriculum demanding a great deal of students who are only just finding their professional identity. He also questions whether IPE is robust enough to withstand the upheaval in education and practice that it may well have contributed to, and asks whether those who support IPE are able to:

> muster arguments, experience and evidence cogently and convincingly to demonstrate that IPE is indeed indispensable in implementing more cost effective policies for education and practice? The jury is out (p. 47).

Whether IPE survives or not, Barr is reminding us that we need to remain research-minded to evaluate both our educational programmes and service delivery to identify how we could undertake both domains more effectively.

Having looked at the rationale for interprofessional practice, it is worthwhile considering the following question: 'If there is such a compelling case for interprofessional practice, why does it not occur more naturally'?

**Activity 4.3**

### Interprofessional practice: A positive or negative experience?

- Given that there is a compelling case for interprofessional practice, why do you think it does not happen as a matter of course?
- Can you think of a case where you tried to work with other agencies and found it a positive experience? Why was this so?
- Can you think of a case where this proved difficult and, if so, why?

## What gets in the way of interprofessional working?

When you considered your ideas of why interprofessional work does not occur naturally, you might have identified some of the issues we are about to discuss: cultural differences, boundary disputes, status differences, communication barriers, complex accountabilities, and disputed decision-making powers (McLaughlin 2013a; Smith 2013).

### Cultural differences

Social services, whether children's services or adult services, have been traditionally expected to work closely with their health colleagues, GPs, district nurses, health visitors, paediatricians, physiotherapists, speech therapists, and so on. One of the key differences between health and social work in the UK is that health is a universal service free at the point of delivery, while social work is not. Social work is a selective service with access and assessment criteria where people may have to pay for their homecare or residential care. Health has well-established, highly regarded professionals like doctors, while social work is a much younger profession, and public regard for the work is much lower, as evidenced in the public inquiries on child deaths.

Within the UK, at least at present, the majority of social workers are employed by local authorities who are governed by local councillors, as opposed to the NHS, which is directly responsible to government without local councillor control. It should also be noted that health is generally associated with a medical model of understanding the world, while social work seeks to work within a social model. These differences create tensions between the two organizations and induce differing cultural expectations that any interprofessional work needs to acknowledge and work to overcome. Of particular interest is the current UK government's devolution agenda which is supporting a devolution of the health and social care budgets to promote the development of an integrated health and social care service in Greater Manchester (Devo Manc). The 10 local authorities, the NHS, public health, and emergency health services are to be integrated as part of a Devo Manc deal. It will be interesting to see how the integration works out, and whether it leads to better outcomes for citizens and patients.

### Boundary disputes

Having already identified that professional boundaries are both a claim for expertise and a political statement, it is not surprising that boundary disputes can concern the nature and extent of each partner's role and responsibilities (Smith 2013). Hudson (2007) has identified that, what is and what is not 'my job' can be a source of conflict in interprofessional working. Also, it is easy to see how others might contribute to helping you achieve your goals; it is not always as easy to accept that you can be called upon by others to achieve their goals.

---

**Activity 4.4**

#### What information would a professional want from another professional?

To help understand this point, consider the issue of a 16-year-old girl who is a substance user, causing problems at both home and school, and whose parents fear that she is also involved in criminal activities.

Consider what a:

- Substance use worker might want from a social worker, school teacher, and youth offending officer.
- Social worker might want from a substance use worker, school teacher, and youth offending officer.
- School teacher might want from a youth offending officer, drugs worker, and a social worker.
- Youth offending officer might want from a drugs worker, school teacher, and social worker?

Whose views do you think should be paramount? What might the parents want from the differing professions? And last, but not least – what about the views of the 16-year-old girl?

Boundary disputes can impact in at least three ways:

1. A 'colonization' of the tasks of one profession by another.
2. The avoidance of some tasks by both professions.

   or:

3. The organization's management decides that neither profession has the desired skill set, or that a non-professionalized skill set could undertake many of the tasks of the professionals more cheaply, thus resulting in the recruitment of more non-professionals and a reduction in the number of professionals.

This third response is not necessarily negative as it may meet the service user and/or carer needs more effectively, but this would have to be a research question rather than a budgetary one.

### Status issues

Inevitably, bringing in different professions with different traditions, different pay structures, and differing organizational arrangements will result in status disputes. Smith (2013) notes that unequal standing can be seen in both highly visible and subtle ways (e.g. look at size of offices in an organization or the titles of those who work there). This also identifies another issue we need to bear in mind which is that it cannot be assumed that all partnerships are, or should be, equal. Within legal firms it is normal to have senior and junior partners.

### Communication barriers

Finding or agreeing a common language to working together has been a long-standing issue for interprofessional practice. McLaughlin (2009) has written about terms such as: 'patient', 'client', 'consumer', 'service user' or 'expert by experience', which are not merely neutral terms but help to construct relationships, and have material consequences between professionals and those they seek to serve. The tendency of professionals to slip into specialist terminology and acronyms between professional colleagues may speed up communication, but with other professions and service users and carers this can be experienced as exclusionary and divisive.

One other aspect of communication worthy of mention here is the challenge of computer systems talking to each other. Differing professional agencies have differing computing requirements, often within a confidentiality and data protection framework, making it difficult both technologically and practically for information sharing, which can slow down interprofessional practice development.

### *Complex accountabilities and decision-making*

Another potential issue for interprofessional teams is the challenge for workers to be managed by someone from a different professional group who they feel does not understand their profession or its uniqueness. This can lead to feelings of favouritism between team members and concerns that their career may be impacted upon negatively by someone who does not appreciate the subtleties of their role or their profession's contribution to the interprofessional team. This can also lead to disputes in decision-making and to who has the ultimate authority to make operational and strategic decisions. This has been an endemic concern of interprofessional working as to whose needs come first. Should the police's need for evidence override a domestic violence situation where a distressed and abused women is in need of care or services?

We have considered some of the internal issues that support and challenge interprofessional practice. Quinney (2006: 22) helpfully summarizes the work of Barrett and Keeping (2005) in identifying key elements that can enable or prevent effective interprofessional practice.

- The need to be aware of the role of the other professionals, as well as having a clear understanding of your own role.
- The need for a motivation and commitment to interprofessional practice.
- The need to be confident, both personally and professionally, about the contribution of your profession.
- The need for honest and open communication.
- The time and opportunity to develop trust and mutual respect.
- The need to develop a model of shared power with clear responsibilities and accountabilities.
- Ground rules for the management of conflict, remembering that conflict is not always bad.
- The need for senior management support and commitment.
- The need to embrace uncertainty as it is inherent in such practice and needs to be recognized and managed.
- The need to recognize that tensions can, and will, arise from envy and rivalry between individuals and organizations when competing for resources and power.
- Being aware that working with people with complex problems in a complex structure can create anxiety that can become displaced onto other team members.

This listing from Quinney (2006) is very helpful in summarizing some of the key elements, but raises issues of its own. The elements are all focused on individual practitioner and organizational issues with no mention of the role of the service user or carer within the process; are they just pawns within this process to be done to, rather than worked with? It is also not clear how many of these have to be in place before success is guaranteed; nor is there a sense of whether all these components are of the same worth, or not? The listing is a useful checklist, and those of you working in multi-agency teams may want to check how many of these preconditions are in place. The next section considers the challenge for service users who experience interprofessional workers.

## The service user perspective

As Watson and West (2006: 144–5) note:

> One of the dangers inherent in a multi-agency approach is that a degree of *collusion* begins to emerge between the workers to the detriment of the service user's perspective. This can emerge from an eagerness on the part of the workers to be seen to be sharing a common set of objectives and for the relationships to be working well.
>
> (italics in original)

Watson and West (2006) suggest that in situations like this good interprofessional practice equals professionals working 'well together' irrespective of whether this creates better outcomes for the service user and carer. Workers become so focused on facilitating joint working they lose sight of the purpose of the joint working. Sharland et al. (2007) also found that this was a theme in qualifying education in social work.

Another aspect of interprofessional practice is the potential for greater surveillance. Surveillance is neither inherently positive nor negative (Lyon 2007). We accept that electronic surveillance makes our cars safer when we park in car parks and shop for the weekly groceries. Surveillance represents a process whereby special attention is paid to particular behaviours, which go beyond what would be termed natural curiosity. However, the single parent may view their increased surveillance by a 'team around the child' of social worker, family support worker, health visitor, teacher, and GP as less supportive and more controlling. As Banks (2010) reminds us, we as workers need to remember that, just because we plan and implement what we view as a supportive act, this may not be the way it is experienced. Our attempts to act in a supportive way might actually be experienced as overly controlling.

## What does distinctly good interprofessional evidence-informed practice look like?

Having considered a range of issues concerned with interprofessional practice, it is clear that there are compelling arguments that we need more interprofessional practice. It is also clear that there are endemic organizational and personal issues that make the achievement of such a position inherently difficult to achieve. Interprofessional work is more complex and contested than it is often given credit for. At this point it might be helpful to ask what would distinctly good interprofessional practice look like?

---

**Activity 4.5**

### What would distinctly good interprofessional practice look like

How do you think you would recognize distinctly good interprofessional work? Thinking of the example of the 16-year-old girl in Activity 4.4, what would you consider distinctly good interprofessional work to look like in this situation?

---

In seeking to answer the question above, we might first want to consider that inherently good interdisciplinary work occurs when it includes the service user and/or carer, and meets their needs. While this is a very attractive answer, and works if there is only one service user or carer, it begs the question of what to do when we have more than one client in the same family. Meeting a parent's needs may be at the cost of a child, or vice versa. Such ethical dilemmas are endemic within social work, and if it is a child and a parent then the decision is made by the legal paramountacy principle that children's needs should come first (Children Act 1989 part 1 Section 1.1). This answer is helpful, but fails to be of help when the needs of two children, or that between a carer and the adult they care for, are in opposition. Such dilemmas will need to be discussed and critically reflected upon at supervision in respect to ethical standpoints, research evidence, and service user and carer preferences. However, by including the service user's and carer's perspective the answer importantly does direct us away from the notion of interprofessional practice as merely about process, and puts the service user and carer back at the centre of the assessment and intervention processes. Importantly for distinctly good interprofessional evidence-informed practice, this also requires social workers and other agency workers to actively engage service users and carers in identifying their needs and how they wish that they may be addressed.

Secondly, distinctly good interprofessional work should be commensurate with the extent and complexity of the assessed need. In so doing, it should challenge the taken-for-granted assumption that, not only is interprofessional practice a good way of working, it is the only way. Practitioners and managers need to challenge themselves as to why this particular case or intervention would benefit from interprofessional practice and could not be delivered effectively from a mono-professional skill set. It is a waste of resources if an interprofessional team is put together to intervene in a case when it really only needs one person to do it.

We need to avoid falling into a mindset that sees all cases as interprofessional ones. As McLaughlin (2013a: 962) states:

> it is as bad to practice mono-professionally when an interprofessional approach is required as to practice in an interprofessional way when a mono-professional approach is required.

On a similar theme we need to consider if a team is required, which roles are needed for the team to deliver a service. If an agency worker does not have a role that would help meet the service user's or carer's needs they should not be in the interprofessional team.

---

**Case study 4.1: Working interprofessionally: some issues to consider**

Dave is an 8-year-old white boy living at home with his mother Anne, a 24-year-old methadone user who has had previous difficulty in managing her substance use, and has also had reported mental health issues in the past. Anne has no support from her family or Dave's father, who is believed to have assaulted her. She doesn't appear to have any friends. Anne is unemployed and has difficulty managing financially, but is very committed to her son. The home is a rented one-bedroom flat, badly in need of repair. Dave's attendance at school has become increasingly erratic and his class teacher has become concerned that Dave's educational attainment and emotional health are being affected by his mother's care.

a) As a child and family social worker allocated this case, which agencies do you consider it would be important to include in assessing the situation? Why? Who do you think are likely to be the key agencies (if any) involved in meeting the needs in this case, and who should coordinate?

b) As a substance use worker allocated this case, which agencies do you consider it would be important to include in assessing the situation? Why? Who do you think are likely to be the key agencies (if any) involved in meeting the needs in this case, and who should coordinate?

c) As a mental health worker allocated this case, which agencies do you consider it would be important to include in assessing the situation? Why? Who do you think are likely to be the key agencies (if any) involved in meeting the needs in this case, and who should coordinate?

d) Compare your answers to (a), (b) and (c), and consider what this tells you about interprofessional practice from differing professional perspectives. Lastly, consider whether it matters for Anne or Dave which agency acts as coordinator for any support offered?

---

Thirdly, on an organizational level, Glasby (2007) identified a hierarchical model of potential relationships ranging from a merger to just sharing information. He also noted that the top of the hierarchy was not necessarily the best point for all organizations, and distinctly good interprofessional work would be based at the lowest level commensurate with the tasks that were required to be completed. This creates a problem with the increasing push towards mergers and the integration of health and social services, which may not be the best model for promoting effective outcomes for service users and carers. This demands that practitioners working towards an evidence-informed practice need to take into account the organizational structures of any interprofessional team to contribute to an holistic evidence base on how structures help or hinder working together to meet service user and carer needs.

Lastly, given the lack of evidence about the impact of interprofessional work at an individual and organizational level, and the lack of evidence about interprofessional education, distinctly good interprofessional work would seek to evaluate its practice to build an evidence base that demonstrated what worked where, and why. In particular, this research evidence would cover the processual issues of working together between professionals and their organizations, but would also include the outcomes for service users and carers and the learning for social workers.

For the evidence-informed practitioner, interprofessional practice offers the potential to streamline assessments, improve communication, and improve the efficiency and effectiveness of the care system. Through coordinating with other workers more effectively it offers holistic and personalized care, and improves the planning and commissioning between services so that organizations complement, rather than disrupt, the flow of each other. If this is done, it will also ensure opportunities to prevent needs from escalating. As we have already noted, one of the key drivers for effective interprofessional practice is sufficient resources, which is a major difficulty for public service organizations – social services, education, the health service, and police – all of whom are being asked to do more with less. In fact, in many areas the drive for greater collaboration between agencies, including mergers, are being fuelled by the need to reduce budgets in the hope that greater collaboration will save the necessary budget reductions. Evidence-informed practitioners thus need to, with fellow interprofessional colleagues, evaluate their practice both from a perspective of whether it has 'worked' for them as practitioners, but also from the service user's and carer's perspective. They also need to be sensitive to the changes organizations are undergoing, and whether the levels of proposed collaboration result in better service delivery or are merely 'a rearrangement of the deckchairs on the Titanic'.

## Summary

In this chapter we have identified the problematic nature of interprofessional practice at both individual and organizational levels. Alongside this, we have suggested that the evidence base for interprofessional working and education is weak. We have also highlighted enablers and barriers for interprofessional working, and highlighted that interprofessional working can pay too much attention to the collaborative workings of practitioners at the expense of service users and carers. Lastly, we have made a plea for evidence-informed practitioners to problematize interprofessional work and to evaluate it, both from the perspective of joint working but also, importantly, from the service user's and carer's perspective.

**Key points**

- Defining interprofessional is problematic.
- Interprofessional practice is seen as the answer to society's wicked problems.
- Interprofessional practice has been driven by increased specialization and professionalization.
- There is not just one type of collaborative organization, and the degree of merging of organizations should be commensurate to the aims of the collaboration.
- The evidence for interprofessional practice and education is currently weak.
- Cultural issues, boundary disputes, status issues, communication, and complex accountabilities can make interprofessional practice difficult.
- Service users' and carers' views can be overlooked in interprofessional practice.
- Distinctly good interprofessional practice includes service users and/or carers as co-creators, and is commensurate with the extent and complexity of the assessed need(s).

**Further resources**

Littlechild, B. and Smith, R. (eds) (2013) *A Handbook for Interprofessional Practice in the Human Services*. Harlow: Pearson.

McLaughlin, H. (2013a) Motherhood, apple pie and interprofessional working, *Social Work Education*, 32(7): 956–63.

Rummery, K. (2009) Healthy partnerships, healthy citizens? An international review of partnerships in health and social care and patient/user outcomes, *Social Science & Medicine*, 69: 1797–804.

# Part 2

## Applying evidence-informed practice for social work

# 5   Creating evidence-informed cultures in practice

**Chapter overview**

By the end of this chapter you should have an understanding of:

- The barriers and facilitators to implementing evidence-informed practice in social work organizations.
- How to assess for barriers and facilitators to social workers and organizations implementing evidence-informed practice.
- Ways in which to tackle barriers and foster facilitators in order to create an evidence-informed culture in social work practice.

## Introduction

The extent to which social workers engage in evidence-informed practice (EIP) is dependent upon both individual and organizational factors. Individual factors include the extent to which social workers subscribe to the principles and practice of EIP, their knowledge and skills in engaging in EIP, and their access to information that enables them to engage in EIP. Individual factors can also include the extent to which the researcher translates and makes available research findings to the social work practice community. Organizational factors include resources (e.g. dedicated staff time to engage in EIP; training in research methods), support from management to access and implement research in practice, and the focus of management on either quantity of outcomes (e.g. managerialism and performance management) or quality of outcomes. In other practice situations, social workers may be 'told' what interventions to use in practice without fully engaging in the EIP process. For example, local authorities may 'prescribe' a particular intervention to be used with every service user (or carer) (e.g. 'Signs of Safety' in child protection), or external funding bodies may stipulate a particular intervention if the agency accepts the funding. As demonstrated, there are multiple and interacting factors that can influence the development and sustainment of evidence-informed cultures in social work practice.

In this chapter we explore the extent to which social workers become evidence-informed practitioners by examining the individual and organizational barriers and facilitators to such a position from the perspective of both practitioners and researchers. We then explore the potential for developing evidence-informed cultures within organizations, and facilitators for integrating research and EIP into social work organizations.

---

**Activity 5.1**

### Rate yourself as an evidence-informed social worker

Using the scale below, rate the extent to which you consider yourself an evidence-informed social worker? Why did you select this number and not one or two numbers below? What would need to happen in order for you to move up one or two numbers on this scale?

| 1 | 2 | 3 | 4 | 5 | 6 | 7 | 8 | 9 | 10 |

Not at all an
evidence-informed
social worker

Absolutely an
evidence-informed
social worker

---

## Barriers to implementing evidence-informed practice

Over the years, many researchers have attempted to identify the barriers and facilitators to implementing EIP in social work. The aim of such research was to develop education, training and support that can break down barriers and strengthen the facilitators to implementing EIP, with the ultimate aim of providing the most efficient and effective services to service users and carers. We will briefly outline the findings from this research on the barriers to implementing EIP based on the individual factors (e.g. the social work practitioner; the researcher) and the organizational factors. Although we present them as distinct categories below, we acknowledge that there is overlap between the individual and organizational factors, and a barrier in one category often creates a barrier in another.

---

**Activity 5.2**

### Individual and organizational barriers to implementing EIP

On a piece of paper, draw three columns and label the first column 'The social work practitioner', the second column 'The researcher', and the third column 'The organization'. Based on your knowledge, experience, or merely an educated guess, create a list of the possible barriers to implementing EIP under each of these three headings.

### The social work practitioner

Social workers are often reluctant to engage in EIP because they do not have the knowledge and skills in the EIP process or in accessing, assessing, and applying research. A review of the literature by Gray et al. (2015), and a subsequent survey of social work practitioners, found that social workers did not receive training on critical research appraisal and application on a par with other disciplines (e.g. psychology social policy, sociology). The review indicated that social workers had an inadequate understanding of what constituted 'evidence', and how to access, assess, and apply research in practice. The subsequent survey of social work practitioners found 22 per cent identified a lack of research knowledge and skills as a barrier to implementing EIP (Gray et al. 2015). Additional studies have found social workers lack an understanding of research methods and findings and, therefore, have inadequate knowledge and skills in critically evaluating research and translating it into practice situations (Mullen and Bacon 2004; Bellamy et al. 2006). Without knowledge of research methodology and data analysis, and the necessary skills to access, assess, and apply research findings to practice, social workers are not able to implement the EIP process, specifically because they are not able to engage in the element of applying 'best research evidence'.

Social workers have also been found to have negative attitudes or perceptions of research and its applicability to practice situations. For example, a review of the literature by Bellamy et al. (2006: 29) found some social workers to have a 'basic distrust for evidence, based on objections related to political, ethical, or control issues'. For these social workers, there is a distrust or resistance to innovation, evidence-based interventions, or intervention protocols (Gibbs 2003) as they are viewed as a 'cost-cutting tool', or as interventions that are popular at the moment without fully considering the best interest of service users and carers (Bellamy et al. 2006). Social workers often feel there is a 'lack of fit' between interventions developed and/or validated by researchers as 'evidence-based interventions', and the realities of practice with service users and carers who are not always similar to those individuals in the research. In this sense, social workers view the interventions as 'cookbook approaches that are too broad and do not speak to the unique contextual or cultural needs of clients' (Bellamy et al. 2006: 29).

---

**Case study 5.1: Social work practitioners' reported barriers and facilitators to implementing EIP**

Bledsoe-Mansori and colleagues (2013) administered the Bringing Evidence for Social Work Training (BEST) programme to 16 social workers across three agencies in New York City, which consisted of 10 teaching modules based on the steps of the EIP process. Qualitative data from focus groups following the 10 teaching modules indicated a general positive experience and attitude to EIP among the social workers, but they expressed worry that time constraints and lack of experience with research would limit their ability to formulate and answer questions in the EIP process. In addition to an expressed lack of experience and skills in accessing evidence, the social workers also indicated a general lack of access to evidence due to the cost of fee-based resources and search engines that provide links to full-text articles. Finally, the social workers also expressed a lack of confidence in interpreting the empirical evidence, particularly in terms of interpreting statistics and the quality of the findings.

### The researcher

The researcher can also serve as a barrier to the implementation of EIP in that they often fail to produce research relevant to the practice community, or, if it is relevant, often fail to disseminate research to the practice community. Researchers based in academic environments (i.e. universities) are often faced with the dilemma of researching, writing, and publishing for the academic community, *or* researching, writing, and disseminating research to the practice community. Researching for the academic community often means obtaining external funding to conduct research that will result in publication of the findings in high-impact, peer-reviewed academic journals. Universities are generally not supportive or rewarding of practitioner, community, or service user or carer involvement in research (McRoy et al. 2012; Palinkas and Soydan 2012), as such research is less likely to be published in high-impact, academic journals. It is also true that, for those seeking to develop an academic research career, 'publish or perish' in peer-reviewed journals is still essential for academic career progression (Robbins et al. 2016).

Universities in the United Kingdom (UK) are ranked and receive funding based on their performance in the Research Excellence Framework (REF) (http://www.ref.ac.uk), which is an exercise consisting of ranking research outputs (i.e. publications) on the following scale: recognized nationally 1*; recognized internationally 2*; internationally excellent 3*; and world-leading 4*. Universities place significant importance on research influence, rather than practice influence, as they would prefer to support and reward research that is published in high-impact, academic journals that can demonstrate international excellence, rather than an unfunded evaluation of a new intervention being implemented in a community-based agency that would not be rated as highly under the REF. Therefore, researchers are left with the tension of conducting and producing research that can directly impact the practice community, *or* meeting the requirements of their employing university in order to ensure job security and promotion. This was partly mitigated in the 2014 REF exercise, which introduced impact as a contributor to a university's overall score. However, impact was weighted at 20 per cent, while publications are weighted at 65 per cent of the overall score. Palinkas and Soydan (2012: 7) argue that such tensions result in:

> deficits in identifying research questions with a high degree of relevance for front-line social work, lack of practitioner and consumer interest in understanding scientific data, and, most seriously, deficits in translating research results to the benefit of end users.

A qualitative study by Teater (2017) of 20 social work academics in the United States (US) also found the 'social work researcher' to be a barrier to research-impacting social work practice. The academics indicated that research often falls short of impacting practice because the actual research is not applicable. One academic stated: 'I'm not sure that the majority of social work researchers are writing for that audience and I don't think what is being put out there is reaching them either.' Again, this is often because academics are disseminating research findings through peer-reviewed academic journals, which many social work practitioners are unable to access. Osterling and Austin (2008) referred to this as 'communication barriers' where researchers are not writing for a practice audience, in that the research is not presented in an easily understandable fashion, reports use statistical analyses that are not understandable to practitioners, and researchers do not clearly specify the implications of research to practice.

Another academic from Teater's study stated: 'I think there's issues of accessibility for people once they're out of school. How in the world are they going to get access to a peer-reviewed journal? That stuff is locked down.' And another academic echoed this concern by stating: 'After they graduate they can't even get into the databases. And so a lot of our literature that we're reproducing are in these secured databases of knowledge that nobody can access.' While this is also true in the UK, there has been a movement with the REF 2021 that all submitted articles must be accessible to the public. This has resulted in universities looking towards open access publishing, or creating repositories of staff publications based on the pre-accepted version of the article, as opposed to the published one. The difficulty here for practitioners is knowing the research they want to access, and where the author is based. Therefore, the researcher can be a barrier to the implementation of EIP in social work as they are not consistently producing and communicating research that has relevance to practice, nor are they disseminating findings freely to the practice community.

### The organization

The organization in which social work is practised can also serve as a barrier to the implementation of EIP. In order for social workers to effectively engage in EIP they must be supported by their organization in terms of providing the resources necessary to engage in the EIP process, and creating a climate that is supportive of this way of working. Resources required to engage in EIP include the following: dedicated staff time, funding support, training, and access to evidence materials, including information technology (IT) to access research databases, such as SCIE, NICE, Cochrane Collaboration, Campbell Collaboration, and other professional research organizations (Bellamy et al. 2006; Osterling and Austin 2008; Gray et al. 2015). A study of social service professionals in the UK ($N$=155) on the implementation of EIP found the main barriers included the lack of time and/or resources (80 per cent), and lack of information and/or training (71 per cent) (Morago 2010). Lack of time has consistently been the most widely cited barrier to social workers engaging in EIP (Osterling and Austin 2008; Gray et al. 2015).

The organizational climate will most likely determine the extent to which resources are provided for social workers to engage in EIP; therefore, the organizational climate has been identified as a potential barrier and facilitator to implementing EIP. According to Aarons and Sawitzsky (2006: 62), organizational climate 'reflects workers' perceptions of, and emotional response to, the characteristics of their work environment'. Workers employed in climates with greater structure and more support are found to perform better, and workers employed in climates that are more open to innovation and use of evidence-based interventions, with more positive agency leadership, guidelines and protocols to help implement EIP, and an investment in IT support, supervision and administrative support have more positive attitudes toward EIP (Osterling and Austin 2008; Gray et al. 2015; Tuten et al. 2016).

As demonstrated, there are numerous barriers to social workers engaging in EIP that can range from social workers' lack of knowledge and skills in accessing, assessing, and applying research findings to practice situations, to researchers failing to disseminate research findings to the practice community, to organizations failing to provide the time and resources necessary to effectively engage in EIP. In fact, it could be argued that it is amazing any social workers do! The questionnaire below was constructed to assess social workers' attitudes, access, and confidence in engaging in evidence-informed practice. We suggest you complete the questionnaire to assess any barriers and facilitators to your own engagement in EIP.

---

**Activity 5.3**

### Attitudes, access, and confidence in engaging in EIP

Please indicate the extent to which you agree or disagree with the following statement about EIP.

| Statement | Strongly disagree 1 | Disagree 2 | Agree 3 | Strongly agree 4 |
|---|---|---|---|---|
| I believe that EIP is valuable in my practice as a social worker. | 1 | 2 | 3 | 4 |
| I personally appreciate the advantages of practising EIP. | 1 | 2 | 3 | 4 |
| EIP should be an integral part of the social work curriculum. | 1 | 2 | 3 | 4 |
| I support EIP principles as an essential approach to practice. | 1 | 2 | 3 | 4 |
| EIP is a routine part of my professional growth as a social worker. | 1 | 2 | 3 | 4 |
| Evidence-informed social work has changed the way I approach my work. | 1 | 2 | 3 | 4 |

| | | | | |
|---|---|---|---|---|
| It has been difficult for me to practise evidence-informed social work. | **1** | **2** | **3** | **4** |
| EIP is 'cook-book' social work that disregards clinical experience in providing the best interventions for clients. | **1** | **2** | **3** | **4** |
| It is feasible to use EIP routinely when providing interventions for clients. | **1** | **2** | **3** | **4** |
| EIP improves the quality of social work client interventions. | **1** | **2** | **3** | **4** |

Please indicate the extent to which you access social work evidence from the following sources. If you feel you cannot respond because of lack of information, lack of experience, or uncertainty, please check the column labelled 'unfamiliar'. How frequently do you access social work evidence from. . .

| Source | Unfamiliar 1 | Never 2 | Rarely 3 | Occasionally 4 | Often 5 | Very often 6 |
|---|---|---|---|---|---|---|
| Colleagues – other social workers or health/social care providers? | 1 | 2 | 3 | 4 | 5 | 6 |
| Textbooks? | 1 | 2 | 3 | 4 | 5 | 6 |
| The internet (excluding Cochrane reviews)? | 1 | 2 | 3 | 4 | 5 | 6 |
| Original research papers published in peer-reviewed journals? | 1 | 2 | 3 | 4 | 5 | 6 |
| The Cochrane Database of Systematic Reviews? | 1 | 2 | 3 | 4 | 5 | 6 |
| *Journal of Evidence-Informed Social Work*? | 1 | 2 | 3 | 4 | 5 | 6 |
| Continuing professional development course/ workshops/post-quali-fying (PQ) courses? | 1 | 2 | 3 | 4 | 5 | 6 |
| Podcasts and web conferences (webinars)? | 1 | 2 | 3 | 4 | 5 | 6 |
| Databases of Critically Appraised Topics (CATS)? | 1 | 2 | 3 | 4 | 5 | 6 |

What does this tell you about your ability to access research evidence?

Please indicate the extent to which you are confident at appraising the following aspects of a published research report:

| Aspect | Not at all confident 1 | Not confident 2 | Moderately confident 3 | Confident 4 | Very confident 5 |
|---|---|---|---|---|---|
| Appropriateness of the study design. | 1 | 2 | 3 | 4 | 5 |
| Bias in the study design or data analysis. | 1 | 2 | 3 | 4 | 5 |
| Adequacy of the sample size. | 1 | 2 | 3 | 4 | 5 |
| Generalizability (or transferability) of the findings. | 1 | 2 | 3 | 4 | 5 |
| Appropriate use of statistical tests. | 1 | 2 | 3 | 4 | 5 |
| Overall value of the research report. | 1 | 2 | 3 | 4 | 5 |

*Scale adapted from: W.D. Hendricson, J.D. Rugh, J.P. Hatch et al. (2011) Validation of an instrument to assess evidence-based practice knowledge, attitudes, access, and confidence in the dental environment, *Journal of Dental Education*, 75: 131–44.

## Facilitators to implementing evidence-informed practice

Williams and Sherr (2013: 106) argue that the development of EIP 'may only be possible in the context of highly-resourced, well-connected networks of institutions and highly-trained individuals with both the commitment and financial reinforcement to pursue EIP development'; yet we believe this is a tall order, and that the development and integration of EIP can be integrated into social work practice at different levels given the barriers and facilitators that exist within that context. We reviewed the individual and organizational barriers in the previous section, and will now turn to the individual and organizational facilitators.

### The social work practitioner

Social workers have reported advantages to using EIP, which have included the following (Bellamy et al. 2006; Aarons and Palinkas 2007):

- Conceptualizing, planning, and guiding interventions.
- Increasing knowledge and skills.

- Improving outcomes for service users and/or carers.
- Integrating and supplementing clinical judgement and knowledge.
- Standardizing service delivery.
- Complying with current practice, values, and professional consensus.

The advantages to using EIP in social work can be enhanced through the individual factors of the social work practitioner. Researchers have attempted to examine what those specific factors may include, yet the research on factors, such as educational level and content, age, attitudes towards EIP, training, and the use of EIP, have remained mixed (Tuten et al. 2016). For example, a study of social work practitioners by Nelson and Steele (2007) found that taking an EIP class during university education, having more positive attitudes towards intervention research, self-identified theoretical orientation, and being employed in a more positive organizational culture were associated with higher levels of EIP use. Yet, although Tuten et al. (2016) found greater organizational innovation and flexibility, and more knowledge of EIP was associated with reporting the use of evidence-based interventions in practice – only one element of EIP – there was no relationship between receiving training and supervisory support and the reported use of evidence-based interventions in practice. Researchers have repeatedly found that the type of social work degree (e.g. undergraduate, graduate, postgraduate) was not associated with the use of EIP or evidence-based interventions (Nelson and Steele 2007; Baker and Ritchey 2009; Pope et al. 2011; Tuten et al. 2016), and years of clinical experience, or years in practice, were not associated with use of EIP (Nelson and Steele 2007; Pope et al. 2011). Age has not been found to be associated with the use of EIP or evidence-based interventions (Pope et al. 2011; Tuten et al. 2016; Teater and Chonody 2016), and although Teater and Chonody's (2016) study of social work practitioners found no difference in use of EIP based on gender, Pope et al. (2011) found men to have more knowledge and use of EIP compared to women. Finally, although two studies have found no difference in field or area of practice or social work setting (clinical versus non-clinical) (Baker and Ritchey 2009; Pope et al. 2011), Teater and Chonody (2016) found social workers within the medical/palliative care fields reported greater use of EIP compared to social workers in other settings.

The key facilitators that are consistently found across the research and literature are the education and training of social workers on research methods and EIP, and positive attitudes towards research and EIP. Therefore, in attempts to foster the facilitators that are found to enhance the use of EIP by social work practitioners, social workers should receive education on research methods and the EIP process in their undergraduate and/or graduate-level social work programmes, as well as continual training in these topics through post-qualifying education and continuing professional development (CPD) training programmes. Through the education and training programmes, social workers should be made aware of the benefits and advantages of EIP – as those listed above – in attempts to create and foster more positive attitudes toward EIP.

**Reflection point 5.1**

## Your social work education and training

Think about your social work education and training on research methods and EIP. What are your initial thoughts, feelings, and beliefs? What were the positive and negative aspects to these modules/trainings? What did you learn from these modules/trainings? And what – if anything – do you think was missing?

It is also important that we consider the potential for social workers to conceptualize their own practice as potential research-in-action, and to consider how they can evidence how their practice has made a difference, as opposed to merely completing the statutory paperwork (as discussed in previous chapters).

### The researcher

The researcher can facilitate the implementation of EIP by presenting research findings in an understandable and user-friendly way, drawing practical and realistic implications from the research findings to 'real-life' practice situations, and creating researcher–practitioner collaborations to assist in identifying areas of social work practice in need of research evidence, assisting in the planning and implementation of research projects, and linking research findings to practice (Osterling and Austin 2008). Although researchers employed within universities have to meet the demands of their employers in terms of publishing articles in peer-reviewed journals, social work academics have identified three specific ways in which they can facilitate the implementation of EIP through their research (Teater 2017):

1. *Asking the question, 'How relevant is my research to practice?'* – Researchers can explore ways in which their research can be applied to and useful to practice, versus accepting that research will only (potentially) influence practice indirectly. For example, research and practice colleagues can work together to figure out *'How we can use this to work with the clients that we're seeing directly.'*
2. *Widen the scope of dissemination* – Researchers need to transfer research findings from the university to the social work field in order to have relevance for practice. Dissemination of research findings to the community could consist of *'presentation in the communities and going out, rather than presenting to each other at conferences but finding ways to do applied training like, this is the research and here's what it means and here's how you could use that'*.
3. *Writing for your audience* – Researchers can tailor the reporting of research findings to the intended audience. For example, one academic stated: *'I am trying to create kind of practice briefs and policy briefs that kind of summarize the research articles that I write into maybe like two-page pretty-looking briefs.'* The academic goes on to state: *'It's like a watered-down version of articles, whatever the takeaway points for practice.'*

---

**Reflection point 5.2**

### Access, assess, and apply research to practice

Thinking about your practice or placement experience, how easy or difficult it is for you to access, assess, and apply research to practice? What do you see as the barriers for you to access, assess, and apply research to practice? How would your manager or supervisor respond if they found you reading a research article? Think about some ways in which the barriers can be overcome.

---

### The organization

As demonstrated, the organization is critical in facilitating an environment in which social workers can implement EIP. Facilitators include providing resources and support in the form of dedicated time to engage in EIP, such as reading research and discussing with colleagues, access to databases and informational sources to explore research evidence, and strong leadership that supports the use of research and is open to change (Osterling and Austin 2008). Additional facilitators can also include in-service training on research methods and the EIP process, and training to enhance knowledge and skills on how to access, assess, and apply research findings to practice (Osterling and Austin 2008).

Given the barriers and facilitators discussed above, we will now consider the ways in which we can create evidence-informed cultures in social work practice, and ways to bridge the divide between research and practice, particularly through creating research–practice partnerships.

## Creating evidence-informed cultures

Creating an evidence-informed culture within social care organizations requires identifying and addressing the potential individual and organizational factors that can act as both barriers and facilitators. Along with the identified barriers and facilitators listed above, Austin and Claassen (2008: 274–7) have identified the following five key components as specific to creating an organizational culture that is supportive of EIP:

1. *Leadership* – Evidence-informed cultures require strong and effective leadership among middle and senior management that demonstrates open and honest communication, is open to learning, and is supportive of change. Although any staff member can initiate and engage in EIP, there needs to be support and leadership from management in order to provide resources and support for staff to engage in EIP and lead in supporting and fostering innovation. Ideally, there should be an EIP Champion.
2. *Involvement of stakeholders* – Along with strong leadership, evidence-informed cultures must have the involvement of all stakeholders or staff members who

will be involved in any of the steps of the EIP process. This may involve including staff members from different levels of management, staff from multiple departments and/or disciplines, and those individuals who champion an EIP culture, as well as those more sceptical to the process. Those individuals who are supportive of an EIP culture can assist in supporting and motivating those individuals who have yet to 'buy in' to EIP. Ideally, service users and carers should be included in the stakeholder group to help prioritize research questions and to contribute their experiences of effective approaches.

3. *A cohesive team* – Merely involving stakeholders in the process is not enough to create an evidence-informed culture, but rather, the stakeholders and staff members must operate as a cohesive team. The team requires a leader who is knowledgeable about group processes and how change occurs to be able to provide and support an environment where staff members can discuss and reflect on their practice, the process of change, and explore any discomfort and long-held assumptions that might be impeding the change process. Teamwork can also help in implementing the EIP where team members can discuss research, reflect on practice experience, and process through decisions on choice of interventions.

4. *Organizational resources* – An evidence-informed culture can only occur if there are adequate resources to support and maintain the implementation of the EIP process. As noted in the previous sections on barriers and facilitators, organizational resources must 'minimally' include access to computers and the internet, library facilities, and journals to access evidence through research databases. Additional resources include an EIP Champion, dedicated staff time to engage in the EIP process, and staff training on how to access, assess, and apply research to practice.

5. *Readiness to become a learning organization* – Finally, change cannot occur unless the organization is ready for change. Therefore, the first step to creating an evidence-informed culture is to assess the readiness to change from organizational, individual, and system levels. Austin and Claassen (2008) suggest four areas to assess: organizational capacity; organizational culture; staff capacity; and the implementation plan (see assessment tools available from Austin and Claassen 2008). Chapter 8 provides an overview of the steps to implementation of EIP at the organizational level, as well as tools to prepare for implementation.

### Bridging the divide between research and practice

A consistent theme across the individual and organizational factors that either support or hinder the creation of an evidence-informed culture is the extent to which social workers access, assess, and apply research to practice. We acknowledge that evaluating and applying the 'best available evidence' is only one of three elements in the EIP process, yet it seems to be the most difficult with which to engage. We acknowledged earlier in this chapter that research may not be reaching or infiltrating practice due to researchers not researching topics that are relevant to practice; and if research is relevant, it is often disseminated through avenues that are not always accessible to social workers. We also acknowledged that social workers often lack the knowledge and skills to assess and apply research to practice. Based on these identified barriers, we provide the following suggestions to bridge the divide between research and practice in attempts to foster the creation of evidence-informed cultures.

*Integration of research and EIP throughout the social work education curriculum.* We acknowledged in Chapter 1 that the *Global Standards for Social Work Education,* as well as social work education regulatory bodies in the US, Australia, and England, call for the integration of research in the social work curriculum; yet social workers still report a lack of knowledge and skills in being able to assess and apply research to practice. To address this deficit there needs to be a stronger integration of evidence-based interventions and the EIP process across the social work curriculum that reinforces research to have relevance within all areas of social work practice. This is in contrast to traditional ways of teaching research, which involves students taking a specific research methods course that 'appears' separate from their social work-based courses and their practice. We believe students should have the opportunity to apply the EIP process to social work situations, such as through their field placements, where students can move through the steps of the EIP process under supervision (Berger 2013; Teater and Chonody 2016). As Teater and Chonody (2016) argue: 'Integrating EIP throughout all social work courses and providing opportunities to practice EIP further integrates the process within practice, which can lead to future social workers seeing the importance and relevance of EIP to their practice.'

*Education and training on research and EIP should continue beyond the social work education curriculum.* The education and training on how to access, assess, and apply research evidence to practice should continue beyond initial qualifying social work education. We argue that aspects of research and EIP should be integrated into the Assessed and Supported Year in Employment (ASYE), every post-qualifying award, and continuing professional development (CPD) training. This will include a review of the best available evidence that most appropriately relates to the practice or educational topic, as well as training on how to access research, assess the reliability, validity, and applicability to the practice situation, and ways in which the research can be applied. The ongoing training and reinforcement of the importance and relevance of research and EIP to practice will enhance the confidence of social workers in engaging in EIP.

*Social workers should participate in research and be supported to engage in research–practice partnerships.* Social workers who are involved in the research process are more inclined to use research findings to improve their practice. Participation can range from no communication or consultation between social work practitioners and researchers, to practitioners being included in the identification of the initial research question, through to the reporting of the research findings. Osterling and Austin (2008) found that practitioners who were involved in the research process from the very beginning, or were able to develop strong collaborations at some point after the research was initiated, were more inclined to welcome the research findings and disseminate them within their practice settings. The practitioners reported the following factors as helpful in supporting their understanding of the research and ensuring the findings were applied to practice:

- Interim reports on study findings.
- Personal contacts with researchers.
- Co-worker involvement in the study.
- Extensive conversations with researchers before dissemination.
- Attitude changes regarding the value and use of research.
- Continuous contact between workers' supervisors and researchers (Osterling and Austin, 2008: 307–9).

Practitioners and agencies should look at ways in which the differing agencies can better collaborate for mutual benefit, whereby practitioners can gain support in researching their key issues while also becoming a living laboratory welcoming to researchers who can demonstrate they are working to develop EIP to improve service user and carer outcomes.

Finally, the results of any research should be translated into sources of information that are meaningful and digestible to social work practitioners, such as specific approaches and tools, toolkits, guidelines, and highlights to apply the research to practice (Bellamy et al. 2006). This could also include attending team meetings, and setting up master classes on different subjects or workshops.

## Summary

In this chapter we identified the numerous individual and organizational factors that can serve as both barriers and facilitators to creating an evidence-informed culture. We also provided two assessment tools to use to assess the attitudes, access, and confidence of social work practitioners to engage in EIP. Overcoming barriers to creating an evidence-based culture requires change on multiple levels, from strengthening the education of social workers, to creating organizations that provide support and leadership, to bridging the barriers between research and practice. The next three chapters attempt to break down such barriers by providing you with the necessary tools to begin to engage in the EIP process within your social work practice.

### Key points

- The extent to which social workers engage in EIP is dependent upon both individual and organizational factors, which can serve as both barriers and facilitators.
- Individual factors for social work practitioners can include the extent to which they subscribe to the principles and practice of EIP, and their knowledge and skills in engaging in EIP.
- Individual factors for researchers can include the extent to which they conduct research relevant to social work practice, and translate and make available research findings to the social work practice community.

- Organizational factors include resources, such as dedicated staff time to engage in EIP and ongoing training, and support from management to implement research in practice.
- Creating an evidence-informed culture within organizations requires strong leadership; involvement of stakeholders; a cohesive team; organizational resources; and readiness to become a learning organization.

## Further resources

Barratt, M. and Hodson, R. (2006) *Firm Foundations: A Practical Guide to Organizational Support for the Use of Research*. Dartington, UK: Research in Practice.

Gray, M., Joy, E., Plath, D. et al. (2015) What supports and impedes evidence-based practice implementation? A survey of Australian social workers, *British Journal of Social Work*, 45: 667–84.

Osterling, K.L. and Austin, M.J. (2008) The dissemination and utilization of research for promoting evidence-based practice, *Journal of Evidence-Based Social Work*, 5: 295–319.

Thyer, B. (2015) Preparing current and future practitioners to integrate research in real practice settings, *Research on Social Work Practice*, 25: 463–72.

# 6 Steps in evidence-informed practice

**Chapter overview**

By the end of this chapter you should have an understanding of:

- The six steps of the evidence-informed practice process.
- How to identify and construct practice-research questions.
- How to engage in a review of the evidence and the different types of evidence.
- How to weigh the three elements of the evidence-informed practice process.

## Introduction

In Chapter 1, evidence-informed practice (EIP) in social work was defined as: 'a decision-making process integrating best research evidence, practitioner experience, and [service user and carer] and/or community characteristics, values, and preferences in a manner compatible with the organizational systems and context in which care delivery occurs' (Manuel et al. 2009: 614) and as 'a process of lifelong learning that involves continually posing specific questions of direct practice importance to [service users and/or carers], searching objectively and efficiently for the current best evidence relative to each question, and taking appropriate action guided by evidence' (Gibbs 2003: 6). We also distinguished EIP from evidence-based interventions. EIP is a *process* that involves social workers engaging in the three aspects of EIP – best available evidence; the service user's and carer's values and wishes; and social worker's knowledge, values, and experiences – to assess, provide interventions, and evaluate practice. Evidence-based inventions are products, tools, or protocols of interventions that have been established as 'evidence-based'. In this sense, evidence-based interventions are tools that social workers would assess when exploring the 'best available evidence' element of the EIP process, and are only one aspect to consider when engaging in EIP.

In this chapter we begin to explore the process of EIP by providing you with a detailed explanation of each of the six steps of the process. We provide a discussion of how you can develop practice-research questions, gather research evidence from primary and secondary sources, critically appraise the research, apply the research evidence given your knowledge and experience as a social worker and the service user's or carer's values and wishes, and evaluate your practice and the outcomes of the intervention. We explore the difficulties in engaging in EIP, and provide examples of when the three elements of EIP may not be considered equally.

## Steps in EIP process

Social workers engaging in EIP consider information from three sources: best available evidence; the service user's and/or carer's values and wishes; and the social worker's knowledge and experience – often referred to as 'practice wisdom'. To effectively engage in EIP, social workers must possess diverse interpersonal and communication skills, as well as skills in critical thinking and critical analysis. In particular, social workers need to communicate and engage with service users or carers to elicit their identified problems or concerns that have resulted in social work intervention. Social workers must then use critical thinking and analysis skills to assess the service user's or carer's situation, find and critique existing literature and research (i.e. 'best available evidence') that can be used to inform the social worker's work with the service user or carer, and identify possible interventions to address the identified problems. The possible interventions then need to be communicated with the service users or carers so that the choice of intervention and work can be as collaborative as possible. Finally, social workers should continually receive feedback from service users or carers, as well as other involved individuals, on the extent to which the intervention and the work together is being effective. This process, from engagement with a service user and/or carer through to evaluation of the effectiveness of the intervention, can take place through the following six steps of the EIP process, as outlined by Sackett (2000) and Rubin and Babbie (2016):

1. Formulate a question to answer practice needs.
2. Search for the evidence to answer the question.
3. Critically appraise the evidence.
4. Determine which evidence-based intervention is most appropriate for your particular service user or carer, along with your professional knowledge and the service user's and/or carer's values and circumstances.
5. Apply the evidence-based intervention.
6. Evaluate the effectiveness and efficiency in carrying out steps one through five, and provide feedback on the process and outcome.

We describe each of the six steps in detail below. We want to acknowledge that the EIP process is not a 'one-size-fits-all' approach to social work practice, but rather a way for you, as a social worker, to consider how to best integrate and consider the best research evidence with your professional knowledge and experience and the service user's and/or carer's values and wishes (Pope et al. 2011). We also want to stress that the process presented below is meant to be flexible; it is not a rigid sequential process. Nevo and Slonim-Nevo (2011: 1194) argue that the 'process itself should be flexible and creative enough to meet the ongoing changing goals, conditions, experiences, and preferences of [service users/carers] and practitioners'.

Before we start, consider the reflective exercise below (Reflection 6.1) to begin thinking about your own practice and the types of questions you may ask in relation to your practice and practice population.

**Reflection point 6.1**

**What problems arise in your practice?**

Think about your professional or practice placement experience. What are the general problems or concerns of the service users and/or carers? Who specifically defines the problems or concerns? How do you know how to assist the service users and carers in answering or addressing these problems or concerns?

### Step 1: Formulate a question to answer practice needs

The first step in the EIP process is to identify what needs to be answered, understood or addressed in order to inform practice decisions and to alleviate or reduce the service user's or carer's identified problem(s). As a social worker, you should first collaborate with the service user or carer to specify the problem as perceived by her or him, identify any contributing factors to the problem, and the aspects of the problem that should be prioritized (Jaynes 2014). The problem should be as specific as possible and measurable – for example, an immeasurable problem of 'lack of health and well-being' versus a more measurable problem of 'losing weight due to not eating'.

Additionally, the questions posed in relation to the identifying problem should be well-structured and answerable, and should fill knowledge gaps within your practice. Monette et al. (2010) acknowledge that not all questions may be answerable – for example, questions that pertain to values or existential questions, such as 'What's the meaning of life?', are not conducive to the EIP process as they are subjective and not supported by empirical evidence. Questions more favourable to the EIP process will have specific relevance to the practice situation along the different stages of social work practice. For example, questions most useful to the EIP process are (Rubin 2008: 43):

- What intervention, programme, or policy has the best effects?
- What factors best predict desirable or undesirable consequences?
- What is it like to have had my client's experiences?
- What assessment tool should be used?

Additionally, McNeece and Thyer (2004: 13) propose that questions more appropriate for the EIP process will contain a verb and information specific to the service user's or carer's situation:

1. A question with a verb, as in:
   a. What has been shown to help. . .? or
   b. What individual-level interventions have worked. . .? or

  c. What group work interventions improve. . .? or
  d. What community-based interventions reduce. . .? or
  e. What policies assist or harm. . .? and

2. A question including some aspect of the service user's or carer's problem or condition, as in:
  a. What individual-level interventions reduce the risk of teenage pregnancy? or
  b. What group work interventions are the most successful in getting clients to stop misusing alcohol? or
  c. How can schools reduce student absenteeism? or
  d. How can communities foster integration of older adults into the community?

In some situations, social workers may have several predetermined interventions from which to choose in the work with service users or carers at a specific agency. For example, a social worker may work in a drug and alcohol treatment centre, which is equipped to provide motivational interviewing and cognitive behavioural group therapy, and the social worker's practice-research question may relate to which intervention would be more effective for a specific service user or carer. Rubin and Babbie (2016) suggest using the acronym CIAO to help in developing questions when a choice of two or more interventions are specified in advance of the work with the service user or carer. CIAO stands for:

- **C**lient characteristics.
- **I**ntervention being considered.
- **A**lternative intervention (if any).
- **O**utcome (Rubin and Babbie 2016: 28).

Based on our example above, we may write our practice-research question as follows:

- **C**: If a 45-year-old white British male who has been ordered by a court to attend a drug and alcohol programme
- **I**: receives cognitive behavioural group therapy
- **A**: or motivational interviewing and individual counselling
- **O**: which is more likely to result in successful completion of the programme?

We want to acknowledge some potential difficulties to engaging in this step of the EIP process. First, we identified numerous individual and organizational factors in Chapter 5 that can serve as barriers to engaging in EIP. In particular, we acknowledged how the organizational climate is critical to helping or hindering engagement with the EIP process. While some organizations may provide freedom to social workers to explore and implement interventions, others may limit interventions to one or a few, based on the values and ethos of the agency or what has been specified through a funding source or through policy and legislation. Therefore, as a social worker, you need to be cognizant of the fact that the extent to which you can formulate a practice-research question may be limited by your organization and the services they are willing to provide. Jaynes (2014: 229) suggests that social workers 'match their question formulation within existing narrative structure, aligned with prevailing culture, and operationalized very similarly to what is in effect at the particular practice setting at hand'. Although this may limit your creativity as a social worker and your ability to fully engage in the EIP process, Jaynes (2014: 229) argues that 'agencies are more likely to move ahead with EIP if the operationalization of variables and the nature of the questions it addresses fit within the agencies' modus operandi'.

Second, although your work with service users or carers should be as collaborative as possible, including problem identification and the formulation of the practice-research question, we need to acknowledge that there are situations in which service users are mandated to receive social work interventions, and they may not acknowledge there is a problem to address, or may disagree with the identified problem. Additionally, the problem may be identified externally (e.g. court mandated) and there is no flexibility for you to modify the identified problem. For example, Stephen is mandated to attend the alcohol and drug centre, yet he does not see that he has a problem with using alcohol. In situations similar to this, the problem can be modified to generate a practice-research question to initiate the EIP process, such as asking what interventions are more effective when service users are mandated to receive services. Yet, at other times, service users such as Stephen may disagree that there is a problem at all, and may refuse to engage in the work together. Under such circumstances you may first need to formulate a question around effective approaches to engagement before moving on to interventions to address the identified problem. Ideally, you should leave a copy of your agreed question with your service user or carer so that they know exactly what you are working on together.

---

### Activity 6.1

**Step 1: Formulate a question to answer practice needs**

Based on your current or recent professional or practice placement, select a service user or carer (or family, or community) with whom you are working/ have worked and consider the following:

- Specify the problem for social work intervention.
- Formulate a question to answer practice needs.
- To what extent is/was the service user or carer in agreement with the problem and focus of work together?

---

*Step 2: Search for the evidence to answer the question*

After you have identified the problem and formulated a practice-research question, the next step is for you to search for information and the 'best available evidence' to answer the question. This could be through primary research using professional journals that present research findings and information directly relevant to social work practice. For example, *Journal of the Society for Social Work and Research, Research on Social Work Practice, Journal of Evidence-Informed Social Work, Adoption & Fostering* (sponsored by CoramBAAF http://corambaaf.org.uk), and *British Journal of Social Work* (sponsored by the British Association of Social Workers https://www.basw.co.uk). In this case, you would search through the journals – often using databases such as social care online or Scopus that enable you to search using key words or phrases – to find information that is relevant to the practice situation.

Yet we identified in Chapter 5 that engaging in EIP can be difficult for social workers if they do not have time dedicated to engage in the process and if they do not have information technology (IT) to access professional research and literature databases – which often requires paid subscriptions. Assuming social workers have access to the internet, we still assume that they have little time to conduct a thorough literature review that requires an exhaustive search of the literature, an assessment of the information collected, and a synthesis of the information into a coherent answer to the practice-research question. In this case, we suggest that you engage in secondary research by accessing databases and sources of information where the literature has already been assessed, critiqued, and synthesized, with the resulting information being presented in a way that is easy to access, read, and apply to social work practice situations. Such sources of information are often called systematic reviews or meta-analyses.

A *systematic review* reports 'comprehensive searches for unpublished as well as published studies that address a particular research question' (Rubin and Babbie 2016: 29), and a *meta-analysis* 'is a type of systematic review that pools the statistical results across studies of particular interventions and generates conclusions about what interventions have the strongest impacts on [service] outcome' (Rubin and Babbie 2016: 30). The most notable, internationally recognized sources of systematic reviews are the Cochrane Collaboration (http://www.cochrane.org) and the Campbell Collaboration (https://www.campbellcollaboration.org). The Cochrane Collaboration publishes systemic reviews of topics related to healthcare – for example, child health, mental health, pregnancy and childbirth, and tobacco, drugs and alcohol. The Campbell Collaboration publishes systemic reviews on topics related to social welfare, education, and criminal justice – for example, the effectiveness of parenting programmes, or therapeutic approaches for children and youth. Both organizations provide information that is free to the public. Additional databases that offer synthesized information are the Social Care Institute for Excellence (SCIE) (http://www.scie.org.uk), which provides information and knowledge on practice approaches specific to social care services and the effectiveness of different approaches, and the National Institute for Health and Care Excellence (NICE) (https://www.nice.org.uk), which provides evidence-based guidelines specific to health and social care services. Table 6.1 provides a list of useful websites to search for evidence. In Chapter 7, we explore in more detail how to conduct a literature search, how to access information, and how to critically appraise the evidence.

**Table 6.1** Useful websites to search for evidence

- Cochrane Collaboration: http://www.cochrane.org
- Campbell Collaboration: https://www.campbellcollaboration.org
- Critical Appraisal Skills Programme (CASP): http://www.casp-uk.net
- Database of Abstracts of Reviews of Effects (DARE): http://www.crd.york.ac.uk/CRDWeb/
- National Institute for Health and Care Excellence (NICE): https://www.nice.org.uk
- NHS Choices: http://www.nhs.uk/pages/home.aspx
- NIHR School for Social Care Research: http://www.lse.ac.uk/LSEHealthAndSocialCare/aboutUs/NIHRSSCR/home.aspx
- PubMed Health: https://www.ncbi.nlm.nih.gov/pubmedhealth/
- Research in Practice: https://www.rip.org.uk
- Social Care Institute for Excellence (SCIE): https://www.scie.org.uk
- Trip Database: https://www.tripdatabase.com

**Activity 6.2**

**Step 2: Search for the evidence to answer the question**

Based on your practice-research question developed in Activity 6.1, go to either the Cochrane Collaboration website (http://www.cochrane.org/evidence) or the Campbell Collaboration website (https://www.campbell-collaboration.org/library.html) and enter a search term that pertains to your question. For example, if you are interested in interventions related to individuals diagnosed with a mental illness and who use substances, type in 'mental illness substance misuse' in the search field. Identify at least one useful review that can assist in answering your practice-research question.

We also want to acknowledge that in some cases you may find that no, or very limited, evidence exists to assist you in answering your practice-research question. In such situations, you still need to determine an intervention or course of action to address the identified problem. This predicament may lead you to 'experiment' with a new intervention, either through individual work or with your colleagues who are working with similar practice-research problems. It is important to seek supervision in such situations, as well as to evaluate the extent to which the intervention is working from your perspective and the service user's or carer's perspective. Your, and the service user's or carer's experience in implementing and receiving the intervention should be recorded and reported back to your colleagues in order for this 'research' to influence future practice and future research to further substantiate the effectiveness of the intervention. Chapter 8 discusses in more detail ways in which to implement interventions and evaluate their effectiveness.

### Step 3: Critically appraise the evidence

Once you have identified and gathered evidence to answer your practice-research question, you now must begin to assess and critically appraise the quality of the research. When conducting primary research – gathering information and research reports from journal articles, policy reports, and government documents – you will need to utilize your knowledge of research methods and analytical skills in order to assess the quality of the quantitative, qualitative, and mixed-methods studies in terms of the overall research designs, sampling methods, approach to data analysis, and the conclusions drawn from the findings. We provide more information on specific aspects and approaches to assessing primary research in Chapter 7.

As stated under Step 2 above, and in Table 6.1, there are useful websites from organizations that assess primary research sources for you and present them through systematic reviews or meta-analysis reports. The intention of the systematic reviews is that the work has already been completed for you in terms of analysing the existing research on a specific topic in terms of quality and the extent to which the findings can be generalized to a broader population. Yet, as Rubin and Babbie (2016) point out, you still need to be cognizant that there can also be flaws in systematic reviews and meta-analyses and, therefore, you must be able to critically appraise these sources.

## Activity 6.3

### Step 3: Critically appraise the evidence

Consider the review that you selected from Activity 6.2 and answer the following questions:

- Were there any potential or reported conflicts of interest among the authors, or personal or professional agendas that could have influenced the findings?
- What type of studies were used in the review, and do you find these to be inclusive or exclusive in terms of the available evidence to be included?
- To what extent does the review critique the methodology of the included studies?
- What is your overall assessment of the review?

### Step 4: Determine which evidence-based intervention is most appropriate

Once you have identified and critically appraised the quality of the 'best available evidence', you must now determine the extent to which the interventions are appropriate and can be applied to the service user or carer with whom you are working. We want to reiterate that this step involves a consideration of the three elements of the EIP process – best available evidence; your knowledge and experience as a social worker; and the service user's or carer's values and wishes.

In terms of the best available evidence obtained and critically assessed in Steps 2 and 3, the intervention that you choose to apply should be applicable to the service user's or carer's situation and circumstances. For the social worker, this step involves making 'a judgement regarding what is applicable to her particular case, what is irrelevant or not, how the different interventions implied by the evidence could be integrated and what relative weight should be assigned to each of them in the understanding and [intervening with a service user/carer]' (Nevo and Slonim-Nevo 2011: 1190). Your search of the 'best available evidence' might have resulted in studies that report the effectiveness of interventions with service users or carers that are similar, but do not hold exactly the same characteristics as your service user or carer. For example, the research was conducted with white British males and females, yet you are working with a service user who is a Somali refugee. In this case, you will need to use your professional knowledge and experience, along with the service user's values and wishes, to determine if the intervention should be applied in this situation. If, when weighing these three elements, you and the service user decide the intervention is the most appropriate to address the identified problem, then you proceed to Steps 5 and 6; if the intervention is found to be ineffective in your work (in Step 6), then you stop the intervention and try something else (revisit Steps 2 and 3).

Rubin and Babbie (2016) provide several factors to consider when engaging in this step of the EIP process:

1. *The quality of the evidence that you appraised in Step 3.* There is no magic number of studies that have to be considered. Instead, it is more important to evaluate the quality of the studies that are available and determine 'which intervention has the best evidence for the time being' (p. 32).
2. *The applicability of the evidence to your specific servicer user or carer.* As with number 1 above, the studies should be considered in terms of how they can apply to the service user or carer with whom you are working. As with our example of the Somali refugee above, a highly rigorous and executed study conducted with white British males may be less appropriate to consider in our work when compared to several less well-executed studies with refugee populations.
3. *There is no evidence directly relevant to your service user or carer or their situation.* When there is no evidence directly relevant to your service user or carer, or their situation, the best course of action may be to apply an intervention that is indirectly relevant. The application can be on a trial basis – in agreement with the service user or carer – and evaluated (as in Step 6).
4. *The values and wishes of the service user or carer.* The selection of the intervention should be decided in collaboration with the service user or carer. Although you do not need to provide full details of how you have arrived at the chosen intervention, what would be helpful to the service user or carer is informing her or him about the 'intervention and the evidence about its potential effectiveness and any possible undesirable side effects, and obtaining informed consent to participate in the intervention' (p. 33).

Finally, this step also involves your knowledge and experience of what you have found to be effective in your past work with service users and carers who are similar. Although you do not rely solely on your 'practice wisdom', you do need to consider this as one of the factors in deciding which intervention to implement. The more experience you gain as a social worker, the more knowledge you will have regarding the extent to which particular interventions are effective with your service user and carer base.

### Step 4: Determine which evidence-based intervention is most appropriate

Determine the intervention that you would like to employ with your service user or carer based on the review of the evidence in Activity 6.3, along with your knowledge and experience as a professional or student social worker, and your service user's or carer's values, wishes, and circumstances. Explain your rationale for choice of intervention.

### Step 5: Apply the evidence-based intervention

Once you have selected the intervention most appropriate for the service user or carer, you can now move to applying the intervention to the practice situation. This step will involve you assessing the extent to which you have the knowledge and skills to implement the intervention while considering any service user or carer characteristics that might affect how the intervention is received and perceived (Jaynes 2014). You may need to seek out training on how to effectively and skilfully execute the intervention, which could be through continuing professional development (CPD) workshops, classes at a local college or university, and/or training and supervision from a skilled colleague. Rubin and Babbie (2016: 34) argue that 'if you are unable to obtain sufficient training or supervision, you should try to refer the client to other practitioners who have the requisite training and experience in the intervention'. To knowingly implement an intervention you do not have the skills to undertake is to act unethically (refer back to Chapter 3).

Implementing the intervention also requires you to combine the *science* from the 'best available evidence' with your knowledge and skills, and the service user's or carer's specific circumstances and personal traits, which involves the *art* of skilfully integrating these three aspects together. The intervention is only one factor in the work together, and you must draw on your assessment and communication skills to determine exactly how you will implement the intervention, at what speed, and to what extent you may need to modify or add additional interventions to the work with the service user or carer. Shlonsky and Stern (2007: 607–8) report on this skilful, yet complicated activity:

> It takes a great deal of clinical skill to successfully integrate current best evidence with [service user and/or carer] preferences/actions, clinical state/circumstances, and the practice context. Indeed, this coming together is the hardest part of the endeavour and is also the one we know the least about. We must be honest about our current limitations. [Evidence-informed practice] is an emerging approach, and it will take considerable time and effort to make it work.

**Reflection point 6.2**

### Assessing your ability to implement the intervention

Assess the extent to which you have the necessary knowledge and skills to implement the intervention you chose in Activity 6.4. If you believe you need training or supervision in applying this intervention, conduct a web search on where you could receive such training. What is the time commitment and cost for such training? What are the barriers and facilitators to you implementing this intervention in your practice?

This step also involves developing an intervention plan with the service user or carer. The care plan should consist of the identified problem, the choice of intervention, and the goals of the work together. The intervention goals should be specified in a manner that is measurable to enable you and the service user or carer to assess the effectiveness of the intervention and work together (in Step 6). The acronym SMART is often used to assist social workers in defining goals that are: **S**pecific, **M**easurable, **A**ttainable, **R**ealistic, and **T**imely. The Social Care Institute for Excellence (SCIE) (2013) provide the following guidance for developing SMART goals:

- *Specific* – Goals are easier to accomplish when they are specific to the problem or goal, versus general and unfocused. For example, 'rejoin my old lunch club and attend twice a week.'
- *Measurable* – The goals should have concrete criteria for measuring their progress. For example, did the individual rejoin the lunch club (yes or no), and how many times did she attend a week?
- *Attainable* – Individuals are more likely to reach goals that they find personally meaningful to them. Therefore, the goals should be developed as collaboratively as possible with the service user or carer. For example, 'Be able to cook Sunday lunch for my family again.'
- *Realistic* – The goals should be realistic in that the service user or carer should be willing and able to work towards the goal.
- *Timely* – The goals should have a clear time frame for completion. For example, 'By the end of the week I will be able to button my own cardigan.'

**Activity 6.5**

### Step 5: Apply the evidence-based intervention

Based on your responses and outputs from Activities 6.1–6.4, develop a plan on how you will implement the intervention in your practice. Devise a care plan identifying the problem and develop 2–5 SMART goals for the work together.

### Step 6: Evaluate the effectiveness and provide feedback

The final step in the EIP process involves evaluating the effectiveness of the intervention implemented in Step 5, receiving feedback from the service user and/or carer, and communicating the findings to your colleagues and other stakeholders. Nevo and Slonim-Nevo (2011: 1193) state that this is one of the most important steps in the EIP process as:

> evaluation is needed for accountability, increased efficiency, determining the direction of the intervention, engaging the [service user or carer] in the [intervention] process and providing data about [service users or carers] and common problems to policy decision makers.

Your evaluation should focus on the extent to which the goals established in Step 5 are being achieved. This could be through formal measures, such as standardized scales (e.g. Beck's depression inventory; Rosenberg's self-esteem scale), data collected from the agency (e.g. number of hours of care received in a week; drug test analysis results; attendance at a parenting programme), or self-reports of service users or carers (e.g. number of alcoholic drinks consumed in a week; self-report on feelings or health and well-being). It is important for you to involve the service user and/or carer in this process in order for them to see and track their progress and for them to provide you with feedback about what they see as working, not working, and what they would like to see happen in the future. If your evaluation and feedback indicates the intervention is not effective, then you should revisit Steps 2 and 3 to determine a new intervention.

The findings from your evaluation with service users and carers should also be relayed to your colleagues and other stakeholders through informal communication or, more formally, through presentations at team meetings, local network meetings, or national conferences. This information is useful to colleagues and stakeholders in that they can learn from your experience of what is effective and what is not, and use this information to inform their practice and future practice or policy decisions. Chapter 8 provides more details on the different forms of evaluation that you can implement in your practice.

## Activity 6.6

### Step 6: Evaluate the effectiveness and provide feedback

Based on the goals you developed in Activity 6.5, devise an evaluation plan and consider the following:

1. How you will measure whether progress is being made on the goals?
2. How you will receive feedback from the service user and/or carer?
3. How you will use your evaluation measures and/or methods to provide feedback to the service user and/or carer?
4. How you will relay your findings to your colleagues?

## Summary

Through this chapter we presented the six steps of the EIP process. Although presented in sequential order, from Step 1 to Step 6, the EIP process should be implemented in a more flexible and creative way that often involves moving back and forth between the steps. The steps involve identifying a practice-research question; searching the literature and published research to answer the question; critically assessing the information ('best available evidence') you've obtained in terms of quality; assessing the appropriateness of the best available evidence for your particular practice situation and service user or carer; implementing the intervention, while designing goals; and evaluating the accomplishment and movement towards achieving the goals to determine the effectiveness of the intervention and work together. Chapters 7 and 8 provide additional information and skills on how to critically assess the 'best available evidence', and how to implement EIP in your practice.

### Key points

- The EIP process consists of six steps that begin with a formulation of an answerable question and end with an evaluation of the intervention and work with the service user and/or carer.
- Although the six steps are presented in sequential order, you will need to be flexible and creative in engaging in the EIP process in order to consider and address changing goals, experiences, and preferences of the service user and/or carer.
- You should construct your practice-research question based on the service user's and/or carer's definition of the identified problem as much as possible.
- There are useful and free websites that house systematic reviews and meta-analyses for you to access when searching for 'best available evidence' to answer your practice-research question.
- All sources of 'evidence' should be critically assessed for the quality of the research – this includes systematic reviews and meta-analyses.
- Choice of intervention should be based on the 'best available evidence', as well as your professional knowledge and experiences and the service user's or carer's values, wishes, and circumstances.
- Your work should continually be evaluated against the SMART goals you develop with the service user or carer. You should change your intervention when it is found to be ineffective.

## Further resources

Mullen, E.J., Bledsoe, S.E. and Bellamy, J.L. (2008) Implementing evidence-based social work practice, *Research on Social Work Practice*, 18: 325–38.

Nevo, I. and Slonim-Nevo, S. (2011) The myth of evidence-based practice: towards evidence-informed practice, *British Journal of Social Work*, 41: 1176–97.

Social Work Policy Institute (2010) *Evidence-Based Practice*. Available at: http://www.social-workpolicy.org/research/evidence-based-practice-2.html [Accessed 6 December 2016].

# 7 Critically appraising the evidence

**Chapter overview**

By the end of this chapter you should have an understanding of:

- The different types of literature reviews, and how to conduct a literature review.
- The 'hierarchy of evidence' in assessing which evidence is the best.
- How to critically appraise research from both a quantitative and qualitative perspective.

## Introduction

In Chapter 6, we presented and discussed the six steps of the evidence-informed practice (EIP) process, which ranged from identifying a practice-research question to evaluating and obtaining feedback on the implementation of an intervention with the service user or carer. Through this chapter, we provide additional information and skills needed to implement Step 2 and Step 3 of the EIP process. Step 2 involves searching for the evidence to answer the practice-research question, and Step 3 involves critically appraising the evidence. We will begin with a presentation of the different types of literature reviews, and then discuss how to conduct a literature review. We then present the 'hierarchy' of best available evidence and discuss and provide tools on how to critically appraise the evidence, particularly when the research involves quantitative and qualitative research methodology.

## Conducting a literature review to search for evidence

Answers to practice-research questions are often found in the existing literature where researchers, practitioners, theorists and/or political analysts have researched or explored topics related to your practice-research question and report what is known, not known, and what needs to be explored further in the future. The literature can be presented in numerous forms, such as peer-reviewed papers, books, research monographs, policy documents, best practice guidance documents, and government legislation. Social work practitioners have varying degrees of access to these different sources of information – as was discussed in

Chapter 5 – which is often dependent on whether social workers have internet access in which to be able to conduct a review of the literature through search engines and online databases.

There are two main ways in which to search for answers (or search for evidence) to practice-research questions. The first is the *bottom-up approach* to conducting a literature review, where you would search through the literature collecting any and all information that is relevant to your practice-research question and topic. Once the information is collected, you would then read each piece of information and critically assess the quality and applicability of the information to your specific practice situation. Based on your assessment of the information collected, you would then decide the best course of action in your practice (Rubin and Babbie 2016). The second is the *top-down approach*, which involves reading already completed reviews of the literature, such as systematic reviews, scoping reviews, books, and meta-analyses. The top-down approach involves you relying on others to conduct a review of the literature and synthesize the material in a useful way.

There are advantages and disadvantages to both the bottom-up and top-down approaches to a literature review. The top-down approach saves you time in conducting a search and critically appraising the literature, yet requires you to trust the author of the literature review in terms of having completed a thorough review, and accurately assessing the material. It also assumes nothing of any relevance to your practice question has been published since the literature review was completed. The bottom-up approach enables you to sift through the literature first-hand, where you can assess the quality of the material and the extent to which the information is applicable to your practice situation. Yet a thorough review of the literature requires a great amount of time and skill in both searching and critiquing the material. Rubin and Babbie (2016) argue for a combination of the bottom-up and top-down approaches. In particular, you should not rely on one specific top-down piece, but rather explore and critique several top-down pieces as they may have contradictory information based on bias of the author or differences in the authors' critical appraisal skills. In critiquing the top-down sources, you should ask the following questions (Rubin and Babbie 2016: 31):

- Did the authors have a vested interest in the particular practice approach?
- What were the evidentiary standards used in the appraisal of the studies?
- Did the studies have to meet certain minimal methodological criteria to quality for inclusion in the review?
- What methodological criteria were used to distinguish studies offering the best evidence from those offering weaker evidence?

Additionally, you can conduct a bottom-up search to complement the material you review from the top-down sources. Bottom-up searches can include conducting traditional or normative literature reviews, scoping reviews, or systematic reviews.

### *Traditional literature reviews*

A traditional literature review involves searching sources of information that can provide answers to your practice-research question. You can easily conduct a literature review with technology and access to the internet through the use of search engines, such as Google and Google Scholar. If you have access to a library, then you may use scholarly databases such as Academic Search Complete, Applied Social Sciences Index, Social Care Online, Scopus, or Social Sciences Citation Index. The steps in a literature review include the following:

1. Define your research question or the general topic of your review.
2. Determine the search engines you will use to conduct the review.
3. Establish key words or phrases related to your research question or topic to input into the search engines.
4. Conduct your search.
5. Review the materials to determine their relevance to the research question or topic.

For example, we are social workers working in adult social care and are interested in determining the appropriateness of reablement for older adults who reside in their own home. We begin our literature review by defining the research question or topic for review, which is as follows: 'Is reablement an effective intervention for older adults who reside in their own home?' We next need to determine the search engine and/or databases we will use to conduct the review, which we specify as Google and Google Scholar because those are the search engines and databases to which we have access. We then specify the search terms of phrases we will input into the search engine that best depict our research topic. We have chosen the following: 'reablement older adults'; 'reablement older adults effectiveness'; and 'reablement older adults home'. We input the phrases one at a time into Google and into Google Scholar. We then review the results from the search in terms of their relevance to the research topic.

The first result from our search of 'reablement older adults' in Google is the following:

> Tuntland, H., Aaslund, M.K., Espehaug, B., et al. (2015) Reablement in community-dwelling older adults: a randomized control trial, *BMC Geriatrics*, 15: 145.

This journal article reports the findings from a randomized control trial where 31 older adults with functional decline were assigned to receive the reablement service (i.e. intervention group) which assists in enabling older adults to participate in activities of daily living that they perceive as difficult. Thirty older adults with functional decline were assigned to receive services as usual (i.e. the control group), which consisted of personal or practical assistance, safety alarms, meals on wheels, or assistive technology. Older adults in both groups were assessed at the beginning of the service (i.e. baseline/pre-test), and again at three and nine months (i.e. post-test) in terms of their self-perceived activity performance, satisfaction with performance, physical capacity, and health-related quality of life. The findings revealed that older adults in the 10-week reablement programme had better activity performance and satisfaction with performance when compared with the control group, yet there were no differences between the intervention and control group on physical capacity and health-related qualify of life.

As part of the literature review, you would sift through the results from your search, read the relevant pieces of information, and conclude with an answer to your research question based on your analysis of the information. From the journal article above, we may conclude that the reablement programme is an effective intervention with older adults who reside in their own home. Yet this is only one piece of information conducted with 61 older adults in Norway. We will discuss in more detail, below, skills in determining the credibility and applicability of the information and in determining which types of information (e.g. primary quantitative, qualitative, or mixed-methods research; systematic reviews; personal accounts; best practice guidelines) are more credible and appropriate to include and assess in your literature review.

### Activity 7.1

**Conducting a literature review**

Think about your current or past professional or practice placement experience and develop a practice-research question or topic to explore. Using Google or Google Scholar, conduct a literature search in order to answer this question. Provide a summary of findings.

*Scoping reviews*

Scoping reviews are more sophisticated literature reviews consisting of a specific methodological approach to the review. A scoping review is defined as 'a form of knowledge synthesis that addresses an exploratory research question aimed at mapping key concepts, types of evidence, and gaps in research related to a defined area or field by systematically searching, selecting, and synthesizing existing knowledge' (Colquhoun et al. 2014: 1292–4). Scoping reviews generally cover broad questions to explore what has been done, or what is known in the field. The methodological approach to a scoping review consists of the following six steps, as outlined by Colquhoun et al. (2014: 1293–4), which has been adapted from the initial framework for conducting scoping reviews by Arksey and O'Malley (2005) and Levac et al. (2010):

1. *Identify the research question* – Although scoping review questions can be quite broad, they should be clearly written to specify the scope of the inquiry, including the concept, target population, and health and/or social care outcomes of interest, and the overall purpose. For example, a scoping review by Sims and Cabrita Gulyurtlu (2014) titled, 'A scoping review of personalisation in the UK: approaches to social work and people with learning disabilities', specified the aim of the review as follows: 'To find out what was known from the existing literature about the use of personalisation by people with learning disabilities and the role of social workers to support it' (p. 15). The specific research questions included the following: 'What has been the impact of

personalisation on service users' lives?'; and 'What has been the role of social workers in this process?' (p. 16).

2. *Identify relevant studies* – This stage involves developing the plan for where to search (e.g. electronic databases, references lists, hand searching of key journals, material produced by professional organizations, and/or conference proceedings), which search terms to use, the parameters around the publication date of materials, and whether any materials will be considered that are published in different languages. Such decisions should also be made against the feasibility of conducting the review, such as time, resources, and expertise of the reviewers. For example, in Sims and Cabrita Gulyurtlu's (2014) review of personalization in the UK, they restricted the publication dates to be between 1996 and 2011, which was due to the official date of the start of direct payments after the Direct Payments Act of 1996. Additionally, they specified their search terms, which included the following: learning disabilities; learning difficulties; intellectual disabilities; social work; personalization; personal budgets; individual budgets; personalized; direct payments; individualized; person-centred; and self-directed support. Finally, they specified their search engines (e.g. EBSCO; PsyINFO; MEDLINE; Web of knowledge), and the other journals and websites they reviewed (e.g. *British Journal of Social Work*; *British Journal of Learning Disabilities*; *Community Care Online*).

3. *Determine the inclusion and exclusion criteria for the studies* – This stage involves reviewing the literature and determining the specific inclusion and exclusion criteria. Although some decisions have already been made in stage 2, other inclusion and exclusion criteria may emerge while reviewing the literature. For example, Sims and Cabrita Gulyurtlu's (2014) review of personalization in the UK included the following: 'the inclusion criteria included UK-based studies, social work, learning disability and synonyms only. The exclusion criteria excluded non-UK studies, non-social work studies including health, IT, education and nursing, people with disabilities, including physical disabilities, and older people' (p. 15).

4. *Chart the data or findings* – This stage involves reading, reviewing and charting the data or findings from the literature. What exactly is recorded on the chart is to be determined by the reviewers and should be directly related to the research questions.

5. *Collect, summarize, and report the results* – This stage involves reporting on the main themes or findings from the review. This should involve the findings in relation to the study's purpose and aim, as well as implications for practice, policy, and future research. Sims and Cabrita Gulyurtlu's (2014) review of personalization in the UK found the limited research on the impact of personalization on the lives of people with learning disabilities centred around two main themes: choice and control; and autonomy and independence (p. 17). And the following three themes emerged in regard to the role of social workers in this process: the impact of personalization on social work and social workers; the potential opportunities personalization represents for changing social work practice; and the critiques and dilemmas impacting on social work practice (p. 18).

6. *Seek consultation* – This final stage is considered optional and involves seeking consultation from stakeholders who can suggest additional references and provide additional insights beyond what was found in the review of the literature. The consultation can provide opportunities for knowledge transfer and exchange of ideas between researchers, practitioners, stakeholders and service users and carers.

---

**Activity 7.2**

### Search for a scoping review

Search for a scoping review that addresses your practice-research question or topic you chose to explore in Activity 7.1. For example, if you explored the topic 'children who witness domestic violence', then input 'scoping review children who witness domestic violence' into Google or Google Scholar. Assess the quality of the scoping review against the six steps as depicted by Colquhoun et al. (2014).

---

### Systematic reviews

A systematic review is an even more sophisticated review of the literature when compared to scoping reviews. As was discussed in detail in Chapter 6, a systematic review involves 'comprehensive searches for unpublished as well as published studies that address a particular research question' (Rubin and Babbie 2016: 29). Scoping reviews are often used to inform future systematic reviews. Whereas both scoping and systematic reviews conduct a thorough review of the literature to answer practice-research questions, there are differences between the two. Table 7.1 highlights the differences between scoping and systematic reviews.

A systematic review aims to explore all the existing literature that meets the inclusion criteria and tends to have a more narrow focus when compared with a scoping review. The review includes a critical analysis of the information and a synthesis of the data (Armstrong et al. 2011). Systematic reviews consist of the following key elements:

a clearly stated set of objectives with predefined eligibility criteria for studies; an explicit, reproducible methodology;
a systematic search that attempts to identify all studies that would meet the eligibility criteria;
an assessment of the validity of the findings of the included studies, and for example through the assessment of risk of bias;
a systematic presentation, and synthesis, of the characteristics and findings of the included studies. (Higgins and Green 2011: 1.2.2).

The Cochrane Collaboration (for healthcare research – www.cochrane.org) and the Campbell Collaboration (for social welfare, education, and criminal justice

**Table 7.1** Differences between scoping and systematic reviews

| Systematic review | Scoping review |
| --- | --- |
| * Focused research question with narrow parameters. | * Research question(s) often broad. |
| * Inclusion/exclusion usually defined at the outset. | * Inclusion/exclusion can be developed post hoc. |
| * Quality filters often applied. | * Quality not an initial priority. |
| * Detailed data extraction. | * May or may not involve data extraction. |
| * Quantitative synthesis often performed. | * Synthesis more qualitative and typically not quantitative. |
| * Formally assesses the quality of studies and generates a conclusion relating to the focused research question. | * Used to identify parameters and gaps in a body of literature. |

*From: R. Armstrong, B.J. Hall, J. Doyle et al. (2011) Cochrane update: 'Scoping the scope' of a Cochrane review, *Journal of Public Health*, 33(1): 147–50.

research – www.campbellcollaboration.org) publish guidelines and protocol outlines for conducting systematic reviews.

Conducting a systematic review is time-consuming, often taking well over a year to complete. The results provide valuable information that is free to access if registered and published with the Cochrane or Campbell collaborations. The reviews detail the methodology for the review of the literature and the main findings presented in both an original research article and in a plain language summary. Text box 7.1 provides an example of the authors' conclusions of a systematic review of research that explores whether providing tobacco cessation interventions targeted to smokers receiving services and recovery for alcohol and other drug dependencies increases tobacco abstinence.

---

### Text box 7.1: Example of a Cochrane review: authors' conclusions

The studies included in this review suggest that providing tobacco cessation interventions targeted to smokers in treatment and recovery for alcohol and other drug dependencies increases tobacco abstinence. There was no evidence that providing interventions for tobacco cessation affected abstinence from alcohol and other drugs. The association between tobacco cessation interventions and tobacco abstinence was consistent for both pharmacotherapy and combined counselling and pharmacotherapy, for participants both in treatment and in recovery, and for people with alcohol dependency or other drug dependency. The evidence for the interventions was low quality due primarily to incomplete reporting of the risks of bias and clinical heterogeneity in the nature of treatment. Certain results were sensitive to the length of follow-up or the type of pharmacotherapy, suggesting that further research is warranted regarding whether tobacco cessation interventions are associated with tobacco abstinence for people in recovery, and the outcomes associated with NRT versus non-NRT or combined pharmacotherapy. Overall, the results suggest that tobacco cessation interventions incorporating pharmacotherapy should be incorporated into clinical practice to reduce tobacco addiction among people in treatment for, or recovery from, alcohol and other drug dependence.

*From: D. Apollonio, R. Philipps and L. Bero (2016) *Interventions for Tobacco Use Cessation in People in Treatment for or Recovery from Substance Use Disorders (Review)*. Available at: http://onlinelibrary.wiley.com/doi/10.1002/14651858.CD010274.pub2/pdf/abstract [Accessed 2 January 2017].

We have discussed both scoping and systematic reviews as a bottom-up approach to conducting a literature review where the reviewer gathers all relevant information and literature, critically assesses the information, and synthesizes it into the main findings and summary form. Yet, as we mentioned earlier in this chapter, completed traditional literature reviews, scoping reviews, and systematic reviews can also serve as top-down sources of information where you access the completed reviews to help in answering your practice-research question, rather than complete a review from scratch. You will need to assess any completed review in terms of the quality, bias, and applicability of the information to your practice situation. Whether completing literature reviews on your own, or relying on the reviews of others, you must be able to assess the quality of the evidence and determine which evidence is the best evidence.

## What kind of evidence is the best evidence?

The steps of the evidence-informed practice (EIP) process, as discussed in Chapter 6, involve you, as the social worker, in reviewing the 'best available evidence' to answer your practice-research question. But what constitutes 'best' available evidence? Within the traditional evidence-based practice model, there is a 'hierarchy of evidence', which assumes that all forms of evidence are not equivalent. Rather, some forms of evidence produced through more 'rigorous' research methods are more highly regarded than others, and, thus, are seen to provide more credible answers to practice-research questions. The hierarchy of evidence is presented below, with the most credible and reliable sources of evidence at the top, and the least credible and reliable at the bottom (McNeece and Thyer 2004; Pooler 2012):

- Systematic reviews/meta-analyses.
- Randomized control trials (RCTs).
- Quasi-experimental studies.
- Case-control and cohort studies.
- Pre-experimental group studies.

- Surveys.
- Qualitative studies.
- Expert opinion.
- Views of colleagues or peers.

Systematic reviews are deemed the most credible sources of evidence as they consist of a rigorous review of all relevant pieces of research – often from randomized control trials – that address a particular research question. More sophisticated systematic reviews incorporate an analysis of the statistical findings across the studies reviewed, called a meta-analysis, which 'pools the statistical results across studies of particular interventions and generates conclusions about what interventions have the strongest impacts on [service] outcome' (Rubin and Babbie 2016: 30). Although the research topics explored through systematic reviews are increasing, there are some areas of social work that have limited research to review and include in a systematic review. For example, we explored the reablement programme with older adults in our discussion above of traditional literature reviews. A systematic review of the literature was conducted, and the results of the effectiveness are inconclusive because there are too few studies to date. Text box 7.2 reports the authors' conclusions on the systematic review.

---

**Text box 7.2: Systematic review of reablement programme: authors' conclusions**

There is considerable uncertainty regarding the effects of reablement as the evidence was of very low quality, according to our GRADE ratings. Therefore, the effectiveness of reablement services cannot be supported or refuted until more robust evidence becomes available. There is an urgent need for high-quality trials across different health and social care systems due to the increasingly high-profile of reablement services in policy and practice in several countries.

*From: A. Cochrane, M. Furlong, S. McGilloway et al. (2016) *Time-limited Home-care Reablement Services for Maintaining and Improving the Functional Independence of Older Adults*. Available at: http://onlinelibrary.wiley.com/doi/10.1002/14651858.CD010825. pub2/abstract [Accessed 3 January 2017].

---

Randomized control trials (RCTs) are studies where service users or carers are randomly assigned to a specific group that receives either: (a) an experimental intervention (i.e. experimental group); (b) services as usual or no intervention (i.e. control group); and/or, in some RCTs, (c) a placebo or a bogus intervention. Well-executed RCTs are able to conclude whether a particular intervention is effective over another intervention or no intervention at all. Random assignment of service users or carers to the intervention or control group limits bias and any naturally occurring differences between service users and carers. RCTs should use valid and reliable measures to test for any differences between the intervention and control groups, both before and after receiving the intervention, and should include a large enough sample size (without client attrition – dropping out, withdrawing from the study) to use inferential statistics with adequate statistical power (McNeece and Thyer 2004). Although RCTs are viewed as the 'gold standard' of research, we want to acknowledge that they are often conducted in restricted (or controlled) environments, which can limit their applicability to real-life social work settings and, at times, fail to take into account the experiences and perspectives of service users or carers for whom the intervention is intended. As Fisher (2016: 502) notes:

> national policy requires more than evidence of effectiveness: we also need to know whether the intervention can be provided in ordinary services (not just under experimental conditions), whether it is acceptable to the people it was designed to assist, and whether it is affordable.

Quasi-experimental research designs are similar to RCTs, the difference being that there is no random assignment of service users or carers to the intervention and control groups. Therefore, there could be naturally occurring differences between the two groups of service users or carers. For example, if service users self-select one type of intervention over another, the two groups may not be similar in terms of demographics or psychosocial factors, which makes it difficult to attribute any changes or differences in the two groups directly to the intervention (McNeece and Thyer 2004). Case-control designs also compare two groups of people who have received different interventions, or have experienced different outcomes from interventions. Yet, in case-control designs, instead of identifying the two different groups and collecting data prospectively, the two groups are identified after having received different interventions, and data are collected retrospectively to explore what past differences might explain the differences in outcomes (Rubin and Babbie 2016). Pre-experimental designs lack a control group, which makes it impossible to directly attribute any changes in service users or carers as a result of receiving an intervention. Such designs may include evaluating any differences in service users or carers from before to after receiving an intervention (pre-test-post-test design), or evaluating service users or carers on particular criteria only after receiving an intervention (post-test only design).

Survey research aims to explore, explain, or describe a phenomenon or experience of a large group of people. Surveys often consist of questionnaires distributed via mail, online, telephone, or face-to-face, which have a number of questions for the respondent to answer. The questions tend to be quantitative, where the researcher is then able to aggregate responses and infer the findings to a larger population with some degree of certainty; yet, as we have mentioned earlier, they can also include qualitative questions to enable respondents to personalize or elaborate their answers. Purely qualitative studies are not often used to test the effectiveness of interventions or outcomes, but are used more to explore service users' or carers' subjective experiences, perspectives, and reactions to a service or intervention, or to examine the process of change (McNeece and Thyer 2004).

Evidence can also come from experts who provide opinions and guidance based on clinical evidence, descriptive studies, or reports from committees, such as the National Institute for Health and Care Excellence (NICE) guidelines, evidence-based local procedures, or care pathways, and from colleagues or peers who have knowledge and expertise in a particular area of practice and whose views are informed by their practice experience, observations, and reflections (Pooler 2012). Best practice guidance documents are one source of information that synthesize research on the effectiveness of different practice approaches, and provide guidelines on how to implement interventions. For example, NICE and SCIE develop best practice guidelines that are based on a thorough review of the best available evidence. The guidelines are completed based on the following process (NICE 2017):

1. Topics chosen – Social care topics are referred from the Department of Health and the Department for Education.
2. Scope produced – The scope addresses why there is a need for the guideline, the areas the guideline will and will not cover, and what it intends to achieve. Stakeholders are consulted during this process.
3. Guidelines developed – The guidelines are developed based on a review of the evidence and literature. A summary of the evidence is prepared, as well as the impact the guidelines will have on costs. The evidence is considered by a committee consisting of practitioners, professionals, care providers, commissioners, and service users and carers.
4. Draft guidelines are sent to stakeholders for consultation – The guidelines are assessed for their impact on equality.
5. Comments are considered and guidelines are revised.
6. Guidelines are signed off and published.
7. Guidelines are updated.

**Activity 7.3**

### NICE guidelines

Visit the NICE website at https://www.nice.org.uk. Click on 'Find NICE guidance' and then click on 'Social care guidelines'. Search for a NICE guidance that relates to your current professional or practice placement experience. Were you aware of this particular guidance? To what extent to do you find the guidance helpful to your practice?

In addition to the sources of evidence listed in the hierarchy of evidence, you may also make use of information from books, which often synthesize research evidence, policy documents and legislation, and detail the powers and duties of social workers within certain practice situations.

Although there is a hierarchy of evidence, you may not always have access to more credible sources of evidence, or such sources of evidence may not exist. If that is the case – for example, if there are no systematic reviews or RCTs on a particular topic, or the topic was not suitable for an RCT, then you would search for evidence from pre-experimental survey or qualitative studies. McNeece and Thyer (2004: 12) provide the following guidance:

> Please note that EBP does NOT mean that one can only make use of systematic reviews or meta-analyses in order to make practice decisions. If these are lacking, EBP suggests that the practitioner then find out what guidance can be obtained from quasi-experimental, cohort studies, or qualitative reports, if these indeed represent the very 'best' outcomes research which is available to inform practice. EBP says that one should rely on the best AVAILABLE evidence, not only on BEST evidence, such as that based on RCTs (because often there is no BEST evidence available).

Finally, the hierarchy of evidence is not without critique. Although we acknowledge that the hierarchy presents the most rigorous types of research as more credible and reliable than other forms of research, we want to point out that a well-executed rigorous study may not always be the most appropriate source of evidence to inform your practice decisions, even when it is available. As we have noted throughout this book, EIP involves not only the best available evidence, but also your knowledge and experience as a social worker and the service user's or carer's wishes, values, and circumstances. As Fisher (2016: 507) argues, within social work we want to take 'a more inclusive approach to what counts as evidence, recognizing that the knowledge of people who use services and of practitioners adds critical elements to the knowledge from research'. Therefore, you must use your critical analysis skills in order to judge the different sources of evidence and determine which is most appropriate for your practice situation.

## Critically appraising the evidence

Once we have searched for the best available evidence to answer our practice-research question, we can then move to the next step in the EIP process of critically appraising the evidence. Your critical appraisal will include determining the validity or credibility of the evidence and its applicability to your practice situation. Pooler (2012: 22) suggests asking the following questions as part of the appraisal:

- Can the evidence or results of the research study be trusted? Have they been formed through an appropriate methodology during the research process?
- What is the evidence telling you and what does it mean?
- Does the research/evidence answer your question?
- Is it all relevant to your clinical practice?

The Critical Appraisal Skills Programme (CASP 2013) further indicates that, where the article or evidence is published, or who the author is, should not determine the quality or trustworthiness of the study. Rather, readers should appraise each piece against the following three criteria (CASP 2013):

1. **Is the study valid?** – You should assess the quality of the research methodology, looking for any bias.

2. **What are the results?** – If you decide the study is valid, then you will assess the study's results. In particular, you are looking for any differences between the intervention (or experimental) group and the control group, the extent of uncertainty in the results, expressed as $p$-values, confidence intervals, and sensitivity analysis – for quantitative research studies.

3. **Are the results useful?** – You will decide the extent to which the study results apply to your practice-research question. You will also assess the extent to which the study's sample characteristics are similar or different to your practice population and specific service user or carer.

In addition to these general questions, there are additional specific questions that can be asked to assist you in critically appraising systematic reviews and different types of quantitative and qualitative studies. Such tools include Gibbs' (2003) Quality of Study Rating Form (QSRF), which is used to rate quantitative-based

**Table 7.2** CASP (2013) checklist for RCTs

**A. Are the results of the trial valid?**

| | | | | |
|---|---|---|---|---|
| 1. | Did the trial address a clearly focused issue? | Yes | Can't tell | No |
| 2. | Was the assignment of participants to interventions randomized? | Yes | Can't tell | No |
| 3. | Were participants, health workers and study personnel blinded? | Yes | Can't tell | No |
| 4. | Were the groups similar at the start of the trial? | Yes | Can't tell | No |
| 5. | Aside from the experimental intervention, were the groups treated equally? | Yes | Can't tell | No |
| 6. | Were all of the participants who entered the trial properly accounted for at its conclusion? | Yes | Can't tell | No |

**B. What are the results?**

7. How large was the intervention effect?
Consider: What outcomes were measured? Is the primary outcome clearly specified? What results were found for each outcome? Is there evidence of selective reporting of outcomes?

8. How precise was the estimate of the intervention effect?
Consider: What are the confidence limits? Were they statistically significant?

**C. Will the results help locally?**

| | | | | |
|---|---|---|---|---|
| 9. | Can the results be applied in your context (or to the local population)? | Yes | Can't tell | No |
| 10. | Were all clinically important outcomes considered? | Yes | Can't tell | No |
| 11. | Are the benefits worth the harms and costs? | Yes | Can't tell | No |

*From: Critical Appraisal Skills Programme (CASP) (2013) *Randomized Controlled Trials Checklist*. Available at: http://media.wix.com/ugd/dded87_40b9ff0bf53840478331915a8ed8b2fb.pdf [Accessed 3 January 2017].

effectiveness studies. The QSRF tool consists of 22 questions that address the quality of the study and the intervention effect size. For example, assessing whether there is a clear description of the intervention in terms of who, what, when, where, and why, and assessing the size (>20 individuals) and equality of characteristics of the intervention and control groups.

Other tools and checklists are available online for free through CASP (http://www.casp-uk.net). CASP provides eight checklists for use in appraising evidence, including systematic reviews, RCTs, case control studies, cohort studies, and qualitative studies. The checklists provide 10–12 questions that address the three broad questions of:

- Are the results valid?
- What are the results?
- Will the results help locally?

Tables 7.2 and 7.3 provide examples of checklists for RCTs and for qualitative research.

**Table 7.3** CASP (2013) checklist for qualitative studies

**A. Are the results of the review valid?**

| | | | |
|---|---|---|---|
| 1. Was there a clear statement of the aims of the research? | Yes | Can't tell | No |
| 2. Is a qualitative methodology appropriate? | Yes | Can't tell | No |
| 3. Was the research design appropriate to address the aims of the research? | Yes | Can't tell | No |
| 4. Was the recruitment strategy appropriate to the aims of the research? | Yes | Can't tell | No |
| 5. Was the data collected used in a way that addressed the research issue? | Yes | Can't tell | No |
| 6. Has the relationship between researcher and participants been adequately considered? | Yes | Can't tell | No |
| 7. Have ethical issues been taken into consideration? | Yes | Can't tell | No |
| 8. Was the data analysis sufficiently rigorous? | Yes | Can't tell | No |

**B. What are the results?**

| | | | |
|---|---|---|---|
| 9. Is there a clear statement of findings? | Yes | Can't tell | No |

**C. Will the results help locally?**

| | | | |
|---|---|---|---|
| 10. How valuable is the research? | | | |

*From: Critical Appraisal Skills Programme (CASP) (2013) *Qualitative Research Checklist*. Available at: http://media.wix.com/ugd/dded87_29c5b002d99342f788c6ac670e49f274.pdf [Accessed 3 January 2017].

## Summary

In this chapter we have explored Steps 2 and 3 of the EIP process in more detail. We examined how to search for evidence using traditional literature reviews, scoping reviews, and systematic reviews. We also presented the 'hierarchy of evidence', which ranges from the lowest on the hierarchy of 'views of colleagues or peers', to the highest on the hierarchy of systematic reviews and meta-analyses. Although the 'hierarchy of evidence' is important in assessing the quality and credibility of the 'best available evidence' in the EIP process, we acknowledge that you need to assess the evidence alongside your practice knowledge and experiences and the service user's or carer's wishes, values, and circumstances. Based on the assessment, you may find that a piece of qualitative research is more appropriate and informative for your practice situation than a systematic review or RCT. Finally, we explored the importance of critically appraising the evidence. We presented initial questions that you can explore when appraising the evidence, as well as additional tools to use in relation to quantitative and qualitative studies.

**Key points**

- There are bottom-up and top-down approaches to a literature search. The bottom-up search involves accessing, reviewing, and assessing all available literature, and a top-down search involves reading already completed reviews.
- Bottom-up searches can include *producing* traditional or normative literature reviews, scoping reviews, or systematic reviews. Top-down searches involve *consuming* existing literature reviews, such as scoping reviews or systematic reviews.
- The 'hierarchy of evidence' assumes that all forms of evidence are not equivalent, and some forms of evidence, such as systematic reviews and RCTs, are more highly regarded and, thus, more credible than other forms of evidence, such as qualitative research and opinions of colleagues and peers.
- Despite the 'hierarchy of evidence', an EIP approach should 'rely on the best AVAILABLE evidence, not only on BEST evidence' (McNeece and Thyer 2004: 12), and should consider your practice knowledge and experiences and the service user's or carer's wishes, values, and circumstances, alongside the best available evidence.
- Critically appraising the evidence involves determining the validity or credibility of the evidence and its applicability to your practice situation.
- Critical appraisal of the evidence should consider: Is the study valid?, What are the results?, and Are the results useful? (CASP 2013).

## Further resources

Campbell Collaboration – www.campbellcollaboration.org
Cochrane Collaboration – www.cochrane.org
Colquhoun, H.L., Levac, D., O'Brien, K.K. et al. (2014) Scoping reviews: time for clarity in definition, methods, and reporting, *Journal of Clinical Epidemiology*, 67: 1291–4.
Critical Appraisal Skills Programme (CASP) – www.casp-uk.net
SCIE – www.scie.org.uk

# 8 Implementing evidence-informed practice and evaluating your practice

---

**Chapter overview**

By the end of this chapter you should have an understanding of:

- How to implement an intervention at the individual practitioner level.
- Different ways to evaluate the effectiveness of the intervention and your practice.
- Ways in which to provide feedback on the effectiveness of the intervention.
- The phases to implementing an intervention at the organizational level.

---

## Introduction

In this chapter we will further explore the evidence-informed practice (EIP) model by providing additional information and skills needed to implement the last two steps of the EIP process. Chapter 7 provided information and skills on how to search for evidence to answer practice-research questions (Step 2), and questions to ask, and tools to use, to critically appraise the evidence (Step 3). Based on your analysis of the evidence in Step 3, you will then complete Step 4 of the EIP process by determining the most appropriate intervention to use, given your practice knowledge and experience and the service user's or carer's values, wishes, and circumstances. This chapter provides additional information and skills needed to implement the intervention within your individual practice or organization (Step 5), evaluate the effectiveness of the work, and provide feedback on the evaluation (Step 6). We will begin the chapter by discussing how to implement an intervention at the individual practitioner level, including tools and techniques used to evaluate the effectiveness of the intervention and ways in which to provide feedback and disseminate the findings from your evaluation. We will conclude with the steps to implementation at the organizational level and tools to prepare for implementation.

## Implementation of the best available evidence and intervention

Step 5 of the EIP model involves implementing the intervention that was selected after your review and appraisal of the best available evidence. Your choice of intervention is not only based on the information from the best available evidence, but also given your practice knowledge and experience and the service user's or carer's values, wishes, and circumstances. Once you have chosen the intervention, the next step is to implement it within your practice. When implementing the intervention, you need to consider the following: '(1) the quality and applicability of evidence; (2) the context or organizational environment; and (3) the process of implementing change' (Bellamy et al. 2006: 34). We will first discuss the skills and considerations for implementing interventions at the individual practitioner level, and then the steps and considerations in implementing interventions at the organizational level.

### Individual level

You may find yourself working in an organization where you have the freedom to determine the type of interventions to employ with individual service users and/ or carers without having the intervention implemented across the whole organization or uniformly across all service users and carers. For example, if you work with children in care, you may be able to select the most appropriate intervention based on the characteristics of the child, versus using a technique that is prescribed by the organization. In such circumstances, you can implement Step 5 of the EIP process as an individual social worker on your own, or as part of a group of social workers – for example, implementing a particular intervention within a specific social work team. Yet we caution you to have the adequate skills and knowledge to implement the intervention, which is often achieved through working with experienced practitioners and gaining appropriate training. We encourage you to review our discussion of Step 5 in Chapter 6.

For example, let us imagine that you are working with a 12-year-old young person who is experiencing difficulties adjusting to a new school after a recent move to a new foster home. The child is experiencing 'externalizing behaviours' exhibited by being disruptive in class by refusing to sit in her chair, arguing with the teacher, and fighting with her classmates. You may explore different types of interventions to use in your one-on-one sessions with the young person and decide that, based on the evidence and circumstances of the young person and your work together, you would employ techniques from solution-focused brief therapy (see Wood et al. 2011 for the appropriateness of this intervention with children and families).

Solution-focused brief therapy (SFBT) is 'a short-term model of practice that seeks to amplify what clients are already doing well and help them realize a future where the problem is no longer a problem' (Kondrat 2014: 170). The intervention consists of the following five stages: (1) describe the problem; (2) develop well-formulated goals; (3) explore exceptions to the problem; (4) end-of-session feedback; and (5) evaluate client progress (see Kondrat 2014 for an overview of SFBT). In implementing the intervention you would want to gain agreement from the young person to work together and use different tools and questions to attempt to help in resolving the identified problem(s) (i.e. goal questions; exception questions; scaling questions). As part of the EIP process, and as a specific stage within SFBT, you will develop goals for the work together with the young person. For example, in Chapter 6 we presented the acronym SMART, which is a tool to develop goals that are **S**pecific, **M**easurable, **A**ttainable, **R**ealistic, and **T**imely. Through specific questioning, you and the young person establish several goals, one of which is to 'sit through one class period quietly once a day for a school week'. You continue to implement the intervention with the young person – while seeking appropriate supervision and training – and move to Step 6 in evaluating the effectiveness of the intervention.

In the situation above you may also wish to consider, if some of your colleagues have similar challenging young people on their caseload, whether it would be better working with the young people as a group, or as individuals. One of the authors during their practice career did do such group work with young offenders, which allowed them to work with two other colleagues and eight young people, rationalizing resources and increasing the author's skills and expertise, while also providing a theoretical-based intervention for eight young people. Group work has some advantages over individual work as it allows the young people to also learn from each other, as well as from the group's social workers, and given the importance of the peer group in adolescence this can be very powerful.

## Evaluating the effectiveness of the work

Evaluating the effectiveness of your work, and/or the intervention, is the final step in the EIP process (Step 6); it takes into account the extent to which you and the service user or carer have met the established goals in Step 5. Practice evaluation involves bringing research tools into practice in that it involves '(1) goal setting; (2) monitoring or tracking of behaviour (using research tools); and (3) a systematic, analytical process of developing insights into the applicability of the specific intervention with the specific client' (Briggs and Rzepnicki 2004: 325). This also takes us right back to Chapter 1 when we argued very strongly that it was critical for social workers to evaluate their practice, or run the risk that they were doing more harm than good.

An evaluation consisting of research within a natural practice setting is often referred to as practice-based research. It consists of utilizing traditional research methods to measure outcomes (i.e. quantitative or qualitative methodologies), but also gathering information and knowledge regarding the broader narrative of social workers and service users and carers that addresses the processes and experiences of delivering the practice (Dirkx 2006).

Programme evaluation is a specific type of evaluation that aims to: (1) assess the ultimate success of a programme; (2) assess how the programme is being implemented; or (3) determine what is needed for programme planning and development (Rubin and Babbie 2016). There are two main types of programme evaluations: summative and formative. Summative evaluations 'assess the ultimate success of programmes and decisions about whether they should be continued or chosen in the first place from among alternative options' (Rubin and Babbie 2016: 286). Summative evaluations aim to determine the extent to which the programme delivering the intervention is achieving successful outcomes. For example, is the programme achieving what it has set out to achieve? Formative evaluations 'focus on obtaining information for planning programmes and improving their implementation and performance' (Rubin and Babbie 2016: 286). Instead of determining whether outcomes are achieved, as in summative evaluations, formative evaluations are more concerned with the process of delivery (e.g. implementation, performance) of the intervention and how the process could run more smoothly, effectively, and efficiently. Whereas summative evaluations tend to be more quantitative in nature, formative evaluations may rely on both quantitative and qualitative methods.

In addition to, or in combination with, programme evaluations, other evaluations can take the form of large-scale research studies that measure effectiveness of interventions or practice at an organizational level, usually through the use of quasi- or pre-experimental designs or mixed-methods which combine elements of quantitative and qualitative methodologies. For example, an evidence-based intervention, multisystemic therapy (MST), was implemented in England after its development and implementation within US social service organizations. MST was developed by two US academics, Dr Scott Henggeler and Dr Charles Borduin, and is a family- and community-based intensive intervention aimed to target the multiple causes of conduct problems and offending in young people aged 12–17 years (Wiggins et al. 2012). The aim of the intervention is to improve the skills of parents and caregivers in order to assist in changing the behaviours of the young person. MST practitioners provide intensive support (on call 24 hours a day, seven days a week) in the home, but also work with schools and communities over a period of three to six months. Because the work of the practitioner is intensive, they typically hold a caseload of four to six families (Wiggins et al. 2012). Text box 8.1 provides an overview of the implementation of this evidence-based practice in England, and highlights the large-scale evaluation of its effectiveness.

---

### Text box 8.1: Implementation and evaluation of MST in England

A recent RCT of the MST programme in England was undertaken by Butler and colleagues (2011) at University College London. This trial was carried out with an ethnically diverse sample of 108 families who were randomized to either MST or usual supportive Youth Offending Team services. Young people were eligible if they were on a court referral order for treatment, a supervision order of at least three months' duration, or, following imprisonment, on licence in the community for at least six months. Participants were predominantly male, half were from Black or minority ethnic groups, and on average they had committed more than two offences in the previous year (more than half of their convictions were for violent offences). Results showed that, compared with the control group, at 18 month follow-up MST provided significantly reduced non-violent offending, youth-reported delinquency and parental reports of aggressive and delinquent behaviours.

The results suggest that there is scope for an MST intervention in addition to the existing multi-agency services on offer for young offenders in the UK.

However, the researchers stressed the need for further examination of its cost-effectiveness, to determine that the costs of delivering the programme are justified by the results achieved.

Alongside this UK trial, qualitative interviews were carried out with both parents and young people assigned to MST, approximately three months after the intervention finished (Tighe et al 2012). These showed that the intervention was valued and acceptable to families in the UK, and that they credited it with improvements in offending and relationships between the parent and young person. The interviews found that in this study population there was a sense that the intervention had come to an end too abruptly or too soon for some. The researchers suggested that future implementation of MST might consider a longer intervention in certain cases, or some follow up sessions after the main intervention is completed (Tighe et al 2012).

(Wiggins et al. 2012: 34–5)

*From: M. Wiggins, H. Austerberry and H. Ward (2012) *Implementing Evidence-Based Programmes in Children's Services: Key Issues for Success*. Available at: https://www.gov.uk/government/uploads/system/uploads/attachment_data/file/183483/DFE-RR245.pdf [Accessed 15 January 2017].

If you or your organization do not have the skills and resources necessary to carry out an evaluation, then you can explore opportunities to collaborate or contract with outside agencies, such as local universities or research firms, to assist in the process (McNeece and Thyer 2004). Additionally, if the cost of the evaluation is too expensive for your organization, then you can seek external funding, such as through governmental bodies and research councils (e.g. ESRC; Department of Health; Department for Education) or research charities (e.g. Leverhulme Trust; Nuffield Foundation; Joseph Rowntree Charitable Trust; Big Lottery). Partnering with individuals or research centres from local universities can ease the application process and enhance the chances of funding. Lastly, you may also want to consider partnering with another service delivery organization as a means to reduce costs and make an evaluation affordable.

### Single-system designs

Alternatively, evaluations can consist of smaller-scale designs, such as single-system designs (SSD), often referred to as single-case designs, that can be implemented by a social worker aiming to evaluate practice with a specific service user or carer. In SSDs, the sample size is one: either one service user, one carer, one family, one community, or one organization. Rubin and Babbie (2016: 260) describe SSDs as follows:

Single-case designs apply the logic of time series designs to the evaluation of practice effectiveness with a single case. Such designs involve obtaining repeated measures of a client system with regard to particular outcome indicators of a target problem. Repeated measures of the trend in the target problem are obtained before a particular intervention is introduced, and these repeated measures are continued after intervention is introduced to see if a sustained pattern of improvement in the target problem commences shortly after the onset of intervention.

The most common type of SSD is the AB design, where the data are collected on the indicators of the target problem before the intervention, and then directly after for a period of time. There are other types of SSDs that you can use in your practice, such as the ABAB design, where the intervention is implemented, then removed (possibly due to the social worker being on holiday or another natural break in services), yet data are still being collected on the target problem, and then the intervention is reinstated. Figure 8.1 depicts the AB design that we conducted with our young person to evaluate whether the use of SFBT was effective in reducing classroom disruptions and achieving the goal: 'sit through one class period quietly once a day for a school week'.

As depicted, we measured the problem by collecting data on how many class disruptions the young person had in each week. For the three weeks prior to implementing the SFBT intervention, the young person had between 8 and 10 class disruptions per week, yet we see that the disruptions per week go down after the intervention was implemented. The decrease ended at 0 disruptions per week for three weeks. The findings from the SSD indicate that the intervention is effective. If the problem behaviour did not change from the baseline to intervention phases, then you would conclude the intervention to be ineffective with the service user or carer, and you would change your choice of intervention.

Additionally, although this is one way in which to evaluate your work with an individual service user or carer, you should also consider other methods of data collection on how the intervention is being perceived and experienced by the service user or carer. For example, you can ask for feedback from the

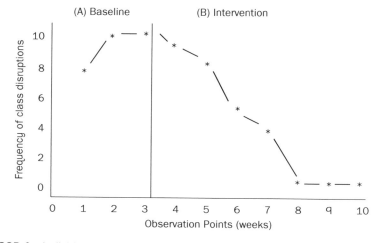

**Figure 8.1** SSD for individual practice

service user or carer verbally, or you can ask service users or carers to keep a diary that documents their experience in making a change and reaching their goals, with a specific focus on what is working well and not so well. You can also incorporate creative aspects in gaining feedback, such as having service users or carers take photographs or draw pictures that illustrate their experiences in overcoming problems and achieving goals. Such information can be extremely useful in helping you critically reflect on what is effective in your work with the particular service user or carer, and can also serve as a therapeutic intervention itself by serving as a point for discussion together. It also provides evidence for you to analyse your practice with your supervisor in supervision, allowing you to have a '360°' perspective of your intervention – bearing in mind that all interventions have both intentional and unintentional consequences.

---

**Activity 8.1**

**Evaluating your work**

Think of an intervention that you would like to implement with the service user or carer population with whom you work. This could be an intervention that you have heard about, read about, discovered through the activities in the previous chapters of this book, or an innovative intervention that you have created. How might you go about evaluating the effectiveness of this intervention in your work? Would an SSD be useful in this situation? Why or why not? What creative ways could you gain feedback from service users or carers?

---

## Feedback and dissemination

The final stage of the EIP process is the dissemination, or sharing, of the feedback received from service users and carers, and the findings of the evaluation conducted in Step 6 in regards to the extent to which the intervention was effective. It is important for social workers to learn from each other in terms of what is effective in practice – how any intervention has been effective, or the ways in which it has been ineffective. Social workers can provide the findings of their feedback and research through team meetings, presentations at local agencies and organizations, local authorities, universities, conferences focused on social work practice, or through writing the findings for professional magazines, journals and/or websites (e.g. *Community Care*, *Practice*). Additionally, we urge social workers to work with local university social work programmes to continually evaluate practice and contribute to the growing knowledge base of social work practice.

Although social workers can implement EIP at the individual practitioner level, or with a small group of like-minded practitioners, social workers will be able to engage more effectively if EIP is adopted and implemented at the organizational level. We conclude this chapter with an overview of the steps in implementing EIP at the organizational level.

### Organizational level

Implementation is the process of putting a plan into effect. As with any change in procedures or ways of working, implementation of a new intervention within an organization is a process that takes time and should be executed over several phases. There is a whole body of literature, including research and theory, which addresses how to effectively and efficiently implement change in organizations, called implementation science, organizational behaviour or change management. And organizations that are open and active in implementing change and learning from the feedback and evaluation of such change are called 'learning organizations'. A learning organization is one that is able to continuously transform itself through the connected learning of its people. In a learning organization, every activity and intervention presents an opportunity to learn (Pedler et al. 1991).

Although we will draw from this literature to describe how to implement EIP interventions in social work practice, we want to acknowledge that we are providing a very brief overview and recommend you explore change management and learning organizations in more detail if you are interested, are seeking to implement an intervention within your organization, and/or becoming a learning organization.

The Ontario Centre of Excellence for Child and Youth Mental Health (OCECYMH) has developed a useful framework and toolkit for implementation of evidence-informed practice. The framework for implementation consists of three phases: (1) planning phase: getting people and systems ready for change; (2) doing phase: training on specific practices, implementing, adapting, and evaluating; and (3) sustaining phase: learning to continually use new evidence to improve practice (OCECYMH 2013: 10). The bulk of the implementation process occurs during the planning phase; therefore, we provide more details and specific tools to assist in the planning phase below.

### Planning phase: getting people and systems ready for change

This is the 'getting started' phase where you need to build leadership support, engage stakeholders, and have a plan on how to manage and lead the change. The first step is to assess the organization's readiness to implement the change, which includes the ability to support and the readiness to make the change, as well as the attitudes and skills of staff in regard to implementing the change (see Chapter 5). Table 8.1 provides an assessment tool adapted from Horsley (1983) to determine the readiness and feasibility of organizations to implement the intervention or change. As you can see, the questions assess the ease of implementation in terms of feasibility, time, and support or buy-in, and the cost-benefit factors in terms of financial cost to implement, the physical and emotional well-being of service

**Table 8.1** Practice change scoring assessment tool

| A. Factors affecting ease of implementation | Score (Circle) |
|---|---|
| 1. How tangible (technological/material) or intangible (interpersonal/ nonmaterial) is the intervention? <br> **1 = Very intangible – 5 = Very tangible** | **1-2-3-4-5** |
| 2. How much change in current social work function(s) would this intervention require? <br> **1 = Extensive – 5 = No change** | **1-2-3-4-5** |
| 3. To what extent does this intervention address a relevant social work practice problem or need in your organization? <br> **1 = There is little concern by anyone – 5 = There is concern by a great many** | **1-2-3-4-5** |
| 4. Would this kind of practice change be acceptable to you and others in your team? <br> **1 = Not acceptable at all – 5 = There is concern by a great many** | **1-2-3-4-5** |
| 5. To what extent is social work in your organization free to decide to carry out this intervention? <br> **1 = Requires organization-wide approval – 5 = Requires no other group's approval** | **1-2-3-4-5** |
| 6. To what extent would this intervention fall under the control of social work in your organization? <br> **1 = Social work would have no control – 5 = Social work would have clear control** | **1-2-3-4-5** |
| 7. To what extent do social work staff have to be involved in implementing the intervention? <br> **1 = All social workers must be involved – 5 = Few social workers need to be involved** | **1-2-3-4-5** |
| 8. To what extent would this intervention require changes in staffing patterns for social work personnel? <br> **1 = Substantial change required – 5 = No change required** | **1-2-3-4-5** |
| 9. To what extent can the intervention be divided into separate phases that can be implemented one step at a time? <br> **1 = Complete and not divisible – 5 = Easily divisible or not necessary** | **1-2-3-4-5** |
| 10. To what extent can the intervention be stopped if it does not prove desirable? <br> **1= Very difficult to stop – 5 = Stopped without any difficulty** | **1-2-3-4-5** |
| 11. To what extent would a trial of this innovation disrupt or interfere with the way social workers currently function? <br> **1 = Would be very disruptive – 5 = Would not interfere or disrupt** | **1-2-3-4-5** |
| 12. What length of time would be required to carry out this intervention, considering the need for training/materials/staff? <br> **1 = 6 months or more – 5 = 2 weeks to 1 month** | **1-2-3-4-5** |

*(Continued)*

**Table 8.1** (continued)

| | |
|---|---|
| 13. How difficult would it be to demonstrate that this intervention has had an effect on service users or carers?<br>**1 = Very difficult – 5 = Easy** | **1-2-3-4-5** |
| 14. How difficult would it be to get appropriate staff (or others) involved in collecting evidence that the intervention is effective?<br>**1 = Very difficult – 5 = Easy** | **1-2-3-4-5** |
| 15. What length of time would be required to evaluate the benefits?<br>**1 = Long time (several months) – 5 = Short time** | **1-2-3-4-5** |
| *Ease of implementation subtotal*<br>*60–75 Very good*<br>*45–59 Good*<br>*Below 45 Questionable* | |
| **B. Cost-benefit factors** | **Score (Circle)** |
| 1. To what extent would the benefits derived from the intervention be visible?<br>**1 = Intangible and not obvious – 5 = Major improvement in service user or carer well-being** | **1-2-3-4-5** |
| 2. To what extent would the benefits of the intervention affect the physical and emotional well-being of the service users or carers?<br>**1 = Minimal improvement well-being – 5 = It will facilitate their work** | **1-2-3-4-5** |
| 3. To what extent would this intervention facilitate or interfere with the work of social workers in your organization?<br>**1 = It will interfere with their work – 5 = It will facilitate their work** | **1-2-3-4-5** |
| 4. To what extent are the materials required by this intervention currently available in your organization?<br>**1 = Not at all available – 5 = Readily available** | **1-2-3-4-5** |
| 5. To what extent would personnel require specialized training in order to implement the intervention?<br>**1 = Extensive training – 5 = Little or no special training** | **1-2-3-4-5** |
| 6. To what extent would the benefits support the time and energy involved in implementing the intervention?<br>**1 = Take months to implement and benefits are obscure for a long time – 5 = Requires no additional staff/materials/equipment** | **1-2-3-4-5** |
| 7. How costly would it be to start this intervention?<br>**1 = Requires extra staff and costly materials/equipment – 5 = Requires no additional staff/materials/equipment** | **1-2-3-4-5** |
| 8. How costly would it be to maintain the intervention once it was started?<br>**1 = Requires ongoing budgeting – 5 = Requires no additional staff/materials/equipment** | **1-2-3-4-5** |
| 9. To what extent would the monetary cost of social work services be altered by implementing this innovation?<br>**1 = Increased costs per service user or carer per day – 5 = Major saving per service user or carer per day** | **1-2-3-4-5** |

**Table 8.1**  (continued)

| | |
|---|---|
| 10. To what extent would the benefits of the intervention be proportional to all the difficulties inherent in implementing this intervention? **1 = Difficulties outweigh any benefits – 5 = Benefits outweigh any difficulties** | **1-2-3-4-5** |
| ***Cost-benefit subtotal*** *40–50 Very good* *30–40 Good* *Below 30 Questionable* | |

*Adapted from: J. Horsley (1983) *Using Research to Improve Nursing Practice: A Guide – CURN Project.* Austin, TX: Pro Ed.

users and/or carers, and the time to complete social work effectively and without interference. The overall scores indicate whether the 'ease of implementation' and 'cost-benefit' is questionable, good, or very good, which are both summed and assessed separately. Although you can complete the assessment on your own, OCECYMH (2013) recommends that three to five people who occupy different roles within the organization complete assessments of implementation capacity. This can allow for comparisons of perspectives from people who will have different expectations and responsibilities within the change process. It is important to note that, if an organization is assessed as questionable or not ready to implement a change, then moving forward will most likely only lead to the implementation being unsuccessful. The assessment tool can highlight areas within the organization, or staff, where preparatory work needs to take place before moving forward with the implementation process.

The scores from this assessment tool are also provided in the worksheet depicted in Table 8.2. This practice change project worksheet, adapted from Sawatzky-Dickson (2010), is used to help map out and plan the implementation steps and processes, which can be used in conjunction with the assessment tool. The worksheet addresses the background and rationale for the implementation of the intervention, a look at current practice and the proposed new practice, potential goals to measure, strategies to evaluate the effectiveness of the intervention, and a consideration of the costs, barriers, risks, and benefits.

## Activity 8.2

### Plan to implement an intervention in your organization

Consider your social work organization, where you either work or are on your practice placement, and complete the following tasks:

- Think of an intervention that you would like to implement with the service user or carer population with whom you work. This can either be the intervention you selected in Activity 8.1, or a different intervention.

- Complete the assessment tool in Table 8.1.
- Complete the practice change project worksheet in Table 8.2.
- Based on your assessment and worksheet response, provide a summary of your thoughts, feelings, and beliefs about implementing this intervention in your organization.

In addition to assessing the organization, this first phase also involves identifying and establishing leadership support. Support from leadership should include an understanding of the need for the implementation, and support to provide resources to make it happen. The drivers of the implementation change process can use the information obtained from the assessment tool and practice change project worksheet to develop a presentation to leadership that covers the need and rational for the intervention, the facilitators, barriers, and costs and benefits to the implementation (OCECYMH 2013).

Equally, you must also engage and involve the stakeholders in planning the implementation of the intervention. Stakeholders include: staff within the organization who will be involved in any aspect of delivering the intervention, or collecting or analysing data as part of the evaluation of the intervention; service users or carers who will be at the receiving end of the intervention; and leaders and policymakers who have the power to implement policies and practices that can either help or hinder the implementation of the new intervention, either currently or in the future. As with gaining the support from leadership within the organization, you should gain support from stakeholders by informing them of the need and rational for the intervention, the facilitators, barriers, costs and benefits to the implementation, including how they will be personally impacted, how the intervention will be evaluated, and how any feedback and evaluation findings will be communicated to them. Involvement of service users and/or carers is also critical to ensure that any changes consider service users' and carers' priorities for change. Service users and carers can be consulted about the best ways in which to keep them informed of changes, or how they could be more involved through being a member of the implementation team (OCECYMH 2013) and how they can contribute to the evaluation of the changes.

**Activity 8.3**

### Involving servicer users and/or carers

Consider the intervention you proposed in Activity 8.2. How could you best inform service users and/or carers of this change, and to what extent could you involve them in the implementation process? Describe the potential benefits and challenges to their involvement.

**Table 8.2** Practice change project worksheet

| Project initiated by: | Project lead: | | | | |
|---|---|---|---|---|---|
| **Problem/Clinical question:** | | | | | |
| **Background:** | | | | | |
| **Recommendation from the literature:** | | | | | |
| **Current practice:** | | | | | |
| **Proposed new practice:** | | | | | |
| **Goal** (e.g. reduced length of stay; obtain housing; reduced levels of depression) | | | | | |
| **How will you measure outcomes?** | | | | | |
| **Is this new practice supported by reputable sources?** (i.e. SCIE; NICE) | | | | | |
| **Whose authority is required to implement this change?** | | | | | |
| **Results of practice change scoring assessment tool:**<br>**Cost-benefit:**  **Ease of implementation:**<br>☐ Very good        ☐ Very good<br>☐ Good            ☐ Good<br>☐ Questionable        ☐ Questionable | | | | | |
| **What do you think needs to be in place?** (equipment, supplies, education, space allocation, policies, guidelines): | | | | | |
| **What time frame might be involved?**<br>☐ Implement in one step<br>☐ Implement gradually<br>☐ Implement in series of steps (outline) | | | | | |
| **What costs are predicted** (if any)? | | | | | |
| **What barriers are anticipated?** | | | | | |
| **What are the risks if this particular practice change does not occur?** | | | | | |
| **What do you propose the next steps to be?** | | | | | |
| **Communication strategy:** | | | | | |
| **List all key stakeholders**: (Check boxes to indicate as communication has been done and support received) | | | | | |
| **Areas involved:** | | | | | |
| **Position/Name** | **Support** | | **Position/Name** | **Support** | |
| | Yes | No | | Yes | No |
| | | | | | |
| | | | | | |
| | | | | | |
| | | | | | |

*Adapted from: D. Sawatzky-Dickson (2010) *Evidence-Informed Practice Resource Package*. Available at: http://www.wrha.mb.ca/osd/files/EIPResourcePkg.pdf [Accessed 14 January 2017].

Some stakeholders may be resistant to any change. In such situations, OCECYMH (2013) provides the following tips on dealing with resistance: (1) 'provide information (the why, what, and how) and what it means to staff; (2) reflect concerns: acknowledge and validate the person's opinion; and (3) roll with resistance: each person's perspective is valuable. It may provide insight into the challenges associated with the change initiative' (p. 21). In such situations, you may need to rely on your social work communication skills and social work theories and methods to work with people in implementing the change (e.g. motivational interviewing) versus 'pushing' them along the process.

The planning phase requires a core group of individuals who either serve on the core team or the implementation team, both of which have involved roles in planning and executing the change. Whereas the core team is established from the beginning, and oversees the entire implementation process, including the implementation plan, the implementation team is established when the planning phase is complete, and assists in carrying out the implementation plan (OCECYMH 2013: 24). The core team is typically comprised of a minimum of three people who represent various roles and positions within the organization (e.g. front-line social worker; social work team manager; executive director). Although some members of the core team may remain on the implementation team, others may not. The implementation team should also include individuals who occupy differing roles within the organization, and who have an interest or role within the implementation of the intervention, such as being responsible for implementing the intervention, providing supervision, participating in the evaluation, or receiving the intervention as a service user or carer (OCECYMH 2013). Regular meetings will need to take place for both the core and subsequent implementation teams.

The final component of the planning phase is the development of the implementation plan. According to OCECYMH (2013: 34):

> The implementation plan lets you anticipate challenges (e.g., cost, commitment, responsibility), create a common understanding among staff (e.g., regardless of level of involvement, everyone understands the goal of the programme), and tie together all of the steps involved in moving from early planning to sustaining a new practice.

The core team should be responsible for constructing the implementation plan, yet this plan should be open for revisions and modifications based on feedback and lessons learned through the actual implementation process. The actual implementation plan can be a document similar to the practice change project worksheet (if implementing a smaller change within the organization), or it can often be an extensive document that takes into account all aspects of the organization, such as the inner setting, outer setting, characteristics of the intervention, characteristics of the service users and carers, and process of implementation (Damschroder et al. 2009). An example implementation framework is provided by OCECYMH at: http://www.excellenceforchildandyouth.ca/sites/default/files/docs/ISStoolkit/25_key_implementation_factors.pdf.

### Doing phase: training on specific practices, implementing, adapting, and evaluating

Once the implementation plan has been devised, the next phase involves executing the plan through the doing phase. This phase involves selecting and training the key staff that will implement the intervention; maintaining communication and access to trainers or consultants of the intervention for consultation, supervision, and/or coaching; providing supervision to staff and avenues for staff and service users and carers to provide feedback on the implementation, as well as any problems or difficulties in implementing the intervention; establishing the methods of evaluation and identifying the data to be collected to measure outcomes; continuing communication with stakeholders, the regular core team, and the implementation team, particularly in regard to what is going well and not so well; and determining ways in which to disseminate the findings from the evaluation (OCECYMH 2013).

### Sustaining phase: learning to continually use new evidence to improve practice

The final phase, the sustaining phase, requires 'learning organizations' to process the evaluation findings and modify interventions based on what has been found to be effective or ineffective. The information from the evaluation

**Table 8.3** Six 'drivers' of successful implementation

---

1. **Staff selection** – Staff recruitment and selection are key components of implementation at practitioner and organizational levels.

2. **Staff training** – Staff members at all levels require training when a new practice is implemented. Effective training involves theory and discussion; demonstration of skills; and opportunities for practice and feedback.

3. **Coaching, mentoring, and supervision** – Whereas skills needed by successful practitioners can be introduced in training, many skills can only really be learned on the job with the help of a consultant or coach.

4. **Internal management support** – Internal management support provides leadership to support implementation, makes use of a range of information to shape decision-making, and provides structures and processes for implementing new practices and keeping staff focused on desired outcomes.

5. **Systems-level partnerships** – Systems-level partnerships involve working with external partners to support programme implementation and the front-line work of practitioners.

6. **Staff and programme evaluation** – Evaluation entails using measures of practitioner performance and adherence to the programme model, along with programme outcomes measures, to assess overall programme performance and develop quality improvement plans.

---

*Adapted from: A.J.R. Metz, K. Blase and L. Bowie (2007) *Implementing Evidence-based Practices: Six 'Drivers' of Success*. Washington, DC: Child Trends.

findings should also be communicated with stakeholders and the core and implementation teams. A sustainability plan should be devised that addresses how the organization will continue providing the intervention, including ongoing supervision, training, resources needed, process and outcome evaluations, and ways in which the organization can assist other organizations in implementing the intervention, if found to be effective. In summary, we present the six 'drivers' of successful implementation in Table 8.3, as provided by Metz et al. (2007).

## Summary

In this chapter we provided more information on the implementation of interventions (Stage 5) and the evaluation of interventions (Stage 6), which are the last two stages of the EIP process. We discussed how implementation can occur at the individual practitioner level, and encouraged you to receive training and supervision when implementing a new intervention. We discussed the importance of evaluation, provided an overview of different types of evaluations, and illustrated how you can evaluate your individual practice through single-system designs. We stressed the importance of gaining feedback from service users and carers, and disseminating the feedback and the findings from your evaluation to the social work community to continue to enhance social work practice. Finally, we discussed the three stages of the implementation process at the organizational level, which includes an extensive planning phase, followed by the doing and sustaining phases.

## In closing

This chapter has taken us full circle, back to the start of this book and why we feel passionately that, for social work to flourish, EIP is essential. We highlighted in Chapter 1 the rationale for EIP, and the range of potential research knowledge, and their importance to our understanding of social work from different perspectives in Chapter 2. We discussed the importance of the ethical nature of social work and social work research in Chapter 3. Not only did this include the importance of what we do, and do not do, it also raised the question of 'Who should be helped?' – a political question which we cannot avoid, as avoiding it is an act of acceptance of the current situation and the conditions under which (many) of social work's challenges are created; but is not the central feature of this book. In Chapter 4 we provided a critical appreciation of the need to work interprofessionally, the challenges this created, and its lack of supporting evidence. Chapters 5–8 set out the systematic practical steps in which you, as practitioners, can become evidence-informed practitioners, and how organizations can become learning organizations and contribute to the development of social work knowledge that is inclusive of service user and carer knowledges, is informed by your own practice, and uses research knowledge critically to help promote better outcomes for service users and carers.

## Key points

- Implementation can occur at the individual practitioner level, but practitioners should ensure they are appropriately trained and skilled in the intervention.
- Evaluating the effectiveness of your work and/or the intervention is the final step in the EIP process (Step 6). It takes into account the extent to which you and the service user or carer have met the defined goals.
- Single-system designs are a tool to evaluate your practice with one service user or one carer.
- Feedback from service users and carers, and the findings from evaluations, should be disseminated to your colleagues and the broader social work community.
- The process of implementation within organizations consists of three phases: (1) planning phase; (2) doing phase; and (3) sustaining phase.
- The planning phase involves building leadership support, engaging stakeholders, and having a plan on how to manage and lead the change.
- The doing phase involves implementing the change, while ensuring staff are trained and supervised, communication is maintained with stakeholders, and establishing evaluation methods.
- The sustaining phase involves processing the evaluation findings and modifying the intervention, based on what has been found to be effective or ineffective.

## Further resources

Nugent, W. (2010) *Analyzing Single-System Design Data*. Oxford: Oxford University Press.

Ontario Centre of Excellence for Child and Youth Mental Health (OCECYMH) (2013) *Implementing Evidence-informed Practice: A Practical Toolkit*. Ottawa, Ontario: OCECYMH.

Royse, D., Padgett, D. and Thyer, B. (2016) *Program Evaluation: An Introduction to an Evidence-Based Approach*, 6th edn. Boston, MA: Cengage Learning.

Wiggins, M., Austerberry, H. and Ward, H. (2012) *Implementing Evidence-Based Programmes in Children's Services: Key Issues for Success*. London: DfE. Available at: https://www.gov.uk/government/uploads/system/uploads/attachment_data/file/183483/DFE-RR245.pdf [Accessed 15 January 2017].

# Appendix

## Abbreviations

| | |
|---|---|
| **AASW** | Australian Association of Social Workers |
| **ASYE** | Assessed and supported year in employment |
| **AYE** | Assessed year in employment |
| **BASW** | British Association of Social Workers |
| **BMJ** | British Medical Journal |
| **CPD** | Continuing Professional Development |
| **CSWE** | Council on Social Work Education |
| **DfE** | Department for Education |
| **DHSSPS** | Department of Health, Social Services and Public Safety in Northern Ireland |
| **DH** | Department of Health |
| **EBP** | Evidence-based practice |
| **EIP** | Evidence-informed practice |
| **ESRC** | Economic and Social Research Council |
| **GSCC** | General Social Care Council |
| **HCPC** | Health and Care Professions Council |
| **HEFCE** | Higher Education Funding Council for England |
| **IASSW** | International Association of Schools of Social Work |
| **IFSW** | International Federation of Social Work |
| **IPE** | Interprofessional education |
| **LGA** | Local Government Association |
| **NICE** | The National Institute for Health and Care Excellence |
| **OCECYMH** | The Ontario Centre of Excellence for Child and Youth Mental Health |
| **PCF** | Professional Capabilities Framework |
| **RCTs** | Randomized control trials |
| **REF** | Research Excellence Framework |
| **RIP** | Research in Practice |
| **RIPfA** | Research in Practice for Adults |
| **RSW** | Residential social work |
| **SCIE** | Social Care Institute for Excellence |
| **SFBT** | Solution-focused brief therapy |
| **SMART** | specific, measurable, attainable, realistic, timely |
| **SSD** | Single-system designs |
| **SSSC** | Scottish Social Services Council |
| **SOP** | Standards of Proficiency |
| **SWAN** | Social Work Action Network |

| | |
|---|---|
| **SWRB** | Social Work Reform Board |
| **TCSW** | The College of Social Work |
| **UK** | United Kingdom |
| **US** | United States |
| **WAG** | Welsh Assembly Government |

# References

Aarons, G.A. and Palinkas, L.A. (2007) Implentation of evidence-based practice in child welfare: service provider perspectives, *Administration and Policy in Mental Health and Mental Health Services Research*, 34(4): 411–19.

Aarons, G.A. and Sawitzky, A. (2006) Organizational culture and climate and mental health provider attitudes toward evidence-based practice, *Psychosocial Services*, 3(1): 71–2.

Arksey, H. and O'Malley, L. (2005) Scoping studies: towards a methodological framework, *International Journal of Social Research Methodology*, 8(1): 19–32.

Armstrong, R., Hall, B.J., Doyle, J. et al. (2011) Cochrane update: 'Scoping the scope' of a Cochrane review, *Journal of Public Health*, 33(1): 147–50.

Austin, M.J. and Claassen, J. (2008) Implementing evidence-based practice in human service organizations: preliminary lessons from the frontlines, *Journal of Evidence-Based Social Work*, 5(1/2): 271–93.

Australian Association of Social Workers (AASW) (2015) *Australian Social Work Education and Accreditation Standards (ASWEAS) 2012 V1.4*. Canberra: AASW. Available at: https://www.aasw.asn.au/document/item/3550 [Accessed 25 November 2016].

Baker, L.R. and Ritchey, F.J. (2009) Assessing practitioner's knowledge of evaluation: initial psychometrics of the practice evaluation knowledge scale, *Journal of Evidence-Based Social Work*, 6(4): 376–89.

Balen, R., Blyth, E., Clabretto, H. et al. (2006) Involving children in health and social care research: 'Human becomings' or 'active beings', *Childhood*, 13(1): 29–48.

Banks, S. (2012) *Ethics and Values in Social Work*, 4th edn. Basingstoke: Palgrave.

Banks, S. (2010) Interprofessional ethics: a developing field? Notes from the Ethics and Social Welfare Conference, Sheffield, UK May, 2010, *Ethics and Social Welfare*, 4(3): 280–94.

Barr, H. (2013) Change and challenge in interprofessional education, in B. Littlechild and R. Smith (eds) *A Handbook for Interprofessional Practice in the Human Services*. Harlow: Pearson.

Barratt, M. and Hodson, R. (2006) *Firm Foundations: A Practical Guide to Organizational Support for the Use of Research*. Dartington, UK: Research in Practice.

Barrett, G. and Keeping, C. (2005) The processes required for effective interprofessional work, in G. Barrett, D. Selman and J. Thomas (eds) *Interprofessional Working in Health and Social Care*. Basingstoke: Palgrave.

Beauchamp, T.L. and Childress, J.F. (1989) *Principles of Biomedical Ethics*, 3rd edn. Oxford: Oxford University Press.

Beddoe, L. (2012) External supervision in social work: power, space, risk, and the search for safety, *Australian Social Work*, 65(2): 197–213.

Bell, L. (2017) *Research Methods for Social Workers*. London: Palgrave.

Bellamy, J.L., Bledsoe, S.E. and Traube, D.E. (2006) The current state of evidence-based practice in social work: a review of the literature and qualitative analysis of expert interviews, *Journal of Evidence-Based Social Work*, 3(1): 23–48.

Beresford, P. (2000) Service users' knowledges and social work theory: conflict or collaboration?, *British Journal of Social Work*, 30(4): 489–503.

Berger, R. (2013) Incorporating EBP in field education: where we stand and what we need, *Journal of Evidence-Based Social Work*, 10(2): 127–35.

Bhaskar, R. (1979) *The Possibility of Naturalism*. Brighton: Harvester.

Biestek, E. (1961) *The Casework Relationship*. London: George Allen & Unwin.

Bledsoe-Mansori, S.E., Manuel, J.I., Bellamy, J.L. et al. (2013) Implementing evidence-based practice: practitioner assessment of an agency-based training program, *Journal of Evidence-Based Social Work*, 10(2): 73–90.

Boddy, J. and Oliver, C. (2010) *Research Governance in Children's Services: The Scope for New Advice*. London: Department for Education.

Brandt, A.M. (1978) *Racism, Research and the Tuskagee Syphilis Report (Report no. 8)*. New York: Hastings Center.

Branfield, F. and Beresford, P. (2006) *Making User Involvement Work: Supporting Service User Networking and Knowledge*. York: Joseph Rowntree Foundation.

Briggs, H.E. and Rzepnicki, T.L. (2004) *Using Evidence in Social Work Practice: Behavioral Perspectives*. Chicago, IL: Lyceum Books.

British Association of Social Workers (BASW) (2016) *Professional Capabilities Framework – End of Last Placement/Qualifying Level*. Available at: https://www.basw.co.uk/pcf/PCF07LastPlacementQualifyingLevelCapabilities.pdf [Accessed 25 November 2016].

British Psychological Association (2010) *Code of Human Research Ethics*. Leicester: BPS. Available at: http://www.bps.org.uk/sites/default/files/documents/code_of_human_research_ethics.pdf [Accessed 7 February 2017].

Butler, I. (2002) A code of ethics for social care and social work research, *British Journal of Social Work Research*, 32(2): 239–48.

Cameron, A., Lart, R. and Bostock, L. (2014) Factors that promote or hinder joint integrated working between health and social care services: a review of research literature, *Health and Social Care*, 22(3): 225–33.

Carers Trust (n.d.) *What is a Carer?* Available at: https://carers.org/what-carer [Accessed 28 May 2017].

Carey, M. and Green, L. (2013) *Practical Social Work Ethics: Complex Dilemmas Within Applied Social Care*. Farnham: Ashgate Publishing Ltd.

Carpenter, J., Webb, C., Bostock, L. and Coomber, C. (2012) *Effective Supervision in Social Work and Social Care: SCI Research Briefing 43*. London: SCIE. Available at: http://www.scie.org.uk/publications/briefings/files/briefing43.pdf [Accessed 23 December 2016].

Clifford, D. (2013) Limitations of virtue ethics in the social professions, *Ethics and Social Welfare*, 8(1): 2–19.

Colquhoun, H.L., Levac, D., O'Brien, K.K. et al. (2014) Scoping reviews: time for clarity in definition, methods, and reporting, *Journal of Clinical Epidemiology*, 67(12): 1291–4.

Community Care (2016) *Government Makes U-Turn on Plan to Control New Social Work Regulator*. Available at: http://www.communitycare.co.uk/2016/10/20/government-makes-u-turn-plans-control-new-social-work-regulator/ [Accessed 3 December 2016].

Council on Social Work Education (CSWE) (2015) *2015 Educational Policy and Accreditation Standards for Baccalaureate and Master's Social Work Programs*. Alexandria, VA: CSWE. Available at: https://www.cswe.org/getattachment/Accreditation/Accreditation-Process/2015-EPAS/2015EPAS_Web_FINAL.pdf.aspx [Accessed 25 November 2016].

Creswell, J.W. (2003) *Research Design: Qualitative, Quantitative and Mixed Methods Approaches*, 2nd edn. London: Sage.

Critical Appraisal Skills Programme (CASP) (2013) *Appraising the Evidence*. Available at: http://www.casp-uk.net/appraising-the-evidence [Accessed 3 January 2017].

Croisdale-Appleby, D. (2014) *Re-visioning Social Work Education: An Independent Review*. Durham: Croisdale-Appleby. Available at: https://www.gov.uk/government/uploads/system/uploads/attachment_data/file/285788/DCA_Accessible.pdf [Accessed 25 November 2016].

Cronin, A. (2001) Focus groups, in N. Gilbert (ed.) *Researching Social Life*, 2nd edn. London: Sage, pp. 164–77.

Crotty, M. (2003) *The Foundations of Social Research*. London: Sage.

Damschroder, L., Aron, D., Keith, R. et al. (2009) Fostering implementation of health services research findings into practice: a consolidated framework for advancing implementation science, *Implementation Science*, 4: 50.

Davys, A. and Beddoe, L. (2010) *Best Practice in Supervision: A Guide for the Helping Professions.* London: Jessica Kingsley.

Dennison, S. (2016) *The UK Government's Brexit Strategy: What we Know so Far.* Commentary, European Council on Foreign Relations website. Available at: http://www.ecfr.eu/article/commentary_the_uk_governments_brexit_strategy_what_we_know_so_far7108 [Accessed 5 December 2016].

Department for Education (DfE) (2014) *Knowledge and Skills for Child and Family Social Work.* London: DfE. Available at: https://www.gov.uk/government/uploads/system/uploads/attachment_data/file/338718/140730_Knowledge_and_skills_statement_final_version_AS_RH_Checked.pdf [Accessed 2 December 2016].

Department of Health (DH) (1998) *Partnerships in Action.* London: Her Majesty's Stationery Office.

Department of Health (DH) (2000) *The NHS Plan: A Plan for Investment a Plan for Reform.* London: Department of Health.

Department of Health (DH) (2005) *Research Governance Framework for Health and Social Care,* 2nd edn. London: Department of Health. Available at: https://www.gov.uk/government/uploads/system/uploads/attachment_data/file/139565/dh_4122427.pdf [Accessed 9 January 2017].

Department of Health (DH) (2010a) *Equity and Excellence: Liberating the NHS.* London: Department of Health.

Department of Health (DH) (2010b) *A Vision for Adult Social Care: Capable Communities and Active Citizens.* London: Department of Health.

Department of Health (DH) (2015) *Knowledge and Skills Statement for Social Workers in Adult Services.* London: Department of Health. Available at: https://www.gov.uk/government/uploads/system/uploads/attachment_data/file/411957/KSS.pdf [Accessed 2 December 2016].

Department of Health, Social Services and Public Safety (DHSSPS) (2012) *Improving and Safeguarding Social Wellbeing: A Strategy for Social Work in Northern Ireland 2012–2022.* Belfast: DHSSPS. Available at: http://www.niscc.info/storage/resources/2012april_dhssps_socialworkstrategy2012-2022_afmck1.pdf [Accessed 6 December 2016].

Dirkx, J.M. (2006) Studying the complicated matter of what works: evidence-based research and the problem of practice, *Adult Education Quarterly*, 56(4): 273–90.

Dixon, J., Biehal, N., Green, J. et al. (2013) Trials and tribulations: challenges and prospects for randomized control trials of social work with children, *British Journal of Social Work*, 44(6): 1563–81.

Dominelli, L. (2005) Social work research: contested knowledge for practice, in R. Adams, L. Dominelli and M. Payne (eds) *Social Work Futures: Crossing Boundaries, Transforming Practice.* Basingstoke: Palgrave Macmillan, pp. 223–36.

Driessens, K., McLaughlin, H. and Van Doorn, L. (2016) The meaningful involvement of service users in social work education: examples from Belgium and the Netherlands, *Social Work Education: The International Journal*, 35(7): 739–51.

ESRC (2015) *ESRC Framework for Research Ethics: Updated January 2015.* Swindon: ESRC. Available at: http://www.esrc.ac.uk/files/funding/guidance-for-applicants/esrc-framework-for-research-ethics-2015/ [Accessed 7 February 2017].

Evans, T. and Hardy, M. (2010) *Evidence and Knowledge for Practice.* Cambridge: Polity Press.

Family Rights Group (2016) *Where and How are Family Group Conferences Used?* Available at: http://www.frg.org.uk/where-and-how-are-family-group-conferences-used [Accessed 29 December 2016].

Fenton, J. (2016) *Values in Social Work: Reconnecting with Social Justice.* London: Palgrave.

Fisher, M. (2016) The Social Care Institute for Excellence and evidence-based policy and practice, *British Journal of Social Work*, 46(2): 498–513.

Fook, J. (2002) *Social Work: Critical Theory and Practice*. London: Sage.

Fouche, C. (2015) *Practice Research Partnerships in Social Work: Making a Difference*. Bristol: Policy Press.

Freeth, D., Hammick, M., Reeves, S. et al. (2005) *Effective Interprofessional Education: Development, Delivery, Evaluation*. Oxford: Blackwell.

Flynn, M.C. (2007) *The Murder of Steven Hoskin: A Serious Case Review*, Cornwall Adult Protection Committee. Available at: http://www.hampshiresab.org.uk/wp-content/uploads/2007-December-Serious-Case-Review-regarding-Steven-Hoskin-Cornwall.pdf [Accessed 28 May 2017).

Galvani, S. (2008) Working together: responding to people with alcohol and drug problems, in K. Morris (ed.) *Social Work and Multi-Agency Working: Making a Difference*. Bristol: Policy Press.

Gambrill, E. (2016) Is social work evidence-based? Does saying so make it so? Ongoing challenges in integrating research, practice and policy, *Journal of Social Work Education*, 52(Suppl. 1): S110–25.

General Medical Council (2009) *Tomorrow's Doctors*. Manchester: General Medical Council. Available at: http://www.gmc-uk.org/Tomorrow_s_Doctors_1214.pdf_48905759.pdf [Accessed 13 December 2016].

Gibbs, L. (2003) *Evidence-Based Practice for the Helping Professions: A Practical Guide with Integrated Multimedia*. Pacific Grove, CA: Brooks/Cole.

Giddens, A. (1977) *Studies in Social and Political Theory*. London: Hutchinson.

Gilgun, J.F. (2010) Methods for enhancing theory and knowledge about problems, policies and practice, in I. Shaw, K. Briar-Lawson, J. Orme and R. Ruckdeschel (eds) *The Sage Handbook of Social Work Research*. London: Sage.

Glasby, J. (2007) *Understanding Health and Social Care*. Bristol: Policy Press.

Gray, M., Joy, E., Plath, D. et al. (2015) What supports and impedes evidence-based practice implementation? A survey of Australian social workers, *British Journal of Social Work*, 45(2): 667–84.

Gredig, D. and Marsh, J.C. (2010) Improving intervention and practice, in I. Shaw, K. Briar-Lawson, J. Orme and R. Ruckdeschel (eds) *The Sage Handbook of Social Work Research*. London: Sage.

Greenhalgh, T., Annadale, E., Ashcroft, R. et al. (2016) An open letter to the BMJ editors on qualitative research, *British Medical Journal*, 35(2): 1957.

Hardwick, L. and Worsley, A. (2011) *Doing Social Work Research*. London: Sage.

Harvey, D., Plummer, D., Pighills, A. et al. (2013) Practitioner research capacity: a survey of social workers in Northern Queensland, *Australian Social Work*, 66(4): 540–54.

Hammersley, M. (1995) *The Politics of Social Research*. London: Sage.

Health and Care Professions Council (HCPC) (2016) *Fitness to Practise Annual Report 2016*. London: HCPC. Available at: http://www.hpcuk.org/assets/documents/100051F3Fitnesstopractiseannualreport2016.pdf [Accessed 16 February 2016].

Health and Care Professions Council (HCPC) (2017) *Standards of Proficiency – Social Workers in England*. London: HCPC. Available at: http://www.hcpcuk.org/assets/documents/10003B-08Standardsofproficiency-SocialworkersinEngland.pdf [Accessed 8 July 2017].

HEFCE (2012) *Ref 2014: Assessment Framework and Guidance on Admissions*. Bristol: HEFCE. Available at: http://www.ref.ac.uk/media/ref/content/pub/assessmentframeworkandguidanceonsubmissions/GOS%20including%20addendum.pdf [Accessed 9 January 2017].

Higgins, M. (2015) The struggle for the soul of social work in England, *Social Work Education: The International Journal*, 34(1): 4–18.

Higgins, J.P.T. and Green, S. (eds) (2011) *Cochrane Handbook for Systematic Reviews of Interventions*, Version 5.1.0. The Cochrane Collaboration. Available at: http://www.handbook.cochrane.org [Accessed 3 January 2017].

Homan, R. (1991) *The Ethics of Social Research*. Harlow: Longman.

Horsley, J. (1983) *Using Research to Improve Nursing Practice: A Guide – CURN Project*. Austin, TX: Pro Ed.

Hudson, B. (2007) Pessimism and optimism in interprofessional working: the Sedgefield Integrated team, *Journal of Interprofessional Care*, 21(1): 3–15.

Husband, C. (1995) The morally active practitioner and the ethics of anti-racist social work, in R. Hugman and D. Smith (eds) *Ethical Issues in Social Work*. London: Routledge.

Huss, E. (2012) *What We See and What We Say: Using Images in Research, Therapy, Empowerment, and Social Change*. London: Routledge.

Huss, E. (2015) *A Theory-based Approach to Art Therapy: Implications for Teaching, Research and Practice*. Abingdon: Routledge.

IASSW/IFSW (2004) *Global Standards for Education and Training of Social Workers*. Adelaide: IASSW/IFSW. Available at: http://cdn.ifsw.org/assets/ifsw_65044-3.pdf [Accessed 25 November 2016].

IFSW/IAASW (2014) *Global Definition of Social Work*. Available at: http://ifsw.org/get-involved/global-definition-of-social-work/ [Accessed 7 December 2016].

Ixer, G. (1999) There's no such thing as reflection, *British Journal of Social Work*, 29(4): 513–27.

Jaynes, S. (2014) Using principles of practice-based research to teach evidence-based practice in social work, *Journal of Evidence-Based Social Work*, 11(1/2): 222–35.

Jessiman, T., Carpenter, J. and O'Donnel, T. (2016) A randomised control trial of a therapeutic intervention for children affected by sexual abuse, in L. Hardwick, R. Smith and A. Worsley (eds) *Innovations in Social Work Research: Using Creative Methods*. London: Jessica Kingsley.

Kline, R. (2009) We need to protect whistleblowing social workers, *The Guardian*, 14 September. Available at: https://www.theguardian.com/society/joepublic/2009/sep/14/social-workers-careers-whistleblowers-whistleblowing [Accessed 21 February 2017].

Kondrat, D. (2014) Solution-focused practice, in B. Teater (ed.) *An Introduction to Applying Social Work Theories and Methods*. Maidenhead: Open University Press.

Laming, H. (2003) *The Victoria Climbié Inquiry: Report*, CM5730. London: The Stationery Office. Available at: https://www.gov.uk/government/uploads/system/uploads/attachment_data/file/273183/5730.pdf [Accessed 23 December 2016].

Leathard, A. (2003) Introduction, in A. Leathard (ed.) *Interprofessional Collaboration: From Policy to Practice in Health and Social Care*. Hove: Brunner-Routledge.

Levac, D., Colquhoun, H. and O'Brien, K.K. (2010) Scoping studies: advancing the methodology, *Implementation Science*, 5: 69.

Local Government Association (2014) *Standards for Employers of Social Workers in England*, Available at: https://www.local.gov.uk/sites/default/files/documents/employer-standards-guide–c8b.pdf [Accessed 8 July 2017].

Lorenzetti, I. (2013) Developing a cohesive emancipatory social work identity: risking an act of love, *Critical Social Work*, 14(2): 48–59.

Lyon, D. (2007) *Surveillance Studies: An Overview*. Cambridge: Policy Press.

Manuel, J., Mullen, F., Bellamy, J. et al. (2009) Preparing social work practitioners to use evidence-based practice: a comparison of experiences from an implementation project, *Research on Social Work Practice*, 19(5): 613–27.

McLaughlin, H. (2009) What's in a name: client, patient, customer, consumer, expert by experience, service user: what's next?, *British Journal of Social Work*, 19(6): 1101–17.

McLaughlin, H. (2012) *Understanding Social Work Research*, 2nd edn. London: Sage.

McLaughlin, H. (2013a) Motherhood, apple pie and interprofessional working, *Social Work Education*, 32(7): 956–63.

McLaughlin, H. (2013b) Keeping interprofessional honest: fads and critical reflections, in B. Littlechild and R. Smith (eds) *A Handbook for Interprofessional Practice in the Human Services*. Harlow: Pearson.

McLaughlin, H., Sadd, J., McKeever, B. et al. (2016) Service user and carer involvement in social work education – where are we now?, *Social Work Education: The International Journal*, 35(8): 863–5.

McLaughlin, H. and Shardlow, S. (2009) Different cultures: different ethics? Research governance and social care, *Ethics and Social Welfare*, 3(1): 4–17.

McNeece, C.A. and Thyer, B.A. (2004) Evidence-based practice and social work, *Journal of Evidence-Based Social Work*, 1(1): 7–25.

McRoy, R.G., Flanzer, J.P. and Zlotnik, J.L. (2012) *Building Research Culture and Infrastructure*. New York: Oxford University Press.

Metz, A.J.R., Blase, K. and Bowie, L. (2007) *Implementing Evidence-based Practices: Six 'Drivers' of Success*. Washington, DC: Child Trends.

Monette, D., Sullivan, T. and De Jong, C. (2010) *Applied Social Research: A Tool for the Human Services*, 8th edn. Belmont, CA: Brooks/Cole.

Morago, P. (2010) Dissemination and implementation of evidence-based practice in the social services: a UK survey, *Journal of Evidence-Based Social Work*, 7(5): 452–65.

Moriarty, J., Baginsky, M. and Manthorpe, J. (2015) *Literature Review of Roles and Issues Within the Social Work Profession in England*. London: Social Care Workforce Research Unit, King's College London. Available at: http://www.professionalstandards.org.uk/docs/default-source/publications/research-paper/literature-review-roles-and-issues-within-the-social-work-profession-in-england-2015.pdf?sfvrsn=6 [Accessed 23 December 2016].

Mullen, E.J. and Bacon, W. (2004) A survey of practitioner adoption and implementation of practice guidelines and evidence-based treatments, in A.R. Roberts and K. Yeager (eds) *Evidence-Based Practice Manual: Research and Outcome Measures in Health and Human Services*. New York: Oxford University Press.

Mullins, L.J. (1989) *Management and Organisational Behaviour*, 2nd edn. London: Longman.

NatCen (2016) *British Social Attitudes 33*. Available at: http://www.bsa.natcen.ac.uk/latest-report/british-social-attitudes-33/welfare.aspx [Accessed 5 December 2016]

National Institute for Health and Care Excellence (NICE) (2017) *How we Develop NICE Guidelines*. Available at: https://www.nice.org.uk/about/what-we-do/our-programmes/nice-guidance/nice-guidelines/how-we-develop-nice-guidelines [Accessed 3 January 2017].

Neary, M. (2014) *Making the Education of Social Workers Consistently Effective: Report of Sir Martin Neary's Independent Review of the Education of Children's Social Workers*. London: DfE. Available at: https://www.gov.uk/government/uploads/system/uploads/attachment_data/file/287756/Making_the_education_of_social_workers_consistently_effective.pdf [Accessed 25 November 2016].

Needham, C. and Carr, S. (2009) *Co-production: An Emerging Evidence Base for Adult Social Care Transformation*, SCIE Research Briefing 31. London: SCIE. Available at: http://www.scie.org.uk/publications/briefings/files/briefing31.pdf [Accessed 29 December 2016].

Nelson, T.D. and Steele, R.G. (2007) Predictors of practitioner self-reported use of evidence-based practices: practitioner training, clinical setting, and attitudes towards research, *Administration and Policy in Mental Health and Mental Health Services Research*, 34(4): 319–30.

Nevo, I. and Slonim-Nevo, S. (2011) The myth of evidence-based practice: towards evidence-informed practice, *British Journal of Social Work*, 41(6): 1176–97.

Ontario Centre of Excellence for Child and Youth Mental Health (OCECYMH) (2013) *Implementing Evidence-informed Practice: A Practical Toolkit*. Ottawa, Ontario: OCECYMH.

Orme, J. and Shemmings, D. (2010) *Developing Research-Based Social Work Practice*. Basingstoke: Palgrave Macmillan.

Osterling, K.L. and Austin, M.J. (2008) The dissemination and utilization of research for promoting evidence-based practice, *Journal of Evidence-Based Social Work*, 5(1/2): 295–319.

Oxford English Dictionary (2016) http://www.oed.com.ezproxy.mmu.ac.uk/view/Entry/65368?rskey=2Z7e08&result=1#eid [Accessed 23 December 2016).

Palinkas, L.A. and Soydan, H. (2012) *Translation and Implementation of Evidence-Based Practice*. New York: Oxford University Press.

Papouli, E. (2016) Teaching and learning for ethical social work practice in social work education, in I. Taylor, M. Bogo, M. Levevre and B. Teater (eds) *Routledge International Handbook of Social Work Education*. Abingdon: Routledge.

Pawson, R., Boaz. R., Grayson, L. et al. (2003) *Types and Quality of Knowledge in Social Care*. London: SCIE.

Peck, E., Gulliver, P. and Towell, D. (2002) *Modernising Partnerships: An Evaluation of Somerset's Innovations in the Commissioning and Organisation of Mental Health Services: Final Report*. London: Institute of Applied Health and Social Policy, King's College.

Pedler, M., Burgoyne, J. and Boydell, T. (1991) *The Learning Company: A Strategy for Sustainable Development*. Maidenhead: McGraw-Hill.

Pence, G.E. (2000) *Classic Cases in Medical Ethics: Accounts of Cases that have Shaped Medical Ethics, with Philosophical, Legal and Historical Backgrounds*, 3rd edn. New York: McGraw-Hill.

Persons, J. (1999) Evidence-based psychotherapy: a graduate course proposal, *Clinical Science*, 2: 12.

Plomer, A. (2005) *The Law and Ethics of Medical Research: International Bioethics and Human Rights*. London: Cavendish Publishing Company.

Pooler, A. (2012) *An Introduction to Evidence-Based Practice in Nursing and Healthcare*. London: Routledge.

Pope, N.D., Rollins, L., Chaumba, J. et al. (2011) Evidence-based practice knowledge and utilization among social workers, *Journal of Evidence-Based Social Work*, 8(4): 349–68.

Popper, K. (1980) *The Logic of Scientific Discovery*. London: Hutchinson.

Powell, K.L. and Dalton, M.M. (2003) Co-production, service exchange networks, and social capital, *Social Policy Journal*, 2(2/3): 89–105.

Pugh, R. (2009) Dual relationships: personal and professional boundaries in rural social work, *British Journal of Social Work*, 37(8): 1405–23.

Quinney, A. (2006) *Collaborative Social Work Practice*. Exeter: Learning Matters.

Redfern, M. (2001) *The Royal Liverpool Children's Inquiry Report*. London: The Stationery Office.

Ritchie, J.H. (1994) *The Report of the Inquiry into the Care and Treatment of Christopher Clunis*. Norwich: HMSO.

Robbins, S., Fogel, S.J., McLaughlin, H. et al. (2016) Publish, don't perish! Strategies for getting published in peer reviewed journals, *Social Work Education: The International Journal*, 35(5): 487–94.

Roe, R. (2006) *Report of the 21st Century Review: Changing Lives*. Edinburgh: Scottish Executive.

Ruch, G. (2002) From triangle to spiral: reflective practice in social work education: practice and research, *Social Work Education*, 21(2): 199–216.

Rubin, A. (2008) *Practitioner's Guide to using Research for Evidence-Based Practice*. Hoboken, NJ: John Wiley & Sons.

Rubin, A. and Babbie, E. (2016) *Essential Research Methods for Social Work*, 4th edn. Boston, MA: Cengage Learning.

Rummery, K. (2009) Healthy partnerships, healthy citizens? An international review of partnerships in health and social care and patient/user outcomes, *Social Science & Medicine*, 69(12): 1797–804.

Sackett, D.L. (2000) *Evidence-Based Medicine: How to Practice and Teach EBM*, 2nd edn. Edinburgh: Churchill Livingstone.

Sackett, D., Rosenberg, W., Gray, J. et al. (1996) Evidence-based medicine: what it is and what it isn't, *British Medical Journal*, 312(7023): 71–2.

Sawatzky-Dickson, D. (2010) *Evidence-Informed Practice Resource Package*. Winnipeg: Winnipeg Regional Health Authority. Available at: http://www.wrha.mb.ca/osd/files/EIPResourcePkg.pdf [Accessed 14 January 2017].

Schön, D. (1983) *The Reflective Practitioner: How Professionals Think in Action*. New York: Basic Books.

Scottish Government (2015) *Social Services in Scotland: A Shared Vision and Strategy 2015–2020*. Scotland: Social Work Services Strategic Forum. Available at: http://www.gov.scot/Resource/0047/00473374.pdf [Accessed 1 July 2017].

Scottish Social Services Council (SSSC) (2015) *Review of Social Work Education: Statement on Progress 2014–2015*. Dundee: SSSC. Available at: http://www.sssc.uk.com/about-the-sssc/multimedia-library/publications/70-education-and-training/76-statistics-and-reports/review-of-social-work-education-statement-of-progress-2014-2015 [Accessed 5 December 2016].

Shardlow, S. (2013) Ethical tensions in social work, in J. Parker and M. Doel (eds) *Professional Social Work*. London: Learning Matters.

Sharland, E., Taylor, I. with Jones, L., Orr, D. and Whiting, R. (2007) *Interprofessional Education for Qualifying Social Work*. London: SCIE.

Shaw, C., Brady, L.-M. and Davey, C. (2011) *Guidelines for Research with Children and Young People*. London: National Children's Bureau.

Sheldon, B. (2001) The validity of evidence-based practice in social work: a reply to Stephen Webb, *British Journal of Social Work*, 31(5): 801–9.

Sheldon, B. and Chilvers, R. (2000) *Evidence-Based Social Care: A Study of Prospects and Problems*. Lyme Regis: Russell House Publishing.

Sheldon, B. and McDonald, G. (2008) *A Textbook of Social Work*. London: Routledge.

Shlonsky, A. and Stern, S.B. (2007) Reflections on the teaching of evidence-based practice, *Research on Social Work Practice*, 17(5): 603–11.

Sims, D. and Cabrita Gulyurtlu, S.S. (2014) A scoping review of personalisation in the UK: approaches to social work and people with learning disabilities, *Health and Social Care in the Community*, 22(1): 13–21.

Social Care Institute for Excellence (SCIE) (2013) *Maximising the Potential of Reablement*. Available at: http://www.scie.org.uk/publications/guides/guide49/goalsetting.asp [Accessed 6 December 2016].

Social Research Association (2003) *Ethical Guidelines*. London: Social Research Association. Available at: http://the-sra.org.uk/wp-content/uploads/ethics03.pdf [Accessed 7 February 2017].

Smith, R. (2009) *Doing Social Research*. Maidenhead: Open University Press.

Smith, R. (2013) Key issues in interprofessional and interagency working in health and social care, in B. Littlechild and R. Smith (eds) *A Handbook for Interprofessional Practice in the Human Services*. Harlow: Pearson.

Snape, D. and Spencer, L. (2003) The foundations of qualitative research, in J. Ritchie and J. Lewis (eds) *Qualitative Research Practice: A Guide for Students and Researchers*. London: Sage.

Taylor, B., Killick, C. and McGlade, A. (2015) *Understanding and Using Research in Social Work*. London: Sage.

Teater, B. (2017) Social work research and its relevance to practice: 'the gap between research and practice continues to be wide', *Journal of Social Service Research, published online 20 July 2017, doi: 10, 1080/01488376.2017.1340393*.

Teater, B. and Chonody, J. (2016) Identifying as an evidence-based social worker: the influence of attitudes, access, confidence, and education, paper presented at the European Conference for Social Work, Aalborg, Denmark (2 April 2016).

Teater, B., Lefevre, M. and McLaughlin, H. (2016) Developing the social work academic workforce: profiles from the United Kingdom and the United States of America, in I. Taylor, M. Bogo, M. Lefevre and B. Teater (eds) *Routledge International Handbook of Social Work Education*. Oxford: Routledge, pp. 355–69.

Trevithick, P. (2008) Revisiting the knowledge base of social work: a framework for practice, *British Journal of Social Work*, 38(6): 1212–37.

Trinder, L. (2000) Evidence-based practice in social work and probation, in L. Trinder and S. Reynolds (eds) *Evidence-Based Practice: A Critical Approach*. Oxford: Blackwell.

Tuntland, H., Aaslund, M.K., Espehaug, B. et al. (2015) Reablement in community-dwelling older adults: a randomised control trial, *BMC Geriatrics*, 15: 145.

Tuten, M., Morris-Compton, D., Abrefa-Gyan, T. et al. (2016) Predictors of the use of evidence-based interventions among National Association of Social Work (NASW) members, *Journal of Evidence-Informed Social Work*, 13(3): 253–62.

United Nations (1948) *The Universal Declaration of Human Rights*. New York: United Nations.

United Nations (1989) *Convention on the Rights of the Child*. New York: United Nations.

Watson, D. and West, J. (2006) *Social Work Process and Practice*. Basingstoke: Palgrave Macmillan.

Webber, M. (2015) Increasing the synergy between research and practice in social work, in M. Webber (ed.) *Applying Research Evidence in Social Work Practice*. London: Palgrave.

Welsh Assembly Government (WAG) (2007) *A Strategy for Social Services in Wales Over the Next Decade*. Cardiff: WAG. Available at: http://gov.wales/dhss/publications/socialcare/strategies/fulfilledlives/fulfilledlivese.pdf?lang=en [Accessed 5 December 2016].

Whittaker, A. and Havard, T. (2016) Defensive practice as 'fear-based' practice: social work's open secret?, *British Journal of Social Work*, 46(5): 1158–74.

Williams, N.J. and Sherr, M.E. (2013) Oh how I try to use evidence in my social work practice: efforts, successes, frustrations, and questions, *Journal of Evidence-Based Social Work*, 10(2): 100–10.

Wilson, K., Ruch, G., Lymbery, M. et al. (2008) *Social Work: An Introduction to Contemporary Practice*. Harlow: Pearson Education Limited.

Wiggins, M., Austerberry, H. and Ward, H. (2012) *Implementing Evidence-Based Programmes in Children's Services: Key Issues for Success*. London: DfE. Available at: https://www.gov.uk/government/uploads/system/uploads/attachment_data/file/183483/DFE-RR245.pdf [Accessed 15 January 2017].

Wilson, G. (1994) Co-production and self-care: new approaches to managing community care services for older people, *Social Policy and Administration*, 28(3): 236–50.

Wilson, K., Ruch, G., Lymbery, M. and Cooper, A. (2008) *Social Work: An Introduction to Contemporary Practice*. Harlow: Pearson Education Limited.

Wood, K., Bond, C., Humphrey, N. et al. (2011) *Systematic Review of Solution Focused Brief Therapy (SFBT) with Children and Families*. Manchester: DfE. Available at: https://www.gov.uk/government/uploads/system/uploads/attachment_data/file/184113/DFE-RR179.pdf [Accessed 15 January 2017].

Zwarenstein, M., Reves, S. and Perrier, L. (2005) Effectiveness of pre-licensure interprofessional education and post-licensure collaborative interventions, *Journal of Interprofessional Care*, 19(Suppl. 1): 148–65.

# Index